$BC = \frac{BA}{2}$ $\frac{6}{2} = 3$

90 6
30 (30)

$\frac{\sin 90}{60} = \frac{\sin 30}{x}$

$\frac{\sin 90}{60} = \frac{\sin \theta}{x}$
51.6

CAMBRIDGE
EDUCATIONAL SERVICES®

AMERICA'S #1 CAMPUS-BASED TESTPREP

ACT® • PLAN® • EXPLORE®*
Victory

Student Text
Volume 1

ACT® • PLAN® • EXPLORE® • SAT • PSAT • GRE® • GMAT® • LSAT® • MCAT® • TOEFL® • GED® • PRAXIS® • PSAE™ • WorkKeys® • Stanford • ITBS • State Tests • CollegePrep™ • Learning Styles • Guidance Services • Professional Development • Motivation & Admissions Workshops • Data Services • Formative Assessments

*ACT®, PLAN®, and EXPLORE® are registered trademarks of ACT, Inc. Cambridge Educational Services has no affiliation with ACT, Inc., and this product is not approved or endorsed by ACT, Inc.

The above-cited marks are the property of their respective owners.

Our Mission: Progress Through Partnership

Cambridge Educational Services partners with educators who share the significant mission of educational advancement for all students. By partnering together, we can best achieve our common goals: to build skills, raise test scores, enhance curriculum, and support instruction. A leading innovator in education for twenty years, Cambridge is the nation's premier provider of school-based test preparation and supplemental curriculum services.

Cambridge Publishing, Inc.
www.CambridgeEd.com

© 1994, 1995, 1996, 1997, 2000, 2003, 2004, 2005, 2009, 2010 by Cambridge Publishing, Inc.
All rights reserved. First edition 1994
Tenth edition 2010

Printed in the United States of America
13 12 11 10   2 3 4 5

ISBN-13: 978-1-58894-097-1

Portions reprinted from ACT
© 2009 by Thomas H. Martinson
All rights reserved

TABLE OF CONTENTS

HOW TO USE THIS BOOK

This book is organized into two parts:

- **Pre-Assessment/Course Planning.** A diagnostic pre-assessment and score reports help you identify your starting point and prepare for the course.

- **Core/Targeted Skills.** Seven skills review chapters serve as a refresher on topics you may not have studied in a while.

The following introduction will briefly explain how to use each part of this volume.

Pre-Assessment/Course Planning

In order to know where to begin preparing for the real test, you have to find out what you already do well and what you could learn to do better. The pre-assessment serves this purpose. First, you will take an official, retired test under actual testing conditions. Then, with the help of your instructor, you will examine your Student Summary report and determine exactly which topics to review, for how long, and in what order.

There are six "Winning Strategies" sections in Pre-Assessment/Course Planning that will help get you started:

- "Pre-Assessment Administration" explains the logistics of taking the pre-assessment. Perforated essay response and bubble sheets for the pre-assessment are located in Appendix B of this book for programs not utilizing the Cambridge Assessment Service.

- "How to Use the Pre-Assessment Report" helps you to make connections between your performance on the pre-assessment and the items in this book that you most need to study.

- "Setting a Test Score Target" helps you to understand the college admissions process and aids you in setting goals for where you should apply.

- "Overcoming Test Anxiety" discusses how to approach test days, from planning to maintaining the right perspective.

- "Overall Time Management" provides strategies for you to use when scheduling your study time.

- "Planning a Schedule for the Course" helps you to develop a study schedule that will aid your success in the course.

Core/Targeted Skills

This text contains skills review lessons and items that will enable you to do three things: (1) review material that you may have forgotten; (2) learn material that you may never have learned; and (3) master the skills required to answer the more difficult multiple-choice items on the real test.

The Core/Targeted Skills portion of this course is divided into seven chapters:

- Grammar and Mechanics

- Diagramming Sentences

- Math

- Reading

- Vocabulary

- Science

- Writing

Each chapter contains concept lessons and corresponding review exercises. For example, the lessons in the Math Skills Review cover the following topics: numbers, fractions, decimals, percents, statistical measures, ratios and proportions, exponents and radicals, algebraic operations, algebraic equations and inequalities, geometry, coordinate geometry, and story problems. The other chapters cover a similar range of topics that are appropriate to each subject.

These exercises do not necessarily contain problems that mimic the items on the real test. The problems are designed to help you learn concepts—not necessarily to help you learn about how the concepts appear on the actual exam. After you have mastered the skills, you will be able to take full advantage of the concepts and test-taking strategies that are developed in volume 2 of this set.

Pre-Assessment/Course Planning

Objectives:

Take an official test under real testing conditions to gain predictive data on which to base your study.

Get tips for setting goals, overcoming test anxiety, managing your time, and creating a study plan.

See what types of items and pacing you will encounter on the ACT®, PLAN®, and EXPLORE® tests.

Snapshot of Pre-Assessment/Course Planning:

You start your course with an official ACT®, PLAN®, or EXPLORE® test so that you know where you stand. This diagnostic test tells you and your instructor where you need to focus to see the greatest improvement. You should complete this test under real testing conditions so you know what to expect when you take an actual test. The structure of the course hinges on your pre-assessment performance, so try hard, but do not be too discouraged if you do not perform as well as you hoped. You will soon be learning the core curricular skills necessary to boost your test scores and enhance your academic achievement.

PRE-ASSESSMENT ADMINISTRATION

WINNING STRATEGIES

At the beginning of the course, you will take a pre-assessment. This pre-assessment consists of an official, retired ACT, PLAN, or EXPLORE test. Perforated bubble and essay response sheets for the pre-assessment are located in Appendix B of this book for programs not utilizing the Cambridge Assessment Service. When you take the pre-assessment, you should bring the following items to the classroom, in addition to anything else your teacher instructs you to bring:

1. Sharpened, soft-lead No. 2 pencils

2. A calculator that is approved for use on the test. This includes any four-function, scientific, or graphing calculator, except for those with the following features:

   - Built-in computer algebra systems

   - Pocket organizers or PDAs

   - Handheld or laptop computers

   - Electronic writing pad or pen-input devices

   - Calculators built into any electronic communication device, such as a cell phone

   - Models with a QWERTY (typewriter) keypad (Calculators with letters on the keys are permitted as long as the keys are not arranged in a QWERTY keypad.)

   You may use the following types of calculators if you make appropriate modifications:

   - Models with paper tape: the paper must be removed.

   - Models that make noise: the sound feature must be turned off.

   - Models that have an infrared data port: the port must be covered with duct tape, electrician's tape, or another heavy, opaque material.

   - Models that have a power cord: the power cord must be removed.

   (For more detailed information on calculator usage, go to www.actstudent.org/faq/answers/calculator.html.)

3. A watch (to pace yourself as you work through each test section)

As you take the test, remember the following points about marking the bubble sheet:

- The bubble for each answer choice must be completely darkened. If the letter within the bubble can be read through the pencil mark, then it is not dark enough. Mechanical pencils, even with No. 2 pencil lead, often fail to leave a dark mark.

- Stay within the lines.

- When erasing pencil marks, be sure to erase the marks completely. Do not leave any stray marks.

- Circle the answer choices in the test booklet. Towards the end of the section, or after each completed group of items, transfer the selected answers as a group to the answer form. Not only does this minimize erasing on the answer form, but it also saves time and minimizes transcription errors.

- When changing an answer, over-darken the final answer choice after completely erasing the original mark. This extra density tends to offset the residue left over from the original answer choice.

Strategic test-taking:

- Code items in the margin of the test booklet as easy or difficult before beginning to answer them. When pressed for time, you can skip to items that you are more likely to answer correctly.

- Make notes and calculations directly in the test booklet.

- Underline key words in Reading passages.

If your program has ordered pre-assessment Student Summary reports, you will receive one of these reports with your pre-assessment results. This report will help you determine the areas in which you need the most study and enable you to target the skills that are necessary to lay a foundation for success in the course. You can then utilize the course time to prepare in those areas so that when you take the real test, you are ready to do your best. You will learn more about how to read and use the Student Summary report in the "How to Use the Pre-Assessment Report" section on page 5.

HOW TO USE THE PRE-ASSESSMENT REPORT

In the transition from Pre-Assessment/Course Planning to Core/Targeted Skills, you and your teacher will use the results of your pre-assessment to recognize your individual strengths and weaknesses. Having this valuable information will allow you to create a realistic study plan for the course so that you can effectively manage your time.

You will receive the results of your official pre-assessment in the form of a Student Summary report approximately 10 days after taking the test. This report provides details about your performance and will help you to determine where to focus your efforts during the course by strategically targeting those skills that will help you to improve in your areas of weakness. Review the details of the sample Student Summary report below so that you are familiar with its contents.

Sample Student Summary Report

On the following pages is a sample ACT Student Summary report. Note that only the ACT report is shown. However, the PLAN and EXPLORE reports follow the same format.

Calculated by counting the number of correct answers per test (raw score) and then applying an ACT conversion factor

Student's percentile ranking compared to others who took the test. 24% scored at or below the Reading score of 16.

The average of the four test scores (English, Mathematics, Reading, and Science) rounded to the nearest whole number

Most colleges look at the highest ACT composite score regardless of the number of times taken. Colleges may even take the best individual test scores from any of a student's test dates and combine them to create a new composite "super score."

The sum of the scores of two readers, reported on a scale of 2–12. If the readers' scores disagree by more than one point, a third reader will resolve the discrepancy.

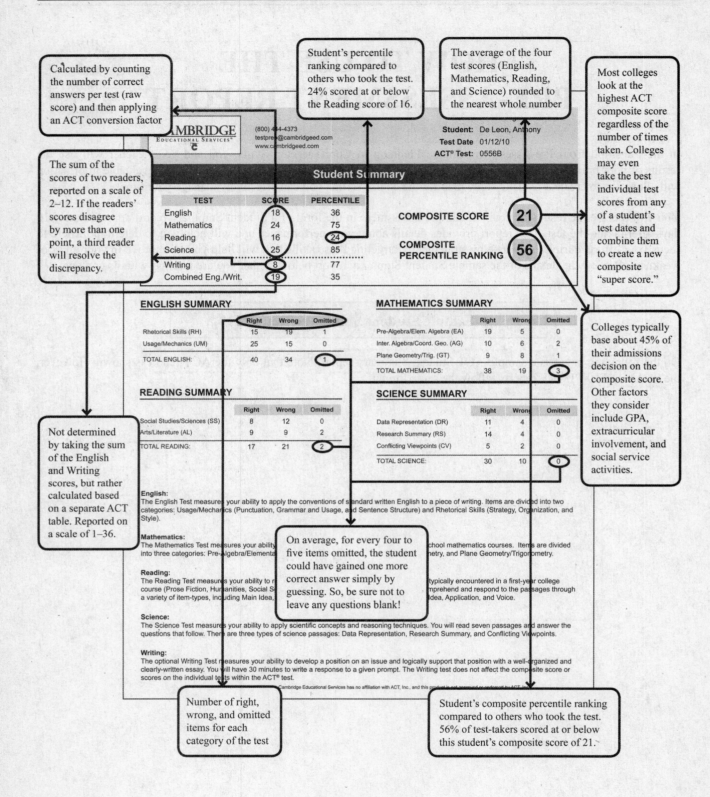

CAMBRIDGE
EDUCATIONAL SERVICES

(800) 444-4373
testprep@cambridgeed.com
www.cambridgeed.com

Student: De Leon, Anthony
Test Date 01/12/10
ACT® Test: 0556B

Student Summary

TEST	SCORE	PERCENTILE
English	18	36
Mathematics	24	75
Reading	16	24
Science	25	85
Writing	8	77
Combined Eng./Writ.	19	35

COMPOSITE SCORE 21

COMPOSITE PERCENTILE RANKING 56

Not determined by taking the sum of the English and Writing scores, but rather calculated based on a separate ACT table. Reported on a scale of 1–36.

Colleges typically base about 45% of their admissions decision on the composite score. Other factors they consider include GPA, extracurricular involvement, and social service activities.

ENGLISH SUMMARY

	Right	Wrong	Omitted
Rhetorical Skills (RH)	15	19	1
Usage/Mechanics (UM)	25	15	0
TOTAL ENGLISH:	40	34	1

MATHEMATICS SUMMARY

	Right	Wrong	Omitted
Pre-Algebra/Elem. Algebra (EA)	19	5	0
Inter. Algebra/Coord. Geo. (AG)	10	6	2
Plane Geometry/Trig. (GT)	9	8	1
TOTAL MATHEMATICS:	38	19	3

READING SUMMARY

	Right	Wrong	Omitted
Social Studies/Sciences (SS)	8	12	0
Arts/Literature (AL)	9	9	2
TOTAL READING:	17	21	2

SCIENCE SUMMARY

	Right	Wrong	Omitted
Data Representation (DR)	11	4	0
Research Summary (RS)	14	4	0
Conflicting Viewpoints (CV)	5	2	0
TOTAL SCIENCE:	30	10	0

English:
The English Test measures your ability to apply the conventions of standard written English to a piece of writing. Items are divided into two categories: Usage/Mechanics (Punctuation, Grammar and Usage, and Sentence Structure) and Rhetorical Skills (Strategy, Organization, and Style).

Mathematics:
The Mathematics Test measures your ability [...] school mathematics courses. Items are divided into three categories: Pre-Algebra/Elementa[...] [...]metry, and Plane Geometry/Trigonometry.

Reading:
The Reading Test measures your ability to r[...] [...] typically encountered in a first-year college course (Prose Fiction, Humanities, Social S[...] [...]mprehend and respond to the passages through a variety of item-types, including Main Idea, [...] [...] Idea, Application, and Voice.

Science:
The Science Test measures your ability to apply scientific concepts and reasoning techniques. You will read seven passages and answer the questions that follow. There are three types of science passages: Data Representation, Research Summary, and Conflicting Viewpoints.

Writing:
The optional Writing Test measures your ability to develop a position on an issue and logically support that position with a well-organized and clearly-written essay. You will have 30 minutes to write a response to a given prompt. The Writing test does not affect the composite score or scores on the individual tests within the ACT® test.

On average, for every four to five items omitted, the student could have gained one more correct answer simply by guessing. So, be sure not to leave any questions blank!

Number of right, wrong, and omitted items for each category of the test

Student's composite percentile ranking compared to others who took the test. 56% of test-takers scored at or below this student's composite score of 21.

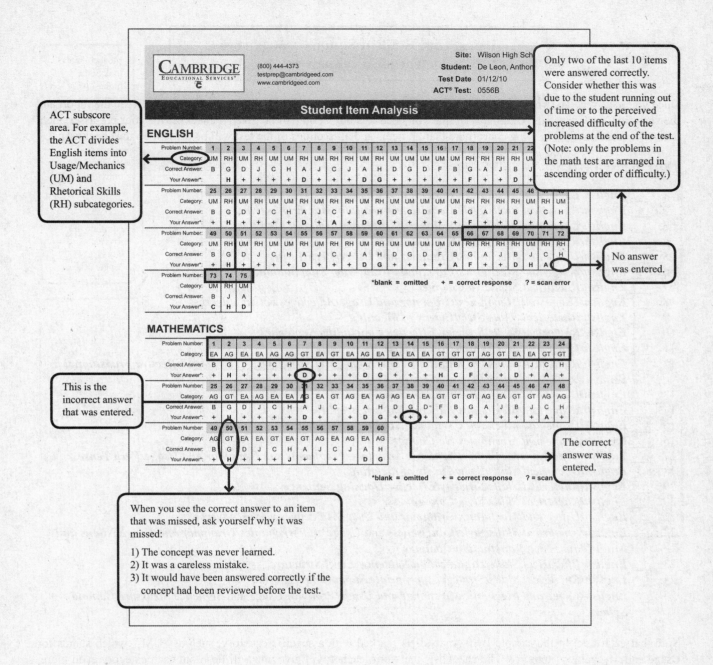

ACT subscore area. For example, the ACT divides English items into Usage/Mechanics (UM) and Rhetorical Skills (RH) subcategories.

Only two of the last 10 items were answered correctly. Consider whether this was due to the student running out of time or to the perceived increased difficulty of the problems at the end of the test. (Note: only the problems in the math test are arranged in ascending order of difficulty.)

No answer was entered.

This is the incorrect answer that was entered.

The correct answer was entered.

When you see the correct answer to an item that was missed, ask yourself why it was missed:

1) The concept was never learned.
2) It was a careless mistake.
3) It would have been answered correctly if the concept had been reviewed before the test.

Using Your Student Summary Report to Target Weaknesses

Once you have received your pre-assessment student summary report, you can make connections between the report and the specific Core/Targeted Skills material that you need to study. You will be given a checklist for your pre-assessment that will resemble the following chart (note that all items and all sections of the test will be present on the checklist):

TEST 1: ENGLISH

1. ___ *English/Usage and Mechanics/Punctuation/Commas.*
2. ___ *English/Rhetorical Skills/Style/Conciseness* and *Idiomatic Expression.*
3. ___ *English/Usage and Mechanics/Sentence Structure/Misplaced Modifiers.*
4. ___ *English/Rhetorical Skills/Style/Conciseness.*
5. ___ *English/Usage and Mechanics/Grammar and Usage/Verb Tense.*
6. ___ *English/Usage and Mechanics/Punctuation/End-Stop Punctuation.*
7. ___ *English/Rhetorical Skills/No Change.*
8. ___ *English/Usage and Mechanics/Grammar and Usage/Adjectives versus Adverbs.*
9. ___ *English/Rhetorical Skills/Style/Clarity of Meaning.*
10. ___ *English/Rhetorical Skills/Strategy/Effective Concluding Sentence.*
11. ___ *English/Usage and Mechanics/No Change.*
12. ___ *English/Rhetorical Skills/Organization/Paragraph-Level Structure* and *Strategy/Effective Transitional Sentence.*
13. ___ *English/Usage and Mechanics/Punctuation/Commas.*
14. ___ *English/Usage and Mechanics/Punctuation/Apostrophes.*
15. ___ *English/Usage and Mechanics/Sentence Structure/Fragments.*
16. ___ *English/Usage and Mechanics/No Change.*
17. ___ *English/Usage and Mechanics/Sentence Structure/Fragments* and *Grammar and Usage/Verb Tense.*
18. ___ *English/Rhetorical Skills/Style/Clarity of Meaning.*
19. ___ *English/Rhetorical Skills/Strategy/Effective Opening Sentence.*
20. ___ *English/Rhetorical Skills/Style/Conciseness.*
21. ___ *English/Usage and Mechanics/Grammar and Usage/Adjectives versus Adverbs.*
22. ___ *English/Rhetorical Skills/Style/Conciseness* and *Usage and Mechanics/Grammar and Usage/Nouns and Noun Clauses* and *Punctuation/Commas.*
23. ___ *English/Rhetorical Skills/Organization/Sentence-Level Structure.*
24. ___ *English/Rhetorical Skills/Strategy/Appropriate Supporting Material.*
25. ___ *English/Usage and Mechanics/Grammar and Usage/Pronoun Usage* and *Sentence Structure/Comma Splices.*

Note that each item in the sample Item Analysis is marked with a specific category, such as "UM," which stands for Usage and Mechanics (item #1). The checklists that your teacher will give you will flesh out each category even more, giving you a very specific idea of the concepts tested by each question on the exam (see example above).

According to the sample Item Analysis, the student missed items #1, 2, and 7 of the first 10 items in section 1 of the test. The categories for these items are *English/Usage and Mechanics/Punctuation/Commas* (#1), *English/Rhetorical Skills/Style/Conciseness* and *Idiomatic Expression* (#2), and *English/Rhetorical Skills/No Change* (#7). (Note that "No Change" items on the ACT English Test are those in which the given item is correct as written.) Based on this information, the student knows to study the "Commas" section of the Grammar Mechanics Skills Review and the section called "Write Concisely, Clearly, and Legibly" in the Composition portion of the Writing Skills Review. As for the "No Change" items, the best way to deal with items of this type is to look back at the original problem and evaluate, with your teacher's help if necessary, why you missed the problem.

In addition to studying related topics in the Core/Targeted Skills part of the book, you can flip to the Item Index at the back of volume 2 and find specific problems in Test Mechanics, Concepts, and Strategies or Practice Test

Reinforcement that test the same topics. Furthermore, you know to pay special attention to these topics as they come up later in the course.

Using both the checklist distributed by your teacher and your Item Analysis report, mark an "X" on your checklist beside the items that you answered incorrectly and a "?" by the items that you do not fully understand. The descriptions on the checklist tell you what topics in the Core/Targeted Skills part of volume 1 of the student text to review. Then, once you have your checklist of items to study, fill in your "to do" list:

Topic	Start Date	Date to Be Completed	Date Completed

SETTING A TEST SCORE TARGET

WINNING STRATEGIES

As a high school student, the next significant hurdle for you in reaching your academic and career goals is applying to and getting accepted into a college or university. This section prepares you to take significant practical steps toward successful admission to the college or university of your choice.

Colleges and universities use a variety of approaches in selecting which students are accepted to attend their schools. To you as a student, the admissions processes may seem complex ("Why must I complete all these forms, tests, and recommendations?"), the criteria for admission may appear mysterious ("Why did the university select student 'A' and not student 'B'?"), and the entire process may be emotionally frustrating ("Why haven't I heard back from college 'X', why did I get denied by university 'Y', and why was I placed on a waiting list by university 'Z'?").

To gain helpful strategies for applying to a college or university, read through this section carefully to see what we have learned over the years. We have advised tens of thousands of students, interviewed college admissions officers across the country, and attended annual college advisors' conferences. In the following pages, we have compiled the most valuable statistics and advice we have gleaned from a variety of sources.

This section is designed for a range of students—from those who are already actively working on their applications to those who are only starting to think about applying to college. Therefore, some of the points that are made are very general, while other points are very specific. You may already be familiar with some of the information, while other points and tips may surprise you. Whatever your current stage in the college application process, the following information and strategies will be helpful for both applying to and getting into the college of your choice.

Embrace the College Application Process as Truly Important

Applying for college is a really big deal! When you embark on the college application process, you take the important first step on a personal and career path that may influence the rest of your life. Decisions that you make about colleges at this stage of your life influence how much money you will make, where you may live, and what jobs will be available to you 5, 10, 20, 30, or even 40 years from now. Just imagine the different pathways that your life might follow depending on whether you do or do not get into college. Compare your career prospects depending on whether you are or are not accepted by your first-choice school. Or consider whether your life satisfaction might change if you can't enter the specialty program in which you have invested your dreams.

Now, this is not to say that not getting into a certain school or a specific program spells ultimate disaster. Not all high school students dream of becoming psychologists, engineers, or biochemists. And not every student needs to receive a degree in an advanced subject from one of the very best schools to achieve personal or career success. But to many high school students, success or failure in the admissions process does influence, to various degrees, future potential. Indeed, you do not have to look far into the future to appreciate the effect that the admissions decision will have on your everyday life. The time, energy, and money that you invest in the college application process at this point may determine, at the very least, where you are likely to live for the next four years, how you will spend your time, and who will become your friends and acquaintances over those years.

Appreciate How Much the Application Process Might Cost You

You must also appreciate the financial commitment that you are making when applying to colleges and universities. Your current dreams most likely include walking in the near future into the college of your choice as a new student. With your high school years falling away, you can fully anticipate a future with challenging academic studies, new friendships, exciting vocational preparation, and a flood of life experiences as a college student. You will live among other students from all over the nation and the world, be introduced to cutting-edge research, experience enthusiasm for college athletics, learn from intelligent instructors and professors, and engage with a variety of new social networks.

But with the dream of attending college comes the sobering reality that a college degree comes with a financial price tag. You must understand the pieces of the financial puzzle and work diligently to piece that puzzle together so the financial system benefits you. While every college maintains a unique system for providing financial aid, most colleges use a basic pattern for establishing costs; determining a student's needs; and providing scholarships, grants, loans, and other financial aid. When you understand the basic system that colleges use to assist college students in paying for college, you can begin to proactively help yourself.

First of all, the fees that you pay to take the ACT test, if you request ten score reports to be sent to schools that interest you, could be almost $100. Furthermore, colleges and universities charge application fees that typically run between $60 and $75. Assuming that you apply to ten schools, you could easily spend over $600 on application fees. In addition, you could spend at least $100 on administrative details, such as document preparation, copying, and postage. When you add approximately $400 for test preparation, you could easily be committed to a total of over $1,200 just to apply to colleges.

On top of the application expenses, you may need to send a non-refundable acceptance deposit by a certain deadline after you receive an acceptance notice. You may find yourself in the uncomfortable position of having to pay this deposit in order to ensure that you have reserved a spot at your chosen college or university even though you have not yet heard from some other schools.

These initial sums of money, however, pale in comparison to the cost of tuition, which can approach nearly $40,000 each year at private institutions (see "Tuition at Top Ranked Liberal Arts Colleges" on the next page). When the expense of room and board for four years is taken into account, for example, the expense to obtain your college degree could easily exceed $160,000. The costs accompanying a college education can be broken down into the following major components. (Your own personal needs may differ depending on your situation.)

- *Tuition*: Tuition is the cost for providing instruction and includes the expenses for professors, classrooms, equipment, learning resources, and an array of support services needed to manage and maintain a college.

- *Room and Board*: Room and board is the expense charged for living in college housing and eating meals provided by the college food service. Students may also have options to provide their own room and board through other means (e.g., renting private housing).

- *Fees*: Fees are special costs assigned for services, activities, or projects that are not covered by tuition. These fees may cover technology enhancements, laboratory needs, student activities, health services, athletic attendance, special building projects, etc. At some colleges, tuition and fees are communicated as a single cost.

- *Transportation*: Transportation costs incurred by students include traveling to or from college at the start or end of each semester, on breaks, or on holidays. Costs may also be realized when acquiring a private vehicle, insurance, maintenance, and parking.

- *Books and Supplies*: Books and supplies include required textbooks, class resources, materials, or equipment. The costs for books and supplies vary per class and academic program.

- *Incidentals:* Other costs to you as a student might include various general living expenses, health insurance, clothing, recreation, etc.

Most colleges provide a breakdown of these expenses for prospective students. Financial aid departments can communicate a detailed estimate of these various costs.

Tuition at Top Ranked Liberal Arts Colleges
(Expenses only—does not include Room and Board)*

Williams College (MA)	$39,490
Amherst College (MA)	$38,928
Swarthmore College (PA)	$37,860
Middlebury College (VT)	$50,780 (comprehensive fee)
Wellesley College (MA)	$38,062

* "Best Colleges 2010," U.S. News & World Report, http://colleges.usnews.rankingsandreviews.com/best-colleges (accessed January 11, 2010).

Do not let these numbers frighten you. We are not trying to dissuade you from pursuing a college or university degree. In fact, we applaud students who accept the challenge of obtaining a college or university education. We are simply trying to dramatize a point—namely, that the decision to apply to college has significant financial implications for you as an individual and perhaps for your family. But for many, the investment in preparing for, applying to, and studying at a college or university will be rewarded by four years of rich college experiences, deep new learning, and a great start on a rewarding career path.

Consider Your Academic, Career, and Personal Goals

Reflection

Write down some thoughts about what academic, career, and personal successes you'd like to achieve in the next 20 years of your life. Include the salary you would like to earn in the next 10 or 20 years. (Use the chart on the following page as a point of reference.)

List some ways that getting into a college or university of your choice might help you achieve these academic, career, and personal goals.

The following chart displays a range of salaries (high, average, low) for several occupations[1].

Occupation	Occupation/Salary Ranges (in USD/year)		
	25th Percentile	Median	75th Percentile
Physician (Family and General Practitioners)	$122,070	$160,530	>$166,400
Lawyer	$76,270	$113,240	>$166,400
Secondary School Teacher	$42,070	$52,200	$66,110
Librarian	$42,980	$53,710	$66,750
Registered Nurse	$52,520	$63,750	$77, 970
Technical Writer	$47,710	$62,730	$80,490
Police Patrol Officer	$40,450	$53,210	$67,990
Electrical Engineer	$65,720	$83,110	$104,060
Marketing Manager	$78,340	$110,030	$149,390
Construction Laborer	$22,700	$29,150	$39,750
Graphic Designer	$33,130	$43,180	$58,140
Customer Service Representative	$23,980	$30,290	$38,480
Administrative Assistant	$33,700	$41,650	$52,240
Accountant	$46,740	$60,340	$79,470
Human Resources Manager	$74,480	$96,550	$127,270

Note that higher paying occupations often require a college or university degree. Recent U.S. Census Bureau information indicates that individuals with a bachelor's degree earn on average almost twice as much annually as high school graduates without further education[2]. For additional salary information, visit www.salary.com or www.payscale.com.

Determine a Path toward Paying for College

Colleges expect students to pay for college using the following basic formula:

College Payment = Family Portion + Student Portion + College Aid + Federal Student Aid + State Student Aid

---

[1]Bureau of Labor Statistics. "National Cross-Industry Estimates." United States Department of Labor. http://www.bls.gov/oes/oes_dl.htm (accessed May 18, 2010).
[2]Weinberg, Daniel H. "Evidence From Census 2000 About Earnings by Detailed Occupation for Men and Women." *Census 2000 Special Reports* CENSR-15 (May 2004):3. http://www.census.gov/prod/2004pubs/censr-15.pdf (accessed May 16, 2010).

And here is a breakdown of its components:

- *Family Portion:* Colleges, often utilizing the Free Application for Federal Financial Aid (FAFSA) forms, determine each student's "Expected Family Contribution." In general, this is a calculation of how much a parent or parents are expected to pay. Among other factors, the "Expected Family Contribution" takes into consideration marital status, income levels, size of family, and current financial assets.

- *Student Portion:* A student's portion is established through a percentage calculated from his or her savings from work, gifts, or other sources.

- *College Aid:* Colleges choose to award grants, scholarships, waivers, assistantships, and work-study funding through their own endowments and financial resources. Colleges have various formulas to determine aid.

- *Federal Student Aid:* The federal government provides a number of resources for college students. Such federal student aid typically comes through grants, work-study, and loans. According to the U.S. Department of Education[3], the federal government provides more than $83 billion in these types of student aid every year to nearly 14 million students. When received from the federal government, financial aid can be used by eligible students not only for tuition, fees, books, supplies, and transportation, but also for such items as dependent child-care expenses.

- *State Student Aid:* States may offer additional financial aid to their legal residents through grants or loans. Each state varies in the type and amounts of aid offered.

The following terms often appear in the context of financial aid:

- *Grants:* Grants do not have to be repaid and are generally awarded based on financial need demonstrated by the family and/or student.

- *Scholarships:* Scholarships do not have to be repaid and are presented based on a variety of factors, including, but not limited to, accomplishments in academics, athletics, or extracurricular activities; musical or artistic talent; or leadership.

- *Loans:* Loans are funds used for education that are repaid to the lending institution, usually with interest. A "Stafford Loan" is administered by the government.

- *Employment:* College students can earn funds by working in exchange for wages. Work-study programs may be subsidized by colleges or by governmental agencies.

Here are some quick tips to assist your search for financial aid:

- Thoroughly explore the FAFSA website immediately. The website is www.fafsa.ed.gov and it contains valuable information about funding sources for college and university. See www.fafsa4caster.ed.gov to anticipate aid levels even if you are not yet applying to schools. Help in understanding the federal aid application process is also available at 1-800-4-FED-AID.

- Determine and maintain your eligibility for federal financial aid, as well as state-sponsored college aid programs. Read thoroughly the FAFSA (or state) guidelines to determine and maintain your eligibility. Among other factors, eligibility is based on the following general criteria: having a high school diploma, GED, or equivalent; being a U.S. citizen or eligible noncitizen; possessing a valid Social Security number; and complying with Selective Service registration. Review all eligibility requirements in full on the FAFSA website.

---

[3]"Funding Education Beyond High School: The Guide to Federal Student Aid 2009–10," Federal Student Aid, http://studentaid.ed.gov/students/attachments/siteresources/FundingEduBeyondHighSchool 0910.pdf (accessed April 7, 2010).

- Submit your FAFSA application and paperwork according to necessary deadlines. There are no exceptions offered by the federal government for the FAFSA application dates and deadlines. Go to www.fafsa.ed.gov to verify the submission schedule for federal aid.

- Check with your high school counselor about financial aid funded by the state in which you claim legal residency. Generally, states maintain websites that provide information about state-funded financial aid.

- Start early to search for available scholarships. Talk to your high school counseling office about scholarship options. Ask a variety of college financial aid offices for a list of scholarships or scholarship websites that they recommend. At www.federalstudentaid.ed.gov, there is a searchable index of available scholarships. Remember to search for any and all possible scholarships for which you might apply. A wide variety of scholarships are granted that target particular groups of students. The following are some general categories which you might consider when searching for a more targeted scholarship (note that this is not an exhaustive list): ethnicity, academic performance level, athletic ability, civic group affiliation, parents' employers, religious affiliation, political connection, local or regional area, gender, community service, and special talent or ability.

- Communicate and negotiate with colleges for financial aid. Directly ask about other financial aid sources if you need them. Be assertive about your own needs. Remember that college-based financial aid counselors deal with thousands of students in a short period of time, so assert yourself, voice your needs, and be persistent. If there are special circumstances in your family that affect your ability to pay for college, clearly articulate those. Depending on your need, move up the organizational chain of command to negotiate for more scholarship and grant money. You may also benefit from talking to multiple colleges.

- Remember that student loans, whether they come from the federal government, state government, or private financial institutions, must ultimately be repaid. Always read repayment information carefully when applying for student loans.

- All colleges address student financial needs and financial aid differently. As with all information in this section, check directly with each school you are considering to obtain unique and necessary information, paperwork, and deadlines for securing financial aid and scholarships.

Solve the Puzzle of How and Why Colleges Select Students for Admission

During the application process, you may for a time feel like a lab specimen placed under a microscope. Why do colleges and universities invest so much time and energy in assessing each and every student who applies? Why do schools ask so many questions, need transcripts and test scores, and require references? Why does it matter to a college or university which students are accepted to study in its programs? Why does it seem some schools open wide their doors for almost anyone to attend while others only allow a select few students to study at their institution? Some answers to these questions are simple, but others are more complex.

First, colleges and universities are selective because of their own financial needs. A college or university has to be run in the same way as any other business. It has paid employees, it owns or rents property, it operates a library, it buys furniture and office equipment, it pays utility bills, etc. As a student, your tuition and fees pay for many of these expenses. A college or university, therefore, is absolutely dependent upon a steady flow of tuition income. At the same time, most colleges and universities must limit the number of students they can allow to attend. This limit may be due to the amount of total spaces available for student housing, the quantity of classrooms on hand, or even the number of students that its board of directors allows based on various college rules and regulations. So, admissions directors make decisions about whether you will be accepted in the context of budgetary constraints. The college needs you as a student to start paying tuition and to continue paying tuition (or to have someone else—parents, a scholarship, state or federal aid, etc.—pay tuition). A college simply cannot afford to have large numbers of students dropping out of school. Therefore, one of the primary concerns of a college admissions officer is to ensure that those applicants who are accepted are committed to completing a course of study.

Second, schools worry about their reputations and how potential students might help or hinder that reputation. Colleges and universities desire future alumni who will make their school look good to others. It should not be surprising to learn that as an applicant, if you show considerable professional promise, you would be considered more favorably than others. A school that graduates successful B.A. and B.S. students gets a reputation for being a good school, and such a reputation tends to attract more highly qualified applicants.

Third, colleges and universities also want to be socially responsible to the needs of individuals and the wider society. They meet this responsibility in some fairly obvious ways, such as by actively seeking applicants from groups who are under-represented in the professional community and by establishing programs to train professionals for positions of special need.

Regardless of the various filters that schools use to evaluate potential students, the admissions process should benefit both the student and the college. The process is ideally designed to create a positive mutual relationship between students and institutions. Unfortunately, for decades, there have been more interested students than available spots at certain accredited colleges and universities. For a great number of schools, especially in specialty programs, there are actually far more applicants than available seats. Given the mismatch between the number of available seats and the number of applicants, the application process has turned into a rigorous competition.

Top Ranked Schools and Percentage of Applicants Accepted (Fall 2008)*

Harvard University	7.9%	California Institute of Technology	17.4%
Princeton University	9.9%	University of Pennsylvania	16.9%
Yale University	8.6%	Columbia University	10.0%
Massachusetts Institute of Technology	11.9%	Duke University	22.4%
Stanford University	9.5%	University of Chicago	27.9%

* "Best Colleges 2010," U.S. News & World Report, http://colleges.usnews.rankingsandreviews.com/best-colleges (accessed January 11, 2010).

With the strategies provided in this section, you will have the information to create a solid college application—that is, an application that will give a college an affirmative reason for accepting you. Each college and university is unique in its admissions criteria. No single source of information (not even this textbook) can guarantee your acceptance to the college or university of your choice. But solid information regarding the process is helpful. In addition to this student textbook, you may also want to consider some other sources. For general information about the accredited colleges in the United States, you should refer to the *College Handbook*. This book can be found in either your school's library or your local bookstore. The *College Handbook* is published by the College Board and contains summaries of approximately 3,800 two- and four-year colleges. Use this handbook for general guidance. Additionally, check out the website or request an information packet from each school in which you have even a passing interest. Read the information carefully; it will provide listings of faculty members and their qualifications, descriptions of any special programs, information about student activities and campus life, financial aid information, and much more. Email or call the admissions department if you desire additional information or have other questions.

Reflection

A. Create a list of ten colleges or universities to which you might consider applying.

    1.

    2.

    3.

    4.

    5.

    6.

    7.

    8.

    9.

    10.

B. Put a star next to each college or university that you consider to be selective (accepts fewer students than apply—use the *College Handbook* for help in this process).

C. Place a check mark next to those colleges or universities that you have a strong desire to attend. Call or email for more information about their admissions and application process.

Making the Admissions Process Work for You

There is no one single admissions process used by every college and university. Rather, each institution has its own customized admissions process, which differs from that of every other college in the country.

There are approximately 2,500 four-year colleges and universities in the U.S. We are unable to talk about the exact details of the admissions process for every school, not only because of the sheer number of institutions but because colleges and universities regard the mechanics of the decision-making process as a highly sensitive, even secretive, matter. As a result, they don't share the details of that process with outsiders. We can, however, help clarify this fuzzy process with a few important generalizations. By researching college and university admissions processes, we have discovered some patterns you can expect. You can also help yourself by researching the specific admissions policies and statistics of the schools in which you are interested. In any event, you are ultimately incapable of exercising much control over the way a college makes its decision. The good news, as you will see, is that you do not need "inside" information to create an effective application.

So, how do colleges or universities select which applicants to accept for enrollment? As a general practice, university personnel make the decision based on some combination of the following:

Selection for Admission

NUMERIC EDUCATIONAL DATA
(GPA, ACT test score, Class Rank)

+ PERSONAL ACHIEVEMENTS (academic and non-academic)
(Extracurricular Activities, Athletics, Clubs, Community Service, Jobs, etc.)

+ REFERENCES FROM KEY PEOPLE
(Teachers, Coaches, Advisors, Administrators, Employers, Clergy, etc.)

+ SPECIAL STATUS CHARACTERISTICS
(Unique Talents, Abilities, Geographical Location, Ethnicity, Socioeconomic Status, State Residency, Family Who Are Alumni, etc.)

+ GOALS AND ASPIRATIONS
(Career Goals, Dreams, or Ambitions Provided Through Personal Statement)

Don't undervalue the importance of your extracurricular activities, especially community service initiatives, in the application process. Currently, the trend indicates that schools are searching for students who have not only achieved academic success but who have balanced school with other interests and activities that have helped them become well-rounded individuals. Involvement in community service, clubs, athletics, the arts, or unique employment may help differentiate you from other students with equivalent ACT test scores and GPA.

Who ultimately makes the decision to accept you as a student? Again, colleges and universities answer this question differently. Faculty committees may be required to gather and make decisions by majority vote or unanimous agreement before an applicant is accepted. A professional admissions officer or a Dean of Admissions may make the decisions. A committee of members drawn from both administration and faculty may choose who receives an acceptance letter. Other students may even have some input into the decisions. However, we encourage you not to dwell on these different possibilities. This particular factor—who makes the decision to accept your application—is completely out of your control. Instead, focus your time and energy on what you *can* control.

In order to successfully compete with your peers, you must portray yourself as an attractive candidate; you must convince those making the admissions decision that you will help them satisfy their need for a qualified and unique student body. This persuasive approach to acceptance must be a guiding force as you create your application.

Because each college and university has a unique admission process and criteria, it is important that you communicate directly with an admission counselor at each school to which you are applying. Discuss the specifics of how the school weighs the factors listed above and what you can do to help yourself in the process.

Reflection

Your ACT test score and GPA are important (see the next section) but so are other life experiences.

Create a list of fifteen unique experiences you have had, personal qualities that you exhibit, or accomplishments you have achieved (awards, community service projects, unique international travel, employment promotions, musical or artistic accomplishments, student government or volunteer positions, etc.)

1.

2.

3.

4.

5.

6.

7.

8.

9.

10.

11.

12.

13.

14.

15.

Determine to Elevate Your ACT Test Score and Your GPA

Despite the variety of formal admissions selection processes, one generalization is significant to remember:

> *"Every college relies to some extent on an applicant's grade point average (GPA) and standardized test score, but there are few (if any) colleges that rely solely on these quantitative factors."*

This statement contains two important ideas; let us examine each of them.

First of all, most colleges do use a student's grade point average and ACT test score to help determine his or her viability as a future student. Schools do differ, though, on how they rely on these numbers. Many schools use a formula that blends the two together into what is called an index. This formula is designed to weigh the two numbers so that they give admissions officers some idea of how applicants stack up against each other.

How each college uses this type of index varies from school to school. Some schools have a fairly mechanical admissions process that places great emphasis on the index or some variation on its form. For example, a school may choose to set a minimum index below which applications receive little or no consideration. Such schools may also have a second, higher minimum that triggers an automatic acceptance. In this case, students with indices that exceed the higher minimum are accepted unless there is some glaring weakness in the application that otherwise disqualifies them. (As you prepare to apply, it would be helpful to research the ACT test score ranges of students who are typically accepted at the institutions with which you have an interest. This will help you determine whether you are already a good fit for these schools as far as test scores are concerned or whether you need to study harder in order to elevate your ACT test score.) On the other hand, there are schools that claim to minimize the importance of the ACT test and the GPA. They claim that the ACT test score is the very last factor at which they look when making decisions. Such schools tend to have a very flexible admissions process.

Most schools fall between the two ends of the spectrum. Typically, schools use the test scores and grades as a screening device to determine how much attention will be given to an application. Applications with very low test scores and grades will receive little attention. The schools reason that unless there is something obvious and compelling in the application to offset the low numbers, the applicant should be rejected. Applications with very high test scores and grades will also receive little attention. The reasoning is that unless there is something obvious and compelling in the application to reject the applicant, he or she should be accepted. Based on this theory, the applications with average test scores and grades will receive the greatest attention. These applications are provided by candidates who are at least competitive enough for that particular school but do not command an automatic acceptance. It is in this pool of candidates that competition is the most intense.

The following table illustrates what happens at most colleges. The fractions represent the total number of accepted applicants divided by the total number of applicants.

GPA	ACT TEST SCORE (Percentile)			
	61–70%	*71–80%*	*81–90%*	*91–100%*
3.75+	$\frac{2}{19}$	$\frac{49}{101}$	$\frac{102}{116}$	$\frac{72}{79}$
3.50–3.74	$\frac{6}{112}$	$\frac{75}{275}$	$\frac{301}{361}$	$\frac{120}{129}$
<3.49	$\frac{10}{160}$	$\frac{90}{601}$	$\frac{375}{666}$	$\frac{201}{250}$

The twelve categories in the table show how this particular college responded to applications with certain ACT test scores (shown in percentile terms) and GPAs. The category in the upper right-hand corner represents candidates who scored above the 90th percentile with GPAs above 3.75. The table shows that 72 of the 79 applicants who satisfy these conditions were accepted and seven were rejected.

What is obvious from the table is that some candidates with higher numbers were rejected in favor of candidates with lower numbers. For example, of those candidates with scores between the 81st and 90th percentiles, 74 more candidates were accepted with a GPA below 3.50 than were accepted with a GPA between 3.50 and 3.74.

Why would a college reject an applicant with higher numbers for one with lower numbers? The answer lies in our analysis of the admissions process. Apparently, there were factors in the applications of those who were accepted that suggested to the admissions committee that such applicants would better meet the social and economic goals of the institution. Those factors are unquantifiable—motivation, commitment, leadership, experience, and so on.

As you prepare your applications, you may already, of course, be saddled with your GPA and your ACT test score. Aside from hard work, there is nothing that you can do to change those factors. If you still have an opportunity, work hard to elevate your GPA. Besides that, the only remaining control you will have over your application will be those unquantifiable factors, and we will advise you on how to maximize their impact.

Send in Your Applications at the Right Time

There is one final point about the mechanics of the application process that you must understand: early and rolling admissions. Early admissions and rolling admissions are devices used by many colleges to regulate the release of acceptance notifications to potential students.

A typical college application season opens in October and closes in May or June. Applications from students are received throughout this season, and decisions are made on an ongoing basis with the intent of targeting an entering class. Based on its admissions history, a college will estimate the expected range of ACT test scores and GPAs of the students that it will accept in the upcoming year. Then, as it receives applications (e.g., on a monthly basis for rolling admissions or by a specific deadline for early admissions), the college or university will act on each application accordingly. Students with very strong applications compared with the target group receive acceptances; students with weak applications receive rejections. Applications in the middle may be carried over, and the applicants will receive either an application pending notification—also know as a deferral notice—or no notification at all.

The early or rolling admissions process has advantages for both the college and the applicant. From the applicant's point of view, the earlier you know the decision about an application, the better. Once you know whether you have been accepted or rejected, you can begin to make additional important decisions about your future. After you've received official notification of your admission into a school and decided to accept that offer, you can move forward in acquiring scholarships and loans, securing housing, making travel plans, looking for student employment opportunities, and scheduling personal trips and opportunities prior to leaving for college. Some students accept an early application simply to relieve the anxiety of waiting to hear from other schools. From the college's point of view, the configuration of the entering class begins to take shape as early as possible and therefore allows the university time for establishing the budget, hiring new faculty or instructors, arranging for student housing needs, and planning for student orientation.

The early or rolling admissions process is also a tool that you can use to your advantage: do apply early. Obviously, for most schools there are more seats available earlier in the admissions season rather than later. We do not mean to imply that you will be rejected if you apply late in the season. In fact, it is impossible to exactly quantify the advantage that earlier applications may have over later applications. Still, if you want to maximize your chances of acceptance, apply early. Also, be aware that if you attempting to acquire a special scholarship for a college or university, the date of admissions application and notification might be tied directly to that scholarship. You should read all scholarship information carefully with this in mind.

Reflection

From the list of colleges that you created earlier, list those schools that allow for early or rolling admissions. You may need to contact the schools directly to determine this.

Utilize a Sophisticated Approach to Determine Where to Send Applications

Given the time, energy, and financial commitment that you will be making to apply to schools, one of the most obvious questions in your mind will be, "Where should I apply?" You should apply to a group of schools that, given your financial resources, will maximize your chances of gaining admission to the schools that will best help you reach your future goals.

To apply to a college, you must send in a non-refundable application fee. Essentially, you are gambling with your money. You pay the application fee in advance of knowing whether you will win or lose (gain admission or not). So, hedge your bets. In such a "gambling" situation, a person has several choices. Some options will be long shots; other options will be almost sure things; and still other options will lie somewhere in between these two extremes. The long shots will pay handsome dividends, and the sure things will pay a reasonable return. The other options will obviously pay somewhere in between.

Given these considerations, you should select two or perhaps three "long shot" schools. As the term "long shot" implies, the odds of your being accepted to these schools are not extremely high, but the potential payoff justifies the gamble. These may be highly selective schools or ones that typically require ACT test scores and GPAs above what you have earned. On the other extreme, you should also select one or two "sure thing" schools. In this case, you may have to apply to either a school in your geographical area that does not enjoy a reputation as a standout school, a school that is located in another part of the country but is looking for students with your characteristics, or a smaller school currently in need of students. Given that you've now gambled on a few "long shot" schools and a few "sure thing" schools, the rest of your applications should go to your "good bet" schools—schools for which the chances for acceptance are 40 to 75 percent.

Now, let us assume that you have the resources to apply to ten schools and that you have both an above average GPA and an above average ACT test score. Depending on your exact GPA and ACT test numbers, you may very well have a chance at one of the top colleges. But those colleges are your "long shot" schools (colleges that are very selective). You are almost a "sure thing" at many schools (colleges that are not selective), and there is a long list of schools in the middle (colleges that are selective) at which your application will likely receive serious consideration but is not guaranteed for acceptance.

This strategy of "stacking" your applications will maximize your chances of acceptance at one of your desired schools, while minimizing your chances of not getting into any school at all. Of course, the details of this strategy will be unique for you as an individual with distinct aspirations. For students who are lucky enough to have a high GPA and a top ACT test score, the middle- and bottom-tier schools collapse into a single tier. At the other extreme, those students who have a GPA and ACT test score that are below what most schools accept will have to work with the second and third tiers.

As you prepare to implement this strategy, make a realistic assessment of your chances. Candidates unfortunately tend to overestimate the importance of what they believe to be their own interesting or unique factors. For example, we often hear candidates who make such statements as, "Well sure my GPA is a little low, but I had to work part-time while I was in school," and "I know my ACT test score is not that good, but I was a member of the high school Student Council." These points are valid and are usually taken into consideration by admissions officers. However, the most important concern is how much weight these points will be given since such statements are true of most everyone who is applying to college. For example, if you are thinking of applying to a program that requires an average GPA of 3.8 and an average ACT test score in the 90th percentile and you do not meet these requirements, then it will be difficult for you to obtain admission to that program unless your application has some other strikingly unique characteristics.

As you consider where to apply, you will probably want to know which undergraduate schools are the best in the country. Since there is no single criterion for "best school" that would be accepted by everyone, it is arguable whether this classification can be made objectively. However, even though no unequivocal classification can be made, it is possible to make an approximation as to the best schools in the nation. The "U.S. News & World Report" 2010 rankings[4] list the top 25 national universities and top 25 national liberal arts colleges. (Entries on the list may change each year, as may the rankings. This particular report is published annually, so check out the most recent one available.)

Top 25 National Universities

1. Harvard University (MA)
1. Princeton University (NJ)
3. Yale University (CT)
4. California Institute of Technology
4. Massachusetts Institute of Technology
4. Stanford University (CA)
4. University of Pennsylvania
8. Columbia University (NY)
8. University of Chicago (IL)
10. Duke University (NC)
11. Dartmouth College (NH)
12. Northwestern University (IL)
12. Washington University in St. Louis (MO)
14. Johns Hopkins University (MD)
15. Cornell University (NY)
16. Brown University (RI)
17. Emory University (GA)
17. Rice University (TX)
17. Vanderbilt University (TN)
20. University of Notre Dame (IN)
21. University of California— Berkeley
22. Carnegie Mellon University (PA)
23. Georgetown University (DC)
24. University of California—Los Angeles
25. University of Virginia

Top 25 National Liberal Arts Colleges

1. Williams College (MA)
2. Amherst College (MA)
3. Swarthmore College (PA)
4. Middlebury College (VT)
4. Wellesley College (MA)
6. Bowdoin College (ME)
6. Pomona College (CA)
8. Carleton College (MN)
8. Davidson College (NC)
10. Haverford College (PA)
11. Claremont McKenna College (CA)
11. Vassar College (NY)
13. Wesleyan University (CT)
14. Grinnell College (IA)
14. Harvey Mudd College (CA)
14. U.S. Military Academy (NY)
14. Washington and Lee University (VA)
18. Smith College (MA)
19. Colgate University (NY)
19. U.S. Naval Academy (MD)
21. Hamilton College (NY)
22. Colby College (ME)
22. Oberlin College (OH)
24. Colorado College
25. Bates College (ME)

[4]"Best Colleges 2010." U.S. News & World Report. http://colleges.usnews.rankingsandreviews.com/best-colleges (accessed January 9, 2010).

Taking the ACT Test

We have already emphasized the important role that the ACT test plays in the admissions process. Therefore, it is only common sense that you do everything you can to maximize your score. You should not take the ACT test until you are certain that you are capable of performing to the best of your abilities. Colleges receive all of your ACT test scores (not just your best score), and many colleges will average multiple scores.

You are already heading in the right direction by taking this course—we will provide you with everything you need to succeed on the ACT test. The rest is up to you. Good luck!

OVERCOMING TEST ANXIETY

Test anxiety can manifest itself in various forms—from the common occurrences of "butterflies" in the stomach, mild sweating, or nervous laughter, to the more extreme occurrences of overwhelming fear, anxiety attacks, and unmanageable worry. It is quite normal for students to experience some mild anxiety before or during testing without being greatly affected. On the other hand, more intense worry, fear, or tension can prevent students from performing successfully on standardized tests. Some experts who study human performance propose that light stress may actually help to focus a person's concentration on the task at hand. However, stress that reaches beyond minimum levels and remains for a long period of time can block a student's ability to quickly recall facts, remember strategies, analyze complex problems, and creatively approach difficult items. When taking a test, being calm and collected promotes clear and logical thinking. Therefore, a relaxed state of mind is essential to you as a test-taker. The following strategies provide practical hints and methods to help alleviate debilitating test anxiety.

Plan—Have a Study Plan and Stick to It

Putting off important test review assignments until the last minute naturally causes high stress for anyone who is seriously anxious about test day. Even the brightest student experiences nervousness when he or she walks into a test site without being fully prepared. Therefore, stress reduction methods should begin weeks or even months in advance. Prepared test-takers are more relaxed, confident, and focused, so you should begin to review materials earlier rather than later in order to reduce anxiety.

Be warned that it is almost impossible to successfully cram for standardized tests. Waiting until the day or week before the test to begin studying will only serve to elevate your anxiety level. While cramming at the last minute may have worked for you in the past with quizzes or less comprehensive tests, it will not work to prepare you for long, comprehensive, standardized tests. Such comprehensive tests require extended and intensive study methods. Trying to cram will leave you feeling frustrated, unprepared, overwhelmed, and nervous about the pending test day.

So, the key to combating test anxiety is to plan ahead so that you are not unprepared. Do not procrastinate—develop a study plan, start early, and stick to it. A study plan is a written set of daily goals that will help you track the content and the sequence of your test review. This plan will help you tell yourself what, when, where, and how much you will study. (See the "Overall Time Management" section on page 32 for a further description of how to organize your time effectively.)

By planning your work and working your plan, you can alleviate any unnecessary anxiety. Here are some tips on how to produce your study plan:

Record a Plan on Paper

A written study plan is more concrete and dependable than one that simply rattles around in your head. So, you should use a piece of paper and a pencil to write out a plan for reviewing all of the materials that are necessary to succeed on the test. Record important items and dates on your calendar (Overall Time Management), and post the study plan in a place where you will see it often (e.g., your bedroom door or your refrigerator). When you accomplish one of the goals on your plan (e.g., taking a timed practice exam or reviewing a certain number of items), designate its completion with a checkmark. This system of recording your goals will give you a sense of achievement.

Break the Test into Pieces

Standardized tests are segmented into multiple sections according to subject-area. However, you should not try to learn all of the material related to a particular subject-area in one sitting. The subject matter that is covered is far too broad to learn in a few short minutes, so you should not try to learn every test strategy at once or review the whole test in one day. Instead, you should break the test into smaller portions and then study a portion until you are confident that you can move on to another. You should also vary the sections that you study in order to ward off boredom. For example, on Monday, study a reasoning section, and on Tuesday, study the reading section.

In addition to breaking the test into smaller portions, you should always remember to review sections that you have already studied. This review will keep all of the sections fresh in your mind for test day. No two students are capable of learning at an identical rate. Some students can learn huge chunks of information at once, while other students need to review smaller amounts of information over a greater period of time. Determine the amount of material that you can comfortably and adequately cover in one day; then, attack that amount of material on each day.

For most students, the study plan is determined by the class schedule. The class schedule and sequence have been developed to help you improve your test score. So, follow the guidance of your class instructor and mold your personal study plan around the schedule.

Do Some Studying or Preparation Every Day

Yes. It is very important that you study something every single day. Once you get the "study snowball" rolling, the momentum will help you overcome the temptation to quit. Be consistent. It is far better to study sixty minutes per day for seven straight days than to study seven straight hours only once per week.

Study at the Same Time and Place

Find somewhere quiet to study, where there are few distractions, the lighting is good, and you feel comfortable. Avoid studying in bed or in a lounge chair; simulate the test conditions by studying at a desk or table. Turn off the television or the radio. Shut down the computer, unless of course you are using it as a study tool. Give yourself uninterrupted quality time to study. Find a consistent time when you can study and lock it into your schedule. Do not let yourself off the hook. Study each day at the same time and place so that you can become accustomed to your work environment.

Set Goals and Reward Yourself

Set a weekly goal for the amount of time that you will study and the amount of material that you will review. When you meet these weekly goals, reward yourself. Offer yourself special incentives that will motivate you to reach your next goal.

Find a Study Partner or Someone to Hold You Accountable for Your Progress

There really is strength in numbers. Find at least one person who will help you stay on course with your goals. Have this person ask you, every few days, whether or not you are sticking to your plan. Consider finding a "study buddy." Push each other to set and reach high test preparation goals.

Early and consistent test preparation means that you will walk calmly and confidently into the testing center on test day, knowing that you have done your very best to prepare for the test.

Prepare Positively—Replace Anxiety with Positivity

Positive thinking helps overcome test anxiety. For years, psychologists have studied how attitudes affect and alter achievement. These studies suggest that students with positive attitudes consistently score higher than students with negative attitudes.

Here are some practical ways to create a positive mindset:

Talk Positively to Yourself

Success comes in a "can," not a "cannot." So, learn to think positively by mentally replacing "cannot" with "can." Negative statements such as "I will never pass this test," "I know I can't get this," or "I'm not smart enough to get a good score," are counterproductive, and they hinder both studying and the test-taking process. In order to eliminate negative thoughts, you must first take note of them when they occur and then take steps to remove them from your mind. As soon as you recognize a negative thought, immediately replace it with a positive thought. It is quite easy. Whenever you hear phrases such as "I can't do this" or "I'm not smart enough," think to yourself, "I *can* do this," "I *will* understand this," or "I *am* smart enough." Furthermore, as you walk into the classroom on the day of the test, repeatedly say to yourself, "I have studied, I will do my best, and I will succeed."

Think Positively About Yourself

Think positively with the help of visualization. Try this: while in a relaxed mood, close your eyes and envision yourself walking into the test room, perfectly calm and confident. Now, imagine yourself taking each section of the test without any difficulty and with great calmness. See yourself answering the items quickly and correctly. Watch yourself exiting the test area with confidence because you know that you performed extremely well. With these visualization techniques, you can mentally and emotionally practice taking the test in a confident and calm manner. You can practice visualizing yourself at any time and for any given situation. Many students find that it works well close to bedtime. Coaches encourage their peak performing athletes to use daily visualization exercises in order to increase their abilities in running, jumping, shooting, etc. Every single day, from now until the test day, practice visualization and picture yourself taking the test quickly, easily, confidently, and calmly. Visualization can help you exude a positive attitude and overcome test anxiety. Get the picture?

Act Positively Toward Yourself

On the day of the test, act positively. Even if you do not "feel" completely confident, you should stride into the test site with your head held high and a bounce in your step. Show both yourself and your peers that you are at ease and in complete control of the situation. Present yourself as someone who knows that he or she will be successful. Acting confidently will actually help you feel confident.

Practice these strategies in order to instill a positive mental attitude. Positive thinking means believing in yourself. Believe that you can achieve your highest goal under any circumstances. Know that you can do it. Dare to try.

Put Away Negative Thoughts—They Fuel Test Anxiety

Since you will be practicing positive thinking, you should also learn to recognize and eliminate distorted, or twisted, thinking. Avoid thinking any of the following distorted things about yourself:

"I must always be perfect." The reality is that everyone makes mistakes. In testing situations, perfectionists mentally fuss and fume about a single mistake instead of celebrating all of the items that they answered correctly. Dwelling on

mistakes wastes time and creates more tension. Push mistakes behind you and move forward to the next set of items. Remember that we all reserve the right to learn and grow.

"I failed the last time, so I'll fail this time." Past failure does not lead to future failure. People do get better the more that they practice. Because you did poorly on something in the past does not guarantee a poor performance either this time or in the future. Use this test as an opportunity for a fresh start. Forget yesterday's failures and realize that today is a brand new beginning.

"People won't like me if I do poorly." It is preferable to have good relations with people and to have them approve of you or even to love you—but it is not necessary. You will not be unhappy unless you make yourself unhappy. Rely on self-approval, not on the approval of others. Do your best because you want to and you can, not because you want to please someone else.

"I have been anxious when taking tests before; therefore, I'll always be anxious." This twisted logic implies that you have no control over your behavior; however, that is not the case. You can change and learn to control your anxiety. It might take time and hard work to build calmness and confidence, but it is certainly within your reach.

Power Up Physically—Release Stress with Physical Exercise

Physical exercise is an excellent way to both reduce anxiety levels and cope with the effects of stress. Start a regular program of physical fitness that includes stretching and cardiovascular activities. If necessary, check with a doctor or a health professional in order to develop a customized fitness program.

Practice Being Calm—Learn to Mentally and Physically Relax

You may not realize that mental and physical relaxation play significant parts in the studying process. By setting aside time for clearing your mind and body of stress and anxiety, you will refresh your mental and physical energy reserves. Spend quality time studying and reviewing for the test. Then, spend time relaxing your mind and body so that you are re-energized for your next study session.

Practice the following relaxation exercises to calm the body and mind:

Physical Relaxation Exercise

Pick a quiet room where there are few distractions. Shut off all intrusive lights. Sit in a chair or lie down in a bed. If you wear glasses, take them off. Get comfortable, loosening any tight or binding clothing. Close your eyes, and take a deep breath. Blow out all of the air in your lungs, and then breathe in deeply. Now, focus on your tense muscles and consciously relax them. Start by focusing on your toes, your feet, and your calves. Tense and release your muscles to fully relax them. Move upward through each muscle group in your body, up to and including your facial muscles. Continue to breathe slowly, steadily, and fully during this exercise. Repeat this process, while consciously relaxing tense muscles, until you relax your entire body. Then, rest in this state for a few minutes. When you are finished, open your eyes, and remain still for another minute or two before rising.

Breathing Exercise

Deep and relaxed breathing will calm your nerves and reduce stress. Whenever you start feeling anxious, take time out to perform this simple breathing exercise. Place your hands upon your stomach and breathe in slowly and deeply through your nose, feeling your rib cage rise. Pause and hold your breath for a second, thinking to yourself, "I am calm." Release your breath slowly and fully, blowing it out through your mouth. Repeat this exercise eight to ten times. Perform this exercise whenever you feel nervous or anxious.

Mental Relaxation Exercise

Meditation, in various forms, has been practiced to allow the mind to release stressful thoughts. Many types of meditation can be learned and then practiced on a regular basis. A popular type of meditation is the passive form. Begin meditating after your body is in a relaxed state. Concentrate on something monotonous until your mind becomes quiet. You may choose to concentrate on a sound, a word, or an object. Observe your thoughts without controlling them. Gently refocus on the sound, word, or object. Passively observe your thoughts when they come, then gently refocus back upon the sound, word, or object.

Prepare—Do Not Leave Important Items Until the Last Minute

You are going to want to remain as relaxed as possible on the day of the test. In order to eliminate the last-minute, frantic rush to find that "one thing" that you cannot locate, make a list of the items that you need for the day of the test. Set out those important items the night before in order to efficiently and effectively speed you on your way toward the testing center.

Determine the Items That You Are Expected to Bring

Carefully read the test materials so that you know exactly what you should and should not bring to the test center.

Gather the Items That You Need

On the night before the test, gather all of the necessary items so that you can avoid the anxiety of trying to find them at the last minute.

Know the Directions to the Test Center

If you have not been to the test center before, make sure that you are provided with clear and specific directions as soon as possible. If you are at all confused about how to get to the test center, call the center immediately and clarify the directions.

Decide Whether to Study the Night Before the Test

Should you study the night before the test? Well, as mentioned earlier, you certainly should not attempt to cram for the test. You may want to review a few strategies, but you do not want to attempt to learn large amounts of new material. Instead, take some time to review, and then find some entertaining activity to occupy your time. Go to the gym or see a movie with friends. Laughing is always a great way to reduce stress, so you may want to find something humorous to do or watch.

Sleep Well

A good night of sleep will help reduce stress on the test day. Do not stay out late on the night before the test.

Get to the Test Site Early

Your anxiety level will increase if you arrive at the test center late. So, arrive early. Take a few minutes to relax and compose yourself. You may also need time to locate the restrooms and drinking fountains. However, do not arrive at the test center too early. Students typically get nervous and anxious when they have to wait for a long period of time with nothing to do except think about the upcoming test. So, find the balance between "too early" and "too late" that works best for you.

Watch Your Diet

What you choose to eat can be a physical cause of stress. Therefore, control your eating habits in order to maintain lower stress levels. Eat a healthy meal on the day of the test. Restrict your intake of sugar, salt, and caffeine. Remember that sugar and caffeine are found in coffee, cola, cocoa, and tea. These substances trigger a stress response in your body. High levels of sugar and caffeine are associated with nervousness, dizziness, irritability, headaches, and insomnia. Additionally, smoking has been found to decrease a person's ability to handle stress. Cigarettes act as a stimulant because of their nicotine content and will serve to increase stress levels.

Dress Comfortably

The good news is that you are going to a test, not a fashion show. So, wear comfortable clothes to the testing center; choose clothes that are not overly binding or tight. Dressing in layers is always a good idea since testing rooms are notoriously either too hot or too cold.

Pause—Release Physical and Mental Anxiety Before the Test

As already stated, relaxation allows you to focus your full attention and energy on the task at hand, rather than be distracted by tension and stress. You must release as much tension and anxiety as possible right before taking the test.

Release and Relax

Having arrived early at the test site, take the last few minutes to relax. Do not attempt to study or review at this point. Instead, use a simple relaxation technique. Close your eyes, and breathe in deeply through your nose. Hold that breath for a few seconds. Next, release that breath through your mouth. Repeat this "in-and-out" breathing cycle. Try to gradually slow the pace of the "in-and-out" motion of your breathing. Visualize yourself at a place that you find peaceful and relaxing, such as the beach, the woods, or some other favorite spot. Continue this technique for a few minutes until you feel yourself becoming relaxed and calm.

Do Some Low-Level Physical Exercise

Take a brisk walk. For many people, walking helps lower high stress levels, while positively easing the mind from worrying about the upcoming test. Others find that stretching exercises help loosen tense muscles. Just be sure to be at the testing center in time.

Massage Tension Away

While waiting for the test, sit comfortably in your chair. Notice places in your body that feel tense—generally the shoulders, neck, or back. Gently massage tense areas for a few minutes.

Press On—Concentrate on the Current Item, Not the Last or Next One

Dwelling on answers to previous items will only elevate test anxiety, so do not worry about those sections or items that you have finished.

Focus on One Item at a Time

Your task on any test is to correctly answer each item, one item at a time. Good test-takers focus only on the item with which they are currently working. Poor test-takers worry about items that they just completed or about items in the upcoming section. Try to stay "in the moment" by concentrating on one item at a time.

Proudly Depart—Walk Out with Your Head Held High

Know That You Have Done Your Best

If you have followed the strategies listed in this section, attended test preparation classes, and spent time reviewing and studying on your own, you have most likely done your very best to prepare for the test. As you walk out of the test site, remind yourself that you have indeed put forth your best effort.

Watch the Labels

After the test, never label yourself as a "failure," "loser," or "underachiever." Instead, if you do not feel that you did as well as you expected, use the experience to learn about the test and about yourself. Students are able to retake standardized tests, so reflect upon what you can do better next time, not upon how poorly you think you did this time.

Perspective—Keep Life in Perspective

Yes, the test you will take is important, but other things in life are important too. Remember that this test is a means to an end—getting into graduate school—and not the end itself.

Note: Some test-takers, even after applying all of the above strategies, still experience debilitating stress. Intense anxiety or stress that causes nausea, headaches, overwhelming emotional fears, or other severe symptoms may need special attention and care that goes beyond the strategies in these pages. If you suffer from these debilitating stress symptoms, ask your counseling office about what resources are available to help overcome severe test anxiety.

OVERALL TIME MANAGEMENT

High school students live hectic and exciting lives. In order to succeed in high school, you must learn how to manage your time, which really means that you must learn how to manage yourself by becoming a proactive student. To be proactive means to act assertively and decisively in order to prepare for upcoming events or situations. To be proactive also means to make wise decisions about how to plan the use of your time. Therefore, a proactive student is a well-prepared student.

Classes and homework take up a great deal of the day, but there are also opportunities for recreation, extracurricular activities, and personal development. While jobs, athletics, friends, clubs, concerts, and other activities may take time away from your academic life, learning to manage your time and juggle multiple responsibilities is essential for succeeding in high school. This section focuses on how to better manage your time by using such powerful tools as the *PLAN* method and pyramid scheduling.

Scheduling for Success—Have a PLAN

The *PLAN* method presents four elements for maximizing your time:

> *PRIORITIZE* tasks according to their long-term benefit.
> *LIST* those tasks according to their priority.
> *ARRANGE* those tasks on a schedule.
> *NEGOTIATE* your schedule if those tasks become overwhelming.

P...Prioritize

Though involvement in many activities is important, it is necessary to determine which of these activities are the most important. Students who *prioritize* their tasks arrange them in an optimum order that is based on level of importance: more important tasks take precedence over less important tasks. So, in order to prioritize, you need to identify activities that will benefit you most in the long run.

Different students have different priorities. While most students do not study during all of their free time, successful students generally prioritize academics over other activities. These students devote a majority of their free time to studying so that they can reinforce what they have already learned in class. In order to effectively prioritize your tasks, you must first identify your own long-term goals. With a better understanding of your goals for the future, you can more effectively prioritize your activities in the present.

Here are some questions that you should ask yourself in order to better determine your long-term goals:

- What clubs or social service organizations would I like to join?
- What sports would I like to play?
- With whom do I want to be friends?
- What type of impact would I like to have on my community?
- What special accomplishments do I want to achieve?
- What types of positive things do I want people to say about me?
- Whom do I want to impress? How will I impress them?
- What will make me a happy and fulfilled person?
- Do I want to go to college? If so, which college and what major might I choose?

- What career would I like to pursue?
- In what additional ways can I prepare for this career?

L...List

Every week, make a *list* of the tasks that you want to accomplish, placing the most important tasks at the top of your list.

A...Arrange

Each day, *arrange* all of your tasks on a daily schedule, prioritizing the most important tasks over tasks that are less important. The key to prioritization is to maintain a clear understanding of what is most important so that you can remain focused on the most significant tasks at hand.

N...Negotiate

In any given term, there are weeks that are especially busy and may prove to be overwhelming. Typically, chapter tests and final exams require considerable amounts of study time. The following are seven tips on how to better *negotiate* the details of your schedule in accordance with the potential added pressures of exam time.

1. Anticipate weeks with heavy workloads and note them on your schedule.
2. Meet with your teachers to discuss any problems that you might have with completing class work.
3. Form a study group to help prepare for tests.
4. Get plenty of rest; you will need rest and energy during stressful times.
5. Do not wait until the last week of the term to complete major projects; procrastination is unproductive.
6. Attempt to get time off from your job during the most hectic times.
7. Say no to distractions such as watching television and reading frivolous books or magazines.

Manage Your Time by Using Pyramid Scheduling

A pyramid consists of a large base, or foundation, which transitions into progressively narrower levels until finally reaching a small point at the top. In a similar fashion, pyramid scheduling begins with organizing your long-term projects and then moves on to your more immediate tasks until finally reaching your daily schedule. Purchase an annual calendar or planner so that you can schedule months, weeks, and days, approaching your scheduling process in the following manner:

Schedule the Entire Term

During the first week of each term, organize all of your major assignments and responsibilities on the calendar. After you have received a syllabus for each of your classes, reference all important dates that coincide with any of the following:

- Class assignments, such as reading selections and projects
- Tests and exams
- Quizzes
- Holidays and vacations
- Personal obligations, such as birthdays and family gatherings
- Job commitments
- Extracurricular activities, such as athletic events and student government meetings

Schedule Each Month

Two days before the beginning of each month, review your monthly schedule for all assignments, tests, and quizzes. Then, reference any important dates for monthly activities that do not already appear on your calendar, such as:

- Additional assignments
- Sporting events or concerts that you plan to attend
- Personal commitments, such as work schedule and social engagements
- Study blocks for major projects, exams, tests, or quizzes

Schedule Each Week

On Sunday night of each week, review your weekly schedule for all assignments, tests, and quizzes. Look for any personal appointments or special commitments that may be scheduled for the upcoming week. Then, on a weekly calendar, outline a schedule for that upcoming week so that you will have sufficient time for studying and completing assignments. Each day of the weekly schedule should be divided up into mornings, afternoons, and evenings so that you can reference the most important times for certain daily activities, such as:

- Classes
- Class assignments, such as reading selections and projects
- Tests and exams
- Quizzes
- Holidays and vacation days
- Personal commitments, such as work schedule and social engagements
- Employment commitments
- Extracurricular activities
- Study sessions

Schedule Each Day

On the night before each school day, create a schedule that outlines important times for the following daily activities:

- Class schedule
- Study times
- Job schedule
- Free time
- Additional appointments, tasks, or responsibilities

Finally, Remember to Stick to Your Schedule

Unless emergencies arise, stick to your schedule. Do not change your schedule unless it is absolutely necessary to accommodate and prioritize new activities. Remember that time management is really about self-management. So, remain disciplined so that you can follow your schedule without falling prey to distractions.

Successful students are able to manage themselves by learning and using valuable time management tools. If you start to use these tools now, you can be successful in high school and beyond. Always remember to schedule your work and work your schedule.

PLANNING A SCHEDULE FOR THE COURSE

The most significant aspect of an effective study plan is that it is a written plan. A written study plan is more concrete than one that you simply draw on from memory. So, when creating your plan, write out a day-by-day schedule for reviewing all of the materials that are necessary for success in the course. This written format will provide a clear and dependable guide for study. The schedule should be prioritized according to the time that you need to devote to each of the different subjects, based on the amount of time that you have.

Consider how you can plan your study time so that it corresponds with the course topics. In addition to assignments given in class, you may wish to devote extra study time to your particular areas of weakness. Use the empty calendars that follow the schedule to develop a plan of action with your teacher, determining what topics you will study each day and allotting time to study those sections of the book and complete the relevant exercises. Remember that it is not necessary for you to do everything all at once. Instead, picking a few things to focus on each week will help you to better manage your time.

Using the following empty calendars, fill in your assignments and study plan for each day. Your teacher can help you set goals for each subject.

Month 1						
Sunday	**Monday**	**Tuesday**	**Wednesday**	**Thursday**	**Friday**	**Saturday**

			Month 2			
Sunday	Monday	Tuesday	Wednesday	Thursday	Friday	Saturday

			Month 3			
Sunday	Monday	Tuesday	Wednesday	Thursday	Friday	Saturday

Month 4						
Sunday	**Monday**	**Tuesday**	**Wednesday**	**Thursday**	**Friday**	**Saturday**

Month 5						
Sunday	**Monday**	**Tuesday**	**Wednesday**	**Thursday**	**Friday**	**Saturday**

Core/Targeted Skills

Objectives:

Build a strong foundation of verbal basics in the Grammar and Mechanics, Diagramming Sentences, Vocabulary, and Reading Skills Reviews.

Practice the components of solid essay writing in the Writing Skills Review.

Review the most commonly tested math concepts in the Math Skills Review.

Recall key science concepts in the Science Skills Review.

Snapshot of Core/Targeted Skills:

The lessons and exercises in each of these chapters are designed to reinforce the core skills that you have already learned in school. Mastery of these skills will boost your performance not only in the classroom but also on the ACT®, PLAN®, or EXPLORE® test. Focus your efforts on the topics that you find the most challenging.

Grammar and Mechanics Skills Review

```
┌─────────────┐
│   COURSE    │
│   CONCEPT   │
│   OUTLINE   │
└─────────────┘
```

What You Absolutely Must Know

Parts of Speech

Nouns

A **noun** is a word that refers to any one of the following items: persons, animals, plants, objects, times, places, and ideas.

Examples:

Persons:	Bob, woman, niece, student, doctor, men, brothers, teachers
Animals:	dog, mouse, cow, cats, elephants, birds
Plants:	grass, tree, bushes, oaks
Objects:	glove, car, building, sidewalk, desks, buses
Times:	hour, 8 o'clock, Thanksgiving, Mondays, weekends
Places:	home, office, city, Puerto Rico, Poland, Africa
Ideas:	democracy, love, youth, sisterhood, dreams

Pronouns

A **pronoun** is a word that can substitute for a noun.

Examples:

Hernandez hit a home run. <u>He</u> waved to the crowd.
The woman went into the store. <u>She</u> bought a book.
My sisters live in St. Louis. <u>They</u> are coming to visit.
The bull escaped from the pasture. The farmer caught <u>him</u>.
The plant seems dry. Julie should water <u>it</u>.

Verbs

A **verb** is a word that expresses activity, change, feeling, or existence.

Examples:

The dog <u>is running</u> down the street.
The weather <u>became</u> cold.
Carl <u>worries</u> that he might not pass the test.
The letter <u>was</u> several days late.

Modifiers

A **modifier** describes a word or makes the meaning of a word more specific. There are two types of modifiers. **Adjectives** modify nouns and pronouns.

Examples:

The <u>blue</u> car ran into the <u>red</u> car.
The <u>tall</u> woman was carrying an <u>expensive</u> umbrella.

Adverbs modify verbs, adjectives, and other adverbs.

Examples:

The farmer <u>patiently</u> waited for the cows.
My house was <u>badly</u> damaged after a large branch fell on the roof in the last thunderstorm.
With a full-time job and raising a child alone, Julie felt like she was <u>almost</u> always busy.

Conjunctions

A ***conjunction*** connects (1) words, (2) phrases, or (3) clauses.

Examples:

1. John <u>and</u> Mary are organizing a walk-a-thon.
   The book is on the table <u>or</u> the counter.
   Alex speaks <u>both</u> English <u>and</u> Spanish.
   Tina can play <u>either</u> offense <u>or</u> defense.
   The cookies contain raisins, currants, <u>and</u> nuts.
   All students must take physics, chemistry, <u>or</u> biology.

2. The tomatoes are packed into jars <u>and</u> shipped to a warehouse.
   Students must enter through the main gate on Elm Street <u>or</u> the side door on Broadway.
   Skimming the trees <u>and</u> banking sharply over the shoreline, the pontoon plane made a safe landing.
   Either the newly appointed dean <u>or</u> the assistant principal will make the presentation.

3. After the storm, the clouds dissipated, <u>and</u> the sun dried the field.
   The book was returned to the library last week, <u>or</u> it is still in the lounge.
   The ant worked hard <u>while</u> the grasshopper played.
   <u>Though</u> Victoria is only 13 years old, she is already a senior.

Prepositions

A ***preposition*** establishes a relationship between an object (usually a noun phrase) and some other part of the sentence, often expressing a location in time or place.

Examples:

Patty sat <u>on</u> the chair.
Cliff gave the apples <u>to</u> Tom.
Geneva is the owner <u>of</u> the diner.
The mop is <u>in</u> the closet <u>beside</u> the broom.

Parts of Speech

DIRECTIONS: In items #1–20, identify each underlined word's part of speech. Use the following key:

      N = Noun
      V = Verb
   Pro = Pronoun
     M = Modifier
      C = Conjunction
Prep = Preposition

Answers are on page 751.

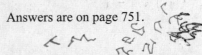

1. The taxi wove in and out of traffic as it hurried to the airport.

   taxi __N__   traffic __N__   it __Pro__

   hurried __V__   airport __N__

2. The movers unloaded the sofa and put it in the living room.

   movers __N__ unloaded __V__   and __C__

   it __Pro__   in __Pro__

3. The dark clouds completely blocked our view of the mountains and the lake.

   dark __M__   clouds __N__   blocked __V__

   our __Pro__   and __C__

4. After dinner, we cleared the dishes from the table, put them in the kitchen sink, and sat down to watch the game.

   dinner __N__   cleared __V__   table __N__

   and __C__   sat __V__

5. One room in the library was filled with books written by authors of Polish ancestry.

   room __N__   was filled __V__   with __Prep__

   authors __N__   Polish __M__

6. Some of the first television shows were adaptations of earlier radio versions of the same programs.

   first __M__   shows __N__   were __V__

   earlier __M__   programs __N__

7. When the waiter arrived, Victor ordered pie with ice cream, chocolate syrup, and a cherry.

   waiter __N__   arrived __V__   Victor __N__

   ordered __V__   and __C__

8. The building inspector finally approved the plans and allowed the construction to continue.

   inspector __N__ finally __M__   approved __V__

   and __Con__   allowed __V__

9. The superintendent notified the tenants in the building that the water would be off for two hours.

   notified __V__   in __Prep__   water __N__

   would be __V__ hours __N__

10. Just as the <u>band</u> <u>finished</u> the number, the <u>crowd</u> <u>burst</u> into <u>loud</u> applause.

band __N__   finished __PV__   crowd __N__

burst __V__   loud __N__

11. Carlos <u>called</u> Iris to tell <u>her</u> that he <u>would be</u> late for <u>their</u> <u>date</u>.

called __V__   her __Pro__   would be __V__

their __Pro__   date __N__

12. The <u>cat</u> <u>slept</u> on the windowsill in the <u>warmth</u> <u>of</u> the afternoon <u>sun</u>.

cat __N__   slept __V__   warmth __N__

of __Prep__   sun __N__

13. As the <u>train</u> <u>pulled</u> into each station, the conductor <u>called</u> out the <u>name</u> of that station <u>and</u> the name of the next station.

train __N__   pulled __V__   called __V__

name __N__   and __Con__

14. By the time <u>we</u> got to Woodstock, the <u>children</u> <u>were</u> sound asleep <u>in</u> the <u>rear</u> of the car.

we __Pro__   children __Noun__   were __V__

in __Pre__   rear __N__

15. Before <u>they</u> <u>leave</u> the camp, the guides <u>teach</u> the <u>hikers</u> how to identify poison ivy <u>and</u> warn them to avoid it.

they __Pro__   leave __V__   teach __N__

hikers __N__   and __Con__

16. Chuck <u>covered</u> the <u>steaming</u> hot pancakes with plenty of <u>melted</u> butter and sweet, <u>sticky</u> <u>syrup</u>.

covered __V__   steaming __M__   melted __M__

sticky __M__   syrup __N__

17. Last <u>weekend</u>, we <u>made</u> a <u>special</u> trip to the mountains to see the <u>brilliant</u> colors of the <u>beautiful</u> fall leaves.

weekend __N__   made __V__   special __M__

brilliant __M__   beautiful __M__

18. After that <u>eventful</u> afternoon, Art <u>wrote</u> to Cathy several times, <u>but</u> <u>his</u> letters all came back <u>unopened</u>.

eventful __M__   wrote __V__   but __Con__

his __Pro__   unopened __M__

19. Through the morning mist, we could just <u>barely</u> <u>make out</u> the headlights of the <u>bus</u> <u>as</u> <u>it</u> turned off the highway.

barely ____   make out __V__   bus __N__

as __Pro__   it __Pro Noun__

20. Our host <u>offered</u> <u>us</u> a choice of coffee <u>or</u> tea and served some little cakes, which <u>were</u> <u>delicious</u>.

offered __V__   us __Pro__   or __Pre__

were __V__   delicious __M__

Common Grammatical Errors

Note: Throughout this Grammar and Mechanics Skills Review, ✓ = correct, and ✘ = wrong.

> ## Subject-Verb Agreement

One common grammatical error is lack of agreement between subject and verb. The simplest subject-verb disagreements are usually obvious, as in the following examples:

Examples:

> The books <u>is</u> on the shelf. ✘
> The books <u>are</u> on the shelf. ✓
>
> My dog <u>eat</u> twice a day and <u>sleep</u> inside. ✘
> My dog <u>eats</u> twice a day and <u>sleeps</u> inside. ✓

In order to test your ability to spot such errors, test-writers may use one of the three following distractions:

WHAT OBSCURES SUBJECT-VERB AGREEMENT?

1. Material Inserted Between Subject and Verb

2. Inverted Sentence Structure

3. Use of Compound Subjects

Material Inserted Between Subject and Verb

Examples:

Star <u>performers</u> in the movies or on television usually <u>earns</u> substantial income from royalties. ✘

One school of thought maintains that the federal <u>deficit</u>, not exorbitant corporate profits or excessively high wages, <u>cause</u> most of the inflation we are now experiencing. ✘

A recent survey shows that a <u>household</u> in which both the wife and the husband are pursuing careers <u>stand</u> a better chance of surviving intact than one in which only the husband works. ✘

In each of these three sentences, the subject and verb do not agree: "performers...earns," "deficit...cause," and "household...stand." However, the errors may not be immediately evident because of the intervening material. In the first sentence, the subject is separated from the verb by prepositional phrases. In the second sentence, the subject and the verb are separated by a parenthetical expression. In the third sentence, a clause intervenes between the subject and the verb.

The plausibility of the incorrect verb choice, and therefore the chance that the error will go unnoticed, is strengthened when there is a word or phrase near the verb that might be mistaken for the subject: "television...earns," "profits and wages…cause," and "careers…stand." If the first word of each of these pairs had been the subject, then there would have been no failure of agreement.

Inverted Sentence Structure

A second common problem of subject-verb agreement is *inverted sentence structure*. In an inverted sentence, the verb precedes the subject. You should pay careful attention to the agreement between subject and verb, no matter how those elements are ordered.

Examples:

> Although the first amendment to the Constitution does guarantee freedom of speech, the Supreme Court has long recognized that there <u>has</u> to be some restrictions on the exercise of this right. ✗

> Jennifer must have been doubly pleased that day, for seated in the gallery to watch her receive the award <u>was</u> her brother, her parents, and her husband. ✗

In both of these sentences, the subjects and verbs do not agree. The relationships are obscured by the order in which the elements appear in the sentence—the verbs come before the subjects. These sentences should read:

> Although the first amendment to the Constitution does guarantee freedom of speech, the Supreme Court has long recognized that there <u>have</u> to be some restrictions on the exercise of this right. ✓

> Jennifer must have been doubly pleased that day, for seated in the gallery to watch her receive the award <u>were</u> her brother, her parents, and her husband. ✓

WATCH FOR INVERTED SENTENCE STRUCTURES

Regardless of the order of the sentence—subject-verb or verb-subject—the verb must always agree with its subject. If a sentence has a complex structure, it often helps to look at each element in isolation.

Use of Compound Subjects

Finally, be alert for *compound subjects*. Usually, when the subject of a sentence consists of two or more elements joined by the conjunction "and," the subject is considered plural and requires a plural verb. Consider the following example:

Example:

> Of the seven candidates, only John, Bill, and Jim <u>was</u> past office holders. ✗

The subject, "John, Bill, and Jim," is compound (joined by "and") and requires the plural verb "were"—even though the individual nouns are singular.

WATCH FOR COMPOUND SUBJECTS

Compound subjects, typically two or more subjects joined by "and," are plural and need a plural verb.

Be careful not to confuse the compound subject with the disjunctive subject. When elements of the subject are joined by "or," the verb must agree with the element nearest to it. Replacing "and" with "or" changes our previous example:

Example:

Of the seven candidates, John, Bill, or Jim is likely to win. ✓

The elements are joined by "or," so the verb must agree with "Jim," which is the element closest to the verb. Therefore, the singular "is," as in "Jim is," is correct.

Additionally, watch out for subjects that are designed to look like plural but which are actually singular. Typically, these subjects are disguised using pronouns.

Example:

Neither one of those fools even <u>know</u> how to change a light bulb. ✗

The subject is not "those fools"; instead, it is the singular subject "Neither one." Thus, the singular verb "knows" is required.

WATCH FOR DISJUNCTIVE AND SINGULAR SUBJECTS

1. If the elements of the subject are joined by "or," the subject is disjunctive. The verb must agree with the closest element of the subject.

2. Be alert for singular subjects that appear to be plural (typically pronouns).

Pronoun Usage

The rules for *pronoun usage* are summarized as follows:

PRONOUN USAGE RULES

1. A pronoun must have an antecedent (referent) to which it refers.

2. The pronoun must refer clearly to the antecedent.

3. The pronoun and antecedent must agree.

4. The pronoun must have the proper case.

Pronouns Must Have Antecedents

A *pronoun* is used as a substitute for a noun. The noun that it replaces is called the *antecedent* (referent). With the exception of certain idioms such as "It is raining," a pronoun that does not have an antecedent is used incorrectly.

Examples:

Although Glen is president of the student body, he has not yet passed his English exam, and because of it, he will not graduate with the rest of his class. ✖

The damage done by Senator Smith's opposition to the policy of equal employment is undeniable, but <u>that</u> is exactly what he attempted to do in his speech on Thursday. ✖

In the first example, what is the antecedent of "it"? It is not "he has not yet passed his English exam," because that is a complete thought, or clause, not just a noun. "It" is not a pronoun substitute for that entire thought. Rather, "it" refers to Glen's "failure" to pass the exam, thereby providing "it" with the required antecedent. However, "failure" does not appear in noun form in the sentence. In other words, "it" wants to refer to a noun, but there is no noun to function as its point of reference. The sentence must be rewritten: "because of that fact, he will not graduate…."

In the second example, "that" functions as a relative pronoun—it relates something in the first clause to the second clause. However, to what does "that" refer? Test possibilities by substituting them for "that" in the second clause. The sentence should make sense when you replace the pronoun with its antecedent. Is the antecedent "damage"?

but <u>damage</u> is exactly what he attempted to do…. ✖

Perhaps, then, the antecedent is "opposition" or "undeniable":

but <u>opposition</u> is exactly what he attempted to do…. ✖
but <u>undeniable</u> is exactly what he attempted to do…. ✖

There are no other candidates for the antecedent, so we must conclude that the use of "that" is incorrect. Most likely, what the writer intended to say was that the Senator attempted to deny the damage:

The damage done by Senator Smith's opposition to the policy of equal employment is undeniable, but he attempted to deny that damage in his speech on Thursday. ✓

+---+
| **PRONOUNS MUST HAVE ANTECEDENTS** |
| |
| Except for a few idiomatic expressions ("It" is getting |
| late, "It" will be sunny today), every pronoun must have |
| an antecedent. An antecedent must be a noun, not a thought |
| or phrase. Identify a pronoun's antecedent and then check |
| that it is correct by substituting it for the pronoun in |
| the sentence. |
+---+

Antecedents Must Be Clear

The antecedent of a pronoun must be made clear from the structure of the sentence. Consider these examples:

Examples:

Edward's father died before <u>he</u> reached his twentieth birthday, so <u>he</u> never finished his education. ✖

In 1980, the University Council voted to rescind Provision 3, <u>which</u> made it easier for some students to graduate. ✖

In the first example, it is not clear whether the father died before he reached the age of 20 or before Edward reached the age of 20. Furthermore, it is not clear whose education remained unfinished. Similarly, in the second example, the antecedent of "which" is not clear. "Which" may refer to Provision 3 or it may refer to the University Council's vote to rescind Provision 3.

WATCH FOR UNCLEAR ANTECEDENTS

The antecedent of a pronoun must be clearly identified by the structure of the sentence.

Example:

> The letter is on the desk <u>that</u> we received yesterday. ✘
> The letter <u>that</u> we received yesterday is on the desk. ✔

Finally, the impersonal use of "it," "they," and "you" tends to produce vague, wordy sentences.

Examples:

> In the manual, <u>it</u> says to make three copies. ✘
> The manual says to make three copies. ✔

> <u>They</u> predict we are in for a cold, wet winter. ✘
> The almanac predicts a cold, wet winter. ✔

Pronoun-Antecedent Agreement

The pronoun must agree with its antecedent. Consider the following example:

Example:

> Historically, the college dean was also a professor, but today <u>they</u> are usually administrators. ✘

In the example, "they" must refer to "dean," but "dean" is singular and "they" is plural. The sentence can be corrected in one of two ways: by changing the first clause to the plural or by changing the second clause to the singular.

> Historically, college deans were also professors, but today they are usually administrators. ✔
> Historically, the college dean was also a professor, but today the dean is usually an administrator. ✔

WATCH FOR PRONOUN-ANTECEDENT AGREEMENT

If the antecedent is singular, the pronoun must be singular; if the antecedent is plural, the pronoun must be plural.

Finally, it is incorrect to use different forms of the same pronoun to refer to an antecedent. This error results in the sentence having different antecedents and therefore a *shifting subject*.

Pronouns Must Have Proper Case

A pronoun must agree with its antecedent in case, number, and person. The pronoun's function in a sentence determines which case should be used. You should be familiar with the following four categories of pronoun case: nominative (or subjective), objective, and possessive.

TYPES OF PRONOUN CASE

1. *Nominative* (*subjective*) case pronouns are used as subjects of sentences.

2. *Objective* case pronouns are used as objects: direct objects, indirect objects, and objects of prepositions.

3. *Possessive* case pronouns are used to show possession. Use a possessive pronoun preceding a gerund. A gerund is the "-ing" form of a verb that is used as a noun.

The following examples illustrate correct usage of pronoun case:

Examples:

Nominative:
I thought he would like the gift we bought. ✓

Objective:
The choice for the part is between Bob and me. ✓ (The object pronoun me follows the preposition between.)

Possessive:
Do you mind my using your computer? ✓ (The possessive pronoun my precedes the gerund using.)

EXAMPLES OF PRONOUN CASE

		1st Person	2nd Person	3rd Person
Nominative	Singular:	I	you	he, she, it
Case	Plural:	we	you	they
Objective	Singular:	me	you	him, her, it
Case	Plural:	us	you	them
Possessive	Singular:	my	your	his, her, its
Case	Plural:	our	your	their

The following are additional examples of the *nominative*, or subjective, pronoun case:

Examples:

John and him were chosen. ✗
John and he were chosen. ✓ (He is the subject of the verb; we certainly would not say that him was chosen.)

It was her who was chosen. ✗
It was she who was chosen. ✓

Us student-workers decided to organize into a union. ✗
We student-workers decided to organize into a union. ✓

He is as witty as <u>her</u>. ✘
He is as witty as <u>she</u>. ✓

The following are additional examples of the *objective* pronoun case:

Examples:

They accused Tom and <u>he</u> of stealing. ✘
They accused Tom and <u>him</u> of stealing. ✓ (<u>Him</u> is the object of the verb <u>accused</u>; they accused <u>him</u>, not <u>he</u>.)

The tickets were given to Bill and <u>I</u>. ✘
The tickets were given to Bill and <u>me</u>. ✓ (<u>Me</u> is the object of <u>to</u>; the tickets were given to <u>me</u>, not to <u>I</u>.)

Finally, personal pronouns that express ownership never require an apostrophe. Also, a pronoun that precedes a gerund ("-ing" verb form used as a noun) is usually the possessive case.

Examples:

This book is <u>your's</u>, not <u>her's</u>. ✘
This book is <u>yours</u>, not <u>hers</u>. ✓

He rejoiced at <u>him</u> going to the party. ✘
He rejoiced at <u>his</u> going to the party. ✓

Some pronouns are either singular or plural, while others can be both. The structure and intended meaning of the sentence indicate whether the pronoun is singular or plural.

SINGULAR AND/OR PLURAL PRONOUNS

Singular: anybody, another, everybody, everything, somebody, something, nobody, one, anyone, everyone, someone, no one, each, every, neither, either, much

Plural: both, few, many, most, several

Singular and Plural: all, any, half, more, none, some

Technically, pronouns are divided into seven formal categories:

> ### FORMAL CATEGORIES OF PRONOUNS
>
> *Personal*:   I, we, my, mine, our, ours, me, us, you, your, yours, he, she, it, they, his, hers, its, their, theirs, him, her, them
>
> *Demonstrative*:   this, these, that, those
>
> *Indefinite*:   all, any, anything, both, each, either, one, everyone, everybody, everything, few, many, more, neither, none, somebody, someone, something
>
> *Relative*:   (subjective) who, which, that; (objective) whom, which, that; (possessive) whose
>
> *Interrogative*:   what, which, who, whom, whose
>
> *Reflexive/Intensive*:   myself, ourselves, yourself, yourselves, himself, herself, itself, themselves
>
> *Reciprocal*:   each other, one another

Adjectives versus Adverbs

Adjectives Modify Nouns; Adverbs Modify Verbs, Adjectives, and Other Adverbs

Adjectives are used to modify nouns, while **adverbs** are used to modify verbs, adjectives, or other adverbs.

Example:

> No matter how <u>quick</u> he played, Rich never beat Julie when playing the card game "Speed." ✘

In the above example, "quick" is intended to modify the speed with which Rich played cards. However, "quick" is an adjective and therefore cannot be used to modify a verb. By adding "-ly" to the end of "quick," we can transform it into an adverb and the sentence reads: "No matter how quickly he played…."

The following examples further illustrate the proper use of adjectives and adverbs:

Examples:

> *Adjectives*:
> Mr. Jackson is a <u>good</u> teacher. ✔
> He is a <u>bad</u> driver. ✔
> There has been a <u>considerable</u> change in the weather. ✔
> My sister is a <u>superb</u> dancer. ✔
> The teacher gave a <u>quick</u> explanation of the problem. ✔
> This is a <u>slow</u> exercise. ✔
>
> *Adverbs*:
> Mr. Jackson teaches <u>well</u>. ✔

He drives <u>badly</u>. ✔
The weather has changed <u>considerably</u>. ✔
My sister dances <u>superbly</u>. ✔
The teacher explained the problem <u>quickly</u>. ✔
This exercise must be done <u>slowly</u>. ✔

The following examples underscore that adjectives, not adverbs, must be used to modify nouns:

Examples:

He said that the medicine tasted <u>terribly</u>. ✘
He said that the medicine tasted <u>terrible</u>. ✔

The dog remained <u>faithfully</u> to its master until the end. ✘
The dog remained <u>faithful</u> to its master until the end. ✔

I felt <u>badly</u> about forgetting the appointment. ✘
I felt <u>bad</u> about forgetting the appointment. ✔

In each of the above, the emphasized word modifies the subject of the sentence and not the verb. The following examples underscore that adverbs, not adjectives, must be used to modify verbs and adjectives:

Examples:

He can do the job <u>easier</u> than you can. ✘
He can do the job more <u>easily</u> than you can. ✔

The problem seemed <u>exceeding</u> complex to me. ✘
The problem seemed <u>exceedingly</u> complex to me. ✔

It rained <u>steady</u> all day yesterday. ✘
It rained <u>steadily</u> all day yesterday. ✔

The professor presented an <u>obvious</u> important point in class. ✘
The professor presented an <u>obviously</u> important point in class. ✔

We all agreed that the new film was <u>real</u> funny. ✘
We all agreed that the new film was <u>really</u> funny. ✔

The students found the physics examination <u>extreme</u> difficult. ✘
The students found the physics examination <u>extremely</u> difficult. ✔

If you speak <u>firm</u>, he will listen to you. ✘
If you speak <u>firmly</u>, he will listen to you. ✔

He made <u>considerable</u> more progress than I did. ✘
He made <u>considerably</u> more progress than I did. ✔

Linking Verbs

Linking verbs are followed by adjectives, not adverbs. The following is a list of common linking verbs:

COMMON LINKING VERBS				
be	become	appear	look	seem
remain	feel	smell	sound	taste

Note that some of the verbs listed as linking verbs may sometimes function as verbs of action. The following examples illustrate this point:

Examples:

Adjectives:
I feel <u>tired</u>. ✓
He looked <u>angry</u>. ✓
The pie tastes <u>delicious</u>. ✓

Adverbs:
I felt my way <u>slowly</u> in the darkness. ✓
He looked about the room <u>angrily</u>. ✓
She tasted the pie <u>cautiously</u>. ✓

Watch for Adjectives Posing as Adverbs

WATCH FOR ADJECTIVE-ADVERB SWITCHING

Be alert for adjectives posing in place of adverbs and vice versa. Adjectives can usually be transformed into adverbs by adding "-ly." However, verbs must be modified by adverbs, not simply an adjective posing as an adverb.

Examples:

1. The girl looks <u>intelligently</u>. ✗
   The girl looks <u>intelligent</u>. ✓

2. That perfume smells <u>sweetly</u>, doesn't it? ✗
   That perfume smells <u>sweet</u>, doesn't it? ✓

3. The physician appeared <u>nervously</u> when he talked to the patient. ✗
   The physician appeared <u>nervous</u> when he talked to the patient. ✓

4. This bed seems very <u>comfortably</u>. ✗
   This bed seems very <u>comfortable</u>. ✓

5. Several people arrived too <u>lately</u> to be admitted to the performance. ✗
   Several people arrived too <u>late</u> to be admitted to the performance. ✓

   ➤ In the incorrect sentence, "lately" is not an adverb for "late." Instead, "lately" means "as of late."

6. The horse ran <u>fastly</u> enough to win the race. ✖
   The horse ran <u>fast</u> enough to win the race. ✓

   ➤ In the incorrect sentence, "fastly" is not a word.

7. The architect worked <u>hardly</u> to finish his drawings by the next day. ✖
   The architect worked <u>hard</u> to finish his drawings by the next day. ✓

   ➤ In the incorrect sentence, "hardly" is not an adverb for "hard." Instead, "hardly" means "barely."

Adjective Forms

Adjectives have three forms: the simple, the comparative, and the superlative. The simple form is used to attribute a characteristic to a noun by modifying it.

Examples:

The <u>blue</u> book is on the shelf.
The book is on the <u>top</u> shelf.

When two things are compared, the comparative form of the adjective should be used. The comparative is formed in one of two ways:

RULES FOR COMPARISONS BETWEEN TWO OBJECTS

1. Two objects can be compared by adding "-er" to the adjective.

   or

2. Two objects can be compared by placing "more" before the adjective.

Examples:

She is <u>more busier</u> than her sister. ✖
She is <u>busier</u> than her sister. ✓
She is <u>more busy</u> than her sister. ✓

Jeremy is <u>more wiser</u> than we know. ✖
Jeremy is <u>wiser</u> than we know. ✓
Jeremy is <u>more wise</u> than we know. ✓

If three or more things are being compared, the superlative form of the adjective is used. The superlative is formed in one of two ways:

> ## RULES FOR COMPARISONS AMONG THREE OR MORE OBJECTS
>
> 1. Three or more objects can be compared by adding "-est" to the adjective.
>
>   *or*
>
> 2. Three or more objects can be compared by placing "most" before the adjective.

Examples:

Mary is the <u>shorter</u> of all of her friends. ✘
Mary is the <u>shortest</u> of all of her friends. ✓

Of all the books, this one is the <u>more</u> difficult. ✘
Of all the books, this one is the <u>most</u> difficult. ✓

This is the <u>most sharpest</u> knife I have. ✘
This is the <u>sharpest</u> knife I have. ✓

Some comparative and superlative modifiers require changing the words themselves. A few of these irregular comparisons are given below. Whenever you are in doubt about the comparative forms of any adjective or adverb, consult your dictionary.

> ## MODIFIERS THAT DO CHANGE
>
> | *Positive* | *Comparative* | *Superlative* |
> |---|---|---|
> | good | better | best |
> | well | better | best |
> | bad (evil, ill) | worse | worst |
> | badly | worse | worst |
> | far | farther, further | farthest, furthest |
> | late | later, latter | latest, last |
> | little | less, lesser | least |
> | many, much | more | most |

Some adjectives and adverbs express qualities that go beyond comparison. These adjective and adverbs describe the highest degree of a given quality and, as a result, they cannot be improved. Some of these words are listed below.

> ## MODIFIERS THAT DO NOT CHANGE
>
> | | | | | |
> |---|---|---|---|---|
> | complete | horizontally | perfectly | squarely | unique |
> | correct | immortally | preferable | square | uniquely |
> | dead | infinitely | round | supreme | universally |
> | exact | perfect | secondly | totally | |

When the comparative form is used in an expression like "This thing is better than any other in the group," remember that "this thing" must be set off from the other members of the group by a word such as "other" or "else."

Example:

Our house is cooler than any house on our block. ✖

Since "our house" belongs to the group of houses on "our block," "our house" must be set off from the other houses by "other" or "else." To correct the above sentence, we could write:

Our house is cooler than any <u>other</u> house on our block. ✓

Example:

He has a better record than any salesman in our group. ✖

Again, since "he" belongs to the group of salesmen, "he" must be set off from the other salesmen by "other" or "else." So, the sentence should read:

He has a better record than any <u>other</u> salesman in our group. ✓

Finally, be aware of incomplete comparisons, which can be both illogical and confusing.

Examples:

The plays of Shakespeare are as good as Marlowe. ✖
The plays of Shakespeare are as good as <u>those</u> of Marlowe. ✓

His skill in tennis is far better than other athletes his age. ✖
His skill in tennis is far better than <u>that</u> of other athletes his age. ✓

His poetry is as exciting, if not more exciting than, the poetry of his instructor. ✖
His poetry is as exciting <u>as</u>, if not more exciting than, the poetry of his instructor. ✓

AVOID INCOMPLETE COMPARISONS

Double-check that the basis of any comparison is explicitly clear. This may include adding words such as "that" or "as" to ensure that the intended comparison is made.

Double Negatives

It is true that we all hear and sometimes say *double negatives* in daily conversation. However, double negatives are NOT acceptable in standard written English.

Example:

I <u>hadn't hardly</u> begun to understand Spanish when I had to move again. ✖

The phrase "hadn't hardly" is a double negative. The sentence should read: "I had hardly begun to understand...."

WATCH FOR DOUBLE NEGATIVES

Watch for double negatives ("not barely," "hardly nothing")—they are always incorrect.

Nouns and Noun Clauses

Nouns are names of people, places, things, or ideas; they are used to indicate the subject of a sentence. Like pronouns, nouns have a case.

TYPES OF NOUN CASE*

1. *Nominative (Subjective)* case is used when the noun is the subject of the sentence.

2. *Objective* case is used when the noun is an indirect or direct object or is the object of a preposition.

3. *Possessive* case is used when nouns are intended to show possession.

*English nouns do not change form between the nominative case and the objective case; however, because pronouns stand in for nouns and have distinct nominative and objective forms, it can be determined that nouns have cases as well.

Sometimes the place of the noun in a sentence is filled by a ***noun clause*** instead of a single noun. A noun clause is a dependent clause.

Example:

That Judy was chosen for the promotion is not surprising. ✓

The failure to properly introduce a noun clause is an error of sentence structure. "That" by itself is not the noun, nor is "Judy was chosen for the promotion" a noun. However, the two combined create a noun clause and function as the noun.

RULE FOR INTRODUCING NOUN CLAUSES

A noun clause is a group of words that functions as the subject (or another noun usage) of a sentence. "That" is often the best word to use to introduce noun clauses.

Examples:

The reason the saxophone is popular is <u>because</u> its timbre can approximate that of the human voice. ✗
The reason the saxophone is popular is <u>that</u> its timbre can approximate that of the human voice. ✓

<u>Why</u> American car manufacturers did not reduce car sizes earlier than they did is a mystery to most market experts. ✗

<u>That</u> American car manufacturers did not reduce car sizes earlier than they did is a mystery to most market experts. ✓

The above examples make the error of introducing noun clauses with "because" and "why." In both sentences, a noun clause is required; "that" should be used in both cases.

WATCH FOR "BECAUSE" AND "WHY" AS NOUN CLAUSE INTRODUCTIONS

Noun clauses must be introduced by "that," not "because" or "why."

Additionally, DO NOT use "where" for "that" in object clauses.

Example:

I saw in the bulletin <u>where</u> Mrs. Wagner's retirement was announced. ✗
I saw in the bulletin <u>that</u> Mrs. Wagner's retirement was announced. ✓

However, if the subject of the sentence actually is about where something is, then use "where."

Examples:

<u>Where</u> he went is not known now. ✓

<u>Where</u> the wedding had initially been scheduled is not where it ended up being held. ✓

All I want to know is <u>where</u> we are supposed to go for homeroom attendance. ✓

Common Grammatical Errors

DIRECTIONS: For items #1–25, circle the letter of the underlined part of the sentence containing the grammatical error. Answers are on page 751.

1. The professor deals <u>harsh</u> with students <u>who are</u>
    A   B

    <u>not prepared</u>, and <u>he is</u> even <u>more severe</u> with
    B   C   D

    those who plagiarize.

2. A recent study <u>indicates</u> that the average person
    F

    <u>ignores</u> most commercial advertising and <u>does</u>
    G   H

    <u>not buy</u> products <u>because of them</u>.
    H   J

3. <u>Despite the fact</u> that New York City is <u>one of the</u>
    A   B

    <u>most</u> densely populated areas in the world, <u>there</u>
    B   C

    <u>are</u> many parks where one can sit on a bench
    C

    under the trees and <u>you can</u> read a book.
    D

4. Charles Dickens <u>wrote</u> about the <u>horrifying</u>
    F   G

    conditions in the English boarding <u>schools that</u> he
    H

    learned about on one <u>of his</u> trips to Yorkshire.
    J

5. André Breton <u>initiated</u> the Surrealist movement
    A

    <u>with the publication</u> of a manifesto, <u>and it</u>
    B   C

    incorporated the theories of Freud <u>as well as</u> his
    D

    own.

6. The review of the concert <u>published</u> in the
    F

    morning's paper mentioned that the soloist <u>is a</u>
    G

    very promising talent and <u>that</u> the orchestra
    H

    <u>played capable</u>.
    J

7. During <u>the war</u>, there were many people in the
    A

    Polish countryside <u>that</u> sheltered <u>those</u> who <u>had</u>
    B   C   D

    <u>escaped</u> from concentration camps.
    D

8. The dean <u>lectured</u> <u>to we students</u> <u>on the privilege</u>
    F   G   H

    <u>and</u> responsibility <u>of attending</u> the university.
    H   J

9. <u>You taking the initiative</u> <u>in the negotiations</u> <u>will</u>
    A   B   C

    <u>profit</u> the company <u>to a great degree</u>.
    C   D

10. The members of the club <u>insisted that</u> <u>I be</u> the
    F   G

    representative of the organization at the

    <u>conference which</u> was something <u>I had hoped</u> to
    H   J

    avoid.

11. No one knows for sure whether there was a real
    A   B
    person about which Shakespeare wrote his
                     C   D
    sonnets.

12. Although the director of the zoo takes great pains
    F   G
    to recreate the natural habitats of the animals, few
    H
    of the exhibits is completely accurate in every
                 J
    detail.

13. Climatic differences between the north and south
    of some countries helps to account for the
       A   B   C
    differences in temperament of the inhabitants of
    C   D
    the two regions.
    D

14. The month of August was particularly cold;
                     F
    hardly no daily temperatures were recorded above
    G   H
    80 degrees, and only one was recorded above 90
                   J
    degrees.

15. The diaries of Stendhal, which make entertaining
                          A
    reading, also provides a great wealth of
    A   B
    information about musical taste and performance
              C
    practice in the last century.
            D

16. Given the evidence of the existence of a
    F
    complicated system of communication used by
                                      G
    whales, it is necessary to acknowledge its
    G   H   J
    intelligence.

17. Him being at the rally does not necessarily mean
    A   B
    that the congressman agrees with the president's
    C   D
    entire platform.

18. Although there is no perfect form of government,
    representative democracy, as it is practiced in
                           F
    America, is a system that is working well and
    F   G   H
    more than satisfactory.
    J

19. George hired a caterer, who he later
          A   B C D
    recommended, after tasting her specialty—spring
    D
    rolls.

20. After driving past Trinity Church, the bus stopped
    F   G
    at the recent constructed Exposition Tower, the
       G
    tallest building in the city, to allow the passengers
    H   J
    to take the special elevators to the observation
    J
    tower.

21. The student senate passed the resolution banning
                      A   B
    smoking in the cafeteria with scarcely any
    B   C
    dissenting votes which angered many members of
              D
    the faculty.

22. Most employers assume that one's professional
                  F
    personality and work habits are formed as a result
                              G   H
    of your early work experience.
    H J

23. Only a small number of taxi drivers fail to insure
         A   **B**

    their vehicles, but usually these are the ones who
                                        C

    need it most.
         D

24. Angered by the double standard society imposed
         F   **G**

    on women, Edna St. Vincent Millay wrote candid
    G   **H**

    about her opinions and her personal life.
    H **J**

25. Unless they hire players who are better hitters, the
           A   **B** **C**

    fans will gradually lose interest in the team
              D

    despite the fine efforts of the pitching staff.

DIRECTIONS: For items #26–41, first identify each answer choice as an adjective or an adverb by writing ADJ (adjective) or ADV (adverb) on the line that follows each choice. Then, circle the adjective or adverb that best fills the blank in the item stem. Answers are on page 751.

26. Kathy does her homework ---------.

    slow _____   (slowly) ___ ADV ___

27. We understand each other ---------.

    (really well ___ ADV ___)   real good _____

28. Students should be --------- to their professors at all times.

    (polite ___ ADJ ___)   politely _____

29. Paula has adjusted to her new school. She is doing ---------.

    good _____   well ___ ADV ___

30. I think the cake is done. It smells ---------.

    good ___ ADV ___   well _____

31. Your room is a --------- mess. Clean it up at once!

    terrible ___ ADJ ___   terribly _____

32. When I found out that the accident was my fault, I felt ---------.

    awfully _____   awful ___ ADJ ___

33. The movie we saw last night wasn't --------- exciting.

    terrible _____   (terribly ___ ADJ ___)

34. Doing a job --------- right away saves time in the long run.

    (well ___ ADV ___)   good _____

35. Cats have a developed sense of smell. They can smell ---------.

    (well ___ ADV ___)   good _____

36. "Mrs. Chang, your son works --------- in class. You can be proud of him."

    (hard ___ ADV ___)   hardly ___ ADJ ___

37. In order to deliver the package on time, the messenger biked ---------.

    (fast ___ ADJ ___)   quick _____

38. The college I will be attending in September is ---------.

    nearly _____   (near ___ ADJ ___)

39. After contracting the disease, Marc's symptoms appeared ---------.

slow _____   slowly _____

40. Doctors need to remain --------- even during an epidemic.

healthy _____   healthily _____

41. Leo's stomach felt --------- after the terrific Thanksgiving feast.

heavy _____   heavily _____

DIRECTIONS: In sentences #42–66, circle the correct verb choice. Answers are on page 752.

42. Each year, many people who did not graduate from high school (receive, receives) GED diplomas.

43. The books on the top shelf (was, were) all written by Emily Brontë.

44. The stores in the downtown sector's newly renovated mall (offer, offers) brand name fashions at reduced prices.

45. Only a few dust-covered bottles of the vintage wine (remain, remains) in the cellar.

46. Each tourist who visits the caverns (is, are) given a guidebook.

47. Underneath the leaf covering (was, were) several different species of insects.

48. The young boys, who had never before been in trouble with the law, (was, were) worried about what their parents would say.

49. Several barrels containing a highly toxic liquid (has, have) been discovered at the abandoned factory.

50. The sponsors of the arts and crafts fair (hope, hopes) that it will attract several thousand visitors.

51. Dawn, Harriet, and Gloria, who have formed their own singing group, (is, are) auditioning for jobs.

52. According to insiders, the mayor, whose administration has been rocked by several crises, (worry, worries) that more layoffs are inevitable.

53. There (has, have) been several acts of vandalism in the cemetery in recent months.

54. Rock musicians who perform in front of large speakers often (loses, lose) part of their hearing.

55. The leaves from the branches of the tree that hang over the fence (falls, fall) into the neighbor's yard.

56. The computer and the printer, which are sitting on James' desk, (has, have) never been used.

57. Theresa, wearing her hip-length waders, (was, were) fishing in the middle of the stream.

58. The film critic for the *New York Times* (write, writes) that the film is very funny and entertaining.

59. Several of the ingredients that are used in the dish (has, have) to be prepared in advance.

60. The computer that controls the temperature of the living quarters of the ship (was, were) malfunctioning.

61. There (has, have) been some support for a proposal to build a new courthouse in the center of town.

62. Bill and Jean (is, are) going to the game tomorrow.

63. There (was, were) several students absent last week.

64. I hope that no one has left (his or her, their) homework at home.

65. Each of the sisters celebrated (her, their) birthday at the Plaza.

66. The music of Verdi's operas (is, are) filled with dramatic sweep.

DIRECTIONS: For items #67–80, analyze the given sentence for grammatical errors. If an error exists, rewrite the sentence correctly. If the sentence is correct as written, write NO CHANGE. Answers are on page 753.

67. My two daughters enjoy different TV shows; the oldest watches game shows, while the youngest prefers talk shows.

My two daughters enjoy different TV shows; the older one watches game shows, while the younger one prefers talk shows.

68. Her present instructor is better of all the ones she has had so far.

Her present instructor is better than all the others she had so far

69. In the technology lab, I choose the computer with the more greater memory.

70. According to the counselor, taking these classes in this order is much beneficial than the other way around.

71. Our school is very unique in many aspects.

72. The fraternity he joined is better than all fraternities.

73. Which of these three sections is better?

74. You will receive your grades no latest than tomorrow at 2 p.m.

75. There is no need for farther negotiation.

76. She is doing so badly in her art class that she could not do any worst.

_____

_____

77. This exercise seems more difficult than all of them.

_____

_____

78. Jeff is taller than any boy in his class.

_____

_____

79. The heroine was unbelievable naive.

_____

_____

80. Drive carefully. There may be ice on the roads.

_____

_____

Analyzing Sentence Structure

When analyzing the structure of a sentence, ask yourself the following five questions:

CHECKLIST FOR ANALYZING SENTENCE STRUCTURE

1. Is the word group a complete sentence?

2. Is the sentence a run-on sentence?

3. Are the elements of the sentence parallel?

4. Are there any incomplete split constructions?

5. Do the verb tenses correctly reflect the sequence of events?

Sentence Fragments

A **sentence fragment** is a group of words that begins with a capital letter and ends with a period. A fragment looks like a sentence but really isn't because it lacks a main verb. Therefore, a fragment is a word grouping but not a complete thought.

Examples:

1. The regulation permitting camping in the state forest but not within 100 feet of a lake or stream. ✘
   The regulation permits camping in the state forest but not within 100 feet of a lake or a stream. ✓

   ➤ In the incorrect sentence, "permitting" is not a main verb.

2. Flights leaving the west coast and the Midwest were delayed. Because of severe thunderstorms in the east. ✘
   Flights leaving the west coast and the Midwest were delayed because of severe thunderstorms in the east. ✓

   ➤ In the incorrect sentence, "because" introduces a dependent, not an independent, clause. In the corrected sentence, the fragment is joined as a dependent clause to a proper independent clause.

3. While the carpenter finished framing the door, and the locksmith installed the hardware. ✘
   The carpenter finished framing the door, and the locksmith installed the hardware. ✓

   ➤ In the incorrect sentence, "while" makes the word group a dependent clause. In the corrected sentence, eliminating the "while" lets the word group stand as two independent clauses, each with its own main verb.

If you are editing your own work and find that you have written a sentence fragment, you have a lot of flexibility in how you eliminate the error. However, on a multiple-choice test, your options are limited. Typically, you have three choices for fixing a sentence fragment:

> ### METHODS FOR FIXING SENTENCE FRAGMENTS
>
> 1. Change a verb form so that it becomes a main verb.
>
> 2. Combine the fragment with a true independent clause (sentence).
>
> 3. Convert a dependent clause into an independent clause.

Run-on Sentences

Be aware of sentences that carelessly run main clauses together without appropriate punctuation or connectors. ***Run-on sentences*** can be corrected in one of three ways: "end-stop" punctuation, a semicolon, or a connector.

The most common way to correct a run-on sentence is to divide the sentence using "end-stop" punctuation.

Examples:

> The lecture was dull you almost fell asleep. ✗
> The lecture was dull. You almost fell asleep. ✓
>
> Was the lecture dull you almost fell asleep. ✗
> Was the lecture dull? You almost fell asleep. ✓
>
> The lecture was incredibly dull you almost fell asleep. ✗
> The lecture was incredibly dull! You almost fell asleep. ✓

The comma is not an end-mark. DO NOT use a comma by itself to separate two sentences.

Example:

> Close the window, there is a draft in the room. ✗
> Close the window. There is a draft in the room. ✓

Sometimes, two sentences are very closely related in meaning, and full "end-stop" punctuation may seem too strong. A semicolon can then be used to divide the two sentences.

Example:

> It was a beautiful day there was not a cloud in the sky. ✗
> It was a beautiful day; there was not a cloud in the sky. ✓

A third way to correct the run-on is to use a connector (conjunction) such as "and," "but," "for," "or," and "nor" if the two sentences are equally important. It is usually advisable to place a comma before these connectors.

Example:

> I like to ski, my friend prefers to sit by the fire. ✗
> I like to ski, but my friend prefers to sit by the fire. ✓

Particular problem words that may cause run-ons are "however," "therefore," "consequently," and "moreover." These words are not sentence connectors, and when they follow a complete thought, either a period or a semicolon should precede them.

Example:

> Many asteroids are far away therefore they appear dim and are difficult to see. ✗
> Many asteroids are far away. Therefore, they appear dim and are difficult to see. ✓
> Many asteroids are far away; therefore, they appear dim and are difficult to see. ✓

Faulty Parallelism

Faulty parallelism is a common grammatical error. Whenever elements of a sentence perform similar or equal functions, they should have the same form. Consider the following faulty sentences; they are missing necessary words:

Examples:

> At most colleges, the dominant attitude among students is that gaining admission to professional graduate school is more important than <u>to obtain</u> a well-rounded education. ✗

> To demand that additional seasonings be placed on the table is <u>insulting</u> the chef's judgment on the proper balance of ingredients. ✗

> The review was critical of the film, citing the poor photography, the weak plot, and the dialogue <u>was stilted</u>. ✗

In the first example, "gaining admission" and "to obtain" must both have the same form. Either both must be in the gerund form or both must be in the infinitive form. For example: "gaining admission…is more important than obtaining…."

In the second example, the subject ("to demand") and the predicate complement ("insulting") must both have the same form: "To demand…is to insult…."

In the last example, the last element of the list of film criticisms is not of the same form as the other two elements. The sentence should read: "…citing the poor photography, the weak plot, and the stilted dialogue."

CHECK THAT ALL ELEMENTS OF A SENTENCE ARE PARALLEL

Check that all elements of a sentence are parallel—including verb forms, noun forms, and word pairs such as "this…that," "either…or," and "neither…nor."

Examples:

> He spends his time playing cards, swimming, going to the theater, and at school. ✗
> He spends his time playing cards, swimming, going to the theater, and <u>going to</u> school. ✓

> He manages his business affairs with knowledge, ease, and confidently. ✗
> He manages his business affairs with knowledge, ease, and <u>confidence</u>. ✓

He was required by the instructor to go to the library, to take out several books on the Vietnam War, and that he should report to the class on what he had learned. ✘
He was required by the instructor to go to the library, to take out several books on the Vietnam War, and <u>to report</u> to the class on what he had learned. ✓

I am studying the sources of educational theory and how educational theory has evolved. ✘
I am studying the sources and <u>the evolution</u> of educational theory. ✓

He was not only sympathetic but also knew when to be considerate. ✘
He was not only sympathetic but also <u>considerate</u>. ✓

Not only did he enjoy the movie but also the play. ✘
<u>He enjoyed</u> not only the movie but also the play. ✓

I was concerned about the price of the car and if it was comfortable. ✘
I was concerned about the price and <u>the comfort</u> of the car. ✓

Neither does he speak Spanish nor Helen. ✘
Neither he nor Helen <u>speaks</u> Spanish. ✓

Incomplete Split Constructions

Split constructions refer to phrases in which a thought, interrupted by intervening material, is completed later in the sentence.

Example:

The officials were not only aware of, but actually encouraged, the misreporting of scores. ✓

This sentence contains a perfectly acceptable split construction. Ordinarily, the object of a preposition closely follows the preposition: "aware of the misreporting." Here, the object of the preposition is separated from the preposition by the phrase "but actually encouraged." This is unobjectionable as long as the thought is properly completed. There is a danger, however, that the intervening material will throw something off in the sentence.

CHECK THAT SPLIT CONSTRUCTIONS ARE COMPLETED

A split construction is a sentence structure in which two otherwise separate ideas are joined together by a later element. Be alert for split constructions and check that any interrupted thought is correctly completed.

Consider the following faulty sentences; they are incomplete split constructions:

Examples:

Her colleagues always speak of Professor Collins as a person who has and will always be sensitive to the needs of younger students. ✘

Judging from the pricing policies of many large corporations, maintaining a stable share of the market is as important, if not more important than, making a large profit. ✘

In the first sentence, the error is in the verb. The auxiliary verb "has" needs the verb "been," but "been" does not appear in the sentence. The sentence could be corrected by completing the construction: "...has been and will always be...." In the second sentence, the error is an incomplete comparison. The sentence should read: "...as important as, if not more important than...."

RULE FOR CHECKING FOR SPLIT CONSTRUCTIONS

The intervening material makes it difficult to spot errors of split construction. Therefore, when checking for split constructions, read the sentence without the intervening material—it should make sense, be grammatically correct, and be a complete sentence.

Examples:

George Washington <u>always has</u> and always will be <u>regarded</u> as the father of this country. ✘
George Washington <u>always has been</u> and always will be <u>regarded</u> as the father of this country. ✓

The smaller stone is just <u>as valuable</u>, and perhaps even more valuable than, <u>the larger stone</u>. ✘
The smaller stone is just <u>as valuable as</u>, and perhaps even more valuable than, <u>the larger stone</u>. ✓

Most television crime shows <u>are aimed</u> and appeal to <u>adults</u> over the age of 30. ✘
Most television crime shows <u>are aimed at</u> and appeal to <u>adults</u> over the age of 30. ✓

Verb Forms

Principal Parts of Verbs

The ***principal parts*** of verbs are the infinitive or present tense, the past tense, and the past participle. Most verbs are called regular verbs because the past tense and the past participle are formed by adding "-d" or "-ed" to the infinitive or present tense form:

Examples:

Present Tense:
borrow, dare, guard, miss, staple

Past Tense:
borrowed, dared, guarded, missed, stapled

Past Participle:
borrowed, dared, guarded, missed, stapled

Some verbs, however, do not follow the usual rule. They are called irregular verbs.

PRINCIPAL PARTS OF COMMON IRREGULAR VERBS

Present	Past	Past Participle	Present	Past	Past Participle
arise	arose	arisen	lead	led	led
be	was, were	been	leave	left	left
bear	bore	borne	lend	lent	lent
become	became	become	lie	lay	lain
begin	began	begun	light	lit, lighted	lit, lighted
bid	bade	bid, bidden	lose	lost	lost
blow	blew	blown	make	made	made
break	broke	broken	meet	met	met
bring	brought	brought	read	read	read
build	built	built	ride	rode	ridden
buy	bought	bought	ring	rang	rung
catch	caught	caught	rise	rose	risen
choose	chose	chosen	run	ran	run
cling	clung	clung	see	saw	seen
come	came	come	send	sent	sent
cut	cut	cut	sew	sewed	sewn
do	did	done	shake	shook	shaken
draw	drew	drawn	sit	sat	sat
drink	drank	drunk	shoot	shot	shot
drive	drove	driven	shrink	shrank, shrunk	shrunk, shrunken
eat	ate	eaten	slay	slew	slain
fall	fell	fallen	sleep	slept	slept
feed	fed	fed	slide	slid	slid
feel	felt	felt	speak	spoke	spoken
fight	fought	fought	spend	spent	spent
find	found	found	spin	spun	spun
flee	fled	fled	spring	sprang, sprung	sprung
fling	flung	flung	stand	stood	stood
fly	flew	flown	steal	stole	stolen
forget	forgot	forgotten	sting	stung	stung
forgive	forgave	forgiven	swear	swore	sworn
freeze	froze	frozen	swing	swung	swung
get	got	gotten	swim	swam	swum
give	gave	given	take	took	taken
go	went	gone	teach	taught	taught
grow	grew	grown	tear	tore	torn
hang (a person)	hanged	hanged	tell	told	told
hang (an object)	hung	hung	think	thought	thought
hear	heard	heard	throw	threw	thrown
hide	hid	hidden	wake	waked, woke	waked, woken
hold	held	held	wear	wore	worn
hurt	hurt	hurt	weave	weaved, wove	woven
keep	kept	kept	win	won	won
know	knew	known	wring	wrung	wrung
lay	laid	laid	write	wrote	written

Present, Past, and Future Tense

The tense of a verb indicates whether the action or condition described by the verb belongs to the present, to the past, or to the future.

Examples:

> *Present Tense:*
> deliver, learn, open, respond
>
> *Past Tense:*
> delivered, learned, opened, responded
>
> *Future Tense:*
> will deliver, will learn, will open, will respond

A problem of logical expression is poor choice of verb tense. The ***verb tenses*** in a correctly written sentence accurately reflect the ***sequence*** and/or ***logic*** of events described. The following examples contain verb tense errors:

Examples:

> As soon as Linda finished writing her dissertation, she <u>will take</u> a well-earned vacation in Paris. ✘
>
> A recent study shows that many mothers re-enter the labor force after their children <u>left</u> home. ✘

The first sentence is incorrect because the initial verb phrase ("As soon as Linda finished") describes an action that was entirely completed in the past; however, the subsequent verb phrase ("she will take") makes it sound as if that first action had not been completed and was instead on-going. Depending on whether Linda has already completed the dissertation, the sentence could be corrected in one of two ways:

> As soon as Linda <u>finishes</u> writing her dissertation, she will take a well-earned vacation in Paris. ✓
> As soon as Linda finished writing her dissertation, she <u>took</u> a well-earned vacation in Paris. ✓

The first corrected version states that neither event has yet occurred and that the writing will precede the vacation. The second corrected version states that both events are completed and that the writing preceded the vacation.

In the second sentence above, the verb "left" is incorrect because the verb "re-enter" describes a present, on-going action. The sentence can be corrected by making it clear that "children leaving home" is also a present, on-going phenomenon:

> A recent study shows that many mothers re-enter the labor force after their children <u>leave</u> home. ✓
> A recent study shows that many mothers re-enter the labor force after their children <u>have left</u> home. ✓

Either sentence is acceptable since both make it clear that leaving home is not a completed past action but an ongoing phenomenon.

WATCH FOR SHIFTING VERB TENSES

Make sure that verb tenses properly reflect the sequence, as well as the duration, of any action described in the sentence.

Examples:

> Charles came to town last week and <u>goes</u> to a resort where he <u>rests</u> for three days. ✘
> Charles came to town last week and <u>went</u> to a resort where he <u>rested</u> for three days. ✓

Joan came home last week and <u>goes</u> to her summer cottage where she <u>spends</u> the last weekend of her vacation. ✗
Joan came home last week and <u>went</u> to her summer cottage where she <u>spent</u> the last weekend of her vacation. ✓

The Perfect Tenses

Use the ***present perfect*** for an action begun in the past and extended to the present.

Example:

I am glad you are here at last; <u>I have waited</u> an hour for you to arrive. ✓

In this case, "I waited" would be incorrect. The action "have waited" (present perfect) began in the past and extended to the present.

Use the ***past perfect*** for an action begun and completed in the past before some other past action.

Example:

The foreman asked what <u>had happened</u> to my eye. ✓

In this case, "happened" would be incorrect. The action "asked" and the action "had happened" (past perfect) are used because one action (regarding the speaker's eye) is "more past" than the other action (the foreman's asking).

Use the ***future perfect*** for an action begun at any time and completed in the future. When there are two future actions, the action completed first is expressed in the future perfect tense.

Example:

When I reach Chicago tonight, my uncle <u>will have left</u> for Los Angeles. ✓

The action "will have left" is going to take place before the action "reach," although both actions will occur in the future.

The Subjunctive Mood

The ***subjunctive*** is used to express a wish, a command, a supposition, or a condition that is contrary to fact. The subjunctive is very important in other languages, but only a few remnants survive in English. The most important forms of the subjunctive are the use of "were" in place of "was" and the use of "be" in place of "am" in clauses requiring the subjunctive.

Example:

I wish that I <u>were</u> on a tropical island lying on the beach. ✓

In this sentence, "were" is used rather than "was" in order express the subjunctive (contrary to fact) idea that the speaker is not lying on the beach of a tropical island.

Example:

The teacher required that all reports <u>be</u> typed. ✓

In this example "be" is used rather than "are" because the teachers wishes or commands that the reports be typed.

EXERCISE 3

Analyzing Sentence Structure

DIRECTIONS: For items #1–28, choose the verb form that completes the sentence correctly. Answers are on page 754.

1. A gentleman is _____ to see you.

   A. comes
   B. came
   C. come
   D. coming
   E. will come

2. Bill was _____ to telephone you last night.

   F. to suppose
   G. supposed
   H. suppose
   J. supposing
   K. will suppose

3. My friend has _____ to get impatient.

   A. to begin
   B. began
   C. begin
   D. beginning
   E. begun

4. He has _____ a serious cold.

   F. catched
   G. caught
   H. catch
   J. catching
   K. will catch

5. He could _____ before large groups if he were asked.

   A. sing
   B. sang
   C. sung
   D. singed
   E. singing

6. She has _____ before large groups several times.

   F. sing
   G. sang
   H. sung
   J. singed
   K. singing

7. They have already _____ to the theater.

   A. go
   B. goes
   C. going
   D. gone
   E. will go

8. He has _____ me excellent advice.

   F. give
   G. gave
   H. gived
   J. giving
   K. given

9. He is _____ to his parents.

   A. to devote
   B. devote
   C. devoted
   D. devoting
   E. will devote

10. The engineer has designed and _____ his own home.

    F. to build
    G. builds
    H. building
    J. built
    K. had built

11. He _____ as he ran onto the stage following the clown and the magician.

    A. to laugh
    B. laughing
    C. laughed
    D. laughs
    E. had laughed

12. She _____ the high-jump so well at trials that she is going to the Olympics this summer.

    F. had jumped
    G. to jump
    H. jumping
    J. jumps
    K. jumped

13. It _____ that she continued to blame me even after she knew it wasn't my fault.

    A. hurt
    B. hurts
    C. has hurt
    D. hurting
    E. will hurt

14. The man _____ the murder occur if he had really been on that street corner when he said he was.

    F. see
    G. sees
    H. would have saw
    J. seen
    K. would have seen

15. The child _____ everywhere now that she is able to stand up by herself.

    A. to walk
    B. walks
    C. walked
    D. walking
    E. had walked

16. Tomorrow morning, Sam _____ his sister.

    F. was calling
    G. called
    H. calling
    J. has called
    K. will call

17. After she had completed her investigation, the state trooper _____ her report.

    A. was writing
    B. wrote
    C. has written
    D. writes
    E. will write

18. When I was growing up, we _____ every summer at my grandmother's home in the country.

    F. spend
    G. will spend
    H. have spent
    J. were spending
    K. spent

19. Whenever we get a craving for a late night snack, we _____ a pizza.

    A. order
    B. ordered
    C. had ordered
    D. have ordered
    E. were ordering

20. For years now, John _____ his milk at the corner grocery.

    F. buys
    G. will buy
    H. has bought
    J. is buying
    K. bought

21. We were just leaving when the telephone _____.

    A. rang
    B. will ring
    C. was ringing
    D. has rung
    E. had rung

22. We arrived at the house by noon, but the wedding _____ over.

    F. is
    G. will be
    H. had been
    J. has been
    K. was

23. We _____ to drive to the game, but the car stalled.

    A. plan
    B. will plan
    C. had planned
    D. are planning
    E. have planned

24. The roofers were putting the last shingles on the house while the plumber _____ the water lines.

    F. is testing
    G. was testing
    H. tests
    J. will test
    K. had tested

25. A large flock of Canadian Geese _____ over the meadow and landed in the pond.

    A. will fly
    B. were flying
    C. fly
    D. flew
    E. are flying

26. Hui worked very hard to complete her course-work before the baby _____ due.

    F. is
    G. are
    H. was
    J. will be
    K. were

27. We _____ to drive from Wisconsin to Washington in two days, but we were late.

    A. want
    B. are wanting
    C. were wanted
    D. wants
    E. had wanted

28. Earl and I _____ to eat lunch together outside if it doesn't rain.

    F. will hope
    G. had hoped
    H. hope
    J. did hope
    K. hoped

DIRECTIONS: For items #29–52, circle the letter of the underlined part of the sentence containing the error. Answers are on page 754.

29. The owner of the collection <u>requested that</u> the
                                        A

    museum <u>require</u> <u>all people with a camera</u> <u>to leave</u>
              B   C   D

    them at the door.

30. The young comic found that capturing the
    F
    audience's attention was easy, but to maintain
                                    G
    their interest was difficult.
    H   J

31. The whale had been laying on the beach for over
                        A
    two hours before the rescue teams were able to
                                      B
    begin moving it back into the water.
    B   C   D

32. The praying mantis is welcomed by homeowners
                       F
    for its ability to control destructive garden pests,
       G   H
    unlike the cockroach, which serves no useful
                           J
    function.
    J

33. The newly purchased picture was hanged on the
        A   B   C
    back wall nearest the bay window.
              D

34. The opening scene of the film was a grainy,
        F   G
    black-and-white shot of an empty town square in
         G   H
    which an outlaw was hung.
    H   J

35. We spent an exhausting day shopping we could
    A   B   C
    hardly wait to get home.
    C   D

36. The fact that she is bright, articulate, and has
                                                 F
    charisma will serve her well in her campaign for
    F   G
    governor, particularly since her opponent has
              H   J
    none of those qualities.
    J

37. Puritans such as William Bradford displaying the
                                       A
    courage and piety needed to survive in the New
                       B
    World, a world both promising and threatening,
                   C
    which offered unique challenges to their faith.
    D

38. The woman to whom I take my clothes for
                 F   G
    tailoring has sewed the hem on this skirt
    G   H
    perfectly.
    J

39. Unfortunately, before cures are found for diseases
                   A
    such as cancer, many lives would have been lost
                                B
    and million of dollars in medical services spent to
                                                C
    treat symptoms rather than to provide a cure.
                   D

40. The house on the corner was completely empty,
        F   G   H
    no one came to the door.
    H   J

41. For many people, it is difficult to accept
                                  A
    compliments graciously and even more difficult
                                B
    taking criticism graciously.
    C   D

42. <u>Due</u> to the <u>extremely warm</u> weather this winter,
    F   G

the water has not <u>froze</u> on the pond <u>sufficiently</u>.
    H   J

43. The French poet Artaud <u>believed</u> <u>that</u>, <u>following</u>
    A   B   C

the climax of a drama, the audience <u>experienced</u> a
    D

violent catharsis and is thereby "reborn."

44. <u>Where</u> had <u>everyone</u> <u>gone all</u> the lights were <u>off</u>.
    F   G   H   J

45. <u>Rather</u> than <u>declaring</u> bankruptcy, he <u>applied</u> for
    A   B   C

a loan, and the bank <u>loaned</u> him the money.
    D

46. <u>Wagering</u> on the Kentucky Derby favorite <u>is</u> a
    F   G

bad <u>betting</u> proposition, for in the last fifteen
    H

years, the horse that has been the crowd favorite

at post time of the Kentucky Derby <u>loses</u> the race.
    J

47. We entered the cave <u>very</u> <u>slowly</u> <u>almost</u> afraid of
    A   B

what we <u>might find</u> <u>there</u>.
    C   D

48. After he <u>had learned of</u> her suicide, he <u>drunk</u> all
    F   G   H

of the poison <u>from the vial</u>.
    J

49. <u>During the years</u> she spent <u>searching for a cure</u>
    A   B

for the disease, Dr. Thompson interviewed

hundreds of patients, ran thousands of tests, and

<u>cross-checking</u> <u>millions of bits of data</u>.
    C   D

50. <u>After struggling with the problem</u> for most of the
    F

afternoon, he finally <u>flinged</u> the papers <u>on</u> the
    G   H

desk and <u>ran out of the room</u>.
    J

51. <u>Suddenly</u>, I felt that something <u>was going to</u>
    A   B

<u>happen my</u> heart began to <u>beat furiously</u>.
    C   D

52. <u>Early in his career</u>, the pianist entertained
    F

thoughts <u>of becoming</u> a composer; but after
    G

receiving bad reviews for his own work, <u>he had</u>
    H J

<u>given up</u>.
    J

DIRECTIONS: For items #53–57, analyze the given sentence for sentence fragment errors. If an error exists, choose the answer choice that best corrects the error. If the sentence is correct as written, choose (A). Answers are on page 754.

53. <u>During the time that I was in the hospital. I read</u> every one of the Sherlock Holmes stories.

  A. NO CHANGE
  B. During the time that I was in the hospital, reading
  C. During the time that I was in the hospital, I read
  D. During the time of being in the hospital. I read
  E. Being in the hospital during the time reading

54. A city ordinance <u>prohibiting the construction of any structure that is</u> taller than the statue of Minerva, the Roman Goddess of Wisdom, on the dome of City Hall.

   F. NO CHANGE
   G. which prohibits the construction of any structure that is
   H. that prohibits the construction of any structure that is
   J. prohibits the construction of any structure that is
   K. prohibiting the construction of any structure being

55. Because the low-lying land was very <u>marshy and the construction of a complex system of drainage ditches was</u> necessary before construction could begin.

   A. NO CHANGE
   B. marshy and the construction of a complex system of drainage ditches being
   C. marshy with the construction of a complex system of drainage ditches
   D. marshy, the construction of a complex system of drainage ditches being
   E. marshy, the construction of a complex system of drainage ditches was

56. The loud noise from the overly sensitive alarm on the car <u>parked in front of the building making</u> it difficult for the audience to understand the speaker.

   F. NO CHANGE
   G. that was parked in front of the building making
   H. which parked in front of the building making
   J. parked in front of the building made
   K. parked in front of the building to make

57. <u>Calling Wyoming the "Equality State," and</u> women were permitted to vote in the territory as early as 1869.

   A. NO CHANGE
   B. Called Wyoming the "Equality State," and
   C. Calling Wyoming the "Equality State, because
   D. Wyoming is called the "Equality State," because
   E. The "Equality State" being the name of Wyoming,

DIRECTIONS: For items #58–75, analyze the given sentence for sentence structure errors. If an error exists, rewrite the sentence correctly. If the sentence is correct as written, write NO CHANGE. Answers are on page 754.

58. When at school, he studies, goes to the library, and he works on the computer.

   _____ No Change

   _____

   _____

59. In order to get eight hours of sleep, the student prefers sleeping in late in the morning to go to bed early in the evening.

   _____

   _____

   _____

60. He could not deliver the supplies. Because the roads had not yet been plowed.

   _____ He could not deliver

   _____ The supplies Because the

   _____ road had not been

   _____ plowed yet.

61. I still need to pass Math 252, English 301, and return two overdue books before I am allowed to graduate.

_____

_____

_____

62. You need to talk to either the teacher or the counselor.

_____

_____

_____

63. Our instructor suggested that we study the assignment carefully, go to the library to research the topic extensively, and we should conduct a survey among 20 subjects.

_____

_____

_____

64. The increase of attrition among community college students is caused by a lack of family support and students have a limited income while attending school.

_____

_____

_____

65. Many non-smokers complained about the health risks associated with second-hand smoke; as a result, smoking is banned in the library, in the cafeteria, and smokers have to leave the building to light a cigarette.

_____

_____

_____

66. Dr. Smydra is not only a captivating lecturer but also an engaging conversationalist.

_____

_____

_____

67. After talking to financial aid and see your advisor, return to the registrar's office.

_____

_____

_____

68. Professor Walker not only helped me, but many of my classmates as well.

_____

_____

_____

69. In his communications class, he can either work in groups or in pairs.

_____

_____

_____

70. I prefer that other geography textbook because of the clear explanations, numerous exercises, and Mrs. Patrick's vivid teaching style.

_____

_____

_____

71. The question is whether to study tonight or should I get up earlier tomorrow morning?

_____

_____

_____

72. I will either graduate this fall or lose out on a great opportunity with IBM.

I will either graduate this fall or lose out on a great opportunity with IBM.

73. Reasons for the latest tuition increase are the upgraded computers, new library and, last but not least, inflation has increased to 6.5 percent.

_____

_____

_____

74. If you want to succeed, one must be willing to work hard.

_____

_____

75. She likes tennis, golf, and to go swimming.

_____

_____

Problems of Logical Expression

Faulty or Illogical Comparisons

One problem of logical expression is faulty or illogical comparisons. A faulty comparison is the attempt to compare two things that cannot logically be compared. Consider the following faulty examples:

Examples:

> Today, life expectancies of both men and women are much higher compared to the turn of the century when living conditions were much harsher. ✘

> The average salary of a professional basketball player is higher than the top-level management of most corporations. ✘

A comparison can only be made between like or similar items. Yet, in the first sentence, we see an attempt to compare "life expectancies" with "the turn of the century"—two dissimilar concepts. The sentence can be corrected simply by adding "life expectancies at" before "the turn of the century." Now we have life expectancies compared to life expectancies, and that is a logical comparison.

The same error occurs in the second sentence. An attempt is made to compare "average salary" to "management." The error can be corrected in the same way as in the first example. In short, we can simply add "the average salary of" before "the top-level management."

WATCH FOR ILLOGICAL COMPARISONS

Be alert for sentences that attempt to make an illogical comparison between two dissimilar concepts.

Unintended Meanings

Another problem of logical expression relates to whether a sentence says what it intends to say. Sometimes, a sentence intends to say one thing but actually says another.

Examples:

> A childless charwoman's daughter, Dr. Roberts was a self-made woman. ✘

> If the present interest rates fall, the dollar will lose some of its value on the foreign exchange. ✘

At first, both sentences may sound plausible. However, a closer reading shows that each contains an error of logical expression.

The first example asserts that Dr. Roberts was the daughter of a childless charwoman. However, this is not possible; if Dr. Roberts' mother had been childless, there would be no Dr. Roberts. Of course, the sentence intends to say that Dr.

Roberts was both childless as well as the daughter of a charwoman ("Childless and a charwoman's daughter, Dr. Roberts was a self-made woman.").

The second example contains a more subtle error. It asserts that "present interest rates" might change. However, that is logically impossible. By definition, a "present rate" cannot change. If the rate changes, the result is a new interest rate; the result is not a changed "present rate." The sentence is corrected simply by deleting the word "present."

There are countless ways in which sentences can include unintended meanings. So, when you review a sentence, always remember to ask yourself if the ideas or actions being described are logically accurate and/or possible.

VERIFY THAT EACH SENTENCE HAS ITS INTENDED MEANING

Use logic to verify that each sentence has its intended meaning.

Conciseness

There are many kinds of conciseness errors. Several examples are below.

Avoid Awkward Sentences

A sentence may be grammatically and logically correct but still be awkward.

Examples:

> The giant condor is able to spread its wings up to 25 feet. ✘
> The giant condor has a wingspan of up to 25 feet. ✓

> Although most students would benefit from further study of the sciences, doing so is frightening to most of them in that science courses are more difficult than liberal arts courses. ✘
> Although most students would benefit from further study of the sciences, most of them are afraid to take science courses because they are more difficult than liberal arts courses. ✓

> Given that the Incas lacked the wheel, the buildings at Machu Picchu are more astonishing than any Greek temples that are comparable as an achievement. ✘
> Given that the Incas lacked the wheel, the buildings at Machu Picchu are more astonishing than any comparable Greek temple. ✓

In each example above, the second sentence is better because it is more concise.

Avoid Passive Verbs

Another common error involves passive verbs. The examples below show how active verbs (instead of passive verbs) produce sentences that are more clear and concise.

Examples:

> One-fourth of the market <u>was captured</u> by the new computer firm. ✘
> The new computer firm <u>captured</u> one-fourth of the market. ✓

The winning lottery ticket <u>was sold</u> by the gas station attendant. ✗
The gas station attendant <u>sold</u> the winning lottery ticket. ✓

The lesson <u>was finished</u> by the teacher, so she let us leave class early. ✗
The teacher <u>finished</u> the lesson, so she let us leave class early. ✓

AVOID PASSIVE VERBS

A passive verb combines a form of the verb "to be" or "to have" with an active verb (e.g., "The ball <u>was thrown</u>."). Avoid passive verbs. Active verbs are stronger and more direct.

Avoid Needlessly Wordy Sentences

Sometimes, a sentence will be incorrect because it is needlessly wordy.

Examples:

The protracted discussion over what route to take continued for a long time. ✗
The discussion over what route to take continued for a long time. ✓

An aim of the proposal is chiefly to ensure and guarantee the academic freedom of students. ✗
An aim of the proposal is to guarantee the academic freedom of students. ✓

In the first example, "protracted" is unnecessary because it means "to continue for a long time." In the second example, "chiefly" is unnecessary because an "aim" is a chief concern. Likewise, "ensure" is unnecessary because it has the same meaning as "guarantee."

Misplaced Modifiers

Another error of logical expression involves misplaced modifiers. A modifier should be as close as possible to what it modifies. If a modifier is too distant from what it is supposed to modify, it can modify the wrong part of the sentence.

Examples:

Stuffed with herb dressing, trussed neatly, and baked to a golden hue, Aunt Fannie served her famous holiday turkey. ✗

The doctor said gently to the patient that there was nothing wrong with a smile. ✗

At the party, Fred served cold lemonade to his thirsty guests in paper cups. ✗

In the first example, the introductory modifier immediately precedes Aunt Fannie. As a result, it sounds like she was stuffed, trussed, and baked. To correct the sentence, simply relocate the introductory modifier: "Aunt Fannie served her famous holiday turkey stuffed with herb dressing, trussed neatly, and baked to a golden hue."

In the second example, there is ambiguity because "with a smile" is improperly placed. As a result, the doctor's meaning is unclear: he either means there is nothing wrong with smiling; or, more likely, the doctor smiled as he informed the patient that nothing was wrong. To correct the sentence, simply relocate the modifier: "With a smile, the doctor said gently to the patient that there was nothing wrong."

Finally, in the third example, there is ambiguity because "in paper cups" is improperly placed. As a result, the sentence implies that the guests themselves are in paper cups. To correct the sentence, simply relocate the modifier: "At the party, Fred served cold lemonade in paper cups to his thirsty guests."

WATCH FOR MISPLACED MODIFIERS

Watch for sentences with ambiguous or incorrect modification. A modifier should be as close as possible to what it's supposed to modify.

Examples:

> I bought a piano from an old lady with intricate carvings. ✘
> I bought a piano with intricate carvings from an old lady. ✓
>
> I read about the destruction of Rome in my history class. ✘
> In my history class, I read about the destruction of Rome. ✓

The word "only" can also cause confusion depending on how it's placed in a sentence.

Examples:

> Only he kissed her. ✓
> He only kissed her. ✓
> He kissed only her. ✓

All of these sentences are logically possible. However, each sentence has a different meaning simply because the word "only" is placed differently in each one.

Finally, participle phrases can create confusion if they're improperly placed.

Examples:

> Answering the doorbell, the cake remained in the oven. ✘
> Answering the doorbell, we forgot to take the cake from the oven. ✓
>
> Falling on the roof, we heard the sound of the rain. ✘
> We heard the sound of the rain falling on the roof. ✓

As with previous examples, we can correct the sentences by moving the modifier (i.e., the participle phrase) as close as possible to what it's supposed to modify.

Problems of Logical Expression

DIRECTIONS: Read the following passage. For items #1–15, choose the best answer that corrects the sentence without changing its meaning or intent. When correcting the sentences, look at them in the context of the passage in order to check for consistency and logical expression. If the sentence is correct as written, choose "NO CHANGE." Answers are on page 755.

(1) When I was a child, my grandmother's kitchen was the scene of feverish activity during the early fall. (2) One morning, she would go to the farmers' market and return with baskets of fruits and vegetables. (3) Then, she would spend the rest of the day preparing the fruits and vegetables for the wide-mouthed canning jars that will be preserved through the winter. (4) Until the late fall, the pantry shelves were lined with rows of jars containing pickled peaches, creamed corn, and many varieties of jams and jellies.

(5) Today, we are able to buy fresh fruits and vegetables at the local grocery store even during the winter. (6) Indeed, years ago, home-canning was a practical solution to one of nature's dilemmas. (7) On the one hand, the harvest produced more fruits and vegetables than could be consumed immediately, so without some way to preserve the produce, it would spoil. (8) On the other hand, during the winter months, fresh produce was not available, so it was important to have preserved foods available.

(9) There is nothing any more mysterious about home-canning than any food preparation. (10) Special canning jars are packed with prepared food, fitted with self-sealing lids, which are submerged in boiling water. (11) The sustained high heat kills dangerous organisms causing the food to spoil. (12) As it gradually cools, a vacuum pulls the lid down against the mouth of the jar to make an airtight seal. (13) Unless the seal is broken, no organisms can enter the jar to cause spoilage.

(14) Although we no longer depend on home-canning, home-canning can be fun. (15) Spread on hot toast on a cold winter morning, a homemade jam just tastes better than a store. (16) You also will enjoy giving jars of homemade preserves to friends and relatives that are both unusual and personal as gifts. (17) All you need to do to get started is to find a book at the local library or bookstore and follow the directions about home-canning.

1. Sentence (2): <u>One</u> morning, she would go to the farmers' market and return with baskets of fruits and vegetables.

   A. NO CHANGE
   B. Some
   C. Each
   D. Once
   E. This

2. Sentence (3): Then, she would spend the rest of the day preparing the fruits and vegetables for the wide-mouthed canning jars that <u>will be preserved</u> through the winter.

   F. NO CHANGE
   G. preserve them
   H. preserved them
   J. were preserved
   K. would be preserved

3. Sentence (4): <u>Until</u> the late fall, the pantry shelves were lined with rows of jars containing pickled peaches, creamed corn, and many varieties of jams and jellies.

   A. NO CHANGE
   B. Since
   C. By
   D. Up to
   E. Then

4. Sentence (6): <u>Indeed,</u> years ago, home-canning was a practical solution to one of nature's dilemmas.

   F. NO CHANGE
   G. Indeed
   H. Furthermore,
   J. Moreover,
   K. However,

5. Sentence (7): On the one hand, the harvest produced more fruits and vegetables than could be consumed immediately, <u>so</u> without some way to preserve the produce, it would spoil.

   A. NO CHANGE
   B. meanwhile
   C. anyway
   D. instead
   E. otherwise

6. Sentence (8): <u>On the other hand,</u> during the winter months, fresh produce was not available, so it was important to have preserved foods available.

   F. NO CHANGE
   G. In fact
   H. Really
   J. Still
   K. Yet

7. Sentence (9): There is nothing any more mysterious about home-canning <u>than any</u> food preparation.

   A. NO CHANGE
   B. than any other
   C. as any
   D. as any other
   E. than

8. Sentence (10): Special canning jars are packed with prepared food, fitted with self-sealing lids, <u>which are submerged</u> in boiling water.

   F. NO CHANGE
   G. that are submerged
   H. submerging
   J. submerged
   K. and submerged

9. Sentence (11): The sustained high heat kills dangerous organisms <u>causing</u> the food to spoil.

   A. NO CHANGE
   B. that caused
   C. that could cause
   D. to cause
   E. which caused

10. Sentence (12): <u>As it gradually cools,</u> a vacuum pulls the lid down against the mouth of the jar to make an airtight seal.

   F. NO CHANGE
   G. As they gradually cool,
   H. Gradually cooling,
   J. Gradually cooled,
   K. As the jars gradually cool,

11. Sentence (13): Unless the seal is broken, no organisms <u>can enter</u> the jar to cause spoilage.

   A. NO CHANGE
   B. are entering
   C. entered
   D. have entered
   E. had entered

12. Sentence (14): Although we <u>no longer</u> depend on home-canning, home-canning can be fun.

   F. NO CHANGE
   G. usually
   H. never
   J. constantly
   K. perhaps

13. Sentence (15): Spread on hot toast on a cold winter morning, a homemade jam just tastes better than <u>a store</u>.

   A. NO CHANGE
   B. a store's
   C. the store
   D. some store
   E. any store

14. Sentence (16): You also will enjoy giving jars of homemade preserves to friends and relatives <u>that are both unusual and personal as gifts</u>.

   F. NO CHANGE
   G. as gifts that are both unusual and personal
   H. being gifts both unusual and personal
   J. which are gifts that are both unusual and personal
   K. that are gifts which are both unusual and personal

15. Sentence (17): All you need to do to get started is to find <u>a book at the local library or bookstore and follow the directions about home-canning</u>.

   A. NO CHANGE
   B. a home-canning book at the local library or bookstore with directions
   C. a book about home-canning at the local library or bookstore and follow the directions
   D. a book with directions about home-canning at the local library or bookstore and follow them
   E. a local library or bookstore with a home-canning book and follow the directions

DIRECTIONS: For items #16–27, circle the letter of the underlined part of the sentence that contains an error. Answers are on page 755.

16. <u>Written in almost total isolation from the world</u>,
            F

   Emily Dickinson <u>spoke of</u> love <u>and</u> death in <u>her</u>
               G   **H**   **J**

   poems.

17. <u>Being highly qualified for the position</u>, the bank
          A

   president <u>will conduct</u> a final interview with the
           B

   new candidate tomorrow, <u>after which</u> <u>he will</u>
                 C   **D**

   <u>make</u> her a job offer.
    E

18. <u>In broken English</u>, the police officer patiently
      F

   listened to the tourist ask for directions to Radio

   City Music Hall, <u>after which</u> she <u>motioned</u> the
               G   **H**

   tourist and his family into the squad car and drove

   <u>them</u> to their destination.
    J

19. <u>Following the recent crash of the stock market</u>,
           A

   Peter <u>bought</u> a book on portfolio management <u>in</u>
        B   **C**

   <u>order to learn</u> methods to protect his investments
      D

   <u>from a well-known investment banker</u>.
          E

20. <u>Recent</u> research indicates that people <u>who</u> lived
    F   **G**

   agrarian lifestyles in the Middle Ages had <u>much</u>
                          H

   <u>more</u> leisure time <u>than people</u> today.
    J   **K**

21. <u>Since</u> we have a <u>broader</u> technological base,
   A   **B**

   American scientists believe that our space

   program <u>will ultimately prove</u> superior <u>to Russia</u>.
        C   **D**

22. Although a person may always represent <u>himself</u>
$\qquad\qquad\qquad\qquad\qquad\qquad\qquad\qquad$ **F**

in a judicial proceeding, licensed lawyers <u>only</u>
$\qquad\qquad\qquad\qquad\qquad\qquad\qquad\qquad$ **G**

may represent <u>others</u> in <u>such</u> proceedings for a
$\qquad\qquad\quad$ **H** $\qquad$ **J**

fee.

23. <u>Unlike the pale and delicately built ballerinas of</u>
$\qquad\qquad\qquad\qquad$ **A**

<u>romantic ballet</u>, Judith Jamison's movement
$\qquad$ **B**

<u>seems more African than</u> European-American,
$\qquad\qquad$ **C**

and her physical appearance <u>reinforces</u> the
$\qquad\qquad\qquad\qquad\qquad\quad$ **D**

contrast.

24. Market experts <u>predict</u> that in ten years, when the
$\qquad\qquad\qquad\quad$ **F**

harmful effects of caffeine become <u>more</u>
$\qquad\qquad\qquad\qquad\qquad\qquad$ **G**

<u>generally known</u>, the number of tons of
$\qquad$ **G**

decaffeinated coffee <u>consumed by</u> Americans
$\qquad\qquad\qquad\qquad$ **H**

each year will exceed <u>coffee containing caffeine</u>.
$\qquad\qquad\qquad\qquad\qquad$ **J**

25. Illiteracy, <u>a widespread problem in the United</u>
$\qquad\qquad\qquad\qquad$ **A**

<u>States</u>, <u>undermines</u> productivity because many
A $\qquad$ **B**

mistakes <u>are</u> made by workers who do not know
$\qquad\qquad$ **C**

how to read <u>on the job</u>.
$\qquad\qquad\qquad$ **D**

26. As sailors <u>are often assigned</u> to ships <u>that remain</u>
$\qquad\qquad\qquad$ **F** $\qquad\qquad\qquad$ **G**

at sea for months at a time, men in the Navy

<u>spend</u> more time away from home <u>than any</u>
H $\qquad\qquad\qquad\qquad\qquad\qquad$ **J**

<u>branch of the service</u>.
J

27. <u>Like A. J. Ayer</u>, much of Gilbert Ryle's
$\quad$ **A**

philosophical argumentation <u>relies</u> on analysis of
$\qquad\qquad\qquad\qquad\qquad$ **B**

the way <u>people</u> <u>ordinarily</u> use language.
$\qquad\quad$ **C** $\qquad$ **D**

DIRECTIONS: For items #28–45, analyze the given sentence for logical expression errors. If an error exists, rewrite the sentence correctly. If the sentence is correct as written, write NO CHANGE. Answers are on page 755.

28. The life of my generation is easier than my parents.

_____

_____

29. Professor Baker's explanations are not as clear as Professor Thomas' explanations.

_____

_____

30. You can learn just as much, if not more, online as in a regular classroom.

_____

_____

31. I am spending more time on the assignments in my management class than all my other classes combined.

_____

_____

32. He tripped on a crack in the pavement going to school.

When he was going to school, he tripped on a crack on the pavement.

33. Mary only failed the test; everyone else in her class passed.

had

34. Did you see the film about the five people on the boat on television?

35. The police officer ordered the man to stop in his patrol car.

36. Upon picking up the phone, the noise became muted.

When you

37. While swimming, a fish nibbled on my toe.

I was

38. Of all his admirers, his wife only loved him.

only

39. He went to the old church to pray for the people on Cemetery Hill.

No change

40. Upon entering the class, the blackboard came into view.

When we

The blackboard came into the view when entering the blackboard

41. The baby was pushed by his mother in a stroller.

42. To get to school, we nearly walked two miles.

43. Leaning out the window, the garden could be seen below.

When   she could see

44. The hotel room was clean and comfortable that we had reserved.

that we had reserved

The hotel room we had reserved was clean and comfortable

45. This book is heavier in weight than that one.

This book weight is heavier than that one

Idioms and Clarity of Expression

Standard English contains numerous idioms and two-word verbs that are perfectly acceptable to use. The following is a list of commonly accepted idioms and two-word verbs:

IDIOMS AND TWO-WORD VERBS

about time, about to
above all
act up
add up (*make sense*)
a good deal of
an arm and a leg
at the drop of a hat
back out (of)
bank on
be about to
be an old hand (at)
be a question of
beat around the bush
be bound to
be broke
be fed up (with)
be off
be out of something
be out of the question
be over
be short for, be short of
be the picture of
be up to someone
be warm
bite off more than one can chew
break down, break the ice
break the news (to)
bring about
broken English
brush up on
by and large
by heart, by no means
call off
call on
care for
catch on, catch up (with)
come across, come down with
come out smelling like a rose
cost an arm and a leg
count on, count out
cut down on, cut it close
cut out, cut out for
day in and day out
die down
do over, do with, do without
dream up
drop in (on), drop off
size up
sleep on it
snap out of
speak up (*say something,*
speak more loudly)
spell out (for)
stand a chance
stand for
stand out
start up
stay out, stay up
a stone's throw (from)
straighten up
take a chance, take advantage (of)
take after, take in, take into account

every other
fall behind, fall through
a far cry from
feel free
feel like a million bucks
feel up to
few and far between
fill in (for)
fly off the handle
follow in someone's footsteps
for good
get the hang of
get in one's blood
get in the way
get off, get on, get over, get to
get rid of
get the better of
get under way
give a hand (to, with)
go on (with)
go without saying
hand in, hand out
hang up
have a heart
have in mind
have over
hear first hand (from)
hear from, hear of
hit it off
hold on (to), hold still, hold up
how come?
in the dark, in hot water
in the long run, in no time
jump to conclusions
keep an eye on, keep an eye out (for)
keep from, keep on one's toes
keep on (with), keep up (with)
knock it off
lay off
learn the ropes
leave out
let (somebody) alone, let (somebody) know
let go of
look after, look for, look forward to
look into, look out (for)
look up (to)
make a difference, make a point of
make ends meet, make out
take it easy, take off (*leave*)
take one's mind off, take one's time
take over, take pains, take turns
talk over
tangle with
tell apart
think much of
think over
throw cold water on
tie up, tie into
trade in
turn down, turn up, turn into
turn off, turn on, turn out, turn in
under the weather

make sense of, make way for
make up, make up one's mind
mark up, mark down
may as well, might as well
mean to
move on, move up
next to nothing
nose something out
now and then
odds and ends
on a shoestring, on its last leg
on the go
on one's last leg, on one's toes
on pins and needles
on second thought
on the mend, on the road, on the run
on the tip of one's tongue
on the whole
open up
out of order, out of sorts
out of this world, out to win
over and over
part with
pass up
pat oneself on the back
pay off, pay someone a visit
pick out, pick up (learn)
pick up the tab (for)
a piece of cake
play by ear
point out
pull one's leg
put aside, put off
put one's best foot forward
put together, put up (with)
rave about
rough it
rule out
run into, run out of, run short (of)
save one's breath
search me
see off, see to
serve one right
set out
settle down, settle on
sing another tune
show around, show up
shut down
up against
ups and downs
up-to-date
use up
wait for, wait on
warm up (to)
watch out (for)
wear out
a whole new ballgame
with flying colors
without a hitch
work out (*exercise, solve*)
write out
zero in (on)

A non-idiomatic expression is not acceptable standard written English for any of the following reasons:

CHECKLIST FOR IDIOMATIC EXPRESSION ERRORS

1. Diction

    a. Wrong Word Choice

    b. Wrong Preposition

    c. Gerund versus Infinitive

2. Ambiguity in Scope

3. Low-Level Usage

Diction

The first category of idiomatic expression errors involves diction, i.e., word choice.

Wrong Word Choice

Sometimes, a word can be used incorrectly and lead to a construction that is non-idiomatic or not acceptable standard written English.

Example:

> The techniques of empirical observation in the social sciences are different <u>than</u> those in the physical sciences. ✗

The above example is wrong because "different than" is a non-idiomatic expression. The correct idiomatic expression is "different from": "The techniques of empirical observation in the social sciences are different <u>from</u> those in the physical sciences."

Sometimes, words whose meanings are very similar can be used incorrectly and lead to a construction that is non-idiomatic or not acceptable standard written English.

Examples:

> John expressed his intention to make the trip, but <u>if</u> he will actually go is doubtful. ✗
> John expressed his intention to make the trip, but <u>whether</u> he will actually go is doubtful. ✓
>
> Herbert divided the cake <u>among</u> Mary and Sally. ✗
> Herbert divided the cake <u>between</u> Mary and Sally. ✓
>
> Herbert divided the cake <u>between</u> Mary, Sally, and himself. ✗
> Herbert divided the cake <u>among</u> Mary, Sally, and himself. ✓
>
> The <u>amount</u> of students in the class declined as the semester progressed. ✗
> The <u>number</u> of students in the class declined as the semester progressed. ✓

There are <u>less</u> students in Professor Smith's class than there are in Professor Jones' class. ✘
There are <u>fewer</u> students in Professor Smith's class than there are in Professor Jones' class. ✓

Finally, some sentences are incorrect because they include words that fail to convey the author's intended meaning. An author sometimes makes this mistake because the wrong word and the correct word are actually quite similar.

The following list is an extended summary of commonly confused word groups:

CONFUSING WORD GROUPS

accede—*to agree with* .... They will *accede* to your request for more information.
exceed—*to be more than* .... Unfortunately, her expenditures now *exceed* her income.
concede—*to yield* (not necessarily in agreement) .... They *concede* that more information is necessary.

accept—*to receive*, or .... I'll *accept* the gift from you.
  to agree to something .... I will lend you the money if you *accept* my conditions.
except—*to exclude* or *excluding* .... Everyone *except* my uncle went home.

access—*availability*, or .... The lawyer was given *access* to the grand jury records.
  to get at .... I could not *access* the files without the proper password.
excess—*state of surpassing specified limits* (noun), or ... Expenditures this month are far in *excess* of income.
  more than usual (adjective) .... The airline charged him fifty dollars for *excess* baggage.

adapt—*to adjust or change* .... Children can *adapt* to changing conditions very easily.
adept—*skillful* .... Proper instruction makes children *adept* in various games.
adopt—*to take as one's own* .... The war orphan was *adopted* by the general and his wife.

adapted to—*original or natural suitability* .... The gills of the fish are *adapted to* underwater breathing.
adapted for—*created suitability* .... Atomic energy is constantly being *adapted for* new uses.
adapted from—*changed to be made suitable* .... Many of Wagner's librettos were *adapted from* Norse sagas.

addition—*the act or process of adding* .... In *addition* to a dictionary, he always used a thesaurus.
edition—*a printing of a publication* .... The first *edition* of Shakespeare's plays appeared in 1623.

advantage—*a superior position* .... He had an *advantage* in experience over his opponent.
benefit—*a favor conferred or earned* .... The rules were changed for his *benefit*.

adverse—*unfavorable* .... He was very upset by the *adverse* decision.
averse—*having a feeling of repugnance or dislike* .... Many writers are *averse* to criticism of their work.

advice—*counsel, opinion* (noun) .... Let me give you some free *advice*.
advise—*to offer advice* (verb) .... I'd *advise* you to see your doctor.

affect—*to influence* (verb) .... The pollution *affected* our health.
effect—*to cause or bring about* (verb), or .... Our lawsuit *effected* a change in the law.
  a result (noun) .... The *effect* of the storm could not be measured.

all ready—*everybody or everything ready* .... They were *all ready* to write when the test began.
already—*previously* .... They had *already* written the letter.

all together—*everybody or everything together* .... The boys and girls stood *all together* in line.
altogether—*completely* .... His action was *altogether* strange for a person of his type.

allude—*to make a reference to* .... In his essay, he *alludes* to Shakespeare's puns.
elude—*to escape from* .... The burglar *eluded* the police.

allusion—*an indirect reference* .... The poem is an *allusion* to one of Shakespeare's sonnets.
illusion—*an erroneous concept or perception* .... My mirror created the *illusion* of space in the narrow hall.

alongside of—*side by side with* .... Bill stood *alongside of* Henry.
alongside—*parallel to the side* .... Park the car *alongside* the curb.

among—*a term used with more than two persons or things* .... The inheritance was equally divided *among* the four kids.
between—*a term used with two persons or things* .... The inheritance was divided *between* the two kids.

angel—*a heavenly creature* .... She has been an *angel* in these difficult times.
angle—*a point at which two lines meet*, or .... A line perpendicular to another line forms a right *angle*.
  an aspect seen from a particular point of view .... From that *angle*, the picture looks completely different.

ante—*a prefix meaning before* .... The *ante*chamber is the small room before the main room.
anti—*a prefix meaning against* .... He is known to be *anti*-American.

assistance—*the act of assisting, aid* .... I needed his *assistance* when I repaired the roof.
assistants—*helpers, aides* .... The chief surgeon has four *assistants*.

breadth—*width* .... The canvas was twice greater in length than in *breadth*.
breath—*an intake of air* .... Before you dive in, take a very deep *breath*.
breathe—*to draw air in and give it out* .... It is difficult to *breathe* when you have a bad cold.

CONFUSING WORD GROUPS

build—*to erect, construct* (verb), or .... I want to *build* a sandcastle.
 the physical makeup of a person (noun).................. She has a very athletic *build*.
built—*the past tense of build* .... We *built* a moat around the sandcastle.

buy—*to purchase*.. I want to *buy* a new tie.
by—*near,*... My bloodhound likes to sleep *by* the door at night.
 by means of, or.. He comes to school *by* public transportation.
 not later than .... Mary said that she would be back at work *by* noon.
bye—*free pass to next round* .... She had a *bye* in the tournament.

canvas—*a heavy, coarse material* .... The *canvas* sails were very heavy.
canvass—*to solicit, conduct a survey* .... The politicians are going to *canvass* our neighborhood.

capital—*place of government,* or .... Paris is the *capital* of France.
 wealth... It takes substantial *capital* to open a restaurant.
capitol—*building that houses legislatures* .... Congress convenes in the *Capitol* in Washington, D.C.

carat—*a unit of weight*.. The movie star wears a ten-*carat* diamond ring.
caret—*a proofreading symbol, indicating where* .... He added a phrase in the space above the *caret*.
 something is to be inserted
carrot—*a vegetable* .... Does he feed his pet rabbit a *carrot* every other day?

click—*a brief, sharp sound* .... The detective drew his gun when he heard the lock *click*.
clique—*an exclusive group of people or set* .... In high school, I was not part of any *clique*.

cease—*to end*.. Please *cease* making those sounds.
seize—*to take hold of*... *Seize* him by the collar as he comes around the corner.

choice—*a selection* .... My *choice* for a career is teaching.
choose—*to select*.. We may *choose* our own advisors.
chose—*the past tense of choose* .... I finally *chose* my wedding dress.

cite—*to quote* .... He enjoys *citing* Shakespeare to illustrate his views.
sight—*seeing, what is seen* .... The *sight* of the accident was appalling.
site—*a place where something is located or occurs* .... We are seeking a new *site* for the baseball field.

cloth—*fabric or material* .... The seats were covered with *cloth*, not vinyl.
clothe—*to put on clothes, to dress*................................ Her job is to *clothe* the actors for each scene.

coarse—*vulgar,* or... He was shunned because of his *coarse* behavior.
 harsh .... The sandpaper was very *coarse*.
course—*a path,* or... The ship took its usual *course*.
 a plan of study.. How many *courses* are you taking this term?

complement—*a completing part*.................................. His wit was a *complement* to her beauty.
compliment—*an expression of praise or admiration* .... He received many *compliments* for his fine work.

confidant—*one to whom private* .... His priest was his only *confidant*.
 matters are confided (noun)
confidence—*a feeling of assurance or certainty* (noun) .... The ballplayer is developing *confidence* in his ability.
confident—*having confidence in oneself* (adjective) .... Her success in business has given her a *confident* manner.

conscience—*the ability to recognize the difference* .... The attorney said the criminal lacked a *conscience*.
 between right and wrong
conscious—*aware* .... He was *conscious* that his actions had consequences.

consul—*a government representative* .... Americans abroad should keep in touch with the *consuls*.
council—*an assembly that meets for deliberation* .... The student *council* met to discuss a campus dress code.
counsel—*advice (counselor)* .... The defendant heeded the *counsel* of his friends.

decent—*suitable* .... The *decent* thing to do is to admit your error.
descent—*going down*.. The *descent* into the cave was dangerous.
dissent—*disagreement* .... Two of the justices filed a *dissenting* opinion.

desert (DEZZ-ert)—*an arid area* .... I have seen several movies set in the Sahara *desert*.
desert (di-ZERT)—*abandon,* or .... The soldier was warned not to *desert* his company.
 a reward or punishment.. We're certain that execution is a just *desert* for his crime.
dessert (di-ZERT)—*the final course of a meal* .... We had strawberry shortcake for *dessert*.

disburse—*to pay out* .... This week the bank has *disbursed* a million dollars.
disperse—*to scatter, distribute widely*............................ The defeated army began to *disperse*.

discomfit—*to upset* .... The general's plan was designed to *discomfit* the enemy.
discomfort—*lack of ease* .... This starched collar causes *discomfort*.

dual—*double*... Dr. Jekyll had a *dual* personality.
duel—*a contest between two persons or groups* .... Aaron Burr and Alexander Hamilton engaged in a *duel*.

elicit—*to draw forth, evoke*....................................... Her performance *elicited* tears from the audience.
illicit—*illegal, unlawful* .... He was arrested because of his *illicit* business dealings.

CONFUSING WORD GROUPS

emigrate—*to leave a country* .... They *emigrated* from Norway in the nineteenth century.
immigrate—*to enter a country* .... Many Irish *immigrated* to the United States.

eminent—*of high rank, prominent, outstanding* .... He was the most *eminent* physician of his time.
imminent—*about to occur, impending* .... His nomination to the board of directors is *imminent*.

epitaph—*an inscription on a tombstone or monument* .... His *epitaph* was taken from a section of the Bible.
epithet—*a term used to describe or characterize* .... The drunk was shouting *epithets* at the passersby.
    the nature of a person or thing

expand—*to spread out* .... As the staff increases, we can *expand* our office space.
expend—*to use up* .... Don't *expend* all your energy on one project.

fair—*light in color,* .... I have a very *fair* complexion.
    reasonable, or .... Your attitude is not a *fair* one.
    beauty .... The *fair* princess rode her horse off into the sunset.
fare—*a set price* .... The *fare* is reduced for senior citizens.

farther—*used to express distance* .... John ran *farther* than Bill walked.
further—*used to express time or degree* .... Please go no *further* in your argument.

faze—*to worry or disturb* .... I tried not to let his mean look *faze* me.
phase—*an aspect* .... A crescent is a *phase* of the moon.

find—*to locate* .... Can you *find* the keys?
fine—*good,* .... He is a *fine* cook.
    well, ... After being very sick for two weeks, now I feel absolutely *fine*.
    precise, or .... The calibration of the scale requires very *fine* measurements.
    a penalty .... I received a parking *fine* for an expired meter.
fined—*penalized* .... The judge *fined* him twenty dollars.

formally—*in a formal way* .... He was dressed *formally* for the dinner party.
formerly—*at an earlier time* .... He was *formerly* a delegate to the convention.

fort (fort)—*a fortified place* .... A small garrison was able to hold the *fort*.
forte (FOR-tay)—*a strong point* .... Conducting Wagner's music was Toscanini's *forte*.
forte (FOR-tay)—*a musical term that means loudly* .... The musical composition was meant to be played *forte*.

idle—*unemployed or unoccupied* .... He didn't enjoy remaining *idle* while he recuperated.
idol—*image or object of worship* .... Rock musicians are the *idols* of many teenagers.

in—indicates *inclusion or location,* or .... The spoons are *in* the drawer.
    motion within limits .... We were walking *in* the room.
into—*motion toward one place from another* .... I put the spoons *into* the drawer.

incidence—*to the extent or frequency of an occurrence* .... The *incidence* of rabies has decreased since last year.
incidents—*occurrences, events* .... Luckily, the accidents were just minor *incidents*.

it's—*the contraction of it is,* or .... *It's* a very difficult assignment.
    the contraction of it has .... *It's* been a very long day.
its—*possessive pronoun meaning belonging to it* .... We tried to analyze *its* meaning.

knew—*the past tense of know* .... I *knew* her many years ago.
new—*of recent origin* .... I received a *new* bicycle for my birthday.

know—*to have knowledge or understanding* .... I *know* your brother.
no—*a negative used to express denial or refusal* .... There are *no* more books available.

later—*after a certain time* .... I'll see you *later*.
latter—*the second of two* .... Of the two speakers, the *latter* was more interesting.

lay—*to put* .... I (*lay, laid, have laid*) the gift on the table.
lie—*to recline* .... I (*lie, lay, have lain*) on my blanket on the beach.

lets—*the third person singular present of let* .... He *lets* me park my car in his garage.
let's—*contraction for let us* .... *Let's* go home early today.

lightening—*making less heavy* .... Removing the books will succeed in *lightening* your bag.
lightning—*electric discharge in the atmosphere,* or .... Thunderstorms often produce startling *lightning* bolts.
    moving with great speed .... The horse raced *lightning* fast.

loose—*not fastened or restrained,* or .... The dog got *loose* from the leash.
    not tight-fitting .... After my diet, the new pants were too *loose* on me.
lose—*to mislay,* .... Try not to *lose* your umbrella.
    to be unable to keep, or .... She *lost* her mind.
    to be defeated .... They can't *lose* with their new strategy.

CONFUSING WORD GROUPS

mind—*human consciousness* (noun),...................................... Make up your *mind* which record you want.
   to object (verb), or .... We don't *mind* if you bring a friend.
    to watch out for.. I cannot go to the movies because I have to *mind* the children.
mine—*a possessive, showing ownership* .... Use your own sled; that one is *mine*.

moral—*good or ethical* (adjective), or .... The trust administrator had a *moral* obligation to the heirs.
   a lesson to be drawn (noun) .... The *moral* of the story is that it pays to be honest.
morale—*spirit*.. The team's *morale* improved after the coach's speech.

passed—*the past tense of to pass* .... The week *passed* very quickly.
past—*just preceding or an earlier time*, or.................................... The *past* week was a very exciting one.
   in a direction going close to and then beyond......................... We walked down the block and *past* the old mansion.

patience—*enduring calmly with tolerant understanding* .... He has very little *patience* with fools.
patients—*people under medical treatment* .... There are twenty *patients* waiting to see the doctor.

personal—used to describe *an individual's character,*.................... He took a *personal* interest in each of the students.
   conduct, or private affairs
personnel—*an organized body of individuals*................................. The store's *personnel* department is on the third floor.

precede—*to come before* .... What events *preceded* the fight?
proceed—*to go ahead*.. We can *proceed* with our next plan.

principal—*chief or main* (adjective),... His *principal* support comes from the real estate industry.
   a leader, or .... The school *principal* called a meeting of the faculty.
   a sum of money (noun).. He earned 10 percent interest on the *principal* he invested.
principle—*a fundamental truth or belief* .... As a matter of *principle*, he didn't register for the draft.

prophecy—*prediction* (noun, rhymes with *sea*) .... What is the fortune-teller's *prophecy*?
prophesy—*to predict* (verb, rhymes with *sigh*)............................. What did the witches *prophesy*?

quiet—*silent, still*.. My brother is very shy and *quiet*.
quit—*to give up or discontinue* .... I *quit* the team last week.
quite—*very, exactly, or to the greatest extent* .... His analysis is *quite* correct.

raise—*to lift, to erect* .... The neighbors helped him *raise* a new barn.
raze—*to tear down*.. The demolition crew *razed* the old building.
rise—*to increase in value*, or .... The price of silver will *rise* again this month.
    to get up or move from a lower to a higher position............... If a judge enters a room, everyone must *rise* from their seats.

seem—*to appear*.. He *seems* to be sleeping.
seen—*the past participle of see* .... Have you *seen* your sister lately?

set—*to place something down* (mainly) .... He (*sets, set, has set*) the lamp on the table.
sit—*to seat oneself* (mainly) .... He (*sits, sat, has sat*) on the chair.

stationary—*standing still* .... Long ago, people thought that the earth was *stationary*.
stationery—*writing material* .... We bought our school supplies at the *stationery* store.

suppose—*to assume or guess*... I *suppose* you will be home early.
supposed—*past tense and past participle of suppose* .... I (*supposed, had supposed*) you would be home early.
supposed—*ought to or should* (followed by *to*)............................. I am *supposed* to be in school tomorrow.

than—*used to express comparison* .... Jim ate more *than* we could put on the large plate.
then—*used to express time*, or .... I knocked on the door, and *then* I entered.
   a result or consequence .... If you go, *then* I will go too.

their—*belonging to them* .... We took *their* books home with us.
there—*in that place* .... Your books are over *there* on the desk.
they're—*the contraction of they are* .... *They're* coming over for dinner.

though—*although* or .... *Though* he's my friend, I can't recommend him.
   as if (preceded by *as*)... He acted *as though* nothing had happened.
thought—*past tense of to think* (verb), or...................................... I *thought* you were serious!
   an idea (noun) .... It is the *thought* that counts.
through—*in one side and out another,*.. We enjoyed running *through* the snow.
   by way of, or... They met each other *through* a mutual friend.
   finished.. My boyfriend and I are completely *through* with one another.

to—*in the direction of* (preposition), or.. We shall go *to* school.
   used before a verb to indicate the *infinitive*............................ I like *to* swim.
too—*very, also* .... It is *too* hot today.
two—*the numeral 2*.. I ate *two* sandwiches for lunch.

CONFUSING WORD GROUPS

use—*to employ or put into service* .... I want to *use* your chair.
used—past tense and the past participle of *to use* .... I *used* your chair.
used—*in the habit of or accustomed to*, ... I am *used* to your comments.
    (followed by *to*)
used— an adjective meaning *not new* .... I bought a *used* car.

weather—*atmospheric conditions* .... I don't like the *weather* in San Francisco.
whether—*introduces a choice* .... He inquired *whether* we were going to the dance.
    (*whether* should not be preceded by *of* or *as to*)

were—*a past tense of to be* .... They *were* there yesterday.
we're—the contraction of *we are* .... *We're* in charge of the decorations.
where—*place or location* .... *Where* are we meeting your brother?

who's—the contraction of *who is*, or .... *Who's* the next batter?
    the contraction of *who has* .... *Who's* already gone to this movie?
whose—*of whom, implying ownership* .... *Whose* notebook is on the desk?

your—a possessive showing *ownership* .... Please give him *your* notebook.
you're—the contraction of *you are* .... *You're* very sweet.

Wrong Preposition

In standard written English, only certain prepositions can be used with certain verbs. As a result of daily conversation and writing in standard written English, you should know which prepositions and verbs can be used together.

Example:

> I asked him repeatedly if he was from <u>about</u> here, but he never answered me. ✘

The phrase "was from about here" is incorrect. From daily conversation, you should recognize the correct phrase: "he was from *around* here."

Gerund versus Infinitive

The **gerund** is the "-ing" form of a verb, and it is used as a noun.

Examples:

> My doctor recommends <u>bicycling</u> as an alternative form of exercise. ✔

> The company discontinued <u>testing</u> on animals. ✔

The **infinitive** is the "to" form of a verb. It is used as a noun.

Examples:

> Our new physics professor prefers <u>to teach</u> by example. ✔

> The restaurant requires men <u>to wear</u> a coat and tie. ✔

In some circumstances, you can use either the gerund or the infinitive.

Examples:

<u>Adding</u> an extra room to the house is the next project. ✓

<u>To add</u> an extra room to the house is the next project. ✓

However, in some circumstances, the gerund and the infinitive are NOT interchangeable. The difference is not a matter of grammar because both the infinitive and the gerund are used as nouns. Instead, the difference is a matter of what fluent English speakers would regard as idiomatic (acceptable).

Examples:

Tania says that <u>to open</u> the window will keep the room cool. ✘ (The infinitive is not idiomatic.)
Tania says that <u>opening</u> the window will keep the room cool ✓ (The gerund is idiomatic.)

She intends <u>calling</u> her mother on Sunday. ✘ (The gerund is not idiomatic.)
She intends <u>to call</u> her mother on Sunday. ✓ (The infinitive is idiomatic.)

WATCH FOR GERUND-INFINITIVE SWITCHING

Sometimes an infinitive can replace a gerund (or vice versa) and the result is non-standard written English.

Ambiguity in Scope

Watch for ***ambiguity in scope***. This occurs when there is not a clear division between two ideas; as a result, two ideas that should be separate seem to merge.

Examples:

After the arrest, the accused was charged with resisting arrest and criminal fraud. ✘

The recent changes in the tax law will primarily affect workers who wait tables in restaurants, operate concessions in public places, and drive taxis. ✘

In the first example, the scope of "resisting" is not clear. As a result, the sentence could be interpreted to mean that the accused was charged with resisting criminal fraud. To correct the sentence, simply insert "with" before "criminal fraud": "…charged with resisting arrest and with criminal fraud." The intended scope of "resisting" is now made clear, and the clear division between the two separate ideas is established.

In the second example, the scope of "workers" is not clear. In short, the sentence uses "and" to join together the three types of workers described: "…workers who wait tables in restaurants, operate concessions in public places, *and* drive taxis." As a result of this word choice, the sentence could be interpreted to mean that the changed tax law will affect only those workers who do all three jobs. Clearly, this is not the intent of the sentence. To correct the sentence, simply change "and" to "or"; or, give the job descriptions in a series of parallel constructions: "…workers who wait tables in restaurants, workers who operate concessions in public places, and workers who drive taxis." If either of these corrections is made, the intended scope of "workers" is made clear.

> ## WATCH FOR AMBIGUITY IN SCOPE
>
> Watch for sentences that run two or more ideas together. Correct the error by adding words that make it clear the two ideas are distinct.

Low-Level Usage

Some expressions heard in daily conversation are regarded as *low-level usage* and are unacceptable in standard written English. You will need to recognize the difference between standard and non-standard written English.

Example:

> She <u>sure</u> is pretty! ✗
> She <u>certainly</u> is pretty! ✓

AVOID LOW-LEVEL USAGE

Instead of:	*Say:*
ain't	am not; are not; is not
aren't I	am I not
around (2 p.m.)	about (2 p.m.)
being that	since
between you and I	between you and me
bunch (of people)	group (of people)
but that	that
cannot seem	seems unable
different than	different from
else than	other than
equally as good	equally good; just as good
have got	have
having took	having taken
in back of	behind
kind of	somewhat; rather
may of	may have
might of	might have
must of	must have
off of	off
on account of	because
plan on	plan to
put in	spend, make, or devote
quite a few	many
same as	in the same way as; just as
should of	should have
sort of	somewhat; rather
theirselves	themselves
try and	try to
unbeknownst to	without the knowledge of
upwards of	more than
worst kind	very badly
would of	would have

EXERCISE 5

Idioms and Clarity of Expression

DIRECTIONS: In sentences #1–99, circle the correct word choice. Answers are on page 755.

1. He is the (principal, principle) backer of the play.

2. I hope your company will (accept, except) our offer.

3. We hope to have good (weather, whether) when we are on vacation.

4. Put the rabbit back (in, into) the hat.

5. The attorney will (advice, advise) you of your rights.

6. She is far taller (than, then) I imagined.

7. Are they (all ready, already) to go?

8. She answered the letter on shocking pink (stationary, stationery).

9. What is the (affect, effect) you are trying to achieve?

10. I want to (set, sit) next to my grandfather.

11. He's going to (lay, lie) down for a nap.

12. I'm (all together, altogether) tired of his excuses.

13. He saluted when the flag (passed, past) by.

14. I'd like another portion of (desert, dessert).

15. Try not to (loose, lose) your good reputation.

16. How much will the final examination (effect, affect) my grade?

17. What is it (you're, your) trying to suggest?

18. She's not (use, used) to such cold weather.

19. The cost of the coat will (raise, rise) again.

20. You are (suppose, supposed) to be home at six o'clock.

21. Her cat ran straight for (its, it's) bowl of food.

22. Are you (conscience, conscious) of what you are doing?

23. It will (seen, seem) that we are afraid.

24. His essays are filled with literary (allusions, illusions).

25. This wine will be a good (complement, compliment) to the meal.

26. It's (later, latter) than you think!

27. My cousin has a swimmer's (build, built).

28. I never (knew, new) him before today.

29. She asked her a (personal, personnel) question.

30. The golf (coarse, course) was very crowded.

31. The costume was made from old (cloth, clothe) napkins.

32. The ball carrier was trying to (allude, elude) the tacklers.

33. There are (know, no) more exhibitions planned.

34. I will wait for you in the (ante, anti) room.

35. Her (moral, morale) is very low.

36. Begin the sentence with a (capital, capitol) letter.

37. The fact that he nearly had an accident did not even (faze, phase) him.

38. He earns royalties in (access, excess) of a million dollars a year.

39. Now, may we (precede, proceed) with the debate?

40. Her (fort, forte) is writing lyrics for musical comedy.

41. They wondered how they were going to (disburse, disperse) the huge crowd.

42. Everyone was dressed (formally, formerly) for the dinner party.

43. I am not (adverse, averse) to continuing the discussion at another time.

44. Can something be done to diminish the (incidence, incidents) of influenza in that area?

45. "Seeing the film in class will serve a (dual, duel) purpose," he explained.

46. I'm not sure I want to (expand, expend) so much energy on that project.

47. Imagine my (discomfit, discomfort) when she showed up at the party too!

48. He was a famous matinee (idle, idol) many years ago.

49. When did they (emigrate, immigrate) from New York to Paris?

50. I think she is part of a (click, clique) of snobs and creeps.

51. She paid little attention to the fortune-teller's (prophecy, prophesy).

52. The lights went out when the (lightning, lightening) hit the house.

53. I'll provide you (what ever, whatever) assistance you require.

54. We are in (eminent, imminent) danger of losing our reservations.

55. Will she be able to (adapt, adopt) to our way of performing the operation?

56. As we went through the old cemetery, we were fascinated by some of the (epitaphs, epithets).

57. He shared the riches (between, among) Laura, Millie, and Ernestine.

58. The housing law was rewritten for his (advantage, benefit).

59. (Alot, A lot) of the time, he falls asleep at nine o'clock.

60. It was difficult to keep track of the (amount, number) of people who visited him last week.

61. I see him in the park (almost, most) every day.

62. Are you certain that he is (alright, all right) now?

63. She is just beginning to (aggravate, annoy) her mother.

64. He is the school's oldest living (alumni, alumnus).

65. He spotted the riverbank and then guided the canoe up (alongside, alongside of).

66. (Being as, Since) it is Wednesday, we are going to a Broadway matinee.

67. He is (anxious, eager) to be finished with the dental treatment.

68. Where do you want to (meet, meet at)?

69. My aunt just went inside to rest (awhile, a while).

70. It was (about, around) noon when we met for lunch.

71. I brought a (couple, couple of) books for you; both are historical novels.

72. Between (you and I, you and me), I think that her hat is very unbecoming.

73. The (continual, continuous) ticking of the clock was very disconcerting.

74. She (cannot seem, seems unable) to get up early enough to eat breakfast with him.

75. I (assume, expect) that you really earned your salary today.

76. I'm (disinterested, uninterested) in seeing that movie.

77. You must be (every bit as, just as) sleepy as I am.

78. I doubt (that, whether) it will snow today.

79. Sam, Joe, Lou, and Artie have worked with (each other, one another) before.

80. She asked him (if, whether) he wanted to have lunch with her or with her sister.

81. All (humans, human beings) need to take a certain amount of water into their bodies every week.

82. We hope to (conclude, finalize) the deal this month.

83. We were upset when she (flaunted, flouted) her mother's orders.

84. His girlfriend only eats (healthful, healthy) foods.

85. He said such terrible things about her that she is suing him for (libel, slander).

86. I would like to see you in (regard, regards) to the apartment you plan to rent.

87. She is always late for work, (irregardless, regardless) of how early she wakes up in the morning.

88. He'll (loan, lend) you a hand carrying the groceries.

89. The media (are, is) doing the job poorly.

90. The art director was taken (off, off of) the most profitable gallery show.

91. I hope that she will (quit, stop) sending us the job applications.

92. The reason the baby is crying is (because, that) she is hungry.

93. Does he (manage, run) the department efficiently?

94. Anyone who wants to have (his or her, their) conference with me today is invited to meet in my office at ten o'clock.

95. She scored more points than (any, any other) player on the team.

96. His room is very neat (but, while) hers is very messy.

97. He will (try and, try to) be more pleasant to his sister.

98. I shall give it to (whoever, whomever) arrives first.

99. This time, we will not wait (for, on) you for more than ten minutes.

DIRECTIONS: In sentences #100–114, determine whether the gerund choice, (A), the infinitive choice, (B), or BOTH the gerund and the infinitive, (C), is the correct answer to fill in the blank. Answers are on page 759.

100. After the break, the teacher continued _____.

    A. lecturing
    B. to lecture
    C. BOTH

101. He forgot _____ me at the party last year, so he introduced himself again.

    A. meeting
    B. to meet
    C. BOTH

102. Please remember _____ five minutes early on the day of the test.

    A. arriving
    B. to arrive
    C. BOTH

103. He hesitated _____ for the assignment.

    A. volunteering
    B. to volunteer
    C. BOTH

104. After her speech, the lecturer proceeded _____ questions.

    A. taking
    B. to take
    C. BOTH

105. The politician continued _____ soft money contributions during his campaign.

    A. accepting
    B. to accept
    C. BOTH

106. "I will not tolerate _____," the professor said.

    A. talking
    B. to talk
    C. BOTH

107. Taking sixteen credit hours, the student has neglected _____ some of her essays.

    A. writing
    B. to write
    C. BOTH

108. She has not even begun _____ for the exam even though it is tomorrow.

    A. preparing
    B. to prepare
    C. BOTH

109. The applicant tried _____ for an extension of the deadline, but his request was turned down.

    A. asking
    B. to ask
    C. BOTH

110. The class has been warned not _____.

    A. cheating
    B. to cheat
    C. BOTH

111. The senior anticipates _____ next month.

    A. graduating
    B. to graduate
    C. BOTH

112. Knowing that the deadline is tomorrow has forced me _____ on the project.

    A. concentrating
    B. to concentrate
    C. BOTH

113. Cats cannot stand _____ the sound of a vacuum cleaner.

    A. hearing
    B. to hear
    C. BOTH

114. I do not want to spend any more time _____ these equations.

    A. solving
    B. to solve
    C. BOTH

DIRECTIONS: For items #115–129, circle the letter of the underlined part of the sentence containing the error and write the correct word or phrase. Answers are on page 759.

115. Economists have established that there is a
                      A

    relation—albeit an indirect one—between the
    B

    amount of oil imported into this country and the
    C

    number of traffic accidents.
    D

    Correct Word/Phrase: _____

116. Ironically, today Elizabeth I and her rival for the
                                     F

    English throne, Mary Stuart, whom Elizabeth had
                         G   **H**

    executed, lay side by side in Westminster Abbey.
            J

    Correct Word/Phrase: _____

117. Although the script is interesting and well-written, it is not clear whether it can be adopted
  A   B
for television since the original story contains
scenes that could not be broadcast over the public
                C   D
airwaves.

Correct Word/Phrase: _____ _Wether_

118. If he had known how difficult law school would
       F
be, he would of chosen a different profession or
      G
perhaps even have followed the tradition of going
            H   J
into the family business.

Correct Word/Phrase: _____

119. When shopping malls and business complexes get
                                                    A
built, quite often the needs of the handicapped are
A   B
not considered; as a result, it later becomes
necessary to make costly modifications to
                   C
structures to make them accessible to persons of
                         D
impaired mobility.

Correct Word/Phrase: _____

120. Researchers have found that children experience
                  F   G
twice as much deep sleep than adults, a fact
                           H   J
which may teach us something about the
  J
connection between age and learning ability.

Correct Word/Phrase: _____

121. Despite the ample evidence that smoking is
        A   B
hazardous to one's health, many people seem to
   B   C
find the warnings neither frightening or
                                        D
convincing.

Correct Word/Phrase: _____ _nor_

122. No matter how many encores the audience
                    F
demands, Helen Walker is always willing to sing
                        G
yet another song which pleases the audience.
H   J

Correct Word/Phrase: _____

123. In light of recent translations of stone carvings
                A
depicting scenes of carnage, scholars are now
   B
questioning as to whether the Incas were really a
            C   D
peace-loving civilization.

Correct Word/Phrase: _____ _despi_

124. In galleries containing works of both Gauguin
and Cézanne, you will find an equal number of
                                        F
admirers in front of the works of each, but most
          G   H
art critics agree that Gauguin is not of the same
artistic stature with Cézanne.
                 J

Correct Word/Phrase: _____

125. The Board of Education <u>will never be</u> <u>fully</u>
                               A   B

     <u>responsive</u> to the needs of Hispanic children in
     C

     the school system so long <u>that</u> the mayor refuses
                             D

     to appoint a Hispanic educator to the Board.

     Correct Word/Phrase: _____ *fulfill* _____

126. The judge <u>sentenced</u> the president of the
               F

     corporation to ten years in prison for <u>embezzling</u>
                                          G

     corporate funds but <u>gave</u> his partner in crime <u>less</u>
                        H   J

     <u>of a sentence</u>.
     J

     Correct Word/Phrase: _____

127. Scientists <u>have recently discovered</u> that mussels
                   A

     <u>secrete</u> a powerful adhesive that allows them
     B

     <u>attaching</u> themselves to rocks, concrete pilings,
     C

     and <u>other</u> stone or masonry structures.
          D

     Correct Word/Phrase: _____ *secret* _____

128. Wall paintings found recently in the caves of

     Brazil are <u>convincing</u> evidence that cave art
                F

     <u>developed</u> in the Americas at an earlier time <u>as</u> <u>it</u>
     G   H J

     did on other continents.

     Correct Word/Phrase: _____

129. The <u>drop</u> in oil prices and the slump in the
          A

     computer industry <u>account for</u> the recent <u>raise</u> in
                     B   C

     unemployment in Texas and the <u>associated</u> decline
                                        D

     in the value of real estate in the region.

     Correct Word/Phrase: _____ *rise* _____

DIRECTIONS: In items #130–143, correct or omit the underlined preposition as necessary. If the preposition is correct as written, select NO CHANGE. Answers are on page 759.

130. Where are you going <u>to</u>?

     F. NO CHANGE
     G. from
     H. in
     J. OMIT the underlined portion.

131. He has not yet taken advantage <u>off</u> the sale.

     A. NO CHANGE
     B. of
     C. from
     D. OMIT the underlined portion.

132. The teacher broke the news <u>to</u> the student.

     F. NO CHANGE
     G. too
     H. two
     J. OMIT the underlined portion.

133. Due to decreased sales, the workers were laid <u>off</u> by the company.

     A. NO CHANGE
     B. of
     C. down
     D. OMIT the underlined portion.

134. The manager promised to look <u>in to</u> the customer's complaint.

    F. NO CHANGE
    G. into
    H. unto
    J. OMIT the underlined portion.

135. The lawyer voiced his objection <u>on</u> the recount of the votes.

    A. NO CHANGE
    B. to
    C. about
    D. OMIT the underlined portion.

136. The office will open sometime <u>in</u> a half hour.

    F. NO CHANGE
    G. within
    H. inside
    J. OMIT the underlined portion.

137. There are many students waiting <u>on</u> the instructor during her office hours.

    A. NO CHANGE
    B. for
    C. to
    D. OMIT the underlined portion.

138. Please save energy by turning <u>of</u> the lights before you leave the house.

    F. NO CHANGE
    G. off
    H. in
    J. OMIT the underlined portion.

139. The dancers swung <u>in</u> motion when the music started.

    A. NO CHANGE
    B. in to
    C. into
    D. OMIT the underlined portion.

140. I work at the bank <u>in</u> the corner of Main and Packard.

    F. NO CHANGE
    G. on
    H. around
    J. OMIT the underlined portion.

141. He took it <u>up on</u> himself to schedule the meeting.

    A. NO CHANGE
    B. on
    C. upon
    D. OMIT the underlined portion.

142. Ralph had difficulty getting to sleep <u>till</u> very late.

    F. NO CHANGE
    G. up to
    H. until
    J. OMIT the underlined portion.

143. This class is different <u>than</u> the other.

    A. NO CHANGE
    B. of
    C. from
    D. OMIT the underlined portion.

Punctuation

It is important to be familiar with the principal rules governing *punctuation*. This section is not intended to give a definitive set of punctuation rules; instead, it provides a basic overview of correct usage.

Commas

USE A COMMA BEFORE COORDINATING CONJUNCTIONS

Coordinating conjunctions ("and," "but," "nor," "or," "for," "yet," "so") join two independent clauses. Use a comma before coordinating conjunctions unless the two clauses are very short.

Examples:

The boy wanted to borrow a book from the library, <u>but</u> the librarian would not allow him to take it until he had paid his fines. ✓

Joe has been diligent about completing his work, <u>but</u> he has had many problems concerning his punctuality. ✓

I sincerely hope that these exercises prove to be of assistance to you, <u>and</u> I believe that they will help you to make a better showing on your examinations. ✓

Generally, a comma is not used before a subordinate clause that ends a sentence. However, in some circumstances a comma can be used to emphasize the point of the subordinate clause.

Examples:

I cannot possibly find the time to study for the test, unless I rearrange my piano lessons and only work on the weekends. ✓

My mother always scolded my brother and me for being loud and obnoxious, even though the silence worried her more. ✓

If there is no subject following the conjunction, a comma cannot be used since this would create a sentence fragment. If there is a subject following the conjunction, the comma can be omitted if the two clauses are very short.

Examples:

She went to the cafe <u>and</u> bought a cup of coffee. ✓

Roy washed the dishes <u>and</u> Helen dried them. ✓

I saw him <u>and</u> I spoke to him. ✓

A restrictive phrase or clause is vital to the meaning of a sentence. DO NOT set off restrictive phrases or clauses with commas.

Example:

> A sailboat, without sails, is useless. ✗
> A sailboat without sails is useless. ✓

USE COMMAS FOR CLARITY

1. Use a comma if the sentence might be subject to different interpretations without it.

2. Use a comma if a pause would make the sentence clearer and easier to read.

The following examples show how commas can change the meaning of a sentence:

Examples:

> The banks that closed yesterday are in serious financial trouble. (Some banks closed yesterday, and those banks are in trouble.)
> The banks, which closed yesterday, are in serious financial trouble. (All banks closed yesterday, and all banks are in trouble.)
>
> My cat Leo fell down the laundry chute. (The implication is that I have more than one cat.)
> My cat, Leo, fell down the laundry chute. (Here, Leo is an appositive. Presumably, he is the only cat.)
>
> Inside the people were dancing. ✗
> Inside, the people were dancing. ✓
>
> After all crime must be punished. ✗
> After all, crime must be punished. ✓

If you read the last two examples aloud, you will hear how a natural pause suggests where a comma should be inserted. This practice of listening for a pause is not infallible. However, it is the best practice when all other rules governing use of the comma seem to fail.

USE COMMAS TO SEPARATE COORDINATE ADJECTIVES, WORDS IN A SERIES, AND NOUNS IN DIRECT ADDRESS

1. Use a comma between coordinate adjectives. Coordinate adjectives are adjectives of equal importance that precede a noun. If the word "and" can be added between two adjectives without changing the sense of the sentence, you are dealing with coordinate adjectives and should separate them with commas.

2. Use commas to separate the words in a series when three or more elements are present. In such a series, use a comma before "and" or "or." If the series ends in "etc.," use a comma before "etc." DO NOT use a comma after "etc." in a series, even if the sentence continues.

3. Use commas to set off nouns in direct address. The name of the person addressed should be separated from the rest of the sentence by commas.

Examples:

The jolly, fat, ruddy man stood at the top of the stairs. ✓
He is a wise, charming man. ✓
She is a slow, careful reader. ✓

Coats, umbrellas, and boots should be placed in the closet at the end of the hall. ✓
Pencils, scissors, paper clips, etc. belong in your top desk drawer. ✓

Bob, please close the door. ✓
I think, José, that you are the one who was chosen. ✓

USE A COMMA TO SEPARATE QUOTATIONS AND INTRODUCTORY PHRASES

1. Use a comma to separate a short, direct quotation from the speaker.

2. Use a comma after an introductory phrase of two or more words.

3. Use a comma after an introductory phrase whenever the comma would aid clarity.

4. Use a comma after introductory gerunds, participles, and infinitives regardless of their length.

However, if a subordinate clause follows the main clause, it is not necessary to set it off with a comma.

Examples:

She said, "I must leave work on time today." ✓
"Tomorrow I begin my summer job," he told us. ✓

As a child, she was a tomboy. ✓
She was a tomboy as a child. ✓

To Dan, Phil was a friend as well as a brother. ✓
Phil was a friend as well as a brother to Dan. ✓

In 1998, hundreds of people lost their lives in an earthquake. ✓
Hundreds of people lost their lives in an earthquake in 1998. ✓

When you come home, please ring the bell before opening the door. ✓
Please ring the bell before opening the door when you come home. ✓

Because the prisoner had a history of attempted jailbreaks, he was put under heavy guard. ✓
The prisoner was put under heavy guard because he had a history of attempted jailbreaks. ✓

Finally, commas must be used to set off certain phrases and elements that interrupt the natural flow of a sentence.

USE PAIRS OF COMMAS TO SET OFF APPOSITIVE, PARENTHETICAL, AND NON-RESTRICTIVE ELEMENTS

1. An appositive phrase follows a noun or pronoun and has the same meaning as that noun or pronoun. For example, "Mrs. Walker, <u>a teacher</u>, walked up the steps."

2. Parenthetical expressions are words that interrupt the flow of the sentence without changing the meaning of the sentence. Examples include "however," "though," "for instance," "by the way," "to tell the truth," "believe me," "it appears to me," "I am sure," and "as a matter of fact."

3. A non-restrictive element introduces material that is not essential to the sentence and, if removed, will not change the meaning of the original sentence. For example, "The blanket, <u>which was red</u>, lay on the grass."

Examples:

Mr. Dias, <u>our lawyer</u>, gave us some great advice. ✓
Bob, <u>an industrious and hard-working student</u>, will run for class treasurer. ✓

This book, <u>I believe</u>, is the best of its kind. ✓
Julie and her three dogs, <u>I am sure</u>, will not easily find an apartment to rent. ✓

Sam, <u>who is a very well behaved dog</u>, never strays from the front yard. ✓
Millie, <u>who is a fine student</u>, has a perfect attendance record. ✓

Read a sentence aloud to determine if commas should be used to set off a parenthetical expression. If you pause before and after the parenthetical expression, use commas to set it off. In general, if material can be omitted without changing the meaning of the main clause, the material is non-restrictive and should be set off by commas.

USE COMMAS TO SEPARATE DATES, ADDRESSES, AND SPECIFIC LOCATIONS

Use commas to separate the different parts of a date and address. Be sure to include a comma after the last item too.

Examples:

The train will arrive on Friday, February 13, 2003, if it is on schedule. ✓

My new address is: 2040 Winnebago Ave., Apt. #2, Madison, WI. ✓

My daughter traveled from Cambridge, Massachusetts, to Albany, New York, in three hours. ✓

The above rules summarize the most important uses of commas. If you follow these rules, you will not make a serious mistake involving commas.

WHEN SHOULD COMMAS NOT BE USED?

1. DO NOT use a comma to separate a subject from its verb.

2. DO NOT use commas to set off a restrictive or necessary clause or phrase. For example, do not write "The dog, that was barking, bothered me."

3. DO NOT use a comma in place of a conjunction.

Semicolons

USE A SEMICOLON TO SEPARATE A SERIES OF NUMBERS OR A SERIES OF PHRASES THAT CONTAIN COMMAS

1. Use a semicolon to avoid confusion with numbers.

2. Use a semicolon to separate a series of phrases or clauses, each of which contains commas.

Examples:

Add the following prices: $.25; $7.50; and $12.89. ✓

The old gentleman's heirs were Margaret Whitlock, his half-sister; James Bagley, the butler; William Frame, companion to his late cousin, Robert Bone; and his favorite charity, the Salvation Army. ✓

USE A SEMICOLON TO SEPARATE TWO INDEPENDENT CLAUSES

A semicolon may be used to separate two independent clauses when they have a close relationship and are NOT connected with a coordinating conjunction.

Example:

The setting sun caused the fields to take on a special glow; all was bathed in a pale light. ✓

A *semicolon* is often used between two or more independent clauses that are connected by conjunctive adverbs. Examples of conjunctive adverbs include "consequently," "therefore," "also," "furthermore," "for example," "however," "nevertheless," "still," "yet," "moreover," and "otherwise." (Note: A comma must follow the adverb.)

USE SEMICOLONS ONLY WITH INDEPENDENT CLAUSES

Use a semicolon only if each clause can function as an independent sentence.

Examples:

He waited at the station for well over an hour. However, no one appeared. ✓
He waited at the station for well over an hour; however, no one appeared. ✓

Anne is working at the front desk on Monday. Ernie will take over on Tuesday. ✓
Anne is working at the front desk on Monday; Ernie will take over on Tuesday. ✓

She waited for her check to arrive in the mail for two weeks. However, the check never appeared. ✓
She waited for her check to arrive in the mail for two weeks; however, the check never appeared. ✓

DO NOT use a semicolon between an independent clause and a phrase or subordinate clause.

Example:

She worked extra hours every night; yet, was not able to finish the project on time. ✗
She worked extra hours every night yet was not able to finish the project on time. ✓

To summarize, there are three different ways to separate two independent clauses: (1) use a comma followed by a conjunction; (2) use a semicolon; or (3) use a period.

Example:

Autumn had come, and the trees were almost bare. ✓
Autumn had come; the trees were almost bare. ✓
Autumn had come. The trees were almost bare. ✓

If you are uncertain about using a semicolon to connect independent clauses, write two sentences instead.

Colons

The *colon* is always used in the following situations:

┌───┐
│ **RULES FOR SITUATIONS REQUIRING A COLON**   │
│   │
│ 1. A colon should be placed after the salutation in a business letter. │
│   │
│ 2. A colon should be used to separate hours from minutes.   │
│   │
│ 3. A colon should be used to precede a list of three or more items or a long quotation. │
│   │
│ 4. A colon should be used to introduce a question.   │
└───┘

Examples:

Dear Board Member: ✓

The eclipse occurred at 10:36 a.m. ✓

There are three branches of government: executive, judicial, and legislative. ✓

My question is this: Are you willing to punch a time clock? ✓

DO NOT use a colon directly after a verb.

Examples:

We played: volleyball, badminton, football, and tag. ✗
We played volleyball, badminton, football, and tag. ✓

We purchased: apples, pears, bananas, and grapes. ✗
We purchased apples, pears, bananas, and grapes. ✓

DO NOT USE COLONS TO CALL ATTENTION TO ELABORATION OR EXPLANATIONS IF ALREADY SIGNALED

A colon may be used to call attention to elaboration or explanation. However, DO NOT use colons after expressions such as "like," "for example," "such as," and "that is." In fact, colons are intended to replace these terms.

Be careful not to use a colon to introduce or call attention to material that is already signaled by some other element of the sentence.

Example:

We did many different things on our vacation, such as: hiking, camping, biking, canoeing, and kayaking. ✗
We did many different things on our vacation, such as hiking, camping, biking, canoeing, and kayaking. ✓
We did many different things on our vacation: hiking, camping, biking, canoeing, and kayaking. ✓

Periods

RULES FOR SITUATIONS REQUIRING A PERIOD

1. Use a period at the end of a sentence that makes a statement, gives a command, or makes a "polite request" in the form of a question that does not require an answer.

2. Use a period after an abbreviation and after the initial in a person's name.

Examples:

He is my best friend. ✓

There are thirty days in September. ✓

Would you please hold the script so that I may see if I have memorized my lines. ✓

Gen. Robert E. Lee led the Confederate forces. ✓

Note: DO NOT use a period in postal service name abbreviations such as AZ (Arizona) or MI (Michigan).

Exclamation and Question Marks

RULES FOR SITUATIONS REQUIRING AN EXCLAMATION MARK

Use exclamation marks after commands or expressions that show strong emotion. Only use exclamation marks to express strong emotion or to imply urgency.

Examples:

Wonderful! You won the lottery! ✓

Oh no! I won't go! ✓

RULES FOR SITUATIONS REQUIRING A QUESTION MARK

Use a question mark after a request for information. A question mark is used after a direct question. A period is used after an indirect question.

Note: A question must end with a *question mark* even if the question does not encompass the entire sentence.

Examples:

At what time does the last bus leave? ✓

"Daddy, are we there yet?" the child asked. ✓

Did you take the examination on Friday? ✓

The instructor wanted to know if you took the examination on Friday. ✓

Dashes

The material following the *dash* usually directs the reader's attention to the content that precedes it. Unless this material ends a sentence, dashes, like parentheses, must be used in pairs.

RULES FOR SITUATIONS REQUIRING A DASH

1. Use a pair of dashes to set off an explanatory group of words. If the group of words appears at the end of a sentence, it can be preceded by a single dash.

2. Use a dash before a word or group of words that indicates a summation or reversal of what preceded it.

3. Use a dash to mark a sudden break in thought that leaves a sentence unfinished.

Examples:

The tools of his trade—probe, mirror, and cotton swabs—were neatly arranged on the dentist's tray. ✓

Patience, sensitivity, understanding, and empathy—these are the marks of a friend. ✓

He was not pleased with—in fact, he was completely hostile toward—the takeover. ✓

Dashes can be used like commas to set off parenthetical remarks. The difference is a matter of emphasis. Dashes mark a more dramatic shift or interruption of thought. DO NOT mix dashes and commas.

Hyphens

RULES FOR SITUATIONS REQUIRING A HYPHEN

1. Use a hyphen when creating a compound modifier that will precede a noun. A compound modifier is an adjective or adverb phrase that consists of two or more words (e.g., "a walk-in closet").

2. Use a hyphen when creating adjective or adverb phrases that involve numbers (e.g., "a three-course meal").

The following examples illustrate when it is correct to use a hyphen and when it is correct to NOT use a hyphen:

Examples:

There was a sit-in demonstration at the office. ✓

We will sit in the auditorium. ✓

I purchased a four-cylinder car. ✓

I purchased a car with four cylinders. ✓

Quotation Marks

WHEN TO USE QUOTATION MARKS

1. Use quotation marks to enclose the actual words of a speaker or writer.

2. Use quotation marks to emphasize words used in a special or unusual sense.

3. Use quotation marks to set off titles of short themes or parts of a larger work.

Examples:

Jane said, "There will be many people at the party." ✓

He kept using the phrase "you know" throughout his conversation. ✓

"Within You, Without You" is my favorite song on the *Sgt. Pepper's Lonely Hearts Club Band* album by The Beatles. ✓

WHEN NOT TO USE QUOTATION MARKS

1. DO NOT use quotation marks for indirect quotations.

2. DO NOT use quotation marks to justify a poor choice of words.

Examples:

He said that "he would be happy to attend the meeting." ✗
He said that he would be happy to attend the meeting. ✓

I gave her research summary article a low score because I didn't think she "got it right." ✗
I gave her research summary article a low score because I didn't think she understood the methods or results. ✓

PUNCTUATION RULES FOR SITUATIONS WITH QUOTATIONS

1. Always place periods and commas inside quotation marks.

2. Place a question mark inside quotation marks if it is part of a quotation. For example, "Do you like ice cream?" Place a question mark outside quotation marks if the entire sentence is a question that involves the quotation. For example:

   Do you think he was serious when he said "I don't like you"?

3. Place an exclamation mark inside quotation marks if it is part of a quotation. For example, "I'm rich!" Place an exclamation mark outside quotation marks if the entire sentence is an exclamation that involves the quotation. For example:

   I can't believe he said "I don't care"!

4. Always place colons and semicolons outside quotation marks.

Examples:

The principal said, "Cars parked in the fire lane will be ticketed." ✓

The first chapter of *The Andromeda Strain* is entitled "The Country of Lost Borders." ✓

My favorite poem is "My Last Duchess," a dramatic monologue written by Robert Browning. ✓

Three stories in Kurt Vonnegut's *Welcome to the Monkey House* are "Harrison Bergeron," "Next Door," and "EPICAC." ✓

Mother asked earlier tonight, "Did you take out the garbage?" ✓

Do you want to go to the movies and see "Jurassic Park"? ✓

The sentry shouted, "Drop your gun!" ✓

Save us from our "friends"! ✓

My favorite poem is "My Last Duchess"; this poem is a dramatic monologue written by Robert Browning. ✓

He was quoted as supporting the investigation in *The Washington Post*: "I don't know of any proof of misappropriation of funds; however, I support a full investigation into any possible wrongdoing by government officials." ✓

Apostrophes

The apostrophe is used for possession and contraction.

> ## USE APOSTROPHES TO INDICATE POSSESSION
>
> Use apostrophes to create the possessive case of nouns. However, DO NOT use apostrophes with possessive pronouns (e.g., "yours," "hers," "ours," "theirs," and "whose").

Examples:

    lady's = belonging to the lady ✓

    ladies' = belonging to the ladies ✓

To determine if an apostrophe has been used properly, read the apostrophe as "of the."

Example:

    childrens' = of the childrens ✗
    children's = of the children ✓

This rule applies at all times, even with compound nouns separated by hyphens and with entities made up of two or more names.

Examples:

    Brown and Sons' delivery truck = the delivery truck of Brown and Sons ✓

    Lansdale, Jackson, and Smith's law firm = the law firm belonging to Lansdale, Jackson, and Smith ✓

If a singular or plural noun doesn't end in "s," simply add " 's " to create the possessive form (e.g., "Smith's farm"). If a singular or plural noun does end in "s," simply add an apostrophe to create the possessive form (e.g., "James' farm").

Examples:

    Socrates's philosophy ✗
    Socrates' philosophy ✓

    Johnsons's house ✗
    Johnsons' house ✓

> ## USE APOSTROPHES FOR CONTRACTIONS
>
> Use an apostrophe when creating a contraction; insert the apostrophe in place of the omitted letter(s). It is NOT acceptable in standard written English to begin a paragraph with a contraction.

Examples:

    haven't = have not ✓

    o'clock = of the clock ✓

class of '85 = class of 1985 ✓

Be careful with "its" and "it's." "It's" is the contraction of "it is." "Its" is the third person possessive pronoun. Also, DO NOT confuse "they're" ("they are"), "their" (possessive), and "there" (preposition).

Examples:

The cat knows when <u>it's</u> time for <u>its</u> bath. ✓

They're happy to be done with <u>their</u> work. ✓

's → not s
's → if the word ends in s
s

Punctuation

DIRECTIONS: Punctuate sentences #1–55 with commas, semicolons, periods, exclamation marks, question marks, quotation marks, dashes, hyphens, and apostrophes as necessary. Answers are on page 759.

1. He was not aware that you had lost your passport

2. Did you report the loss to the proper authorities

3. I suppose you had to fill out many forms

4. What a nuisance

5. I hate doing so much paper work

6. Did you ever discover where the wallet was

7. I imagine you wondered how it was misplaced

8. Good for you

9. At least you now have your passport

10. What will you do if it happens again

11. I dont know if they are coming though I sent them an invitation weeks ago

12. Neurology is the science that deals with the anatomy physiology and pathology of the nervous system

13. Nursery lore like everything human has been subject to many changes over long periods of time

14. Bob read Joyces *Ulysses* to the class everyone seemed to enjoy the reading

15. In order to provide more living space we converted an attached garage into a den

16. Because he is such an industrious student he has many friends

17. I dont recall who wrote *A Midsummer Nights Dream*

18. In the writing class students learned about coordinating conjunctions and but so or yet for and nor

19. Those who do not complain are never pitied is a familiar quotation by Jane Austen

20. Howard and his ex wife are on amicable terms

21. Her last words were Call me on Sunday and she jumped on the train

22. He is an out of work carpenter

23. This is what is called a pregnant chad

24. Come early on Monday the teacher said to take the exit exam

25. The dog mans best friend is a companion to many

26. The winner of the horse race is to the best of my knowledge Silver

27. Every time I see him the dentist asks me how often I floss

28. The officer was off duty when he witnessed the crime

29. *Anna Karenina* is my favorite movie

30. Red white and blue are the colors of the American flag

31. Stop using stuff in your essays its too informal

32. She was a self made millionaire

33. The Smiths who are the best neighbors anyone could ask for have moved out

34. My eighteen year old daughter will graduate this spring

35. Dracula lived in Transylvania

36. The students were told to put away their books

37. Begun while Dickens was still at work on *The Pickwick Papers Oliver Twist* was published in 1837 and is now one of the authors most widely read works

38. Given the great difficulties of making soundings in very deep water it is not surprising that few such soundings were made until the middle of this century

39. Did you finishing writing your thesis prospectus on time

40. The root of modern Dutch was once supposed to be Old Frisian but the general view now is that the characteristic forms of Dutch are at least as old as those of Old Frisian

41. Moose once scarce because of indiscriminate hunting are protected by law and the number of moose is once again increasing

42. He ordered a set of books several records and a film almost a month ago

43. Perhaps the most interesting section of New Orleans is the French Quarter which extends from North Rampart Street to the Mississippi River

44. Writing for a skeptical and rationalizing age Shaftesbury was primarily concerned with showing that goodness and beauty are not determined by revelation authority opinion or fashion

45. We tried our best to purchase the books but we were completely unsuccessful even though we went to every bookstore in town

46. A great deal of information regarding the nutritional requirements of farm animals has been accumulated over countless generations by trial and error however most recent advances have come as the result of systematic studies at schools of animal husbandry

47. *Omoo* Melvilles sequel to *Typee* appeared in 1847 and went through five printings in that year alone

48. Go to Florence for the best gelato in all of Italy said the old man to the young tourist

49. Although the first school for African Americans was a public school established in Virginia in 1620 most educational opportunities for African Americans before the Civil War were provided by private agencies

50. As the climate of Europe changed the population became too dense for the supply of food obtained by hunting and other means of securing food such as the domestication of animals were necessary

51. In Faulkners poetic realism the grotesque is somber violent and often inexplicable in Caldwells writing it is lightened by a ballad like humorous sophisticated detachment

52. The valley of the Loire a northern tributary of the Loire at Angers abounds in rock villages they occur in many other places in France Spain and northern Italy

53. The telephone rang several times as a result his sleep was interrupted

54. He has forty three thousand dollars to spend however once that is gone he will be penniless

55. Before an examination do the following review your work get a good nights sleep eat a balanced breakfast and arrive on time to take the test

Diagramming Sentences Skills Review

**COURSE
CONCEPT
OUTLINE**

What You Absolutely Must Know

Subjects and Verbs

Subjects

Subjects are difficult to define simply. Here is one incomplete definition: the subject of a sentence is the noun, pronoun, phrase, or clause about which the sentence says or asks something.

Examples:

1. Susan finished her report and handed it in.

   ➢ The sentence says something about Susan. It tells the reader what Susan did. "Susan" is the subject of the sentence.

2. Is patience a virtue?

   ➢ The sentence asks the reader something about patience.

So far so good; nevertheless, this definition has its weaknesses. Let's examine a few more sentences.

Examples:

1. Carla's blatant impatience caused everyone in the restaurant to laugh.

   ➢ The sentence tells the reader something about Carla and something about her impatience. Is "Carla's" or "impatience" the subject? "Carla's" is a possessive, so it cannot be a subject.

2. It is raining.

   ➢ "It" is the subject. But does the sentence really tell something about "it"?

3. You know that mighty Casey struck out.

   ➢ Is the subject of the sentence "you" or "Casey"? "You know" is the main clause (which always contains the subject of the sentence, in this case "you"), and the rest of the sentence is a dependent clause (which never contains the subject of the sentence, but like all clauses has a subject, in this case "Casey").

As you can see, we need a better definition. So, here is a more helpful one: the subject of a sentence is the word with which the verb agrees. This definition is more helpful than you may at first realize. Consider the following:

Examples:

1. On the lake they see a sailboat.

   ➢ What is the subject of the sentence—"lake," "they," or "sailboat"? It can only be "they" because "see" does not agree with either of the other words.

2. Across from the library there will be state-of-the-art tennis courts.

> If a verb is in the future tense, you may want to change it mentally to the present tense before looking for agreement. In this case, the change would be from "will be" to "are." You can see that the verb agrees with "tennis courts," not with "library."

In standard prose, the subject of a sentence usually comes before the verb. There are two main exceptions:

SITUATIONS IN WHICH THE VERB COMES BEFORE THE SUBJECT

1. When "there" or "here" is used to announce the delayed appearance of the subject (e.g., "Next week there will be a birthday party at school.")

2. With questions (e.g., "Have you seen the toys in the attic?")

An *expletive* is a word that has a syntactic function but really doesn't contribute to the meaning of a sentence. In the sentence, "There are two books on the table," "there" doesn't add anything to the meaning of the sentence, as you can prove by dropping it: "Two books are on the table." "There" does, however, fill the usual place of the subject and announce to the reader or listener that the order of words in the sentence may be different from what is expected. So, "there" announces that the verb will precede the subject.

Verbs

Let's consider the tenses (present, past, future, present perfect, past perfect, and future perfect), voices (active and passive), and forms (simple, progressive, and emphatic) of two *verbs*: "play" and "sell."

ACTIVE VOICE OF THE VERB "PLAY"

1. *Simple Present:* plays, play
2. *Simple Past:* played
3. *Simple Future:* will play, shall play
4. *Simple Present Perfect:* has played, have played
5. *Simple Past Perfect:* had played
6. *Simple Future Perfect:* will have played, shall have played
7. *Present Progressive:* am playing, is playing, are playing
8. *Past Progressive:* was playing, were playing
9. *Future Progressive:* will be playing, shall be playing
10. *Present-Perfect Progressive:* has been playing, have been playing
11. *Past-Perfect Progressive:* had been playing
12. *Future-Perfect Progressive:* will have been playing, shall have been playing
13. *Present Emphatic:* does play, do play
14. *Past Emphatic:* did play

PASSIVE VOICE OF THE VERB "PLAY"

1. *Simple Present:* am played, is played, are played
2. *Simple Past:* was played, were played
3. *Simple Future:* will be played, shall be played
4. *Simple Present Perfect:* has been played, have been played
5. *Simple Past Perfect:* had been played
6. *Simple Future Perfect:* will have been played, shall have been played
7. *Present Progressive:* am being played, is being played, are being played
8. *Past Progressive:* was being played, were being played

ACTIVE VOICE OF THE VERB "SELL"

1. *Simple Present:* sells, sell
2. *Simple Past:* sold
3. *Simple Future:* will sell, shall sell
4. *Simple Present Perfect:* has sold, have sold
5. *Simple Past Perfect:* had sold
6. *Simple Future Perfect:* will have sold, shall have sold
7. *Present Progressive:* am selling, is selling, are selling
8. *Past Progressive:* was selling, were selling
9. *Future Progressive:* will be selling, shall be selling
10. *Present-Perfect Progressive:* has been selling, have been selling
11. *Past-Perfect Progressive:* had been selling
12. *Future-Perfect Progressive:* will have been selling, shall have been selling
13. *Present Emphatic:* does sell, do sell
14. *Past Emphatic:* did sell

PASSIVE VOICE OF THE VERB "SELL"

1. *Simple Present:* am sold, is sold, are sold
2. *Simple Past:* was sold, were sold
3. *Simple Future:* will be sold, shall be sold
4. *Simple Present Perfect:* has been sold, have been sold
5. *Simple Past Perfect:* had been sold
6. *Simple Future Perfect:* will have been sold, shall have been sold
7. *Present Progressive:* am being sold, is being sold, are being sold
8. *Past Progressive:* was being sold, were being sold

The *imperative* mood includes the verb forms used to command someone to do something.

Examples:

1. Go!

2. Run!

3. Sit!

4. Speak!

In each case, the imperative has the same form as the present infinitive (e.g., "to go," "to run," "to sit," "to speak") but without the particle "to." This is even true of the infinitive "to be," whose imperative form is "be" (as in "Be good!" or "Be quiet!"). Imperatives do not have to be followed by an exclamation mark, but they often are.

Diagramming Subjects and Verbs

Every diagram of a sentence has at least two lines. First, there is a horizontal base line, which is used for subjects, main verbs, direct objects, predicate nominatives, predicate adjectives, and objective complements. Second, there is a vertical line that passes through the base line and divides the subject of the sentence from the predicate of the sentence (the predicate is the main verb and its objects or complements).

All finite verbs (verbs that can serve as main verbs) are diagrammed in the space provided for the verb. This space starts immediately to the right of the line that divides the subject from the predicate. This is true for all finite verbs regardless of tense (present, past, future, present perfect, past perfect, and future perfect), voice (active and passive), mood (indicative, imperative, and subjunctive), and form (simple, progressive, and emphatic). This does not apply, however, to so-called "verbals," which cannot serve as main verbs in a sentence (infinitives, gerunds, and participles).

Note: As you work through the Diagramming Sentences Skills Review, you may want to check the Glossary of Grammatical Terms and Diagramming Symbols at the end of the Diagramming Sentence Skills Review (pp. 221–231) for the meanings of words and expressions that you do not understand.

In diagramming, the subject is always placed on the far left of the horizontal base line. As mentioned above, the vertical line passing through the base line serves to separate the subject from the verb. The examples that follow are very simple sentences that include only a subject and verb; these diagrams will help you to understand the basics of diagramming sentences.

SUBJECT AND VERB DIAGRAMMING MODEL

Subject | verb

Examples:

1. Children play.

Children | play

The noun "children" is the subject of the sentence. The verb "play" is in the present tense.

2. They were selling.

They	were selling

The personal pronoun "they" is the subject of the sentence. The past progressive "were selling" is the verb. The nominative (subject) forms of the personal pronouns are "I," "you," "he," "she," "it," "we," "you," and "they."

3. It had been played.

It	had been played

The subject of the sentence is the personal pronoun "it." The verb "had been played" is in the past-perfect tense, passive voice.

4. Sandwiches are being sold.

Sandwiches	are being sold.

The subject of the sentence is the plural noun "sandwiches." The verb "are being sold" is a progressive form in the present tense, passive voice.

Subjects and Verbs

DIRECTIONS: Create a diagram for each of the following sentences. Answers are on page 763.

1. Ducks quack.

2. Mosquitoes are buzzing.

3. People have been talking.

4. They will be captured.

5. Money had been collected.

Modal Auxiliary Verbs

Authorities differ as to which verbs should be called *modal auxiliary verbs*. In this lesson, the list of modal auxiliary verbs will include "can," "could," "may," "might," "must," "should," and "would." It is impossible to discuss modal verbs without referring to the indicative and the subjunctive moods, so let's be sure we have a clear understanding of those terms.

Indicative

The *indicative* mood is used for pointing out, describing, or asking. Most verb forms are indicative. Here are some sentences whose verbs are in the indicative mood.

Examples:

1. It is snowing.

2. That has been my house for the last ten years.

3. When does the movie begin?

4. I had a headache.

5. Will you be my friend?

Three modal forms, "can," "may," and "must," are always indicative.

Examples:

1. Ronald <u>can</u> run fast.

   ➢ This sentence says simply that Ronald has the ability to run fast.

2. The children <u>may</u> go with us.

   ➢ This sentence says either that the children have permission to accompany us or that it is possible they will go with us.

3. Stella <u>must</u> stay home this evening.

   ➢ This sentence tells of a particular obligation incumbent upon Stella.

In the first of these examples, if we talk about Ronald's ability to run fast in the past, we would say "When he was young, Ronald could run fast." However, if we want to talk about the characters in the other sentences in the past, we must use altogether different verbs. For the second sentence, we would say "The children were permitted to go with us. And for the third sentence, we would say "Stella had to stay home that evening."

Subjunctive

The modal auxiliary verb "could" is used not only in the past indicative but also in the present *subjunctive*.

Examples:

1. If Ronald had not injured his foot, he <u>could</u> run fast.

   ➤ In this sentence, "could" does not refer to an actual ability. Instead, it refers to an ability Ronald would have if he hadn't hurt himself. This sentence rules out Ronald's ability to run fast here and now.

2. If Ronald wanted to do so, he <u>could</u> run fast.

   ➤ This sentence has two possible meanings. The first meaning is that it's impossible for Ronald to run fast because he doesn't want to do so. The second meaning is that it's improbable Ronald can run fast because it's improbable he wants to do so. If you make a small change and use the indicative in this sentence, its meaning becomes less ambiguous: "Ronald can run fast if he wants to do so."

"Might" is the present subjunctive form of "may." Note the difference between the following sentences:

Examples:

1. If she is here, she <u>may</u> be able to help us.

   ➤ In this sentence, her ability to help is possible (because it is possible that she is here).

2. If she were here, she <u>might</u> be able to help us.

   ➤ In this sentence, her ability to help is purely speculative (because she is not here).

"Would" is used in unreal (contrary-to-fact) conditional sentences.

Example:

If I had time, I <u>would</u> help you.

Contrast the above example with a sentence containing a real condition.

Example:

If I have time, I <u>will</u> help you.

"Would" is also used to express habitual action in the past (e.g., "Back then, people would often sit on their front porch and talk with passing neighbors.").

"Should" is seldom used these days as a future-tense indicator.

Example:

Next year I <u>should</u> like to visit my cousin in New York.

Instead, it is more widely used to express obligation and expectation.

Examples:

1. I really <u>should</u> do my homework.

2. You <u>should</u> be able to find our house.

"Must" has no past tense and no subjunctive form. If we want to use the verb "must" in the past or as a subjunctive, we have to choose another verb.

Examples:

1. They had to leave early. (past)

2. If he had to work harder, he would. (subjunctive)

All seven modals can be used with basic present-perfect forms (present-perfect infinitives without "to").

Examples:

1. He <u>cannot</u> have finished so soon.

2. She <u>could</u> have pouted, but she didn't.

3. If she was there, she <u>may</u> have been able to help them.

4. If she had been there, she <u>might</u> have been able to help them.

5. If I had had time, I <u>would</u> have helped you.

   ➢ This is an unreal conditional sentence in past time.

6. I really <u>should</u> have done my homework.

7. They <u>must</u> have left.

   ➢ This sentence is not the same as "They had to leave."

Notice that in the third and fourth examples, the use of "may" and "might," respectively, helps to distinguish between real and unreal situations.

Finally, with regard to the subjunctive mood, many grammarians claim that it is almost dead in English. They say it is used only in an occasional expression such as "If I were you." For example, if you were asked the verb tense of "gave" and "lived," you would likely say that both are past tense verbs. You would be half right. These verbs are past indicative forms, but they are also present subjunctive forms: "If we gave him five dollars [right now], he would be able to eat"; "If you lived closer [right now], we could get together more often."

Diagramming Modal Auxiliary Verbs

A modal auxiliary verb and the verb it modulates are considered a single verb phrase. In a sentence diagram, this verb phrase is placed in the normal position of the verb (i.e., right after the vertical line that follows the subject):

MODAL AUXILIARY VERB DIAGRAMMING MODEL

Subject | verb

Examples:

1. This must leak.

This | must leak

The demonstrative pronoun "this" is the subject of the sentence. The complete verb consists of the modal auxiliary verb "must" and the present infinitive of the intransitive verb "leak." Intransitive verbs have no passive voice.

2. They should have hurried.

They | should have hurried

The subject of the sentence is the personal pronoun "they." The complete verb consists of the modal auxiliary verb "should" and the basic present perfect form of "hurry."

3. Homes may have been destroyed.

Homes | may have been destroyed

The subject of the sentence is "homes." The verb phrase "may have been destroyed" consists of the modal auxiliary verb "may" and the basic present perfect passive form of "destroy."

Every sentence has a subject and a predicate. The predicate is everything in the sentence that is not the subject, modifiers of the subject, or independent elements. Up to this point, you have only been asked to diagram sentences that have unmodified subjects and predicates that consist only of a verb or verb phrase. As you proceed through this skills review, you will be asked to diagram increasingly complex sentences. Regardless of how complex the sentences become, though, remember that every diagram must include a horizontal base line and a vertical line passing through that base line.

EXERCISE **2**

Modal Auxiliary Verbs

DIRECTIONS: Create a diagram for each of the following sentences. Answers are on page 763.

1. You may stay.

2. They should be scolded.

3. She must have been delayed.

4. That could have been done.

5. They might be coming.

Conjunctions

Coordinating Conjunctions

Coordinating conjunctions connect words, phrases, and clauses of equal importance. Almost always, they connect words, phrases, and clauses of the same kind (i.e., nouns with nouns, verbs with verbs, etc.). Coordinating conjunctions include "and," "but," "or," and "nor."

Examples:

1. Hansel and Gretel marked the trail through the forest. (*compound subject*)

2. The children laughed and played. (*compound verb*)

3. The stepmother commanded, "Hansel and Gretel, wait here until your father and I return." (*compound vocative*)

4. In which song is America called "the land of the free and the home of the brave"? (*compound predicate nominative*)

5. They have a mountain of money but a thimbleful of time. (*compound direct object*)

6. Would you call a tadpole a fish or a reptile? (*compound objective complement*)

7. The project manager was excited but too exhausted to think straight. (*compound predicate adjective*)

8. The students were urged to express their ideas clearly and concisely. (*compound adverb*)

9. Ours is a government by and for the people. (*compound preposition*)

10. She yearned to go to Colorado and ski all winter. (*compound infinitive phrase*)

11. She went shopping but he stayed home. (*compound sentence*)

Subordinating Conjunctions

Subordinating conjunctions are conjunctions that introduce dependent clauses. Subordinating conjunctions include "because," "since," "although," and "if."

Example:

If you take Brenda, and Josh rides with Amelie, I'll see to it that Johanna and Natalie find a way. (*compound adverb clause*)

Correlative Conjunctions

Correlative conjunctions are paired conjunctions that link balanced words, phrases, and clauses. Correlative conjunctions include "both...and," "either...or," "just as...so," "neither...nor," and "whether...or."

Examples:

1. She likes to ride the roller coaster with <u>either her parents or her grandparents</u>. (*compound object of a preposition*)

2. The meet director gave <u>both the winner and the runner-up</u> a large trophy. (*compound indirect object*)

3. He could live <u>neither with her nor without her</u>. (*compound prepositional phrase*)

Diagramming Conjunctions

When diagramming a compound subject, place the individual subjects on parallel horizontal lines and put the coordinating conjunction on a broken vertical line between the two horizontal lines. In the diagramming model below, the "c.c." stands for "coordinating conjunction":

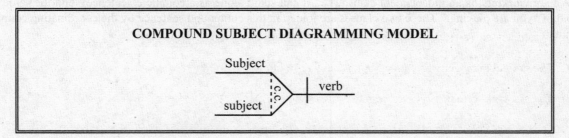

Example:

Jack and Jill are falling.

"Jack and Jill" is a compound subject. "And" is a coordinating conjunction.

Do the same with compound verbs.

To diagram a compound sentence, diagram the first main clause above the second, and put the coordinating conjunction on a broken-line step-down between the verbs of the two diagrams:

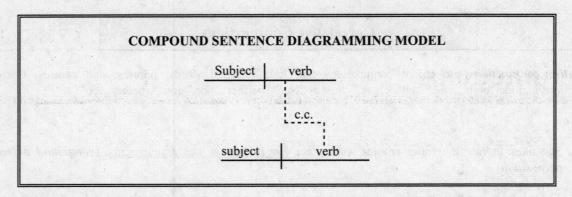

COMPOUND SENTENCE DIAGRAMMING MODEL

Example:

We are working but you are playing.

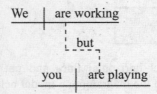

"We are working" is an independent clause (i.e., it can stand alone as a complete sentence), and the same can be said of "you are playing." These two clauses are joined in this compound sentence by the coordinating conjunction "but."

Conjunctions

DIRECTIONS: Create a diagram for each of the following sentences. Answers are on page 764.

1. Buses come and go.

2. Deer were running and jumping.

3. Children run, jump, and play.

4. Doctors and nurses are scurrying.

5. Bombs fell and people died.

Articles, Attributive Adjectives, and Direct Objects

Articles

Although not all languages have *articles*, English has three: "the" (definite article), "a" (indefinite article), and "an" (indefinite article).

Adjectives

Adjectives modify nouns; in other words, they describe or limit nouns in some way. If we call something "a house," we don't differentiate it from any other house. If we call a house "a beautiful house," we restrict the house to that subset of houses that are beautiful. If we call the house "a beautiful white house," we further restrict or modify it by the addition of the adjective "white"; in other words, we restrict the house to that subset of houses that are both beautiful and white.

Attributive Adjectives

Attributive adjectives usually appear right before nouns or pronouns, either following an article ("a beautiful house," "the beautiful house") or not preceded by an article ("beautiful houses"). Sometimes, a noun is modified by two or more attributive adjectives.

Examples:

1. We entered the beautiful white house.

2. A tall, dark, and handsome stranger approached us in the living room.

Attributive adjectives are distinguished from predicate adjectives, which come after linking verbs.

Example:

The house is white.

Occasionally, though, an attributive adjective follows its noun.

Examples:

1. There will be time enough to finish the gardening.

2. The boys were waiting for something else to happen.

Direct Objects

Direct objects receive the action of a verb directly; however, not all verbs take direct objects. Verbs that do are called transitive verbs; verbs that do not are called intransitive verbs. The following are examples of intransitive verbs: all forms of the verbs "be," "become," "seem," "come," aspire," and "squirm."

Here is a way to identify direct objects: as you read a sentence, ask "whom?" or "what?" immediately after a non-linking verb. The answer, if you get one, is a direct object.

Examples:

1. That is a tree.

    ➢ If you ask "what?" right after "is," you get the answer "tree"; however, "tree" is a predicate nominative since it follows the linking verb "is."

2. They saw a tree.

    ➢ If you ask "what?" right after "saw," the answer is "tree." "Saw" is not a linking verb, so "tree" is a direct object.

3. In college she studied economics.

    ➢ Is there a direct object in this sentence? To find out, ask "what?" right after "studied" (i.e., "In college she studied what?" ⇒ "In college she studied economics."). "Studied" is not a linking verb, so "economics" is a direct object.

4. In college she sometimes studied until two in the morning.

    ➢ Is there a direct object in this sentence? If you ask "She sometimes studied whom?" or "She sometimes studied what?", you see that the answer is not present in the sentence; therefore, the sentence has no direct object. Not every non-linking verb will have a direct object.

5. They like Amy but dislike her friend.

    ➢ Are there direct objects in this sentence? To find out, ask "whom?" right after the verb "like" (i.e., "They like whom?" ⇒ "They like Amy."). Similarly, ask "whom?" right after the verb "dislike" (i.e., "They dislike whom?" ⇒ "They dislike her friend."). Neither "like" nor "dislike" is a linking verb, so both "Amy" and "her friend" are direct objects (the noun that serves as the direct object is "friend"; "her friend" is referred to as the complete direct object).

6. He has been an accountant for nine years.

    ➢ If you ask "what?" right after the verb "has been," the answer is "accountant"; however, "accountant" is a predicate nominative since it follows the linking verb "has been," a form of "be."

7. They hiked out into the country and enjoyed the sights.

    ➢ There are two verbs in this sentence: "hiked" and "enjoyed." Does either have a direct object? If you ask "They hiked what?" or "They hiked whom?", you see that the answer is not present in the sentence. In contrast, if you ask "They enjoyed what?", the answer to the question is "sights"; so, "sights" is a direct object.

8. We planted flowers and vegetables in our garden.

   ➢ If you ask "what?" after the verb "planted," the answer is "flowers and vegetables." "Planted" is not a linking verb, so "flowers and vegetables" is a direct object.

9. She can read and write French, but she does not speak the language well.

   ➢ There are three verbs in this sentence: "read," "write," and "speak." Do they all have direct objects? If you ask "She can read and write what?", you see that the answer is present in the sentence (i.e., "She can read and write French."). Similarly, if you ask "She does not speak what?", you see that the answer is "language." None of the verbs are linking verbs, so "French" and "language" are direct objects.

> ### Diagramming Articles, Attributive Adjectives, and Direct Objects

---

An article is diagrammed on a slanted line below the noun it modifies. The top of the slanted line touches the horizontal line underneath the noun:

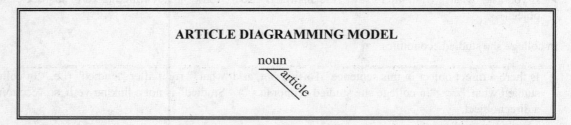

ARTICLE DIAGRAMMING MODEL

Example:

The flowers are blooming.

flowers | are blooming

An attributive adjective is diagrammed on a slanted line below the noun it modifies. It is placed to the right of an article:

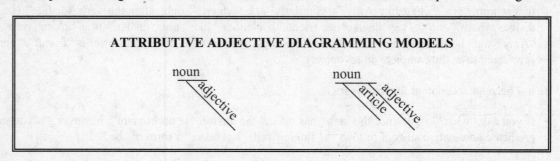

ATTRIBUTIVE ADJECTIVE DIAGRAMMING MODELS

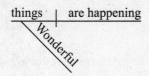

Examples:

1. Wonderful things are happening.

2. A full moon shone.

A direct object is diagrammed after its verb. A vertical line touching the base line from above separates the verb from the direct object:

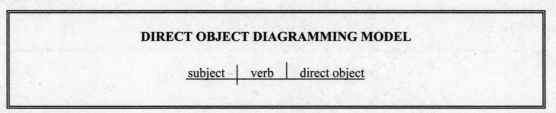

Examples:

1. Most people saw the comet.

2. They have a cat and a small dog.

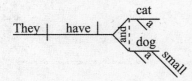

3. The agency feeds unwanted dogs and cats.

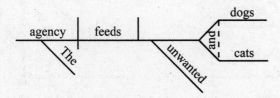

"Unwanted" modifies both "dogs" and "cats." Therefore, it must be placed on a segment of the direct object line that pertains to both direct objects.

4. They splurged and bought a house.

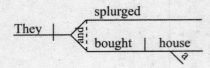

5. She mowed and watered the lawn.

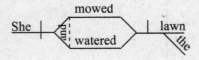

Both verbs have the same direct object.

Articles, Attributive Adjectives, and Direct Objects

DIRECTIONS: Create a diagram for each of the following sentences. Answers are on page 765.

1. We must consider a different plan.

2. Either the county or the city must assume primary responsibility.

3. The new store sells athletic clothing and equipment.

4. Employers appreciate honest and diligent employees.

5. She buys and restores old furniture.

Adverbs

In general, **adverbs** modify verbs, adjectives, and other adverbs. Less frequently, they are also used to modify prepositions, prepositional phrases, conjunctions, clauses, and sentences. There are transitional adverbs, which function both as conjunctions and as adverbs, and there are independent adverbs, which modify nothing at all. So, how does one recognize an adverb?

Adverbs that End in "-ly"

The list of **adverbs that end in "-ly"** extends into the thousands. Here are just a few: "thoroughly," "pleasantly," "helpfully," "dearly," "horribly," and "astutely." However, some words that end in "-ly" aren't adverbs at all but are adjectives (e.g., "manly," "costly," and "portly"), as illustrated in the first three of the following examples:

Examples:

1. She speaks <u>friendly</u> to everyone. ✘
   She is a <u>friendly</u> person. ✓

2. He smiles <u>manly</u>. ✘
   They admire his <u>manly</u> qualities. ✓

3. She listens to her patients <u>motherly</u>. ✘
   She shows a <u>motherly</u> concern for her patients. ✓

4. The assistant principal spoke softly, patiently, and supportively to the troubled student.

   ➤ The adverbs "softly," "patiently," and "supportively" modify the verb "spoke." They tell how the assistant principal spoke.

5. Honestly, I don't care.

   ➤ "Honestly" is an independent adverb; it does not modify any word in the sentence.

Adverbs that Do Not End in "-ly"

And then there are **adverbs that do not end in "-ly,"** e.g., "also," "too," "quite," "very," "here," and "there."

Examples:

1. The motives of the exceedingly gracious hostess were quite political.

   ➤ The adverb "exceedingly" modifies the attributive adjective "gracious." The adverb "quite" modifies the predicate adjective "political."

2. Ray answered the question quite hastily and altogether incorrectly.

   ➤ The adverb "quite" modifies the adverb "hastily." The adverb "altogether" modifies the adverb "incorrectly."

Adjectives that Also Function as Adverbs

What's more, there are quite a few *adjectives that also function as adverbs*, e.g., "fast," "high," "low," "long," "right," "left," "late," and "early."

Examples:

1. Only racecar drivers need <u>fast</u> cars. ✓ (adjective)
   He drives too <u>fast</u>. ✓ (adverb)

2. It was a <u>long</u> wait. ✓ (adjective)
   They had to wait <u>long</u>. ✓ (adverb)

3. She made a <u>right</u> turn. ✓ (adjective)
   She turned <u>right</u>. ✓ (adverb)

4. The <u>early</u> bird gets the worm. ✓ (adjective)
   That bird arrives <u>early</u>. ✓ (adverb)

Diagramming Adverbs

Every adverb is diagrammed on a slanted line. If the adverb modifies a verb or a predicate adjective (predicate adjectives are introduced in the next lesson), the slanted line is extended down from the horizontal line under the verb or predicate adjective:

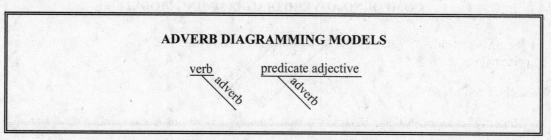

ADVERB DIAGRAMMING MODELS

Example:

The neighbor talks incessantly.

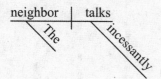

If the adverb modifies an attributive adjective or another adverb, the slanted line underneath the adverb is placed on the left of and parallel to the slanted line of the attributive adjective or of the adverb and is hooked at the top onto this line:

ADVERB MODIFYING ATTRIBUTIVE ADJECTIVE DIAGRAMMING MODEL

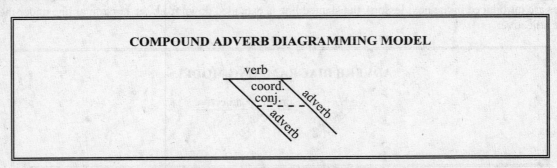

Example:

The thoroughly bored students were fidgeting.

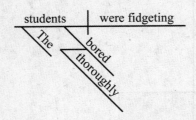

If two adverbs or a compound adverb modify a verb, two slanted lines are extended down from the horizontal line underneath the verb:

COMPOUND ADVERB DIAGRAMMING MODEL

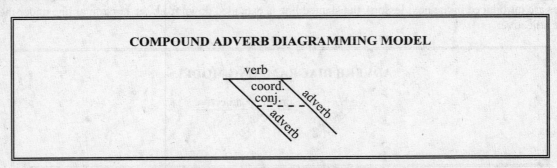

Examples:

1. We awoke very early.

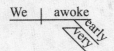

2. She walked swiftly and silently.

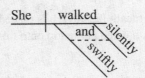

3. The strikingly but superficially beautiful antagonist entered.

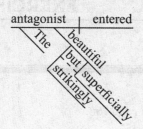

4. Quickly he showered and dressed.

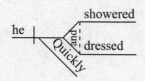

Some adverbs are independent words, modifying nothing at all. Such an adverb is placed on a horizontal line above and separate from the rest of the sentence, as in the following example:

Example:

Not surprisingly, the fatuous man loves a diffident woman.

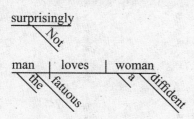

Adverbs

DIRECTIONS: Create a diagram for each of the following sentences. Answers are on page 766.

1. Angrily and inexorably the storm devastated the coastal regions.

2. Not all Americans favor bigger and more expensive cars.

3. I did the assignment fast and inattentively.

4. She wrote an exceedingly but unexpectedly beautiful poem.

5. This subdivision has about fifty residences.

Subjective Complements: Predicate Nominatives and Predicate Adjectives

Subjective complements are nouns or adjectives (or the equivalent of either) that complete linking verbs. Such nouns and equivalent expressions are called *predicate nominatives*; such adjectives and equivalent expressions are called *predicate adjectives*. Subjective complements can also follow certain intransitive verbs as well as passive-voice forms of factitive verbs.

Predicate Nominatives

Examples:

1. The woman in the blue dress is my sister.

   ➤ The predicate nominative is the noun "sister," which follows a form of the verb "be."

2. It is I.

   ➤ The predicate nominative is the personal pronoun "I."

3. Have you ever been a lifeguard?

   ➤ The predicate nominative is "lifeguard." The verb "have been" is a present-perfect form of the verb "be."

4. This could be an important clue.

   ➤ As you would probably expect, modal forms of the verb "be" (such as "may be," "should be," "could have been," and "must have been") can take subjective complements.

5. She was elected president.

   ➤ "President," a predicate nominative, follows a passive-voice form of the factitive verb "elect." Factitive verbs, such as "make," "choose," "appoint," and "designate," are used to make someone something. Predicate nominatives can also be preceded by the expletive "as" (e.g., "He was chosen as leader of the small delegation."). (An expletive is a word with a function but with little or no meaning.)

Predicate Adjectives

Examples:

1. I had been sick for a week.

   ➤ "Sick" is a predicate adjective. "Had been" is a past-perfect form of the verb "be."

2. She felt sad.

   ➤ "Sad" is a predicate adjective. In addition to "feel," the verbs "seem," "become," "look," "remain," "taste," and other similar verbs can be followed by predicate adjectives. You can test them with the adjective "good" (e.g., "it seems good," "he is becoming good," "you look good," "we want to remain good," or "the water tastes good").

3. Blackberries grow wild along the south edge of the woods.

   ➤ "Wild" is a predicate adjective. In this sentence, the verb "grow" is intransitive; in other words, it has a meaning in this sentence ("to thrive" or "to become larger") that does not take a direct object. In other contexts, "grow" can function as a transitive verb meaning "to cause to grow" (e.g., "She likes to grow green beans and tomatoes.").

4. They left angry but arrived happy.

   ➤ "Angry" and "happy" are predicate adjectives; each follows an intransitive verb. "Arrive" is always intransitive. "Leave" can be either intransitive or transitive depending on the context. For example, it is transitive in the sentence "Most customers and employees have already left the building."

5. Tom was made livid by the derogatory remark about his daughter.

   ➤ The predicate adjective "livid" follows a passive form of the factitive verb "make."

Diagramming Subjective Complements

In a sentence diagram, a back slash is used to separate verbs from subjective complements (predicate nominatives and predicate adjectives):

SUBJECTIVE COMPLEMENT DIAGRAMMING MODEL

verb \ subjective complement

Examples:

1. One uncle is an attorney.

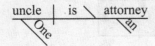

2. The best student became a philosophy professor.

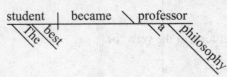

"Became" is a linking verb. "Philosophy" is a noun used as an adjective.

3. Two seniors were made co-captains.

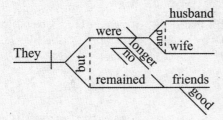

"Were made" is a passive form of a factitive verb.

4. They were no longer husband and wife but remained good friends.

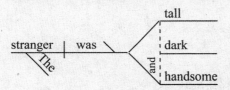

This sentence has a compound predicate and a compound predicate nominative.

5. The stranger was tall, dark, and handsome.

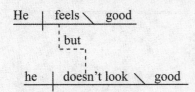

Note the tripartite predicate adjective.

6. He feels good, but he doesn't look good.

He | feels \ good
    but
he | doesn't look \ good

7. I am getting sick.

I | am getting \ sick

When "get" means "become," as it does in this sentence, it is a linking verb.

8. Here the corn grows tall.

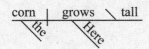

The intransitive verb "grows" is followed in this sentence by a predicate adjective, "tall."

9. She is just playing stupid.

$$\underline{\text{She}\ \Big|\ \text{is playing}\ \diagdown\ \text{stupid}}$$
$$\diagdown\underset{\text{just}}{}$$

When "play" means "pretend to be," it can be followed by a subjective complement.

Subjective Complements: Predicate Nominatives and Predicate Adjectives

DIRECTIONS: Create a diagram for each of the following sentences. Answers are on page 767.

1. Our waiter was both efficient and courteous.

2. She was feeling happy, but he was feeling sad.

3. He is a truly remarkable scholar but a lousy poet.

4. He became angry and silent and left the room.

5. She has been, is, and will be a very effective mayor.

Appositives

Appositives are words, phrases, or clauses that identify or explain other words in the same sentence. Appositives are said to be in apposition with the words they identify or explain. Most appositives are nouns in apposition with preceding nouns; however, they can also be pronouns, verbs, adjectives, adverbs, prepositions, phrases, or clauses. Occasionally, they can also precede the word or words with which they are in apposition. Appositives are set off with parentheses or commas.

Examples:

1. We planned to travel (fly) to Seattle.

   ➤ This sentence contains a verb in apposition with a verb.

2. These flowers are for my best friend, you.

   ➤ This sentence contains a personal pronoun in apposition with a noun.

3. She regrets the disappearance of many feral (wild) animals.

   ➤ This sentence contains an adjective in apposition with an adjective.

4. He removed the books clandestinely (secretly).

   ➤ This sentence contains an adverb in apposition with an adverb.

5. We live on (beside) a river.

   ➤ This sentence contains a preposition in apposition with a preposition.

6. The office workers were told to be less officious (to mind their own business).

   ➤ This sentence contains an infinitive phrase in apposition with an infinitive phrase.

7. On Friday evenings we go out to eat (the only excitement of the week), and then we work all weekend.

   ➤ This sentence contains a noun phrase in apposition with a clause.

In English, when a proper name is in apposition with a possessive noun, only the proper name has a possessive ending.

Example:

I borrowed my friend Melvin's car.

Restrictive and Non-Restrictive Appositives

There is an important distinction between ***restrictive and non-restrictive appositives***: the former are necessary for identification, and the latter are unnecessary for identification.

RESTRICTIVE VERSUS NON-RESTRICTIVE APPOSITIVES

Restrictive: "My cousin Alan broke his arm." (noun in apposition with a noun)

Non-restrictive: "My father, a skiing instructor, broke his arm." (noun in apposition with a noun)

Intensifying Pronouns

Certain pronouns are both reflexive and intensifying. As *intensifying pronouns*, they are appositives: "myself," "yourself," "himself," "herself," "itself," "ourselves," "yourselves," and "themselves."

Examples:

1. The author herself will be there to sign copies of her new book.

   ➤ This sentence contains an intensifying pronoun ("herself") in apposition with a noun ("the author").

2. They themselves will be there.

   ➤ This sentence contains an intensifying pronoun ("themselves") in apposition with a pronoun ("they").

Diagramming Appositives

Appositives are placed in parentheses immediately after the word or words with which they are in apposition:

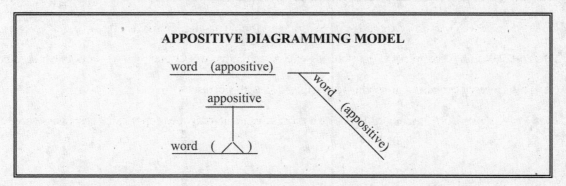

APPOSITIVE DIAGRAMMING MODEL

You can disregard the appositive on a pedestal for now. It is a topic for later consideration.

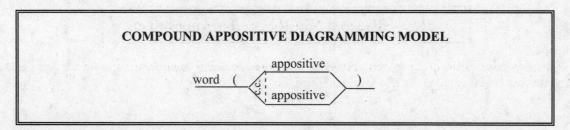

COMPOUND APPOSITIVE DIAGRAMMING MODEL

Examples:

1. Everyone likes my friend Jacob.

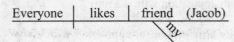

   "Jacob" is in apposition with the direct object, "friend."

2. That's her son Al's car.

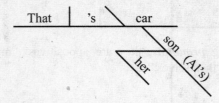

   The sentence has two possessives: the pronoun "her" and the noun "Al's." If the appositive "Al's" is omitted, one says "her son's car."

3. Two seniors, namely Isabel and Latoya, were chosen as co-captains.

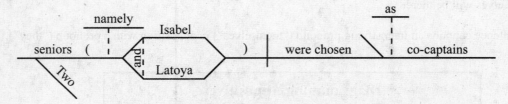

   The sentence has two expletives: "namely," which introduces the compound appositive "Isabel and Latoya," and "as," which introduces the predicate nominative "co-captains."

Appositives

DIRECTIONS: Create a diagram for each of the following sentences. Answers are on page 769.

1. Her cousins Jack and Jill climbed a hill.

2. J. J., a four-year band member, was chosen as the most outstanding musician.

3. The renters altered, that is, nearly destroyed, the apartment.

4. They have strength, speed, and mental toughness—the right qualities.

5. Have you met my friend Marcy?

Prepositional Phrases

Prepositions

Prepositions are particles (small, uninflected words) that show relationships between their objects and other words. You can name many prepositions by thinking of any place a mouse can go: "in," "into," "around," "up," "down," "over," "under," and "through." Many prepositions, however, have nothing to do with place: "with," "without," "for," "besides," "since," "of," and "except."

When used in a sentence, a preposition must have an object. If a particular word does not have an object, it is not a preposition. It may look exactly like a preposition (i.e., it may be spelled the same), but without an object it functions as an adverb, a conjunction, or as part of a phrasal verb.

Examples:

1. Jack Horner was sitting <u>in</u> a corner.

   ➢ The preposition "in" has the object "corner."

   They just walked <u>in</u>.

   ➢ Here, "in" is an adverb. Adverbs do not have objects.

2. Poor Jethro had to stay <u>after</u> school.

   ➢ The preposition "after" has the object "school."

   He stayed for an hour <u>after</u> the other students had left.

   ➢ Here, "after" is a subordinating conjunction, introducing an entire clause ("the other students had left").

3. The dog chased the cat <u>around</u> the house.

   ➢ The object of the preposition "around" is "house."

   The flu is going <u>around</u>.

   ➢ Here, "around" is an adverb.

4. There is no one here <u>but</u> us.

   ➢ The object of the preposition "but" is the pronoun "us."

   She went to school <u>but</u> her brother stayed home.

   ➢ Here, "but" is a coordinating conjunction.

For now, only nouns and pronouns will be used as objects of prepositions; later, however, you will see how gerunds and gerund phrases, infinitives and infinitive phrases, as well as noun clauses can be objects of prepositions. It is even possible for prepositional phrases to be used as objects of prepositions.

Some prepositions consist of more than one word. Examples of these phrasal prepositions are "out of," "along with," "as for," and "by means of."

Adverbs, too, can modify prepositions and prepositional phrases.

Examples:

1. The fireworks display will begin right after the game.

   ➤ The adverb "right" modifies the preposition "after."

2. The food arrived just in time for the party.

   ➤ The adverb "just" modifies the prepositional phrase "in time."

Adverbial Prepositional Phrases

Most prepositional phrases are adverbial or adjectival. *Adverbial prepositional phrases* modify verbs, adjectives, and adverbs.

Examples:

1. Carolyn and Barbara strolled through the park.

   ➤ The prepositional phrase "through the park" modifies the verb "strolled." It tells where Carolyn and Barbara strolled.

2. Transparent in the middle, the glass is increasingly opaque as it approaches the frame.

   ➤ The prepositional phrase "in the middle" modifies the adjective "transparent."

3. Everyone moved closer to the storyteller.

   ➤ The prepositional phrase "to the storyteller" modifies the adverb "closer."

Adjectival Prepositional Phrases

Adjectival prepositional phrases modify nouns and pronouns.

Examples:

1. All eyes were focused on the woman on the tightrope.

   ➤ The prepositional phrase "on the tightrope" modifies the noun "woman."

2. Someone in the corner stood up.

   ➤ The prepositional phrase "in the corner" modifies the pronoun "someone."

3. As far as anyone knew, he was in good health.

➤ The prepositional phrase "in good health" functions as a predicate adjective, modifying the pronoun "he."

Diagramming Prepositional Phrases

To diagram a prepositional phrase, place the preposition on a diagonal line connected to the horizontal or diagonal line of the word or words modified. From a point near the bottom of this diagonal line, draw a horizontal line to the right, and put the object of the preposition on this line. Any modifiers of the object are diagrammed in the expected manner:

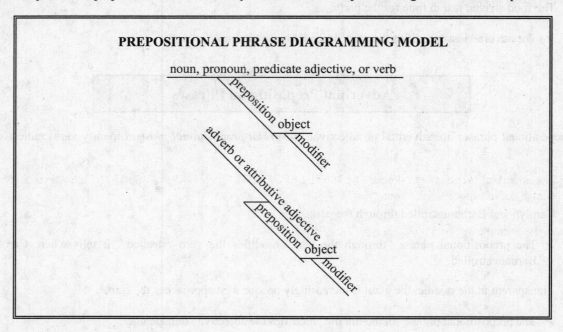

PREPOSITIONAL PHRASE DIAGRAMMING MODEL

noun, pronoun, predicate adjective, or verb

preposition / object / modifier

adverb or attributive adjective / preposition / object / modifier

Examples:

1. A porter carried our baggage to the car.

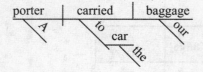

The prepositional phrase "to the car" is adverbial; it modifies the verb "carried."

2. Late for her doctor's appointment, Susan was driving dangerously.

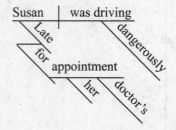

The adverbial prepositional phrase "for her doctor's appointment" modifies the attributive adjective "late."

3. He is of sound mind and body.

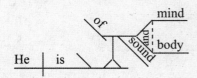

"Of sound mind and body," a prepositional phrase with a compound object, serves in this sentence as a predicate adjective, modifying the pronoun "he."

4. She eats too fast for the rest of us.

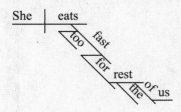

The adverbial prepositional phrase "for the rest of us" modifies the adverb "fast." The adjectival prepositional phrase "of us" modifies the noun "rest."

5. In the evening we went out for a ride.

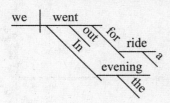

"In the evening" and "for a ride" are prepositional phrases modifying the verb "went." "Out," which looks like a preposition, is an adverb in this sentence.

6. I can live with or without television.

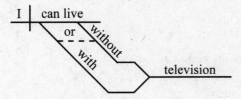

The adverbial prepositional phrase "with or without television" features two prepositions and a single prepositional object.

7. Everyone but Jay ran right out of the house.

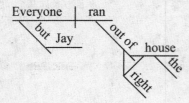

In this sentence, "but" is a preposition. "Out of" is a phrasal preposition. The adverb "right" modifies the prepositional phrase "out of the house."

Prepositional Phrases

DIRECTIONS: Create a diagram for each of the following sentences. Answers are on page 770.

1. Early in the week, friends of ours are coming for dinner.

2. They approach every new challenge with enthusiasm and determination.

3. We can go through the narrow tunnel or over the narrow bridge.

4. The principal is taking a group of teachers out for lunch.

5. She acted in accordance with the express wishes of her clients.

Indirect Objects and Objective Complements

Indirect Objects

Indirect objects tell to whom or for whom direct objects are given, said, or shown. In the sentence "He showed them the picture," the direct object is "picture." The indirect object (i.e., the people to whom the picture was shown) is "them." An indirect object is not preceded by a preposition. "He showed them the picture" means the same thing as "He showed the picture to them." However, in the latter sentence, "them" is not an indirect object; instead, it is the object of the preposition "to."

Examples:

1. Fred gave his sister a present.

   ➤ "Present" is a direct object. The indirect object is "sister."

2. Will you lend me a dollar?

   ➤ "Dollar" is a direct object. The indirect object is "me."

3. She is telling her students a story.

   ➤ "Story" is a direct object. The indirect object is "students."

Remember: Not every sentence that has a direct object has an indirect object as well. Indirect objects are found only in sentences that have verbs of giving, telling, or showing, such as "offer," "hand," "teach," "lend," "promise," "bring," and "get." Even verbs like "sing" and "find" can take indirect objects if they imply a kind of giving or offering, as in "Will you sing us a song?" and "Find me a pretty flower!" In the previous sentences, the indirect objects are "us" and "me." "Do" doesn't seem to be a verb of giving, but it is in a sentence like "Please do me a favor."

Objective Complements

Objective complements are nouns or adjectives (or the equivalent of nouns or adjectives, like pronouns or participles) that complete verbs with respect to direct objects. The verb in a sentence with an objective complement is often factitive (i.e., it makes someone or something someone or something else): "elect," "appoint," "choose," "render," "name," "call," "entitle," "color," "dye," and "make."

Examples:

1. They called their mascot Herbie.

   ➤ The noun "Herbie" is an objective complement; the verb "called" is factitive.

2. The summer job will make him strong.

   ➤ The adjective "strong" is an objective complement; the verb "make" is factitive.

3. The shock of standing in front of the class has rendered the poor boy speechless.

    ➤ The adjective "speechless" is an objective complement; the verb "rendered" is factitive.

4. The parents named their daughter Aphrodite.

    ➤ The noun "Aphrodite" is an objective complement; the verb "named" is factitive.

5. One of my classmates dyed his hair purple.

    ➤ The adjective "purple" is an objective complement; the verb "dyed" is factitive.

Like predicate nominatives, some objective complements are introduced by the expletive "as."

Example:

The European travelers chose a bilingual woman as their spokesperson.

Objective complements appear only in active sentences. To change a sentence with an objective complement into its corresponding passive sentence, one takes the direct object of the sentence and makes it the subject. The passive factitive verb acts as a linking verb, and the objective complement of the original sentence becomes a subjective complement (either a predicate nominative or a predicate adjective). To see how this works, let's change the five example sentences above into their corresponding passive forms.

Examples:

1. Their mascot was called Herbie.

    ➤ "Herbie" is a predicate nominative.

2. He will be made strong by the summer job.

    ➤ "Strong" is a predicate adjective.

3. The poor boy has been rendered speechless by the shock of standing in front of the class.

    ➤ "Speechless" is a predicate adjective.

4. The hair of one of my classmates was dyed purple.

    ➤ "Purple" is a predicate adjective.

5. A bilingual woman was chosen as spokesperson by the European travelers.

    ➤ "Spokesperson" is a predicate nominative.

The above rules hold when the objective complement is a noun, a pronoun, or an adjective. We will see in the next lesson that it does not apply when the objective complement is an infinitive.

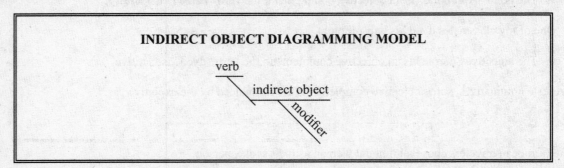

Diagramming Indirect Objects and Objective Complements

An indirect object is diagrammed like an object of a preposition, on a horizontal line that extends to the right from a point near the bottom of a diagonal line whose top touches the base line under the verb. Leave the diagonal line empty:

INDIRECT OBJECT DIAGRAMMING MODEL

verb

indirect object

modifier

Examples:

1. Show Jenny the letter from Theresa.

x | Show | letter
the
Jenny
from
Theresa

The noun "Jenny," which indicates the person to whom something is to be shown, is an indirect object. The "*x*" represents the unexpressed subject "you." The prepositional phrase "from Theresa" is adjectival.

2. She gave him her phone number.

She | gave | number
him
her
phone

The personal pronoun "him" is an indirect object. "Phone" is a noun used as an adjective.

3. I told William and Sarah the news.

I | told | news
the
William
and
Sarah

"William and Sarah" is a compound indirect object.

4. Play me my favorite melody.

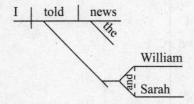

x | Play | melody
me
my
favorite

In this context, playing is a kind of giving; thus the verb "play" can have an indirect object.

There are two acceptable ways of diagramming objective complements. The one has tradition on its side, while the other is more appealing to most people today:

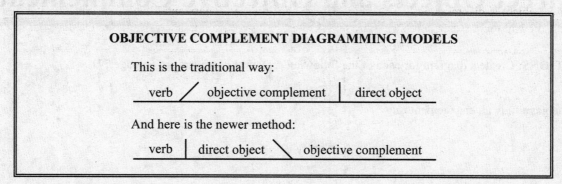

OBJECTIVE COMPLEMENT DIAGRAMMING MODELS

This is the traditional way:

| verb / objective complement | direct object |

And here is the newer method:

| verb | direct object \ objective complement |

The following examples utilize the newer method:

Examples:

1. The class elected him treasurer.

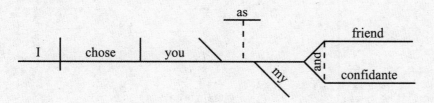

The noun "treasurer" is an objective complement.

2. I chose you as my friend and confidante.

"Friend and confidante" is a compound objective complement. "As" is an expletive.

Indirect Objects and Objective Complements

DIRECTIONS: Create a diagram for each of the following sentences. Answers are on page 771.

1. John gave Judy an engagement ring.

2. The governor gave each distinguished student and his or her mentor a monetary award.

3. The rescue team found the campers alive and declared them extremely fortunate.

4. Jamie told Shanika, her next-door neighbor, the news about their friend Pam.

5. Humpty-Dumpty was found in pieces, and neither the king's horses nor the king's men could make him whole again.

Infinitives

Transitive Infinitives

The basic form of a verb—the form that is usually preceded by the particle "to"—is called an infinitive. All *infinitives* have tense, and *transitive infinitives* have voice as well as progressivity; however, they do not have person and number.

INFINITIVES OF THE TRANSITIVE VERB "FIND"

1. *Present Active:* to find

2. *Present Passive:* to be found

3. *Present-Perfect Active:* to have found

4. *Present-Perfect Passive:* to have been found

5. *Progressivity:* to be finding, to have been finding

An infinitive with its modifiers and objects is called an infinitive phrase. Like simple infinitives, infinitive phrases can be used as adverbs, adjectives, or nouns.

Examples:

1. They are playing <u>to win</u>. (as an *adverb*)

2. We drove fifty miles <u>to see the performance</u>. (as an *adverb*)

3. You have nothing <u>to do</u>. (as an *adjective*)

4. I am looking for something <u>to read on vacation</u>. (as an *adjective*)

5. Who doesn't want <u>to succeed</u>? (as a *noun*)

6. The children are learning <u>to write correctly</u>. (as a *noun*)

When used as nouns, infinitives and infinitive phrases can be subjects, direct objects, predicate nominatives, appositives, objects of prepositions, and objective complements.

Examples:

1. <u>To die</u> is our common destiny. (as a *subject*)

2. <u>To fly</u> is fun for a while. (as a *subject*)

3. <u>To stand up for the rights of the underprivileged</u> is admirable. (as a *subject*)

4. <u>To drive a car properly</u> requires practice and a respect for the rights of others. (as a *subject*)

5. Do you want <u>to rest</u>? (as a ***direct object***)

6. Children like <u>to run and play</u>. (as a ***direct object***)

7. She tried <u>to read a good book</u>. (as a ***direct object***)

8. Would you prefer <u>to go to a movie today or to eat out tomorrow</u>? (as a ***direct object***)

9. Their goal will be <u>to survive</u>. (as a ***predicate nominative***)

10. Her job was <u>to hire the best people available</u>. (as a ***predicate nominative***)

11. To strive is <u>to succeed</u>. (as a ***predicate nominative***)

12. It was not my idea <u>to leave early</u>. (as an ***appositive***)

13. Sometimes it is necessary <u>to stand and fight</u>. (as an ***appositive***)

14. Nothing remained except <u>to fold our tents and go home</u>. (as the ***object of the preposition "except"***)

15. The waiter did everything but <u>pay the bill</u>. (a "*to*-less" infinitive as the ***object of the preposition "but"***)

16. Do you really have nothing to do except <u>disturb others</u>? (a "*to*-less" infinitive as the ***object of the preposition "except"***)

17. She made them <u>stay after school</u>. (a "*to*-less" infinitive as an ***objective complement***)

18. He heard someone <u>come in the back door</u>. (a "*to*-less" infinitive as an ***objective complement***)

19. We watched the red sun <u>sink below the horizon</u>. (a "*to*-less" infinitive as an ***objective complement***)

In these cases where the infinitive is used as an objective complement, the infinitive is quite often "*to*-less."

One might consider the phrase "to be honest" as an objective complement in the sentence "I believe him to be honest." However, a better analysis of this sentence might be to consider the phrase "him to be honest" as an objective-case subject with a verb in the infinitive form (a construction akin to the subject accusative with infinitive in Latin). The sentence can be restated as "I believe <u>that he is honest</u>" (i.e., with the indirect statement underlined), which is precisely the kind of construction that is rendered as a subject accusative with infinitive in Latin.

Complementary Infinitives

The modal auxiliary verbs "may," "might," "can," "could," "should," and "must" are so closely tied to their complements (the verbs that complete them) that the two (modal auxiliary and complement) are considered single verb forms ("may arrive," "can help," "should wait," "must have seen," etc.) and are so diagrammed. Other verbs achieve this same closeness with their complements ("ought to hurry," "am going to meet," "used to watch," etc.). In such constructions, the infinitives that complement the introductory words are usually preceded by the particle "to" and are called ***complementary infinitives***.

Examples:

1. Students <u>have to stay</u> in their homerooms until the bell rings.

2. Students <u>ought to stay</u> in their homerooms until the bell rings.

3. Students <u>are to stay</u> in their homerooms until the bell rings.

4. Students <u>are going to stay</u> in their homerooms until the bell rings.

5. Students <u>used to stay</u> in their homerooms until the bell rang.

Do not confuse complementary infinitives with direct objects. In general, sentences that contain transitive verbs (i.e., verbs that take direct objects) are able to be restated in the passive voice. Even though "have" and "used" can take direct objects, they can't do so in the above sentences because their meanings there do not allow them to be used passively. If you try to express these sentences in the passive voice, you get nonsense.

Example:

To stay in homerooms until the bell rings is had by students. (Nonsense, right?)

Above, you were introduced to infinitives and infinitive phrases used as predicate nominatives; now, you will meet infinitives and infinitive phrases used as predicate adjectives. The infinitives may be preceded by forms of the verb "to be," but they can also follow other linking verbs (e.g., "seem," "appear," and certain passive verbs).

Examples:

1. He seemed <u>to have all his ducks in a row</u>. (as a ***predicate adjective***)

2. One contestant appears <u>to lack self-confidence</u>. (as a ***predicate adjective***)

3. The Royal Library of Alexandria is thought <u>to have contained more than 500,000 books</u>. (as a ***predicate adjective***)

4. This is said <u>to be the best Vietnamese restaurant in town</u>. (as a ***predicate adjective***)

In a peculiar construction, the particle "for" is used as an expletive to introduce an infinitive phrase used as a subject, a direct object, a predicate nominative, or an appositive. Such infinitive phrases have subjects.

Examples:

1. For us to deny our common humanity would be harmful to society. (subject of infinitive: "us")

2. The old man does not like for others to do his work for him. (subject of infinitive: "others")

3. The plan was for him to read the script first. (subject of infinitive: "him")

4. It is essential to the success of the company for all employees to contribute their time and talents. (subject of infinitive: "employees")

An infinitive phrase can also be used as the object of the preposition "for."

Examples:

1. The salespeople were itching for the last customers to leave the store. (subject of infinitive: "customers")

2. The boss bought a second car for the staff to use. (subject of infinitive: "staff")

Finally, infinitives and infinitive phrases can also be used as independent expressions.

Examples:

1. To tell the truth, I've never caught a really big fish in my life.

2. Kay made a good impression, to say the least.

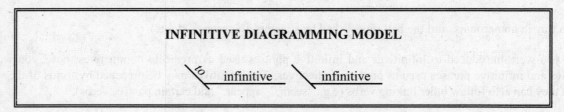

Diagramming Infinitives

Most infinitives are preceded by the particle "to"; however, some are "*to*-less":

INFINITIVE DIAGRAMMING MODEL

to infinitive   infinitive

Examples:

1. To own her own car has long been her desire.

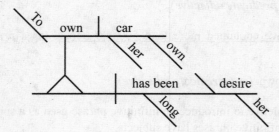

The infinitive phrase "to own her own car" is the subject of the sentence.

2. He hates to wash dishes and take out the garbage.

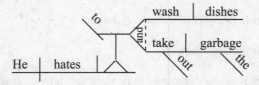

This sentence features a compound infinitive phrase used as a direct object.

3. To love is to live fully.

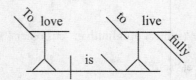

The subject of the sentence is the infinitive "to love"; the infinitive phrase "to live fully" is a predicate nominative.

4. We have nothing to do, we are ready to go, and we can't wait to leave.

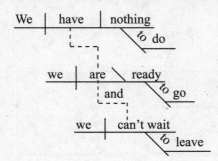

"To do" is an adjectival infinitive; it modifies the noun "nothing." "To go" is an adverbial infinitive; it modifies the adjective "ready." "To leave" is an adverbial infinitive; it modifies the verb "can't wait."

5. The weather forced him to head south.

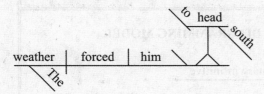

The infinitive phrase "to head south" is an objective complement. Don't forget the other way of diagramming objective complements, as follows:

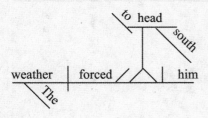

6. It is difficult to watch television and to study effectively at the same time.

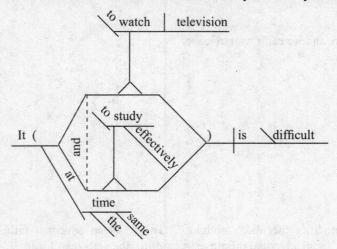

The compound infinitive phrase "to watch television and to study effectively at the same time" is in apposition with the subject of the sentence, "it."

COMPLEMENTARY INFINITIVE DIAGRAMMING MODEL

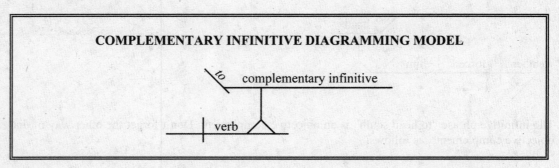

Examples:

1. The wedding is to be held in an azalea garden.

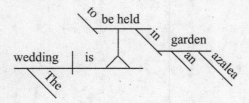

The complementary infinitive "to be held" is in the present tense, passive voice.

2. You ought to have been there.

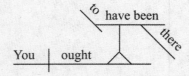

"To have been" is a complementary infinitive. It is in the present perfect tense.

3. We are going to go to the game and scream.

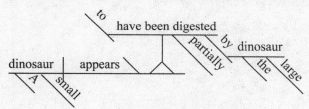

"To go to the game and scream" is a compound complementary infinitive phrase.

4. She is about to speak.

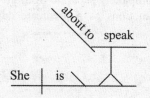

"About to" is a phrasal particle.

5. A small dinosaur appears to have been partially digested by the large dinosaur.

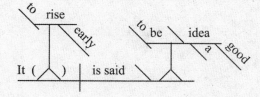

The infinitive phrase introduced by the present perfect passive infinitive "to have been digested" functions as a predicate adjective after the linking verb "appears."

6. It is said to be a good idea to rise early.

It ( ) | is said

The passive verb "is said" functions as a linking verb. The infinitive phrase "to rise early" is in apposition with the subject, "it."

7. To be sure, the second computer is for the children to use.

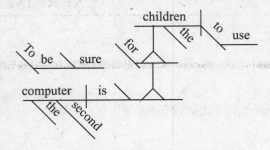

"To be sure" is an independent infinitive phrase; therefore, its diagram is completely separate from the rest of the diagram. "For the children to use" is a prepositional phrase that functions as a predicate adjective. "Children" is the subject of the infinitive "to use."

Infinitives

DIRECTIONS: Create a diagram for each of the following sentences. Answers are on page 773.

1. Their plan was to fly to Seattle and rent a car.

2. That is easy to promise but hard to do.

3. She spoke too softly to be understood.

4. He walks three miles every day to stay cardiovascularly healthy.

5. Domestic responsibilities compelled them to stay at home.

6. The students are to go immediately to their desks.

7. For them to become angry is not helpful to our cause.

8. To have to be told three times to behave is a sign of immaturity.

9. She said for the children to be ready to leave in ten minutes.

10. They are thought to have been kidnapped by insurgents.

Gerunds

Gerunds are verbal nouns; in other words, they are both nouns and verbs. As a noun, a gerund can function as other nouns function (i.e., as the subject of a sentence, as a direct object, as a predicate nominative, etc.). As a verb, a gerund can have several different functions. If the gerund is a linking verb, it can be followed by a predicate nominative or a predicate adjective. A transitive gerund can take a direct object. Finally, if it is a verb of saying, giving, or showing, a gerund can take an indirect object. With regard to how a gerund can be modified, again there are two different possibilities. As a noun, a gerund can be modified by adjectives and by words functioning as adjectives (i.e., nouns, prepositional phrases, etc.). As a verb, a gerund can be modified by adverbs and by words functioning as adverbs (i.e., adverbial objectives, prepositional phrases, etc.).

Like infinitives, gerunds have tense and (in the case of transitive gerunds) voice; however, gerunds do not have person or number. If a verb is intransitive (i.e., a verb that does NOT transfer action to an object), it has only two gerund forms. For example, the intransitive verb "be" has only two gerund forms: present ("being") and present-perfect ("having been"). These two gerunds could be used in a sentence like "Being in love is better than having been in love." If a verb is transitive (i.e., a verb that does transfer action to an object), it has two active forms and two corresponding passive forms. For example, the transitive verb "to see" has not only a present active gerund ("seeing") and a present-perfect active gerund ("having seen") but also a present passive gerund ("being seen") as well as a present-perfect passive gerund ("having been seen").

Gerund Phrases

A gerund with its complements, objects, and modifiers constitutes a gerund phrase. *Gerund phrases* can, like simple gerunds, function as subjects, predicate nominatives, appositives, direct objects, objects of prepositions, objective complements, and adverbial objectives (the last of which are mostly limited to modifiers of "worth").

Examples:

1. Waiting is not fun. (as a *subject*)

2. Walking for at least thirty minutes daily is healthy. (as a *subject*)

3. Eating out can get boring. (as a *subject*)

4. Her hobby is running. (as a *predicate nominative*)

5. Giving free food to friends is regarded by the manager as stealing. (as a *predicate nominative*)

6. Learning to walk is putting one foot in front of the other. (as a *predicate nominative*)

7. These are a few of my grandchildren's favorite things: coloring, listening to stories, and watching videos. (as an *appositive*)

8. It was a pleasure getting to know you. (as an *appositive*)

9. This is the life for me, just lying on the sand and soaking up the sun. (as an *appositive*)

10. She doesn't like hitting. (as a *direct object*)

11. Do you enjoy their ranting and raving? (as a *direct object*)

12. Have you tried <u>starting at the beginning</u>? (as a ***direct object***)

13. In the wintertime you can lower your heating bill by <u>freezing</u>. (as the ***object of a preposition***)

14. Sunday afternoons are reserved for <u>doing fun things with their children</u>. (as the ***object of a preposition***)

15. Since his heart surgery, he has given much thought to <u>eating and drinking healthfully</u>. (as the ***object of a preposition***)

16. Do you call that <u>dancing</u>? (as an ***objective complement***)

17. The judge condemned their door-to-door sales as <u>taking advantage of the elderly</u>. (as an ***objective complement***)

18. Anyone in his right mind would consider that strategy <u>manipulating the books</u>. (as an ***objective complement***)

19. Anything worth <u>doing</u> is worth <u>doing right</u>. (as an ***adverbial objective***)

Diagramming Gerunds

GERUND DIAGRAMMING MODEL

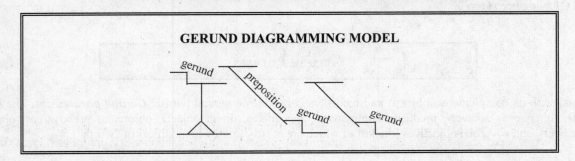

Examples:

1. Diagramming is a symbolic way of showing grammatical relationships between the words of a sentence.

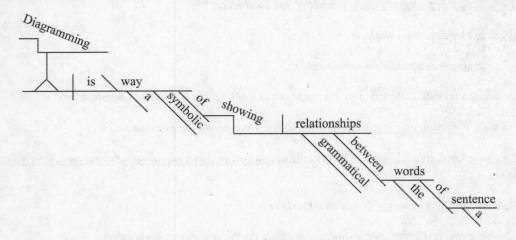

In this sentence, the gerund "diagramming" is the subject. Another gerund, "showing," introduces a gerund phrase that serves as the object of the preposition "of."

2. His basketball strong points are rebounding and blocking shots.

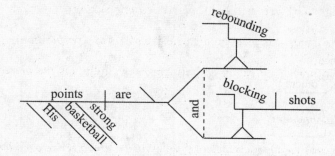

The compound predicate nominative comprises a gerund and a gerund phrase. Because gerunds are not only nouns but also verbs, some of them take direct objects.

3. Everyone in the family teases him about his snoring during our favorite TV programs.

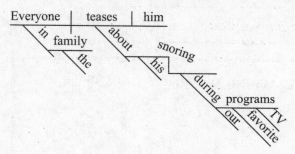

Adjective modifiers of gerunds (i.e., "his") hang from the upper horizontal line of the gerund step-down, whereas adverbial modifiers (i.e., the prepositional phrase "during our favorite TV programs") hang from the lower line.

4. It is usually delightful listening to children at play.

The gerund phrase "listening to children at play" is in apposition with the subject of the sentence, "it."

5. He does sometimes utter well-intentioned untruths about the appearance of others, but he doesn't consider that lying.

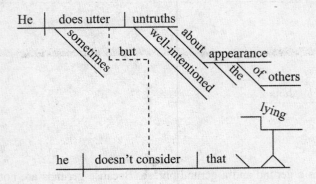

"That" is a demonstrative pronoun that functions as a direct object while the gerund "lying" is an objective complement.

Gerunds

DIRECTIONS: Create a diagram for each of the following sentences. Answers are on page 776.

1. Ms. Shelby, a teacher at our school, calls her friendship with Mr. Moss, a teacher at a rival school, "fraternizing with the enemy."

2. Something worth quoting is worth quoting accurately.

3. The landlord increased his profit by raising the rent and reducing the amenities.

4. The men are playing golf and the women are going shopping.

5. The joylessness in Mudville is the result of Casey's not having hit a home run.

Participles

Participles are verbal adjectives; in other words, they are both verbs and adjectives. Like infinitives and gerunds, participles have tense and voice but no person and number. There are five participial forms of most transitive verbs:

PARTICIPIAL FORMS OF THE VERB "CARRY"

1. *Present Active:* carrying

2. *Present Passive:* being carried

3. *Present-Perfect Active:* having carried

4. *Present-Perfect Passive:* having been carried

5. *Simple Past:* carried

Participles can function both as attributive adjectives and as predicate adjectives. They can also serve as objective complements. They have an essential role in nominative absolutes, and they have an independent use.

Participles and participial phrases can modify subjects, predicate nominatives, direct objects, indirect objects, objects of prepositions, appositives, objective complements, and adverbial objectives.

Examples:

1. Lost, the puppy wandered from house to house in search of food. (as an *attributive adjective*)

   ➤ A past participle modifies a subject.

2. Having run all the way from Marathon to Athens, the messenger died. (as an *attributive adjective*)

   ➤ A participial phrase introduced by a present-perfect participle modifies a subject.

3. Having been shot, he was rushed to a nearly hospital. (as an *attributive adjective*)

   ➤ A present-perfect passive participle modifies a subject.

4. The first thing they saw was a uniformed man riding a white horse. (as an *attributive adjective*)

   ➤ A participial phrase introduced by a present active participle modifies a predicate nominative.

5. Do you know the person being arrested? (as an *attributive adjective*)

   ➤ A present passive participle modifies a direct object.

6. They gave the girl sleeping in the corner an award for honesty. (as an *attributive adjective*)

   ➤ A participial phrase introduced by a present participle modifies an indirect object.

7. The children found all the eggs except the one <u>hidden in an old flower pot</u>. (as an ***attributive adjective***)

  ➢ A participial phrase introduced by a past participle modifies an object of a preposition.

8. Mary's life was saved by her sister, the woman <u>standing next to her</u>. (as an ***attributive adjective***)

  ➢ A participial phrase introduced by a present participle modifies an appositive.

9. Thomas Heywood considered Mistress Frankford a woman <u>killed with kindness</u> and so titled his play. (as an ***attributive adjective***)

  ➢ A participial phrase introduced by a past participle modifies an objective complement.

10. The finished product did not seem to be worth the time and effort <u>invested in it</u>. (as an ***attributive adjective***)

  ➢ A participial phrase introduced by a past participle modifies a compound adverbial objective.

11. The children came <u>running</u>. (as a ***predicate adjective***)

  ➢ The intransitive verb "came" functions as a linking verb in this sentence.

12. You were seen <u>lying on a park bench across from the train station</u>. (as a ***predicate adjective***)

  ➢ The passive verb "were seen" acts as a linking verb.

13. They feel themselves <u>being drawn through a tunnel</u>. (as an ***objective complement***)

14. Each morning, the neighbors heard him <u>whistling the same tune</u>. (as an ***objective complement***)

Nominative Absolutes

Nominative absolutes are grammatically independent expressions consisting of nouns or pronouns modified by participles.

Examples:

  1. <u>Their funds exhausted</u>, they knew one of them had to find a job fast.

  2. <u>Victory having been accomplished at a terrible price</u>, the homecoming was bittersweet at best.

Dangling Participles

While careful speakers of English avoid ***dangling participles*** like the plague, they typically allow themselves to dangle the present participle "speaking."

Example:

  <u>Speaking of food</u>, it's time to head home and light the grill.

> The participle "speaking" is used independently with nothing to modify; one can argue that it functions here as a preposition.

Diagramming Participles

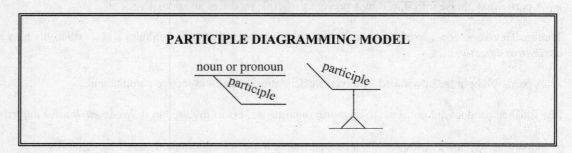

PARTICIPLE DIAGRAMMING MODEL

Examples:

1. Letting the guests wait, she kept talking on the phone.

"Letting" and "talking" are present participles. The former serves as an attributive adjective, the latter as a predicate adjective after the verb "kept," which in this sentence is a linking verb. The "*to*-less" infinitive "wait" is an objective complement.

2. Speaking of superfluity, you will find at least forty boxes stacked in the closet.

"Speaking of superfluity" is an independent participial phrase. "Stacked" is a past participle. The participial phrase "stacked in the closet" modifies "boxes," a direct object.

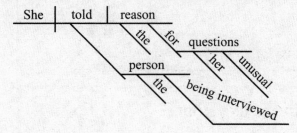

3. She told the person being interviewed the reason for her unusual questions.

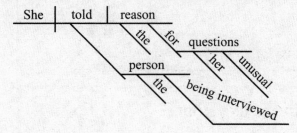

The present passive participle "being interviewed" modifies the indirect object, "person."

4. Her eyes turned toward two people sitting in the corner.

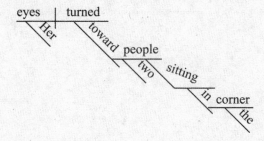

"Sitting" is a present participle. The participial phrase "sitting in the corner" modifies "people," the object of the preposition "toward."

5. Upon awakening, Gretchen saw the witch attempting to light the oven.

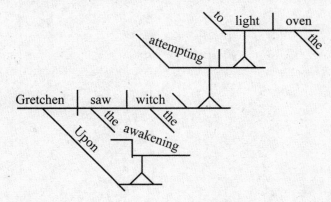

"Awakening," the object of the preposition "upon," is a gerund, not a participle. The participial phrase "attempting to light the oven" is an objective complement. Within this phrase, the infinitive phrase "to light the oven" functions as the direct object of the present active participle "attempting."

6. With her chores finished, she went outside to play.

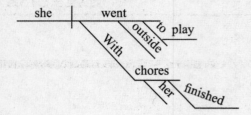

"With her chores" is a prepositional phrase modifying the verb. "Finished" is a past participle modifying "chores."

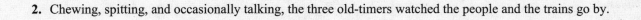

Participles

DIRECTIONS: Create a diagram for each of the following sentences. Answers are on page 777.

1. Still running smoothly after twenty-five miles, she left the park and headed for the finish line.

2. Chewing, spitting, and occasionally talking, the three old-timers watched the people and the trains go by.

3. Having reached the end of her twelve-hour shift, the exhausted nurse heaved a sigh of relief.

4. The bridge having collapsed, some interstate commuters were forced to drive much farther each day.

5. Speaking of rascals, Oscar just knocked at the door.

Adverb Clauses

A clause is a group of words that has a subject and a predicate (i.e., the verb, its objects, and the modifiers of the verb and of its objects). An independent, or main, clause is a clause that can stand alone as a complete sentence. Every sentence must have at least one main clause. A dependent, or subordinate, clause cannot stand alone as a complete sentence but is dependent upon another clause.

Up until now, we have been considering (and diagramming) only independent clauses. There are three types of dependent clauses: *adverb clauses*, adjective clauses, and noun clauses. In this lesson, you will be introduced to adverb clauses.

Subordinating Conjunctions

Some adverb clauses are introduced by subordinating conjunctions (e.g., "because," "since," "although," and "if").

Examples:

1. Stacy stayed home on Derby day because it was raining.

2. Since none of us has a basketball, we can't play basketball.

  ➤ For "since" to be a subordinating conjunction, it must be causal (i.e., it must mean "because").

3. Although she had just bought a new dress, she decided to wear an old one.

4. I would have left earlier if I hadn't had to clean my room.

  ➤ "If" is a subordinating conjunction only when it is conditional.

Relative Adverbs

Other adverb clauses are introduced by *relative adverbs* (e.g., "when," "where," "after," "before," "while," "since," and "as"). Relative adverbs are adverbs because they modify the kinds of words that adverbs modify. They are called relative adverbs because, in part, they function as prepositions with relative-pronoun objects. This will become clear as you examine the following examples:

Examples:

1. We can do our homework when we return.

  ➤ The relative adverb "when" can be expressed as "at the time at which." This expression comprises two prepositional phrases: "at the time" and "at which," the former modifying the verb "do" and the latter modifying the verb "return." "Which" in "at which" is a relative pronoun. Relative pronouns and relative clauses are discussed in the lesson that immediately precedes Exercise 14.

2. Dorothy wanted to go where her friends were going.

  ➤ The relative adverb "where" is the equivalent of "to the place to which."

3. When we retire, we can go hiking whenever the weather is accommodating.

   ➤ Both "when" and "whenever" are relative adverbs. The latter is the equivalent to "at any time at which." "When" and "where" can also be interrogative adverbs and, as such, introduce direct and indirect questions (the latter being noun clauses, which is the topic of the lesson that immediately precedes Exercise 15).

4. Make hay while the sun shines.

   ➤ "While," a relative adverb, can be restated as "during the time at which."

5. After he had worked in the garden for an hour, he sat down and fell asleep.

   ➤ The relative adverb "after" can be restated as "after the time at which." Notice that "after" in the expression "after the time at which" is not a relative adverb but a preposition.

6. He hasn't stopped talking since he got here.

   ➤ The relative adverb "since" is temporal, not causal. It is the equivalent of "since the time at which." The latter "since" is a preposition.

Equal and Unequal Comparisons

There are two types of comparison: equal and unequal. Both are expressed by using relative adverbs and (often elliptical) subordinate clauses. *Equal comparisons* require the positive (or basic) form of an adjective or adverb preceded by "as" or "so" (ordinary adverbs) and followed by "as" (a relative adverb). *Unequal comparisons* require the comparative form of an adjective or adverb followed by the relative adverb "than."

Adjectives and adverbs have three gradations:

POSITIVE, COMPARATIVE, AND SUPERLATIVE ADJECTIVES AND ADVERBS

1. *Adjectives:* tall, taller, tallest; good, better, best; beautiful, more beautiful, most beautiful

2. *Adverbs:* soon, sooner, soonest; well, better, best; awkwardly, more awkwardly, most awkwardly

---

The sentence "You are as tall as she" expresses an equal comparison (i.e., the two people being compared are equal in height). Every comparison contains a subordinate clause, which is usually expressed elliptically. For example, "You are as tall as she" in its expanded form is "You are as tall as she is tall." The first "as" of the correlatives "as...as" is a regular adverb; it modifies the adjective "tall" (the first one). The second "as" is a relative adverb and modifies the second (or unexpressed) "tall." To see why the second "as" is not an ordinary adverb but a relative adverb, consider this equivalent restatement: "You are tall in the degree in which she is tall." The first "as" is rendered by "in the degree," the second by "in which." Since this "which" is a relative pronoun, the second "as" is called a relative adverb.

Examples:

1. Jessica can run as fast as her brother.
   Expanded sentence: Jessica can run as fast as her brother can run fast.
   Equivalent sentence: Jessica can run fast in the degree in which her brother can run fast. ("Fast" is an adverb in this sentence.)

2. The Smiths are not so wealthy as the Joneses.
   Expanded sentence: The Smiths are not so wealthy as the Joneses are wealthy.
   Equivalent sentence: The Smiths are not wealthy in the degree in which the Joneses are wealthy.

3. They are as honest as they are kind. (This sentence is not elliptical.)
   Equivalent sentence: They are honest in the degree in which they are kind.

The sentence "You are taller than she" expresses an unequal comparison (i.e., the two people being compared are unequal in height). The expanded form of this elliptical sentence is "You are taller than she is tall." This is equivalent to "You are tall beyond the degree in which she is tall." In this restatement, "taller" is rendered as "tall beyond the degree," and "than" is expressed as "in which," a prepositional phrase containing a relative pronoun; thus, "than" is called a relative adverb.

Examples:

1. Her work is more difficult than his.
   Expanded sentence: Her work is more difficult than his is difficult.
   Equivalent sentence: Her work is difficult beyond the degree in which his is difficult.

2. Jack was hurt worse than Jill.
   Expanded sentence: Jack was hurt worse than Jill was hurt badly.
   Equivalent sentence: Jack was hurt badly beyond the degree in which Jill was hurt badly.

3. I would rather write a report than read one.
   Expanded sentence: I would rather write a report than I would gladly read one.
   Equivalent sentence: I would write a report gladly beyond the degree in which I would gladly read one.

You have been introduced to the correlatives "as…as" and "so…as" and have noted that they are used with the positive degree of adjectives and adverbs (in so-called equal comparisons). Another correlative expression, "the…the," is used with the comparative degree. In the sentence "The bigger they are, the harder they fall," which can be rephrased as "They fall harder in the degree in which they are bigger," "the" in "the bigger" is a relative adverb, while "the" in "the harder" is a regular adverb.

In the sentence "We were so tired that we fell asleep right away," "so…that" (always with an intervening word or words) is a correlative expression expressing result. It is not to be confused with "so that" (written together), which expresses purpose (e.g., "She turned off the TV so that she could study better."); "so that" is a phrasal subordinating conjunction. In the case of "so…that," "so" is a regular adverb and "that" is a relative adverb. The sentence "We were so tired that we fell asleep right away" can be restated as "We were tired to the degree at which we fell asleep right away."

Diagramming Adverb Clauses

Adverb clauses are introduced by subordinating conjunctions and relative adverbs:

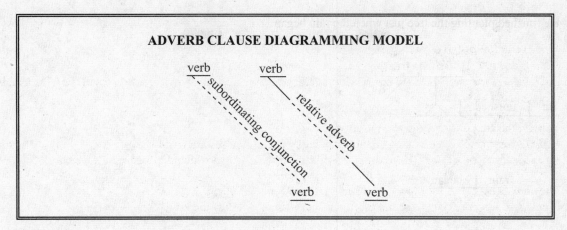

ADVERB CLAUSE DIAGRAMMING MODEL

Examples:

1. They want to climb Mt. Everest because it is the world's highest mountain.

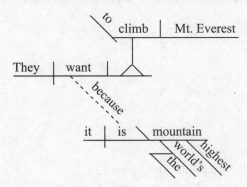

The subordinating conjunction "because" introduces a dependent clause (everything from "because" on). The infinitive phrase "to climb Mt. Everest" is a direct object. "Mountain" is a predicate nominative. "The" modifies "world's," not "mountain." (For example, in the phrase "my teacher's grade book," "my" modifies "teacher's," so it must follow that "the" would also modify "teacher's" if the phrase were changed to "the teacher's grade book.")

2. Although school had been dismissed early, we got home late.

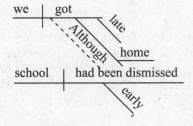

In sentence diagrams, dependent clauses are placed below independent clauses regardless of word order. "Home" is diagrammed as an adverbial objective here. It can also be construed and diagrammed as a simple adverb.

3. He finished planting the tree just when the rain began.

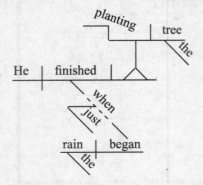

The solid lines at both ends of the broken line show that "when" modifies both "finished" and "began." The relative adverb "when" is modified by the adverb "just." The gerund phrase "planting a tree" functions as a direct object.

4. She volunteers whenever and wherever her help is needed.

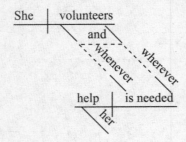

The dependent clause is introduced by the compound relative adverb "whenever and wherever."

5. Although the store is closed on weekends, we will arrange to deliver on Saturdays if the customer agrees to pay a delivery charge.

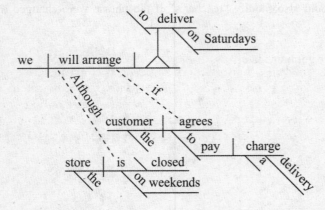

This sentence has two subordinate clauses, each introduced by a subordinating conjunction. "Closed" is not a participle in this sentence but a simple adjective.

> ## Diagramming Equal and Unequal Comparisons

EQUAL AND UNEQUAL COMPARISON DIAGRAMMING MODELS

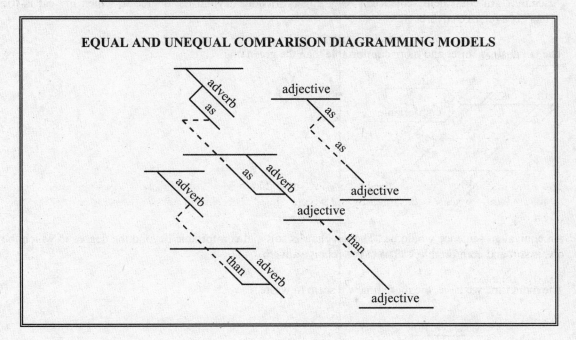

Examples:

1. This store is as large as that one.

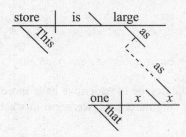

The sentence expresses an equal comparison. Like most comparative sentences, it is elliptical. The expanded sentence is "This store is as large as that one is large." The instances of "*x*" in the diagram represent the words "is" and "large." The sentence can be restated as "This store is large in the degree in which that store is large." The first adverb is a regular adverb; it modifies the first "large." The second "as" is a relative adverb. In the rephrased sentence, it is expressed by "in which," a prepositional phrase containing a relative pronoun.

2. My dog is friendlier than my cat.

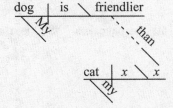

This sentence, which expresses an unequal comparison, is elliptical. The expanded sentence is "My dog is friendlier than my cat is friendly"; hence, the instances of "*x*" in the diagram represent the words "is" and "friendly." An equivalent sentence is "My dog is friendly beyond the degree in which my cat is friendly." "Than" is a relative adverb.

3. The tan chair is softer and more comfortable than the green one.

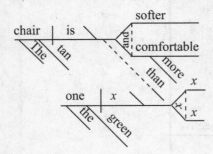

An equivalent sentence would be "The tan chair is soft and comfortable beyond the degree in which the green one is soft and comfortable." "Than" is a relative adverb.

4. The more time we have, the more time we seem to waste.

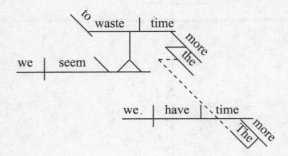

This sentence can be rephrased as "We seem to waste more time in the degree in which we have more time." "The" in "the more time we have" is a relative adverb, and "the" in "the more time we seem to waste" is a regular adverb.

5. I was so hungry that I ate ten pancakes.

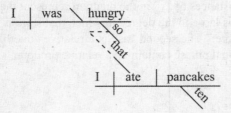

This sentence is equivalent to "I was hungry to the degree at which I ate ten pancakes." "So" is a regular adverb, and "that" is a relative adverb.

Adverb Clauses

DIRECTIONS: Create a diagram for each of the following sentences. Answers are on page 779.

1. Although snow was expected later in the day, most schools were open.

2. She knows a lot about the world because she travels a lot.

3. When they entered the theater, they went to their seats immediately.

4. She arrived after the party had begun but before the food had been served.

5. Whenever she crossed the old bridge, she thought of a night many years ago.

6. The more it rains, the faster the grass grows.

7. It was so late that no more trick-or-treaters were expected.

8. After the guests arrive, but before the food is brought out, let's remind them of the reason for the party.

9. He is kinder and more generous than his sister.

10. When our family does a jigsaw puzzle, the children always put in more pieces than the parents.

Adjective Clauses

Adjective clauses are clauses that modify nouns or any words that substitute for nouns. There are two kinds of adjective clauses: those introduced by relative pronouns and those introduced by relative adverbs.

Relative Clauses

Adjective clauses introduced by relative pronouns (e.g., "who," "whom," "whose," "which," and "that," among other words) are called *relative clauses*. Every relative pronoun has an antecedent (i.e., a preceding word or words to which the relative pronoun refers). A relative pronoun agrees with its antecedent in number and gender but not in case. It takes its case from its use in its own clause. A good understanding of this idea allows one to choose confidently between "who" and "whom."

Examples:

1. That is the man whom (or that) we saw at the game.

    ➤ The relative pronoun "whom" (or "that") is the direct object in its clause. "Man," the antecedent, is a predicate nominative. Careful speakers and writers do not use "who" in the objective case.

2. Do you know the person who (or that) wrote this book?

    ➤ The relative pronoun "who" (or "that") is the subject of its clause. Its antecedent, "person," is a direct object. One never uses "whom" in the nominative case.

3. They are the neighbors whose cat was stolen.

    ➤ "Neighbors," a predicate nominative, is the antecedent of "whose," a relative pronoun in the possessive case.

4. Distracted, Joe nearly pulled out in front of a fast-moving truck, which made him look twice at the next intersection.

    ➤ The antecedent of the relative pronoun "which" is not "truck" but the entire clause "he nearly pulled out in front of a fast-moving truck." In other words, it wasn't the truck itself but instead his experience of nearly pulling out in front of the truck that made him look twice at the next intersection. "Which" is the subject of the relative clause.

Sometimes, when the relative pronoun "whom" or "that" is a direct object or the object of a preposition, we omit it. Of the previous examples, only the first can be expressed without an expressed relative pronoun: "That is the man we saw at the game." Another example would be "Those are the tools I work with every day." In this sentence, the relative pronoun "that," the object of the preposition "with," is unexpressed.

The indefinite relative pronouns "whoever," "whomever," "whichever," and "whatever" (along with those with an inserted "so," such as "whosoever") ordinarily do not have expressed antecedents.

Examples:

1. "I'll give a bonus point to whoever can tell me what page we're on," said the frustrated French teacher.

   ➤ Many people, even many educated people, would say "whomever" here, thinking (incorrectly) that the indefinite relative pronoun is the object of the preposition "to." It isn't. The unexpressed antecedent "anyone" is the object of the preposition; "whoever" is the subject of the relative clause.

2. They plan to give the money to whomever they find in the shelter.

   ➤ This time "whomever" is correct because it is the direct object in its own clause. The object of the preposition "to" is the unexpressed antecedent "anyone."

The word "what" can mean "that which." When it does, it is considered a relative pronoun.

Example:

They did what the lieutenant ordered.

➤ In this sentence, an unexpressed "that," the direct object of the verb "did," is the antecedent of "what," a relative pronoun. "What" is the direct object of the verb "ordered."

Relative pronouns also agree with their antecedents in person. Notice the subject-verb agreement in the following:

Example:

You, who <u>are</u> my child, love me, and I, who <u>am</u> your father, love you.

Adjective Clauses Introduced by Relative Adverbs

Examples:

1. That is the reason why I was late.

   ➤ Since "why" is equivalent here to the prepositional phrase "for which," it is called a relative adverb. Notice that this sentence can be expressed without an expressed "why" (i.e., "That is the reason I was late.").

2. From here you can see the hospital where our children were born.

   ➤ "Where," a relative adverb, is equivalent to "in which."

3. Clayton remembers a time when candy bars cost five cents.

   ➤ The relative adverb "when" is equivalent to "at which."

Diagramming Adjective Clauses

In diagramming, one draws a broken line between a relative pronoun and its antecedent. Like all other dependent clauses, a relative clause is diagrammed below its main clause:

ADJECTIVE CLAUSE DIAGRAMMING MODEL

antecedent

relative pronoun

Examples:

1. I have to see the shipment that came in today.

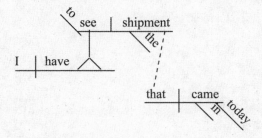

The relative pronoun "that" is the subject of its clause. Its antecedent, "shipment," is a direct object. "To see" is a complementary infinitive.

2. I know the person whose ring was stolen.

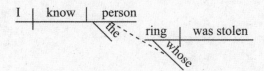

"Person," a direct object in its clause, is the antecedent of the possessive relative pronoun "whose."

3. That's the book that I've been waiting for.

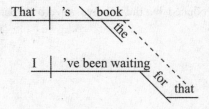

"That," the object of the preposition "for," is a relative pronoun. Its antecedent is "book," a predicate nominative. The second "that" could be omitted (i.e., "That's the book I've been waiting for."). In diagramming this sentence, one would represent the missing relative pronoun with an "*x*":

4. Tell whoever asks.

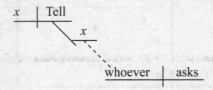

The first "*x*" stands for the unexpressed subject, "you." The second "*x*" stands for "anyone," the unexpressed antecedent of the indefinite relative pronoun "whoever."

5. They read into the text whatever they want to find.

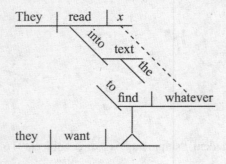

The indefinite relative pronoun "whatever" is equivalent to "anything that." The antecedent is represented in the diagram by an "*x*."

6. I know a place where we can have the reunion.

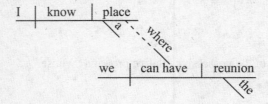

The adjective clause "where we can have the reunion" is introduced by the relative adverb "where" (the equivalent of "at which").

Adjective Clauses

DIRECTIONS: Create a diagram for each of the following sentences. Answers are on page 782.

1. Choose carefully the person in whom you place your full trust.

2. The guy whose car is parked illegally may soon be looking for a ride.

3. The accident happened on the day they arrived in Miami.

4. The other prizes will be given to whoever answers correctly.

5. I have already told you the reason I can't be there.

Noun Clauses

Noun clauses are clauses that function as nouns. Noun clauses are used as subjects, predicate nominatives, direct objects, objects of prepositions, adverbial objectives, and appositives. They may be introduced by the expletives "that," "whether," and "if" (in the sense of "whether"); by the interrogative pronouns "who," "whom," "whose," "which," and "what"; by the interrogative adjectives "which" and "what"; and by the interrogative adverbs "how," "when," "where," and "why." Some noun clauses have no special introductory word or words.

Noun Clauses Introduced by the Expletive "That"

Examples:

1. He knew that he had forgotten something.

   ➤ The noun clause "that he had forgotten something" functions as a direct object. The same sentence can be expressed without "that": "He knew he had forgotten something."

2. That they scored so few points is a source of great embarrassment to the team, which prides itself on its potent offense.

   ➤ The noun clause "that they scored so few points" is the subject of the sentence.

3. Why doesn't it bother the teacher that most of her students are talking?

   ➤ The noun clause "that most of her students are talking" serves as an appositive. It is in apposition with the subject "it."

4. The answer is that she encourages group work at certain times of the day.

   ➤ The noun clause "that she encourages group work at certain times of the day" is a predicate nominative.

5. I'm sorry that we can't wait that long.

   ➤ The noun clause "that we can't wait that long" functions as an adverbial objective. It modifies the predicate adjective "sorry." The same sentence can be expressed with an understood "that": "I'm sorry we can't wait that long."

Noun Clauses Introduced by the Expletives "Whether" and "If"

Examples:

1. Whether we succeed or not often depends on how much effort we are willing to expend.

   ➤ "Whether we succeed or not" is the subject of the sentence. "Whether or not" is a phrasal expletive.

2. Can you tell me if the Kramers live on this street?

   ➤ "If the Kramers live on this street" is a direct object. "If" can sometimes be used as an introductory expletive instead of "whether."

3. The big question was whether it was going to rain.

   ➤ The noun clause "whether it was going to rain" functions as a predicate nominative. "Whether" is an expletive.

4. The two brothers disagree about whether the Pope is infallible.

   ➤ "Whether the Pope is infallible," a noun clause, is used here as the object of the preposition "about."

Noun Clauses Introduced by Interrogative Words

Noun clauses can be introduced by interrogative pronouns, interrogative adjectives, and interrogative adverbs.

Examples:

1. Who was required to attend the meeting had never been clarified.

   ➤ The noun clause "who was required to attend the meeting" acts as the subject of the sentence. "Who" is an interrogative pronoun.

2. They asked what they could do to help and what tools were available.

   ➤ The noun clauses form a compound direct object. The first "what" is an interrogative pronoun, and the second "what" is an interrogative adjective.

3. We are puzzled about why we have to stay.

   ➤ The noun clause "why we have to stay" is the object of the preposition "about." "Why" is an interrogative adverb.

4. It is amazing how long she can remain under water.

   ➤ The noun clause "how long she can remain under water" is an appositive. It is in apposition with the subject of the sentence, "it." "How" is an interrogative adverb.

Diagramming Noun Clauses

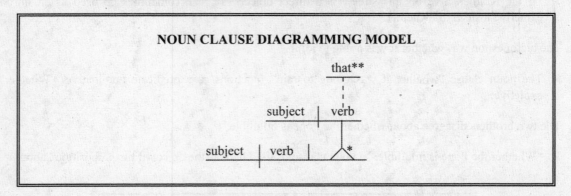

NOUN CLAUSE DIAGRAMMING MODEL

*This particular noun clause is a direct object; however, noun clauses can also function as subjects, predicate nominatives, objects of prepositions, appositives, and adverbial objectives.

**If the expletive "that" is unexpressed, an "*x*" represents it in a diagram. Other words that can introduce noun clauses are the expletives "whether" and "if" as well as interrogative pronouns, adjectives, and adverbs.

Examples:

1. The trouble is that she doesn't do her homework.

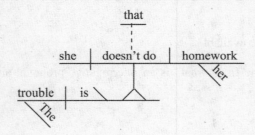

   The noun clause "that she doesn't do her homework" functions as a predicate nominative. "That" is an expletive.

2. She wondered whether he was sorry he had hurt her.

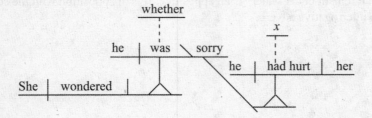

   This sentence features a noun clause within a noun clause. The larger noun clause, "whether he was sorry he had hurt her," functions as a direct object. The smaller noun clause, "he had hurt her," is an adverbial objective. The expletive "that" is unexpressed. It is represented in the diagram by an "*x*."

3. Robert is always uncertain about which pages he should study.

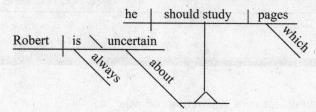

The noun clause "which pages he should study" is the object of the preposition "about." "Which" is an interrogative adjective.

4. It has never been disclosed why they did what they did.

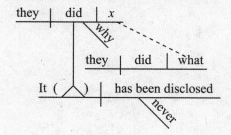

The noun clause "why they did what they did" is in apposition with the subject of the sentence, "it." The relative pronoun "what" is the equivalent of "that which."

5. You are not as big as you think.

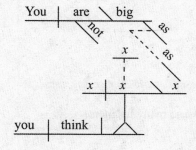

This elliptical sentence ends with the unexpressed noun clause "that you are big." These four words are represented by instances of "x" in the diagram. The sentence contains a so-called equal comparison. The second "as" is a relative adverb; it introduces an adverb clause, of which the unexpressed noun clause is a part.

EXERCISE **15**

Noun Clauses

DIRECTIONS: Create a diagram for each of the following sentences. Answers are on page 784.

1. An unintended result of the experiment was that many birds died.

2. It is a widespread belief that poinsettias are poisonous.

3. The professor attempted to find out who damaged his car.

4. The station manager claimed to be uncertain as to why the station had lost so many listeners.

5. How many angels could fit on the head of a pin was a question that some medieval theologians are said to have found intriguing.

Glossary of Grammatical Terms and Diagramming Symbols

Absolute phrase – a phrase that has a logical, but not a grammatical, connection to the rest of the sentence (see "nominative absolute").

Active voice – a characteristic of transitive verbs that indicates the relationship of the verb to the subject as doer or performer. A transitive verb is in the active voice when the subject of the sentence is the agent (i.e., when the subject is doing something).

Adjective – a word that modifies (qualifies, describes, limits) a noun, pronoun, or equivalent expression. One differentiates between attributive adjectives and predicate adjectives according to their position relative to the modified nouns and pronouns.

Adjective clause – a clause that functions as an adjective by modifying (qualifying, describing, limiting) a noun, pronoun, or equivalent expression. There are two types of adjective clauses: 1) relative clauses and 2) clauses linked to nouns in other clauses by means of a relative adverb.

Adverb – a word that modifies verbs, adjectives, other adverbs, prepositions, prepositional phrases, conjunctions, clauses, and sentences.

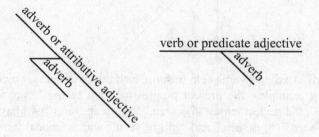

Adverbial objective – a noun or pronoun used as an adverb (indirect objects are included among adverbial objectives).

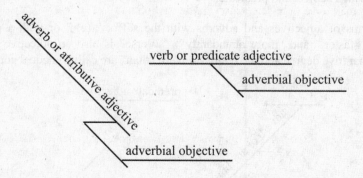

Antecedent – a word, phrase, or clause to which a pronoun refers (for which a pronoun stands).

Appositive – a word or group of words whose purpose is to identify or explain another word or group of words in the same sentence. The appositive usually follows the word(s) with which it is in apposition. Appositives can be restrictive or non-restrictive. An example of a restrictive appositive is the word "John" in "his brother John." In this first example, there is more than one brother (e.g., "His brother John, his brother Sam, and his brother Will are all tall"); so, no comma is used between "brother" and "John." An example of a non-restrictive appositive is the word "John" in "his brother,

John" (e.g., "His brother, John, is a good man."). In this second example, John is the only brother; so, a comma separates "brother" and "John."

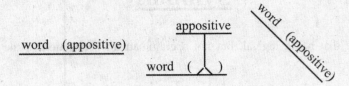

Article – definite ("the") and indefinite ("a," "an").

Attributive adjective – an adjective that either precedes the noun or pronoun it modifies (e.g., "a <u>pleasant</u> evening," "a <u>certain</u> someone") or comes immediately after it (e.g., "there will be time <u>enough</u> for that tomorrow" or "let's do something <u>different</u>").

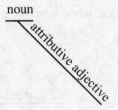

Auxiliary verb – a helping verb. Auxiliary verbs help to form such things as tense, voice, emphasis, and mood. They are underlined in the following examples: the present progressive "<u>am</u> seeing," "<u>are</u> seeing," and "<u>is</u> seeing"; the emphatic "<u>do</u> see" and "<u>did</u> see"; the perfect tenses "<u>has</u> seen," "<u>had</u> seen," and "<u>will have</u> seen"; the future "<u>will</u> see" and "<u>shall</u> see"; the passive "<u>is</u> seen," "<u>was</u> seen," and "<u>will be</u> seen"; and the modal forms "<u>must</u> see," "<u>can</u> see," and "<u>may</u> see."

Clause – a group of words with a subject and predicate.

Comparative degree – forms of adjectives and adverbs with the suffix "-(e)r" or with a preceding "more" (e.g., "larger," "more beautiful," "faster," and "more abundantly"). "Worse" is also an adjective of comparative degree. Comparisons using the comparative degree and the relative adverb "than" are called unequal comparisons.

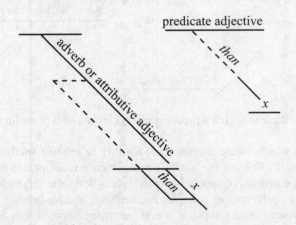

Complement – a term that includes subjective complement (predicate nominative and predicate adjective), direct object, indirect object, objective complement, and retained object.

Complementary infinitive – an infinitive used to complete certain verbs. The complementary infinitives are underlined in the following examples: "They ought to study," "She used to collect stamps," "I have to prepare a speech," "He is going to announce the winners," and "You are to travel to London."

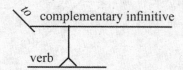

Complex sentence – a sentence containing at least one dependent (subordinate) clause.

Compound sentence – a sentence containing at least two independent (main) clauses.

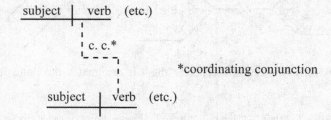

Compound-complex sentence – a sentence containing two or more independent (main) clauses and at least one dependent (subordinate) clause.

Conjunction – a word that connects words, phrases, and clauses. One distinguishes between two kinds of conjunctions: coordinating conjunctions and subordinating conjunctions.

Conjunctive adverb – a word that connects (like a conjunction) and modifies (like an adverb). There are two kinds of conjunctive adverbs: transitional adverbs (e.g., "however," "moreover," "therefore," etc.) and relative adverbs (e.g., "when," "while," "where," etc.).

Coordinating conjunction – a word that connects words, phrases, and clauses of equal importance. The principal coordinating conjunctions are "and," "or," "but," and "nor." (See "compound sentence.")

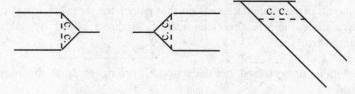

Correlative adverbs – the adverb pairs "as...as," "so...as," "so...that," "then...when," "there...where," and "the...the." Each of these adverb pairs can be restated as a pair of prepositional phrases, with the second of the two containing a relative pronoun (thus, the second adverb is called a relative adverb) and the first containing the antecedent (e.g., "as...as" can be restated as "in the degree in which").

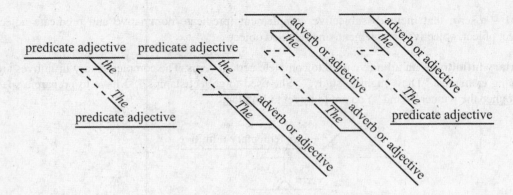

Correlative conjunctions – two-part conjunctions, such as "both…and," "either…or," and "neither…nor."

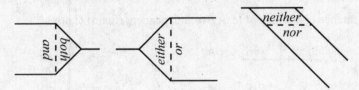

Definite article – English has only one definite article: "the." It designates the noun it modifies as specific or as previously mentioned.

Demonstrative adjective – "this," "that," "these," "those." These adjectives are used to point out someone or something.

Demonstrative pronoun – "this," "that," "these," "those." Like all pronouns, they are used as noun substitutes.

Dependent clause – also called subordinate clause. A dependent clause functions as an adverb, an adjective, or a noun; it is dependent upon, or subordinate to, an independent (main) clause.

Direct address – a noun or phrase indicating the person(s) spoken to; sometimes called a vocative.

```
        vocative
_____
subject  |  verb
```

Direct object – a noun, pronoun, or equivalent expression that names the direct recipient of the action of a transitive verb. Not all sentences have direct objects. You can identify a direct object by asking "Whom?" or "What?" immediately after a non-linking verb.

Elliptical clause – a clause with an unexpressed, but understood, word or words. In diagrams, the variable x represents an unexpressed word or words.

Equal comparison – a comparison using the positive degree of the adjective or adverb and the correlatives "as…as" or "so…as."

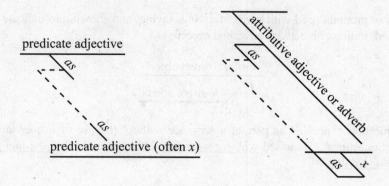

Expletive – a word with a function but with little or no meaning. For example, in the following sentences, "there," "that," and "whether" are expletives: "<u>There</u> is a cat on the roof." "Did you hear <u>that</u> the game has been canceled?" "I don't know <u>whether</u> she will be able to attend."

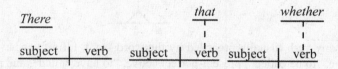

Finite verb – a verb that has person and number. Participles, gerunds, and infinitives are non-finite verbs.

Future tense – a tense that is formed by combining the auxiliary verbs "shall" and "will" with the present infinitive (without "to").

Future-perfect tense – a tense that is formed by combining the auxiliary verbs "shall" and "will" with the present-perfect infinitive (without "to").

Gerund – a verbal noun; a word ending in "-ing" that is both verb and noun.

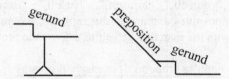

Imperative sentence – a sentence that expresses a command or a request. The subject, "you," is usually unexpressed.

$$x \quad | \quad verb$$

Indefinite article – English has only two forms of the indefinite article: "a" and "an."

Indefinite pronoun – a word like "each," "every," "enough," "much," "any," "either," and "some."

Indefinite relative pronoun – "whoever," "whomever," "whosever," "whichever," and "whatever," as well as "whosoever," "whomsoever," "whosesoever," "whichsoever," "whatsoever," and "what." Indefinite relative pronouns refer to unexpressed indefinite antecedents, such as "anyone" or "anything."

Independent expression – a word or group of words with no grammatical connection to the rest of the sentence. Independent expressions include vocatives, interjections, nominative absolutes, and pleonasms. Not only nouns, but also adverbs, infinitives, infinitive phrases, participles, participial phrases, and prepositional phrases can be used independently.

Indirect object – a noun or pronoun used with verbs of giving, saying, and showing to indicate to whom or for whom the direct object is intended. Indirect objects are adverbial objectives.

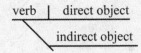

Indirect question – a question expressed as part of a sentence without the use of a question mark. The following sentences contain indirect questions: "He asked <u>why we were late</u>." "She wondered <u>if she had to go to school</u>." "The teacher wants to know <u>who said that</u>."

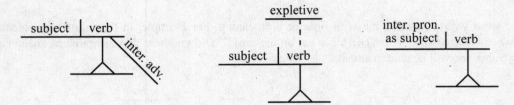

Infinitive – the basic form of any verb (usually preceded by the word "to"). Infinitives have tense and voice (present active, "to call"; present passive, "to be called"; present-perfect active, "to have called"; and present-perfect passive, "to have been called") as well as progressivity ("to be calling," "to have been calling"). Infinitives can function as adverbs ("they are running <u>to win</u>"), as adjectives ("you have nothing <u>to do</u>"), and as nouns ("we all want <u>to succeed</u>").

Infinitive phrase – an infinitive with its modifiers and objects. Like simple infinitives, infinitive phrases can be used as adverbs, adjectives, or nouns.

Intensive pronouns – pronouns that intensify or identify nouns and other pronouns. In form, they are indistinguishable from reflexive pronouns: "myself," "yourself," "himself," "herself," "itself," "ourselves," "yourselves," and "themselves." Intensive pronouns are appositives and are so diagrammed. Examples: "she <u>herself</u> made the dress" (or "she made the dress <u>herself</u>"), "we met with the manager <u>herself</u> to discuss the problem."

noun or pronoun   (intensive pronoun)

Interjection – a word or group of words with no grammatical connection to the rest of the sentence, used to express feeling or emotion (e.g., "wow," "holy Toledo," "for crying out loud," "hurrah").

interjection

subject | verb

Interrogative adjectives – adjectives used in direct and indirect questions: "which," "what."

Interrogative pronouns – pronouns used to ask direct and indirect questions: "who," "whom," "whose," "which," "what."

Intransitive verb – a verb that does not need a direct object. Some intransitive verbs are "go," "sleep," "grin," and "travel." Many intransitive verbs can also be transitive; for example, a tent can "sleep three people," a boss can "grin his approval," and one can "travel the world."

Linking verb – a verb that requires a predicate nominative or a predicate adjective for completion. The most common linking verb is "be," including the participles and gerunds "being" and "having been" as well as the finite forms "is," "am," "are," "was," "were," etc. Some other verbs that can be linking verbs are "seem," "become," "feel," "look," "remain," and "taste." Factitive verbs (e.g., "make," "call," "elect," etc.) can function in the passive voice as linking verbs: "He <u>was made</u> rich," "She <u>is called</u> Kathy," and "You <u>will be elected</u> president." Some scholars put the verb "be" in a category of its own and do not include it among the linking verbs.

Modal auxiliary – a verb used with a main verb to add a note of necessity, possibility, permissibility, or the like: "can," "could," "may," "might," "must," "should," "would."

Nominative absolute – a substantive (noun or noun substitute) modified by a participle or a participial phrase and having no grammatical connection to the rest of the sentence. The participle "being" is sometimes unexpressed (e.g., "His money [being] safely in the bank, he relaxed at last.").

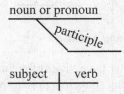

Noun – the name of anything (e.g., "Mr. Smith," "John," "woman," "principal," "student," "Atlanta," "country," "kindness," "hatred," "dawn," "darkness," "sound," "loudness," "lion," "lemur," "book," "computer," "alertness," "curiosity," "weight," "water," "wish," and thousands of others).

Noun clause – a clause that functions as a noun.

Noun phrase – a noun and its modifiers (including articles, adjectives, prepositional phrases, relative clauses, and infinitives).

Nouns as adjectives – a noun placed before another noun such that the former modifies the latter (e.g., "<u>wastepaper</u> basket," "<u>K-Mart</u> special," "<u>holiday</u> blues," "<u>cabin</u> fever").

Number – singular or plural. Nouns and pronouns have number (they are singular or plural), and so do verbs. The number of the subject of a sentence must agree with the number of the verb. If one says, "They eats later," one makes an agreement error involving number.

Objective complement – a noun, adjective, or equivalent expression (prepositional phrase, infinitive, infinitive phrase, participle, participial phrase, gerund, or gerund phrase) that completes the action of the verb and in some way either repeats (i.e., is identical with) or describes the direct object. Consider these sentences:

"They named their baby daughter <u>Estelle</u>."
"That makes me <u>angry</u>."
"We found the book <u>difficult</u>."
"I saw them <u>leaving</u>."
"The weather forced him <u>to stay at home</u>."
"She asked him <u>to help with the groceries</u>."

Most authorities agree that the first four sentences contain objective complements; however, there is significant disagreement concerning the last two. In this skills review, all underlined words above are considered objective complements. One way to recognize an objective complement, when it is a substantive, is this: if a verb seems to have two direct objects, and the first of the two is not an indirect object, then the second is an objective complement.

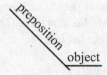

Object of a preposition – a noun or other substantive that follows a preposition and completes it. Without an object, a particle cannot be a preposition.

Participial phrase – a participle with its objects and modifiers

Participle – a verbal adjective. Transitive verbs have five different kinds of participles: present active ("giving," "speaking"), present passive ("being given," "being spoken"), present-perfect active ("having given," "having spoken"), present-perfect passive ("having been given," "having been spoken"), and past ("given," "spoken").

Particle – a subordinate word that is uninflected (i.e., does not change its form to reflect changes in tense, number, or the like). In English, nouns, pronouns, verbs, adjectives, and adverbs are inflected; prepositions, conjunctions, interjections, articles, and expletives are not.

Passive voice – a characteristic of transitive verbs that indicates the relationship of the verb to the subject as receiver of the action. A transitive verb is said to be in the passive voice when the subject of the sentence is acted upon (i.e., when something is done to the subject). (See "active voice.")

Past participle – a verb form used with various tenses of the verb "have" to form the perfect tenses (e.g., "driven," "called," "gone," and "seen").

Past tense – This tense is subdivided into three groups: 1) **simple past** (e.g., "saw," "gave," "hunted," "was (were) seen," "was (were) given," and "was (were) hunted"; 2) **past progressive** (e.g., "was (were) seeing," "was (were) giving," "was (were) hunting," "was (were) being seen," "was (were) being given," and "was (were) being hunted"; 3) **emphatic past** (e.g., "did see," "did give," and "did hunt."

Past-perfect tense – the tense in which verbs use "had" as an auxiliary verb (e.g., "had worked," "had been reading," "had been planted").

Person – an expression used to distinguish among the speaker (or writer), the person spoken (or written) to, and the person spoken (or written) about. There is first person ("I," "we"), second person ("you"), and third person ("he," "she," "it," "they"). The person of the subject must agree with the person of the verb. If one says, "I likes him," one makes an error in subject-verb agreement.

Personal pronouns – pronouns that denote person (first, second, third) and, in some instances, number (singular, plural), gender (masculine, feminine, neuter), and case (nominative, objective, possessive). There are nominative forms (e.g., "I," "you," "he," "she," "it," "we," and "they"), objective forms (e.g., "me," "you," "him," "her," "it," "us," and "them"), and possessive forms (e.g., "my," "mine," "your," "yours," "his," "her," "hers," "its," "our," "ours," "their," and "theirs").

Phrasal prepositions – prepositions that consist of more than one word (e.g., "out of," "because of," "instead of," "along with," "as for," "by means of," "in addition to," "in spite of," etc.).

Phrasal verb – a verb-particle combination with an idiomatic meaning such that the meaning cannot be known from the separate meanings of the verb and the particle (e.g., "she looked up the word" or "he carried out the command"). Notice that one cannot say "the word up which she looked" or "the command out which he carried," which shows that "up" and "out" are not prepositions here.

Phrase – a group of words in a sentence that forms a unit but that does not have a subject or a predicate.

Pleonasm – the deliberate repetition within a sentence of an important element (e.g., "Coney Island, what a magical place it was.").

Possessive – the inflected forms of nouns (e.g., "Mary's," "the workers'," "the men's") and pronouns (e.g., "my," "mine," "your," "yours," "his," "her," "hers," "its," "our," "ours," "their," "theirs") used to show possession or the idea of belonging to.

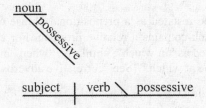

Predicate – the verb together with its modifiers and complements.

Predicate adjective – an adjective or equivalent expression that follows a linking verb and refers to the subject.

$$\text{subject} \mid \text{linking verb} \setminus \text{predicate adjective}$$

Predicate nominative – a substantive that follows a linking verb and refers to the subject.

$$\text{subject} \mid \text{linking verb} \setminus \text{predicate nominative}$$

Preposition – a particle that requires an object (noun, pronoun, or the equivalent) for completion. Prepositions usually precede their objects.

Prepositional phrase – a preposition with its object (including article and adjectives, if any). Prepositional phrases function as adverbs and as adjectives. (See "object of a preposition.")

Present participle – a verb form ending in "-ing" that can function 1) both as a verb and as an adjective (e.g., "a woman wearing a blue skirt," "lovers holding hands"); 2) as a verb only (e.g., "the deer were running through the woods," "we are planning a party"); 3) as an adjective only (e.g., "a sinking ship," "the loving mother").

Present-perfect tense – the tense in which verbs use "has" or "have" as an auxiliary verb (e.g., "has (have) held," "has (have) woven," "has (have) been holding," "has (have) been weaving," "has (have) been held," "has (have) been woven").

Present tense – This tense is subdivided into three groups: 1) **simple present** (e.g., "see," "give," "hunt," "am (are, is) seen," "am (are, is) given," and "am (are, is) hunted"); 2) **present progressive** (e.g., "am (are, is) seeing," "am (are, is) giving," "am (are, is) hunting," "am (are, is) being seen," "am (are, is) being given," and "am (are, is) being hunted"); 3) **emphatic present** (e.g., "do (does) see," "do (does) give," and "do (does) hunt").

Progressive verb forms – verb forms in various tenses used to show action going on or a state continuing. These forms occur in all six tenses of finite verbs (e.g., "is showing," "was showing," "will be showing," "has been showing," "had been showing," "will have been showing") and in the present and past tenses of the passive voice (e.g., "is being shown," "was being shown"). Infinitives have progressive forms in the present and present-perfect tenses (e.g., "to be showing," "to have been showing").

Pronoun – a word that takes the place of a noun. There are various kinds of pronouns: **personal pronouns** (e.g. "I," "you," "he," "she," "it," etc.); **relative pronouns** (e.g., "who," "whom," "whose," "which," "that," etc.); **interrogative pronouns** (e.g., "who," "whom," "whose," "which," "what"); **demonstrative pronouns** (e.g., "this," "that," "these," "those"); **reflexive and intensive pronouns** (e.g., "myself," "yourself," "himself," "herself," etc.); **indefinite pronouns** (e.g., "someone," "anyone," etc.); and **reciprocal pronouns** (e.g., "each other," "one another").

Reflexive pronouns – "myself," "yourself," "himself," "herself," "itself," "ourselves," "yourselves," "themselves." A reflexive pronoun can be used as a predicate nominative, a direct object, an indirect object, or an object of a preposition to refer to the subject of the sentence.

Relative adverb – an adverb that can be restated as a prepositional phrase containing a relative pronoun, or as two prepositional phrases, the second of which contains a relative pronoun. For example, "where" in the expression "the hotel where we are staying" can be restated as "in which"; similarly, "when" in the sentence "We can go when the light turns green" can be restated as "at the time at which." (See "correlative adverbs.")

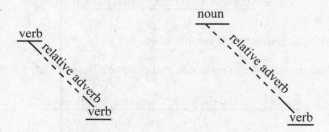

Relative clause – an adjective clause introduced by a relative pronoun. (See "relative pronoun.")

Relative pronoun – a pronoun that introduces a dependent clause and has an antecedent (a previously mentioned noun, pronoun, or the equivalent to which it refers) within the same sentence. The principal relative pronouns are "who," "whom," "whose," "which," and "that." Additional relative pronouns include the indefinite forms "what," "whoever," "whomever," "whosever," "whichever," "whatever," "whosoever," "whomsoever," "whosesoever," "whichsoever," and "whatsoever"; these have an unexpressed antecedent. "As" can be a relative pronoun (e.g., "He liked the same songs as his parents had liked when they were young.").

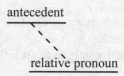

Retained object – a direct object that continues to function as a direct object when the indirect object of a sentence in the active voice becomes the subject of a corresponding sentence in the passive voice. The retained object is underlined in the following example: "Someone gave the youngster a new baseball glove" (active). "The youngster was given <u>a new baseball glove</u>" (passive).

Sentence – an independent clause that begins with a capital letter and ends with a period, a question mark, or an exclamation point. (See "clause.")

Sentence modifier – a word, phrase, or clause that modifies an entire sentence or a major portion thereof, like a clause or an entire predicate.

Subject – a noun, pronoun, or equivalent word, phrase, or clause about which the sentence says something.

$$\text{subject} \mid \text{verb}$$

Subjective complement – a noun, adjective, or the equivalent of either, that completes a linking verb. Such substantives are called "predicate nominatives"; such adjectives and equivalent expressions are called "predicate adjectives."

Subjunctive mood – the modification of verbs used for contrary-to-fact conditions (e.g., "if she were here," "if I had a million dollars"), unreal wishes (e.g., "I wish I were an astronaut," "he wishes he could fly"), and indirect commands and suggestions (e.g., "she insists that he go along"), etc. (e.g., "Be it ever so difficult").

Subordinate clause – (See "dependent clause.")

Substantive – a noun or a noun substitute (such as a pronoun, adjective, phrase, or clause).

Tenses – present, past, future, present perfect, past perfect, future perfect. Tense has a lot to do with time but is not synonymous with it.

Transitional adverb – an adverb used to join clauses. Examples are "consequently," "furthermore," "however," "moreover," "nevertheless," "therefore," etc.

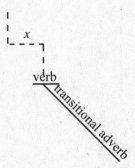

Transitive verb – a verb that needs a direct object for completion. (See "intransitive verb.")

Unequal comparison – (See "comparative degree," "equal comparison.")

Verb – a word expressing action or state. Most verbs end in "-s" in the third person singular of the simple (one-word) present tense. An "-ing" ending is used to express verbs as participles and gerunds. The simple past of most verbs differs in form from the present tense, as does the past participle.

Verbals – non-finite verb forms: gerunds, participles, and infinitives.

Vocative – (See "direct address.")

Voice – a term that refers to the relation of the verb to the subject as doer of the action of the verb or as recipient of the action. A transitive verb is said to be either in the active voice (when the subject of the sentence is acting) or in the passive voice (when the subject is acted upon).

Math Skills Review

```
 ┌──────────────┐
 │   COURSE     │
 │   CONCEPT    │
 │   OUTLINE    │
 └──────────────┘
```

What You Absolutely Must Know

Numbers

Real Number System

All *real numbers* correspond to points on the number line and vice versa. Real numbers include whole numbers, integers, fractions, decimals, and irrational numbers. All real numbers, except zero, are either positive or negative. On the number line, numbers corresponding to points to the left of zero are negative and numbers corresponding to points to the right of zero are positive.

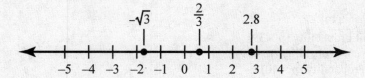

For any two numbers on the number line, the number to the left is *less than* the number to the right. Note that this is the same as saying that for any two numbers on the number line, the number to the right is *greater than* the number to the left. The symbol "<" is used to mean "less than," and the symbol ">" is used to mean "greater than." If a number n is "between 1 and 3" on the number line, then $n > 1$ and $n < 3$; that is, $1 < n < 3$.

Examples:

1. $-5 < -\dfrac{5}{2}$

2. $-0.8 < \dfrac{3}{2} < 2$

3. $2.4 > -\dfrac{1}{4}$

4. $1 > 0.2 > -\sqrt{2}$

The symbol "≤" is used to mean "less than or equal to," and the symbol "≥" is used to mean "greater than or equal to." Therefore, if a number n is "between 1 and 3, inclusive" on the number line, $1 \le n \le 3$.

The following diagram outlines the subsets of the *real number system*. You should be familiar with the terminology and numbers contained in several of these subsets. Each set is a subset of the one above it; for example, the set of natural numbers is a subset of the set of whole numbers, integers, rational numbers, and real numbers. Natural numbers are whole numbers, integers, rational numbers, and real numbers. Refer back to this diagram as often as necessary.

Real Numbers

Real numbers are all the numbers on the number line including fractions, integers, radicals, negatives, and zero.

Rational Numbers

Rational numbers can be expressed as a ratio of two integers (e.g., $\frac{2}{7}$, $-\frac{8}{2}$, $\frac{9}{10}$). A rational number can be expressed as a number that terminates (e.g., -1, 0, 35, -5.25, 8.0262) or as a non-terminating decimal that repeats a series of digits (e.g., $4.333\ldots$, $3.2525\ldots$, $-0.19621962\ldots$). Also, $\sqrt{4}$ is a rational number since it can be expressed as $\frac{2}{1}$, or 2.

Irrational Numbers

Irrational numbers cannot be expressed as a ratio of two integers. No pattern exists when irrational numbers are expressed as decimals and they do not terminate (e.g., $\sqrt{2}$, $-\sqrt{3}$, π).

Integers

Integers are signed (positive and negative) whole numbers and the number zero: $\{\ldots, -2, -1, 0, 1, \ldots\}$.

Whole Numbers

Whole numbers are the numbers used for counting and the number zero: $\{0, 1, 2, 3, \ldots\}$.

Natural or Counting Numbers

Natural numbers are the numbers used for counting: $\{1, 2, 3, \ldots\}$.

Terms and Operations

For simplicity, we will introduce the terms and operational concepts associated with all numbers using *whole numbers*. *Whole numbers* are the numbers used for counting, plus the number zero: $\{0, 1, 2, 3, 4, \ldots\}$. Later we will return to the other numbers of the real number system, including fractions, signed numbers, and irrational numbers.

Basic Terms

sum (total): The result of adding numbers together. The *sum*, or total, of 2 and 3 is 5: $2 + 3 = 5$.

difference: The result of subtracting one number from another. The *difference* between 5 and 2 is 3: $5 - 2 = 3$.

product: The result of multiplying numbers together. The *product* of 2 and 3 is 6: $2 \cdot 3 = 6$.

quotient: The result of dividing one number by another. The *quotient* when 6 is divided by 2 is 3: $6 \div 2 = 3$.

remainder: In division, if the quotient is not itself a whole number, the result can be written as a whole number quotient plus a whole number remainder. For example, $7 \div 3 = 2$, plus a *remainder* of 1.

Symbols of Inclusion

Sets of *parentheses*, *brackets*, and *braces* indicate the order in which operations are to be performed. The innermost symbol of inclusion indicates which operation should be executed first. Generally, operations in parentheses are done first, operations in brackets are done second, and operations in braces are done third. Parentheses, brackets, and braces have the same meaning—three different symbols are used for clarity.

Examples:

1. $(2 + 3) \cdot 4 = 20$

2. $2 + (3 \cdot 4) = 14$

3. $\dfrac{(2 \cdot 3) \cdot (2 + 1)}{3 \cdot (5 - 4)} = \dfrac{(6) \cdot (3)}{3 \cdot (1)} = \dfrac{18}{3} = 6$

A particularly complex statement might use parentheses, brackets, and even braces if necessary. With problems such as these, work from the inside out. Start with the operations within parentheses; then do the operations within the brackets; and finally complete the indicated operations.

Example:

$\{[(2 \cdot 3) - 5] \cdot 1\} + [2 \cdot (4 - 1)] = [(6 - 5) \cdot 1] + (2 \cdot 3) = (6 - 5) + 6 = 1 + 6 = 7$

Order of Operations

Parentheses, brackets, and braces eliminate ambiguity, but they do not always dictate the order in which operations must be done. Use this mnemonic to remember the order of operations for simplifying expressions: *Please Excuse My Dear Aunt Sally*.

Please:	**Parentheses, brackets, braces**
Excuse:	**Exponents, radicals**
My:	**Multiplication***
Dear:	**Division***
Aunt:	**Addition***
Sally:	**Subtraction***

*Remember: add/subtract and multiply/divide in expressions as the operations occur from left to right.

Examples:

1. $6 + 4 \cdot 3 - 5 = 6 + 12 - 5 = 18 - 5 = 13$

2. $[2(3 + 4)](3 \cdot 2) = [2(7)](6) = (14)(6) = 84$

3. $\{(2+7)-[(8\cdot6)\div2]+25\}\{[2+3(2-1)]\div5\} = [(2+7)-(48\div2)+25]\{[2+3(1)]\div5\} = [(2+7)-24+25](5\div5) = (9-24+25)(1) = (-15+25) = 10$

Factoring and Canceling

An important point to make is that even when multiplication and addition are combined, you have a choice about order of operations. In the following example, most people would probably do the addition first and then the multiplication. It is also permissible, however, to do the multiplication first.

Example:

$5(2+3+4) = 5(9) = 45$
$5(2+3+4) = 5(2)+5(3)+5(4) = 10+15+20 = 45$

Thus, $10+15+20$ is equal to $5(2)+5(3)+5(4)$, which in turn equals $5(2+3+4)$. This reverse multiplication process is called *factoring*. Factoring can be a tremendous labor-saving device. It is almost always more efficient to first simplify expressions by factoring.

Example:

$(723)(34)-(723)(33) = 24,582-23,859 = 723$
$(723)(34)-(723)(33) = 723(34-33) = 723(1) = 723$

Factoring can be combined with division for even greater simplifying power. Division of factors common to both the numerator and the denominator is called *canceling*.

Example:

$$\frac{24+36}{12} = \frac{12(2+3)}{12} = (1)(2+3) = 5$$

➢ In this case, 12 can be factored from both 24 and 36. It is then possible to divide 12 by 12, which is 1.

Properties of the Integers 0 and 1

The integers 0 and 1 have special properties that differ from other integers. First, the integer 0 is neither positive nor negative. If n is any number, then $n\pm0 = n$ and $n\cdot0 = 0$. Also, division by 0 is not defined. Therefore, it is never allowable to divide anything by 0. The integer 1 multiplied by any number n is equal to the original number; that is, $1\cdot n = n$. Also, for any number $n \neq 0$, $n\cdot\dfrac{1}{n} = 1$. Note that the number 1 can be expressed in many ways; for example, $\dfrac{n}{n} = 1$ for any number $n \neq 0$. Finally, multiplying or dividing an expression by 1, in any form, does not change the value of that expression.

Examples:

1. $4 + 0 = 4$

2. $4 - 0 = 4$

3. $3 \cdot 0 = 0$

4. $1 \cdot 5 = 5$

5. $2 \cdot \dfrac{1}{2} = 1$

6. $\dfrac{4}{4} = 1$

Factors, Multiples, and Primes

Numbers that evenly divide another number are called the *factors* of that number. If a number is evenly divisible by another number, it is considered a *multiple* of that number. 1, 2, 3, 4, 6, and 12 are all factors of 12: 12 is a multiple of 2, a multiple of 3, and so on. Some numbers are not evenly divisible except by 1 and themselves. A number such as this is called a *prime* number. For example, 13 is evenly divisible by 1 and 13 but not by 2 through 12. <u>Note:</u> 1 is NOT considered a prime number even though it is not evenly divisible by any other number. The following are examples of prime numbers: 2, 3, 5, 7, 11, 13, 17, 19, and 23.

Example:

Let $D = 120$. How many positive factors, including 1 and 120, does D have?

➤ Express 120 using prime factors: $120 = 2(2)(2)(3)(5) = 2^3(3)(5)$. The exponents of the prime factors 2, 3, and 5, are 3, 1, and 1, respectively. Add 1 to each exponent and multiply the results together: $(3+1)(1+1)(1+1) = (4)(2)(2) = 16$.

Odd and Even Numbers

An *odd number* is not evenly divisible by 2; an *even number* is a number that is divisible by 2. Any number with a last digit that is 0, 2, 4, 6, or 8 is divisible by 2 and is even. Any number with a last digit that is 1, 3, 5, 7, or 9 is not evenly divisible by 2 and is odd. Zero is considered an even number. The following are important principles that govern the behavior of odd and even numbers.

PRINCIPLES OF ODD AND EVEN NUMBERS	
1. $\text{EVEN} \pm \text{EVEN} = \text{EVEN}$	5. $\text{EVEN} \cdot \text{EVEN} = \text{EVEN}$
2. $\text{EVEN} \pm \text{ODD} = \text{ODD}$	6. $\text{EVEN} \cdot \text{ODD} = \text{EVEN}$
3. $\text{ODD} \pm \text{EVEN} = \text{ODD}$	7. $\text{ODD} \cdot \text{EVEN} = \text{EVEN}$
4. $\text{ODD} \pm \text{ODD} = \text{EVEN}$	8. $\text{ODD} \cdot \text{ODD} = \text{ODD}$

Examples:

1. $2 + 4 = 6$; $2 - 4 = -2$

2. $4 + 3 = 7$; $4 - 3 = 1$

3. $3 + 4 = 7$; $3 - 4 = -1$

4. $3 + 5 = 8$; $3 - 5 = -2$

5. $2 \cdot 4 = 8$

6. $2 \cdot 3 = 6$

7. $3 \cdot 2 = 6$

8. $3 \cdot 5 = 15$

The rules for multiplication DO NOT apply to division. For example, if you divide the even number 4 by the even number 8, the result is $\frac{1}{2}$. Odd and even are characteristics of whole numbers and negative integers, but not fractions. A fraction is neither odd nor even.

Consecutive Integers

Consecutive integers immediately follow one another. For example, 3, 4, 5, and 6 are consecutive integers, but 3, 7, 21, and 45 are not. In a string of consecutive integers, the next number is always one more than the preceding number. Thus, if n is the first number in a string of consecutive integers, the second number is $n+1$, the third number is $n+2$, the fourth number is $n+3$, and so on.

1ˢᵗ	2ⁿᵈ	3ʳᵈ	4ᵗʰ
n	$n+1$	$n+2$	$n+3$
3	4	5	6

We can also speak of *consecutive even integers* and *consecutive odd integers*. 2, 4, 6, and 8 are consecutive even integers; 3, 5, 7, and 9 are consecutive odd integers. If n is the first number in a string of consecutive even or odd integers, the second number is $n+2$, the third number is $n+4$, the fourth number is $n+6$, and so on.

1ˢᵗ	2ⁿᵈ	3ʳᵈ	4ᵗʰ
n	$n+2$	$n+4$	$n+6$
3	5	7	9
4	6	8	10

Do not be confused by the fact that the sequence for consecutive odd integers proceeds as n, $n+2$, $n+4$, etc. Even though 2, 4, etc. are even numbers, $n+2$, $n+4$, etc. will be odd numbers when the starting point, n, is odd.

Working with Signed Numbers

Numbers are just positions in a linear system. Each whole number is one greater than the number to its left and one less than the number to its right. The following number line represents the *integer number system*, which consists of the signed (positive and negative) whole numbers and zero:

With both positive and negative integers, each position is one more than the position before it and one less than the position after it: −1 is one less than zero and one more than −2; −2 is one less than −1 and one more than −3. The minus sign indicates the direction in which the number system is moving with reference to zero. If you move to the right, you are going in the positive direction; to the left, in the negative direction.

It is natural to use negative numbers in everyday situations, such as games and banking: An overdrawn checking account results in a minus balance. You can manipulate negative numbers using the basic operations (addition, subtraction, multiplication, and division). To help explain these operations, we introduce the concept of absolute value.

Absolute Value

The **absolute value** of a number is its value without any sign and so it is always a positive numerical value: $|x| \geq 0$. Therefore, $|x| = x$ if $x \geq 0$ and $|x| = -x$ if $x < 0$. A number's absolute value is its distance on the number line from the origin, without regard to direction: $|x| = |-x|$.

Examples:

1. $|4| = 4$

2. $|-10| = 10$

3. $|5| - |3| = 5 - 3 = 2$

4. $|-2| + |-3| = 2 + 3 = 5$

This idea of value, without regard to direction, helps to clarify negative number operations.

Adding Negative Numbers

To add negative numbers to other numbers, subtract the absolute value of the negative numbers.

Example:

$10 + (-4) = 10 - |-4| = 10 - 4 = 6$

➤ The number line illustrates the logic: Start at 10 and move the counter four units in the negative direction. The result is 6:

Follow this procedure even if you wind up with a negative result, as illustrated in the following example.

Example:

$10 + (-12) = 10 - |-12| = 10 - 12 = -2$

➤ Start at 10 and move the counter 12 units in a negative direction. The result is two units to the left of zero, or −2.

Similarly, the procedure works when you add a negative number to another negative number.

Example:

$$-3+-2 = -3 - \left|-2\right| = -3 - 2 = -5$$

➤ Begin at –3, and move the counter two units in the negative direction. The result is –5:

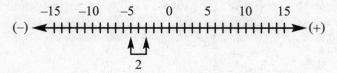

Any addition of a negative number is equivalent to subtraction of a positive number.

Examples:

1. $5 + (-2) = 5 - 2 = 3$

2. $7 + (-7) = 7 - 7 = 0$

Subtracting Negative Numbers

Subtracting negative numbers is a little different. When you subtract a negative number, you are really adding, since the number itself has a negative value. It is like a double negative: "It is not true that Bob's not here" means that Bob is here. To subtract a negative number from another quantity, add the absolute value of the negative number to the other quantity.

Example:

$$10 - (-5) = 10 + \left|-5\right| = 10 + 5 = 15$$

➤ Start at 10: Since the minus signs cancel each other out, move the counter in the positive direction. The result is 15:

Follow this procedure no matter where you start, even if you are subtracting a negative number from zero or from another negative number.

Example:

$$-5 - (-10) = -5 + \left|-10\right| = -5 + 10 = 5$$

➤ Start at –5: Since the minus signs cancel each other out, move the counter in the positive direction. The result is 5:

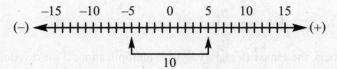

Any subtraction of a negative number is equivalent to addition of a positive number.

Examples:

   1. $4-(-4) = 4+4 = 8$

   2. $0-(-7) = 0+7 = 7$

   3. $-8-(-4) = -8+4 = -4$

Multiplying Negative Numbers

We can also explain the rules for multiplying negative numbers through the concept of absolute value. To multiply a positive number by a negative number, simply multiply together the absolute values of the two numbers, and then make the sign of the resultant value negative. The product of two numbers with the same sign is always positive, and the product of two numbers with different signs is always negative.

Examples:

   1. $3 \cdot -6 = -(|3| \cdot |-6|) = -(3 \cdot 6) = -18$

   2. $-2 \cdot 4 = -(|-2| \cdot |4|) = -(2 \cdot 4) = -8$

A way of remembering this is to think that the minus sign has "tainted" the problem, so the result must be negative.

To multiply a negative number by a negative number, multiply together the absolute values of the two numbers. The product of two negative numbers is always positive.

Example:

   $-3 \cdot -6 = |-3| \cdot |-6| = 3 \cdot 6 = 18$

This is like saying that two wrongs DO make a right—a negative times a negative produces a positive.

Any product involving an odd number of negatives will be negative. Any product involving an even number of negatives will be positive.

Examples:

   1. $-1 \cdot -2 = 2$

   2. $-1 \cdot -2 \cdot -3 = -6$

   3. $-1 \cdot -2 \cdot -3 \cdot -4 = 24$

   4. $-1 \cdot -2 \cdot -3 \cdot -4 \cdot -5 = -120$

Dividing Negative Numbers

When dividing negative numbers, the same rules apply as with multiplication. If the division involves a positive number and a negative number, divide using the absolute values of the numbers, and then make the sign of the resultant value negative.

Examples:

1. $6 \div -3 = -\left(|6| \div |-3|\right) = -(6 \div 3) = -2$

2. $-8 \div 2 = -\left(|-8| \div |2|\right) = -(8 \div 2) = -4$

For division involving two negative numbers, divide using the absolute values of the numbers, and then make the sign of this value positive.

Example:

$$-8 \div -4 = |-8| \div |-4| = 8 \div 4 = 2$$

Any quotient involving an odd number of negatives will be negative. Any quotient involving an even number of negatives will be positive.

Examples:

1. $\dfrac{4}{-2} = -2$

2. $\dfrac{(-2)(6)}{-4} = \dfrac{-12}{-4} = 3$

3. $\dfrac{(3)(-2)(-4)}{(-1)(2)} = -(3 \cdot 4) = -12$

Summary of Signed Numbers

PRINCIPLES FOR WORKING WITH NEGATIVE NUMBERS

1. *Subtraction* of a *negative* number is equivalent to *addition* of a *positive* number.

2. *Addition* of a *negative* number is equivalent to *subtraction* of a *positive* number.

3. *Multiplication* or *division* involving an *odd* number of *negative* numbers always results in a *negative* number.

4. *Multiplication* or *division* involving an *even* number of *negative* numbers always results in a *positive* number.

These rules govern operations with all signed numbers. Be careful how you apply the rules to complicated expressions; just take each item step by step.

Example:

$$\frac{(2 \cdot -3) - (-2 + -12)}{(-8 \div 2) \cdot (2 + -4)} = \frac{(-6) - (-14)}{(-4) \cdot (-2)} = \frac{-6 + 14}{4 \cdot 2} = \frac{14 - 6}{8} = \frac{8}{8} = 1$$

Properties of Real Numbers

The following is a list of the properties of real numbers encountered in this review. Note that these properties apply to all real numbers, not just whole and signed numbers.

PROPERTIES OF REAL NUMBERS
(x, y, and z represent real numbers)

1. $x + y = y + x$ and $xy = yx$.

2. $(x + y) + z = x + (y + z)$ and $(xy)z = x(yz)$

3. $x(y + z) = xy + yz$

4. If x and y are both positive, then $x + y$ and xy are positive

5. If x and y are both negative, then $x + y$ is negative and xy is positive

6. If x is positive and y is negative, then xy is negative

7. If $xy = 0$, then $x = 0$ or $y = 0$

8. $|x + y| \le |x| + |y|$

Examples:

1. $2 + 4 = 4 + 2 = 6$

2. $(2)(4) = (4)(2) = 8$

3. $(3 + 5) + 6 = 3 + (5 + 6) = 3 + 11 = 14$

4. $\left(2\sqrt{3}\right)(3) = 3\left(2\sqrt{3}\right) = 6\sqrt{3}$

5. $\frac{1}{2}(2 + 4) = \frac{1}{2}(2) + \frac{1}{2}(4) = 1 + 2 = 3$

6. $2x = 0 \Rightarrow x = 0$

7. $|5 + 2| \le |5| + |2| \Rightarrow |7| \le 7 \Rightarrow 7 = 7$

8. $|3 + (-2)| \le |3| + |-2| \Rightarrow |3 - 2| \le 3 + 2 \Rightarrow 1 \le 5$

Numbers

DIRECTIONS: Choose the correct answer to each of the following items. Answers are on page 786.

1. Subtracting 1 from which digit in the number 12,345 will decrease the value of the number by 1,000?

   A. 1   C. 3   E. 5
   B. 2   D. 4

2. Adding 3 to which digit in the number 736,124 will increase the value of the number by 30,000?

   A. 7   C. 6   E. 4
   B. 3   D. 2

3. Adding 1 to each digit of the number 222,222 will increase the value of the number by how much?

   A. 333,333   C. 100,000   E. 1
   B. 111,111   D. 10

4. $(1 \cdot 10,000) + (2 \cdot 1,000) + (3 \cdot 100) + (4 \cdot 10) + (5 \cdot 1) = ?$

   A. 5,000   C. 12,345   E. 543,210
   B. 15,000   D. 54,321

5. $(1 \cdot 1) + (1 \cdot 10) + (1 \cdot 100) + (1 \cdot 1,000) + (1 \cdot 10,000) = ?$

   A. 5   C. 11,111   E. 1,111,100
   B. 5,000   D. 111,110

6. $(1 \cdot 100,000) + (2 \cdot 10,000) + (3 \cdot 1,000) = ?$

   A. 123   C. 12,300   E. 1,230,000
   B. 1,230   D. 123,000

7. $(2 \cdot 1,000) + (3 \cdot 100) + (1 \cdot 10,000) + (2 \cdot 10) + 1 = ?$

   A. 11,223   C. 12,321   E. 32,121
   B. 12,132   D. 23,121

8. $(9 \cdot 10,000) + (9 \cdot 100) = ?$

   A. 99   C. 90,009   E. 90,900
   B. 9,090   D. 90,090

9. $(2 \cdot 10,000) + (8 \cdot 1,000) + (4 \cdot 10) = ?$

   A. 284   C. 2,084   E. 28,040
   B. 482   D. 2,840

10. What is the sum of 2 and 3?

    A. 1   C. 6   E. 10
    B. 5   D. 8

11. What is the sum of 5, 7, and 8?

    A. 12   C. 20   E. 28
    B. 15   D. 25

12. What is the sum of 20, 30, and 40?

    A. 60   C. 80   E. 100
    B. 70   D. 90

13. What is the difference between 8 and 3?

    A. 24   C. 8   E. 3
    B. 11   D. 5

14. What is the difference between 28 and 14?

    A. 2   C. 14   E. 392
    B. 7   D. 42

15. What is the product of 2 and 8?

    A. 4   C. 10   E. 24
    B. 6   D. 16

16. What is the product of 20 and 50?

    A. 70   C. 1,000   E. 100,000
    B. 100   D. 10,000

17. What is the product of 12 and 10?

    A. 2   C. 120   E. 300
    B. 22   D. 240

18. What is the sum of $(5 + 1)$ and $(2 + 3)$?

    A. 4   C. 24   E. 40
    B. 11   D. 33

19. What is the difference between $(5+2)$ and $(3 \cdot 2)$?

    A. 0   C. 3   E. 14
    B. 1   D. 10

20. What is the product of the sum of 2 and 3 and the sum of 3 and 4?

    A. 6   C. 35   E. 72
    B. 12   D. 48

21. What is the sum of the product of 2 and 3 and the product of 3 and 4?

    A. 6   C. 18   E. 72
    B. 12   D. 35

22. What is the difference between the product of 3 and 4 and the product of 2 and 3?

    A. 2   C. 6   E. 36
    B. 3   D. 12

23. What is the remainder when 12 is divided by 7?

    A. 1   C. 3   E. 5
    B. 2   D. 4

24. What is the remainder when 18 is divided by 2?

    A. 0   C. 3   E. 9
    B. 1   D. 6

25. What is the remainder when 50 is divided by 2?

    A. 0   C. 3   E. 50
    B. 1   D. 25

26. What is the remainder when 15 is divided by 8?

    A. 0   C. 4   E. 89
    B. 1   D. 7

27. What is the remainder when 15 is divided by 2?

    A. 0   C. 7   E. 14
    B. 1   D. 8

28. When both 8 and 13 are divided by a certain number, the remainder is 3. What is the number?

    A. 4   C. 6   E. 8
    B. 5   D. 7

29. When both 33 and 37 are divided by a certain number, the remainder is 1. What is the number?

    A. 4   C. 10   E. 18
    B. 9   D. 16

30. When both 12 and 19 are divided by a certain number, the remainder is 5. What is the number?

    A. 3   C. 5   E. 9
    B. 4   D. 7

31. $(4 \cdot 3) + 2 = ?$

    A. 6   C. 12   E. 26
    B. 9   D. 14

32. $(2 \cdot 3) \div (2 + 1) = ?$

    A. 0   C. 2   E. 6
    B. 1   D. 3

33. $[2 \cdot (12 \div 4)] + [6 \div (1 + 2)] = ?$

    A. 4   C. 8   E. 24
    B. 6   D. 18

34. $[(36 \div 12) \cdot (24 \div 3)] \div [(1 \cdot 3) - (18 \div 9)] = ?$

    A. 3   C. 16   E. 24
    B. 8   D. 20

35. $[(12 \cdot 3) - (3 \cdot 12)] + [(8 \div 2) \div 4] = ?$

    A. 0   C. 4   E. 16
    B. 1   D. 8

36. $(1 \cdot 2 \cdot 3 \cdot 4) - [(2 \cdot 3) + (3 \cdot 6)] = ?$

    A. 0   C. 6   E. 24
    B. 1   D. 16

37. Which of the following statements is (are) true?

    I. $(4 + 3) - 6 = 4 + (6 - 2)$
    II. $3(4 + 5) = (3 \cdot 4) + (3 \cdot 5)$
    III. $(3 + 5) \cdot 4 = 4 \cdot (5 + 3)$

    A. I only   D. II and III only
    B. II only   E. I, II, and III
    C. III only

38. $12 + 24 + 36 = ?$

    A. $3 \cdot 12$ D. $6(2) + 6(3) + 6(4)$
    B. $12(1 + 2 + 3)$ E. $12 \cdot 24 \cdot 36$
    C. $12(3 + 4 + 5)$

39. $25 + 50 + 100 = ?$

    A. $5(1 + 2 + 3)$ D. $25(1 + 2 + 4)$
    B. $5(1 + 2 + 4)$ E. $25(1 + 5 + 10)$
    C. $25(1 + 2 + 3)$

40. $\dfrac{99(121) - 99(120)}{33} = ?$

   A. 1   **C.** 33   **E.** 120
   B. 3   **D.** 99

41. $1,234(96) - 1,234(48) = ?$

   A. $1,234 \cdot 48$ **D.** $(1,234 \cdot 1,234)$
   B. $1,234 \cdot 96$ **E.** $2 \cdot 1,234$
   C. $1,234(48+96)$

42. How many prime numbers are greater than 20 but less than 30?

   A. 0   **C.** 2   **E.** 4
   B. 1   **D.** 3

43. How many prime numbers are greater that 50 but less than 60?

   A. 0   **C.** 2   **E.** 4
   B. 1   **D.** 3

44. Which of the following numbers is (are) prime?

   I. 11
   II. 111
   III. 1,111

   A. I only   **D.** I and III only
   B. II only   **E.** I, II, and III
   C. I and II only

45. Which of the following numbers is (are) prime?

   I. 12,345
   II. 999,999,999
   III. 1,000,000,002

   A. I only   **D.** I, II, and III
   B. III only   **E.** Neither I, II, nor III
   C. I and II only

46. What is the largest factor of both 25 and 40?

   A. 5   **C.** 10   **E.** 25
   B. 8   **D.** 15

47. What is the largest factor of both 6 and 9?

   A. 1   **C.** 6   **E.** 12
   B. 3   **D.** 9

48. What is the largest factor of both 12 and 18?

   A. 6   **C.** 36   **E.** 216
   B. 24   **D.** 48

49. What is the largest factor of 18, 24, and 36?

   A. 6   **C.** 12   **E.** 18
   B. 9   **D.** 15

50. What is the largest factor of 7, 14, and 21?

   A. 1   **C.** 14   **E.** 35
   B. 7   **D.** 21

51. What is the smallest multiple of both 5 and 2?

   A. 7   **C.** 20   **E.** 40
   B. 10   **D.** 30

52. What is the smallest multiple of both 12 and 18?

   A. 36   **C.** 72   **E.** 216
   B. 48   **D.** 128

53. Which of the following is (are) even?

   I. 12
   II. 36
   III. 101

   A. I only   **D.** I and III only
   B. II only   **E.** I, II, and III
   C. I and II only

54. Which of the following is (are) odd?

   I. $24 \cdot 31$
   II. $22 \cdot 49$
   III. $33 \cdot 101$

   A. I only   **D.** I and III only
   B. II only   **E.** I, II, and III
   C. III only

55. Which of the following is (are) even?

   I. $333,332 \cdot 333,333$
   II. $999,999 + 101,101$
   III. $22,221 \cdot 44,441$

   A. I only   **D.** I and III only
   B. II only   **E.** I, II, and III
   C. I and II only

56. If n is an even number, then which of the following MAY NOT be even?

   A. $(n \cdot n) + n$ **C.** $n + 2$ **E.** $\dfrac{n}{2}$
   B. $n \cdot n - n$ **D.** $3(n+2)$

57. For any whole number n, which of the following MUST be odd?

   I. $3(n+1)$
   II. $3n+2n$
   III. $2n-1$

   A. I only
   B. II only
   C. III only
   D. I and II only
   E. I, II, and III

58. If 8 is the third number in a series of three consecutive whole numbers, what is the first number in the series?

   A. 0
   B. 1
   C. 6
   D. 7
   E. 11

59. If 15 is the fifth number in a series of five consecutive odd numbers, what is the third number in the series?

   A. 5
   B. 7
   C. 9
   D. 11
   E. 13

60. If m, n, and o are consecutive whole numbers that total 15, what is the largest of the three numbers?

   A. 4
   B. 5
   C. 6
   D. 14
   E. 17

61. If $A = 2^2(3)(7) = 84$, how many positive factors, including 1 and 84, does A have?

   A. 12
   B. 24
   C. 36
   D. 42
   E. 84

62. If $B = 5(8)(11) = 440$, how many positive factors, including 1 and 440, does B have?

   A. 8
   B. 10
   C. 12
   D. 16
   E. 24

63. If $ab(c-d+2e) = -6$, which of the numbers a, b, c, d, and e CANNOT be 0?

   A. a and b only
   B. b only
   C. c only
   D. d only
   E. c and d only

64. If $[a-2(b+c-3d)]e = 3$, which of the numbers a, b, c, d, and e CANNOT be 0?

   A. a
   B. b
   C. c
   D. d
   E. e

Items #65–79: Each of the following items includes a number line and a counter. Select the letter of the correct position for the counter after the indicated operations. Note that for some items, a letter choice is included for the original position, indicating that the position may or may not have changed following the indicated operations.

Example:

   $2+3=?$

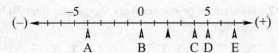

The original position of the counter is 2. If you move it three units in the positive direction, the result is 5, (D).

65. $3+1=?$

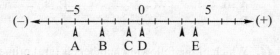

66. $5-2=?$

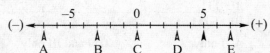

67. $5+(-2)=?$

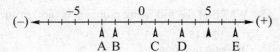

68. $3+2+(-7)=?$

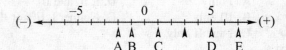

69. $2+(-4)=?$

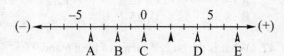

70. $-2+(-2)=?$

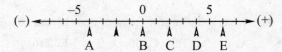

71. $4+(-2)+(-2)=?$

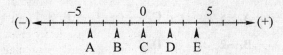

72. $-4+(-1)+(-1)=?$

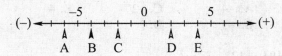

73. $-4+8=?$

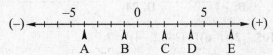

74. $-2+2+(-1)=?$

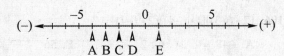

75. $2-(-1)=?$

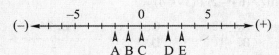

76. $5-(-2)=?$

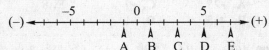

77. $0-(-4)=?$

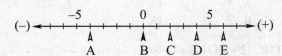

78. $-2-(-1)=?$

79. $-3-(-1)-(-2)=?$

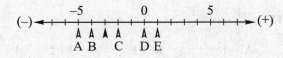

Items #80–120: Determine the correct answer for each of these problems without the aid of a number line.

80. $5+8+(-2)+(-1)=?$

A. 3   C. 10   E. 23
B. 7   D. 13

81. $12-7+6+(-1)=?$

A. 2   C. 10   E. 18
B. 6   D. 14

82. $3+(-3)=?$

A. −6   C. 0   E. 6
B. −3   D. 3

83. $0+(-12)=?$

A. −12   C. −1   E. 12
B. −6   D. 0

84. $-3+1=?$

A. −4   C. 2   E. 8
B. −2   D. 4

85. $-2+(-6)=?$

A. −8   C. −2   E. 4
B. −4   D. 2

86. $-2+(-3)+(-4)=?$

A. −24   C. −6   E. 6
B. −9   D. 0

87. $100+(-99)=?$

A. −199   C. −1   E. 99
B. −99   D. 1

88. $14-(-2)=?$

A. 16   C. 4   E. −14
B. 12   D. −2

89. $2-(-5)=?$

A. 7   C. −2   E. −7
B. 3   D. −3

90. $0-(-4)=?$

A. −8   C. 0   E. 8
B. −4   D. 4

91. $-2-(-3)=?$

    A. -6 **C.** -1 **E.** 3
    B. -5 **D.** 1

92. $-5-(-1)-1=?$

    A. -7 **C.** -3 **E.** 2
    B. -5 **D.** -1

93. $(5-1)+(1-5)=?$

    A. -5 **C.** 0 **E.** 5
    B. -3 **D.** 3

94. $[2-(-6)]-[-2+(-1)]=?$

    A. -2 **C.** 1 **E.** 11
    B. -1 **D.** 5

95. $1 \cdot -2=?$

    A. -2 **C.** $-\dfrac{1}{2}$ **E.** 2
    B. -1 **D.** 1

96. $-8 \cdot 6=?$

    A. -48 **C.** 2 **E.** 48
    B. -2 **D.** 14

97. $-10 \cdot -10=?$

    A. -100 **C.** 0 **E.** 100
    B. -20 **D.** 20

98. $-2 \cdot -1 \cdot 1=?$

    A. -3 **C.** 1 **E.** 4
    B. -2 **D.** 2

99. $-10 \cdot -10 \cdot -10=?$

    A. $-1,000$ **C.** -1 **E.** $1,000$
    B. -30 **D.** 1

100. $-2 \cdot -2 \cdot -2 \cdot -2=?$

    A. -32 **C.** 4 **E.** 32
    B. -8 **D.** 16

101. $-1 \cdot -1 \cdot -1 \cdot -1 \cdot -1 \cdot -1 \cdot -1 \cdot -1 \cdot -1 \cdot -1=?$

    A. -10 **C.** 0 **E.** 10
    B. -1 **D.** 1

102. $4 \div -2=?$

    A. -8 **C.** $-\dfrac{1}{2}$ **E.** 8
    B. -2 **D.** 2

103. $-12 \div 4=?$

    A. -4 **C.** -2 **E.** 4
    B. -3 **D.** 3

104. $-12 \div -12=?$

    A. -144 **C.** 1 **E.** 144
    B. -1 **D.** 24

105. $[7-(-6)]+[3 \cdot (2-4)]=?$

    A. -2 **C.** 7 **E.** 23
    B. 0 **D.** 12

106. $[2 \cdot (-3)][1 \cdot (-4)][2 \cdot (-1)]=?$

    A. -48 **C.** 2 **E.** 56
    B. -16 **D.** 28

107. $(6 \cdot -2) \div (3 \cdot -4)=?$

    A. -12 **C.** 1 **E.** 24
    B. -1 **D.** 3

108. $\{[4-(-3)]+[7-(-1)]\}[-3-(-2)]=?$

    A. -25 **C.** -7 **E.** 8
    B. -15 **D.** -1

109. $[(2 \cdot -1)+(4 \div -2)][(-6+6)-(2-3)]=?$

    A. 5 **C.** -2 **E.** -23
    B. 2 **D.** -4

110. $(2-3)(3-2)(4-3)(3-4)(5-4)(4-5)=?$

    A. -625 **C.** 1 **E.** 625
    B. -1 **D.** 50

111. $[2(3-4)]+[(125 \div -25)(1 \cdot -2)]=?$

    A. -12 **C.** 2 **E.** 125
    B. -8 **D.** 8

112. $-\dfrac{1}{2} \cdot 2 \cdot -\dfrac{1}{2} \cdot 2 \cdot -\dfrac{1}{2} \cdot 2=?$

    A. -16 **C.** -1 **E.** 2
    B. -8 **D.** 1

113. $[(2 \cdot 3) \div (-6 \cdot 1)]\left[(21 \div 7) \cdot \dfrac{1}{3}\right] = ?$

    A. −5　　　C. 1　　　E. 36
    B. −1　　　D. 12

114. $(-5 \cdot -2) - (-2 \cdot -5) = ?$

    A. 0　　　C. 10　　　E. 18
    B. 2　　　D. 12

115. $[-3 - (-3)] - [-2 - (-2)] - [-1 - (-1)] = ?$

    A. −12　　　C. 0　　　E. 12
    B. −6　　　D. 6

116. If n is any negative number, which of the following must also be negative?

    I. $n + n$
    II. $n \cdot n$
    III. $n - n$

    A. I only　　　D. II and III only
    B. II only　　　E. I, II, and III
    C. I and III only

117. If n is any negative number, which of the following must also be negative?

    I. $n \cdot -n$
    II. $-n \cdot -n$
    III. $-n + n$

    A. I only　　　D. II and III only
    B. II only　　　E. I, II, and III
    C. III only

118. If n is any positive number, which of the following must be negative?

    I. $n \cdot -n$
    II. $-n + -n$
    III. $n - (-n)$

    A. I only　　　D. I and III only
    B. II only　　　E. I, II, and III
    C. I and II only

119. If n is any positive number, which of the following must be positive?

    I. $-n - (-n)$
    II. $-n \cdot -n$
    III. $n \div (-n \cdot -n)$

    A. I only　　　D. I and III only
    B. II only　　　E. II and III only
    C. III only

120. Given any number such that $n \neq 0$, which of the following must be equal to 0?

    I. $-n \cdot -n \cdot -n \cdot -n \cdot -n \cdot -n$
    II. $[(n - n) - n] - [(n - n) - n]$
    III. $n \div [(n \div n) \div n]$

    A. I only　　　D. I and III only
    B. II only　　　E. I, II, and III
    C. I and II only

121. In the figure below, what point between A and B is two times as far from A as from B?

    A. 7　　　C. 17　　　E. 31
    B. 10　　　D. 24

122. In the figure below, what point between A and B is three times as far from A as from B?

    A B
    −12　　　28

    A. 12　　　C. 20　　　E. 24
    B. 18　　　D. 21

123. $|1| + |-2| + |3| + |-4| + |5| + |-6| + |7| + |-8| + |9| + |-10| + |11| + |-12| = ?$

    A. −12　　　C. 6　　　E. 78
    B. −6　　　D. 12

Fractions

When one whole number is divided by another whole number and the result is not a third whole number, the result is a *fraction*. For example, when 2 is divided by 3, the result is not a whole number, but rather it is the fraction $\frac{2}{3}$. Note that any whole number can also be expressed as a fraction; e.g., $\frac{12}{3} = 4$, $7 = \frac{7}{1}$.

The number above the division line in the fraction is called the *numerator*; the number below the line is called the *denominator*. In a *proper fraction*, the numerator is less than the denominator, so the fraction has a value of less than 1, e.g., $\frac{1}{2}$ and $\frac{3}{4}$, which are both less than 1. In an *improper fraction*, the numerator is greater than the denominator, so the fraction has a value greater than 1, e.g., $\frac{3}{2}$ and $\frac{4}{3}$, which are both greater than 1. A *mixed number* consists of both a whole number and a fraction written together. For example, $2\frac{1}{2}$ is equivalent to $2 + \frac{1}{2}$, and $3\frac{4}{5}$ is equivalent to $3 + \frac{4}{5}$.

Converting Mixed Numbers to Improper Fractions

Before you add, subtract, multiply, or divide, convert *mixed numbers* to *improper fractions*. To convert a mixed number to an improper fraction, use the following procedure:

Step 1: Use the denominator of the old fractional part of the mixed number as the new denominator.
Step 2: Multiply the whole number part of the mixed number by the denominator of the old fractional part and add to that product the numerator of the old fractional part. This is the new numerator.

Examples:

1. Rewrite $2\frac{3}{7}$ as an improper fraction.

   ➤ The denominator of the improper fraction is 7. The numerator is determined by multiplying 7 by 2 and adding 3 to the result. To summarize: $2\frac{3}{7} \Rightarrow \frac{(2 \cdot 7) + 3}{7} = \frac{14 + 3}{7} = \frac{17}{7}$.

2. $3\frac{1}{4} = \frac{(3 \cdot 4) + 1}{4} = \frac{13}{4}$

3. $6\frac{2}{5} = \frac{(6 \cdot 5) + 2}{5} = \frac{32}{5}$

4. $2\frac{12}{13} = \frac{(2 \cdot 13) + 12}{13} = \frac{38}{13}$

Converting Improper Fractions to Mixed Numbers

To convert an improper fraction to a mixed number, reverse the process described above.

Step 1: Divide the denominator into the numerator. The quotient becomes the whole number part of the mixed number.

Step 2: Use the same denominator for the fraction; the numerator is the remainder of the division process in Step 1.

Examples:

1. Convert $\dfrac{30}{7}$ into a mixed number.

    ➤ Divide 7 into 30; the result is 4 with a remainder of 2. The 4 is the whole number part of the mixed number. Next, the numerator of the fraction is the remainder 2, and the denominator is 7. Therefore, $\dfrac{30}{7} = 4\dfrac{2}{7}$.

2. $\dfrac{29}{5} = 29 \div 5 = 5$ with a remainder of $4 = 5\dfrac{4}{5}$

3. $\dfrac{31}{6} = 31 \div 6 = 5$ with a remainder of $1 = 5\dfrac{1}{6}$

4. $\dfrac{43}{13} = 43 \div 13 = 3$ with a remainder of $4 = 3\dfrac{4}{13}$

Reducing Fractions to Lowest Terms

For reasons of convenience, it is customary to reduce all fractions to their lowest terms. When you reduce a fraction to lowest terms, you really are doing nothing but rewriting it in an equivalent form. This is accomplished by eliminating common factors in both the numerator and the denominator of the fraction.

Example:

$$\frac{8}{16} = \frac{1(8)}{2(8)} = \frac{1}{2}$$

➤ There are various ways of describing what goes on when you reduce a fraction. You might think of taking out a common factor, such as 8 in this example, and then dividing 8 into 8 (canceling). It is also possible to think of the process as dividing both the numerator and the denominator by the same number: $\dfrac{8}{16} = \dfrac{8 \div 8}{16 \div 8} = \dfrac{1}{2}$.

It does not matter how you describe the process, so long as you know how to reduce a fraction to its lowest terms. A fraction is expressed in lowest terms when there is no number (other than 1) that can be evenly divided into both the numerator and the denominator. For example, the fraction $\dfrac{8}{15}$ is in lowest terms, since there is no number (other than 1) that evenly goes into 8 that also evenly goes into 15. On the other hand, the fraction $\frac{8}{12}$ is not in lowest terms, since both 8 and 12 can be evenly divided by 4. Reducing $\frac{8}{12}$ by a factor of 4 gives $\frac{2}{3}$, which is in lowest terms since nothing (other than 1) evenly divides into both 2 and 3.

Examples:

1. $\dfrac{12}{36} = \dfrac{1 \cdot 12}{3 \cdot 12} = \dfrac{1}{3}$

2. $\dfrac{42}{48} = \dfrac{7 \cdot 6}{8 \cdot 6} = \dfrac{7}{8}$

3. $\dfrac{50}{125} = \dfrac{2 \cdot 25}{5 \cdot 25} = \dfrac{2}{5}$

If a fraction is particularly large, you may need to reduce it in steps. The process is largely a matter of trial and error, but there are a couple of rules that can guide you. Remember that if both the numerator and the denominator are even numbers, you can reduce the fraction by a factor of 2. Also, if both the numerator and the denominator end in either 0 or 5, they are both divisible by 5.

Examples:

1. $\dfrac{32}{64} = \dfrac{16(2)}{32(2)} = \dfrac{8(2)}{16(2)} = \dfrac{4(2)}{8(2)} = \dfrac{2(2)}{4(2)} = \dfrac{1(2)}{2(2)} = \dfrac{1}{2}$

2. $\dfrac{55}{100} = \dfrac{11(5)}{20(5)} = \dfrac{11}{20}$

Common Denominators

A ***common denominator*** is a number that is a multiple of the denominators of two or more fractions. For example, 12 is a multiple of both 3 and 4 (both 3 and 4 divide evenly into 12), so it is a suitable common denominator for $\frac{1}{3}$ and $\frac{1}{4}$. Converting a fraction to one with another denominator is the reverse of reducing it to lowest terms. When you multiply both the numerator and the denominator by the same number, you are really just multiplying the fraction by 1, so its value is not changed; e.g., $\frac{3}{3} = 1$.

In grade school, you were taught to find the lowest common denominator for fractions. In truth, any common denominator will work. The easiest way to find a common denominator is to multiply the different denominators together. For example, a common denominator for 2 and 3 is $2 \cdot 3$, or 6; a common denominator for 3 and 4 is $3 \cdot 4$, or 12; a common denominator for 2 and 5 is $2 \cdot 5$, or 10.

What was the big deal about lowest common denominators? It is the same as reducing fractions to lowest terms: It is easier to work with smaller numbers. A common denominator for 2 and 8 is 16, but 8 is also a possibility. It is easier to deal with a fraction of denominator 8 than 16. In the final analysis, you can use any common denominator, because you can always reduce a fraction to its lowest terms.

Operations of Fractions

Adding Fractions

The procedure for adding fractions depends on whether or not the fractions share the same denominator. To add fractions with the same denominator, create a new fraction using that denominator. The new numerator is the sum of the old numerators.

Examples:

1. $\dfrac{3}{7} + \dfrac{2}{7} = \dfrac{5}{7}$

2. $\dfrac{2}{5} + \dfrac{2}{5} = \dfrac{4}{5}$

3. $\dfrac{1}{7} + \dfrac{2}{7} + \dfrac{3}{7} = \dfrac{6}{7}$

To add fractions with different denominators, you must first find a common denominator and convert the fractions in the manner described above. For example, $\dfrac{1}{3}$ and $\dfrac{1}{5}$. Since these fractions have unlike denominators, you must find a common denominator such as 15. Next, you convert each fraction to a fraction with a denominator of 15.

Examples:

1. $\dfrac{1}{3} + \dfrac{1}{5} = \dfrac{1(5)}{3(5)} + \dfrac{1(3)}{5(3)} = \dfrac{5}{15} + \dfrac{3}{15} = \dfrac{8}{15}$

2. $\dfrac{1}{3} + \dfrac{2}{7} = \dfrac{1(7)}{3(7)} + \dfrac{2(3)}{7(3)} = \dfrac{7}{21} + \dfrac{6}{21} = \dfrac{13}{21}$

3. $\dfrac{2}{9} + \dfrac{4}{5} = \dfrac{2(5)}{9(5)} + \dfrac{4(9)}{5(9)} = \dfrac{10}{45} + \dfrac{36}{45} = \dfrac{46}{45}$

To add a fraction and a whole number, you can treat the whole number as a fraction with a denominator of 1.

Example:

$2 + \dfrac{1}{5} + \dfrac{1}{2} = \dfrac{2}{1} + \dfrac{1}{5} + \dfrac{1}{2} = \dfrac{2(10)}{1(10)} + \dfrac{1(2)}{5(2)} + \dfrac{1(5)}{2(5)} = \dfrac{20}{10} + \dfrac{2}{10} + \dfrac{5}{10} = \dfrac{27}{10}$

To add a fraction and a mixed number, add the fractional parts and then add the whole parts.

Example:

$2\dfrac{1}{3} + \dfrac{1}{3} = 2 + \left(\dfrac{1}{3} + \dfrac{1}{3} \right) = 2 + \dfrac{2}{3} = 2\dfrac{2}{3}$

Subtracting Fractions

Follow the same procedures for subtraction of fractions as for addition, except subtract rather than add. When the fractions have the same denominators, simply subtract one numerator from the other.

Examples:

1. $\dfrac{5}{7} - \dfrac{2}{7} = \dfrac{3}{7}$

2. $\dfrac{4}{5} - \dfrac{3}{5} = \dfrac{1}{5}$

When fractions have different denominators, it is first necessary to find a common denominator.

Examples:

1. $\dfrac{7}{8} - \dfrac{3}{5} = \dfrac{7(5)}{8(5)} - \dfrac{3(8)}{5(8)} = \dfrac{35}{40} - \dfrac{24}{40} = \dfrac{11}{40}$

2. $\dfrac{5}{6} - \dfrac{1}{5} = \dfrac{5(5)}{6(5)} - \dfrac{1(6)}{5(6)} = \dfrac{25}{30} - \dfrac{6}{30} = \dfrac{19}{30}$

3. $2 - \dfrac{7}{6} = \dfrac{2}{1} - \dfrac{7}{6} = \dfrac{2(6)}{1(6)} - \dfrac{7(1)}{6(1)} = \dfrac{12}{6} - \dfrac{7}{6} = \dfrac{5}{6}$

"Flying-X" Method

You do not need to worry about finding a lowest common denominator as long as you remember to reduce the result of an operation to lowest terms. This sets up a little trick for adding and subtracting fractions that makes the process a purely mechanical one—one you do not even have to think about. The trick is called the "flying-x."

To add (or subtract) any two fractions with unlike denominators use the following procedure:

Step 1: Multiply the denominators to get a new denominator.
Step 2: Multiply the numerator of the first fraction by the denominator of the second.
Step 3: Multiply the denominator of the first fraction by the numerator of the second.
Step 4: The new numerator is the sum (or difference) of the results of Steps 2 and 3.

Once again, it is more difficult to describe the process than it is to do it. Perhaps the easiest way to learn it is to see it done. To add two fractions: $\dfrac{a}{b} + \dfrac{c}{d} = \dfrac{a}{b} \diagdown\kern-0.6em\diagup\; + \;\diagup\kern-0.6em\diagdown\, \dfrac{c}{d} = \dfrac{ad + bc}{bd}$.

Example:

$\dfrac{2}{7} + \dfrac{1}{5} = \dfrac{2}{7} \diagdown\kern-0.6em\diagup\; + \;\diagup\kern-0.6em\diagdown\, \dfrac{1}{5} = \dfrac{10 + 7}{35} = \dfrac{17}{35}$

As you can see, the connecting arrows make a figure that looks like an "x" floating above the ground, or a "flying x."

The "flying-x" method also works for subtracting fractions.

Examples:

1. $\dfrac{3}{5} - \dfrac{1}{3} = \dfrac{3}{5} \underset{\longrightarrow}{\overset{\longleftarrow}{\times}} \dfrac{1}{3} = \dfrac{9-5}{15} = \dfrac{4}{15}$

2. $\dfrac{6}{7} - \dfrac{5}{6} = \dfrac{6}{7} \underset{\longrightarrow}{\overset{\longleftarrow}{\times}} \dfrac{5}{6} = \dfrac{36-35}{42} = \dfrac{1}{42}$

Of course, this may not give you the lowest terms of the fractions, so it may be necessary to reduce.

Examples:

1. $\dfrac{3}{4} - \dfrac{1}{8} = \dfrac{3}{4} \underset{\longrightarrow}{\overset{\longleftarrow}{\times}} \dfrac{1}{8} = \dfrac{24-4}{32} = \dfrac{20}{32} = \dfrac{5}{8}$

2. $\dfrac{2}{3} - \dfrac{1}{6} = \dfrac{2}{3} \underset{\longrightarrow}{\overset{\longleftarrow}{\times}} \dfrac{1}{6} = \dfrac{12-3}{18} = \dfrac{9}{18} = \dfrac{1}{2}$

Multiplying Fractions

Multiplication of fractions does not require a common denominator. To multiply fractions, just multiply numerators to create a new numerator, and multiply denominators to create a new denominator.

Examples:

1. $\dfrac{3}{4} \cdot \dfrac{1}{5} = \dfrac{3 \cdot 1}{4 \cdot 5} = \dfrac{3}{20}$

2. $\dfrac{2}{3} \cdot \dfrac{2}{5} = \dfrac{2 \cdot 2}{3 \cdot 5} = \dfrac{4}{15}$

Dividing Fractions

Division of fractions is the opposite of multiplication. To divide by a fraction, you invert the divisor (the fraction by which you are dividing) and then multiply the two together.

Examples:

1. $2 \div \dfrac{1}{4} = \dfrac{2}{1} \cdot \dfrac{4}{1} = \dfrac{8}{1} = 8$

2. $\dfrac{\frac{2}{3}}{\frac{5}{6}} = \dfrac{2}{3} \cdot \dfrac{6}{5} = \dfrac{12}{15} = \dfrac{4}{5}$

3. $\dfrac{1}{3} \div \dfrac{5}{6} = \dfrac{1}{3} \cdot \dfrac{6}{5} = \dfrac{6}{15} = \dfrac{2}{5}$

4. $\dfrac{2}{7} \div 2 = \dfrac{2}{7} \div \dfrac{2}{1} = \dfrac{2}{7} \cdot \dfrac{1}{2} = \dfrac{2}{14} = \dfrac{1}{7}$

5. $\dfrac{1}{5} \div \dfrac{1}{2} = \dfrac{1}{5} \cdot \dfrac{2}{1} = \dfrac{2}{5}$

6. $3 \div \dfrac{1}{5} = \dfrac{3}{1} \cdot \dfrac{5}{1} = \dfrac{15}{1} = 15$

Comparing Fractions

Comparing Decimal Equivalents

We can compare the values of fractions in several different ways. The first method is the one most commonly used but which often takes up valuable time. Convert the fractions to decimal equivalents and compare these values.

Example:

Find the largest value of the following fractions: $\dfrac{1}{2}, \dfrac{2}{3}, \dfrac{1}{8}$, and $\dfrac{2}{11}$.

➤ Convert the fractions to decimal equivalents: 0.5, $0.6\overline{6}$, 0.125, and $0.18\overline{18}$. Compare the values: $0.6\overline{6}$ is the largest.

Upward Cross-Multiplication

The second method of comparing fractions is often faster. We use ***upward cross-multiplication***—multiply the denominator of the one fraction with the numerator of the other fraction in an upward direction. The fraction with the greatest product above it has the greatest value.

Example:

Find the largest value of the following fractions: $\dfrac{1}{2}, \dfrac{2}{3}, \dfrac{1}{8}$, and $\dfrac{2}{11}$.

➤ Compare $\dfrac{1}{2}$ with $\dfrac{2}{3}$ by multiplying (3)(1) and (2)(2) and place the value above each fraction: $\overset{③}{\dfrac{1}{2}} \times \overset{④}{\dfrac{2}{3}} \Rightarrow 4$ is larger than 3, so $\dfrac{2}{3}$ is larger than $\dfrac{1}{2}$. Now, compare $\dfrac{2}{3}$ with the other two remaining fractions:

$\overset{⑯}{\dfrac{2}{3}} \times \overset{③}{\dfrac{1}{8}} \Rightarrow \dfrac{2}{3}$ is larger. $\overset{㉒}{\dfrac{2}{3}} \times \overset{⑥}{\dfrac{2}{11}} \Rightarrow \dfrac{2}{3}$ is larger. Therefore, $\dfrac{2}{3}$ is the largest value.

Alternatively, you can directly compare fractions by converting all of the fractions to fractions with the same denominator. The fraction with the largest numerator is then the largest value.

Example:

Find the smallest value of the following fractions: $\dfrac{1}{4}, \dfrac{5}{14}, \dfrac{3}{7}$, and $\dfrac{1}{2}$.

➤ Convert the fractions to fractions with the same denominator: $\frac{1}{4} \cdot \frac{7}{7} = \frac{7}{28}$; $\frac{5}{14} \cdot \frac{2}{2} = \frac{10}{28}$; $\frac{3}{7} \cdot \frac{4}{4} = \frac{12}{28}$; $\frac{1}{2} \cdot \frac{14}{14} = \frac{14}{28}$. Since $\frac{7}{28}$ is the rewritten fraction with the smallest numerator, the fraction equivalent $\frac{1}{4}$ is the smallest value of the given fractions.

Fractions

DIRECTIONS: Choose the correct answer to each of the following items. Answers are on page 786.

1. $5\frac{3}{8} = ?$

A. 1

B. $\frac{15}{8}$

C. $\frac{23}{8}$

D. $\frac{35}{8}$

E. $\frac{43}{8}$

2. $2\frac{3}{4} = ?$

A. $\frac{1}{4}$

B. $\frac{3}{4}$

C. $\frac{9}{4}$

D. $\frac{11}{4}$

E. $\frac{15}{4}$

3. $3\frac{1}{12} = ?$

A. $\frac{13}{2}$

B. $\frac{37}{12}$

C. $\frac{41}{12}$

D. $\frac{53}{12}$

E. $\frac{71}{12}$

4. $1\frac{1}{65} = ?$

A. $\frac{64}{65}$

B. $\frac{65}{66}$

C. $\frac{66}{65}$

D. $\frac{66}{64}$

E. $\frac{67}{66}$

5. $5\frac{2}{7} = ?$

A. $\frac{5}{14}$

B. $\frac{35}{7}$

C. $\frac{37}{7}$

D. $\frac{70}{7}$

E. $\frac{110}{7}$

6. $\frac{12}{8} = ?$

A. 4

B. 3

C. $2\frac{1}{2}$

D. $1\frac{1}{2}$

E. $1\frac{1}{4}$

7. $\frac{20}{6} = ?$

A. $3\frac{1}{3}$

B. $3\frac{2}{3}$

C. $4\frac{1}{6}$

D. $4\frac{1}{3}$

E. 6

8. $\frac{23}{13} = ?$

A. 10

B. $7\frac{7}{13}$

C. $1\frac{10}{13}$

D. $\frac{13}{23}$

E. $\frac{7}{13}$

9. $\frac{25}{4} = ?$

A. $\frac{4}{25}$

B. $\frac{4}{12}$

C. $1\frac{1}{8}$

D. $1\frac{1}{4}$

E. $6\frac{1}{4}$

10. $\frac{201}{100} = ?$

A. $1\frac{1}{100}$

B. $1\frac{1}{50}$

C. $2\frac{1}{100}$

D. $2\frac{1}{50}$

E. 101

11. $\frac{3}{12} = ?$

   A. $\frac{1}{6}$ C. $\frac{1}{3}$ E. $\frac{3}{4}$

   B. $\frac{1}{4}$ D. $\frac{1}{2}$

12. $\frac{27}{81} = ?$

   A. $\frac{1}{9}$ C. $\frac{1}{3}$ E. $\frac{2}{3}$

   B. $\frac{2}{9}$ D. $\frac{4}{9}$

13. $\frac{125}{625} = ?$

   A. $\frac{1}{10}$ C. $\frac{2}{5}$ E. $\frac{4}{5}$

   B. $\frac{1}{5}$ D. $\frac{7}{10}$

14. $\frac{39}{52} = ?$

   A. $\frac{1}{5}$ C. $\frac{1}{3}$ E. $\frac{3}{4}$

   B. $\frac{1}{4}$ D. $\frac{1}{2}$

15. $\frac{121}{132} = ?$

   A. $\frac{1}{11}$ C. $\frac{9}{10}$ E. $\frac{11}{12}$

   B. $\frac{1}{10}$ D. $\frac{10}{11}$

16. Which of the following is equal to $\frac{4}{25}$?

   A. $\frac{8}{50}$ C. $\frac{12}{150}$ E. $\frac{200}{250}$

   B. $\frac{8}{100}$ D. $\frac{160}{200}$

17. Which of the following is NOT equal to $\frac{3}{8}$?

   A. $\frac{6}{16}$ C. $\frac{31}{81}$ E. $\frac{120}{320}$

   B. $\frac{15}{40}$ D. $\frac{33}{88}$

18. Which of the following is NOT equal to $\frac{3}{4}$?

   A. $\frac{6}{8}$ C. $\frac{20}{24}$ E. $\frac{300}{400}$

   B. $\frac{12}{16}$ D. $\frac{36}{48}$

19. Which of the following is NOT equal to $\frac{5}{6}$?

   A. $\frac{25}{30}$ C. $\frac{50}{60}$ E. $\frac{100}{120}$

   B. $\frac{45}{50}$ D. $\frac{55}{66}$

20. Which of the following is NOT equal to $\frac{1}{6}$?

   A. $\frac{2}{12}$ C. $\frac{4}{24}$ E. $\frac{6}{40}$

   B. $\frac{3}{18}$ D. $\frac{5}{30}$

21. $\frac{1}{7} + \frac{2}{7} = ?$

   A. $\frac{2}{7}$ C. $\frac{6}{7}$ E. $\frac{12}{7}$

   B. $\frac{3}{7}$ D. $\frac{8}{7}$

22. $\frac{5}{8} + \frac{1}{8} = ?$

   A. $\frac{1}{2}$ C. $\frac{7}{8}$ E. $\frac{4}{3}$

   B. $\frac{3}{4}$ D. $\frac{8}{5}$

23. $\frac{12}{13} + \frac{12}{13} = ?$

   A. 0   C. $\frac{12}{26}$ E. $\frac{26}{13}$

   B. 1   D. $\frac{24}{13}$

24. $\frac{3}{8} + \frac{5}{8} = ?$

   A. $\frac{2}{8}$ C. $\frac{5}{4}$ E. $\frac{12}{5}$

   B. 1   D. $\frac{8}{5}$

25. $\frac{1}{11} + \frac{2}{11} + \frac{7}{11} = ?$

   A. $\frac{4}{11}$ C. $\frac{10}{11}$ E. $\frac{11}{7}$

   B. $\frac{7}{11}$ D. $\frac{11}{10}$

26. $\frac{3}{8} + \frac{5}{6} = ?$

   A. $\frac{8}{48}$ C. $\frac{29}{24}$ E. $\frac{14}{8}$

   B. $\frac{8}{14}$ D. $\frac{3}{2}$

27. $\frac{1}{8} + \frac{1}{7} = ?$

   A. $\frac{1}{56}$ C. $\frac{1}{15}$ E. $\frac{15}{56}$

   B. $\frac{1}{27}$ D. $\frac{1}{5}$

28. $\frac{1}{12} + \frac{1}{7} = ?$

   A. $\frac{19}{84}$ C. $\frac{10}{19}$ E. $\frac{5}{4}$

   B. $\frac{19}{42}$ D. $\frac{20}{19}$

29. $\frac{3}{5} + \frac{2}{11} = ?$

   A. $\frac{43}{110}$ C. $\frac{54}{55}$ E. $\frac{100}{43}$

   B. $\frac{43}{55}$ D. $\frac{55}{54}$

30. $\frac{1}{2} + \frac{1}{3} + \frac{1}{6} = ?$

   A. $\frac{1}{36}$ C. 1   E. $\frac{7}{3}$

   B. $\frac{1}{12}$ D. $\frac{7}{6}$

31. $\frac{2}{3} + \frac{3}{6} + \frac{4}{6} = ?$

   A. $\frac{9}{20}$ C. $\frac{7}{6}$ E. $\frac{16}{3}$

   B. $\frac{6}{7}$ D. $\frac{11}{6}$

32. $\frac{2}{3} - \frac{1}{3} = ?$

   A. $\frac{1}{6}$ C. $\frac{2}{3}$ E. $\frac{6}{3}$

   B. $\frac{1}{3}$ D. $\frac{4}{3}$

33. $\frac{5}{7} - \frac{4}{7} = ?$

   A. $\frac{9}{7}$ C. $\frac{5}{7}$ E. $\frac{1}{49}$

   B. 1   D. $\frac{1}{7}$

34. $\frac{9}{10} - \frac{1}{5} = ?$

   A. $\frac{7}{10}$ C. $\frac{10}{7}$ E. $\frac{20}{7}$

   B. $\frac{7}{5}$ D. $\frac{18}{7}$

35. $\frac{3}{2} - \frac{1}{4} = ?$

   A. $\frac{5}{4}$ **C.** $\frac{3}{4}$ **E.** $\frac{1}{3}$

   B. $\frac{4}{5}$ **D.** $\frac{2}{3}$

36. $2\frac{1}{2} - \frac{7}{8} = ?$

   A. $\frac{9}{2}$ **C.** $\frac{13}{8}$ **E.** $\frac{4}{5}$

   B. $\frac{5}{2}$ **D.** $\frac{5}{4}$

37. $2\frac{2}{3} - 1\frac{1}{6} = ?$

   A. $1\frac{1}{6}$ **C.** $1\frac{1}{2}$ **E.** 2

   B. $1\frac{1}{3}$ **D.** $1\frac{2}{3}$

38. $\frac{1}{2} \cdot \frac{2}{3} = ?$

   A. $\frac{1}{6}$ **C.** $\frac{1}{2}$ **E.** $\frac{3}{4}$

   B. $\frac{1}{3}$ **D.** $\frac{2}{3}$

39. $\frac{2}{7} \cdot \frac{1}{4} = ?$

   A. $\frac{1}{63}$ **C.** $\frac{1}{4}$ **E.** $\frac{5}{9}$

   B. $\frac{1}{14}$ **D.** $\frac{3}{8}$

40. $\frac{1}{3} \cdot \frac{1}{3} = ?$

   A. $\frac{1}{9}$ **C.** $\frac{1}{3}$ **E.** $\frac{3}{2}$

   B. $\frac{1}{6}$ **D.** $\frac{2}{3}$

41. $\frac{1}{2} \cdot \frac{1}{2} \cdot \frac{1}{2} = ?$

   A. $\frac{1}{16}$ **C.** $\frac{3}{16}$ **E.** $\frac{2}{3}$

   B. $\frac{1}{8}$ **D.** $\frac{3}{8}$

42. $\frac{2}{3} \cdot \frac{3}{4} \cdot \frac{4}{5} = ?$

   A. $\frac{2}{5}$ **C.** $\frac{2}{3}$ **E.** $\frac{4}{5}$

   B. $\frac{3}{5}$ **D.** $\frac{3}{4}$

43. $\frac{1}{4} \cdot \frac{1}{8} \cdot 3 = ?$

   A. $\frac{3}{32}$ **C.** $\frac{1}{4}$ **E.** $\frac{3}{4}$

   B. $\frac{1}{8}$ **D.** $\frac{1}{2}$

44. $\frac{1}{3} \cdot \frac{1}{6} \cdot 12 = ?$

   A. $\frac{1}{3}$ **C.** 1 **E.** 2

   B. $\frac{2}{3}$ **D.** $\frac{3}{2}$

45. $\frac{7}{8} \div \frac{3}{4} = ?$

   A. $\frac{7}{6}$ **C.** $\frac{3}{4}$ **E.** $\frac{1}{8}$

   B. 1 **D.** $\frac{1}{3}$

46. $\frac{5}{7} \div \frac{1}{7} = ?$

   A. $\frac{1}{7}$ **C.** 5 **E.** 12

   B. $\frac{1}{5}$ **D.** 7

47. $\dfrac{1}{12} \div \dfrac{1}{12} = ?$

 A. $\dfrac{1}{144}$ **C.** 12   **E.** 144

 B. 1   **D.** 18

48. $2 \div \dfrac{1}{11} = ?$

 A. 22   **C.** $\dfrac{11}{2}$ **E.** $\dfrac{1}{22}$

 B. 11   **D.** $\dfrac{11}{22}$

49. $\dfrac{8}{9} \div \dfrac{7}{8} = ?$

 A. $\dfrac{64}{63}$ **C.** $\dfrac{7}{9}$ **E.** $\dfrac{1}{3}$

 B. $\dfrac{9}{7}$ **D.** $\dfrac{1}{2}$

50. $\dfrac{1}{10} \div \dfrac{3}{5} = ?$

 A. $\dfrac{1}{6}$ **C.** $\dfrac{3}{10}$ **E.** $\dfrac{5}{3}$

 B. $\dfrac{1}{5}$ **D.** $\dfrac{3}{5}$

51. $\left(\dfrac{1}{4} + \dfrac{2}{3}\right) \cdot \left(\dfrac{3}{2} + \dfrac{1}{4}\right) = ?$

 A. $\dfrac{21}{47}$ **C.** $\dfrac{51}{48}$ **E.** $\dfrac{105}{51}$

 B. $\dfrac{33}{49}$ **D.** $\dfrac{77}{48}$

52. $\left(\dfrac{2}{3} \cdot \dfrac{1}{6}\right) \div \left(\dfrac{1}{2} \cdot \dfrac{1}{4}\right) = ?$

 A. $\dfrac{1}{18}$ **C.** $\dfrac{8}{9}$ **E.** $\dfrac{15}{75}$

 B. $\dfrac{2}{9}$ **D.** $\dfrac{11}{8}$

53. $\left[\left(\dfrac{1}{3} + \dfrac{1}{2}\right) \cdot \left(\dfrac{2}{3} - \dfrac{1}{3}\right)\right] \cdot 18 = ?$

 A. 5   **C.** $\dfrac{5}{6}$ **E.** $\dfrac{2}{3}$

 B. $\dfrac{7}{8}$ **D.** $\dfrac{4}{5}$

54. $\left[\left(\dfrac{1}{3} \div \dfrac{1}{6}\right) \cdot \left(\dfrac{2}{3} \div \dfrac{1}{3}\right)\right] \cdot \left(\dfrac{1}{2} + \dfrac{3}{4}\right) = ?$

 A. 5   **C.** 3   **E.** 1

 B. 4   **D.** 2

55. $8\left(\dfrac{1}{3} + \dfrac{3}{4}\right) = ?$

 A. $\dfrac{1}{3}$ **C.** $\dfrac{16}{3}$ **E.** $\dfrac{26}{3}$

 B. $\dfrac{4}{3}$ **D.** $\dfrac{19}{3}$

56. $\dfrac{1}{4} - \dfrac{1}{5} = ?$

 A. $\dfrac{1}{5}$ **C.** $\dfrac{1}{20}$ **E.** $\dfrac{4}{5}$

 B. $\dfrac{1}{3}$ **D.** $\dfrac{3}{4}$

57. $\dfrac{\dfrac{4}{9}}{\dfrac{2}{5}} = ?$

 A. $\dfrac{1}{2}$ **C.** $\dfrac{8}{45}$ **E.** $1\dfrac{1}{9}$

 B. $\dfrac{3}{4}$ **D.** $\dfrac{11}{9}$

58. $\left(-\dfrac{1}{2}\right)^2 + \left(\dfrac{1}{4}\right)^2 + (-2)\left(\dfrac{1}{2}\right)^2 = ?$

 A. $-\dfrac{3}{16}$ **C.** $\dfrac{1}{3}$ **E.** $\dfrac{4}{5}$

 B. $-\dfrac{1}{5}$ **D.** $\dfrac{3}{4}$

59. Which fraction is the largest?

A. $\frac{9}{16}$ C. $\frac{5}{8}$ E. $\frac{1}{2}$

B. $\frac{7}{10}$ D. $\frac{4}{5}$

60. Jughead eats $\frac{2}{5}$ of a pound of cake each day. How many pounds of cake does Jughead eat in 3 weeks?

A. $4\frac{1}{2}$ C. $5\frac{1}{5}$ E. 10

B. $5\frac{3}{4}$ D. $8\frac{2}{5}$

61. Chompa eats $\frac{3}{8}$ of a bag of candy per day. How many weeks will 42 bags of candy last Chompa?

A. 4   C. 9   E. 16
B. 5   D. 12

62. If Bruce can eat $2\frac{1}{2}$ bananas per day, how many bananas can Bruce eat in 4 weeks?

A. 70   C. 80   E. 90
B. 75   D. 85

63. One brass rod measures $3\frac{5}{16}$ inches long and another brass rod measures $2\frac{3}{4}$ inches long. What is the total length, in inches, of the two rods combined?

A. $6\frac{9}{16}$ C. $5\frac{1}{2}$ E. $5\frac{1}{32}$

B. $6\frac{1}{16}$ D. $5\frac{1}{16}$

64. Which of the following equals the number of half-pound packages of tea that can be taken out of a box that holds $10\frac{1}{2}$ pounds of tea?

A. 5   C. 11   E. 21

B. $10\frac{1}{2}$ D. $20\frac{1}{122}$

65. If each bag of tokens weighs $5\frac{3}{4}$ pounds, how many pounds do 3 bags weigh?

A. $7\frac{1}{4}$ C. $16\frac{1}{2}$ E. $17\frac{1}{2}$

B. $15\frac{3}{4}$ D. $17\frac{1}{4}$

66. During one week, a man traveled $3\frac{1}{2}$, $1\frac{1}{4}$, $1\frac{1}{6}$, and $2\frac{3}{8}$ miles. The next week, he traveled $\frac{1}{4}$, $\frac{3}{8}$, $\frac{9}{16}$, $3\frac{1}{16}$, $2\frac{5}{8}$, and $3\frac{3}{16}$ miles. How many more miles did he travel the second week than the first week?

A. $1\frac{37}{48}$ C. $1\frac{3}{4}$ E. $\frac{47}{48}$

B. $1\frac{1}{2}$ D. 1

67. A certain type of board is sold only in lengths of multiples of 2 feet. The shortest board sold is 6 feet and the longest is 24 feet. A builder needs a large quantity of this type of board in $5\frac{1}{2}$-foot lengths. To minimize waste, which of the following board lengths should be ordered?

A. 6-foot   C. 22-foot   E. 26-foot
B. 12-foot   D. 24-foot

68. A man spent $\frac{15}{16}$ of his entire fortune in buying a car for $7,500. How much money did he possess?

A. $6,000   C. $7,000   E. $8,500
B. $6,500   D. $8,000

69. The population of a town was 54,000 in the last census. Since then it has increased by two-thirds. Which of the following equals its present population?

A. 18,000   C. 72,000   E. 108,000
B. 36,000   D. 90,000

70. $\dfrac{1}{3}$ of the liquid contents of a can evaporates on the first day and $\dfrac{3}{4}$ of the remainder evaporates on the second day. Which of the following equals the fractional part of the original contents remaining at the close of the second day?

A. $\dfrac{5}{12}$ C. $\dfrac{1}{6}$ E. $\dfrac{4}{7}$

B. $\dfrac{7}{12}$ D. $\dfrac{1}{2}$

71. A car is run until the gas tank is $\dfrac{1}{8}$ full. The tank is then filled to capacity by putting in 14 gallons. What is the gas tank's capacity, in gallons?

A. 14   C. 16   E. 18

B. 15   D. 17

Decimals

A *decimal* is nothing more than a special way of writing fractions using a denominator of ten, or one hundred, or one thousand, and so on. Decimals are written with a decimal point to the left of the decimal digits in order to distinguish them from whole numbers.

Examples:

1. The fraction $\dfrac{3}{10}$ written as a decimal is 0.3.

2. The fraction $\dfrac{72}{100}$ written as a decimal is 0.72.

The positions to the right of the decimal point are called decimal places. Decimal places are analogous to the positions of the digits in whole numbers (units column, tens column, etc.). The number of decimal places indicates the denominator of the fraction. One decimal place indicates a denominator of 10; two places indicate a denominator of 100; three indicate a denominator of 1,000; and so on. 0.335 is read as three hundred thirty-five thousandths and 0.12345 as twelve thousand three hundred forty-five hundred thousandths.

$$0 \quad . \quad 1 \quad 2 \quad 3 \quad 4 \quad 5$$

- 1 — TENTHS
- 2 — HUNDREDTHS
- 3 — THOUSANDTHS
- 4 — TEN THOUSANDTHS
- 5 — HUNDRED THOUSANDTHS

When a decimal does not include a positive or negative whole number, a zero is placed to the left of the decimal point. This has no mathematical significance; it is there just to make the decimals more readable. Without the zero, someone might fail to see the decimal and read .335 as 335. On the exam, all decimals that do not include a positive or negative whole number are written with a zero to the left of the decimal point.

Converting Fractions to Decimals

If the fraction already has a denominator that is ten, one hundred, one thousand, etc., the conversion is very easy. The numerator of the fraction becomes the decimal. The number of zeros in the denominator governs the placement of the decimal point. Starting just to the right of the last digit of the numerator, you count over one digit to the left for each zero in the denominator. For example, to express $\dfrac{127}{1,000}$ in decimal form, take the numerator, 127, as the decimal. Then, starting just to the right of the 7, count over three places to the left (one for each zero in 1,000). The decimal equivalent is 0.127.

Examples:

1. $\dfrac{3}{10} = 0.3$ (One zero in the denominator indicates one decimal place.)

2. $\dfrac{13}{100} = 0.13$ (Two zeros in the denominator indicate two decimal places.)

3. $\dfrac{522}{1,000} = 0.522$ (Three zeros in the denominator indicate three decimal places.)

If there are fewer digits in the numerator than zeros in the denominator, add zeros to the left of the number until you have enough decimal places. For example, consider $\dfrac{53}{1,000}$: the denominator contains three zeros, but 53 is only a two-digit number. Therefore, add one zero to the left of the 5: $\dfrac{53}{1,000} = 0.053$.

Examples:

1. $\dfrac{3}{100} = 0.03$ (Two zeros mean two decimal places.)

2. $\dfrac{71}{10,000} = 0.0071$ (Four zeros mean four decimal places.)

3. $\dfrac{9}{100,000} = 0.00009$ (Five zeros mean five decimal places.)

To convert a proper fraction with a denominator other than 10, 100, etc., convert the fraction to an equivalent form using a denominator such as ten, one hundred, etc. For example, to convert $\dfrac{3}{4}$ to a decimal, change it into a fraction with a denominator of 100: $\dfrac{3}{4} = \dfrac{3 \cdot 25}{4 \cdot 25} = \dfrac{75}{100}$. Then, $\dfrac{75}{100}$ is written as 0.75, as described in the previous section.

Examples:

1. $\dfrac{2}{5} = \dfrac{2 \cdot 2}{5 \cdot 2} = \dfrac{4}{10} = 0.4$

2. $\dfrac{1}{4} = \dfrac{1 \cdot 25}{4 \cdot 25} = \dfrac{25}{100} = 0.25$

3. $\dfrac{3}{8} = \dfrac{3 \cdot 125}{8 \cdot 125} = \dfrac{375}{1,000} = 0.375$

4. $\dfrac{1}{50} = \dfrac{1 \cdot 2}{50 \cdot 2} = \dfrac{2}{10} = 0.02$

To determine which denominator you should use, divide the denominator of the fraction into 10, then into 100, then into 1,000, until you find the first denominator that is evenly divisible by the denominator of the fraction. For example, $\frac{3}{8}$ does not have an equivalent form with a denominator of 10, but it does have an equivalent form with a denominator of 1,000. This is the same process used above to find common denominators for fractions. (Note: You can also convert a fraction into a decimal by dividing the numerator of the fraction by its denominator. However, this method obviously presupposes that you know how to divide decimals. We will come back to the topic of converting to decimals when we discuss how to divide decimals.)

Converting Mixed Numbers to Decimals

To change a mixed number to a decimal, convert the fractional part of the mixed number to a decimal as discussed above, and then place the whole number part of the mixed number to the left of the decimal point.

Examples:

1. Convert the mixed number $2\frac{3}{4}$ to a decimal.

    ➤ First, convert $\frac{3}{4}$ to a decimal: $\frac{3}{4} = 0.75$. Then, place the whole-number part to the left of the decimal point: 2.75. Notice that the extra zero is dropped—there is no reason to write 02.75.

2. $6\frac{1}{10} = 6.1$

3. $12\frac{1}{2} = 12.5$

4. $3\frac{7}{8} = 3.875$

Converting Improper Fractions to Decimals

To convert an improper fraction to a decimal, just treat the improper fraction as a mixed number and follow the procedure just outlined.

Examples:

1. $\frac{9}{4} = 2\frac{1}{4} = 2.25$

2. $\frac{7}{2} = 3\frac{1}{2} = 3.5$

3. $\frac{8}{5} = 1\frac{3}{5} = 1.6$

It is also possible, and often easier, to convert improper fractions to decimals by dividing the numerator by the denominator. Again, we will postpone this part of the discussion until we have studied division of decimals.

Converting Decimals to Fractions and Mixed Numbers

To convert a decimal back to a fraction, it is necessary only to create a fraction using the digits of the decimal number as a numerator and a denominator of 1 followed by a number of zeros equal to the number of decimal places.

Examples:

1. Convert 0.125 to a fraction.

    ➤ Use 125 as the numerator and 1,000 as the denominator: $\frac{125}{1,000}$. Reduce the fraction to lowest terms:

    $$\frac{125}{1,000} = \frac{1}{8}.$$

2. $0.04 = \frac{4}{100} = \frac{1}{25}$

3. $0.25 = \frac{25}{100} = \frac{1}{4}$

4. $0.005 = \frac{5}{1,000} = \frac{1}{200}$

Finally, if the decimal consists of both a whole part and a fraction, the conversion will result in a mixed number. The whole part of the mixed number will be the whole part of the decimal. Then, convert the fractional part of the decimal as just shown.

Examples:

1. Convert 2.05 to a mixed number.

    ➤ Write 0.05 as a fraction: $0.05 = \frac{5}{100} = \frac{1}{20}$. The whole number part is 2, so $2.05 = 2\frac{1}{20}$.

2. $1.75 = 1 + \frac{75}{100} = 1 + \frac{3}{4} = 1\frac{3}{4}$

3. $32.6 = 32 + \frac{6}{10} = 32 + \frac{3}{5} = 32\frac{3}{5}$

4. $2.05 = 2 + \frac{5}{100} = 2 + \frac{1}{20} = 2\frac{1}{20}$

5. $357.125 = 357 + \frac{125}{1,000} = 357 + \frac{1}{8} = 357\frac{1}{8}$

Operations of Decimals

Adding and Subtracting Decimals

Decimals can be manipulated in very much the same way as whole numbers. You can add and subtract decimals.

Examples:

1. $0.2 + 0.3 + 0.1 = 0.6$

2. $0.7 - 0.2 = 0.5$

Adding zeros to the end of a decimal number does not change the value of that number. If the decimals do not have the same number of decimal places, add zeros to the right of those that do not until every number has the same number of decimal places. Then, line up the decimal points and combine the decimals as indicated. Follow the same process for subtracting decimals.

Examples:

1. $0.75 - 0.1125 \Rightarrow$ 0.7500
$$-0.1125$$
$$0.6375$$

2. $0.125 + 0.6 + 0.115 \Rightarrow$ 0.125
$$0.600$$
$$+0.115$$
$$0.840$$

3. $0.999 - 0.000001 \Rightarrow$ 0.999000
$$-0.000001$$
$$0.998999$$

4. $2.14 + 0.125 + 0.0005 \Rightarrow$ 2.1400
$$0.1250$$
$$+0.0005$$
$$2.2655$$

5. $0.8 - 0.1111 \Rightarrow$ 0.8000
$$-0.1111$$
$$0.6889$$

6. $0.11 + 0.9 + 0.033 \Rightarrow$ 0.110
$$0.900$$
$$+0.033$$
$$1.043$$

Multiplying Decimals

As with fractions, there is no need to find a common denominator when multiplying decimals: The multiplication process generates its own. Simply multiply as with whole numbers and then adjust the decimal point. To find the correct position for the decimal point first, count the total number of decimal places in the numbers that are being multiplied. Then, in the final product, place the decimal point that many places to the left, counting from the right side of the last digit.

Examples:

1. $0.25 \cdot 0.2 = ?$

   ➢ Ignore the decimals and multiply: $25 \cdot 2 = 50$. Now, adjust the decimal point. Since 0.25 has two decimal places, and 0.2 has one decimal place, count three places to the left, starting at the right side of the 0 in 50; the final product is $0.050 = 0.05$.

2. $0.1 \cdot 0.2 \cdot 0.3 = 0.006$ ($1 \cdot 2 \cdot 3 = 6$, and there are three decimal places in the multiplication.)

3. $0.02 \cdot 0.008 = 0.00016$ ($2 \cdot 8 = 16$, and there are five decimal places in the multiplication.)

4. $2 \cdot 0.5 = 1$ ($2 \cdot 5 = 10$, and there is one decimal place in the multiplication.)

5. $2.5 \cdot 2.5 = 6.25$ ($25 \cdot 25 = 625$, and there are two decimal places in the multiplication.)

6. $0.10 \cdot 0.10 \cdot 0.10 = 0.001$ ($10 \cdot 10 \cdot 10 = 1,000$, and there are six decimal places in the multiplication.)

To simplify the process of multiplying decimals, drop any final zeros before multiplying. Thus, in the case of the last example, $0.10 \cdot 0.10 \cdot 0.10 = 0.1 \cdot 0.1 \cdot 0.1 = 0.001$ since there are three decimal places in the multiplication.

Dividing Decimals

Like multiplication, division generates a common denominator by a suitable adjustment of zeros. However, there are two situations in which division of decimals is a little tricky. Let's review them one at a time.

First, when the divisor (the number doing the dividing) is a whole number, place the decimal point in the quotient (result of division) immediately above the decimal point in the dividend (the number being divided). Then, keep dividing until there is no remainder, adding zeros as needed to the right of the dividend. This is the procedure whenever the divisor is a whole number—even if the dividend is also a whole number.

Examples:

1. $0.25 \div 5 \Rightarrow$
$$5\overline{)0.25} = 0.05$$
$$-25$$
$$\overline{0}$$

2. $2.5 \div 2 \Rightarrow$
$$2\overline{)2.50} = 1.25$$
$$-2$$
$$\overline{0\,5}$$
$$-4$$
$$\overline{10}$$
$$-10$$
$$\overline{0}$$

3. $1.75 \div 25 \Rightarrow$
$$25\overline{)1.75} = 0.07$$
$$-1\,75$$
$$\overline{0}$$

4. $1.44 \div 12 \Rightarrow$
$$12\overline{)1.44} = 0.12$$
$$-1\,2$$
$$\overline{24}$$
$$-24$$
$$\overline{0}$$

5. $0.1 \div 250 \Rightarrow$
$$250\overline{)0.1000} = 0.0004$$
$$-1000$$
$$\overline{0}$$

6. $9 \div 2 \Rightarrow$
$$2\overline{)9.0} = 4.5$$
$$-8$$
$$\overline{10}$$
$$-10$$
$$\overline{0}$$

The second tricky situation occurs when the divisor is a decimal. In these cases, "clear" the fractional part of the decimal by moving the decimal point to the right. For example, if dividing by 0.1, change 0.1 to 1; if dividing by 2.11, convert that to 211 by moving the decimal point two places to the right. However, you must also move the decimal point of the dividend by the same number of places to ensure that their relative values are not changed. Notice that in the following examples both decimal points are moved the same number of places to the right.

Examples:

1. $5 \div 2.5 \Rightarrow$

$$2.5. \overline{)5.0.}$$
$$\underline{-5\ 0}$$
$$0$$

2. $10 \div 1.25 \Rightarrow$

$$1.25. \overline{)10.00.}$$
$$\underline{-10\ 00}$$
$$0$$

3. $50 \div 0.05 \Rightarrow$

$$0.05. \overline{)50.00.}$$
$$\underline{-50\ 00}$$
$$0$$

There are two final things to say about dividing decimals. First, as mentioned previously, you can use division of decimals to convert fractions to decimals. For example, to convert $\dfrac{9}{2}$ to a decimal number, simply divide 9 by 2.

Examples:

1. $\dfrac{9}{2} = 2\overline{)9} \Rightarrow$

$$2\overline{)9.0}$$
$$\underline{-8}$$
$$1\ 0$$
$$\underline{-1\ 0}$$
$$0$$

2. $\dfrac{3}{4} = 4\overline{)3} \Rightarrow$

$$4\overline{)3.00}$$
$$\underline{-2\ 8}$$
$$2\ 0$$
$$\underline{-2\ 0}$$
$$0$$

Second, some fractions do not have exact decimal equivalents. Try converting $\dfrac{1}{3}$ to a decimal using the division route.

You will be at it forever, because you get an endless succession of "3"s. Try converting $\dfrac{1}{9}$ a decimal using the division method. Again, you will get an endless succession, this time of repeating "1"s. By convention, repeating decimals are indicated using an overbar: $0.1\overline{1}$.

Decimals

DIRECTIONS: Choose the correct answer to each of the following items. Answers are on page 787.

1. What is $\frac{7}{10}$ expressed as a decimal?

   A. 70   **C.** 0.7   **E.** 0.0007
   B. 7   **D.** 0.007

2. What is $\frac{73}{100}$ expressed as a decimal?

   A. 73   **C.** 0.73   **E.** 0.0073
   B. 7.3   **D.** 0.073

3. What is $\frac{21}{1,000}$ expressed as a decimal?

   A. 0.21   **C.** 0.0021   **E.** 0.000021
   B. 0.021   **D.** 0.00021

4. What is $\frac{557}{1,000}$ expressed as a decimal?

   A. 5.57   **C.** 0.0557   **E.** 0.00057
   B. 0.557   **D.** 0.0057

5. What is $\frac{34}{10,000}$ expressed as a decimal?

   A. 0.00034   **C.** 0.034   **E.** 3.4
   B. 0.0034   **D.** 0.34

6. What is $\frac{1}{1,000,000}$ expressed as a decimal?

   A. 0.01   **C.** 0.0001   **E.** 0.000001
   B. 0.001   **D.** 0.00001

7. What is $\frac{30}{100}$ expressed as a decimal?

   A. 3   **C.** 0.03   **E.** 0.0003
   B. 0.3   **D.** 0.003

8. What is $\frac{1,000}{4,000}$ expressed as a decimal?

   A. 0.25   **C.** 0.0025   **E.** 0.000025
   B. 0.025   **D.** 0.00025

9. Which of the following is (are) equal to $\frac{1}{10}$?

   I. 1.0
   II. 0.1
   III. 0.1000

   A. I only   **D.** II and III only
   B. II only   **E.** I, II, and III
   C. III only

10. Which of the following is (are) equal to $\frac{25}{100}$?

    I. 0.25
    II. 0.025
    III. 0.0025

    A. I only   **D.** II and III only
    B. I and II only   **E.** I, II, and III
    C. I and III only

11. What is $\frac{257}{100}$ expressed as a decimal?

    A. 25.7   **C.** 0.257   **E.** 0.00257
    B. 2.57   **D.** 0.0257

12. What is $\frac{57}{10}$ expressed as a decimal?

    A. 57   **C.** 0.57   **E.** 0.0057
    B. 5.7   **D.** 0.057

13. What is $\frac{5}{8}$ expressed as a decimal?

    A. 0.125   **C.** 0.850   **E.** 5.80
    B. 0.625   **D.** 1.25

14. What is $\frac{4}{5}$ expressed as a decimal?

A. 0.4   **C.** 0.8   **E.** 2.4
B. 0.6   **D.** 1.2

15. What is $\frac{1}{20}$ expressed as a decimal?

A. 0.05   **C.** 0.0005   **E.** 0.000005
B. 0.005   **D.** 0.00005

16. What is $\frac{1}{50}$ expressed as a decimal?

A. 0.2   **C.** 0.002   **E.** 0.00002
B. 0.02   **D.** 0.0002

17. What is $\frac{3}{200}$ expressed as a decimal?

A. 0.15   **C.** 0.0015   **E.** 0.000015
B. 0.015   **D.** 0.00015

18. What is $\frac{9}{500}$ expressed as a decimal?

A. 0.000018   **C.** 0.0018   **E.** 0.18
B. 0.00018   **D.** 0.018

19. What is $\frac{17}{500}$ expressed as a decimal?

A. 0.175   **C.** 0.0175   **E.** 0.00034
B. 0.034   **D.** 0.0034

20. What is $\frac{123}{200}$ expressed as a decimal?

A. 0.615   **C.** 0.0615   **E.** 0.00615
B. 0.256   **D.** 0.0256

21. $0.1 + 0.1 = ?$

A. 0.002   **C.** 0.2   **E.** 20
B. 0.02   **D.** 2

22. $0.27 + 0.13 + 0.55 = ?$

A. 0.21   **C.** 0.47   **E.** 0.95
B. 0.36   **D.** 0.85

23. $0.528 + 0.116 + 0.227 = ?$

A. 0.871   **C.** 0.243   **E.** 0.0012
B. 0.583   **D.** 0.112

24. $0.7 + 0.013 + 0.028 = ?$

A. 0.741   **C.** 1.02   **E.** 2.553
B. 0.988   **D.** 1.224

25. $1.23 + 0.00001 = ?$

A. 1.24   **C.** 1.23001   **E.** 1.230000001
B. 1.2301   **D.** 1.2300001

26. $57.1 + 23.3 + 35.012 = ?$

A. 412.115   **C.** 115.0412   **E.** 1.15412
B. 115.412   **D.** 11.5412

27. $0.01 + 0.001 + 0.0001 + 0.00001 = ?$

A. 1   **C.** 0.1111   **E.** 0.001111
B. 0.10   **D.** 0.01111

28. $0.9 + 0.09 + 0.009 + 0.0009 = ?$

A. 0.9999   **C.** 0.009999   **E.** 0.0000999
B. 0.09999   **D.** 0.0009999

29. $0.27 + 0.36 + 2.1117 + 3.77777 + 1.42 = ?$

A. 5.44   **C.** 8.11143   **E.** 14.002785
B. 7.93947   **D.** 12.223479

30. $12,279.1 + 3,428.01 + 3,444.99 = ?$

A. 19,151.99   **C.** 19,152.09   **E.** 19,152.11
B. 19,152   **D.** 19,152.1

31. $0.7 - 0.3 = ?$

A. 0.004   **C.** 0.04   **E.** 0.4
B. 0.021   **D.** 0.21

32. $0.75 - 0.25 = ?$

A. 5   **C.** 0.5   **E.** 0.005
B. 1   **D.** 0.25

33. $1.35 - 0.35 = ?$

A. 1   **C.** 0.1   **E.** 0.00001
B. 0.35   **D.** 0.0035

34. $25.125 - 5.357 = ?$

A. 19.768   **C.** 12.115   **E.** 2.288
B. 15.432   **D.** 4.108

35. $1 - 0.00001 = ?$

A. 0.9   **C.** 0.999   **E.** 0.99999
B. 0.99   **D.** 0.9999

36. $0.2 \cdot 0.1 = ?$

   A. 0.3   **C.** 0.1   **E.** 0.006
   B. 0.2   **D.** 0.02

37. $0.1 \cdot 0.1 \cdot 0.1 = ?$

   A. 0.3   **C.** 0.01   **E.** 0.0001
   B. 0.1   **D.** 0.001

38. $1.1 \cdot 1.1 \cdot 1.1 = ?$

   A. 1.331   **C.** 0.111   **E.** 0.00111
   B. 1.111   **D.** 0.0111

39. $0.11 \cdot 0.33 = ?$

   A. 0.363   **C.** 0.00363   **E.** 0.0000363
   B. 0.0363   **D.** 0.000363

40. $0.2 \cdot 0.5 \cdot 0.2 \cdot 0.5 = ?$

   A. 0.1   **C.** 0.001   **E.** 0.00001
   B. 0.01   **D.** 0.0001

41. $5 \cdot 0.25 = ?$

   A. 1.25   **C.** 0.0125   **E.** 0.000125
   B. 0.125   **D.** 0.00125

42. $10 \cdot 0.000001 = ?$

   A. 0.00001 **C.** 0.001   **E.** 0.1
   B. 0.0001   **D.** 0.01

43. $100 \cdot 0.00052 = ?$

   A. 0.0052   **C.** 5.2   **E.** 520
   B. 0.052   **D.** 52

44. $1.2 \cdot 1.2 = ?$

   A. 0.144   **C.** 14.4   **E.** 1,444
   B. 1.44   **D.** 144

45. $1.000 \cdot 1.000 \cdot 1.000 \cdot 1.000 = ?$

   A. 1   **C.** 0.01   **E.** 0.0001
   B. 0.1   **D.** 0.001

46. $6 \div 0.2 = ?$

   A. 0.03   **C.** 3   **E.** 300
   B. 0.3   **D.** 30

47. $0.2 \div 5 = ?$

   A. 0.4   **C.** 0.004   **E.** 0.00004
   B. 0.04   **D.** 0.0004

48. $1 \div 0.001 = ?$

   A. 10,000   **C.** 100   **E.** 0.0001
   B. 1,000   **D.** 0.001

49. $25.1 \div 2.51 = ?$

   A. 100   **C.** 0.1   **E.** 0.001
   B. 10   **D.** 0.01

50. $0.25 \div 8 = ?$

   A. 4   **C.** 0.03125   **E.** 0.003125
   B. 0.4   **D.** 0.004

51. $0.005 \div 0.005 = ?$

   A. 1   **C.** 0.005   **E.** 0.00005
   B. 0.5   **D.** 0.0005

52. $2 \div 2.5 = ?$

   A. 8   **C.** 0.8   **E.** 0.008
   B. 5   **D.** 0.5

53. $111 \div 0.111 = ?$

   A. 1   **C.** 11   **E.** 1,000
   B. 10   **D.** 110

54. $0.12345 \div 0.012345 = ?$

   A. 100   **C.** 1   **E.** 0.01
   B. 10   **D.** 0.1

55. $0.002 \div 0.00002 = ?$

   A. 100   **C.** 0.1   **E.** 0.001
   B. 10   **D.** 0.01

56. Express as a decimal: $\dfrac{3}{5} + \dfrac{5}{8}$.

   A. 1.00   **C.** 1.225   **E.** 1.75
   B. 1.115   **D.** 1.50

57. Find the average of $\dfrac{2}{3}$ and 0.75.

   A. $\dfrac{9}{24}$ **C.** $\dfrac{17}{24}$ **E.** $\dfrac{23}{24}$
   B. $\dfrac{14}{24}$ **D.** $\dfrac{21}{24}$

58. Find the average of 0.1, 0.01, and $\dfrac{1}{4}$.

   A. 0.10   **C.** 0.50   **E.** 1.0
   B. 0.12   **D.** 0.75

59. $\dfrac{12\frac{1}{3}}{0.2} = ?$

- **A.** $\dfrac{1}{50}$
- **C.** $\dfrac{85}{2}$
- **E.** $\dfrac{225}{4}$
- **B.** $\dfrac{3}{40}$
- **D.** $\dfrac{185}{3}$

60. $0.1\left[\dfrac{1}{3} - 2\left(\dfrac{1}{2} - \dfrac{1}{4}\right)\right] = ?$

- **A.** $-\dfrac{2}{15}$
- **C.** $-\dfrac{1}{90}$
- **E.** $\dfrac{3}{4}$
- **B.** $-\dfrac{1}{60}$
- **D.** $\dfrac{1}{2}$

61. For three months, Pete saved part of his monthly allowance. He saved $4.56 the first month, $3.82 the second month, and $5.06 the third month. How much did Pete save altogether?

- **A.** $12.04
- **C.** $13.04
- **E.** $14.44
- **B.** $12.44
- **D.** $13.44

62. From an employee's salary of $190.57, an employer deducts $3.05 for social security and $5.68 for pension. What is the final amount of the check?

- **A.** $180.84
- **C.** $181.84
- **E.** $182.84
- **B.** $181.04
- **D.** $182.04

63. If the outer radius of a metal pipe is 2.84 inches and the inner radius is 1.94 inches, what is the thickness, in inches, of the metal?

- **A.** 0.85
- **C.** 1.00
- **E.** 1.25
- **B.** 0.90
- **D.** 1.18

64. Pete earns $20.56 on Monday, $32.90 on Tuesday, and $20.78 on Wednesday. He spends half of all that he earned during the 3 days. How much does he have left?

- **A.** $36.12
- **C.** $37.12
- **E.** $38.12
- **B.** $36.72
- **D.** $37.72

65. What is the total cost of $3\frac{1}{2}$ pounds of meat at $1.69 per pound and 20 lemons at $0.60 per dozen?

- **A.** $5.92
- **C.** $6.92
- **E.** $7.92
- **B.** $6.42
- **D.** $7.42

66. A reel of cable weighs 1,279 pounds. If the empty reel weighs 285 pounds and the cable weighs 7.1 pounds per foot, how many feet of cable are on the reel?

- **A.** 140
- **C.** 160
- **E.** 180
- **B.** 150
- **D.** 170

67. How much will 345 fasteners at $4.15 per hundred cost?

- **A.** $13.12
- **C.** $14.12
- **E.** $14.82
- **B.** $13.82
- **D.** $14.32

Percents

A *percent* is a special type of fraction that always has a denominator equal to 100. The percent sign, "%," is shorthand for "$\frac{x}{100}$." For example, $67\% = \frac{67}{100}$.

Converting to and from Percents

Since percents are simply a special type of fraction, both fractions and decimals can be converted to percents, and vice versa. The easiest conversion is to change a decimal to a percent: move the decimal point two places to the right and add the percent sign.

Examples:

    1. $0.27 = 27\%$

    2. $0.50 = 50\%$

    3. $0.275 = 27.5\%$

This substitutes "%" for two decimal places—simply a matter of changing things from one form into an equivalent form, which is a process we have already used in several ways. To change a percent back to a decimal, move the decimal point two places to the left and drop the percent sign.

Examples:

    1. $27\% = 0.27$

    2. $50\% = 0.50$

    3. $27.5\% = 0.275$

You already know the rules for converting fractions to decimals, and vice versa. To convert a fraction to a percent, just convert the fraction to a decimal and follow the rule above.

Examples:

    1. $\frac{3}{4} = 0.75 = 75\%$

    2. $\frac{5}{8} = 0.625 = 62.5\%$

    3. $\frac{1}{10} = 0.10 = 10\%$

To reverse the process, follow the rule given above for turning percentages back into decimals, and then use the procedure outlined in the previous section for converting decimals to fractions.

Examples:

1. $75\% = 0.75 = \dfrac{75}{100} = \dfrac{3}{4}$

2. $62.5\% = 0.625 = \dfrac{625}{1,000} = \dfrac{5}{8}$

3. $10\% = 0.1 = \dfrac{1}{10}$

There are two tricky types of percents: those greater than 100% and those less than 1%. First, it is possible to have a percent that is larger than 100. This would be the result of converting a mixed number, such as $2\dfrac{3}{4}$, to a percent: $2\dfrac{3}{4} = 2.75 = 275\%$. Second, percents can also be less than 1, in which case they are written with decimals; for example, 0.5%. However, these numbers follow the general rules outlined above. To convert 0.5% to a fraction: $0.5\% = 0.005 = \dfrac{5}{1,000} = \dfrac{1}{200}$. Similarly, fractions smaller than $\dfrac{1}{100}$ will yield a percent less than 1: $\dfrac{1}{2,500} = 0.0004 = 0.04\%$.

Operations of Percents

Adding and Subtracting Percents

Percents are fractions, so they can be manipulated like other fractions. All percents have 100 as the denominator. It is easy to add and subtract percents because you already have a common denominator.

Examples:

1. Paul originally owned 25% of the stock of a certain company. He purchased another 15% of the stock privately, and he received a gift of another 10% of the stock. What percent of the stock of the company does Paul now own?

   ➢ $25\% + 15\% + 10\% = 50\%$

2. In a certain election, Peter and Mary received 50% of all the votes that were cast. If Peter received 20% of the votes cast in the election, what percent of the votes did Mary receive?

   ➢ $50\% - 20\% = 30\%$

Multiplying Percents

To multiply percents, first convert them to decimals and then multiply. For example, $60\% \cdot 80\% = 0.60 \cdot 0.80 = 0.48 = 48\%$.

Example:

In a certain group, 80% of the people are wearing hats. If 60% of those wearing hats are also wearing gloves, what percent of the entire group is wearing both a hat and gloves?

➤ 60% of 80% = 60% • 80% = 0.60 • 0.80 = 0.48 = 48%

Dividing Percents

To divide percents, first convert them to decimals and then divide. For example, $\frac{100\%}{12.5\%} = \frac{1}{0.125} = 8$.

Example:

Peter is purchasing an item on a lay-away plan. If he pays weekly installments of 8% of the purchase price, how many weeks will it take for Peter to payoff the entire purchase price?

➤ $100\% \div 8\% = 1 \div 0.08 = 12.5$ weeks

Percent Story Problems

Four basic variations of percent problems appear on the exam as story problems:

- What is x percent of something?
- This is what percent of that?
- This is a given percent of what?
- What is the percent change from this quantity to that quantity?

Notice that in each of the first three question forms, there is the phrase "of that" and the phrase "is this" ("this is"). When you set up a fraction for the percent, always place the "is this" value over the "of that" value. This allows us to write the following equation for percents: $\frac{is}{of} = \frac{\%}{100}$. We call this the "is-over-of" equation.

"What Is X Percent of Some Quantity?"

Percents are fractions, so in the question, "What is x percent of some quantity?", the "of" indicates multiplication.

Examples:

1. A certain class is made up of 125 students. If 60% of the students are men, how many men are in the class?

    ➤ 60% of 125 = 60% • 125 = 0.60 • 125 = 75.

2. If Sam originally had $25 and gave 25% of that amount to his friend Samantha, how much money did Sam give to Samantha?

    ➤ 25% of $25 = 25% • 25 = 0.25 • 25 = $6.25.

3. If Paula had 50 marbles and gave 20% of them to her friend Paul, how many marbles did Paula give to Paul?

    ➤ 20% of 50 = 20% • 50 = 0.20 • 50 = 10.

Noting the slight variation in phrasing, "is this" can be represented by "what number." Therefore, you can use the "is-over-of" equation to solve for the unknown value.

Examples:

1. What number is 20% of 25?

> x is 20% of 25: $\dfrac{\text{is}}{\text{of}} = \dfrac{\%}{100} \Rightarrow \dfrac{x}{25} = \dfrac{20}{100} \Rightarrow x = \dfrac{20 \cdot 25}{100} = \dfrac{20}{4} = 5$.

2. If Paula had 50 marbles and gave 20% of them to her friend Paul, how many marbles did Paula give to Paul?

> Simplify the item stem: "x is 20% of 50." Thus, $\dfrac{\text{is}}{\text{of}} = \dfrac{\%}{100} \Rightarrow \dfrac{x}{50} = \dfrac{20}{100} \Rightarrow x = \dfrac{20 \cdot 50}{100} = \dfrac{20}{2} = 10$.

"What Percent Is This of That?"

A second common item involving percents has the form, "What percent is this of that?"

Example:

What percent is 3 of 12?

> Convert $\dfrac{3}{12}$ to a decimal by dividing 3 by 12 and then change that decimal number to a percent: $\dfrac{3}{12} = \dfrac{1}{4} = 0.25 = 25\%$.

There are other ways of phrasing the same question:

- 3 is what percent of 12?
- Of 12, what percent is 3?

Note that all three of the above questions are equivalent and represent the three following general forms:

- What percent is this of that?
- This is what percent of that?
- Of that, what percent is this?

Again, you can set up an "is-over-of" equation and solve for the unknown value.

Example:

5 is what percent of 25? Of 25, what percent is 5? What percent is 5 of 25?

> Notice that all three of these questions are equivalent: "5 is x% of 25." Set up the "is-over-of" equation and solve for the unknown: $\dfrac{\text{is}}{\text{of}} = \dfrac{\%}{100} \Rightarrow \dfrac{5}{25} = \dfrac{x}{100} \Rightarrow x = \dfrac{5 \cdot 100}{25} = \dfrac{100}{5} = 20\%$.

As long as you place the "is this" value in the numerator and the "of that" value in the denominator, you cannot make a mistake.

Examples:

1. What percent is 20 of 50?

> 20 is x% of 50: $\dfrac{\text{is}}{\text{of}} = \dfrac{\%}{100} \Rightarrow \dfrac{20}{50} = \dfrac{x}{100} \Rightarrow x = \dfrac{20 \cdot 100}{50} = 20 \cdot 2 = 40\%$.

2. Of 125, what percent is 25?

➤ 25 is x% of 125: $\dfrac{\text{is}}{\text{of}} = \dfrac{\%}{100} \Rightarrow \dfrac{25}{125} = \dfrac{x}{100} \Rightarrow x = \dfrac{25 \cdot 100}{125} = \dfrac{100}{5} = 20\%$.

3. 12 is what percent of 6?

➤ 12 is x% of 6: $\dfrac{\text{is}}{\text{of}} = \dfrac{\%}{100} \Rightarrow \dfrac{12}{6} = \dfrac{x}{100} \Rightarrow x = \dfrac{12 \cdot 100}{6} = 2 \cdot 100 = 200\%$.

No matter how wordy or otherwise difficult such items get, you can still use the "is-over-of" method by first simplifying the item stem.

Example:

John received a paycheck for $200. Of that amount, he paid Ed $25. What percent of the paycheck did John give Ed?

➤ Simplify the item stem: "$25 is x% of $200." Thus, $\dfrac{\text{is}}{\text{of}} = \dfrac{\%}{100} \Rightarrow \dfrac{\$25}{\$200} = \dfrac{x}{100} \Rightarrow x = \dfrac{25 \cdot 100}{200} = \dfrac{25}{2} = 12.5\%$.

"This Is X Percent of What?"

In the third type of percent problem, the task is to manipulate a given value and percent to determine the unknown total value. Again, you can use the "is-over-of" equation for this variation as well—simply solve for the unknown value.

Examples:

1. 5 is 20% of what number?

➤ 5 is 20% of x: $\dfrac{\text{is}}{\text{of}} = \dfrac{\%}{100} \Rightarrow \dfrac{5}{x} = \dfrac{20}{100} \Rightarrow x = \dfrac{5 \cdot 100}{20} = 5 \cdot 5 = 25$.

2. Seven students attended a field trip. If these 7 students were $6\frac{1}{4}$% of all the 9th-graders, find the total number of 9th-graders.

➤ Simplify the item stem: "7 is 6.25% of x." Thus, $\dfrac{\text{is}}{\text{of}} = \dfrac{\%}{100} \Rightarrow \dfrac{7}{x} = \dfrac{6.25\%}{100} \Rightarrow x = \dfrac{7 \cdot 100}{6.25} = 7 \cdot 16 = 112$.

3. A television set discounted by 18% was sold for $459.20. What was the price of the set before the discount?

➤ If you take 18% off, then $100\% - 18\% = 82\%$ remains. Simplify the item stem: "$459.20 is 82% of x."
Thus, $\dfrac{\text{is}}{\text{of}} = \dfrac{\%}{100} \Rightarrow \dfrac{\$459.20}{x} = \dfrac{82\%}{100} \Rightarrow x = \dfrac{459.20 \cdot 100}{82} = 5.6 \cdot 100 = \$560$.

Percent Change

The fourth percent item involves a quantity change over time. This type of item asks you to express the relationship between the change and the original amount in percent terms. To solve, create a fraction that is then expressed as a percent. Think of this as the "change-over-original" trick, because the fraction places the change over the original amount.

Examples:

1. The price of an item increased from $20 to $25. What was the percent increase in the price?

   ➢ $\dfrac{\text{Change}}{\text{Original Amount}} = \dfrac{25 - 20}{20} = \dfrac{5}{20} = \dfrac{1}{4} = 0.25 = 25\%.$

2. Mary was earning $16 per hour when she received a raise of $4 per hour. Her hourly wage increased by what percentage?

   ➢ $\dfrac{\text{Change}}{\text{Original Amount}} = \dfrac{4}{16} = 0.25 = 25\%.$

The "change-over-original" trick works for decreases as well.

Examples:

1. A stock's value declined from $50 per share to $45 per share. What was the percent decrease in the value of a share?

   ➢ $\dfrac{\text{Change}}{\text{Original Amount}} = \dfrac{5}{50} = \dfrac{1}{10} = 0.10 = 10\%.$

2. Student enrollment at City University dropped from 5,000 students in 1990 to 4,000 students in 2000. What was the percent decrease in the number of students enrolled at City University?

   ➢ $\dfrac{\text{Change}}{\text{Original Amount}} = \dfrac{1,000}{5,000} = \dfrac{1}{5} = 0.20 = 20\%.$

Percents

DIRECTIONS: Choose the correct answer to each of the following items. Answers are on page 787.

1. What is 0.79 expressed as a percent?

   A. 0.0079%   C. 0.79%   E. 79%
   B. 0.079%   D. 7.9%

2. What is 0.55 expressed as a percent?

   A. 55%   C. 0.55%   E. 0.0055%
   B. 5.5%   D. 0.055%

3. What is 0.111 expressed as a percent?

   A. 111%   C. 1.11%   E. 0.0111%
   B. 11.1%   D. 0.111%

4. What is 0.125 expressed as a percent?

   A. 125%   C. 1.25%   E. 0.0125%
   B. 12.5%   D. 0.125%

5. What is 0.5555 expressed as a percent?

   A. 5,555%   C. 55.55%   E. 0.555%
   B. 555.5%   D. 5.555%

6. What is 0.3 expressed as a percent?

   A. 30%   C. 0.30%   E. 0.003%
   B. 3%   D. 0.03%

7. What is 0.7500 expressed as a percent?

   A. 7,500%   C. 75%   E. 0.75%
   B. 750%   D. 7.5%

8. What is 2.45 expressed as a percent?

   A. 2,450%   C. 24.5%   E. 0.245%
   B. 245%   D. 2.45%

9. What is 1.25 expressed as a percent?

   A. 125%   C. 1.25%   E. 0.0125%
   B. 12.5%   D. 0.125%

10. What is 10 expressed as a percent?

    A. 1,000%   C. 10%   E. 0.1%
    B. 100%   D. 1%

11. What is 0.015 expressed as a percent?

    A. 15%   C. 0.15%   E. 0.0015%
    B. 1.5%   D. 0.015%

12. What is 0.099 expressed as a percent?

    A. 99%   C. 0.99%   E. 0.0099%
    B. 9.9%   D. 0.099%

13. What is 0.0333 expressed as a percent?

    A. 3.33%   C. 0.0333%   E. 0.000333%
    B. 0.333%   D. 0.00333%

14. What is 0.001 expressed as a percent?

    A. 0.1%   C. 0.001%   E. 0.00001%
    B. 0.01%   D. 0.0001%

15. What is 0.0100 expressed as a percent?

    A. 1%   C. 0.001%   E. 0.1%
    B. 0.01%   D. 0.0001%

16. What is 25% expressed as a decimal?

    A. 25.0   C. 0.25   E. 0.0025
    B. 2.5   D. 0.025

17. What is 56% expressed as a decimal?

    A. 5.6   C. 0.056   E. 0.00056
    B. 0.56   D. 0.0056

18. What is 10% expressed as a decimal?

    A. 100.0   C. 1.0   E. 0.001
    B. 10.0   D. 0.1

19. What is 100% expressed as a decimal?

    A. 100.0   C. 1.0   E. 0.001
    B. 10.0   D. 0.1

20. What is 250% expressed as a decimal?

    A. 250.0   C. 2.5   E. 0.025
    B. 25.0   D. 0.25

21. What is 1,000% expressed as a decimal?

    A. 1,000.0   C. 10.0   E. 0.01
    B. 100.0   D. 1.0

22. What is 0.25% expressed as a decimal?

    A. 25.0   C. 0.025   E. 0.00025
    B. 0.25   D. 0.0025

23. What is 0.099% expressed as a decimal?

    A. 99   C. 0.099   E. 0.00099
    B. 0.99   D. 0.0099

24. What is 0.0988% expressed as a decimal?

    A. 0.988   C. 0.00988   E. 9.8
    B. 0.0988   D. 0.000988

25. What is 0.00100% expressed as a decimal?

    A. 0.01   C. 0.0001   E. 0.000001
    B. 0.001   D. 0.00001

26. What is $\frac{1}{10}$ expressed as a percent?

    A. 100%   C. 1%   E. 0.01%
    B. 10%   D. 0.1%

27. What is $\frac{3}{100}$ expressed as a percent?

    A. 300%   C. 3%   E. 0.03%
    B. 30%   D. 0.3%

28. What is $\frac{99}{100}$ expressed as a percent?

    A. 99%   C. 0.99%   E. 0.0099%
    B. 9.9%   D. 0.099%

29. What is $\frac{100}{1,000}$ expressed as a percent?

    A. 0.1%   C. 10%   E. 1,000%
    B. 1.0%   D. 100%

30. What is $\frac{333}{100}$ expressed as a percent?

    A. 333%   C. 3.33%   E. 0.0333%
    B. 33.3%   D. 0.333%

31. What is $\frac{9}{1,000}$ as a percent?

    A. 9%   C. 0.09%   E. 0.0009%
    B. 0.9%   D. 0.009%

32. What is $\frac{3}{4}$ expressed as a percent?

    A. 0.0075%   C. 0.75%   E. 75%
    B. 0.075%   D. 7.5%

33. What is $\frac{4}{5}$ expressed as a percent?

    A. 4.5%   C. 45%   E. 450%
    B. 8%   D. 80%

34. What is $\frac{3}{50}$ expressed as a percent?

    A. 60%   C. 0.6%   E. 0.0006%
    B. 6%   D. 0.006%

35. What is $\frac{3}{75}$ expressed as a percent?

    A. 0.004%   C. 0.4%   E. 40%
    B. 0.04%   D. 4%

36. What is $\frac{6}{500}$ expressed as a percent?

    A. 0.012%   C. 1.2%   E. 120%
    B. 0.12%   D. 12%

37. What is $\frac{111}{555}$ expressed as a percent?

    A. 222%   C. 22%   E. 2%
    B. 200%   D. 20%

38. What is $\frac{8}{5,000}$ expressed as a percent?

    A. 16%   C. 0.016%   E. 0.00016%
    B. 0.16% D. 0.0016%

39. What is $1\frac{1}{10}$ expressed as a percent?

    A. 110%   C. 1.1%   E. 0.011%
    B. 11%   D. 0.11%

40. What is $9\frac{99}{100}$ expressed as a percent?

    A. 999%   C. 9.99%   E. 0.0999%
    B. 99.9%   D. 0.999%

41. What is $3\frac{1}{2}$ expressed as a percent?

    A. 0.35%   C. 35%   E. 3,500%
    B. 3.5%   D. 350%

42. What is $1\frac{3}{4}$ expressed as a percent?

    A. 175%   C. 17.5%   E. 1.75%
    B. 134%   D. 13.4%

43. What is $10\frac{1}{5}$ expressed as a percent?

    A. 10.02%   C. 100.2%   E. 1,020%
    B. 10.2%   D. 102%

44. What is $3\frac{1}{50}$ expressed as a percent?

    A. 302%   C. 3.02%   E. 0.00302%
    B. 30.2%   D. 0.0302%

45. What is $\frac{111}{100}$ expressed as a percent?

    A. 1,110%   C. 11.1%   E. 0.0111%
    B. 111%   D. 1.11%

46. What is $\frac{7}{2}$ expressed as a percent?

    A. 0.35%   C. 35%   E. 3,500%
    B. 3.5%   D. 350%

47. What is $\frac{13}{5}$ expressed as a percent?

    A. 260%   C. 2.6%   E. 0.026%
    B. 26%   D. 0.26%

48. What is $\frac{9}{8}$ expressed as a percent?

    A. 1,125%   C. 11.25%   E. 0.1125%
    B. 112.5%   D. 1.125%

49. What is $\frac{22}{5}$ expressed as a percent?

    A. 440%   C. 4.4%   E. 0.044
    B. 44%   D. 0.44%

50. What is $\frac{33}{6}$ expressed as a percent?

    A. 550%   C. 5.5%   E. 0.55%
    B. 53%   D. 5.3%

51. Which of the following is equal to 18%?

    A. $\frac{18}{1}$ C. $\frac{18}{100}$ E. $\frac{18}{10,000}$
    B. $\frac{18}{10}$ D. $\frac{18}{1,000}$

52. Which of the following is equal to 80%?

    A. 80   C. 0.8   E. 0.008
    B. 8   D. 0.08

53. Which of the following is equal to 45%?

    A. $\frac{1}{9}$ C. $\frac{11}{19}$ E. $\frac{9}{10}$
    B. $\frac{9}{20}$ D. $\frac{3}{4}$

54. Which of the following is equal to 7%?

    A. 0.007   C. 0.7   E. 70
    B. 0.07   D. 7

55. Which of the following is equal to 13.2%?

    A. 0.0132   C. 1.32   E. 132
    B. 0.132   D. 13.2

56. Which of the following is equal to 1.111%?

    A. 0.001111 C. 0.11111   E. 11.11
    B. 0.01111   D. 1.111

57. Which of the following is equal to 10.101%?

    A. 0.0010101 C. 0.10101   E. 10.101
    B. 0.010101   D. 1.0101

58. Which of the following is equal to 33%?

    A. $\frac{1}{3}$ C. $\frac{33}{111}$ E. $\frac{33}{10,000}$
    B. $\frac{33}{100}$ D. $\frac{33}{1,000}$

59. Which of the following is equal to 80.1%?

   A. $80\dfrac{1}{10}$ C. $\dfrac{801}{1,000}$ E. 0.00801

   B. 8.01   D. 0.0801

60. Which of the following is equal to 0.02%?

   A. $\dfrac{1}{5}$ C. $\dfrac{1}{500}$ E. $\dfrac{1}{50,000}$

   B. $\dfrac{1}{50}$ D. $\dfrac{1}{5,000}$

61. Which of the following is equal to 250%?

   A. $\dfrac{25}{1,000}$ C. $\dfrac{1}{4}$ E. 25

   B. $\dfrac{25}{100}$ D. 2.5

62. Which of the following is equal to 1,000%?

   A. $\dfrac{1}{10}$ C. 10   E. 1,000

   B. 1   D. 100

63. $37\% + 42\% = ?$

   A. 6%   C. 106%   E. 154%

   B. 79%   D. 110%

64. $210\% + 21\% = ?$

   A. 21,021%   C. 23.1%   E. 0.231%

   B. 231%   D. 2.31%

65. $8\% + 9\% + 10\% + 110\% = ?$

   A. 17%   C. 180%   E. 18,000%

   B. 137%   D. 1,800%

66. $254\% + 166\% + 342\% = ?$

   A. 900%   C. 432%   E. 92%

   B. 762%   D. 111%

67. $0.02\% + 0.005\% = ?$

   A. 7%   C. 1%   E. 0.025%

   B. 2.5%   D. 0.07%

68. $33\% - 25\% = ?$

   A. 0.08%   C. 8%   E. 800%

   B. 0.8%   D. 80%

69. $100\% - 0.99\% = ?$

   A. 1%   C. 11%   E. 99.99%

   B. 9.9%   D. 99.01%

70. $222\% - 22.2\% = ?$

   A. 221.88%   C. 22.188%   E. 1.998%

   B. 199.8%   D. 19.98%

71. If John read 15% of the pages in a book on Monday and another 25% on Tuesday, what percent of the book did he read on Monday and Tuesday combined?

   A. 7.5%   C. 55%   E. 80%

   B. 40%   D. 75%

72. If from 9:00 a.m. to noon Mary mowed 35% of a lawn, and from noon to 3:00 p.m. she mowed another 50% of the lawn, what percent of the lawn did she mow between 9:00 a.m. and 3:00 p.m.?

   A. 17.5%   C. 74.3%   E. 98%

   B. 60%   D. 85%

Items #73–75 refer to the following table:

Schedule for Completing Project X					
	Mon.	Tues.	Wed.	Thurs.	Fri.
% of work to be completed each day	8%	17%	25%	33%	17%

73. By the end of which day is one-half of the work scheduled to be completed?

   A. Monday   C. Wednesday   E. Friday

   B. Tuesday   D. Thursday

74. By the end of Tuesday, what percent of the work is scheduled to be completed?

   A. 8%   C. 25%   E. 88%

   B. 17%   D. 50%

75. If production is on schedule, during which day will $\dfrac{2}{3}$ of the project have been completed?

   A. Monday   C. Wednesday   E. Friday

   B. Tuesday   D. Thursday

76. A bucket filled to 33% of its capacity has an amount of water equal to $\frac{1}{4}$ of the bucket's capacity added to it. The bucket is filled to what percent of its capacity?

   A. 8%   **C.** 33%   **E.** 75%
   B. 25%   **D.** 58%

77. If Edward spends 15% of his allowance on a book and another 25% on food, what percent of his allowance remains?

   A. 10%   **C.** 45%   **E.** 80%
   B. 40%   **D.** 60%

78. 50% of 50% = ?

   A. 1%   **C.** 25%   **E.** 250%
   B. 2.5%   **D.** 100%

79. 1% of 100% = ?

   A. 0.01% **C.** 1%   **E.** 100%
   B. 0.1%   **D.** 10%

80. If a jar contains 100 marbles and 66% of those marbles are red, how many marbles in the jar are red?

   A. 6   **C.** 66   **E.** 6,660
   B. 34   **D.** 660

81. If 75% of 240 cars in a certain parking lot are sedans, how many of the cars in the parking lot are sedans?

   A. 18   **C.** 60   **E.** 210
   B. 24   **D.** 180

82. If 0.1% of the 189,000 names on a certain mailing list have the initials *B.D.*, how many names on the list have the initials *B.D.*?

   A. 1.89   **C.** 189   **E.** 189,000
   B. 18.9   **D.** 18,900

83. What percent of 10 is 1?

   A. 0.1%   **C.** 10%   **E.** 1,000%
   B. 1%   **D.** 100%

84. What percent of 12 is 3?

   A. 2.5%   **C.** 25%   **E.** 400%
   B. 3.6%   **D.** 36%

85. 50 is what percent of 40?

   A. 125%   **C.** 80%   **E.** 8%
   B. 90%   **D.** 12.5%

86. What number is 10% of 100?

   A. 0.01   **C.** 1   **E.** 1,000
   B. 0.1   **D.** 10

87. What number is 250% of 12?

   A. 3   **C.** 24   **E.** 36
   B. 15   **D.** 30

88. If Patty's age is 48 and Al's age is 36, then Al's age is what percent of Patty's age?

   A. 7.5%   **C.** 75%   **E.** 175%
   B. 25%   **D.** $133\frac{1}{3}$%

89. If 25 of the employees at a bank are women and 15 are men, then what percent of the bank's employees are women?

   A. 37.5% **C.** 60%   **E.** 90%
   B. 40%   **D.** 62.5%

90. If the price of an item increases from $5.00 to $8.00, the new price is what percent of the old price?

   A. 20%   **C.** 62.5%   **E.** 160%
   B. 60%   **D.** 92.5%

91. If the price of an item increases from $5.00 to $8.00, the old price is what percent of the new price?

   A. 20%   **C.** 62.5%   **E.** 160%
   B. 60%   **D.** 92.5%

92. If the price of a share of stock drops from $200 to $160, the new price is what percent of the old price?

   A. 20%   **C.** 50%   **E.** 125%
   B. 25%   **D.** 80%

93. If the price of a share of stock drops from $200 to $160, the old price is what percent of the new price?

   A. 20%   **C.** 50%   **E.** 125%
   B. 25%   **D.** 80%

94. If the price of a share of stock drops from $200 to $160, what was the percent decrease in the price?

A. 20%   C. 50%   E. 125%
B. 25%   D. 80%

Items #95–99 refer to the following table:

Enrollments for a One-Week Seminar	
Week Number	Number of Enrollees
1	10
2	25
3	20
4	15
5	30

95. The number of people who enrolled for the seminar in Week 1 was what percent of the number of people who enrolled in Week 2?

A. 5%   C. 50%   E. 250%
B. 40%   D. 80%

96. The number of people who enrolled for the seminar in Week 4 was what percent of the number of people who enrolled in Week 5?

A. 15%   C. 50%   E. 200%
B. 25%   D. 100%

97. The number of people who enrolled for the seminar in Week 5 was what percent of the number of people who enrolled in Week 4?

A. 15%   C. 50%   E. 200%
B. 25%   D. 100%

98. What was the percent increase in the number of people enrolled for the seminar from Week 1 to Week 2?

A. 40%   C. 100%   E. 250%
B. 80%   D. 150%

99. What was the percent decrease in the number of people enrolled for the seminar from Week 3 to Week 4?

 A. 25%   C. 75%   E. $133\frac{1}{3}$%

B. $33\frac{1}{3}$%   D. 125%

100. If a textbook costs $35, what is 8% sales tax on the textbook?

A. $1.20   C. $2.00   E. $3.20
B. $1.80   D. $2.80

101. If a textbook costs $30 plus 8.5% sales tax, what is the total cost of one textbook?

A. $3.55   C. $23.55   E. $33.55
B. $12.55   D. $32.55

102. How much is 25% of 80?

A. 2   C. 20   E. 45
B. 8   D. 40

103. How much is 2.3% of 90?

A. 1.07   C. 2.17   E. 2.3
B. 2.07   D. 2.7

104. On a test that had 50 items, Gertrude got 34 out of the first 40 correct. If she received a grade of 80% on the test, how many of the last 10 items did Gertrude have correct?

A. 6   C. 10   E. 34
B. 8   D. 12

105. The number of the question you are now reading is what percent of 1,000?

A. 0.1%   C. 10.5%   E. 1,050%
B. 10%   D. 100%

106. 40 is what percent of 50?

A. 5%   C. 80%   E. 95%
B. 25%   D. 90%

107. 80 is what percent of 20?

A. 4%   C. 40%   E. 400%
B. 8%   D. 200%

108. In the junior class, 300 enrolled in a test preparation course, while 500 did not. What percent of the junior class did not enroll in a test preparation course?

A. 7%   C. 62.5%   E. 90%
B. 35%   D. 75%

109. Mary's factory produces pencils at a cost to her company of $0.02 per pencil. If she sells them to a wholesaler at $0.05 each, what is her percent of profit based on her cost of $0.02 per pencil?

    A. 25%   C. 75%   E. 150%
    B. 50%   D. 100%

110. In a certain class of 30 students, 6 received A's. What percent of the class did not receive an A?

    A. 8%   C. 60%   E. 90%
    B. 40%   D. 80%

111. If the Wildcats won 10 out of 12 games, to the nearest whole percent, what percentage of their games did the Wildcats win?

    A. 3   C. 38   E. 94
    B. 8   D. 83

112. On Thursday, Hui made 86 out of 100 free throws. On Friday, she made 46 out of 50 free throws. What was Hui's free throw percentage for the two days?

    A. 8.8%   C. 28%   E. 88%
    B. 12.8%   D. 82%

113. A stereo was discounted by 20% and sold at the discount price of $256. Which of the following equals the price of the stereo before the discount?

    A. less than $300
    B. between $300 and $308
    C. between $308 and $316
    D. between $316 and $324
    E. more than $324

114. In a bag of red and black jellybeans, 136 are red jellybeans and the remainder are black jellybeans. If 15% of the jellybeans in the bag are black, what is the total number of jellybeans in the bag?

    A. 151   C. 175   E. 906
    B. 160   D. 200

115. The regular price of a TV set is $118.80. Which of the following equals the price of the TV set after a sale reduction of 20%?

    A. $158.60   C. $138.84   E. $29.70
    B. $148.50   D. $95.04

116. A circle graph of a budget shows the expenditure of 26.2% for housing, 28.4% for food, 12% for clothing, 12.7% for taxes, and the balance for miscellaneous items. Which of the following equals the percent for miscellaneous items?

    A. 79.3   C. 68.5   E. 20.7
    B. 70.3   D. 29.7

117. Two dozen shuttlecocks and four badminton rackets are to be purchased for a playground. The shuttlecocks are priced at $0.35 each and the rackets at $2.75 each. The playground receives a discount of 30% from these prices. Which of the following equals the total cost of this equipment?

    A. $7.29   C. $13.58   E. $19.40
    B. $11.43   D. $18.60

118. A piece of wood weighing 10 ounces is found to have a weight of 8 ounces after drying. Which of the following equals the moisture content?

    A. 80%   C. $33\frac{1}{3}$%   E. 20%
    B. 40%   D. 25%

119. A bag contains 800 coins. Of these, 10% are dimes, 30% are nickels, and the rest are quarters. Which of the following equals the amount of money in the bag?

    A. less than $150
    B. between $150 and $300
    C. between $301 and $450
    D. between $450 and $800
    E. more than $800

120. Six quarts of a 20% solution of alcohol in water are mixed with 4 quarts of a 60% solution of alcohol in water. Which of the following equals the alcoholic strength of the mixture?

    A. 80%   C. 36%   E. 10%
    B. 40%   D. 25%

121. A man insures 80% of his property and pays a $2\frac{1}{2}$% premium amounting to $348. What is the total value of his property?

    A. $19,000   C. $18,000   E. $13,920
    B. $18,400   D. $17,400

122. A clerk spent his 35-hour work week as follows: $\frac{1}{5}$ of his time he sorted mail, $\frac{1}{2}$ of his time he filed letters, and $\frac{1}{7}$ of the time he did reception work. The rest of his time was devoted to messenger work. Which of the following approximately equals the percent of time spent on messenger work by the clerk during the week?

   A. 6%   **C.** 14%   **E.** 20%
   B. 10%   **D.** 16%

123. In a school in which 40% of the enrolled students are boys, 80% of the boys are present on a certain day. If 1,152 boys are present, which of the following equals the total school enrollment?

   A. 1,440   **C.** 3,600   **E.** 5,760
   B. 2,880   **D.** 5,400

124. Mrs. Morris receives a salary raise from $25,000 to $27,500. Find the percent increase.

   A. 19%   **C.** 90%   **E.** $12\frac{1}{2}$%
   B. 10%   **D.** 151%

125. The population of Stormville has increased from 80,000 to 100,000 in the last 20 years. Find the percent increase.

   A. 20%   **C.** 80%   **E.** 10%
   B. 25%   **D.** 60%

126. The value of Super Company Stock dropped from $25 a share to $21 a share. Find the percent decrease.

   A. 4%   **C.** 12%   **E.** 20%
   B. 8%   **D.** 16%

127. The Rubins bought their home for $30,000 and sold it for $60,000. Find the percent increase.

   A. 100%   **C.** 200%   **E.** 150%
   B. 50%   **D.** 300%

128. During the pre-holiday rush, Martin's Department Store increased its sales staff from 150 to 200 persons. By what percent must it now decrease its sales staff to return to the usual number of salespersons?

   A. 25%   **C.** 20%   **E.** 75%
   B. $33\frac{1}{3}$%   **D.** 40%

129. If enrollment at City University grew from 3,000 to 12,000 in the last 10 years, what was the percent increase in enrollment?

   A. 25%   **C.** 300%   **E.** 400%
   B. 125%   **D.** 330%

Statistical Measures

Mean (or average), *median*, *mode*, *range*, *standard deviation*, and *frequency distribution* are types of statistics that can be determined for a given set of numbers. These statistics provide particular information about a particular set of data.

Mean

Calculating a Mean (Average)

To calculate an *average (arithmetic mean)*, just add the quantities contributing to the average and then divide that sum by the number of quantities involved. For example, the average of 3, 7, and 8 is 6: $3 + 7 + 8 = 18$, and $18 \div 3 = 6$. Typically, on the exam, the term "average" is used instead of "mean" or "arithmetic mean."

Example:

A student's final grade is the average of her scores on five exams. If she receives scores of 78, 83, 82, 88, and 94, what is her final grade?

➤ To find the average, add the five grades and divide that sum by 5: $\dfrac{78 + 83 + 82 + 88 + 94}{5} = \dfrac{425}{5} = 85$.

It is possible that an easy item might ask that you find the average of a few numbers, as above; however, items about averages can take several other forms. The generalized formula for an average (arithmetic mean) is given by the following equation.

EQUATION FOR FINDING AN AVERAGE

$$\text{Average (Arithmetic Mean)} = \bar{x} = \frac{x_1 + x_2 + x_3 + \ldots + x_n}{n}$$

Determining Missing Elements

Some items provide the average of a group of numbers and some—but not all—of the quantities involved. You are then asked to find the *missing element(s)*. For example, if the average of 3, 8, and x is 6, what is the value of x? Since the average of the three numbers is 6, the sum or total of the three numbers is $3 \cdot 6 = 18$. The two given numbers are equal to $3 + 8 = 11$, so the third number must be $18 - 11 = 7$. Check the solution by averaging 3, 8, and 7: $3 + 8 + 7 = 18$, and $18 \div 3 = 6$.

Examples:

1. For a certain five-day period, the average high temperature (in degrees Fahrenheit) for Chicago was 30°. If the high temperatures recorded for the first four of those days were 26°, 32°, 24°, and 35°, what was the high temperature recorded on the fifth day?

➤ The sum of the five numbers is $5 \cdot 30 = 150$. The sum for the four days we know about is: $26 + 32 + 24 + 35 = 117$. Thus, the fifth day must have had a high temperature of $150 - 117 = 33$. Note that this is the same as setting up an equation for the average and solving for the missing element: $\frac{26+32+24+35+x}{5} = 30 \Rightarrow x = (30 \cdot 5) - (26+32+24+35) = 150 - 117 = 33$.

2. The average of Jose's scores on four tests is 90. If three of those scores are 89, 92, and 94, what is his fourth score?

> The sum of all four scores must be $4 \cdot 90 = 360$. The three known scores sum to: $89 + 92 + 94 = 275$. Thus, the remaining score must be $360 - 275 = 85$. Note that this is the same as setting up an equation for the average and solving for the missing element: $\frac{89+92+94+x}{4} = 90 \Rightarrow x = (90 \cdot 4) - (89+92+94) = 360 - 275 = 85$.

3. The average of a group of eight numbers is 9. If one of these numbers is removed from the group, the average of the remaining numbers is 7. What is the value of the number removed?

> The sum of the original numbers is $8 \cdot 9 = 72$. The sum of the remaining numbers is $7 \cdot 7 = 49$, so the value of the number that was removed must be $72 - 49 = 23$.

A variation on this type of an item might ask about more than one missing element.

Example:

In a group of children, three of the children are ages 7, 8, and 10, and the other two are the same age. If the average of the ages of all five children is 7, what is the age of the other two children?

> The total sum of the five ages must be $5 \cdot 7 = 35$. The known ages total only $7 + 8 + 10 = 25$, so the ages of the two other children must total 10. Since there are two of them, each one must be 5 years old.

Calculating Weighted Averages

In the average problems discussed thus far, each element in the average has been given equal weight. Sometimes, averages are created that give greater weight to one element than to another.

Example:

Cody bought 4 books that cost $6.00 each and 2 books that cost $3.00 each. What is the average cost of the 6 books?

> The average cost of the 6 books is not just the average of $6.00 and $3.00, which is $4.50. He bought more of the higher priced books, so the average must reflect that fact. One method is to treat each book as a separate expense: $\frac{6+6+6+6+3+3}{6} = \frac{30}{6} = 5$. Another method is to "weigh" the two different costs: $6(4) + 3(2) = 30$ and $\frac{30}{6} = 5$.

Median

The *median* of an odd number of data values is the middle value of the data set when it is arranged in ascending or descending order. The median of an even number of data values is the average of the two middle values of the data set when it is arranged in ascending or descending order.

Examples:

1. What is the median of {1, 1, 2, 3, 4, 5, 6, 7, 7, 7, 8, 8, 9}?

   ➤ The set contains an odd number of data values, so the median is the middle value: 6.

2. What is the median of {7, 9, 10, 16}?

   ➤ The set contains an even number of data values, so the median is the average of the two middle values: $\dfrac{9+10}{2}=9.5$.

Mode

The *mode* is the value that appears most frequently in a set of data. Some data sets have multiple modes, while other data sets have no modes.

Examples:

1. The mode of {2, 4, 5, 5, 5, 6, 6, 19, 2} is 5.

2. The group of numbers {−3, 5, 6, −3, −2, 7, 5, −3, 6, 5, 5, −3} is bimodal since −3 and 5 each occur four times.

Range

There are several ways to measure the degree to which numerical data are spread out or dispersed. The *range* of a set of numbers is the simplest measure of the spread of the data. The range is the difference between the highest and lowest numbers in the set. Note that the range depends on only these two values in the data. The greater the range, the greater the spread in the data.

Example:

The range of {5, 10, 3, 24, 11, 4} is $24-3=21$.

Standard Deviation

Another common measure of dispersion is *standard deviation*. Generally, the greater the spread of the data away from the mean, the greater the standard deviation. The standard deviation of n numbers can be calculated using the following steps.

Step 1: Calculate the arithmetic mean (average) of the n numbers.
Step 2: Calculate the differences between the mean and each of the n numbers.
Step 3: Square each of the differences.
Step 4: Calculate the average of the squared differences.
Step 5: Take the nonnegative square root of the average from Step 4. This is the standard deviation of the n numbers.

Unlike the range of a data set, the standard deviation depends on every data value, though it depends most on values that are farthest from the mean. Therefore, a data set distributed closely around the mean will have a smaller standard deviation than will data spread far from the mean.

Example:

What is the standard deviation of the data set $\{0, 2, 2, 5, 7, 8\}$?

➤ Calculate the average of the 6 numbers: $\text{average}_{\text{data set}} = \dfrac{0+2+2+5+7+8}{6} = \dfrac{24}{6} = 4$. Next, calculate the differences between the average (4) and each of the 6 numbers, and square each of these differences:

$x = 0$: $0 - 4 = -4 \Rightarrow (-4)^2 = 16$
$x = 2$: $2 - 4 = -2 \Rightarrow (-2)^2 = 4$
$x = 5$: $5 - 4 = 1 \Rightarrow 1^2 = 1$
$x = 7$: $7 - 4 = 3 \Rightarrow 3^2 = 9$
$x = 5$: $5 - 4 = 1 \Rightarrow 1^2 = 1$
$x = 8$: $8 - 4 = 4 \Rightarrow 4^2 = 16$

Calculate the average of the 8 squared differences: $\text{average}_{\text{squared differences}} = \dfrac{16+4+4+1+9+16}{6} = \dfrac{50}{6} = \dfrac{25}{3}$.

The standard deviation is equal to the nonnegative square root of this average: $\text{standard deviation} = \sqrt{\dfrac{25}{3}} \approx 2.9$.

Note that on the actual exam, it is unlikely that knowledge of the formula for standard deviation will be tested. Rather, understanding of the concept behind standard deviation—that it is a measure of how the data values vary from the mean—is tested.

Example:

Arrange the following data sets from greatest standard deviation to least standard deviation: $\{12, 13, 14, 15, 16\}$, $\{14, 14, 14, 14, 14\}$, and $\{6, 14, 14, 14, 24\}$.

➤ The second data set has no variation, so the standard deviation is 0. The first data set has small deviations from the mean of 14, so the standard deviation in this set is greater than in the second set. Because of the extreme values 6 and 24, the variation in the third set is clearly greater than the variation in the first set. Thus, the standard deviation in the third set is greater than the standard deviation in 1.

Frequency Distribution

Finally, a frequency distribution is a simple way of displaying how numerical data are distributed. This method arranges the data according to the varying frequencies with which the data occurs.

Example:

Display the following 15 numbers using a frequency distribution: $\{-2, 0, 2, 0, 1, -1, 2, -1, 4, 0, -2, 2, -1, -1, 1\}$.

➢ Simply create a table that lists the different numerical values, x, in the data set and the frequencies, f, with which they occur:

x	F
−2	2
−1	4
0	3
1	2
2	3
4	1
Total	15

Statistical Measures

DIRECTIONS: Choose the correct answer to each of the following items. Answers are on page 788.

1. What is the average of 8, 6, and 16?

    A. 10   C. 13   E. 18
    B. 12   D. 15

2. What is the average of 0 and 50?

    A. 0   C. 10   E. 50
    B. 5   D. 25

3. What is the average of 5, 11, 12, and 8?

    A. 6   C. 9   E. 12
    B. 8   D. 10

4. What is the average of 25, 28, 21, 30, and 36?

    A. 25   C. 29   E. 44
    B. 28   D. 34

5. What is the average of $\frac{1}{4}$, $\frac{3}{4}$, $\frac{5}{8}$, $\frac{1}{2}$, and $\frac{3}{8}$?

    A. $\frac{3}{32}$ C. $\frac{1}{2}$ E. $\frac{27}{32}$

    B. $\frac{5}{16}$ D. $\frac{5}{8}$

6. What is the average of $0.78, $0.45, $0.36, $0.98, $0.55, and $0.54?

    A. $0.49   C. $0.56   E. $0.61
    B. $0.54   D. $0.60

7. What is the average of 0.03, 0.11, 0.08, and 0.5?

    A. 0.18   C. 0.28   E. 1.0
    B. 0.25   D. 0.50

8. What is the average of 1,001, 1,002, 1,003, 1,004, and 1,005?

    A. 250   C. 1,003   E. 5,000
    B. 1,000   D. 2,500

9. What is the average of −8, −6, and −13?

    A. −8   C. −13   E. −9
    B. −15   D. −12

10. Jordan receives test scores of 79, 85, 90, 76, and 80. What is the average of these test scores?

    A. 82   C. 84   E. 86
    B. 83   D. 85

11. Mr. Whipple bought five different items costing $4.51, $6.25, $3.32, $4.48, and $2.19. What is the average cost of the five items?

    A. $3.40   C. $3.90   E. $4.15
    B. $3.80   D. $4.00

12. Nadia received scores of 8.5, 9.3, 8.2, and 9.0 in four different gymnastics events. What is the average of her scores?

    A. 8.5   C. 8.9   E. 9.1
    B. 8.75   D. 9

13. Five people have ages of 44, 33, 45, 44, and 29 years. What is the average of their ages in years?

    A. 36   C. 40   E. 43
    B. 39   D. 41

14. In a certain government office, if 360 staff hours are needed to process 120 building permit applications, on the average how long (in hours) does it take to process one application?

    A. 3   C. 12   E. 36
    B. 6   D. 24

15. In a chemical test for Substance X, a sample is divided into five equal parts. If the purity of the five parts is 84%, 89%, 87%, 90%, and 80%, then what is the overall purity of the sample (expressed as a percent of Substance X)?

    A. 83   C. 86   E. 88
    B. 84   D. 87

16. The average of three numbers is 24. If two of the numbers are 21 and 23, what is the third number?

    A. 20   C. 26   E. 30
    B. 24   D. 28

17. The average of three numbers is 5. If two of the numbers are zero, what is the third number?

    A. 1   C. 5   E. 15
    B. 3   D. 10

18. The average of the weight of four people is 166 pounds. If three of the people weigh 150 pounds, 200 pounds, and 180 pounds, what is the weight of the fourth person?

    A. 134   C. 155   E. 165
    B. 140   D. 161

19. For a certain student, the average of five test scores is 83. If four of the scores are 81, 79, 85, and 90, what is the fifth test score?

    A. 83   C. 81   E. 79
    B. 82   D. 80

20. Sue bought ten items at an average price of $3.60. The cost of eight of the items totaled $30. If the other two items were the same price, what was the price she paid for each?

    A. $15.00   C. $6.00   E. $1.50
    B. $7.50   D. $3.00

21. In a certain shipment, the weights of twelve books average 2.75 pounds. If one of the books is removed, the weights of the remaining books average 2.70 pounds. What was the weight, in pounds, of the book that was removed?

    A. 1.7   C. 3.0   E. 4.5
    B. 2.3   D. 3.3

22. The average of a group of seven test scores is 80. If the lowest and the highest scores are thrown out, the average of the remaining scores is 78. What is the average of the lowest and highest scores?

    A. 100   C. 90   E. 85
    B. 95   D. 88

23. In a certain group, twelve of the children are age 10, and eight are age 15. What is the average of the ages of all the children in the group?

    A. 9.5   C. 11   E. 12
    B. 10.5   D. 11.5

24. Robert made the following deposits in a savings account:

Amount	Frequency
$15	4 times
$20	2 times
$25	4 times

    What was the average of all the deposits Robert made?

    A. $18.50   C. $21.50   E. $22.50
    B. $20.00   D. $22.00

25. The average of the weights of six people sitting in a boat is 145 pounds. After a seventh person gets into the boat, the average of the weights of all seven people in the boat is 147 pounds. What is the weight, in pounds, of the seventh person?

    A. 160   C. 155   E. 147
    B. 159   D. 149

26. Find the mean of the following 5 numbers: 2, 3, 13, 15, and 1.

    A. 4.6   C. 6.8   E. 16.8
    B. 6.2   D. 8.6

27. Find the mean of the following 6 numbers: −3, 2, 6, 5, 2, and 0.

    A. 1   C. 5   E. 8
    B. 2   D. 6

28. If the mean of 6 numbers is 10, what is the sixth number if the five given numbers are −3, 5, 6, 13, and 17?

    A. 12   C. 18   E. 22
    B. 16   D. 20

29. The average of 5 numbers is 56. If two new numbers are added to the list, the average of the 7 numbers is 58. Which of the following equals the average of the two new numbers?

    A. 64   C. 62   E. 60
    B. 63   D. 61

30. Arranged in some order, $3x+1$, $2x+4$, and $x+10$ represent 3 consecutive whole numbers. If x represents a whole number and the average of the 3 numbers is 13, then solve for x.

    A. 2   **C.** 6   **E.** 10
    B. 4   **D.** 8

31. Arthur interviewed 100 female corporate officers and found that 34 of them were 55 years old, 28 were 45 years old, 26 were 35 years old, and 12 of them were 25 years old. What was the average of the women's ages?

    A. 16   **C.** 43.4   **E.** 45
    B. 43   **D.** 44.3

Items #32–34 refer to the following information:

During the last 14 games, a basketball player scored the following points per game: 42, 35, 29, 42, 33, 37, 26, 38, 42, 47, 51, 33, 30, and 40.

32. What is the median score?

    A. 35.4   **C.** 36   **E.** 38
    B. 35.7   **D.** 37.5

33. What is the mode?

    A. 35.4   **C.** 38   **E.** 44
    B. 37.5   **D.** 42

34. If after one more game, the player's average for points per game is exactly 37, how many points did the player score in the fifteenth game?

    A. 30   **C.** 37.5   **E.** 44
    B. 37   **D.** 42

35. Find the median of the following 5 numbers: 1, 3, 7, 2, and 8.

    A. 1   **C.** 3   **E.** 7
    B. 2   **D.** 4.2

36. Find the median for the following data set: $\{2, -3, 8, 4, 9, -16, 12, 0, 4, 2, 1\}$.

    A. 4   **C.** 2   **E.** 0
    B. 2.1   **D.** 1

37. Find the median for the following data set: $\{2, -3, 8, 4, 9, -16, 12, 8, 4, 2\}$.

    A. 2   **C.** 3.5   **E.** 4.2
    B. 3   **D.** 4

38. Find the mode of the following 5 numbers: 4, 8, 10, 8, and 15.

    A. 4   **C.** 9   **E.** 15
    B. 8   **D.** 10

39. Find the mode of the following data set: $\{6, 8, 10, 2, -2, 2, 8, 4, 2\}$.

    A. 6   **C.** 4   **E.** 1
    B. 4.4   **D.** 2

40. A set of seven numbers contains the numbers: 1, 4, 5, and 6. The other three numbers are represented by $2x+8$, $x-4$, and $7x-4$. If the mode of these seven numbers is a negative even integer, then what is a possible value for x?

    A. 0   **C.** 2   **E.** 5
    B. 1   **D.** 4

41. The grades received on a test by twenty students were 100, 55, 75, 80, 65, 65, 95, 90, 80, 45, 40, 50, 85, 85, 85, 80, 80, 70, 65, and 60. What is the average of these grades?

    A. 70.5   **C.** 77   **E.** 100
    B. 72.5   **D.** 80.3

42. Arthur purchased 75 six-inch rulers costing 15¢ each, 100 one-foot rulers costing 30¢ each, and 50 one-yard rulers costing 72¢ each. What was the average price per ruler?

    A. $26\frac{1}{8}$¢   **C.** 39¢   **E.** $77\frac{1}{4}$¢

    B. $34\frac{1}{3}$¢   **D.** 42¢

43. What is the average grade for a student who received 90 in English, 84 in algebra, 75 in French, and 76 in music, if the subjects have the following weights: English 4, algebra 3, French 3, and music 1?

    A. 81   **C.** 82   **E.** 83
    B. $81\frac{1}{2}$ **D.** $82\frac{1}{2}$

Items #44–46 refer to the following information:

A census shows that on a certain neighborhood block the number of children in each family is 3, 4, 4, 0, 1, 2, 0, 2, and 2, respectively.

44. Find the average number of children per family.

A. 4   **C.** $3\frac{1}{2}$ **E.** $1\frac{1}{2}$

B. 3   **D.** 2

45. Find the median number of children.

A. 1   **C.** 3   **E.** 5
B. 2   **D.** 4

46. Find the mode of the number of children.

A. 0   **C.** 2   **E.** 4
B. 1   **D.** 3

47. The diameter of a rod is required to be 1.51 ± 0.015 inches. Which of the following represents the possible range of measurements for the rod's diameter?

A. 1.490 inches to 1.520 inches
B. 1.495 inches to 1.520 inches
C. 1.495 inches to 1.525 inches
D. 1.495 inches to 1.530 inches
E. 1.500 inches to 1.530 inches

48. A is a set containing 5 different numbers, B is a set containing 4 different numbers, all of which are members of A. Which of the following statements CANNOT be true?

A. The mean of A is equal to the mean of B.
B. The median of A is equal to the median of B.
C. The range of A is equal to the range of B.
D. The mean of A is greater than the mean of B.
E. The range of A is less than the range of B.

49. If a set of data values has a mean of 10.0 and a standard deviation of 1.5, which of the following values is less than 1.0 standard deviations from the mean?

A. 8.0   **C.** 9.5   **E.** 12.0
B. 8.5   **D.** 11.5

50. The arithmetic mean and standard deviation of a certain normal distribution are 15.5 and 3.0, respectively. What value is exactly 1.5 standard deviations less than the mean?

A. 10.5   **C.** 12.5   **E.** 14
B. 11.0   **D.** 13.0

51. If the variables A, B, and C take on only the values 1, 2, 3, 4, or 5 with frequencies indicated by the shaded regions below, for which of the frequency distributions is the mean equal to the median?

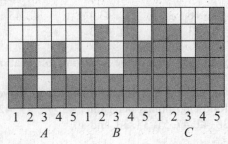

$$1\ 2\ 3\ 4\ 5 \quad 1\ 2\ 3\ 4\ 5 \quad 1\ 2\ 3\ 4\ 5$$
$$A \qquad\qquad B \qquad\qquad C$$

A. A only
B. B only
C. C only
D. A and C only
E. A, B, and C

Ratios and Proportions

Working with Ratios

Two-Part Ratios

A *ratio* is a statement about the relationship between any two quantities, or we might say a ratio is a statement that compares any two quantities. Suppose that in an English class there are five girls and eight boys. We can compare those quantities by saying that the ratio of girls to boys is 5 to 8. Conversely, the ratio of boys to girls is 8 to 5. Notice that order is very important in stating a ratio. The order of the numbers in the ratio must reflect the order of the categories being compared. In our example, it would be incorrect to say that the ratio of girls to boys is 8 to 5.

A phrase such as "5 to 8" is one way of stating a ratio, but there are several other ways. A ratio can also be described using a colon: "the ratio of girls to boys is $5:8$" or "the ratio of boys to girls is $8:5$." Alternatively, the ratio can be written in fraction form: "the ratio $\dfrac{girls}{boys}$ is $\dfrac{5}{8}$," and "the ratio $\dfrac{boys}{girls}$ is $\dfrac{8}{5}$."

Ratios of the form $a:b$ or a/b can also refer to numbers instead of a number of objects. We can speak abstractly of the ratio $5:8$, which is the ratio of any set of five things to any set of eight things. Consequently, ratios can be manipulated in the same way as fractions. Just as you could rewrite a fraction to get a form with a different denominator, you can convert a ratio to an equivalent form by multiplying both terms of the ratio by the same number. For example, $\dfrac{5}{8} = \dfrac{5 \cdot 2}{8 \cdot 2} = \dfrac{10}{16}$ and $\dfrac{8}{5} = \dfrac{8 \cdot 3}{5 \cdot 3} = \dfrac{24}{15}$.

It is customary to reduce a ratio to its lowest terms just as you would reduce fractions to their lowest terms. For example, in a certain classroom, there are ten girls and sixteen boys; the ratio of girls to boys is $\dfrac{10}{16}$, which is $\dfrac{5}{8}$.

Although you may not be aware of it, you probably also use ratios informally in ordinary conversation. A common phrase that signifies a ratio is "for every (number)...there are (number)...." For example, in the classroom just described, for every 10 girls there are 16 boys, or in lowest terms, for every 5 girls there are 8 boys, and for every 8 boys there are 5 girls.

Finally, a ratio can also be stated as a rate using the word "per." If a car travels 200 miles and uses 10 gallons of fuel, the car gets 200 miles per 10 gallons, or 20 miles per gallon. Cost, too, is often described as a ratio. If it is possible to purchase a dozen greeting cards for $2.40, the cost of the cards is $2.40 per dozen, or 20 cents per card.

Three-Part Ratios

When three quantities are to be compared, they can be stated using ordinary ratios. For example, if a bowl of fruit contains two apples, three pears, and five oranges, the ratio of apples to pears is $2:3$; the ratio of apples to oranges is $2:5$; and the ratio of pears to oranges is $3:5$. This same information can also be conveyed in a single statement. The ratio of apples to pears to oranges is $2:3:5$.

A *three-part ratio* depends on the middle term to join the two outside terms. Above, the ratio of apples to pears is $2:3$, and the ratio of pears to oranges is $3:5$. Since 3 is common to both ratios, it can be the middle term. Sometimes it will be necessary to find a common middle term.

Example:

On a certain day, a bank has the following rates of exchange: $\frac{\text{dollar}}{\text{mark}} = \frac{1}{3}$ and $\frac{\text{mark}}{\text{pound}} = \frac{6}{1}$. What is the ratio of dollars to pounds?

➤ To find the ratio dollars : pounds, we will use marks as the middle term. However, the ratio of dollars to marks is $1:3$, and the ratio of marks to pounds is $6:1$. We must change the first ratio to express it in terms of six marks rather than three marks. This is like finding a common denominator before adding fractions: $\frac{1}{3} = \frac{1 \cdot 2}{3 \cdot 2} = \frac{2}{6}$, so the ratio of dollars to marks is $2:6$, and the ratio of dollars to marks to pounds is $2:6:1$. Thus, the ratio of dollars to pounds is $2:1$.

Using Ratios to Divide Quantities

An item may require that you divide a quantity according to a certain ratio.

Examples:

1. A $100 prize is divided between two contestants according to the ratio $2:3$. How much does each contestant receive?

➤ Add the terms of the ratio to determine by how many parts the prize is to be divided. Divide the prize by that many parts, and multiply the result by the number of parts to be given to each contestant. $2 + 3 = 5$, so the prize is to be divided into five parts. Each part is: $100 \div 5 = 20$. One contestant gets $2 \cdot 20 = 40$, and the other contestant receives $3 \cdot 20 = 60$.

2. Bronze is 16 parts tin and 9 parts copper. If a bronze ingot weighs 100 pounds, how much does the tin weigh (in pounds)?

➤ First, the number of parts in the ratio is: $16 + 9 = 25$. Second, $100 \div 25 = 4$, so each part is worth 4 pounds. Since there are 16 parts of tin, the tin must weigh $16 \cdot 4 = 64$ pounds.

Working with Proportions

A *proportion* is the mathematical equivalent of a verbal analogy. For example, $2:3::8:12$ is equivalent to "two is to three as eight is to twelve." The main difference between an analogy and a proportion is the precision. A verbal analogy depends upon words that do not have unique and precise meanings, while mathematical proportions are made up of numbers, which are very exact.

In a mathematical proportion, the first and last terms are called the "extremes" of the proportion because they are on the extreme outside, and the two middle terms are called the "means" (mean can mean "middle"). In a mathematical proportion, the product of the extremes is always equal to the product of the means. For example, $2:3::8:12$ and $2 \cdot 12 = 3 \cdot 8$.

Determining the Missing Elements in Proportions

Since any ratio can be written as a fraction, a proportion, which states that two ratios are equivalent, can also be written in fractional form as an equation. This is the foundation for the process called cross-multiplication, a process that is useful in solving for an unknown element in a proportion.

Examples:

1. $\dfrac{2}{3} = \dfrac{8}{12} \Rightarrow \dfrac{2}{3} \succ=\prec \dfrac{8}{12} \Rightarrow 2 \cdot 12 = 3 \cdot 8$

2. $\dfrac{6}{9} = \dfrac{12}{x} \Rightarrow \dfrac{6}{9} \succ=\prec \dfrac{12}{x} \Rightarrow 6x = 108 \Rightarrow x = \dfrac{108}{6} = 18$

    ➤ After cross-multiplying, divide both sides of the equality by the numerical coefficient of the unknown. Then, check the correctness of this solution by substituting 18 back in to the original proportion: $\dfrac{6}{9} = \dfrac{12}{18} \Rightarrow \dfrac{6}{9} \succ=\prec \dfrac{12}{18} \Rightarrow 6 \cdot 18 = 9 \cdot 12$.

3. $\dfrac{3}{15} = \dfrac{x}{45} \Rightarrow \dfrac{3}{15} \succ=\prec \dfrac{x}{45} \Rightarrow 3 \cdot 45 = 15x \Rightarrow x = \dfrac{135}{15} = 9$

    ➤ Check the solution by substitution: $\dfrac{3}{15} = \dfrac{9}{45} \Rightarrow \dfrac{3}{15} \succ=\prec \dfrac{9}{45} \Rightarrow 3 \cdot 45 = 15 \cdot 9 \Rightarrow 135 = 135$.

Direct Proportions

The use of proportions can be a powerful problem-solving tool. **Direct proportions** equate ratios of two quantities having a direct relationship. The more there is of one quantity, the more there is of the other quantity, and vice versa.

Example:

If the cost of a dozen donuts is \$3.60, what is the cost of 4 donuts? Assume there is no discount for buying in bulk.

➤ One method for solving this item is to calculate the cost of one donut (\$3.60 ÷ 12 = \$0.30), and then multiply that cost by four (\$0.30 • 4 = \$1.20). While this approach is not incorrect, the same result can be reached in a conceptually simpler way. The more donuts being purchased, the greater the total cost, and vice versa. Relate the quantities using a direct proportion: $\dfrac{\text{Total Cost } X}{\text{Total Cost } Y} = \dfrac{\text{Number } X}{\text{Number } Y} \Rightarrow \dfrac{\$3.60}{x} = \dfrac{12}{4} \Rightarrow 12x = \$3.60 \cdot 4 \Rightarrow$ $x = \dfrac{\$14.40}{12} = \$1.20$.

In the previous example, we set up the proportion by grouping like terms: "cost" is on one side of the proportion and "number" is on the other side. It is equally correct to set up the proportion as $\dfrac{\text{Total Cost } X}{\text{Number } X} = \dfrac{\text{Total Cost } Y}{\text{Number } Y}$. Additionally, it does not matter which quantity is on top or bottom: $\dfrac{\text{Number } X}{\text{Total Cost } X} = \dfrac{\text{Number } Y}{\text{Total Cost } Y}$ is equally correct. However, it is generally a good idea to group like terms to avoid confusion.

The LONGER the travel time, the GREATER the distance traveled (assuming a CONSTANT speed).

Example:

If a plane moving at a constant speed flies 300 miles in 6 hours, how far will the plane fly in 8 hours?

➤ Group like terms:

$\dfrac{\text{Time } X}{\text{Time } Y} = \dfrac{\text{Output } X}{\text{Output } Y} \Rightarrow \dfrac{6}{8} = \dfrac{300}{x} \Rightarrow \dfrac{6}{8} \succ=\prec \dfrac{300}{x} \Rightarrow 6x = 8 \cdot 300 \Rightarrow x = \dfrac{2,400}{6} = 400$.

The LONGER the time of operation, the GREATER the output.

Example:

If an uninterrupted stamping machine operating at a constant rate postmarks 320 envelopes in 5 minutes, how long will it take the machine to postmark 480 envelopes?

➤ Group like terms:

$$\frac{\text{Time } X}{\text{Time } Y} = \frac{\text{Output } X}{\text{Output } Y} \Rightarrow \frac{5}{x} = \frac{320}{480} \Rightarrow \frac{5}{x} \gtrless \frac{320}{480} \Rightarrow 5(480) = x(320) \Rightarrow x = \frac{5(480)}{320} = 7.5 \text{ minutes.}$$

The GREATER the number of items, the GREATER the weight.

Example:

If 20 jars of preserves weigh 25 pounds, how much do 15 jars of preserves weigh?

➤ Group like terms:

$$\frac{\text{Weight of Jars } X}{\text{Weight of Jars } Y} = \frac{\text{Jars } X}{\text{Jars } Y} \Rightarrow \frac{25}{x} = \frac{20}{15} \Rightarrow \frac{25}{x} \gtrless \frac{20}{15} \Rightarrow 25(15) = x(20) \Rightarrow x = \frac{25(15)}{20} = 18.75 \text{ pounds.}$$

Inverse Proportions

In some situations, quantities are related inversely; that is, an increase in one results in a decrease in the other. For example, the more workers, or machines, doing a job, the less time it takes to finish. In this case, quantities are related inversely to each other. To solve problems involving inverse relationships, use the following procedure to set up an inverse proportion.

Step 1: Set up an ordinary proportion—make sure to group like quantities.
Step 2: Invert the right side of the proportion.
Step 3: Cross-multiply and solve for the unknown.

Example:

Traveling at a constant rate of 150 miles per hour, a plane makes the trip from Phoenix to Grand Junction in 4 hours. How long will the trip take if the plane flies at a constant rate of 200 miles per hour?

➤ First, set up a proportion, grouping like terms: $\frac{\text{Speed } X}{\text{Speed } Y} = \frac{\text{Time } X}{\text{Time } Y} \Rightarrow \frac{150}{200} = \frac{4}{x}$. Then, invert the right side of

the proportion: $\frac{150}{200} = \frac{x}{4} \Rightarrow \frac{150}{200} \gtrless \frac{x}{4} \Rightarrow 150(4) = 200(x) \Rightarrow x = \frac{150(4)}{200} = 3 \text{ hours.}$

While it is possible, though not advised, to set up a direct proportion without grouping like terms, with an inverse proportion, it is essential to group like terms. This is sufficient reasoning to always group like terms: You will not make a mistake if the item involves an inverse proportion.

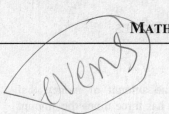

EXERCISE 6

Ratios and Proportions

DIRECTIONS: Choose the correct answer to each of the following items. Answers are on page 788.

1. If a jar contains 3 blue marbles and 8 red marbles, what is the ratio of blue marbles to red marbles?

   A. 3:11   C. 8:3   E. 4:1
   B. 3:8   D. 11:3

2. If a school has 24 teachers and 480 students, what is the ratio of teachers to students?

   A. $\frac{1}{20}$ C. $\frac{1}{48}$ E. $\frac{1}{200}$

   B. $\frac{1}{24}$ D. $\frac{1}{56}$

3. If a library contains 12,000 works of fiction and 3,000 works of nonfiction, what is the ratio of works of fiction to works of nonfiction?

   A. $\frac{1}{9}$ C. $\frac{1}{4}$ E. $\frac{5}{1}$

   B. $\frac{1}{5}$ D. $\frac{4}{1}$

4. Which of the following is (are) equivalent to $\frac{1}{3}$?

   I. $\frac{40}{120}$

   II. $\frac{75}{100}$

   III. $\frac{120}{360}$

   A. I only   D. II and III only
   B. III only   E. I, II, and III
   C. I and III only

Items #5–6 refer to the following table:

Students at Tyler Junior High School		
	7th Grade	8th Grade
Girls	90	80
Boys	85	75

5. What is the ratio of seventh-grade girls to the total number of girls at Tyler Junior High School?

   A. $\frac{9}{17}$ C. $\frac{18}{17}$ E. $\frac{17}{9}$

   B. $\frac{8}{9}$ D. $\frac{9}{8}$

6. What is the ratio of eighth-grade girls to the total number of students at Tyler Junior High School?

   A. $\frac{8}{33}$ C. $\frac{8}{15}$ E. $\frac{17}{30}$

   B. $\frac{9}{33}$ D. $\frac{8}{17}$

7. If an airplane flies 275 miles on 25 gallons of fuel, then what is the average fuel consumption for the entire trip expressed in miles per gallon?

   A. 25   C. 15   E. 7
   B. 18   D. 11

8. An assortment of candy includes 12 chocolates, 6 caramels, and 9 mints. What is the ratio of chocolates : caramels : mints

   A. 4:3:2   C. 3:4:2   E. 2:4:3
   B. 4:2:3   D. 3:2:4

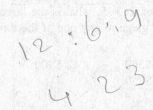

9. If Lucy has twice the amount of money that Ricky has, and Ricky has three times the amount of money that Ethel has, then what is the ratio of the amount of money Ethel has to the amount of money Lucy has?

A. $\frac{1}{8}$ C. $\frac{1}{4}$ E. $\frac{2}{1}$

B. $\frac{1}{6}$ D. $\frac{1}{2}$

10. If three farkels buy two kirns, and three kirns buy five pucks, then nine farkels buy how many pucks?

A. 2   C. 8   E. 17
B. 5   D. 10

11. If Machine X operates at twice the rate of Machine Y, and Machine Y operates at $\frac{2}{3}$ the rate of Machine Z, then what is the ratio of the rate of operation of Machine X to the rate of operation of Machine Z?

A. $\frac{4}{1}$ C. $\frac{4}{3}$ E. $\frac{1}{3}$

B. $\frac{3}{1}$ D. $\frac{3}{4}$

12. If 48 marbles are to be divided between Bill and Carl in the ratio of 3:5, how many marbles should Bill get?

A. 6   C. 18   E. 30
B. 8   D. 24

13. If $10 is to be divided between Janeway and Nelix so that Nelix receives $\frac{1}{4}$ of what Janeway receives, then how much should Janeway receive?

A. $10.00   C. $7.50   E. $2.00
B. $8.00   D. $6.00

14. If a $1,000 reward is to be divided among three people in the ratio of 2:3:5, what is the largest amount that will be given to any one of the three recipients?

A. $200   C. $500   E. $900
B. $300   D. $750

15. If $\frac{6}{8}=\frac{x}{4}$, then $x=$?

A. 12   C. 4   E. 2
B. 6   D. 3

16. If $\frac{14}{x}=\frac{2}{7}$, then $x=$?

A. 7   C. 28   E. 343
B. 14   D. 49

17. If $\frac{3}{4}=\frac{4}{x}$, then $x=$?

A. $\frac{3}{16}$ C. $\frac{4}{3}$ E. $\frac{16}{3}$

B. $\frac{3}{4}$ D. $\frac{7}{3}$

18. If 240 widgets cost $36, what is the cost of 180 widgets?

A. $8   C. $24   E. $32
B. $16   D. $27

19. If a kilogram of a certain cheese costs $9.60, what is the cost of 450 grams of the cheese? (1 kilogram = 1,000 grams)

A. $2.78   C. $3.88   E. $5.12
B. $3.14   D. $4.32

20. If 50 feet of electrical wire cost $4.80, then $10.80 will buy how many feet of the wire?

A. 60   C. 67.25   E. 112.5
B. 62.5   D. 75

21. In a certain group of people, 100 people have red hair. If only 25% of the people have red hair, then how many people do not have red hair?

A. 75   C. 300   E. 500
B. 125   D. 400

22. If a certain fundraising project has raised $12,000, which is 20% of its goal, how much money will have been raised when 50% of the goal has been reached?

A. $60,000   C. $18,000   E. $4,800
B. $30,000   D. $15,000

23. If 48 liters of a certain liquid weigh 50 kilograms, then how much, in kilograms, will 72 liters of the liquid weigh?

    A. 25   C. 75   E. 120
    B. 60   D. 90

24. If the trip from Soldier Field to Wrigley Field takes two hours walking at a constant rate of four miles per hour, how long (in hours) will the same trip take walking at a constant rate of five miles per hour?

    A. 2.5   C. 1.6   E. 1.25
    B. 1.75   D. 1.5

25. A swimming pool is filled by either of two pipes. Pipe A supplies water at the rate of 200 gallons per hour and takes eight hours to fill the pool. If Pipe B can fill the pool in five hours, what is the rate (in gallons per hour) at which Pipe B supplies water?

    A. 125   C. 360   E. 575
    B. 320   D. 480

26. What is the ratio of 3 to 8 expressed as a decimal?

    A. 0.125   C. 0.375   E. 1
    B. 0.25   D. 0.50

27. If the ratio of 3 to 4 is the same as the ratio of 15 to x, find x.

    A. 5   C. 15   E. 25
    B. 10   D. 20

28. Annika can solve 10 math problems in 30 minutes. At this rate, how many math problems can she solve in 48 minutes?

    A. 8   C. 32   E. 56
    B. 16   D. 46

29. Seung can walk up 6 flights of stairs in 4 minutes. At this rate, how many flights of stairs could he walk up in 18 minutes?

    A. 4   C. 14   E. 27
    B. 10   D. 20

30. If 4 candy bars cost $1.04, how much should 6 candy bars cost?

    A. $0.96   C. $1.56   E. $2.06
    B. $1.25   D. $1.85

31. If Baby Andrew takes 8 steps to walk 2 yards, how many steps will he take to walk 5 yards?

    A. 5   C. 15   E. 25
    B. 10   D. 20

32. If a 40-inch stick is divided in a $3:5$ ratio, how long, in inches, is the shorter piece?

    A. 5   C. 15   E. 25
    B. 10   D. 20

33. Orville claims that 3 bags of his popcorn will yield 28 ounces when popped. If this is the case, how many ounces will 5 bags of his popcorn yield when popped?

    A. 23   C. $54\frac{1}{2}$ E. $64\frac{2}{3}$

    B. $46\frac{2}{3}$ D. 64

34. In a poll of 1,000 people, 420 said they would vote for Mason. Based on this poll, how many people would be expected to vote for Mason if 60,000,000 people actually vote?

    A. 25,200,000   C. 26,000,000   E. 26,500,000
    B. 25,500,000   D. 26,200,000

35. In 4 days, a worm grew from 5 centimeters to 12 centimeters. At this rate, how long, in centimeters, will the worm be in another 6 days?

    A. 21   C. 22.25   E. 23
    B. 22   D. 22.5

36. Elan can mow 3 lawns in 85 minutes. At this rate, how long would he need to mow 5 lawns?

    A. 140 minutes, 20 seconds
    B. 141 minutes
    C. 141 minutes, 40 seconds
    D. 142 minutes
    E. 142 minutes, 50 seconds

37. Sarah does $\frac{1}{5}$ of a job in 6 minutes. At this rate, what fraction of the job will she do in 10 minutes?

    A. $\frac{1}{4}$ C. $\frac{1}{2}$ E. $\frac{3}{2}$

    B. $\frac{1}{3}$ D. $\frac{3}{4}$

38. A snapshot measures $2\frac{1}{2}$ inches by $1\frac{7}{8}$ inches. If it is enlarged so that the longer dimension is 4 inches, what is the length, in inches, of the enlarged shorter dimension?

    A. $2\frac{1}{2}$ C. $3\frac{3}{8}$ E. 5

    B. 3   D. 4

39. Three of the men's white handkerchiefs cost $2.29. How much will a dozen of those handkerchiefs cost?

    A. $27.48   C. $9.16   E. $4.58
    B. $13.74   D. $6.87

40. A certain pole casts a 24-foot-long shadow. At the same time another pole that is 3 feet high casts a 4-foot-long shadow. How high, in feet, is the first pole, given that the heights and shadows are in proportion?

    A. 18   C. 20   E. 24
    B. 19   D. 21

41. If a drawing is scaled $\frac{1}{8}$ inch to the foot, what is the actual length, in feet, represented by $3\frac{1}{2}$ inches on the drawing?

    A. 3.5   C. 21   E. 120
    B. 7   D. 28

42. Aluminum bronze consists of copper and aluminum, usually in the ratio of 10:1 by weight. If an object made of this alloy weighs 77 pounds, how many pounds of aluminum does it contain?

    A. 0.7   C. 7.7   E. 77.0
    B. 7.0   D. 70.7

43. It costs 31 cents per square foot to lay vinyl flooring. How much will it cost to lay 180 square feet of flooring?

    A. $16.20   C. $55.80   E. $180.00
    B. $18.60   D. $62.00

44. If Tuvak earns $352 in 16 days, how much will he earn in 117 days?

    A. $3,050   C. $2,285   E. $1,170
    B. $2,574   D. $2,080

45. Assuming that on a blueprint $\frac{1}{8}$ inch equals 12 inches of actual length, what is the actual length, in inches, of a steel bar represented on the blueprint by a line $3\frac{3}{4}$ inches long?

    A. $3\frac{3}{4}$ C. 36   E. 450
    B. 30   D. 360

46. Blake, James, and Staunton invested $9,000, $7,000, and $6,000, respectively. Their profits were to be divided according to the ratio of their investments. If James uses his share of the firm's profit of $825 to pay a personal debt of $230, how much will he have left?

    A. $30.50   C. $34.50   E. $37.50
    B. $32.50   D. $36.50

47. If on a road map $1\frac{5}{8}$ inches represents 10 miles, how many miles does 2.25 inches represent?

    A. $\frac{180}{13}$ miles   C. $\frac{57}{4}$ miles   E. 3 miles

    B. $\frac{53}{4}$ miles   D. $\frac{27}{2}$ miles

48. Jake and Jessie are standing next to each other in the sun. If Jake's shadow is 48 inches long, and he is 72 inches tall, how long is Jessie's shadow, in inches, if she is 66 inches tall?

    A. 42   C. 44   E. 46
    B. 43   D. 45

49. A blueprint allows 1 inch for every 12 feet. At that rate, 7 inches represents how many yards?

    A. $\frac{28}{3}$ C. 84   E. 336

    B. 28   D. 252

50. A bug crawls clockwise around the outside rim of a clock from the 12 to the 4 and travels 7 inches. If a second bug crawls around the outside rim from the 6 to the 11, in the same direction, how many inches did the bug travel?

    A. 7.75   C. 8.25   E. 8.75
    B. 8   D. 8.5

Exponents and Radicals

Powers and Exponents

Powers of Numbers

A *power* of a number indicates repeated multiplication. For example, "3 to the fifth power" means $3 \cdot 3 \cdot 3 \cdot 3 \cdot 3$, which equals 243. Therefore, 3 raised to the fifth power is 243.

Examples:

1. 2 to the second power $= 2 \cdot 2 = 4$.

2. 2 to the third power $= 2 \cdot 2 \cdot 2 = 8$.

3. 2 to the fourth power $= 2 \cdot 2 \cdot 2 \cdot 2 = 16$.

4. 3 to the second power $= 3 \cdot 3 = 9$.

5. 3 to the third power $= 3 \cdot 3 \cdot 3 = 27$.

The second power of a number is also called the square of the number. This refers to a square with sides equal in length to the number; the square of the number is equal to the area of the aforementioned square.

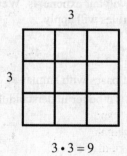

$$3 \cdot 3 = 9$$

The third power of a number is also called the cube of the number, which refers to a cube with sides equal in length to the number; the cube of the number is equal to the volume of the cube with sides equal in length to that number.

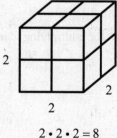

$$2 \cdot 2 \cdot 2 = 8$$

Beyond the square and the cube, powers are referred to by their numerical names, e.g., fourth, fifth, sixth, and so on.

Exponential Notation

The notation system for designating the power of a number is a superscript following the number. The number being multiplied is the **base,** and the superscript is the **exponent**. The exponent indicates the operation of repeated multiplication.

Examples:

1. The third power of 2 is written as 2^3: base $\rightarrow 2^3 \leftarrow$ exponent $= 2 \cdot 2 \cdot 2$.

2. The fifth power of 3 is written as 3^5: base $\rightarrow 3^5 \leftarrow$ exponent $= 3 \cdot 3 \cdot 3 \cdot 3 \cdot 3$.

A base without an exponent is unchanged and represents the ***first power*** of the number. Since $x^1 = x$, the exponent 1 is not explicitly noted.

Examples:

1. $2^1 = 2$

2. $1,000^1 = 1,000$

Operations Involving Exponents

There are special rules that apply to operations involving exponents. When you begin working with radicals (fractional exponents) and algebraic expressions, these same rules will apply.

Multiplication Involving Exponents

The ***product rule*** is used to multiply two identical bases with similar or different exponents. To multiply powers of the same base, add the exponents: $x^m \cdot x^n = x^{m+n}$. To better understand this rule, explicitly write out the multiplication indicated by the exponents.

Example:

$$2^2 \cdot 2^3 = 2^{2+3} = 2^5 = (2 \cdot 2)(2 \cdot 2 \cdot 2)$$

➤ Writing out the expression and using the product rule give you the same result, but it is much faster to apply the latter.

Therefore, the product rule provides an easy shortcut for multiplying identical bases with exponents.

Examples:

1. $3^2 \cdot 3^5 = 3^{(2+5)} = 3^7$

2. $5^2 \cdot 5^3 \cdot 5^5 = 5^{(2+3+5)} = 5^{10}$

3. $x^3 \cdot x^4 = x^{(3+4)} = x^7$

4. $y^7 \cdot y^2 \cdot y^4 = y^{(7+2+4)} = y^{13}$

Notice that each of these examples has only one base. The product rule does NOT apply to terms with different bases.

Example:

$2^4 \cdot 3^4 = ?$

➤ The product rule cannot be used since 2 and 3 are not equal bases. You must explicitly multiply all of the numbers: $2^4 \cdot 3^4 = (2 \cdot 2 \cdot 2 \cdot 2)(3 \cdot 3 \cdot 3 \cdot 3 \cdot) = 16 \cdot 81 = 1,296$.

Finally, the product rule does NOT apply to addition or subtraction of bases with exponents, even if the bases are identical.

Example:

$2^2 + 2^3 \neq 2^5$, since $2^2 + 2^3 = (2 \cdot 2) + (2 \cdot 2 \cdot 2) = 4 + 8 = 12$ and $2^5 = 2 \cdot 2 \cdot 2 \cdot 2 \cdot 2 = 32$.

Division Involving Exponents

The *quotient rule* is used for division involving identical bases with exponents. When dividing similar bases, subtract the exponent in the denominator from the exponent in the numerator: $\dfrac{x^m}{x^n} = x^{m-n}$. As with the product rule, the quotient rule can be verified by explicitly carrying out the indicated operations, as illustrated in the first of the following examples.

Examples:

1. $\dfrac{2^5}{2^3} = 2^{(5-3)} = 2^2$

   ➤ Writing out the expression and using the quotient rule give you the same result: $\dfrac{2^5}{2^3} = \dfrac{2 \cdot 2 \cdot 2 \cdot 2 \cdot 2}{2 \cdot 2 \cdot 2} = \dfrac{32}{8} = 4 = 2^2$.

2. $\dfrac{5^{10}}{5^9} = 5^{(10-9)} = 5^1 = 5$

3. $\dfrac{x^8}{x^6} = x^{(8-6)} = x^2$

4. $\dfrac{y^3}{y^2} = y^{(3-2)} = y^1 = y$

An *exponent of zero* results whenever a quantity is divided into itself. Since a quantity divided into itself is equal to 1, any base (except zero) with an exponent of zero is also equal to 1: $x^0 = 1$ if $x \neq 0$. 0^0 is an undefined operation in math.

Examples:

1. $\dfrac{5^3}{5^3} = 5^{(3-3)} = 5^0 = 1$

2. $\dfrac{x^{12}}{x^{12}} = x^{(12-12)} = x^0 = 1$

Raising a Power to a Power

The *power rule* is used when a power of a number is raised to another power. This is done by multiplying the exponents together: $\left(x^m\right)^n = x^{mn}$. Again, we can prove the validity of this shortcut by explicitly carrying out the indicated multiplications.

Examples:

1. $\left(2^2\right)^3 = 2^{(2 \cdot 3)} = 2^6$

   ➤ Writing out the expression and using the power rule give you the same result: $\left(2^2\right)^3 = (2 \cdot 2)^3 = 4^3 = 4 \cdot 4 \cdot 4 = 64 = 2^6$.

2. $\left(x^3\right)^4 = x^{(3 \cdot 4)} = x^{12}$

Raising a Product to a Power

The *product power rule* is used when a product with exponents is raised to a power. The exponent outside the parentheses governs all the factors inside the parentheses. When raising a product to a power, first multiply the exponent on the outside by each exponent on the inside: $\left(x^m y^p\right)^n = x^{mn} \cdot y^{pn}$.

Examples:

1. $(2 \cdot 3)^2 = 2^2 \cdot 3^2 = 4 \cdot 9 = 36$

   ➤ Writing out the expression and using the product power rule give you the same result: $(2 \cdot 3)^2 = (6)^2 = 36$.

2. $\left(2^2 \cdot 3^3\right)^2 = 2^{(2 \cdot 2)} \cdot 3^{(3 \cdot 2)} = \left(2^4\right)\left(3^6\right) = (16)(729) = 11,664$

3. $\left(x^2 \cdot y^3\right)^4 = x^{(2 \cdot 4)} \cdot y^{(3 \cdot 4)} = x^8 y^{12}$

Raising a Quotient to a Power

The *quotient power rule* is used when a quotient with exponents is raised to a power. It is essentially the same as the previous rule for determining the power of a product. The exponent outside the parentheses governs all the factors inside the parentheses. Determine the power of a quotient by multiplying the exponent on the outside by each exponent on the inside: $\left(\dfrac{x^m}{y^p}\right)^n = \dfrac{x^{mn}}{y^{pn}}$.

Examples:

1. $\left(\dfrac{2}{3}\right)^3 = \dfrac{2^3}{3^3} = \dfrac{8}{27}$

> ➤ Writing out the expression and using the quotient power rule give you the same result: $\left(\dfrac{2}{3}\right)^3 = \dfrac{2}{3} \cdot \dfrac{2}{3} \cdot \dfrac{2}{3} = \dfrac{2 \cdot 2 \cdot 2}{3 \cdot 3 \cdot 3} = \dfrac{8}{27}$.

2. $\left(\dfrac{1^2}{3^3}\right)^2 = \dfrac{1^{(2 \cdot 2)}}{3^{(3 \cdot 2)}} = \dfrac{1^4}{3^6} = \dfrac{1}{729}$

3. $\left(\dfrac{x^2}{y^3}\right)^2 = \dfrac{x^{(2 \cdot 2)}}{y^{(3 \cdot 2)}} = \dfrac{x^4}{y^6}$

Negative Exponents

Negative exponents do not signify negative numbers. Instead, they signify fractions. Specifically, a negative exponent indicates the power of the **reciprocal** of the base: $x^{-n} = \dfrac{1}{x^n}$.

Examples:

1. $\dfrac{2^2}{2^3} = 2^{(2-3)} = 2^{-1} = \dfrac{1}{2^1} = \dfrac{1}{2}$

2. $\dfrac{2^2}{2^3} = \dfrac{2 \cdot 2}{2 \cdot 2 \cdot 2} = \dfrac{4}{8} = \dfrac{1}{2}$

3. $3^{-2} = \left(\dfrac{1}{3}\right)^2 = \dfrac{1}{9}$

4. $x^{-3} = \left(\dfrac{1}{x}\right)^3 = \dfrac{1}{x^3}$

Rational (Fractional) Exponents

Exponents are not restricted to integer values. **Rational (fractional) exponents** are also possible. Later in this chapter, we will use rational exponents when working with radicals. Rational exponents also appear in algebraic expressions, functions, and equations. The rules for working with rational exponents are the same as those for integer exponents.

Examples:

1. $2^{\frac{1}{2}} \cdot 2^{\frac{1}{2}} = 2^{\frac{1}{2}+\frac{1}{2}} = 2^1 = 2$

2. $\left(x^2 y^4\right)^{\frac{1}{4}} = x^{2 \cdot \frac{1}{4}} y^{4 \cdot \frac{1}{4}} = x^{\frac{1}{2}} y$

Working with Exponents

Complex expressions may require the application of two or more operations involving exponents. No matter how complex an item gets, it can be solved by a series of simple steps following the five rules that are explained above for working with exponents. Remember to follow the rules for order of operations. Also, be careful when negative signs are involved.

Examples:

1. $\left(2^3 \cdot 3^2\right)^2 = 2^{3 \cdot 2} \cdot 3^{2 \cdot 2} = 2^6 \cdot 3^4$

2. $\left(\dfrac{3^3 \cdot 5^5}{3^2 \cdot 5^2}\right)^2 = \left(3^{3-2} \cdot 5^{5-2}\right)^2 = \left(3^1 \cdot 5^3\right)^2 = 3^2 \cdot 5^6$

3. $\left(\dfrac{x^2 \cdot y^3}{x \cdot y^2}\right)^2 = \left(x^{2-1} \cdot y^{3-2}\right)^2 = (x \cdot y)^2 = x^2 y^2$

4. $(-3)^3 (-2)^6 = (-27)(64) = -1,728$

5. $-2^4 (-3)^2 = -(2^4)(-3)^2 = -(16)(9) = -144$

These rules for working with exponents provide simple shortcuts, as verified by explicitly executing all indicated operations. When you begin to manipulate algebraic expressions, not only will these same shortcuts apply, but they will become indispensable.

SUMMARY OF OPERATIONS INVOLVING EXPONENTS

1. $x^1 = x$
2. $x^0 = 1$, if $x \neq 0$
3. Product Rule: $x^m \cdot x^n = x^{m+n}$
4. Quotient Rule: $\dfrac{x^m}{x^n} = x^{m-n}$
5. Power Rule: $\left(x^m\right)^n = x^{m \cdot n}$
6. Product Power Rule: $\left(x^m \cdot y^p\right)^n = x^{mn} \cdot y^{pn}$
7. Quotient Power Rule: $\left(\dfrac{x^m}{y^p}\right)^n = \dfrac{x^{mn}}{y^{pn}}$
8. Negative Exponents: $x^{-n} = \left(\dfrac{1}{x}\right)^n = \dfrac{1}{x^n}$

Roots and Radicals

Roots of Numbers

A ***square root*** of a number x is a solution to the equation $\sqrt{x} = b$, in which $x = b^2$. When you perform the multiplication indicated by an exponent, you are in effect answering the question, "What do I get when I multiply this number by itself so many times?" Now ask the opposite question, "What number, when multiplied by itself so many times, will give me a certain value?" For example, when you raise 2 to the third power, you find out that $2^3 = 8$. Now, ask the question in the other direction. What number, when raised to the third, is equal to 8?

This reverse process is called "finding the root of a number." Why roots? Look at the following diagram; since $2^6 = 64$, the sixth root of 64 is 2. The picture resembles plant roots.

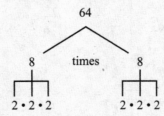

Of course, we rarely deal with sixth roots. Mostly, we deal with two roots: $2 \cdot 2 = 4$, so the second or ***square root*** of 4 is 2; and occasionally with numbers having three roots: $2 \cdot 2 \cdot 2 = 8$, so the third or ***cube root*** of 8 is 2.

The operation of taking a square root of a number is signaled by the ***radical*** sign, $\sqrt{}$. ***Radical*** comes from the Latin word "rad," which means "root."

Examples:

1. $\sqrt{1} = 1$ 4. $\sqrt{16} = 4$ 7. $\sqrt{49} = 7$ 10. $\sqrt{100} = 10$

2. $\sqrt{4} = 2$ 5. $\sqrt{25} = 5$ 8. $\sqrt{64} = 8$ 11. $\sqrt{121} = 11$

3. $\sqrt{9} = 3$ 6. $\sqrt{36} = 6$ 9. $\sqrt{81} = 9$ 12. $\sqrt{144} = 12$

The symbol $\sqrt{}$ always denotes a positive number. Later, when we get to the topic of quadratic equations in algebra, we will run across a "$\pm$" sign preceding the radical; this signifies both the positive and negative values of the root.

If a radical sign is preceded by a superscript number, then the number, or *index*, indicates a root other than the square root. In the notation $\sqrt[n]{a}$, n is the root or index, $\sqrt{}$ is the radical, and a is the radicand.

Examples:

1. $\sqrt[3]{8} = 2 \Rightarrow$ The cube root of 8 is 2.

2. $\sqrt[4]{81} = 3 \Rightarrow$ The fourth root of 81 is 3.

3. $\sqrt[6]{64} = 2 \Rightarrow$ The sixth root of 64 is 2.

Determining Square Roots

If a number is a perfect square (e.g., 4, 9, 16, etc.), then extracting its square root is easy. Simply use the values given in the examples of square roots above. Not every number, however, has an exact square root. In such cases, you can do one of two things. First, you may be able to find in the number a factor that does have an exact square root and extract that factor from under the radical sign.

Examples:

1. $\sqrt{125} = ?$

   ➤ 125 does not have a perfect square root. However, 25 has a perfect square and is a factor of 125, so factor 125 into 25 and 5: $\sqrt{125} = \sqrt{25 \cdot 5}$. Then, take the square root of 25, which is 5; $\sqrt{25} \cdot \sqrt{5} = 5 \cdot \sqrt{5}$. The final expression is $5\sqrt{5}$, which means 5 multiplied by the square root of 5: $\sqrt{125} = 5\sqrt{5}$.

2. $\sqrt{27} = \sqrt{9 \cdot 3} = \sqrt{9} \cdot \sqrt{3} = 3 \cdot \sqrt{3} = 3\sqrt{3}$

3. $\sqrt{32} = \sqrt{16 \cdot 2} = \sqrt{16} \cdot \sqrt{2} = 4 \cdot \sqrt{2} = 4\sqrt{2}$

4. $\sqrt{52} = \sqrt{4 \cdot 13} = \sqrt{4} \cdot \sqrt{13} = 2 \cdot \sqrt{13} = 2\sqrt{13}$

For the purposes of the exam, knowledge of the approximate values for common square roots may save valuable test time. For example, it is useful to know that $\sqrt{2}$ is approximately 1.4 and that $\sqrt{3}$ is approximately 1.7. Other values can be approximated by using ranges; e.g., $\sqrt{7}$ must be between 2 and 3 ($\sqrt{4} < \sqrt{7} < \sqrt{9}$). Since 7 is closer to 9 than to 4, a good approximation of $\sqrt{7}$ is 2.6 to 2.7.

Operations Involving Radicals
(Rational Exponents)

Radicals can be rewritten using *rational (fractional) exponents*. This simplifies the process of working with radicals, since all of the rules for exponents apply to fractional exponents and thus to radicals. The relationship between a rational exponent and the radical representing a given root is: $\sqrt[n]{x^m} = x^{\frac{m}{n}}$, where m and n are integers, and $n \neq 0$.

Examples:

1. $\sqrt{4} = 4^{\frac{1}{2}} = 2$

2. $\sqrt[3]{8} = 8^{\frac{1}{3}} = 2$

When you multiply a square root by itself, the result is the radicand: $\left(\sqrt{x}\right)\left(\sqrt{x}\right) = x$. This can be explained using the product rule for exponents as illustrated in the following example.

Example:

$$\left(\sqrt{2}\right)\left(\sqrt{2}\right) = 2^{\frac{1}{2}} \cdot 2^{\frac{1}{2}} = 2^1 = 2$$

The power rules for working with exponents are the ones you are most likely to use when working with radicals. The following example illustrates how the product power rule applies to radicals.

Example:

$$\sqrt{125} = 125^{\frac{1}{2}} = (25 \cdot 5)^{\frac{1}{2}} = 25^{\frac{1}{2}} \cdot 5^{\frac{1}{2}} = \left(\sqrt{25}\right)\left(\sqrt{5}\right) = 5\sqrt{5}$$

Notice that this is just the process of extracting a square root by finding a factor, but what makes this process work is the product power rule of exponents. The quotient power rule is used in the following example.

Example:

$$\sqrt{\frac{4}{9}} = \left(\frac{4}{9}\right)^{\frac{1}{2}} = \frac{4^{\frac{1}{2}}}{9^{\frac{1}{2}}} = \frac{\sqrt{4}}{\sqrt{9}} = \frac{2}{3}$$

Importantly, since radicals are fractional exponents and obey the rules for exponents, you cannot simply add radicals. $\sqrt{4} + \sqrt{9}$ is not equal to $\sqrt{13}$, and you can prove this by taking the square root of 4, which is 2, and the square root of 9, which is 3. $2 + 3$ is 5, which does not equal $\sqrt{13}$.

OPERATIONS INVOLVING RADICALS (RATIONAL EXPONENTS)

1. Product Rule: $\sqrt{x} \cdot \sqrt{x} = x^{\frac{1}{2}} x^{\frac{1}{2}} = x^1 = x$

2. Quotient Rule: $\dfrac{\sqrt[m]{x}}{\sqrt[n]{x}} = \dfrac{x^{\frac{1}{m}}}{x^{\frac{1}{n}}} = x^{\left(\frac{1}{m} - \frac{1}{n}\right)}$

3. Power Rule: $\left(\sqrt[m]{x}\right)^n = \left(x^{\frac{1}{m}}\right)^n = x^{\frac{n}{m}}$

4. Product Power Rule: $\sqrt[m]{x^n y^p} = \left(x^n y^p\right)^{\frac{1}{m}} = x^{\frac{n}{m}} y^{\frac{p}{m}} = \sqrt[m]{x^n} \cdot \sqrt[m]{y^p}$

5. Quotient Power Rule: $\sqrt[m]{\dfrac{x^n}{y^p}} = \left(\dfrac{x^n}{y^p}\right)^{\frac{1}{m}} = \dfrac{x^{\frac{n}{m}}}{y^{\frac{p}{m}}} = \dfrac{\sqrt[m]{x^n}}{\sqrt[m]{y^p}}$

Exponents and Radicals

DIRECTIONS: Choose the correct answer to each of the following items. Answers are on page 788.

1. What is the third power of 3?
    A. 1   **C.** 9   **E.** 27
    B. 3   **D.** 15

2. What is the fourth power of 2?
    A. 2   **C.** 8   **E.** 32
    B. 4   **D.** 16

3. What is the first power of 1,000,000?
    A. 0   **C.** 1   **E.** 1,000,000
    B. $\dfrac{1}{1,000,000}$ **D.** 10

4. $100^0 = ?$
    A. 0   **C.** 10   **E.** 100,000
    B. 1   **D.** 100

5. $2^3 \cdot 2^2 = ?$
    A. 6   **C.** 2^5 **E.** 4^6
    B. 8   **D.** 2^6

6. $3^{10} \cdot 10^3 = ?$
    I. 30^{30}
    II. $300 \cdot 1,000$
    III. $30 + 30$
    A. I only   **D.** II and III only
    B. II only   **E.** Neither I, II, nor III
    C. I and III only

7. $5^4 \cdot 5^9 = ?$
    A. 25^{36} **C.** 5^{13} **E.** 5
    B. 5^{36} **D.** 5^5

8. $2^3 \cdot 2^4 \cdot 2^5 = ?$
    A. 2^{12} **C.** 8^{12} **E.** 8^{60}
    B. 2^{60} **D.** 4^{60}

9. $(2+3)^{20} = ?$
    A. 5^{20} **C.** 6^{20} **E.** 20^6
    B. $2^{20} + 3^{20}$ **D.** 20^5

10. $\dfrac{2^5}{2^3} = ?$
    A. 2^2 **C.** 2^8 **E.** 2^{15}
    B. 4^4 **D.** 4^8

11. $\dfrac{3^{10}}{3^8} = ?$
    A. 3   **C.** 9^2 **E.** 3^{80}
    B. 3^2 **D.** 3^{18}

12. $\dfrac{5^2}{5^2} = ?$
    I. 0
    II. 1
    III. 5^0
    A. I and II only   **D.** III only
    B. I and III only   **E.** Neither I, II, nor III
    C. II and III only

13. $\dfrac{3^2}{3^3} = ?$
    I. 3^{-1}
    II. $\dfrac{1}{3}$
    III. -1
    A. I only   **D.** I and III only
    B. II only   **E.** I, II, and III
    C. I and II only

14. $\left(2^2\right)^3 = ?$
    A. 2^5 **C.** 4^5 **E.** 6^5
    B. 2^6 **D.** 4^6

15. $\left(5^2\right)^6 = ?$

    A. 5^8 **C.** 10^4 **E.** 10^{12}
    B. 5^{12} **D.** 10^8

16. $\left(7^7\right)^7 = ?$

    A. 21   **C.** 7^{49} **E.** 49^{49}
    B. 7^{14} **D.** 21^7

17. $(3 \cdot 2)^2 = ?$

    I. 36
    II. $3 \cdot 3 \cdot 2 \cdot 2$
    III. $3^2 \cdot 2^2$

    A. I only   **D.** I and III only
    B. II only   **E.** I, II, and III
    C. III only

18. $(5 \cdot 3)^2 = ?$

    I. 15^2
    II. $5^2 \cdot 3^2$
    III. 8^2

    A. I only   **D.** I and II only
    B. II only   **E.** I, II, and III
    C. III only

19. $\left(\dfrac{8}{3}\right)^2 = ?$

    I. $\dfrac{64}{9}$
    II. $\dfrac{8^2}{3^2}$
    III. 11^2

    A. I only   **D.** I and III only
    B. II only   **E.** I, II, and III
    C. I and II only

20. $\left(\dfrac{4}{9}\right)^2 = ?$

    A. $\dfrac{2}{3}$ **C.** $\dfrac{16}{81}$ **E.** $\dfrac{4}{9^2}$
    B. $\dfrac{4}{9}$ **D.** $\dfrac{4^2}{9}$

21. $\left(2^1 \cdot 2^2 \cdot 2^3\right)^2 = ?$

    A. 2^8 **C.** 2^{12} **E.** 2^{18}
    B. 2^{10} **D.** 2^{16}

22. $\left(\dfrac{2^4 \cdot 5^4}{2^2 \cdot 5^2}\right)^2 = ?$

    A. $2^4 \cdot 5^4$ **C.** 4^6 **E.** 24
    B. $2^6 \cdot 2^6$ **D.** 4^8

23. $\dfrac{3^6 \cdot 5^3 \cdot 7^9}{3^4 \cdot 5^3 \cdot 7^8} = ?$

    A. $3^2 \cdot 5 \cdot 7$ **C.** $3 \cdot 5 \cdot 7$ **E.** $3^2 \cdot 7$
    B. $3^2 \cdot 5 \cdot 7^2$ **D.** $3^2 \cdot 5$

24. $\left(\dfrac{5^{12} \cdot 7^5}{5^{11} \cdot 7^5}\right)^2 = ?$

    A. 25   **C.** 5^7 **E.** 7^5
    B. 49   **D.** 5^{11}

25. $\left(\dfrac{12^{12} \cdot 11^{11} \cdot 10^{10}}{12^{12} \cdot 11^{11} \cdot 10^9}\right)^2 = ?$

    A. 0   **C.** 10   **E.** 1,000
    B. 1   **D.** 100

26. $\sqrt{36} = ?$

    I. 6
    II. −6
    III. $3\sqrt{3}$

    A. I only   **D.** II and III only
    B. I and II only   **E.** I, II, and III
    C. I and III only

27. $\sqrt{81} + \sqrt{4} = ?$

    I. $\sqrt{85}$
    II. $\sqrt{9} + \sqrt{2}$
    III. 11

    A. I only   **D.** I and II only
    B. II only   **E.** II and III only
    C. III only

28. $\sqrt{27} = ?$

    A. 3   C. $3\sqrt{9}$ E. 81

    B. $3\sqrt{3}$ D. 27

29. $\sqrt{52} = ?$

    A. $\sqrt{5} + \sqrt{2}$ C. $2\sqrt{13}$ E. 13^2

    B. 7   D. $13\sqrt{4}$

30. $\sqrt{\dfrac{9}{4}} = ?$

    A. $\dfrac{\sqrt{3}}{2}$ C. $\dfrac{3}{2}$ E. $\sqrt{5}$

    B. $\dfrac{3}{\sqrt{2}}$ D. 5

31. $\dfrac{\sqrt{81}}{\sqrt{27}} = ?$

    A. $\sqrt{3}$ C. $3\sqrt{3}$ E. $9\sqrt{3}$

    B. 3   D. 9

32. $2\sqrt{2}$ is most nearly equal to which of the following?

    A. 2.8   C. 4   E. 12

    B. 3.4   D. 7

33. $\sqrt{27}$ is approximately equal to which of the following?

    A. 3   C. 4.5   E. 9

    B. 4   D. 5.1

34. $\sqrt{12}$ is approximately equal to which of the following?

    A. 2   C. 4   E. 8

    B. 3.4   D. 6

35. $\sqrt{23}$ is approximately equal to which of the following?

    A. 4   C. 6   E. 8

    B. 4.8   D. 7

36. $\sqrt{45}$ is approximately equal to which of the following?

    A. 5   C. 6.6   E. 7.5

    B. 5.5   D. 7

37. $\left(7 + \sqrt{5}\right)\left(3 - \sqrt{5}\right) = ?$

    A. $4 + 4\sqrt{5}$ C. $16 + 4\sqrt{5}$ E. 16

    B. $4 - \sqrt{5}$ D. $16 - 4\sqrt{5}$

38. $\left(5 - \sqrt{2}\right)\left(3 - \sqrt{2}\right) = ?$

    A. $17 + \sqrt{2}$ C. $17 + \sqrt{8}$ E. 25

    B. $17 - 8\sqrt{2}$ D. $17 + 8\sqrt{2}$

39. $\left(\sqrt{3} + 1\right)\left(2 - \sqrt{3}\right) = ?$

    A. -1 C. $-1 + \sqrt{3}$ E. $1 + \sqrt{3}$

    B. $-1 - \sqrt{3}$ D. 1

40. $\sqrt{2} \cdot 2\sqrt{3} = ?$

    A. $-2\sqrt{6}$ C. 2   E. $2\sqrt{6}$

    B. $-\sqrt{6}$ D. $\sqrt{6}$

41. $\sqrt{8} + \sqrt{50} = ?$

    A. $-7\sqrt{2}$ C. $\sqrt{2}$ E. 7

    B. $-\sqrt{2}$ D. $7\sqrt{2}$

42. $\sqrt{3^2 + 5^2} = ?$

    A. 6   C. 7   E. 8

    B. $\sqrt{34}$ D. $\sqrt{51}$

43. $\sqrt{\left(2\sqrt{3}\right)^2 + 2^2} = ?$

    A. 1   C. 3   E. 5

    B. 2   D. 4

44. $\dfrac{\sqrt{2}}{2}\left(\sqrt{6} + \dfrac{\sqrt{2}}{2}\right) = ?$

    A. $\sqrt{3} + \dfrac{1}{2}$ C. $\sqrt{6} + 1$ E. $\sqrt{6} + 2$

    B. $\dfrac{\sqrt{3}}{2}$ D. $2\sqrt{3} + \dfrac{1}{2}$

45. $\dfrac{15\sqrt{96}}{5\sqrt{2}} = ?$

    A. $7\sqrt{3}$ C. $11\sqrt{3}$ E. $40\sqrt{3}$

    B. $7\sqrt{12}$ D. $12\sqrt{3}$

46. Which of the following radicals is a perfect square?

    A. $\sqrt{0.4}$ **C.** $\sqrt{0.09}$ **E.** $\sqrt{0.025}$
    B. $\sqrt{0.9}$ **D.** $\sqrt{0.02}$

47. $\left(-\dfrac{1}{3}\right)^4 = ?$

    A. $-\dfrac{1}{81}$ **C.** $-\dfrac{1}{12}$ **E.** $-\dfrac{1}{64}$

    B. $\dfrac{1}{81}$ **D.** $\dfrac{1}{12}$

48. $-4^4 = ?$

    A. -256 **C.** -16 **E.** -8
    B. 256 **D.** 16

49. $\sqrt[12]{x^6} = ?$

    A. x^6 **C.** x^2 **E.** x^{-2}

    B. x^{-6} **D.** $x^{\frac{1}{2}}$

50. $\sqrt[k]{6^{2km}}$ MUST be a positive integer if:

    A. k is a positive integer
    B. k is a multiple of 3
    C. $k < 0$
    D. m is a non-negative common fraction
    E. m is a non-negative integer

51. If n is an integer and 0.012345×10^n is greater than 10,000, what is the least possible value of n?

    A. 2   **C.** 4   **E.** 6
    B. 3   **D.** 5

Algebraic Operations

Algebra is the branch of mathematics that uses letter symbols to represent numbers. The letter symbols are, in essence, placeholders. They function somewhat like "someone" or "somewhere." For example, in the sentence "Someone took the book and put it somewhere," neither the identity of the person in question nor the new location of the book is known. We can rewrite this sentence in algebraic terms: "x put the book in y place." The identity of x is unknown, and the new location of the book is unknown. It is for this reason that letter symbols in algebra are often referred to as "unknowns."

Algebra, like English, is a language, and for making certain statements, algebra is much better than English. For example, the English statement "There is a number such that, when you add 3 to it, the result is 8" can be rendered more easily in algebraic notation: $x + 3 = 8$. In fact, learning the rules of algebra is really very much like learning the grammar of any language. Keeping this analogy between algebra and English in mind, let's begin by studying the components of the algebraic language.

Elements of Algebra

Algebraic Terms

The basic unit of the English language is the word. The basic unit of algebra is the ***term***. In English, a word consists of one or more letters. In algebra, a term consists of one or more letters or numbers. For example, x, $2z$, xy, N, 2, $\sqrt{7}$, and π are all algebraic terms. A term can be a product, quotient, or single symbol.

In English, a word may have a root, a prefix, a suffix, an ending, and so on. In algebra, a term may have a coefficient, an exponent, and a sign, etc. Of course, algebraic terms also include a variable, also referred to as the base.

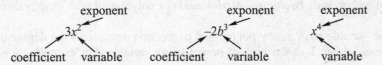

Just as with numbers, when the sign of an algebraic term is positive, the "$+$" is not written; e.g., $3x$ is equivalent to $+3x$. Additionally, when the coefficient is 1, it is understood to be included and is not written out; e.g., x rather than $1x$.

The elements in an algebraic term are all joined by the operation of multiplication. The coefficient and its sign are multiplied by the variable. For example: $-3x = (-3)(x)$; $5a = (+5)(a)$; and $\frac{1}{2}N = (+\frac{1}{2})(N)$.

The exponent, as you have already learned, also indicates multiplication. Thus, x^2 means x times x; a^3 means a times a times a; and N^5 means N times N times N times N times N. Be careful not to confuse the coefficient with the exponent. $3x$ means "$+3$ times x," while x^3 means "x times x times x." Of course, many terms have both a coefficient and an exponent. Thus, $3x^2$ means "$+3$ times x times x," and $-5a^3$ means "-5 times a times a times a."

Algebraic Expressions

In English, words are organized into phrases. In algebra, terms are grouped together in ***expressions***. An expression is a collection of algebraic terms that are joined by addition, subtraction, or both.

Examples:

1. $x + y$

2. $-2x + 3y + z$

3. $3x^2 - 2y^2$

4. $x^2 + y^{20}$

A *rational expression* is a fraction containing algebraic terms. In other words, rational expressions are algebraic fractions.

Examples:

1. $\dfrac{1}{x}$

2. $\dfrac{x^2}{xy - y^2}$

3. $\dfrac{3 + \dfrac{1}{x}}{9 - \dfrac{1}{x^2}}$

Algebraic expressions are classified according to the number of terms the expression contains. A *monomial* is an algebraic expression with exactly one term. A *polynomial* is an algebraic expression with more than one term. A *binomial* is a polynomial with exactly two terms. A *trinomial* is a polynomial with exactly three terms.

The highest power of the variable term in any polynomial expression determines the degree of the polynomial. A *first degree* (or *linear*) *polynomial* has 1 as the highest power of its variable. For example, $y + 3$ is a linear polynomial because the highest power of y is 1. A *second degree* (or *quadratic*) *polynomial* has 2 as the highest power of its variable. For example, $3x^2 - 8x - 3$ is a quadratic polynomial because the highest power of x is 2.

Algebraic Equations

In algebra, a complete sentence is called an equation. An equation asserts that two algebraic expressions are equal. Equations involving rational expressions are called *rational equations.*

Examples:

1. $2x + 4 = 3x - 2$

2. $\dfrac{y^2 - 5y}{y^2 - 4y - 5} = \dfrac{y}{y + 1}$

Operations of Algebraic Terms

Adding and Subtracting Algebraic Terms

Addition and subtraction are indicated in algebra, as they are in arithmetic, with the signs "+" and "−." In arithmetic, these operations combine the numbers into a third number. For example, the addition of 2 and 3 is equivalent to combining 2 and 3 to form the number 5: $2 + 3 = 5$.

In algebra, however, only *similar (like) terms* may be combined. Similar terms are terms with the same variables having the same exponent values. Coefficients do not factor into whether or not terms are similar.

Examples:

1. $3x^2$, $40x^2$, $-2x^2$, and $\sqrt{2}x^2$ are similar terms.

2. xy, $5xy$, $-23xy$, and πxy are similar terms.

3. $10xyz$, $-xyz$, and xyz are similar terms.

4. $3x$ and $3x^2$ are NOT similar terms.

5. xy and x^2y are NOT similar terms.

6. xy, yz, and xz are NOT similar terms.

To simplify an algebraic expression, group similar terms and add/subtract the numerical coefficients of each group. Variables and exponents of combined similar terms remain unchanged.

Examples:

1. $x^2 + 2x^2 + 3x^2 = ?$

   ➤ All three terms are similar since each includes x^2. Combine the terms by adding the coefficients: $1 + 2 + 3 = 6$. Thus, the result is $6x^2$.

2. $y + 2x + 3y - x = ?$

   ➤ With two different types of terms, group the similar terms together: $(2x - x) + (y + 3y)$. Add the coefficients for each type of term. For the x terms, the combined coefficient is $2 - 1 = 1$; for the y terms, $1 + 3 = 4$. The result is $x + 4y$.

3. $x - 3x + 5x - 2x = (1 - 3 + 5 - 2)x = x$

4. $2x - y - 3x + 4y + 5x = (2x - 3x + 5x) + (4y - y) = 4x + 3y$

5. $5x^2 + 3x^3 - 2x^2 + 4x^3 = \left(5x^2 - 2x^2\right) + \left(3x^3 + 4x^3\right) = 3x^2 + 7x^3$

Notice that when you have combined all similar terms, it is not possible to carry the addition or subtraction any further.

Multiplying and Dividing Algebraic Terms

Use the arithmetic **rules of exponents** to multiply or divide algebraic terms. Remember that $x^0 = 1$ when $x \neq 0$, and $x^1 = x$.

OPERATIONS OF ALGEBRAIC TERMS

1. Product Rule: $x^m \cdot x^n = x^{m+n}$ and $ax^m \cdot bx^n = abx^{m+n}$

2. Quotient Rule: $\dfrac{x^m}{x^n} = x^{m-n}$

3. Power Rule: $\left(x^m\right)^n = x^{mn}$

4. Product Power Rule: $\left(x^m \cdot y^p\right)^n = x^{mn} \cdot y^{pn}$

5. Quotient Power Rule: $\left(\dfrac{x^m}{y^p}\right)^n = \dfrac{x^{mn}}{y^{pn}}$

6. Negative Exponents: $x^{-n} = \dfrac{1}{x^n}$

Examples:

1. *Product Rule:*

 a. $\left(x^2\right)\left(x^3\right) = x^{(2+3)} = x^5$

 b. $\left(3x^2\right)(xy) = (3 \cdot 1)\left(x^2 \cdot xy\right) = 3 \cdot x^{(2+1)} \cdot y = 3x^3y$

 c. $(2xyz)(3xy)(4yz) = (2 \cdot 3 \cdot 4)(xyz \cdot xy \cdot yz) = 24 \cdot x^{(1+1)} \cdot y^{(1+1+1)} \cdot z^{(1+1)} = 24x^2y^3z^2$

2. *Quotient Rule:*

 a. $\dfrac{x^3}{x^2} = x^{(3-2)} = x^1 = x$

 b. $\dfrac{2x^4y^3}{x^2z} = \dfrac{2}{1} \cdot \dfrac{x^4y^3}{x^2z} = 2 \cdot \dfrac{x^{(4-2)}y^3}{z} = \dfrac{2x^2y^3}{z}$

3. *Power Rule:* $(x^2)^3 = x^{(2)(3)} = x^6$

4. *Product Power Rule:* $\left(x^2y^3\right)^2 = x^{(2)(2)}y^{(3)(2)} = x^4y^6$

5. *Quotient Power Rule:* $\left(\dfrac{x^2}{y^3}\right)^2 = \dfrac{x^{(2)(2)}}{y^{(3)(2)}} = \dfrac{x^4}{y^6}$

Operations of Algebraic Fractions

Adding and Subtracting Algebraic Fractions

Adding and subtracting algebraic fractions, like adding and subtracting numerical fractions, require common denominators. If the denominators are the same, simply add/subtract the numerators: $\dfrac{a}{x} \pm \dfrac{b}{x} = \dfrac{a \pm b}{x}$.

*Example*s:

1. $\dfrac{5}{x} + \dfrac{3}{x} = \dfrac{5+3}{x} = \dfrac{8}{x}$

2. $\dfrac{2x}{y} - \dfrac{x}{y} = \dfrac{2x-x}{y} = \dfrac{x}{y}$

3. $\dfrac{a}{cd} + \dfrac{x}{cd} = \dfrac{a+x}{cd}$

To add or subtract algebraic fractions with unlike denominators, you must first find a common denominator. Usually, this can be accomplished by using the same method as with numerical fractions: $\dfrac{a}{x} \pm \dfrac{b}{y} = \dfrac{ay}{xy} \pm \dfrac{bx}{xy} = \dfrac{ay \pm bx}{xy}$.

Example:

$$\dfrac{2x}{y} + \dfrac{3y}{x} = \dfrac{2x}{y} \underset{\displaystyle\geq}{\overset{\displaystyle\geq}{+}} \dfrac{3y}{x} = \dfrac{2x^2 + 3y^2}{xy}$$

Multiplying and Dividing Algebraic Fractions

To multiply algebraic fractions, follow the rule for multiplying numeric fractions. Multiply terms in the numerators to create a new numerator, and multiply terms in the denominator to create a new denominator: $\dfrac{a}{c} \cdot \dfrac{b}{d} = \dfrac{ab}{cd}$.

*Example*s:

1. $\dfrac{2}{x} \cdot \dfrac{3}{y} = \dfrac{6}{xy}$

2. $\dfrac{x^2 y^3}{z} \cdot \dfrac{x^3 y^2}{wz} = \dfrac{x^5 y^5}{wz^2}$

To divide algebraic fractions, follow the rule for dividing numeric fractions. Invert the divisor, or second fraction, and multiply: $\dfrac{a}{c} \div \dfrac{b}{d} = \dfrac{a}{c} \cdot \dfrac{d}{b} = \dfrac{ad}{cb}$.

*Example*s:

1. $\dfrac{2}{y} \div \dfrac{3}{x} = \dfrac{2}{y} \cdot \dfrac{x}{3} = \dfrac{2x}{3y}$

2. $\dfrac{2x^2}{y} \div \dfrac{y}{x} = \dfrac{2x^2}{y} \cdot \dfrac{x}{y} = \dfrac{2x^3}{y^2}$

Multiplying Algebraic Expressions

A *polynomial* is an algebraic expression with one or more terms involving only the operations of addition, subtraction, and multiplication of variables. Polynomial means "many terms," although it is possible to get a monomial by adding two polynomials. A multiplication item such as $(x+y)(x+y)$ requires a special procedure. The fundamental rule for multiplying is that every term of one expression must be multiplied by every term of the other expression.

Distributive Property

First, let's look at the case in which a polynomial is to be multiplied by a single term. One way of solving the item is to first add and then multiply. Alternatively, we can use the ***distributive property*** to multiply every term inside the parentheses by the term outside the parentheses, and then we can add the terms: $x(y+x) = xy + xz$. The result is the same regardless of the method used. The following example illustrates these two methods using real numbers.

Example:

$2(3+4+5) = 2(12) = 24$

➤ The distributive property returns the same result: $2(3+4+5) = (2 \cdot 3) + (2 \cdot 4) + (2 \cdot 5) = 6 + 8 + 10 = 24$.

When working with algebraic expressions, use the distributive property, since you cannot add unlike terms. The following examples apply the distributive property to algebraic expressions.

*Example*s:

1. $x(y+z) = xy + xz$

2. $a(b+c+d) = ab + ac + ad$

To multiply two polynomials, either add the polynomials before multiplying them, or reverse the order of operations using the distributive property.

Example:

$(2+3)(1+3+4) = (5)(8) = 40$

➤ The distributive property returns the same result:

$(2+3)(1+3+4) = (2 \cdot 1) + (2 \cdot 3) + (2 \cdot 4) + (3 \cdot 1) + (3 \cdot 3) + (3 \cdot 4) = 2 + 6 + 8 + 3 + 9 + 12 = 40$.

FOIL Method

To multiply two binomials using the ***FOIL method***, follow these steps for combining the binomial terms: (1) multiply the first terms, (2) multiply the outer terms, (3) multiply the inner terms, (4) multiply the last terms, and (5) combine like terms. The FOIL method is simply a mnemonic shortcut derived from the distributive property. The following diagram illustrates application of the FOIL method.

> **MULTIPLYING TWO BINOMIALS**
> **(FOIL: First, Outer, Inner, Last)**
>
> $$(x+y)(x+y) = x^2 + xy + xy + y^2 = x^2 + 2xy + y^2$$

*Example*s:

1. $(x+y)(x-y) = ?$

   ➤ First: $(x)(x) = x^2$.
   Outer: $(x)(-y) = -xy$.
   Inner: $(y)(x) = xy$.
   Last: $(y)(-y) = y^2$.
   Add: $x^2 - xy + xy + y^2 = x^2 + y^2$.

2. $(x-y)(x-y) = ?$

   ➤ First: $(x)(x) = x^2$.
   Outer: $(x)(-y) = -xy$.
   Inner: $(-y)(x) = -xy$.
   Last: $(-y)(-y) = y^2$.
   Add: $x^2 - xy - xy + y^2 = x^2 - 2xy + y^2$.

Three situations, one in addition to the two illustrated in the previous examples, arise with such frequency that you should memorize the results to simplify the calculation.

> **THREE COMMON MULTIPLICATIONS INVOLVING POLYNOMIALS**
>
> 1. $(x+y)^2 = (x+y)(x+y) = x^2 + 2xy + y^2$
>
> 2. $(x-y)^2 = (x-y)(x-y) = x^2 - 2xy + y^2$
>
> 3. $(x+y)(x-y) = x^2 - y^2$

You might be asked to multiply something more complex than two binomials. The process is tedious and time-consuming, but ultimately it is executed the same way.

Example:

$(x+y)^3 = ?$

➤ Apply the FOIL method to the first two binomials, then multiply the last binomial to the resultant trinomial of the first two binomials:

$$(x+y)^3 = (x+y)(x+y)(x+y)$$
$$= \left(x^2 + 2xy + y^2\right)(x+y)$$
$$= x\left(x^2\right) + x(2xy) + x\left(y^2\right) + y\left(x^2\right) + y(2xy) + y\left(y^2\right)$$
$$= x^3 + 2x^2y + xy^2 + x^2y + 2xy^2 + y^3$$
$$= x^3 + 3x^2y + 3xy^2 + y^3$$

Factoring Algebraic Expressions

Although the term *factoring* intimidates many students, factoring is really nothing more than reverse multiplication. For example, if $(x+y)(x+y) = x^2 + 2xy + y^2$, then $x^2 + 2xy + y^2$ can be factored into $(x+y)(x+y)$. Fortunately, for the purposes of taking the test, any factoring you might need to do will fall into one of three categories.

Finding a Common Factor

If all the terms of an algebraic expression contain a common factor, then that term can be factored out of the expression.

Examples:

1. $ab + ac + ad = a(b + c + d)$

2. $abx + aby + abz = ab(x + y + z)$

3. $x^2 + x^3 + x^4 = x^2\left(1 + x + x^2\right)$

4. $3a + 6a^2 + 9a^3 = 3a\left(1 + 2a + 3a^2\right)$

Reversing a Known Polynomial Multiplication Process

Three patterns recur with such frequency on the exam that you should memorize them. These patterns are the same as the ones you were encouraged to memorize in the discussion of the FOIL method.

THREE COMMON POLYNOMIAL MULTIPLICATION REVERSALS

1. Perfect square trinomial: $x^2 + 2xy + y^2 = (x + y)(x + y)$

2. Perfect square trinomial: $x^2 - 2xy + y^2 = (x - y)(x - y)$

3. Difference of two squares: $x^2 - y^2 = (x + y)(x - y)$

Reversing an Unknown Polynomial Multiplication Process

Occasionally, you may find it necessary to factor an expression that does not fall into one of the three categories presented above. The expression will most likely have the form $ax^2 + bx + c$; e.g., $x^2 + 2x + 1$. To factor such expressions, set up a blank diagram: ( )( ). Then, fill in the diagram by answering the following series of questions.

Step 1: What factors will produce the first term, ax^2?

Step 2: What possible factors will produce the last term, c?

Step 3: Which of the possible factors from step 2, when added together, will produce the middle term, bx?

*Example*s:

1. Factor $x^2 + 3x + 2$.

   ➤ What factors will produce the first term, ax^2, where $a = 1$? x times x yields x^2, so the factors, in part, are $(x\ \ )(x\ \ )$. What possible factors will produce the last term? The possibilities are $\{2, 1\}$ and $\{-2, -1\}$. Which of the two sets of factors just mentioned, when added together, will produce a result of $+3x$? The answer is $\{2, 1\}$: $2 + 1 = 3$, as the FOIL method confirms: $(x + 2)(x + 1) = x^2 + x + 2x + 2 = x^2 + 3x + 2$.

2. Factor $x^2 + 4x - 12$.

   ➤ What factors will generate ax^2? $(x\ \ )(x\ \ )$. What factors will generate -12? $\{1, -12\}$, $\{12, -1\}$, $\{2, -6\}$, $\{6, -2\}$, $\{3, -4\}$, and $\{4, -3\}$. Which factors, when added together, will produce the middle term of $+4x$? The answer is $\{6, -2\}$: $6 + (-2) = 4$. Thus, the factors are $(x + 6)$ and $(x - 2)$, as the FOIL method confirms: $(x + 6)(x - 2) = (x + 6)(x - 2) = x^2 - 2x + 6x - 12 = x^2 + 4x - 12$.

Absolute Value in Algebraic Expressions

Algebraic terms involving absolute values are treated the same way as numeric absolute values. Remember that the absolute value of any term is always a positive numerical value.

PRINCIPLES OF ABSOLUTE VALUE

1. $|x| = x$ if $x \geq 0$; $|x| = -x$ if $x < 0$

2. $|x| = |-x|$

3. $|x| \geq 0$

4. $|x - y| = |y - x|$

---

*Example*s:

1. If $w = -3, |w| = ?$

   ➤ Since the value of w is less than zero, $|w| = -w = -(-3) = 3$.

2. Let x be a member of the following set: $\{-11, -10, -9, -8, -7, -6, -5, -4, -3, -2, -1, 0, 1, 2, 3, 4\}$. $\dfrac{|2x - |x||}{3}$ is a positive integer for how many different numbers in the set?

➤ If $x < 0$, then $|x| = -x$: $\dfrac{|2x - |x||}{3} = \dfrac{|2x - (-x)|}{3} = \dfrac{|2x + x|}{3} = \dfrac{|3x|}{3} = |x|$, which is always a positive. Therefore, $\dfrac{|2x - |x||}{3}$ is a positive integer for all numbers in the set less than zero. If $x \geq 0$, then $|x| = x$: $\dfrac{|2x - |x||}{3} = \dfrac{|2x - x|}{3} = \dfrac{|x|}{3} = \dfrac{x}{3}$. Thus, the only other number in the set that returns a positive integer is 3. The total number of values in the set that satisfy the condition is: $11 + 1 = 12$.

Radicals in Algebraic Expressions

Radicals in algebraic expressions are manipulated in the same way as numeric radicals using the rules of exponents.

Example:

Does $\dfrac{3\sqrt{x} + \sqrt{x^3}}{x} = \dfrac{3}{\sqrt{x}} + \sqrt{x}$?

➤ $\dfrac{3\sqrt{x} + \sqrt{x^3}}{x} = \dfrac{3\sqrt{x}}{x} + \dfrac{\sqrt{x^3}}{x} = \dfrac{3x^{\frac{1}{2}}}{x} + \dfrac{x^{\frac{3}{2}}}{x} = 3x^{\left(\frac{1}{2} - 1\right)} + x^{\left(\frac{3}{2} - 1\right)} = 3x^{-\frac{1}{2}} + x^{\frac{1}{2}} = \dfrac{3}{\sqrt{x}} + \sqrt{x}$.

When simplifying expressions containing roots and radicals that are inverse operations of one another, it is important to note that the sign of the variable impacts the sign of the result. Consider $\sqrt{x^2}$. If $x \geq 0$, then $\sqrt{x^2} = x$; if $x < 0$, then $\sqrt{x^2} = -x$.

*Example*s:

1. $\sqrt{2^2} = 2$.

2. $\sqrt{(-2)^2} = -(-2)^2 = 2$.

EXERCISE **8**

Algebraic Operations

DIRECTIONS: Choose the correct answer to each of the following items. Answers are on page 789.

1. Which of the following is (are) like terms?

 I. $34x$ and $-18x$

 II. $2x$ and $2xy$

 III. x^3 and $3x$

 A. I only   **D.** II and III only

 B. II only   **E.** I, II, and III

 C. I and III only

2. Which of the following is (are) like terms?

 I. $\sqrt{2x}$ and $\sqrt{3x}$

 II. π and 10

 III. x^2 and $2x^2$

 A. I only   **D.** I and III only

 B. II only   **E.** I, II, and III

 C. I and II only

3. $x + 2x + 3x = ?$

 A. $6x^6$ **C.** $6x$ **E.** $x - 6$

 B. x^6 **D.** $x + 6$

4. $2x + 3x - x + 4x = ?$

 A. $8x^8$ **C.** $8x$ **E.** $x - 8$

 B. x^8 **D.** $x + 8$

5. $a^3 + a^2 + a = ?$

 A. $3a^3$ **C.** $2a^2$ **E.** $a^3 + a^2 + a$

 B. a^3 **D.** a^2

6. $z^2 + 2z^2 - 5z^2 = ?$

 A. $-9z^2$ **C.** 0 **E.** $2z^2$

 B. $-2z^2$ **D.** $2z^2$

7. $a^3 - 12a^3 + 15a^3 + 2a^3 = ?$

 A. $6a^3$ **C.** $6a$ **E.** a

 B. $2a^2$ **D.** $3a$

8. $3c + 2a - 1 + 4c - 2a + 1 = ?$

 A. $2a + 4c + 12$ **D.** $2a + 1$

 B. $4a + 3c - 2$ **E.** $7c$

 C. $a + c - 1$

9. $-7nx + 2nx + 2n + 7x = ?$

 A. 0 **D.** $9nx + 9xn$

 B. $-5nx + 2n + 7x$ **E.** $4nx$

 C. $18nx$

10. $c^2 + 2c^2d^2 - c^2 = ?$

 A. $4c^2d^2$ **C.** c^2d^2 **E.** cd

 B. $2c^2d^2$ **D.** $2cd$

11. $2x^2 + 2x^2 + 2x^2 = ?$

 A. $6x^6$ **C.** $6x^2$ **E.** 6

 B. $2x^6$ **D.** $6x$

12. $3xy + 3x^2y - 2xy + y = ?$

 A. $6xy - y$ **D.** $x^2y^2 + xy$

 B. $x + xy + y$ **E.** $3xy + x$

 C. $3x^2y + xy + y$

13. $x^2 + 2xy - 3x + 4xy - 6y + 2y^2 + 3x - 2xy + 6y = ?$

 A. $x^2 - 2xy + y^2$

 B. $x^2 + y^2 + 3x + 2y$

 C. $x^2 + 2y^2 + 4xy + 6x + 6y$

 D. $x^2 + 2y + 4xy + 6x$

 E. $x^2 + 2y^2 + 4xy$

14. $8p + 2p^2 + pq - 4p^2 - 14p - pq = ?$

 A. $-2p^2 - 6p$

 B. $-p^2 + 6p$

 C. $2p^2 + 6p$

 D. $p^2 + 3pq$

 E. $3p^2 - pq$

15. $pqr + qrs + rst + stu = ?$

    A. $pqrst$

    B. $pq + qr + rs + st + tu$

    C. $pqr + rst$

    D. $4pqrst$

    E. $pqr + qrs + rst + stu$

16. $\left(x^2\right)\left(x^3\right) = ?$

    A. $x^{\frac{2}{3}}$ C. $x^{\frac{3}{2}}$ E. x^6

    B. x D. x^5

17. $(a)\left(a^2\right)\left(a^3\right)\left(a^4\right) = ?$

    A. $10a$ C. a^5 E. a^{24}

    B. $24a$ D. a^{10}

18. $y^5 \div y^2 = ?$

    A. $3y$ C. $y^{\frac{5}{2}}$ E. y^7

    B. $7y$ D. y^3

19. $\left(x^2 y\right)\left(xy^2\right) = ?$

    A. $4xy$ C. xy^4 E. xy^{16}

    B. $x^3 y^3$ D. $x^4 y^4$

20. $(abc)\left(a^2 bc^2\right) = ?$

    A. $4abc$ C. $a^3 b^2 c^3$ E. abc^6

    B. $a^2 bc^2$ D. $a^3 b^3 c^3$

21. $\left(xy^2\right)\left(x^2 z\right)\left(y^2 z\right) = ?$

    A. $8xyz$ C. $x^3 y^4 z^2$ E. $x^3 y^3 z^3$

    B. $x^2 y^4 z$ D. $x^3 y^3 z^2$

22. $\dfrac{x^2 y^4}{xy} = ?$

    A. y^3 C. $x^2 y^3$ E. xy^8

    B. xy^3 D. $x^3 y^5$

23. $\dfrac{a^3 b^4 c^5}{abc} = ?$

    A. $a^2 b^3 c^4$ C. $(abc)^3$ E. $(abc)^{60}$

    B. $a^3 b^4 c^5$ D. $(abc)^{12}$

24. $\left(x^2 y^3\right)^4 = ?$

    A. $(xy)^9$ C. $x^8 y^{12}$ E. xy^{24}

    B. $x^6 y^7$ D. xy^{20}

25. $\left(\dfrac{a^2}{b^3}\right)^3 = ?$

    A. $\dfrac{a^5}{b}$ C. $a^5 b$ E. $a^6 b^9$

    B. $\dfrac{a^6}{b^9}$ D. $a^6 b$

26. $\dfrac{x^3 y^4 z^5}{x^4 y^2 z} = ?$

    A. $y^2 z^4$ C. $\dfrac{y^2 z^4}{x}$ E. $\dfrac{y^6 z^6}{x}$

    B. $xy^2 z^4$ D. $\dfrac{y^2 z^5}{x}$

27. $\left(\dfrac{c^4 d^2}{c^2 d}\right)^3 = ?$

    A. $c^5 d^3$ C. $c^6 d^3$ E. $c^6 d^6$

    B. $c^5 d^5$ D. $c^6 d^4$

28. $\left(\dfrac{x^2 y^3}{xy}\right)\left(\dfrac{x^3 y^4}{xy}\right) = ?$

    A. $x^2 y^3$ C. $x^3 y^5$ E. $x^6 y^7$

    B. $x^3 y^4$ D. $x^5 y^6$

29. $\left(\dfrac{abc^2}{abc^3}\right)\left(\dfrac{a^2 b^2 c}{ab}\right) = ?$

    A. $\dfrac{ab}{c}$ C. ab E. 1

    B. $\dfrac{bc}{a}$ D. c

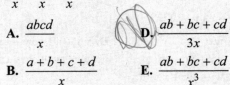

30. $\left(\dfrac{x^5 y^3 z^2}{x^4 y^2 z}\right)^2 \left(\dfrac{x^2 y^3 z^5}{xy^2 z^4}\right)^3 = ?$

A. xyz **C.** $x^5 y^5 z^5$ **E.** xyz^{12}

B. $x^2 y^2 z^2$ **D.** $x^6 y^6 z^6$

31. $\dfrac{a}{c} + \dfrac{b}{c} = ?$

A. $\dfrac{ab}{c}$ **C.** $\dfrac{a+b}{2c}$ **E.** $\dfrac{a+b}{abc}$

B. $\dfrac{a+b}{c}$ **D.** $\dfrac{a+b}{c^2}$

32. $\dfrac{x}{2} + \dfrac{y}{2} + \dfrac{z}{2} = ?$

A. $\dfrac{x+y+z}{2}$ **C.** $\dfrac{x+y+z}{8}$ **E.** $\dfrac{xyz}{8}$

B. $\dfrac{x+y+z}{6}$ **D.** $\dfrac{xyz}{2}$

33. $\dfrac{ab}{x} + \dfrac{bc}{x} + \dfrac{cd}{x} = ?$

A. $\dfrac{abcd}{x}$ **D.** $\dfrac{ab+bc+cd}{3x}$

B. $\dfrac{a+b+c+d}{x}$ **E.** $\dfrac{ab+bc+cd}{x^3}$

C. $\dfrac{ab+bc+cd}{x}$

34. $\dfrac{x^2}{k} + \dfrac{x^3}{k} + \dfrac{x^4}{k} = ?$

A. $\dfrac{x^9}{k}$ **D.** $\dfrac{x^2 + x^3 + x^4}{k}$

B. $\dfrac{x^9}{3k}$ **E.** $\dfrac{x^2 + x^3 + x^4}{3k}$

C. $\dfrac{x^{24}}{k}$

35. $\dfrac{2x}{z} - \dfrac{y}{z} = ?$

A. $\dfrac{2x-y}{z}$ **C.** $\dfrac{2x-y}{x^2}$ **E.** $\dfrac{2xy}{2z}$

B. $\dfrac{2x-y}{2z}$ **D.** $\dfrac{2xy}{z}$

36. $\dfrac{x}{y} + \dfrac{y}{x} = ?$

A. $\dfrac{xy}{x+y}$ **C.** $\dfrac{x+y}{xy}$ **E.** $\dfrac{x^2 + y^2}{xy}$

B. $\dfrac{x+y}{y+x}$ **D.** $\dfrac{xy+yx}{xy}$

37. $\dfrac{a}{b} - \dfrac{b}{a} = ?$

A. $\dfrac{ab}{a-b}$ **C.** $\dfrac{a-b}{ab}$ **E.** $\dfrac{a^2 - b^2}{ab}$

B. $\dfrac{a-b}{b-a}$ **D.** $\dfrac{ab-ba}{ab}$

38. $\dfrac{x^2}{y} + \dfrac{x^3}{z} = ?$

A. $\dfrac{x^2 + x^3}{yz}$ **C.** $\dfrac{x^6}{yz}$ **E.** $\dfrac{x^2 z + x^3 y}{yz}$

B. $\dfrac{x^5}{yz}$ **D.** $\dfrac{x^2 + x^3}{yz}$

39. $\dfrac{x}{a} + \dfrac{y}{b} + \dfrac{z}{c} = ?$

A. $\dfrac{xyz}{abc}$ **D.** $\dfrac{xbc + yac + zab}{a+b+c}$

B. $\dfrac{x+y+z}{a+b+c}$ **E.** $\dfrac{xa+yb+zc}{abc}$

C. $\dfrac{xbc + yac + zab}{abc}$

40. $\dfrac{x^2}{y^2} - \dfrac{y^3}{x^3} = ?$

A. $\dfrac{x^2 - x^3}{y^5}$ **C.** $\dfrac{x^2 - y^3}{x^2 - y^2}$ **E.** $\dfrac{x^6 - y^6}{x^3 y^2}$

B. $\dfrac{x^3 - x^2}{y^6}$ **D.** $\dfrac{x^5 - y^5}{x^3 y^2}$

41. $2(x+y) = ?$

A. $2xy$ **C.** $2 + x + 2y$ **E.** $2x^2 + 2y^2$

B. $2x + 2y$ **D.** $4x$

42. $a(b+c) = ?$

A. $ab+bc$ C. $2abc$ E. $ab+ac+bc$

B. $ab+ac$ D. ab^2+b^2c

43. $3(a+b+c+d) = ?$

A. $3abcd$

B. $3a+b+c+d$

C. $3a+3b+3c+3d$

D. $3ab+3bc+3cd$

E. $12a+12b+12c+12d$

44. $2x\left(3x+4x^2\right) = ?$

A. x^{10} C. $5x^2+6x^3$ E. $6\left(x^2+x^3\right)$

B. $6x+8x^2$ D. $6x^2+8x^3$

45. $3a^2(ab+ac+bc) = ?$

A. $3a^3b^2c$ D. $3a^3b+3a^3c+3a^2bc$

B. $3a^3+3b^3+3c$ E. $3a^5b+3a^5c$

C. $3a^2b+3a^2c+3a^2bc$

46. $(x+y)(x+y) = ?$

A. x^2+y^2 D. $x^2-2xy+y^2$

B. x^2-y^2 E. $x^2+2xy+y^2$

C. $x^2+2xy-y^2$

47. $(a+b)^2 = ?$

A. a^2+b^2 D. $a^2-2ab+b^2$

B. a^2-b^2 E. $a^2+2ab+b^2$

C. $a^2+2ab-b^2$

48. $(x-y)^2 = ?$

A. $x^2+2xy-y^2$ D. $x^2-2xy-y^2$

B. $x^2+2xy+y^2$ E. x^2+y^2

C. $x^2-2xy+y^2$

49. $(a+b)(a-b) = ?$

A. a^2-b^2 D. $a^2-2ab+b^2$

B. a^2+b^2 E. $a^2+2ab-b^2$

C. $a^2+2ab+b^2$

50. $(x-2)^2 = ?$

A. $2x$ C. x^2-4 E. x^2-4x-4

B. $4x$ D. x^2-4x+4

51. $(2-x)^2 = ?$

A. $4-x^2$ C. x^2+4x+4 E. x^2-4x-4

B. x^2+4 D. x^2-4x+4

52. $(ab+bc)(a+b) = ?$

A. $a^2b+ab^2+b^2c+abc$

B. a^2b+ab^2+abc

C. $a^2b+ab^2+a^2bc$

D. $a^2b+ab+bc+abc$

E. $a^2+b^2+c^2+abc$

53. $(x-y)(x+2) = ?$

A. $x^2+2xy+2y$ D. $x^2-xy+2x-2y$

B. $x^2+2xy+x+y$ E. $x^2+2x+2y-2$

C. $x^2+2xy+x-2y$

54. $(a+b)(c+d) = ?$

A. $ab+bc+cd$ D. $ac+ad+bc+bd$

B. $ab+bc+cd+ad$ E. $ab+ac+ad$

C. $ac+bd$

55. $(w+x)(y-z) = ?$

A. $wxy-z$ D. $wy+wz+xy-xz$

B. $wy+xy-yz$ E. $wy-wz+xy-xz$

C. $wy-wz+xy+xz$

56. $(x+y)(w+x+y) = ?$

A. $x^2+wx+wy+xy$

B. $x^2+y^2+wx+wy+2xy$

C. x^2+y^2+wxy

D. $x^2+y^2+wx^2y^2$

E. x^2y^2+wxy

57. $(2+x)(3+x+y) = ?$

A. $x^2+6xy+6$

B. $x^2+6xy+3x+2y+6$

C. $x^2+2xy+6x+6y+6$

D. $x^2+xy+5x+2y+6$

E. $x^2+3xy+2x+y+6$

58. $(x+y)^3 = ?$

A. $x^3 + 5x^2y + y^2z + xyz$

B. $x^3 + 3x^3y + 3xy^3 + y^3$

C. $x^3 + 3x^2y + 3xy^2 + y^3$

D. $x^3 + 6x^2y^2 + y^3$

E. $x^3 + 12x^2y^2 + y^3$

59. $(x-y)^3 = ?$

A. $x^3 - 3x^2y + 3xy^2 - y^3$

B. $x^3 + 3x^3y + 3xy^3 + y^3$

C. $x^3 + 3x^2y - 3xy^2 - y^3$

D. $x^3 + 6x^2y^2 + y^3$

E. $x^2 + 6x^2y^2 - y^3$

60. $(a+b)(a-b)(a+b)(a-b) = ?$

A. 1 **D.** $a^4 - 2a^2b^2 + b^4$

B. $a^2 - b^2$ **E.** $a^4 + 2a^2b^2 + b^4$

C. $a^2 + b^2$

61. $2a + 2b + 2c = ?$

A. $2(a+b+c)$ **D.** $6(a+b+c)$

B. $2(abc)$ **E.** $8(a+b+c)$

C. $2(ab+bc+ca)$

62. $x + x^2 + x^3 = ?$

A. $x(x+2x+3x)$ **D.** $x\left(1+x+x^2\right)$

B. $x(1+2x+3x)$ **E.** $x(1+3x)$

C. $x(1+2+3)$

63. $2x^2 + 4x^3 + 8x^4 = ?$

A. $2x^2\left(1+2x+4x^2\right)$ **D.** $2x^2\left(x+2x^2+4x^3\right)$

B. $2x^2\left(1+2x+4x^3\right)$ **E.** $2x^2\left(x^2+2x^3+4x^4\right)$

C. $2x^2\left(x+2x+4x^2\right)$

64. $abc + bcd + cde = ?$

A. $ab(c+d+e)$ **D.** $c(ab+bd+de)$

B. $ac(b+e)$ **E.** $d(a+b+c+e)$

C. $b(a+c+de)$

65. $x^2y^2 + x^2y + xy^2 = ?$

A. $(x+y)^2$ **D.** $xy(xy+x+y)$

B. $x^2 + y^2$ **E.** $xy(x+y+1)$

C. $x^2y^2(x+y)$

66. $p^2 + 2pq + q^2 = ?$

A. $(p+q)(p-q)$ **D.** $p^2 + q^2$

B. $(p+q)(p+q)$ **E.** $(p-q)^2$

C. $p^2 - q^2$

67. $144^2 - 121^2 = ?$

A. 23

B. $(144+121)(144-121)$

C. $(144+121)(144+121)$

D. 23^2

E. $(144+121)^2$

68. $x^2 - y^2 = ?$

A. $(x+y)(x-y)$ **D.** $x^2 + y^2$

B. $(x+y)(x+y)$ **E.** $2xy$

C. $(x-y)(x-y)$

69. $x^2 + 2x + 1 = ?$

A. $(x+1)(x-1)$ **D.** $x^2 - 1$

B. $(x+1)(x+1)$ **E.** $x^2 + 1$

C. $(x-1)(x-1)$

70. $x^2 - 1 = ?$

A. $(x+1)(x+1)$ **D.** $(x-1)^2$

B. $(x-1)(x-1)$ **E.** $(x+1)^2$

C. $(x+1)(x-1)$

71. $x^2 + 3x + 2 = ?$

A. $(x+1)(x-2)$ **D.** $(x-2)(x-1)$

B. $(x+2)(x+1)$ **E.** $(x+3)(x-1)$

C. $(x+2)(x-1)$

72. $a^2 - a - 2 = ?$

A. $(a+2)(a-1)$ **D.** $(a+2)(a-2)$

B. $(a-2)(a+1)$ **E.** $(a+1)(a-1)$

C. $(a+1)(a+2)$

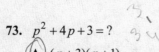

73. $p^2 + 4p + 3 = ?$

   A. $(p+3)(p+1)$　　**D.** $(p+3)(p+4)$
   B. $(p+3)(p-1)$　　**E.** $(p+3)(p-4)$
   C. $(p-3)(p-1)$

74. $c^2 + 6c + 8 = ?$

   A. $(c+2)(c+4)$　　**D.** $(c+3)(c+5)$
   B. $(c+2)(c-4)$　　**E.** $(c+8)(c-1)$
   C. $(c+4)(c-2)$

75. $x^2 + x - 20$

   A. $(x+5)(x-4)$　　**D.** $(x+10)(x-2)$
   B. $(x+4)(x-5)$　　**E.** $(x+20)(x-1)$
   C. $(x+2)(x-10)$

76. $p^2 + 5p + 6 = ?$

   A. $(p+1)(p+6)$　　**D.** $(p-3)(p-2)$
   B. $(p+6)(p-1)$　　**E.** $(p+5)(p+1)$
   C. $(p+2)(p+3)$

77. $x^2 + 8x + 16 = ?$

   A. $(x+2)(x+8)$　　**D.** $(x+4)(x-4)$
   B. $(x+2)(x-8)$　　**E.** $(x+4)(x+4)$
   C. $(x-4)(x-4)$

78. $x^2 - 5x - 6 = ?$

   A. $(x+1)(x+6)$　　**D.** $(x-6)(x+1)$
   B. $(x+6)(x-1)$　　**E.** $(x-2)(x-3)$
   C. $(x+2)(x+3)$

79. $a^2 - 3a + 2 = ?$

   A. $(a-2)(a-1)$　　**D.** $(a-3)(a+1)$
   B. $(a-2)(a+1)$　　**E.** $(a+3)(a+1)$
   C. $(a+1)(a-2)$

80. $x^2 + x - 12 = ?$

   A. $(x+6)(x+2)$　　**D.** $(x-4)(x-3)$
   B. $(x+6)(x-2)$　　**E.** $(x+12)(x+1)$
   C. $(x+4)(x-3)$

81. $x^2 - 8x + 16 = ?$

   A. $x+2$　　**C.** $(x+2)^2$　　**E.** $(x+4)^3$
   B. $x+4$　　**D.** $(x-4)^2$

82. What number must be added to $12x + x^2$ to make the resulting trinomial expression a perfect square?

   A. 4　　**C.** 25　　**E.** 49
   B. 16　　**D.** 36

83. What number must be added to $4x^2 - 12x$ to make the resulting trinomial expression a perfect square?

   A. 2　　**C.** 9　　**E.** 16
   B. 4　　**D.** 12

84. $x^2 - 8x + 15 = ?$

   A. $(x+5)(x+3)$　　**D.** $(x-5)(x-3)$
   B. $(x-5)(x+3)$　　**E.** $(x-15)(x-1)$
   C. $(x+5)(x-3)$

85. $2x^2 + 5x - 3 = ?$

   A. $(x-1)(x+3)$　　**D.** $(3x+1)(x+3)$
   B. $(2x-1)(x+3)$　　**E.** $(3x-1)(2x+3)$
   C. $(2x+1)(x-3)$

86. $21x + 10x^2 - 10 = ?$

   A. $(5x-2)(2x+5)$　　**D.** $(8x+2)(4x+5)$
   B. $(5x+2)(2x+5)$　　**E.** $(10x-4)(2x-5)$
   C. $(5x+2)(2x-5)$

87. $ax^2 + 3ax = ?$

   A. $3ax$　　**C.** $ax(x+3)$　　**E.** $ax^2(x+3)$
   B. $ax(x-3)$　　**D.** $ax^2(-3)$

88. $2x^2 - 8x + 3 - \left(x^2 - 3x + 9\right) = ?$

   A. $(x-6)(x-1)$　　**D.** $(2x-6)(x-1)$
   B. $(x-6)(x+1)$　　**E.** $(2x+6)(x-1)$
   C. $(x+6)(x+1)$

89. If $15x^2 + ax - 28 = (5x-4)(3x+7)$, then $a = ?$

   A. 7　　**C.** 23　　**E.** 33
   B. 14　　**D.** 28

   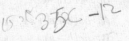

90. $x^2 - 9 = ?$

   A. $x^2 - 3$　　**D.** $(x+3)(x-3)$
   B. $(x-3)(x-3)$　　**E.** $x-3$
   C. $(x+3)(x+3)$

91. $x^2 - 9y^4 = ?$

   A. $\left(x + 3y^2\right)\left(x - 3y^2\right)$

   B. $\left(x - 3y^2\right)\left(x - 3y^2\right)$

   C. $\left(x + 3y^2\right)\left(x + 3y^2\right)$

   D. $\left(2x + 3y^2\right)\left(2x + 3y^2\right)$

   E. $\left(2x - 3y^2\right)\left(2x - 3y^2\right)$

92. $x^2 + 6x - 27 = ?$

   A. $(x-9)(x-9)$ **D.** $(x+9)(x+3)$

   B. $(x-9)(x-3)$ **E.** $(x+9)(x-3)$

   C. $(x-3)(x-3)$

93. $\dfrac{8x^{-4}}{2x^{1}} = ?$

   A. $\dfrac{2}{x^5}$ **C.** $\dfrac{3}{x^5}$ **E.** $\dfrac{8}{x^5}$

   B. $\dfrac{4}{x^4}$ **D.** $\dfrac{4}{x^5}$

94. $\dfrac{3^{-1}x^5 y^2}{2xy} = ?$

   A. $\dfrac{x^2 y}{6}$ **C.** $\dfrac{x^6 y^2}{8}$ **E.** $\dfrac{x^6 y^2}{10}$

   B. $\dfrac{x^4 y}{6}$ **D.** $\dfrac{x^6 y^4}{6}$

95. $\dfrac{6x^{-5}y^2}{3^{-1}x^{-4}y} = ?$

   A. $\dfrac{12y^4}{x^4}$ **C.** $\dfrac{16y^5}{x^4}$ **E.** $\dfrac{18y^5}{x^6}$

   B. $\dfrac{16y^4}{x^5}$ **D.** $\dfrac{18y}{x}$

96. $\dfrac{9^2 x^3 y}{3^{-1}x^{-4}y} = ?$

   A. $243x^7$ **C.** $248x^7$ **E.** $256x$

   B. $244x^3$ **D.** $252x^2$

97. If $x = -2$, $x^2 = ?$

   A. -4 **C.** 6   **E.** 10

   B. 4   **D.** 8

98. If $x = -3$ and $y = 5$, then $x^2 y = ?$

   A. -50 **C.** 45   **E.** 55

   B. -45 **D.** 50

99. If $x = -2$ and $y = -3$, then $x^2 - 4xy - x = ?$

   A. -24 **C.** -18 **E.** -14

   B. -20 **D.** -16

100. $(x - y)\left(x^2 - 2x + 5\right) = ?$

   A. $x^3 - 2x^2 + 5x - x^2 y + 2xy - 5y$

   B. $x^3 + 2x^2 + 5x - x^2 y + 2xy - 5y$

   C. $x^3 - 2x^2 - 5x - x^2 y + 2xy - 5y$

   D. $x^3 - 2x^2 + 5x + x^2 y + 2xy - 5y$

   E. $x^3 - 2x^2 + 5x - x^2 y - 2xy - 5y$

101. $\left(2x + \sqrt{3}\right)^2 = ?$

   A. $3x^2 + 3x\sqrt{3} + 3$ **D.** $-4x^2 + 4x\sqrt{3} + 3$

   B. $4x^2 - 4x\sqrt{3} + 3$ **E.** $4x^2 + 4x\sqrt{3} + 3$

   C. $4x^2 - 4x\sqrt{3} - 3$

102. If $x = -2$ and $y = 3$, then $2x^2 - xy = ?$

   A. 10   **C.** 14   **E.** 18

   B. 12   **D.** 16

103. $\left(\dfrac{x^2 y^3 x^5}{2^{-1}}\right)^2 = ?$

   A. $4x^{12}y^4$ **C.** $4x^{14}y^4$ **E.** $4x^{14}y^6$

   B. $4x^{12}y^{66}$ **D.** $4x^{12}y^6$

104. $\sqrt{x^2 + y^2} = ?$

   A. $x + y$

   B. $x - y$

   C. $x^2 + y^2$

   D. $x^{\frac{1}{2}} + y^{\frac{1}{2}}$

   E. None of the above.

105. $\sqrt{(x+y)^2} = ?$

  A. $\sqrt{x^2 + y^2}$

  B. $\sqrt{x^2 + 2xy + y^2}$

  C. $x^2 + y^2$

  D. $x^2 + 2xy + y^2$

  E. None of the above.

106. $\dfrac{x}{\sqrt{2x-y}} = ?$

  A. $x\sqrt{2x-y}$

  B. $x\sqrt{2x+y}$

  C. $\dfrac{x\sqrt{2x+y}}{2x-y}$

  D. $\dfrac{x\sqrt{2x+y}}{2x+y}$

  E. None of the above.

107. $\dfrac{6}{\sqrt{2a-3c}} = ?$

  A. $\dfrac{6\sqrt{2a-3c}}{2a-3c}$

  B. $\dfrac{6\sqrt{2a+3c}}{2a+3c}$

  C. $\dfrac{6\sqrt{2a+3c}}{2a-3c}$

  D. $\dfrac{6\sqrt{2a-3c}}{2a+3c}$

  E. None of the above.

108. $\dfrac{n}{6} + \dfrac{2n}{5} = ?$

  A. $\dfrac{13n}{30}$ C. $\dfrac{3n}{30}$ E. $\dfrac{3n}{11}$

  B. $17n$ D. $\dfrac{17n}{30}$

109. $1 - \dfrac{x}{y} = ?$

  A. $\dfrac{1-x}{y}$ C. $\dfrac{x-y}{y}$ E. $\dfrac{y-x}{xy}$

  B. $\dfrac{y-x}{y}$ D. $\dfrac{1-x}{1-y}$

110. $\dfrac{x-y}{x+y} \div \dfrac{y-x}{y+x} = ?$

  A. 1 C. $\dfrac{(x-y)^2}{(x+y)^2}$ E. 0

  B. -1 D. $-\dfrac{(x-y)^2}{(x-y)^2}$

111. $\dfrac{1 + \dfrac{1}{x}}{\dfrac{y}{x}} = ?$

  A. $\dfrac{x+1}{y}$ C. $\dfrac{x+1}{xy}$ E. $\dfrac{y+1}{y}$

  B. $\dfrac{x+1}{x}$ D. $\dfrac{x^2+1}{xy}$

112. $\left(\dfrac{2x^2}{y}\right)^3 = ?$

  A. $\dfrac{8x^5}{3y}$ C. $\dfrac{6x^5}{y^3}$ E. $\dfrac{8x^6}{y^3}$

  B. $\dfrac{6x^6}{y^3}$ D. $\dfrac{8x^5}{y^3}$

113. $\dfrac{\dfrac{1}{x} + \dfrac{1}{y}}{3} = ?$

  A. $\dfrac{3x+3y}{xy}$ C. $\dfrac{xy}{3}$ E. $\dfrac{y+x}{3}$

  B. $\dfrac{3xy}{x+7}$ D. $\dfrac{y+x}{3xy}$

114. If $b \geq 0$, then $\dfrac{\sqrt{32b^3}}{\sqrt{8b}} = ?$

  A. $2\sqrt{b}$ C. $2b$ E. $b\sqrt{2b}$

  B. $\sqrt{2b}$ D. $\sqrt{2b^2}$

115. If $x \geq 0$, then $\sqrt{\dfrac{x^2}{9} + \dfrac{x^2}{16}} = ?$

  A. $\dfrac{25x^2}{144}$ C. $\dfrac{5x^2}{12}$ E. $\dfrac{7x}{12}$

  B. $\dfrac{5x}{12}$ D. $\dfrac{x}{7}$

116. $\sqrt{36y^2 + 64x^2} = ?$

 A. $6y + 8x$

 B. $10xy$

 C. $10x^2y^2$

 D. $10x^2y^2$

 E. None of these

117. If $x \geq 0$, then $\sqrt{\dfrac{x^2}{64} - \dfrac{x^2}{100}} = ?$

 A. $\dfrac{x}{40}$ C. $\dfrac{x}{2}$ E. $\dfrac{3x}{80}$

 B. $-\dfrac{x}{2}$ D. $\dfrac{3x}{40}$

118. If $y \geq 0$, then $\sqrt{\dfrac{y^2}{2} - \dfrac{y^2}{18}} = ?$

 A. $\dfrac{2y}{3}$ D. $\dfrac{y\sqrt{3}}{6}$

 B. $\dfrac{y\sqrt{5}}{5}$ E. None of these

 C. $\dfrac{10y}{3}$

119. $\sqrt{a^2 + b^2} = ?$

 A. $a + b$ D. $(a+b)(a-b)$

 B. $a - b$ E. None of these

 C. $\sqrt{a^2} + \sqrt{b^2}$

120. Given every pair (x, y) of negative numbers and

 resulting value $\dfrac{x}{|x|} + \dfrac{xy}{|xy|}$, what is the set of all

 numbers formed?

 A. $\{0\}$ C. $\{2\}$ E. $\{0, 2\}$

 B. $\{-2\}$ D. $\{0, -2\}$

121. When factored as completely as possible with

 respect to the integers, $16x^4 - 81y^{16} = ?$

 A. $\left(4x^2 + 9y^4\right)\left(4x^2 - 9y^4\right)$

 B. $\left(4x^2 + 9y^8\right)\left(4x^2 - 9y^8\right)$

 C. $\left(4x^2 + 9y^4\right)(2x + 3y)(2x - 3y)$

 D. $\left(4x^2 + 9y^8\right)\left(2x + 3y^4\right)\left(2x - 3y^4\right)$

 E. $16x^4 - 81y^{16}$

Algebraic Equations and Inequalities

Pursuing the analogy between English and algebra as a language, the algebraic analogue of a complete sentence in English (with subject and verb) is an equation. An *algebraic equation* is a statement that two algebraic expressions are equivalent.

Examples:

English	*Algebra*
Ed is three years older than Paul..	$E = P + 3$
Paul is twice as old as Mary	$P = 2M$
Ned has \$2 more than Ed...	$N = E + \$2$
Bill has three times as much money as does Ted............................	$B = 3T$

Solving Algebraic Formulas

An *algebraic formula* is an equation that typically involves a relationship between literal quantities. Problems that involve formulas often ask you to solve for a particular unknown (variable) using substitution. Algebraic formulas can take many different forms, including functions, scientific equations, geometric formulas, and story problems. Regardless of the format, the concept is the same: replace the variables with the values that are given and solve for the unknown variable.

Examples:

1. For all real numbers x and y, $x \oplus y = 2x + y^2$. What is the value of $3 \oplus 7$?

    ➤ Substitute 3 for x and 7 for y in the given expression: $x \oplus y = 2x + y^2 \Rightarrow 3 \oplus 7 = 2(3) + (7)^2 = 6 + 49 = 55$.

2. The formula that relates Fahrenheit temperature to Celsius temperature is: $F = 1.8C + 32$, where F is Fahrenheit degrees (°F) and C is Celsius degrees (°C). What is the temperature, in Fahrenheit degrees, if the temperature is 25°C?

    ➤ Substitute 25 for C in the given equation and solve for F: $F = 1.8C + 32 = 1.8(25) + 32 = 45 + 32 = 77°F$.

3. The volume of a sphere is: $V = \dfrac{4\pi r^3}{3}$, where r is the radius of the sphere. Find the volume of a sphere with a radius of 6.

    ➤ Substitute 6 for r in the given formula and solve for V: $V = \dfrac{4\pi r^3}{3} = \dfrac{4\pi(6)^3}{3} = 4\pi \cdot 72 = 288\pi$.

4. If a person must pick one object from a group of x objects and then one object from a group of y objects, the number of possible combinations is xy. Jan must select 1 candy bar from 7 different candy bars and 1 pack of gum from 3 different packs of gum. What is the maximum number of combinations available to Jan?

    ➤ Substitute 7 for x and 3 for y in the given expression: number of combinations $= xy = (7)(3) = 21$.

Formulas that represent real life situations often involve variables with units of measure, such as inches or gallons. You must ensure that all variables have similar units on both sides of the equation in order for the equality to remain true. To maintain consistency, it may be necessary to convert units using equivalent expressions (e.g., 12 inches/foot, 1 foot/12 inches, 60 minutes/hour, 1 hour/60 minutes). Thus, when dealing with quantities given in units of any type, it helps to explicitly write out the units in the expressions.

Example:

If string costs k cents per foot at the hardware store, how much will w feet and j inches of the string cost, in dollars?

➤ Explicitly write out the units in the expression and cancel like units in the numerator and denominator:

$$\text{Cost of string (dollars)} = \frac{k \text{ cents}}{1 \text{ ft. of string}} \cdot \text{length of string (ft.)} \cdot \frac{1 \text{ dollar}}{100 \text{ cents}}$$

$$= \frac{k \text{ cents}}{1 \text{ ft.}} \cdot \left[w \text{ ft.} + \left(j \text{ in.} \cdot \frac{1 \text{ ft.}}{12 \text{ in.}} \right) \right] \cdot \frac{1 \text{ dollar}}{100 \text{ cents}}$$

$$= \frac{k \text{ cents}}{1 \text{ ft.}} \cdot \left[w \text{ ft.} + \left(j \text{ in.} \cdot \frac{1 \text{ ft.}}{12 \text{ in.}} \right) \right] \cdot \frac{1 \text{ dollar}}{100 \text{ cents}}$$

$$= \frac{k \text{ cents}}{1 \text{ ft.}} \cdot \left(w + \frac{j}{12} \right)(\text{ft.}) \cdot \frac{1 \text{ dollar}}{100 \text{ cents}}$$

$$= k \text{ cents} \cdot \left(w + \frac{j}{12} \right) \cdot \frac{1 \text{ dollar}}{100 \text{ cents}}$$

$$= \frac{k}{100} \left(w + \frac{j}{12} \right)$$

Therefore, the cost of the string, in dollars, is: $\frac{k}{100} \left(w + \frac{j}{12} \right)$.

Basic Principle of Equations

The fundamental rule for working with any equation is: Whatever you do to one side of an equation, you must do exactly the same thing to the other side of the equation. This rule implies that you can add, subtract, multiply, and divide both sides of the equality by any value without changing the statement of equality. The only exception is that you cannot divide by zero. The following example illustrates the validity of this principle using an equation containing only real numbers.

Example:

$5 = 5$

➤ This is obviously a true statement. You can add any value to both sides of the equation, say 10, and the statement will remain true. Add 10: $5 + 10 = 5 + 10 \Rightarrow 15 = 15$. You can also subtract the same value from both sides, e.g., 7: $15 - 7 = 15 - 7 \Rightarrow 8 = 8$. You can multiply both sides by the same value, e.g., –2: $8 \cdot -2 = 8 \cdot -2 \Rightarrow -16 = -16$. Finally, you can divide both sides by the same value (except zero); e.g., –4: $-16 \div -4 = -16 \div -4 \Rightarrow 4 = 4$.

This principle for manipulating equations applies to algebraic equations with variables, as the following example illustrates.

Example:

$5 + x = 5 + x$

➤ Add x: $5 + x + x = 5 + x + x \Rightarrow 5 + 2x = 5 + 2x$. Whatever x is, since it appears on both sides of the equation, both sides of the equation must still be equal. Now, subtract a value, e.g., y: $5 + 2x - y = 5 + 2x - y$. Again, since y appears on both sides of the equation, the statement that the two expressions are equal remains true.

DO NOT multiply both sides of an equation by zero if the equation contains a variable. You may lose special characteristics of the variable. For example, the equation $2x = 8$ is true only if $x = 4$. However, the equation $0(2x) = 0(8)$ is true for any value of x.

Solving Linear Equations

Equations that have only variables of the first power are called equations of the first degree or **linear equations**. While a linear equation can have any number of different variables, equations with one or two variables are most common on the exam.

The fundamental rule of equations is the key to solving linear equations. To solve for an unknown variable, identically manipulate both sides of the equation to isolate the variable on one side. Be sure to reduce the other side of the equation by combining similar terms.

*Example*s:

1. If $2x + 3 = x + 1$, then what is the value of x?

   ➤ To solve for x, manipulate the equation to isolate x. Subtract x from both sides: $2x + 3 - x = x + 1 - x \Rightarrow x + 3 = 1$. Next, subtract 3 from both sides: $x + 3 - 3 = 1 - 3 \Rightarrow x = -2$.

2. If $4x + 2 = 2x + 10$, then what is the value of x?

   ➤ Subtract $2x$ from both sides of the equation: $4x + 2 - 2x = 2x + 10 - 2x \Rightarrow 2x + 2 = 10$. Then, subtract 2 from both sides: $2x + 2 - 2 = 10 - 2 \Rightarrow 2x = 8$. Divide both sides by 2: $2x \div 2 = 8 \div 2 \Rightarrow x = 4$.

3. If $3y - 2x = 12$, then what is the value of y?

   ➤ Add $2x$ to both sides of the equation: $3y - 2x + 2x = 12 + 2x \Rightarrow 3y = 12 + 2x$. Divide both sides by 3: $y = \dfrac{2x}{3} + 4$.

So far, we have been very formal in following the fundamental rule for working with equations. The process is simplified using a shortcut called ***transposition***. Transposing is the process of moving a term or a factor from one side of the equation to the other by changing it into its mirror image. Perform these "inverse operations" until the variable is isolated. Note that this shortcut does not change the fundamental rule or its outcome: it simply bypasses the formal steps.

To transpose a term that is added or subtracted, move it to the other side of the equation and change its sign. Thus, a term with a positive sign on one side is moved to the other side and becomes negative, and vice versa. It is imperative when using transposition that you do not forget to change signs when terms change sides.

*Example*s:

1. $x + 5 = 10$

   ➤ Rather than going through the formal steps of subtracting 5 from both sides of the equality, simply transpose the 5: move it from the left side to the right side and change its sign from "+" to "−": $x = 10 - 5 \Rightarrow x = 5$.

2. $x - 5 = 10 \Rightarrow x = 10 + 5 \Rightarrow x = 15$

3. $3x = 5 + 2x \Rightarrow 3x - 2x = 5 \Rightarrow x = 5$

To transpose a multiplicative factor, move the factor to the opposite side of the equation and invert it; that is, replace it with its reciprocal.

Example:

$$\frac{2x + 5}{3} = 9$$

➤ $2x$ and 5 are both divided by 3; in other words, they are both multiplied by $\frac{1}{3}$. Therefore, the $\frac{1}{3}$ must be transposed first. Move it to the opposite side of the equation and invert it: $2x + 5 = 9(3) = 27$. Now the 5 can be transposed: $2x = 27 - 5 = 22$. Finally, solve for x by transposing the 2: $x = 22 \cdot \frac{1}{2} = 11$.

Solving Simultaneous Equations

Ordinarily, if an equation has more than one variable, it is not possible to determine the unique numeric solution for any individual variable. For example, the equation $x + y = 10$ does not have one unique solution set for x and y: x and y could be 1 and 9, 5 and 5, −2 and 12, and so on. However, if there are as many equations as there are variables, the equations can be manipulated as a system to determine the value of each variable. This technique is called *solving simultaneous equations* because the equations are taken to be true at the same time, or simultaneously, in order to determine the variable value. On the exam, simultaneous equations are typically limited to two equations and two unknowns.

Example:

Given $x + y = 10$ and $x - y = 6$, solve for x and y.

➤ If we treat both of the equations as making true statements at the same time, then there is only one solution set for x and y, for there is only one pair of numbers that will satisfy both equations, $x = 8$ and $y = 2$.

It is easy to see the answer to the previous example, but solutions will not always be this obvious. How do you find the specific solution for a given set of equations? There are two methods for solving simultaneous equations: substitution and linear combination (elimination).

Substitution

The steps for *substitution* are as follows:

Step 1: Pick one of the two given equations and define one variable in terms of the other.
Step 2: Substitute the defined variable into the other equation and solve.
Step 3: Substitute the solution back into either equation and solve for the remaining variable.

Examples:

1. If $2x + y = 13$ and $x - y = 2$, what are the values of x and y?

   ➤ Redefine one variable in terms of the other. Since y is already a single variable in both equations, define y in terms of x: $y = 13 - 2x$. Substitute $13 - 2x$ for y in the second equation and solve for x: $x - (13 - 2x) = 2 \Rightarrow x - 13 + 2x = 2 \Rightarrow 3x = 15 \Rightarrow x = 5$. Finally, solve for y by substituting 5 for x in either equation: $2x + y = 13 \Rightarrow 2(5) + y = 13 \Rightarrow y = 3$.

2. If $3x + 2y = 16$ and $2x - y = 6$, what are the values of x and y?

   ➤ Since y is a simple term in the second equation, define y in terms of x: $2x - y = 6 \Rightarrow y = 2x - 6$. Substitute this expression for y in the first equation and solve for x: $3x + 2(2x - 6) = 16 \Rightarrow 3x + 4x - 12 = 16 \Rightarrow 7x = 28 \Rightarrow x = 4$. Finally, solve for y by substituting 4 for x in either equation: $2x - y = 6 \Rightarrow 2(4) - y = 6 \Rightarrow y = 2$.

3. If $y = 7 + x$ and $3x + 2y = 4$, what are the values of x and y?

   ➤ Substitute $7 + x$ for y in the second equation and solve for x: $3x + 2y = 4 \Rightarrow 3x + 2(7 + x) = 4 \Rightarrow 3x + 14 + 2x = 4 \Rightarrow 5x = -10 \Rightarrow x = -2$. Substitute -2 for x in the first equation and solve for y: $y = 7 + x = 7 - 2 = 5$.

Linear Combination (Elimination)

The second method for solving simultaneous equations is *linear combination* or *elimination*. Eliminate one of the two variables by adding or subtracting the two equations. If necessary, division of one equation by another may eliminate one of two variables.

Examples:

1. If $2x + y = 8$ and $x - y = 1$, what are the values of x and y?

   ➤ In this pair of simultaneous equations, there is a "$+y$" term in one equation and a "$-y$" term in the other. Since $+y$ and $-y$ added together yields zero, eliminate the y term by adding the two equations together. (Actually, you will be adding the left side of the second equation to the left side of the first equation and the right side of the second to the right side of the first, but it is easier to speak of the process as "adding equations.") $[2x + y = 8] + [(x - y = 1)] = [3x = 9] \Rightarrow x = 3$. Find the value of y by substituting 3 for x in either equation: $2x + y = 8 \Rightarrow 2(3) + y = 8 \Rightarrow y = 8 - 6 = 2$.

2. If $4x + 3y = 17$ and $2x + 3y = 13$, what are the values of x and y?

   ➤ In this pair, each equation has a $+3y$ term, which you can eliminate by subtracting the second equation from the first. $[4x + 3y = 17] - [2x + 3y = 13] = [2x = 4] \Rightarrow x = 2$. Solve for y by substituting 2 for x in either equation: $4x + 3y = 17 \Rightarrow 4(2) + 3y = 17 \Rightarrow 8 + 3y = 17 \Rightarrow 3y = 9 \Rightarrow y = 3$.

3. $x^5 = 6y$ and $x^4 = 2y$; x is a real number such that $x \neq 0$ and y is a real number. Solve for x.

   ➤ The system of equations is reduced to one equation and one variable by dividing the first equation by the second equation: $\dfrac{x^5}{x^4} = \dfrac{6y}{2y} \Rightarrow x = 3$.

If a system of equations has more variables than equations, then not every variable value can be determined. Instead, you will be asked to solve for one or more variables in terms of another variable.

Examples:

1. If $y = 2a$ and $3x + 8y = 28a$, find x in terms of a.

   ➢ Substitute $2a$ for y and solve for x: $3x + 8(2a) = 28a \Rightarrow 3x = 28a - 16a \Rightarrow 3x = 12a \Rightarrow x = \dfrac{12a}{3} = 4a$.

2. In terms of a, solve the following pair of equations for x and y: $3x - 4y = 10a$ and $5x + 2y = 8a$.

   ➢ First, solve for either x or y in terms of a alone. To solve for x, multiply the second equation by 2 and add the result to the first equation. $[2(5x + 2y = 8a)] + [3x - 4y = 10a] = [10x + 4y = 16a] + [3x - 4y = 10a] = 13x = 26a \Rightarrow x = 2a$. To find y in terms of a, substitute $2a$ for x in either equation: $5x + 2y = 8a \Rightarrow y = \dfrac{8a - 5(2a)}{2} \Rightarrow y = \dfrac{-2a}{2} = -a$.

Solving Quadratic Equations

Equations that involve variables of the second power (e.g., x^2) are called **quadratic equations**. Unlike a linear equation with a single variable, which has a single solution, a quadratic may have two solutions. By convention, quadratic equations are written so that the right side of the equation is equal to zero. The general form is: $ax^2 + bx + c = 0$.

Example:

Solve for x: $x^2 + x - 2 = 0$.

➢ To solve the quadratic equation, factor the left side of the equation: $x^2 + x - 2 = 0 \Rightarrow (x + 2)(x - 1) = 0$. For the equality to hold true, $x + 2$ or $x - 1$ must equal zero. Therefore, $x = -2$ or 1, so this quadratic equation has two solutions.

This last example illustrates the **zero product property**: if $xy = 0$, then $x = 0$ or $y = 0$.

Example:

$x^2 - 3x - 4 = 0$

➢ Factor the left side of the equation: $(x + 1)(x - 4) = 0$. Either $x + 1 = 0$, in which case $x = -1$, or $x - 4 = 0$, in which case $x = 4$. Therefore, the solution set for this quadratic equation is $\{-1, 4\}$.

However, not every quadratic equation has two different solutions.

Example:

$x^2 + 2x + 1 = 0$

➢ Factor the left side of the equation: $(x + 1)(x + 1) = 0$. Since the two factors are the same, the equation has one solution: -1.

For quadratic equations not in standard form, you must first group like terms and rearrange the equation into standard form.

*Example*s:

1. Solve for x: $2x^2 + 12 - 3x = x^2 + 2x + 18$.

    ➢ Rewrite the equation by grouping like terms and simplifying:

    $$2x^2 + 12 - 3x = x^2 + 2x + 18$$
    $$\left(2x^2 - x^2\right) + (-3x - 2x) + (12 - 18) = 0$$
    $$x^2 - 5x - 6 = 0$$
    $$(x - 6)(x + 1) = 0$$

    Either $x - 6 = 0$ or $x + 1 = 0$. Therefore the set of all possible values for x is $\{-1, 6\}$.

2. Solve for x: $x(8 + x) = 2x + 36 + 6x$.

    ➢ Rewrite the equation by grouping like terms and simplifying:

    $$x(8 + x) = 2x + 36 + 6x$$
    $$8x + x^2 = 8x + 36$$
    $$x^2 = 36$$

    Since squaring a negative number yields a positive and squaring a positive number yields a positive, $x = \pm 6$.

Some higher degree equations can also be solved if they can be written in quadratic form.

Example:

Solve for x: $x^4 - 13x^2 + 36 = 0$.

➢ Factor: $\left(x^2 - 9\right)\left(x^2 - 4\right) = 0$. Factor again: $(x + 3)(x - 3)(x + 2)(x - 2) = 0$. To find the four possible values of x, set each factor equal to zero and solve each for x: $x + 3 = 0 \Rightarrow x = -3$; $x - 3 = 0 \Rightarrow x = 3$; $x + 2 = 0 \Rightarrow x = -2$; and $x - 2 = 0 \Rightarrow x = 2$. Therefore, the solution set is: $\{-3, 3, -2, 2\}$.

Alternatively, you can use the quadratic formula, $x = \dfrac{-b \pm \sqrt{b^2 - 4ac}}{2a}$, to solve quadratic equations.

Example:

Solve for x: $3 - x = 2x^2$.

➢ $3 - x = 2x^2 \Rightarrow 2x^2 + x - 3 = 0$. $a = 2, b = 1, c = -3$. Substitute these values into the quadratic formula and solve for x: $x = \dfrac{-b \pm \sqrt{b^2 - 4ac}}{2a} = \dfrac{-1 \pm \sqrt{1^2 - 4(2)(-3)}}{2(2)} = \dfrac{-1 \pm \sqrt{1 + 24}}{4} = \dfrac{-1 \pm 5}{4}$. So, $x = \left\{1, -\dfrac{3}{2}\right\}$.

Solving Equations by Factoring

Factoring is an alternative short-cut method for solving some equations. Before factoring, rewrite the equation with all of the terms on one side of the equation and 0 on the other side. If the nonzero side of the equation can be factored into a product of expressions, then use the following property to yield simpler equations that can be solved: if $xy = 0$, then $x = 0$ or $y = 0$. The solutions of the simpler equations will be solutions of the factored equation. The solutions of an equation are also called the **roots** of the equation.

*Example*s:

1. $\dfrac{\left(4x^2 - 1\right)(x + 2)}{x + 4} = 0$

   ➢ Either $4x^2 - 1 = 0$ or $x + 2 = 0$. In each instance, solve for *x*:

   $4x^2 - 1 = 0$

   $x^2 = \dfrac{1}{4}$

   $x = \pm\dfrac{1}{2}$

   $x + 2 = 0$

   $x = -2$

   Therefore, the set of all possible values for *x* is $\left\{-2, -\dfrac{1}{2}, \dfrac{1}{2}\right\}$.

2. Solve for *x*: $x^3 + 2x^2 + x = 3(x+1)^2$.

   ➢ Move all the terms to one side of the equality and simplify by factoring like terms:

   $x^3 + 2x^2 + x - 3(x+1)^2 = 0$

   $x\left(x^2 + 2x + 1\right) - 3(x+1)^2 = 0$

   $x(x+1)^2 - 3(x+1)^2 = 0$

   $(x - 3)(x+1)^2 = 0$

   $x - 3 = 0$ or $x + 1 = 0$

   $x = \{-1, 3\}$

Algebraic Inequalities

An **inequality** is very much like an equation except, as the name implies, it is a statement that two quantities are not equal. Four different symbols are used to make statements of inequality:

- $>$ greater than
- $<$ less than
- $\geq$ greater than or equal to
- $\leq$ less than or equal to

*Example*s:

$5 > 1$ ....5 is greater than 1.
$2 > -2$ ....2 is greater than -2.
$x > 0$ ....x is greater than zero.
$x > y$ ....x is greater than y.
$8 < 9$ ....8 is less than 9.
$-4 < -1$ .....-4 is less than -1.
$x < 0$ ....x is less than zero.
$y < x$ ....y is less than x.
$x \geq 0$ ....x is greater than or equal to zero. (x could be zero or any number larger than zero.)
$x \geq y$ ....x is greater than or equal to y. (Either x is greater than y, or x and y are equal.)
$x \leq 0$ ....x is less than or equal to zero. (x could be zero or any number less than zero.)
$x \leq y$ ....x is less than or equal to y. (Either x is less than y, or x and y are equal.)

The fundamental rule for working with inequalities is similar to that for working with equalities: Treat each side of the inequality exactly the same. You can add or subtract the same value to each side of an inequality without changing the inequality, and you can multiply or divide each side of an inequality by any *positive* value without changing the inequality.

Example:

$$5 > 2$$
Add 25 to both sides. $5 + 25 > 2 + 25$
$$30 > 27$$
Subtract 6 from both sides. $30 - 6 > 27 - 6$
$$24 > 21$$
Multiply both sides by 2. $24 \cdot 2 > 21 \cdot 2$
$$48 > 42$$
Divide both sides by 6. $48 \div 6 > 42 \div 6$
$$8 > 7$$

However, if you multiply or divide an inequality by a *negative* number, the direction of the inequality is reversed. Therefore, remember to change the direction of the inequality when multiplying or dividing by a negative number.

Example:

$$4 > 3$$
Multiply both sides by -2. $4(-2) < 3(-2)$
$$-8 < -6$$

These properties hold true for inequalities containing variables, as the following two examples illustrate.

*Example*s:

1. For what values of x is $3(2-x) + 7x > 30$?

    ➤ Solve for x:

$$3(2-x)+7x>30$$
$$6-3x+7x>30$$
$$6+4x>30$$
$$4x>24$$
$$x>6$$

2. For what values of x is $3(2-x)+x>30$?

> Solve for x:

$$3(2-x)+x>30$$
$$6-3x+x>30$$
$$6-2x>30$$
$$-2x>24$$
$$x<-12$$

Exponents in Equations and Inequalities

Integer and Rational Exponents

Algebraic equations and inequalities can include terms with integer and rational exponents. The rules of exponents apply when manipulating these terms.

*Example*s:

1. If $x=2$, then what is the value of $\left(x^{-2x}\right)^{x^{-x}}$?

> Substitute $x=2$ into the given expression: $\left(x^{-2x}\right)^{x^{-x}}=\left[(2)^{-2(2)}\right]^{2^{-2}}=\left[(2)^{-4}\right]^{\left(\frac{1}{2}\right)^{2}}=2^{(-4)\left(\frac{1}{4}\right)}=2^{-1}=\frac{1}{2}$.

2. Find the value of $2x^0+x^{\frac{2}{3}}+x^{-\frac{2}{3}}$ when $x=27$.

> Substitute $x=27$: $2x^0+x^{\frac{2}{3}}+x^{-\frac{2}{3}}=2(27)^0+(27)^{\frac{2}{3}}+(27)^{-\frac{2}{3}}=2(1)+\left(\sqrt[3]{27}\right)^2+\dfrac{1}{27^{\frac{2}{3}}}=2+9+\frac{1}{9}=11\frac{1}{9}$.

Algebraic Exponentials

When solving equations that involve algebraic exponential terms, try to find a common base to use throughout the problem.

Example:

Solve for x: $4^{x+2}=8^{3x-6}$

> Since $4=2^2$ and $8=2^3$, the common base in this item is 2. Thus:

$$4^{x+2} = 8^{3x-6}$$

$$\left(2^2\right)^{x+2} = \left(2^3\right)^{3x-6}$$

$$2^{2x+4} = 2^{9x-18}$$

Now, drop the common base and solve for x:

$$2x + 4 = 9x - 18$$

$$22 = 7x$$

$$x = \frac{22}{7}$$

Exponential Growth

Items that involve exponential growth test knowledge of exponential growth sequences, also called geometric sequences. In a geometric sequence, the **ratio**, r, of any term to its preceding term is constant. If the terms of a geometric sequence are designated by a_1, a_2, a_3, ..., a_n, then $\boldsymbol{a_n = a_1 r^{n-1}}$. Sequences that involve exponential growth have real-life applications, such as determining population growth over a specific period.

*Example*s:

1. Find the 5th term of the geometric sequence $\{4, 12, 36, ...\}$.

   ➤ In this geometric sequence, the ratio between the terms is $\frac{12}{4} = 3$. The 5th term is: $a_n = a_1 r^{n-1} \Rightarrow a_5 = 4(3)^{5-1} = 4(3)^4 = 4 \cdot 81 = 324$.

2. On June 1, 1990, the population of Grouenphast was 50,250. If the population is increasing at an annual rate of 8.4%, what is the approximate population of Grouenphast on June 1, 2010?

   ➤ An annual increase of 8.4% means that each year the population will be 108.4% of the previous year's population. Thus, the ratio between terms, r, is 1.084. The population on June 1, 1990 is the starting term: $a_1 = 50,250$. Since June 1, 2010 is 20 years later, the population at that time is the 21st term in the sequence: $n = 21$. So the population on June 1, 2010 is: $a_n = a_1 r^{n-1} \Rightarrow a_{21} = 50,250(1.084)^{20} \approx 252,186$.

The previous example involving growth over time suggests an alternate form of the geometric sequence equation called the **exponential growth equation**: $a_t = a_0 r^{\frac{t}{T}}$. In this equation, a_t is the amount after time t; a_0 is the initial amount ($t = 0$), r is the proportionality constant, t is the total period of growth, and T is the time per cycle of growth. Note that this equation also applies to exponential decay, where the initial amount is larger than the amount after time t.

Example:

The number of rabbits in a certain population doubles every 3 months. Currently, there are 5 rabbits in the population. How many rabbits will there be 3 years from now?

➤ In this case, the total time of growth is 3 years. Since the population doubles every 3 months, the time per cycle of growth is one-fourth of a year. Using the formula for exponential growth: $a_t = a_0 r^{\frac{t}{T}} \Rightarrow a_3 = (5)(2)^{\frac{3}{0.25}} = (5)(2)^{12} = 20,450$. We can verify this solution by working out the values, allowing the population to double every 3 months.

Period (months)	0	3	6	9	12	15	18	21	24	27	30	33	36
Population Size	5	10	20	40	80	160	320	640	1,280	2,560	5,120	10,240	20,480

Properties of Functions

A function is a set of ordered pairs (x, y) such that for each value of x, there is exactly one value of y. By convention, we say that "y is a function of x," which is written as: $y = f(x)$ or $y = g(x)$, etc. The set of x-values for which the set is defined is called the **domain** of the function. The set of corresponding values of y is called the **range** of the function.

Example:

What are the domain and range of the function $y = |x|$?

➤ The function is defined for all real values of x. Hence the domain is the set of all real numbers. Since $y = |x|$ can only be a positive number or zero, the range of the function is given by the set of all real numbers equal to or greater than zero.

When we speak of $f(a)$, we mean the value of $y = f(x)$ when $x = a$ is substituted in the expression for $f(x)$. If $z = f(y)$ and $y = g(x)$, we say that $z = f[g(x)]$. Thus, z is in turn a function of x.

This function notation is a short way of writing the result of substituting a value for a variable. Once a function $f(x)$ is defined, think of the variable x as an input and $f(x)$ as the corresponding output. In any function, there can be no more than one output for a given input. Note, however, that there may be more than one input that returns the same output.

*Example*s:

1. If $f(x) = 2x^x - 3x$, find the value of $f(3)$.

   ➤ Substitute 3 for x in the given expression: $f(x) = 2x^x - 3x \Rightarrow f(3) = 2(3)^3 - 3(3) = 2(27) - 9 = 54 - 9 = 45$.

2. If $f(x) = 2x - 9^{\frac{1}{x}}$, what is $f(-2)$?

   ➤ $f(-2) = 2(-2) - 9^{-\frac{1}{2}} = -4 - \frac{1}{\sqrt{9}} = -4 - \frac{1}{3} = -\frac{13}{3}$.

3. If $z = f(y) = 3y + 2$ and $y = g(x) = x + 2$, then $z = ?$

   ➤ $z = f[g(x)] = 3[g(x)] + 2 = 3(x + 2) + 2 = 3x + 6 + 2 = 3x + 8$.

In the previous chapter we introduced geometric sequences as an example of working with exponents. Note that a geometric sequence ($a_n = a_1 r^{n-1}$) is actually a function. In general, a **sequence**, a_n, is any function $a(n)$ with a domain consisting of only the positive integers and possibly zero; that is, $n = 0, 1, 2, 3, \ldots$, or $n = 1, 2, 3, \ldots$. Note that a sequence is often written by listing its values in the order $a_1, a_2, a_3, \ldots, a_n, \ldots$. For example, $a_n = (-1)^n (n!)$ for $n = 1, 2, 3, \ldots$, is written as $-1, 2, -6, \ldots, (-1)^n (n!), \ldots$.

Example:

1. What is the fifth term of the sequence defined by $a_n = 3n^2 + 2$ for $n = 1, 2, 3, \ldots$?

   ➤ The fifth term of the sequence is for $n = 5$. Substitute 5 for n in the function $3n^2 + 2$: $3(5)^2 + 2 = 77$.

2. Find the fourth term of the sequence with values $-1, 2, -6, \ldots, (-1)^n(n!), \ldots$.

   ➤ The values of n for any sequence are consecutive integers, so determine the value of n for the fourth term of the sequence by finding the first n value. Test $n = 1$: $(-1)^1(1) = -1$. Therefore, the fourth value of n must be 4: $(-1)^4(4!) = 4 \cdot 3 \cdot 2 \cdot 1 = 24$.

Rational Equations and Inequalities

Algebraic equations and inequalities may include rational (fractional) expressions. When manipulating rational expressions, follow the same rules as discussed with equations, inequalities, and algebraic fractions.

Examples:

1. If $\dfrac{x}{x+6} = \dfrac{y^3 - 1}{(y+1)(y^2 - y + 1) + 4}$, then $x = ?$

   ➤ $\dfrac{x}{x+6} = \dfrac{y^3 - 1}{y^3 - y^2 + y + y^2 - y + 1 + 4} = \dfrac{y^3 - 1}{y^3 + 5} = \dfrac{y^3 - 1}{y^3 - 1 + 6} = \dfrac{y^3 - 1}{(y^3 - 1) + 6}$. Therefore, $x = y^3 - 1$.

2. Let x represent a positive whole number. Given the two inequalities, $\dfrac{1}{x} > \dfrac{1}{4}$ and $\dfrac{x-3}{x^2 - 3x} > \dfrac{1}{7}$, how many more values for x satisfy the second equality than satisfy the first inequality?

   ➤ For the first inequality: $\dfrac{1}{x} > \dfrac{1}{4} \Rightarrow x < 4$. Thus, the set of satisfying values for x is $\{1, 2, 3\}$. For the second inequality, $\dfrac{x-3}{x^2 - 3x} > \dfrac{1}{7} \Rightarrow \dfrac{x-3}{x(x-3)} > \dfrac{1}{7}$. Since it is not possible to divide by zero, $x \neq 3$. Reduce the equation: $\dfrac{x-3}{x(x-3)} > \dfrac{1}{7} \Rightarrow \dfrac{1}{x} > \dfrac{1}{7} \Rightarrow 7 > x$. Since $x < 7$ and $x \neq 3$, the set of satisfying values for the second inequality is $\{1, 2, 4, 5, 6\}$. Thus, two more whole numbers satisfy the second inequality than the first.

Radical Equations and Inequalities

Expressions in algebraic equations and inequalities may include radicals. The same principles for working with equations and inequalities apply when manipulating radicals.

Example:

$5\sqrt{x-4} - 28 = 12$ for what value of *x*?

➤ Solve for *x*:

$$5\sqrt{x-4} - 28 = 12$$
$$5\sqrt{x-4} = 40$$
$$\sqrt{x-4} = 8$$
$$\left(\sqrt{x-4}\right)^2 = 8^2$$
$$x - 4 = 64$$
$$x = 68$$

Absolute Value in Equations and Inequalities

Expressions in algebraic equations and inequalities may include absolute values. The same principles for working with equations and inequalities apply when manipulating absolute values.

*Example*s:

1. What is the sum of all different integers that can be substituted for *x* such that $|x| + |x-3| = 3$?

   ➤ The absolute value of any real number, including integers, is always zero or more. Therefore, try only -3, -2, -1, 0, 1, 2, 3. The last four work in the equality: $|0| + |0-3| = 0 + 3 = 3$; $|1| + |1-3| = 1 + 2 = 3$; $|2| + |2-3| = 2 + 1 = 3$; $|3| + |3-3| = 3 + 0 = 3$. Thus, $0 + 1 + 2 + 3 = 6$.

2. If *x* represents an integer, $|x-3| + |x+2| < 7$ for how many different values of *x*?

   ➤ Absolute values are always equal to or greater than zero. Thus, if $x = -4$, $|x-3| = |-4-3| = 7$; there is no need to try any integers less than -3. Similarly, if $x = 5$, $|x+2| = |5+2| = 7$, there is no need to try any integers greater than 4. Therefore, test only the integers between -3 and 4. Six integers satisfy the inequality: $\{-2, -1, 0, 1, 2, 3\}$.

Algebraic Equations and Inequalities

DIRECTIONS: Choose the correct answer to each of the following items. Answers are on page 790.

1. If $3x = 12$, then $x = ?$

   A. 2   C. 4   E. 10
   B. 3   D. 6

2. If $2x + x = 9$, then $x = ?$

   A. 0   C. 3   E. 9
   B. 1   D. 6

3. If $7x - 5x = 12 - 8$, then $x = ?$

   A. 0   C. 2   E. 4
   B. 1   D. 3

4. If $3x + 2x = 15$, then $x = ?$

   A. 2   C. 5   E. 9
   B. 3   D. 6

5. If $a - 8 = 10 - 2a$, then $a = ?$

   A. -2   C. 2   E. 6
   B. 0   D. 4

6. If $p - 11 - 2p = 13 - 5p$, then $p = ?$

   A. -4   C. 1   E. 6
   B. -1   D. 2

7. If $12x + 3 - 4x - 3 = 8$, then $x = ?$

   A. -5   C. 0   E. 5
   B. -1   D. 1

8. If $5x - 2 + 3x - 4 = 2x - 8 + x + 2$, then $x = ?$

   A. -5   C. 1   E. 6
   B. 0   D. 3

9. If $a + 2b - 3 + 3a = 2a + b + 3 + b$, then $a = ?$

   A. -1   C. 2   E. 6
   B. 0   D. 3

10. If $4y + 10 = 5 + 7y + 5$, then $y = ?$

    A. -2   C. 0   E. 8
    B. -1   D. 4

11. If $-4 - x = 12 + x$, then $x = ?$

    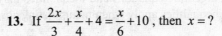

    A. -8   C. 1   E. 4
    B. -2   D. 2

12. If $\dfrac{x}{2} + x = 3$, then $x = ?$

    A. $\dfrac{1}{2}$ C. 1   E. 3

    B. $\dfrac{2}{3}$ D. 2

13. If $\dfrac{2x}{3} + \dfrac{x}{4} + 4 = \dfrac{x}{6} + 10$, then $x = ?$

    A. $\dfrac{11}{12}$ C. 5   E. 20

    B. $\dfrac{3}{2}$ D. 8

14. If $\dfrac{a}{2} - \dfrac{a}{4} = 1$, then $a = ?$

    A. $\dfrac{1}{2}$ C. 1   E. 4

    B. $\dfrac{2}{3}$ D. 2

15. If $\dfrac{1}{p} + \dfrac{2}{p} + \dfrac{3}{p} = 1$, then $p = ?$

    A. $\dfrac{2}{3}$ C. 1   E. 6

    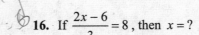

    B. $\dfrac{3}{4}$ D. 2

16. If $\dfrac{2x - 6}{3} = 8$, then $x = ?$

    A. 1   C. 6   E. 18
    B. 3   D. 15

17. If $\dfrac{5-x}{5}=1$, then $x=?$

    A. −5   **C.** 0   **E.** 5

    B. −1   **D.** 1

18. If $\dfrac{2-x}{10}=1$, then $x=?$

    A. −8   **C.** $-\dfrac{1}{5}$ **E.** 5

    B. −1   **D.** 1

19. If $\dfrac{5}{x+1}+2=5$, then $x=?$

    A. $-\dfrac{2}{7}$ **C.** $\dfrac{7}{2}$ **E.** 10

    B. $\dfrac{2}{3}$ **D.** 7

20. If $\dfrac{x}{2}+\dfrac{x}{3}=\dfrac{1}{2}+\dfrac{1}{3}$, then $x=?$

    A. $\dfrac{1}{3}$ **C.** 1   **E.** 3

    B. $\dfrac{2}{3}$ **D.** 2

21. If $3x+y=10$ and $x+y=6$, then $x=?$

    A. 1   **C.** 3   **E.** 5

    B. 2   **D.** 4

22. If $2x+y=10$ and $x+y=7$, then $y=?$

    A. 3   **C.** 5   **E.** 9

    B. 4   **D.** 6

23. If $x+3y=5$ and $2x-y=3$, then $x=?$

    A. 2   **C.** 5   **E.** 9

    B. 4   **D.** 6

24. If $x+y=2$ and $x-y=2$, then $y=?$

    A. −2   **C.** 0   **E.** 2

    B. −1   **D.** 1

25. If $a+b=5$ and $2a+3b=12$, then $b=?$

    A. 1   **C.** 3   **E.** 6

    B. 2   **D.** 4

26. If $5x+3y=13$ and $2x=4$, then $y=?$

    A. 1   **C.** 3   **E.** 5

    B. 2   **D.** 4

27. If $k-n=5$, and $2k+n=16$, then $k=?$

    A. −3   **C.** 1   **E.** 7

    B. 0   **D.** 5

28. If $t=k-5$ and $k+t=11$, then $k=?$

    A. 2   **C.** 8   **E.** 14

    B. 3   **D.** 11

29. If $a+5b=9$ and $a-b=3$, then $a=?$

    A. 1   **C.** 5   **E.** 11

    B. 4   **D.** 7

30. If $8+x=y$ and $2y+x=28$, then $x=?$

    A. 2   **C.** 6   **E.** 18

    B. 4   **D.** 12

31. If $\dfrac{x+y}{2}=4$ and $x-y=4$, then $x=?$

    A. 1   **C.** 4   **E.** 8

    B. 2   **D.** 6

32. If $\dfrac{x+y}{2}=7$ and $\dfrac{x-y}{3}=2$, then $x=?$

    A. 2   **C.** 8   **E.** 14

    B. 4   **D.** 10

33. If $x+y+z=10$ and $x-y-z=4$, then $x=?$

    A. 2   **C.** 6   **E.** 12

    B. 3   **D.** 7

34. If $x+2y-z=4$ and $2x-2y+z=8$, then $x=?$

    A. −2   **C.** 4   **E.** 8

    B. 0   **D.** 6

35. If $x+y+z=6$, $x+y-z=4$, and $x-y=3$, then $x=?$

    A. −2   **C.** 4   **E.** 8

    B. 0   **D.** 6

36. If $x^2-5x+4=0$ then $x=?$

    A. −2 or 1   **C.** −1 or 2   **E.** 4 or 2

    B. 4 or 1   **D.** −4 or −1

37. If $x^2 - 3x - 4 = 0$, then $x = ?$

    A. −4 or 1   **C.** −1 or 2   **E.** 6 or −1
    B. −2 or 2   **D.** 4 or −1

38. If $x^2 + 5x + 6 = 0$, then $x = ?$

    A. −3 or −2   **C.** −1 or 6   **E.** 6 or −2
    B. −3 or 2   **D.** 1 or −6

39. If $x^2 - 3x + 2 = 0$, then $x = ?$

    A. −2 or −1   **C.** 1 or 2   **E.** 3 or 5
    B. −1 or 2   **D.** 2 or 3

40. If $x^2 + 3x + 2 = 0$, then which of the following values is (are) possible for x?

    I. 1
    II. −1
    III. −2

    A. I only   **D.** I and II only
    B. II only   **E.** II and III only
    C. III only

41. If $x^2 + 5x = -4$, then $x = ?$

    A. −1 or −4   **C.** 1 or 2   **E.** 2 or 6
    B. −1 or −2   **D.** 1 or 4

42. If $x^2 - 8 = 7x$, then $x = ?$

    A. −8 and −1   **C.** −1 and 8   **E.** 1 and 8
    B. −4 and 1   **D.** 1 and 4

43. If $k^2 - 10 = -3k$, then $k = ?$

    A. −10 and −1   **C.** −5 and 3   **E.** 2 and −5
    B. −10 and 1   **D.** −3 and 5

44. If $x^2 = 12 - x$, then $x = ?$

    A. −4 and −3   **C.** −3 and 4   **E.** 1 and 6
    B. −4 and 3   **D.** −2 and 6

45. If $3x^2 = 12x$, then $x = ?$

    A. 0 or 3   **C.** −2 or 2   **E.** 3 or 12
    B. 0 or 4   **D.** 2 or 4

46. If $4(5 - x) = 2(10 - x^2)$, then $x = ?$

    A. 0 or 2   **C.** −2 or 4   **E.** 4 or 5
    B. 2 or 4   **D.** 0 or −2

47. For what values of x is $3 + 4x < 28$?

    A. $x < 4$ **C.** $x < 6.25$ **E.** $x \geq 0$
    B. $x > 4$ **D.** $x > 6.25$

48. For what values of x is $5(3x - 2) \geq 50$?

    A. $x \geq 4$ **C.** $x \geq 10$ **E.** $x > 8$
    B. $x \leq 4$ **D.** $x \leq 10$

49. For what values of x is $8 - 3x > 35$?

    A. $x > 0$ **C.** $x \geq 0$ **E.** $x \geq 9$
    B. $x > -3$ **D.** $x < -9$

50. If $x^2 = 6x - 8$, then $x = ?$

    A. −8 and −2   **C.** −2 and 2   **E.** 2 and 8
    B. −4 and −2   **D.** 2 and 4

51. If $(x - 8)(x + 2) = 0$, then $x = ?$

    A. −8 or −2   **C.** 4 or −2   **E.** 10 or −5
    B. −4 or −2   **D.** 8 or −2

52. If $9 - 3(6 - x) = 12$, then $x = ?$

    A. 4 or −2   **C.** 4   **E.** 7
    B. 7 or −2   **D.** 6

53. If $\dfrac{x + 5}{4} = 17$, then $x = ?$

    A. 13 or 25   **C.** 63   **E.** 124
    B. 54   **D.** 75 or −24

54. If $\dfrac{x}{2} - \dfrac{x - 2}{3} = 0.4$, then $x = ?$

    A. −1 or 1.4   **C.** 2 or −1.6   **E.** 2.6
    B. −1.6   **D.** 2.4

55. If $0.02x + 1.44 = x - 16.2$, then $x = ?$

    A. 18   **C.** 14   **E.** 10
    B. 16   **D.** 12

56. If $3 - 2(x - 5) = 3x + 4$, then $x = ?$

    A. $\dfrac{1}{2}$ or $\dfrac{1}{4}$ **C.** $\dfrac{9}{5}$ **E.** 5

    B. $-\dfrac{9}{5}$ **D.** 1 or 3

57. If $x^2 - 9x = 22$, then $x = ?$

A. -11 or 2 **C.** 2 or 3 **E.** 11
B. 3 **D.** 11 or -2

58. If $(x+8)(x+1) = 78$, then $x^2 + 9x = ?$

A. 50 **C.** 60 **E.** 70
B. 55 **D.** 65

59. If $2x + 3y = 12$ and $x = -6$, then $y = ?$

A. 2 **C.** 8 **E.** 12
B. 4 **D.** 10

60. At what point does the line $5x + 2y = 20$ intersect the x-axis? (Hint: What must the y-coordinate be?)

A. $(-4,0)$ **C.** $(0,0)$ **E.** $(4,2)$
B. $(-2,0)$ **D.** $(4,0)$

61. If $3x + 5y = 10$, then $y = ?$

A. $-0.6x - 2$ **C.** $0.5x - 4$ **E.** $-0.6x + 2$
B. $-0.4x + 2$ **D.** $0.6x - 2$

62. If $x = ay + 3$, then $y = ?$

A. $\dfrac{x-2}{4a}$ **C.** $\dfrac{a}{x-3}$ **E.** $\dfrac{a}{3x}$

B. $\dfrac{x-3}{a}$ **D.** $\dfrac{x+a}{3}$

63. If $8x + 16 = (x+2)(x+5)$, then $x = ?$

A. 3 or -2 **C.** -2 **E.** 3
B. -3 **D.** 2 or 3

64. If $\dfrac{x+5}{0.2} = 0.3x$, then $x = ?$

A. $-\dfrac{125}{23}$ **C.** $-\dfrac{250}{47}$ **E.** $\dfrac{250}{47}$

B. -76 **D.** $\dfrac{47}{250}$

65. If $\dfrac{0.2 + x}{3} = \dfrac{\frac{5}{6}}{4}$, then $x = ?$

A. $-\dfrac{40}{17}$ **C.** 0 **E.** $\dfrac{40}{17}$

B. $-\dfrac{17}{40}$ **D.** $\dfrac{17}{40}$

66. If x is an integer and $6 < x < 8$, then what is the value of x?

A. 4 **C.** 7 **E.** 10
B. 5 **D.** 9

67. If x is an integer and $5 \le x \le 7$, then which of the following values is (are) possible for x?

   I. 5
   II. 6
   III. 7

A. II only   **D.** II and III only
B. I and II only   **E.** I, II, and III
C. I and III only

68. If x and y are integers, $2 < x < 4$, and $8 > y > 6$, then what is the value of xy?

A. 12 **C.** 21 **E.** 32
B. 16 **D.** 24

69. If x and y are integers, $5 > x \ge 2$, and $6 < y \le 9$, then which of the following is the *minimum* value of xy?

A. 14 **C.** 20 **E.** 54
B. 18 **D.** 45

70. If $1 \le x \le 3$, then which of the following values is (are) possible for x?

   I. $\dfrac{5}{2}$

   II. $\dfrac{7}{2}$

   III. $\dfrac{3}{2}$

A. I only   **D.** I and III only
B. II only   **E.** I, II, and III
C. I and II only

71. If $3^{8x+4} = 27^{2x+12}$, then $x = ?$

A. $\dfrac{1}{4}$ C. 4   E. 16

B. $\dfrac{1}{9}$ D. 9

72. If $(3+x)x = 2x + x + 16$, then which of the following is (are) the possible value(s) for x?

A. 2   C. 2 or –2   E. 8 or –8
B. 4   D. 4 or –4

73. If $10x^2 = 30$ and $(6+y)y = 6y + 52$, then $2x^2 + 2y^2 = ?$

A. 110   C. 82   E. 55
B. 96   D. 72

74. If $|x| = 5$, then $x = ?$

A. 5
B. 5 or –5
C. Any real number less than 5
D. No real number
E. Any real number greater than zero

75. The commutative property states that if a final result involves two procedures or objects, then the final result is the same regardless of which procedure or object is taken first and which is taken second. Which of the following is an example of the commutative property of addition?

A. $xy = yx$ D. $7 - 3 = 3 - 7$

B. $5 + 4 = 4 + 5$ E. $\dfrac{x}{y} = \dfrac{y}{x}$

C. $2a + b = 2b + a$

76. If $x = 3a$ and $y = 5x + 6$, then $y = ?$

A. 21   C. $6a + 15$ E. $21a$
B. $15a + 6$ D. $3a + 15$

77. If $2(x+3) = 18a + 10$, then $x = ?$

A. $9a + 2$ C. $16a + 4$ E. 11
B. $9a + 5$ D. $9a + 3.5$

78. The formula that relates Fahrenheit temperature to Celsius temperature is $F = 1.8C + 32$, where F is the temperature in Fahrenheit degrees and C is the temperature in Celsius degrees. What is the temperature, in Celsius degrees, if the temperature in Fahrenheit degrees is 41°?

A. 5   C. 9   E. 73
B. 7.2   D. 10.8

79. If x is a real number such that $x \neq 0$, y is a real number, $x^5 = 8y$, and $x^4 = y$, then which of the following is true?

A. $x = 7y$ C. $x = 8y^2$ E. $x = 8$

B. $x = 8y$ D. $x = 7y^2$

80. The commutative property states that if a final result involves two procedures or objects, then the final result is the same regardless of which procedure or object is taken first and which is taken second. Which of the following is an example of the commutative property of multiplication?

A. $xy = yx$ D. $7 - 3 = 3 - 7$

B. $5 + 4 = 4 + 5$ E. $\dfrac{x}{y} = \dfrac{y}{x}$

C. $2a + b = 2b + a$

81. What is the tenth term of the sequence {1, 4, 9, 16, ...}?

A. 25   C. 49   E. 100
B. 36   D. 81

82. If a sequence is defined by the rule $a_n = (a_{n-1} - 3)^2$, what is a_4 (the fourth term of the sequence) if a_1 is 1?

A. 1   C. 3   E. 5
B. 2   D. 4

83. A geometric sequence is a sequence of numbers formed by continually multiplying by the same number; e.g., {81, 27, 9, 3, ...} is a geometric sequence formed by continually multiplying by $\dfrac{1}{3}$. What is the next term in the geometric sequence of {2, 8, 32, 128, ...}?

A. 132   C. 384   E. 1,024
B. 256   D. 512

84. A sequence is formed by substituting consecutive whole numbers in the expression $x^3 + x^2 - 2x + 1$. What is the next term in the sequence of $\{1, 9, 31, 73, \ldots\}$?

A. 115 C. 135 E. 141
B. 125 D. 137

85. Which of the following values for c returns two distinct real solutions to the equation $x^2 - 8x + c = 0$?

A. −20 C. 18 E. 20
B. 17 D. 19

86. Which of the following values for b returns two distinct real solutions to the equation $x^2 + bx + 8 = 0$?

A. 6 C. 4 E. 1
B. 5 D. $\sqrt{2}$

87. The cost of buying a certain material is k cents per yard. What is the cost, in cents, of x yards and y inches of the material?

A. $kx + y$ C. $x + 36y$ E. $xk + 26yk$

B. $36x + y$ D. $xk + \dfrac{yk}{36}$

88. If $x^2 - 14k^2 = 5kx$, what are the 2 solutions for x in terms of k?

A. $2k$ and $7k$ C. k and $5k$ E. k and $-5k$
B. $-2k$ and $7k$ D. $-k$ and $5k$

89. An arithmetic sequence is a sequence of numbers formed by continually adding the same number; e.g., $\{1, 3, 5, 7, 9, 11, \ldots\}$ is an arithmetic sequence formed by continually adding 2. What is the ninth term in the arithmetic sequence of $\{1, 4, 7, 10, 13, \ldots\}$?

A. 16 C. 19 E. 25
B. 17 D. 21

90. $\dfrac{1}{a} + \dfrac{1}{b} = 7$ and $\dfrac{1}{a} - \dfrac{1}{b} = 3$ Find $\dfrac{1}{a^2} - \dfrac{1}{b^2}$.

A. 10 C. 3 E. 4
B. 7 D. 21

91. If $\dfrac{3x}{4} = 1$, then $\dfrac{2x}{3} = ?$

A. $\dfrac{1}{3}$ C. $\dfrac{2}{3}$ E. 2

B. $\dfrac{1}{2}$ D. $\dfrac{8}{9}$

92. If $x = \dfrac{y}{7}$ and $7x = 12$, then $y = ?$

A. 3 C. 7 E. 72
B. 5 D. 12

93. If $x = k + \dfrac{1}{2} = \dfrac{k+3}{2}$, then $x = ?$

A. $\dfrac{1}{3}$ C. 1 E. $\dfrac{5}{2}$

B. $\dfrac{1}{2}$ D. 2

94. If $7 - x = 0$, then $10 - x = ?$

A. −3 C. 3 E. 10
B. 0 D. 7

95. If $x = 7 - \sqrt{3}$ and $y = 7 + \sqrt{3}$, which of the following must be rational?

I. xy
II. $x + y$

III. $\dfrac{x}{y}$

A. I only D. I and II only
B. III only E. I, II, and III
C. I and III only

96. $\dfrac{2^{x+4} - 2(2^x)}{2(2^{x+3})} = ?$

A. $\dfrac{1}{2}$ C. $\dfrac{3}{4}$ E. $\dfrac{7}{8}$

B. $\dfrac{1}{4}$ D. $\dfrac{5}{8}$

97. Let $y = 2^x$ and $w = 8^x$. For what value of x does $w = 2y$?

A. a rational number between 0 and 2
B. a whole number between 2 and 8
C. a irrational number between 2 and 8
D. no such value of x exists
E. more than one such value of x exists

98. A population that starts at 16 and doubles every 30 months can be expressed as $16\left(2^{\frac{2x}{5}}\right)$, where x is the number of elapsed years. What is the approximate population size after 105 months have elapsed?

A. $11\sqrt{2}$ C. 128   E. 192
B. 27   D. $128\sqrt{2}$

99. Let n be a member of the set $\{5, 6, 7, 8, 9, 10, 11, 12, 13, 14, 15, 16\}$. For how many different values of n is the following equation true?

$$\frac{1 + 2 + \ldots + n}{2 + 4 + \ldots + 2n} = \frac{1}{2}$$

A. 0   C. 6   E. 12
B. 1   D. 11

100. Which of the following statements is always correct?

A. If $x < 0$, then $x^2 > -x$
B. If $x > 0$, then $(x+3)(x+2) > x^2 + 4x + 3$
C. If $x > 0$, then $x^3 + 8 > (x+2)\left(x^2 - 2x + 4\right)$
D. If $x = 8$, then $1 + 2 + 3 + \ldots + x > x(x+1)$
E. If $x = 6$, then $\dfrac{2^x}{2^{x-1}} > 4$

101. A prime number is defined as a whole number that is greater than 1 whose only divisors are 1 and the number itself. Examples of prime numbers are 13, 17, and 29. What is the smallest prime number that divides the sum of $3^3 + 5^5 + 7^7 + 11^{11}$?

A. 2   C. 5   E. 11
B. 3   D. 7

102. Let x represent a positive odd integer. The smallest value of x such that $3^{\frac{1}{4}}, 3^{\frac{3}{4}}, 3^{\frac{5}{4}}, \ldots, 3^{\frac{x}{4}}$ is greater than 2^x is:

A. a multiple of 3
B. a multiple of 5 but not a multiple of 3
C. a multiple of 7 but not a multiple of either 3 or 5
D. 11
E. 13

103. If x represents a real number, how many different values of x satisfy the equation $x^{128} = 16^{32}$?

A. 0
B. 1
C. 2
D. more than 2, but not infinite
E. infinite

104. How many of the following five numerical expressions represent whole numbers?

$$8^0, \ 9^{-2}, \ \left(\frac{1}{9}\right)^{-2}, \ \left(\frac{1}{8}\right)^{\frac{2}{3}}, \ \left(\frac{1}{16}\right)^{-\frac{1}{4}}$$

A. 0   C. 3   E. 4
B. 2   D. 4

105. If $y = 3^x$, $3^{x+2} = ?$

A. y^2 C. $y + 3$ E. $y + 9$
B. 2^y D. $9y$

106. How many real values of x exist such that $x = \sqrt{x + 20}$?

A. 0
B. 1
C. 2
D. more than 2, but not infinite
E. infinite

107. Let x be an element of $\{-6, -5, -4, -3, -2, -1, 0, 2, 6, 8, 10, 12\}$ and $x = 3k$, where k is an integer. Find the sum of all different values of x such that $\sqrt{2x + 8} = \sqrt{y}$ for some value of y if y is an element of $\{-2, 0, 2, 4, 6, 8, 10, 12, 14, 16, 18, 20, 22, 24, 26, 28\}$.

A. 3   C. 9   E. 15
B. 6   D. 12

108. Let k be a positive whole number such that $11 < k < 15$. If $\sqrt{8x} + k = 18$, for how many different values of k will the solution set for x contain an even integer?

   A. 0   **C.** 2   **E.** 4
   B. 1   **D.** 3

109. Let $f(x) = \dfrac{x-2}{2x-13}$. If x represents a whole number, what is the largest value of x such that $f(x) < 0$?

   A. −1   **C.** 1   **E.** 8
   B. 0   **D.** 6

110. If $f(x) = kx + w$, $f(2) = 8$, and $f(6) = 20$, what is the value of $k + w$?

   A. 2   **C.** 5   **E.** 20
   B. 4   **D.** 8

111. If $-5 < x < -1$, and $f(x) = \big|14 - |1 + 2x|\big|$, then $f(x)$ equals:

   A. $13 - 2x$ **C.** $13 + 2x$ **E.** $13 + 3x$
   B. $15 + 2x$ **D.** $2x - 13$

112. If $f(x) = 3 + 2^x$ and $g(x) = (2+3)^x$, then what is the value of $f(2) + g(3)$?

   A. 36   **C.** 150   **E.** 300
   B. 132   **D.** 225

113. If $f(x) = \dfrac{kx}{3x+5}$, $x \ne -\dfrac{5}{3}$, k is a constant, and $f(x)$ satisfies the equation $f(f(x)) = x$ for all real values of x except for $x = -\dfrac{5}{3}$, what is the value of k?

   A. k cannot be uniquely determined.
   B. k does not equal any real value.
   C. $k = -\dfrac{5}{3}$

   D. $k = -\dfrac{3}{5}$

   E. $k = -5$

114. The range of the relation $\{(x, y) | y^2 = 4x\}$ is {0, 9, 16}. Which of the following is the domain?

   A. {0, 20.25, 64}
   B. {0, 3, 4}
   C. {0, 36, 64}
   D. {−4, −3, 0, 3, 4}
   E. {0, 2.25, 4}

115. If $y = 2x + 1$ and the domain for x is the set of all non-negative integers, then the range for y is the set of which of the following?

   A. non-negative integers
   B. non-negative even integers
   C. odd integers
   D. positive odd integers
   E. real numbers equal to or greater than 1

116. If $7x + 4y = 218$, and both x and y are positive integers, what is the sum of the two largest values in the range of y?

   A. 433   **C.** 427   **E.** 95
   B. 428   **D.** 101

117. How many whole numbers are not in the domain of values for x if $y = \dfrac{(x-1)(x-2)(x-3)}{x^2 - 11 + 30}$?

   A. 1   **C.** 3   **E.** 5
   B. 2   **D.** 4

118. If $f(x) = 17x + 14$, then $f(2) + f(3) + f(4)$ is:

   A. 195   **C.** 126   **E.** 51
   B. 153   **D.** 102

119. $f(x)$ and $g(x)$ represent linear functions. If $f(x) = 5$ for $x = 1$, $g(x) = 3x + 8$, and $f(x) = g(x)$ for $x = 2$, then what is the value of $f(4)$?

   A. 12   **C.** 20   **E.** 32
   B. 16   **D.** 24

Geometry

If you have ever taken a basic course in geometry, you probably remember having to memorize theorems and do formal proofs. Fortunately, you will not be asked to do any formal proofs on the exam, and the formulas you need to know are few and relatively simple. Most often, test items ask you to find the measure of an angle, the length of a line, or the area of a figure.

Geometric Notation

You should be familiar with basic geometric notation. The line segment with points P and Q as endpoints is represented by $\overline{PQ}$. PQ represents the length of $\overline{PQ}$. A line passing through points P and Q is represented by $\overleftrightarrow{PQ}$. $\overrightarrow{PQ}$ represents the ray beginning at point P and passing through point Q. Finally, the symbol "$\cong$" is used to represent the term "congruent."

Example:

If $\overleftrightarrow{AB}$ does not contain point C, but it does contain point D, what is the maximum number of points in the intersection of $\overleftrightarrow{AB}$ and $\overleftrightarrow{CD}$?

➤ $\overleftrightarrow{AB}$ and $\overleftrightarrow{CD}$ are different lines, so the maximum number of points at which they can intersect is one point, point D.

Line and Angle Properties

For the purposes of this review and the test, the word *line* means a straight line:

$$P \qquad Q$$
$$\bullet\!\!-\!\!-\!\!-\!\!-\!\!-\!\!-\!\!\bullet\!\!-\!\!-\!\!-\ l$$

The line above is designated line *l*. The portion of line *l* from point P to point Q is called "line segment PQ," or "$\overline{PQ}$."

When two lines intersect, they form an ***angle***, and their point of intersection is called the ***vertex*** of that angle.

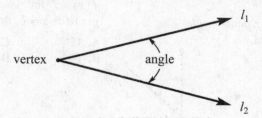

The size of an angle is measured in *degrees*. Degrees are defined in reference to a circle. By convention, a circle is divided into 360 equal parts, or degrees.

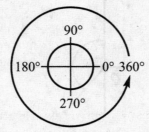

A 90° angle is also called a ***right angle***. A right angle is often indicated in the following way:

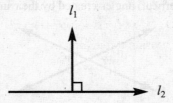

Two right angles form a straight line:

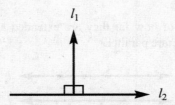

Since two right angles form a straight line, the degree measure of the angle of a straight line is $90° + 90° = 180°$:

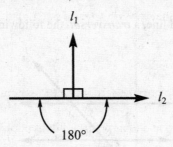

An angle that is less than 90° is called an ***acute angle***:

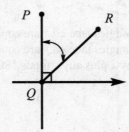

In the figure above, $\angle PQR$ is an acute angle.

An angle that is greater than 90° but less than 180° is called an *obtuse angle*:

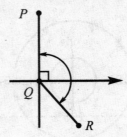

In the figure above, $\angle PQR$ is an obtuse angle.

When two lines intersect, the opposite (or vertical) angles created by their intersection are congruent, or equal:

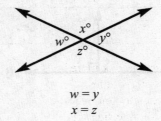

$$w = y$$
$$x = z$$

Two lines that do not intersect regardless of how far they are extended are *parallel* to each other. In the following figure, the symbol $\parallel$ indicates that l_1 and l_2 are parallel.

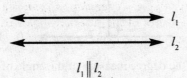

$$l_1 \parallel l_2$$

When parallel lines are intersected by a third line, a *transversal*, the following angle relationships are created:

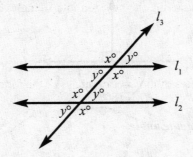

All angles labeled x are equal.
All angles labeled y are equal.
Any x plus any y totals 180.

Two lines that are **perpendicular** to the same line are parallel to each other:

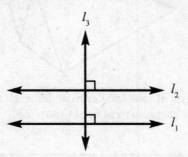

Since l_1 and l_2 are both perpendicular to l_3, we can conclude that l_1 and l_2 are parallel to each other.

Polygon Properties

- A **polygon** is a closed figure created by three or more lines.
- A **triangle** is any polygon with exactly three sides.
- A **quadrilateral** is any polygon with exactly four sides.
- A **pentagon** is any polygon with exactly five sides.
- A **hexagon** is any polygon with exactly six sides.

A polygon with more than six sides is usually referred to as a polygon with a certain number of sides; for example, a polygon with ten sides is called a ten-sided polygon. A **regular polygon** is a polygon with equal sides and equal angles (e.g., a square). The sum of the degree measures of the **exterior angles** of a polygon is 360. The sum of the degree measures of the **interior angles** of a polygon can be expressed as $180(n-2)$, where n is the number of sides in the polygon.

Furthermore, note that any polygon is made up of a number of smaller triangles: a quadrilateral consists of two triangles, a pentagon consists of three triangles, an octagon consists of six triangles, etc. Therefore, the sum of the angles of a polygon can be found by partitioning the polygon into triangles and summing the angle measures of those triangles, each of which is equal to 180°.

Example:

What is the sum of the degree measures of the interior angles of the following six-sided polygon?

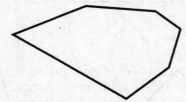

➢ If you remember the formula, use it: $180(n-2) = 180(6-2) = 180 \cdot 4 = 720°$. Otherwise, partition the polygon into smaller triangles:

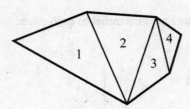

Since the six-sided polygon consists of four smaller triangles, each of which has an interior degree measure of 180°, the polygon's interior degree measure must be $4 \cdot 180 = 720°$.

Triangle Properties and Formulas

Properties of Triangles

A *triangle* is a three-sided figure. Within a given triangle, the larger an angle is, the longer the opposite side of the angle is; conversely, the longer a side is, the larger the opposite angle is.

Examples:

1. In the following figure, since $\overline{PR} > \overline{QR} > \overline{PQ}$, $\angle Q > \angle P > \angle R$.

2. In the following figure, since $\angle P > \angle Q > \angle R$, $\overline{QR} > \overline{PR} > \overline{PQ}$.

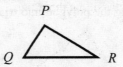

Within a given triangle, if two sides are equal, then the angles opposite the two sides are equal, and vice versa:

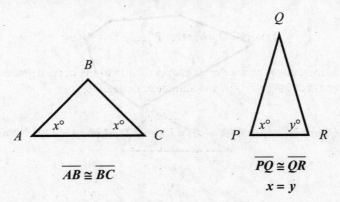

$$\overline{AB} \cong \overline{BC}$$

$$\overline{PQ} \cong \overline{QR}$$
$$x = y$$

A triangle with exactly two equal sides is called an *isosceles triangle*. A triangle with exactly three equal sides is called an *equilateral triangle*.

Example:

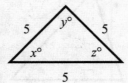

➤ An equilateral triangle has three equal sides and therefore three equal angles: $x = y = z$. Thus, each angle must be $60°$.

A triangle with a right angle is called a *right triangle*. The longest side of the right triangle, which is opposite the 90° angle, is called the *hypotenuse*.

Pythagorean Theorem

The sides of every right triangle fit a special relationship called the *Pythagorean theorem*: the square of the hypotenuse is equal to the sum of the squares of the other two sides. This is easier to understand when it is summarized in a formula.

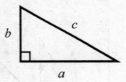

Pythagorean Theorem: $c^2 = a^2 + b^2$

Formulas of Triangles

The *perimeter* of a triangle is the sum of the lengths of the three sides:

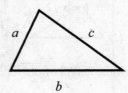

Triangle Perimeter: $P_{triangle} = a + b + c$

The *altitude* of a triangle is a line drawn from a vertex perpendicular to the opposite side. The formula for finding the *area* of a triangle is equal to one-half multiplied by the altitude and the base.

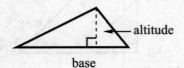

Triangle Area: $A_{triangle} = \dfrac{ab}{2}$

Example:

In the following figure, what is the area of the triangle?

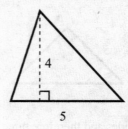

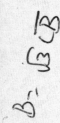

➤ $A_{\text{triangle}} = \dfrac{ab}{2} = \dfrac{4 \cdot 5}{2} = 10$

Special Properties of 45°-45°-90° Triangles

The sides of **45°-45°-90° triangles** share special relationships. In a triangle with angles of 45°-45°-90°, the length of the hypotenuse is equal to the length of either side multiplied by the square root of two. Conversely, the length of each of the two sides is equal to one-half the length of the hypotenuse multiplied by the square root of two.

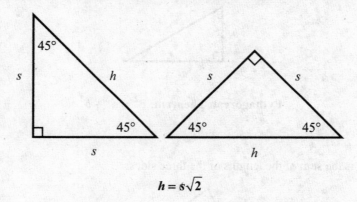

$$h = s\sqrt{2}$$

Examples:

1. In $\triangle ABC$, both $\angle A$ and $\angle C$ are 45°. If the length of $\overline{AB}$ is 3, what is the length of $\overline{AC}$?

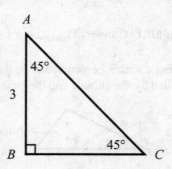

➤ $h = s\sqrt{2} \Rightarrow AC = AB\left(\sqrt{2}\right) = 3\sqrt{2}$

2. In $\triangle LMN$, both $\angle L$ and $\angle N$ are $45°$. If the length of $\overline{LN}$ is 4, what is the length of $\overline{MN}$?

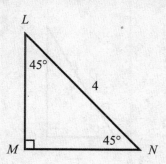

➤ $h = s\sqrt{2} \Rightarrow 4 = s\sqrt{2} \Rightarrow s = \dfrac{4}{\sqrt{2}} = \dfrac{4}{\sqrt{2}} \cdot \dfrac{\sqrt{2}}{\sqrt{2}} = \dfrac{4\sqrt{2}}{2} = 2\sqrt{2}$

Special Properties of 30°-60°-90° Triangles

Similarly, the sides of **30°-60°-90° triangles** also share special relationships. In triangles with angles of 30°-60°-90°, the length of the side opposite the 30° angle is equal to one-half the length of the hypotenuse, and the length of the side opposite the 60° angle is equal to one-half the length of the hypotenuse multiplied by $\sqrt{3}$.

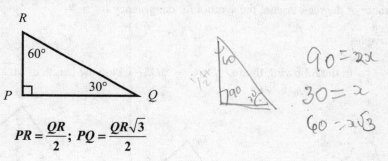

$$PR = \frac{QR}{2}; \quad PQ = \frac{QR\sqrt{3}}{2}$$

*Example*s:

1. In $\triangle ABC$, $\angle A = 60°$ and $\angle C = 30°$. If the length of $\overline{AC}$ is 6, what are the lengths of $\overline{AB}$ and $\overline{BC}$?

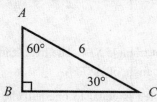

➤ $AB = \dfrac{AC}{2} = \dfrac{6}{2} = 3 \Rightarrow BC = \dfrac{AC\sqrt{3}}{2} = \dfrac{6\sqrt{3}}{2} = 3\sqrt{3}$

2. In $\triangle FGH$, $\angle F = 60°$. If the length of $\overline{FH}$ is 14, what is the length of $\overline{FG}$?

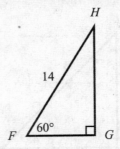

➤ The length of the side opposite the 30° angle, $\overline{FG}$, is equal to one-half the length of the side opposite the 90° angle, $\overline{FH}$: $FG = \dfrac{FH}{2} = \dfrac{14}{2} = 7$.

Similar Triangles

"Real world" items such as blueprints, scale drawings, microscopes, and photo enlargements involve similar figures. **Similar triangles** are frequently encountered on the exams. The symbol for similarity is "~." If two triangles are similar, the corresponding sides have the same ratio, and their matching angles are **congruent**; that is, they have the same number of degrees. Again, the symbol for congruency is "$\cong$."

*Example*s:

1. In the following figure, $\triangle ABC \sim \triangle DEF$. Find the length of $\overline{AC}$.

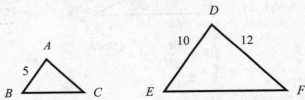

➤ The triangles are similar, so create a proportion relating the similar sides: $\dfrac{AC}{5} = \dfrac{12}{10} \Rightarrow 10(AC) = 5(12) \Rightarrow$
$10AC = 60 \Rightarrow AC = 6$.

2. Right triangle PQR is similar to right triangle STV. The hypotenuse of $\triangle PQR$ is 12 units long and one of the legs is 6 units long. Find the smallest angle of $\triangle STV$.

➤ Any right triangle in which one leg is equal to one-half the hypotenuse must be a 30°-60°-90° triangle. Since the two triangles are similar, the matching angles are congruent. Therefore, the smallest angle of $\triangle STV$ is 30°.

Quadrilateral Properties and Formulas

A **quadrilateral** is a closed, four-sided figure in two dimensions. Common quadrilaterals are the parallelogram, rectangle, and square. The sum of the four angles of a quadrilateral is 360°. A **parallelogram** is a quadrilateral in which both pairs of opposite sides are parallel. Opposite sides of a parallelogram are equal, or congruent. Similarly, opposite angles of a parallelogram are also equal, or congruent. Again, the symbol for congruency is " $\cong$."

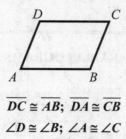

$$\overline{DC} \cong \overline{AB}; \ \overline{DA} \cong \overline{CB}$$
$$\angle D \cong \angle B; \ \angle A \cong \angle C$$

The area of a parallelogram is found by multiplying the base times its height. The height must be measured at a right angle to the base.

Example:

In the following figure, find the area of the parallelogram.

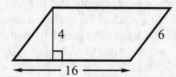

> The base of the parallelogram is 16 and the height is 4 (not 6). Remember, the height must be measured at a right angle to the base. Therefore, the area is: $16 \cdot 4 = 64$.

A *trapezoid* is a quadrilateral with only two parallel sides. The area of a trapezoid is equal to one-half of the height times the sum of the two bases, which are the two parallel sides. Alternatively, a trapezoid can be broken down into triangles and rectangles, and the sum of these areas equals the trapezoid's area. The following example illustrates both methods.

Example:

In the following figure, find the area of the trapezoid.

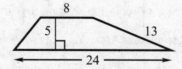

> The area of a trapezoid is: $\dfrac{(b_1 + b_2)h}{2} = \dfrac{(8 + 24)(5)}{2} = 80$. However, if you do not remember the formula, simply break down the trapezoid into two triangles and a rectangle:

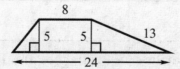

Use the Pythagorean theorem to find the base of the right-hand triangle: $x^2 + 5^2 = 13^2 \Rightarrow x = \sqrt{169 - 25} = \sqrt{144} = 12$. This implies that the base of the left-hand triangle is: $24 - 12 - 8 = 4$. Thus, the left-hand triangle's area is: $\dfrac{4 \cdot 5}{2} = 10$; the right-hand triangle's area is: $\dfrac{12 \cdot 5}{2} = 30$; and the rectangle's area $= 8 \cdot 5 = 40$. The trapezoid area is: $10 + 30 + 40 = 80$.

FORMULAS FOR PARALLELOGRAMS AND TRAPEZOIDS

Parallelogram Area: $A_{parallelogram} = b \cdot h$

Trapezoid Area: $A_{trapezoid} = \dfrac{(b_1 + b_2)h}{2}$

A **rectangle** is any four-sided figure that has four right angles. Since the opposite sides of a rectangle are congruent, it is customary to speak of the two dimensions of a rectangle: width and length. A **square** is a rectangle with four congruent sides.

To find the **perimeter** of either a rectangle or a square, simply add the lengths of the four sides. To find the **area** of a rectangle, multiply the width times the length. In a square, the sides are all congruent, so there is no difference between length and width. To find the area of a square, just square the length of one side.

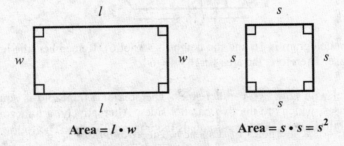

Area $= l \cdot w$ Area $= s \cdot s = s^2$

FORMULAS FOR RECTANGLES AND SQUARES

Rectangular Perimeter: $P_{rectangle} = 2(\text{width}) + 2(\text{length})$
$$= 2w + 2l = 2(w + l)$$

Rectangular Area: $A_{rectangle} = w \cdot l$

Square Perimeter: $P_{square} = 4(\text{side}) = 4s$

Square Area: $A_{square} = s \cdot s = s^2$

Circle Properties and Formulas

Properties of Circles

A *circle* is a closed plane curve, all points of which are equidistant from the center. A complete circle contains 360°, and a semicircle contains 180°. The distance from the center of the circle to any point on the circle is called the *radius*.

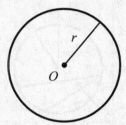

A line segment that passes through the center of the circle and that has endpoints on the circle is called the *diameter*. The diameter of a circle is twice the radius.

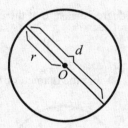

A *chord* is a line segment that connects any two points on a circle. A *secant* is a chord that extends in either one or both directions. A *tangent* is a line that touches a circle at one and only one point. A line that is tangent to a circle is perpendicular to a radius drawn to the point of tangency. The *circumference*, or perimeter, is the curved line that bounds the circle. An *arc* of a circle is any part of the circumference. The symbol for arc is " ⌒ ."

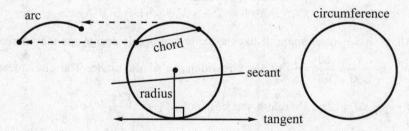

Example:

Two different circles lie in a flat plane. The circles may or may not intersect, but neither circle lies entirely within the other. What is the difference between the minimum and maximum number of lines that could be common tangents to both circles?

➤ Three cases are possible for the orientation of the two circles:

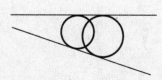  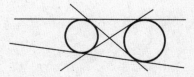

The difference between the minimum and maximum number of tangents that could be common to both circles is: $4 - 2 = 2$.

A ***central angle***, such as $\angle AOB$ in the next figure, is an angle with a vertex at the center of the circle and with sides that are radii. A central angle is equal to, or has the same number of degrees as, it's intercepted arc. An ***inscribed angle***, such as $\angle MNP$, is an angle with a vertex on the circle and with sides that are chords. An inscribed angle has half the number of degrees of its intercepted arc. $\angle MNP$ intercepts $\overset{\frown}{MP}$ and has half the degrees of $\overset{\frown}{MP}$.

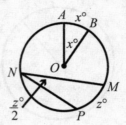

Since the number of degrees of arc in an entire circle is 360, the length of the intercepted arc of a central angle is $\dfrac{x}{360}$ of the circumference of the circle, where x is the degree measure of the central angle.

Example:

In the following circle with center O, if $x = 60$ and the diameter of the circle is 12, what is the length of $\overset{\frown}{MN}$?

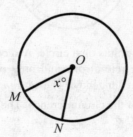

➤ Since the $\angle MON$ is a central angle, it has the same number of degrees as the intercepted $\overset{\frown}{MN}$. Thus, the length of $\overset{\frown}{MN}$ is: $\dfrac{x}{360} = \dfrac{60}{360} = \dfrac{1}{6}$ of the circumference of the circle. The circumference of the circle is:

$C = 2\pi r = 2\pi \cdot \dfrac{d}{2} = \pi d = 12\pi$. Therefore, the length of $\overset{\frown}{MN}$ is: $\dfrac{12\pi}{6} = 2\pi$.

If each side of a polygon is tangent to a circle, the polygon is ***circumscribed*** about the circle and the circle is ***inscribed*** in the polygon. Conversely, if each vertex of a polygon lies on a circle, then the polygon is ***inscribed*** in the circle and the circle is ***circumscribed*** about the polygon.

Example:

In the following figure, $\triangle ABC$ is circumscribed about a circle and square $DEFG$ is inscribed in a circle.

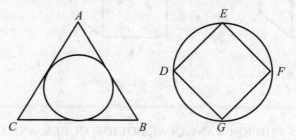

An angle inscribed in a semicircle is a right angle because the semicircle has a measure of 180°.

Example:

In the following figure, $\overset{\frown}{NP}$ has a degree measure of 180°; therefore, the degree measure of $\angle NMP$ must be 90°.

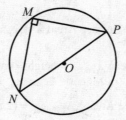

Formulas for Circles

FORMULAS FOR CIRCLES

Circle Circumference: $C_{circle} = 2\pi r = \pi d$; $r = $ radius, $d = $ diameter

Circle Area: $A_{circle} = \pi r^2$

$$\pi(\text{pi}) \approx \frac{22}{7} \approx 3.14$$

Surface Area and Volume of Solids

In a three-dimensional figure, the total space contained within the figure is called the *volume*; it is expressed in *cubic denominations* (e.g., cm^3). The total outside surface is called the *surface area*; it is expressed in *square denominations* (e.g., cm^2). In computing volume and surface area, express all dimensions in the same denomination.

A *rectangular solid* is a figure of three dimensions having six rectangular faces that meet each other at right angles. The three dimensions are length, width, and height. A *cube* is a rectangular solid whose edges are equal. A *cylinder* is a solid composed of two circular, parallel planes joined at the edges by a curved surface. The centers of the circular planes both lie in a line perpendicular to both planes.

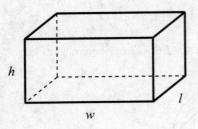 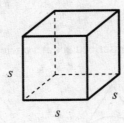 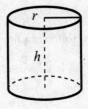

Volume = $w \cdot l \cdot h$ Cube Volume = s^3 Cylinder Volume = $h\pi r^2$

FORMULAS FOR RECTANGULAR SOLIDS, CUBES, AND CYLINDERS

Rectangular Solid Volume: $V_{\text{rectangular solid}} = \text{width} \cdot \text{length} \cdot \text{height} = w \cdot l \cdot h$

Rectangular Solid Surface Area: $A_{\text{rectangular solid}} = 2(w \cdot l) + 2(l \cdot h) + 2(h \cdot w)$

Cube Volume: $V_{\text{cube}} = \text{side}^3 = s^3$

Cube Surface Area: $SA_{\text{cube}} = 6s^2$

Cylinder Volume: $V_{\text{cylinder}} = \text{height} \cdot \text{end area} = h\left(\pi r^2\right)$

Cylinder Surface Area: $SA_{\text{cylinder}} = (2\pi r \cdot h) + 2\left(\pi r^2\right)$

---

*Example*s:

1. What is the volume and surface area of the following rectangular solid?

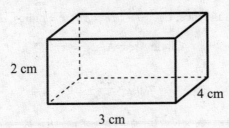

➤ Volume = $w \cdot l \cdot h = 3 \cdot 4 \cdot 2 = 24 \text{ cm}^3$

   Surface Area = $2(w \cdot l) + 2(l \cdot h) + 2(h \cdot w) = 2(3 \cdot 4) + 2(4 \cdot 2) + 2(2 \cdot 3) = 24 + 16 + 12 = 52 \text{ cm}^2$

2. What is the volume and surface area of the following cube?

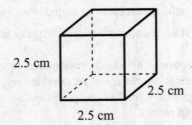

$\quad\blacktriangleright\quad$ Volume $= s^3 = (2.5)^3 = 15.625$ cm^3

$\qquad$ Surface Area $= 6s^2 = 6(2.5)^2 = 37.5$ cm^2

3. What is the volume and surface area of the following cylindrical solid?

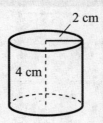

$\quad\blacktriangleright\quad$ Volume $= h\left(\pi r^2\right) = 4\left(\pi \cdot 2^2\right) = 16\pi$ cm^3

$\qquad$ Surface Area $= (2\pi r \cdot h) + 2\left(\pi r^2\right) = (2\pi \cdot 2 \cdot 4) + 2\left(\pi \cdot 2^2\right) = 16\pi + 8\pi = 24\pi$ cm^2

The *surface area of a sphere* is 4π multiplied by the radius squared. The *volume of a sphere* is $\dfrac{4\pi}{3}$ multiplied by the radius cubed.

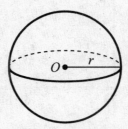

FORMULAS FOR SPHERES

Sphere Surface Area: $SA_{sphere} = 4\pi r^2$

Sphere Volume: $V_{sphere} = \dfrac{4\pi r^3}{3}$

EXERCISE **10**

Geometry

DIRECTIONS: Choose the correct answer to each of the following items. Answers are on page 791.

1. In the figure below, $x = ?$

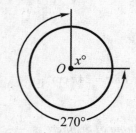

270°

O is the center of the circle.

   A. 30   **C.** 90   **E.** 270
   B. 60   **D.** 120

2. In the figure below, $x = ?$

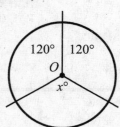

O is the center of the circle.

   A. 45   **C.** 90   **E.** 150
   B. 60   **D.** 120

3. In the figure below, $x = ?$

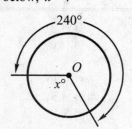

   A. 60   **C.** 120   **E.** 180
   B. 90   **D.** 150

4. In the figure below, $x = ?$

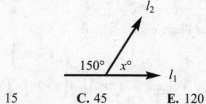

   A. 15   **C.** 45   **E.** 120
   B. 30   **D.** 90

5. In the figure below, $x = ?$

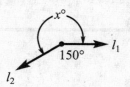

   A. 15°   **C.** 45   **E.** 120
   B. 30   **D.** 90

6. In the figure below, $x = ?$

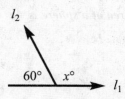

   A. 210   **C.** 150   **E.** 120
   B. 180   **D.** 135

7. In the figure below, $x = ?$

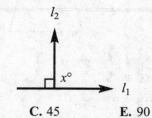

   A. 15   **C.** 45   **E.** 90
   B. 30   **D.** 60

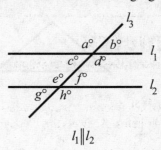

8. In the figure below, $x = ?$

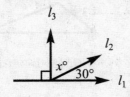

   A. 15   C. 45   E. 90
   B. 30   D. 60

9. In the figure below, $x = ?$

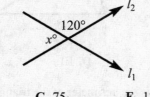

   A. 45   C. 75   E. 120
   B. 60   D. 90

10. In the figure below, $x = ?$

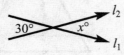

   A. 30   C. 55   E. 80
   B. 45   D. 65

11. Which of the following is (are) true of the figure below?

   I. $\overline{AB} \cong \overline{BC}$
   II. $\overline{BC} \cong \overline{AC}$
   III. $\overline{AC} \cong \overline{AB}$

   A. I only   D. I and III only
   B. II only   E. I, II, and III
   C. I and II only

Items #12–16 are based on the following figure:

$l_1 \| l_2$

12. Which of the following is (are) necessarily true?

   I. $a = b$
   II. $b = c$
   III. $g = h$

   A. I only   D. II and III only
   B. II only   E. I, II, and III
   C. I and II only

13. Which of the following is (are) necessarily true?

   I. $b = c$
   II. $d = c$
   III. $g = e$

   A. I only   D. II and III only
   B. III only   E. I, II, and III
   C. I and III only

14. Which of the following is (are) necessarily true?

   I. $c + d = 180$
   II. $c + a = 180$
   III. $b + g = 180$

   A. I only   D. II and III only
   B. III only   E. I, II, and III
   C. I and II only

15. If $e = 120$, then $g = ?$

   A. 60   C. 120   E. 180
   B. 90   D. 150

16. If $h = 60$, then $d = ?$

   A. 60   C. 120   E. 180
   B. 90   D. 150

17. Which of the following is (are) true of the figure below?

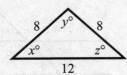

   I. $x = y$
  II. $y = z$
 III. $z = x$

A. I only
B. II only
C. III only
D. I and II only
E. I, II, and III

18. Which of the following is (are) true of the figure below?

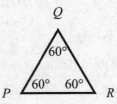

   I. $\overline{PQ} \cong \overline{QR}$
  II. $\overline{QR} \cong \overline{PR}$
 III. $\overline{PR} \cong \overline{PQ}$

A. I only
B. III only
C. I and II only
D. II and III only
E. I, II, and III

19. Which of the following is (are) true of the figure below?

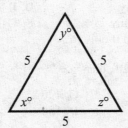

   I. $x = y$
  II. $y = z$
 III. $z = x$

A. I only
B. I and II only
C. I and III only
D. II and III only
E. I, II, and III

20. What is the perimeter of the triangle below?

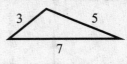

A. 3
B. 5
C. 15
D. 20
E. 30

21. What is the perimeter of the triangle below?

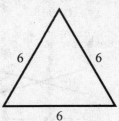

A. 20
B. 18
C. 12
D. 10
E. 8

22. What is the perimeter of the triangle below?

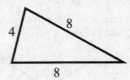

A. 6
B. 12
C. 18
D. 21
E. 24

23. What is the area of the triangle below?

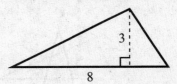

A. 3
B. 6
C. 12
D. 18
E. 24

24. What is the area of the triangle below?

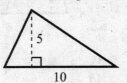

A. 5
B. 10
C. 12
D. 15
E. 25

25. What is the area of the triangle below?

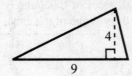

A. 6   **C.** 15   **E.** 24
B. 12   **D.** 18

26. In the figure below, what is the length of $\overline{RS}$?

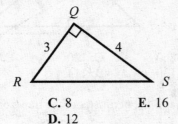

A. 3   **C.** 8   **E.** 16
B. 5   **D.** 12

27. In the figure below, what is the length of $\overline{AB}$?

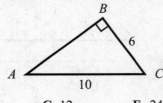

A. 4   **C.** 12   **E.** 24
B. 8   **D.** 16

28. In the figure below, what is the length of $\overline{PR}$?

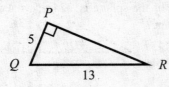

A. 12   **C.** 27   **E.** 48
B. 23   **D.** 36

29. In the figure below, what is the length of $\overline{AC}$?

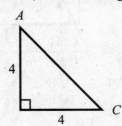

A. 2   **C.** 4   **E.** 8
B. $2\sqrt{2}$ **D.** $4\sqrt{2}$

30. In the figure below, what is the length of $\overline{JL}$?

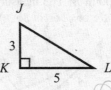

A. $\sqrt{2}$ **C.** $\sqrt{15}$ **E.** $\sqrt{34}$
B. $2\sqrt{2}$ **D.** $2\sqrt{6}$

31. What is the area of the parallelogram below?

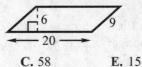

A. 180   **C.** 58   **E.** 15
B. 120   **D.** 29

32. What is the area of the parallelogram below?

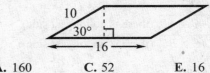

A. 160   **C.** 52   **E.** 16
B. 80   **D.** 26

33. What is the area of the parallelogram below?

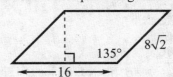

A. $128\sqrt{3}$ **C.** 128   **E.** 64
B. $128\sqrt{2}$ **D.** $64\sqrt{2}$

34. In the figure below, $\overline{AC}$ and $\overline{BD}$ are diameters, and the measure of $\angle ABO$ is 70°. What is the measure of $\angle COD$?

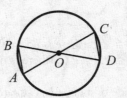

A. 110°   **C.** 40°   **E.** 30°
B. 70°   **D.** 35°

35. In the figure below, $\overline{AC}$ and $\overline{DE}$ bisect each other at point B. The measure of $\angle A$ is 20° and the measure of $\angle D$ is 86°. What is the measure of $\angle DBC$?

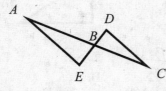

A. 106°   C. 66°   E. 33°
B. 74°   D. 45°

36. In $\triangle ABC$, the measure of $\angle A$ is 23° and the measure of $\angle B$ is 84°. What is the longest side of $\triangle ABC$?

A. $\overline{AC}$
B. $\overline{AB}$
C. $\overline{BC}$
D. $\overline{AC} \cong \overline{AB}$ (there is no longest side)
E. $\overline{AC} \cong \overline{BC}$ (there is no longest side)

37. In $\triangle ABC$, the measure of $\angle A$ is 40° and the measure of $\angle B$ is 70°. What is the longest side of $\triangle ABC$?

A. $\overline{AC}$
B. $\overline{AB}$
C. $\overline{BC}$
D. $\overline{AC} \cong \overline{AB}$ (there is no longest side)
E. $\overline{AC} \cong \overline{BC}$ (there is no longest side)

38. $\triangle ABC$ has three sides with lengths $\overline{AB} = 19$, $\overline{BC} = 20$, and $\overline{AC} = 21$. What is the smallest angle of $\triangle ABC$?

A. $\angle A$
B. $\angle B$
C. $\angle C$
D. $\angle A \cong \angle B$ (there is no smallest angle)
E. $\angle A \cong \angle B \cong \angle C$ (there is no smallest angle)

39. Each side of a cube is a square with an area of 49 square centimeters. What is the volume of the cube, in cubic centimeters?

A. 49   C. 7^4 E. 7^{49}
B. 7^3 D. 49^7

40. Each side of a cube is a square. The total surface area of all sides of this cube is 54 square inches. What is the volume of the cube, in cubic inches?

A. 54^3 C. 9^3 E. 9
B. $\left(\sqrt{54}\right)^3$ D. 27

41. What is the area of the trapezoid below?

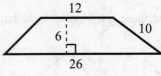

A. 260   C. 120   E. 58
B. 130   D. 114

42. What is the perimeter of the trapezoid below?

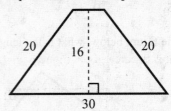

A. 70   C. 80   E. 100
B. 76   D. 90

43. The volume of a sphere is: $V_{\text{sphere}} = \frac{4}{3}\pi r^3$, where r is the radius of the sphere. If the surface area of the sphere is 324π, what is the sphere's volume?

A. 243π C. 729π E. $1,296\pi$
B. 324π D. 972π

44. What is the perimeter of the figure below?

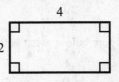

A. 6   C. 10   E. 16
B. 8   D. 12

45. What is the perimeter of the figure below?

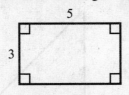

A. 8   C. 14   E. 16
B. 12   D. 15

46. What is the area of the figure below?

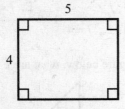

A. 10   C. 16   E. 20
B. 15   D. 18

47. What is the area of the figure below?

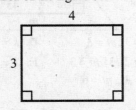

A. 6   C. 12   E. 24
B. 8   D. 16

48. What is the area of the figure below?

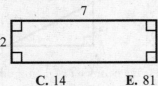

A. 5   C. 14   E. 81
B. 9   D. 25

49. In the figure below, $\overline{AB} = 5$. What is the area of square *ABCD*?

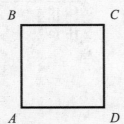

A. 5   C. 20   E. 40
B. 10   D. 25

50. If the radius of a circle is 2, what is the diameter?

A. 1   C. 3   E. 8
B. 2   D. 4

51. If the diameter of a circle is 10, what is the radius?

A. 2   C. 8   E. 20
B. 5   D. 15

52. If the radius of a circle is 3, what is the circumference?

A. 2π C. 6π E. 12π
B. 3π D. 9π

53. If the radius of a circle is 5, what is the circumference?

A. 5π C. 15π E. 24π
B. 10π D. 20π

54. If the diameter of a circle is 8, what is the circumference?

A. 8π C. 4π E. π
B. 6π D. 2π

55. If the radius of a circle is 3, what is the area?

A. π C. 6π E. 12π
B. 3π D. 9π

56. If the radius of a circle is 5, what is the area?

A. 25π C. 18π E. π
B. 21π D. 2π

57. If the diameter of a circle is 8, what is the area?

A. 16π C. 10π E. 4π
B. 12π D. 8π

58. If the diameter of a circle is 12, what is the area?

A. 18π C. 30π E. 36π
B. 24π D. 32π

59. In the figure below, what are *a* and *b*?

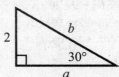

A. $a = \sqrt{3}$, $b = 2$ D. $a = 4$, $b = 2\sqrt{3}$
B. $a = 2\sqrt{3}$, $b = 4$ E. $a = 4$, $b = 4\sqrt{3}$
C. $a = 2$, $b = 2$

60. In the figure below, what are c and d?

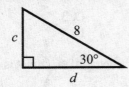

- **A.** $c = 2$, $d = \sqrt{3}$
- **B.** $c = 2\sqrt{2}$, $d = 3$
- **C.** $c = 4$, $d = 4\sqrt{3}$
- **D.** $c = 4\sqrt{2}$, $d = 2$
- **E.** $c = 3$, $d = 2\sqrt{3}$

61. In the figure below, what are e and f?

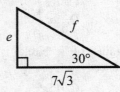

- **A.** $e = 2$, $f = 6$
- **B.** $e = \sqrt{2}$, $f = 8$
- **C.** $e = 4$, $f = 3\sqrt{5}$
- **D.** $e = 7$, $f = 10$
- **E.** $e = 7$, $f = 14$

62. In the figure below, what are g and h?

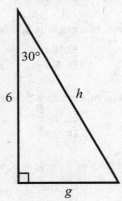

- **A.** $g = \sqrt{3}$, $h = \sqrt{3}$
- **B.** $g = 2\sqrt{2}$, $h = 2\sqrt{3}$
- **C.** $g = 2\sqrt{3}$, $h = 4\sqrt{3}$
- **D.** $g = 4$, $h = 4\sqrt{3}$
- **E.** $g = 6$, $h = 7$

63. What is the altitude of an equilateral triangle with a perimeter of 24?

- **A.** $2\sqrt{3}$
- **B.** $4\sqrt{3}$
- **C.** 6
- **D.** $4\sqrt{5}$
- **E.** 8

64. In the figure below, what are i and j?

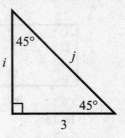

- **A.** $i = 3$, $j = 3\sqrt{2}$
- **B.** $i = 3$, $j = 3$
- **C.** $i = 4\sqrt{2}$, $j = 4$
- **D.** $i = 5$, $j = 3\sqrt{3}$
- **E.** $i = 4$, $j = 5$

65. In the figure below, what are k and m?

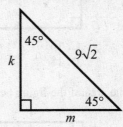

- **A.** $k = 3$, $m = 3$
- **B.** $k = 2\sqrt{3}$, $m = 3$
- **C.** $k = 4$, $m = 6$
- **D.** $k = 9$, $m = 9$
- **E.** $k = 3$, $m = 9$

66. In the figure below, $AB = BC = \sqrt{6}$. What is the length of $\overline{AC}$? Note that the triangle is not drawn to scale.

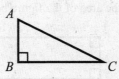

- **A.** 2
- **B.** $2\sqrt{3}$
- **C.** 3
- **D.** $3\sqrt{2}$
- **E.** 4

67. If the perimeter of a square is equal to 40, what is the length of the diagonal?

- **A.** $10\sqrt{2}$
- **B.** $5\sqrt{3}$
- **C.** 10
- **D.** $3\sqrt{5}$
- **E.** 14

68. In the figure below, what is p equal to?

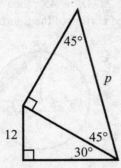

A. $2\sqrt{2}$ **C.** $10\sqrt{2}$ **E.** $24\sqrt{2}$
B. $2\sqrt{3}$ **D.** $20\sqrt{3}$

69. In the circle below, $\overline{RS}$ is parallel to diameter $\overline{PQ}$, and $\overline{PQ}$ has a length of 12. What is the length of minor arc $\overset{\frown}{RS}$?

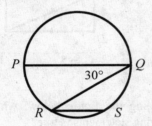

A. $\dfrac{\pi}{2}$ **C.** 2π **E.** $\dfrac{7\pi}{2}$

B. π **D.** $\dfrac{3\pi}{2}$

70. What is the number of degrees in the angle formed by the minute and hour hands of a clock at 2:20?

A. 90 **C.** 60 **E.** 30
B. 70 **D.** 50

71. What is the radius of a circle with an area of 49?

A. 7 **C.** $\dfrac{7}{\sqrt{\pi}}$ **E.** π^2

B. 7π **D.** $\dfrac{7}{\pi}$

72. What is the area of a circle with a circumference of $\dfrac{22\pi}{3}$?

A. $\dfrac{484\pi}{9}$ **C.** $\dfrac{121\pi}{3}$ **E.** $\dfrac{556\pi}{4}$

B. $\dfrac{121\pi}{9}$ **D.** $\dfrac{484\pi}{3}$

73. A circle has an area of $36\pi^3$. What is the radius of the circle?

A. 6 **C.** $6\pi^2$ **E.** $6\pi^4$
B. 6π **D.** $6\pi^3$

74. If the radius of a circle is 8, what is the circumference of the circle?

A. 4π **C.** 12π **E.** 16π
B. 8π **D.** 14π

75. In the figure below, what is the value of the shaded area?

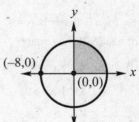

A. 16π **C.** 64π **E.** $16\pi^2$
B. 32π **D.** 66π

76. In the figure below, the length of $\overline{OA}$ is 2 and the length of $\overline{OB}$ is 3. What is the area between the two circles?

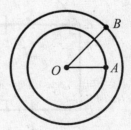

A. 4π **C.** 6π **E.** 8π
B. 5π **D.** 7π

77. In the figure below, a circle with an area of 144π is inscribed in a square. What is the area of the shaded region?

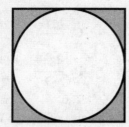

A. $576-144\pi$ D. $1,728-144\pi$
B. $216-72\pi$ E. $256-24\pi$
C. $144-24\pi$

78. A square has a perimeter of 40. A second square has an inscribed circle with an area of 64π. What is the ratio of the length of a side of the first square to the length of a side of the second square?

A. $5:8$ C. $5:16$ E. $12:\pi$
B. $5:4$ D. $10:8\pi$

79. The area of a square is $64x^2y^{16}$. What is the length of a side of the square?

A. $8xy^8$ C. $8x^2y^{16}$ E. $20x^2y^4$
B. $8xy^4$ D. $16x^2y^{16}$

80. In the figure below, what is the area of square $BCDE$?

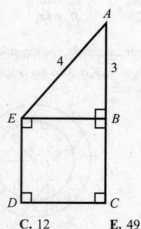

A. 5   C. 12   E. 49
B. 7   D. 24

81. What is the area of a right triangle with legs of lengths 4 and 5?

A. 6   C. 12   E. 24
B. 10   D. 20

82. In the figure below, assume O is the center of the circle. If $\angle OAB$ is $45°$, then what is the area of the shaded portion of the figure?

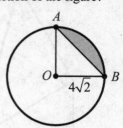

A. $32\pi-16\sqrt{2}$ D. $8\pi-16$
B. $32\pi-8$ E. $8\pi-8$
C. $4\pi-8$

83. In the figure below, rectangle $ABCD$ has an area of 15. What is the length of the diagonal $\overline{AC}$?

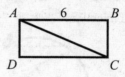

A. 4   C. 6.5   E. 7.5
B. 5   D. 7

84. Regarding the figure below, which one of the following statements is true?

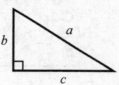

A. $a^2+b^2=c^2$ D. $b^2+c^2=a^2$
B. $a+b=c$ E. $a+c=b$
C. $b+c=a$

85. At 12 cents per square foot, how much will it cost to paint the rectangular slab in the figure below?

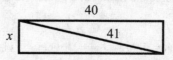

A. $43.20   C. $98.40   E. $201.50
B. $46.40   D. $196.80

86. In the figure below, what is the length of $\overline{BC}$?

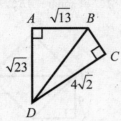

A. 1   **C.** 3   **E.** 5
B. 2   **D.** 4

87. If the diagonal of a square is $5\sqrt{2}$, what is the area of the square?

A. 10   **C.** 25   **E.** 35
B. 20   **D.** 30

88. What is the area of the rectangle in the figure below?

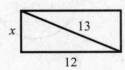

A. 156   **C.** 72   **E.** 60
B. 78   **D.** 66

89. In the figure below, what is x equal to?

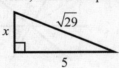

A. $\sqrt{29}-5$ **C.** 24   **E.** $\sqrt{2}$
B. $\sqrt{24}$ **D.** 2

90. If $2\sqrt{3}$ is the diagonal of a square, then what is the perimeter of the square?

A. $4\sqrt{6}$ **C.** $6\sqrt{3}$ **E.** 14
B. 8   **D.** 12

91. In the figures below, what is the ratio of the perimeter of $\triangle ABC$ to the perimeter of $\triangle DEF$?

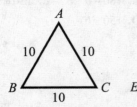

A. 1:1   **C.** 15:16   **E.** 7:3
B. 5:6   **D.** 6:5

92. In terms of π, what is the area of a circle whose radius is $2\sqrt{5}$?

A. π **C.** 10π **E.** 40π
B. 4π **D.** 20π

93. What is the radius of a circle whose area is 12π?

A. 40π **C.** $2\sqrt{3}$ **E.** 3
B. 1   **D.** 2

94. What is the radius of a circle if the distance to walk halfway around the rim of the circle is $\sqrt{6}\pi$?

A. $\sqrt{2}$ **C.** 2   **E.** 3
B. $\sqrt{3}$ **D.** $\sqrt{6}$

95. If the legs of a right triangle are 2 and 5, what is the hypotenuse?

A. $\sqrt{22}$ **C.** $5\sqrt{2}$ **E.** 6
B. $\sqrt{29}$ **D.** $\sqrt{35}$

96. If the hypotenuse of a right triangle is 37 and one leg is 35, what is the length of the other leg?

A. $4\sqrt{3}$ **C.** 12   **E.** 16
B. $6\sqrt{2}$ **D.** $14\sqrt{2}$

97. If $2\sqrt{12}$, $3\sqrt{6}$, and $4\sqrt{3}$ are the dimensions of a rectangular solid, what is the volume of the solid?

A. $216\sqrt{24}$ **C.** $144\sqrt{6}$ **E.** $\sqrt{24}$
B. $\sqrt{5,184}$ **D.** 5,184

98. What is the volume of a cylinder with an altitude of 10 and a circumference of $\sqrt{128}\pi$?

A. $\sqrt{1,280}\pi$ **C.** 640π **E.** $3,460\pi$
B. 320π **D.** $1,280\pi$

99. In the figure below, what is x equal to?

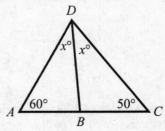

A. 30   **C.** 35   **E.** 70
B. 32   **D.** 40

100. If the ratio of the sides of a triangle are $x : x\sqrt{3} : 2x$, and the length of the smallest side is 5, what is the length of the largest side?

A. 10   **C.** $8\sqrt{3}$ **E.** 20
B. 12   **D.** 15

101. In the figure below, what is the length of $\overline{JK}$?

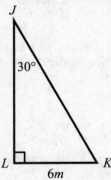

A. $6m\sqrt{3}$ **C.** $12m$ **E.** $14m$
B. $9m$ **D.** $12m\sqrt{3}$

102. In the figure below, $\triangle DEF$ is an isosceles triangle. What is the length of $\overline{DF}$?

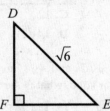

A. $2\sqrt{6}$ **C.** $\sqrt{3}$ **E.** $12\sqrt{2}$
B. $6\sqrt{2}$ **D.** 12

103. If the longest side of a 30°-60°-90° triangle is $2\sqrt{3}$, what is the area of the triangle?

A. 8   **C.** $1.5\sqrt{3}$ **E.** 1
B. 4   **D.** 2

104. In the figure below, what is the length of the diagonal $\overline{AC}$ of square $ABCD$?

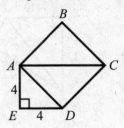

A. $4\sqrt{2}$ **C.** $8\sqrt{2}$ **E.** $32\sqrt{2}$
B. 8   **D.** 16

105. In the figure below, if $\overset{\frown}{BC}$ equals 60°, then what is the area of $\triangle ABC$?

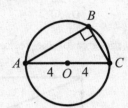

A. 16   **C.** $8\sqrt{3}$ **E.** $10\sqrt{2}$
B. $4\sqrt{3}$ **D.** 12

106. In the figure below, what is $2x - 60$ equal to?

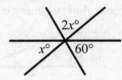

A. 80   **C.** 30   **E.** 10
B. 40   **D.** 20

107. In the figure below, a equals all of the following EXCEPT

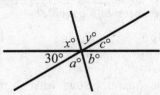

A. y **C.** $180 - b - c$ **E.** $180 - x - y$
B. $150 - x$ **D.** $150 - b$

108. In the figure below, $\overline{EC} \| \overline{AB}$ and $\overline{AD} \cong \overline{BD}$. What is the sum of the degree measures of $\angle A + \angle B + \angle BCE$?

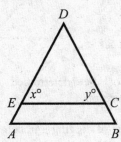

A. $(x+y)°$ **C.** $(180+x)°$ **E.** $(90-y)°$
B. $3x°$ **D.** $-2x°$

109. In the figure below, if $\overline{AE} \| \overline{BD}$ and $\overline{BD} \cong \overline{DC}$, then what is $\angle BDC$ equal to?

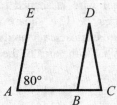

A. $10°$ **C.** $18°$ **E.** $24°$
B. $15°$ **D.** $20°$

110. In the figure below, if $l_1 \| l_2$ and $\angle d = 117°$, which other angles must also equal $117°$?

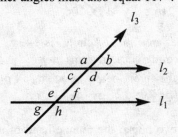

A. a, e, h **C.** c, e, f **E.** a, c, e, g
B. a, c, b **D.** h, f, b

111. In the figure below, what is the value of x?

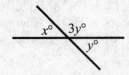

A. 30   **C.** 60   **E.** 80
B. 45   **D.** 65

112. In the figure below, which of the following statements is true?

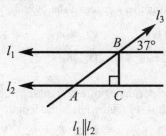

$$l_1 \| l_2$$

A. $\overline{AC} > \overline{BC}$ **D.** $\overline{AC} + \overline{BC} = \overline{AB}$
B. $\overline{AC} < \overline{BC}$ **E.** $\overline{AC} - \overline{BC} = \overline{AB}$
C. $\overline{AC} = \overline{BC}$

113. In the figure below, $\overline{OM} \| \overline{PJ}$, and $\overline{FG}$ and $\overline{EG}$ divide $\angle CGO$ into 3 congruent angles. What is the degree measure of $\angle EGC$?

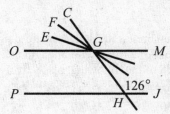

A. $18°$ **C.** $42°$ **E.** $63°$
B. $36°$ **D.** $54°$

114. In the figure below, $\triangle ABE \sim \triangle ACD$. What is the length of $\overline{CD}$?

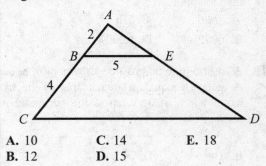

A. 10   **C.** 14   **E.** 18
B. 12   **D.** 15

115. A triangle with sides of 12, 14, and 20 is similar to a second triangle that has one side with a length of 40. What is the smallest possible perimeter of the second triangle?

A. 48   **C.** 120   **E.** 180
B. 92   **D.** 160

116. A right circular cylinder has a base whose diameter is $8x$; the height of the cylinder is $3y$. What is the volume of the cylinder?

    A. $24xy$ C. $48\pi xy$ E. $48\pi x^2 y$

    B. $24\pi x^2 y$ D. $96\pi xy$

117. If the perimeter of a rectangle is 68 yards and the width is 48 feet, what is the length?

    A. 10 yards   C. 20 feet   E. 54 feet
    B. 18 feet   D. 46 feet

118. What is the total length of fencing, in yards, needed to enclose a rectangular area that measures 46 feet long by 34 feet wide?

    A. $26\frac{1}{3}$ C. 48   E. $53\frac{1}{3}$

    B. $26\frac{2}{3}$ D. $52\frac{2}{3}$

119. An umbrella 50" long can lie diagonally on the bottom of a trunk with a length and width that are which of the following, respectively?

    A. 26", 30"   C. 31", 31"   E. 40", 30"
    B. 30", 36"   D. 40", 21"

120. A road runs 1,200 feet from A to B, and then makes a right angle going to C, a distance of 500 feet. A new road is being built directly from A to C. How many feet shorter will the new road be than the old road?

    A. 400   C. 850   E. 1,300
    B. 609   D. 1,000

121. A certain triangle has side lengths of 6, 8, and 10. A rectangle equal in area to that of the triangle has a width of 3. What is the perimeter of the rectangle?

    A. 11   C. 22   E. 30
    B. 16   D. 24

122. A ladder 65 feet long is leaning against a wall. Its lower end is 25 feet away from the wall. How many more feet away from the wall will the ladder be if the upper end is moved down 8 feet?

    A. 60   C. 14   E. 8
    B. 52   D. 10

123. A rectangular bin 4 feet long, 3 feet wide, and 2 feet high is solidly packed with bricks whose dimensions are 8 inches by 4 inches by 2 inches What is the number of bricks in the bin?

    A. 54
    B. 320
    C. 648
    D. 848
    E. Cannot be determined from the given information

124. If the cost of digging a trench is $2.12 per cubic yard, what would be the cost of digging a trench that is 2 yards long, 5 yards wide, and 4 yards deep?

    A. $21.20   C. $64.00   E. $104.80
    B. $40.00   D. $84.80

125. A piece of wire is shaped to enclose a square, whose area is 121 square inches. It is then reshaped to enclose a rectangle whose length is 13 inches. What is the area of the rectangle, in square inches?

    A. 64   C. 117   E. 234
    B. 96   D. 144

126. What is the area, in square feet, of a 2-foot-wide walk around the outside of a garden that is 30 feet long and 20 feet wide?

    A. 104   C. 680   E. 1,416
    B. 216   D. 704

127. The area of a circle is 49π. What is its circumference, in terms of π?

    A. 14π C. 49π E. 147π
    B. 28π D. 98π

128. In two hours, the minute hand of a clock rotates through an angle equal to which of the following?

    A. 90°   C. 360°   E. 1,080°
    B. 180°   D. 720°

129. A box is 12 inches in width, 16 inches in length, and 6 inches in height. How many square inches of paper would be required to cover it on all sides?

    A. 192   C. 720   E. 1,440
    B. 360   D. 900

130. If the volume of a cube is 64 cubic inches, the sum of the lengths of its edges is how many inches?

   A. 48   **C.** 24   **E.** 12

   B. 32   **D.** 16

131. In the figure below, $x = ?$

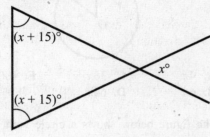

   A. 20   **C.** 50   **E.** 90

   B. 35   **D.** 65

132. What is the difference between the areas of two squares with sides of 5 and 4, respectively?

   A. 3   **C.** 9   **E.** 91

   B. 4   **D.** 16

133. A triangle with sides of 4, 6, and 8 has the same perimeter as an equilateral triangle with sides of length equal to which of the following?

   A. 2   **C.** 3   **E.** 8

   B. $\dfrac{3}{2}$ **D.** 6

134. In the figure below, $x = ?$

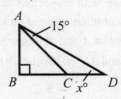

$$\overline{AB} \cong \overline{BC}$$

   A. 15   **C.** 40   **E.** 75

   B. 30   **D.** 60

135. If the area of the rectangle shown below is equal to 1, then $l = ?$

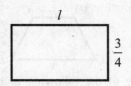

   A. $\dfrac{4}{9}$ **C.** $\dfrac{4}{3}$ **E.** 2

   B. 1   **D.** $\dfrac{9}{4}$

136. A semicircle is divided into three arcs with respective lengths 2π, 6π, and 14π. The semicircle is a part of a circle with which of the following radii?

   A. 44   **C.** 22   **E.** 6

   B. 33   **D.** 11

137. In the figure below, $x = ?$

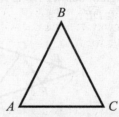

   A. 15   **C.** 45   **E.** 90

   B. 30   **D.** 60

138. In the figure below, $\angle A \cong \angle B$.

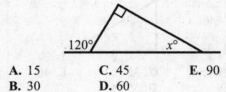

Which of the following statements must be true?

   A. $\angle A \cong \angle B \cong \angle C$

   B. $\angle A \not\cong \angle C$

   C. $\overline{AC} \cong \overline{BC}$

   D. $\overline{BC} \cong \overline{AB}$

   E. $\overline{AB} \cong \overline{AC}$

139. In the figure below, which is not necessarily drawn to scale, $\angle A \cong \angle C$ and $\angle B \cong \angle D$.

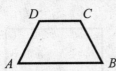

How many of the following four statements of congruence must be true?

$\angle A \cong \angle B$

$\overline{AB} \cong \overline{DC}$

$\overline{AD} \cong \overline{BC}$

$\overline{AB} \cong \overline{BC} \cong \overline{CD} \cong \overline{AD}$

A. 0	**C.** 2	**E.** 4
B. 1	**D.** 3	

140. In the diagram below, $\angle ABC = 90°$, $\overline{AC} = 10\sqrt{2}$, and $\overline{AB} + \overline{BC} = 3\sqrt{38}$. What is the area of $\triangle ABC$?

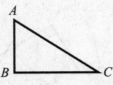

A. 19	**C.** 32	**E.** 40
B. 29	**D.** 35.5	

141. In the diagram below, $\overline{AD} \cong \overline{AE}$ and $\overline{AB} \cong \overline{BF} \cong \overline{CE} \cong \overline{CF} \cong \overline{DE}$.

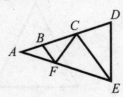

What is the degree measure of $\angle DAE$?

A. 20°	**C.** 25°	**E.** 35°
B. 24°	**D.** 30°	

142. In the figure below, $\triangle ABC$ intersects a circle with center O. $\overline{AB}$ is tangent to the circle at A. If $\overline{AB} = 8$ and $\overline{BO} = 10$, what is the area of the circle?

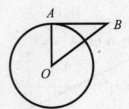

A. 4π	**C.** 36π	**E.** 100π
B. 6π	**D.** 64π	

143. The figure below shows a circle with center O, two radii $\overline{OA}$ and $\overline{OB}$, and two tangents $\overline{AC}$ and $\overline{BC}$. What is the area of the shaded region?

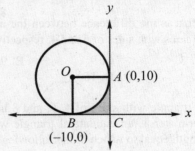

A. $100 - 100\pi$	**C.** $50 - 50\pi$	**E.** $100 - 25\pi$
B. $50 - 100\pi$	**D.** $50 - 25\pi$	

144. The figure below shows two circles lying in the same plane with respective centers at O and P. $\overline{AB}$ is a common external tangent segment to the two circles at A and B, respectively. If $\overline{OA} = 13$, $\overline{PB} = 3$, and $\overline{OP} = 26$, then what is the length of $\overline{AB}$?

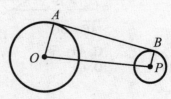

A. 26	**C.** 24	**E.** 18
B. 25	**D.** 20	

145. The figure below shows a circle of area 144π square inches with a radius drawn to the point of tangency of the circle on the x-axis.

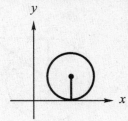

If this point of tangency is 16 inches from the origin, then the number of inches from the origin to the center of the circle is:

A. 12   **C.** 16   **E.** 20

B. $12\sqrt{2}$ **D.** $16\sqrt{2}$

146. In the figure below, $\overline{TP} \cong \overline{RA}$, and $\overline{TR} \| \overline{PA}$.

$\overline{TR} = 12$, $\overline{PA} = 44$. If $\angle P = 45°$, what is the area of *TRAP*?

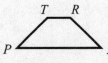

A. 448   **C.** 520   **E.** 1,792

B. 464   **D.** 896

147. In the figure below, which is not necessarily drawn to scale, $\angle ABC = 90°$, $\overline{AB} = 10$, and $\dfrac{\overline{AB}}{\overline{BC}} = 1$. What is the length of $\overline{AC}$?

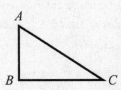

A. 10   **C.** $10\sqrt{2}$ **E.** $20\sqrt{3}$

B. 20   **D.** $10\sqrt{3}$

148. In the figure below, B and E lie on $\overline{AC}$ and $\overline{AD}$, respectively, of $\triangle ACD$, such that $\overline{BE} \| \overline{CD}$. $\overline{BD} \perp \overline{AC}$, and $\overline{BC} \cong \overline{ED}$. If $\overline{BC} = 10$ and $\overline{CD} = 20$, what is the area of $\triangle ABE$?

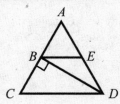

A. 100

B. $50\sqrt{3}$

C. 50

D. $25\sqrt{3}$

E. Cannot be determined from the given information

149. The figure below shows three acute angles and two obtuse angles.

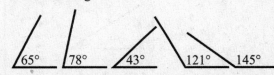

If two different angles are created randomly using the five angles shown, what is the probability that both angles are acute?

A. $\dfrac{1}{10}$ **C.** $\dfrac{2}{5}$ **E.** $\dfrac{3}{10}$

B. $\dfrac{1}{5}$ **D.** $\dfrac{3}{5}$

150. The perimeter of a regular hexagon is given by the formula: $P_{hexagon} = 6s$, where s is the length of one side. If one side of a regular hexagon has a length of 3, what is the perimeter?

A. 12   **C.** 18   **E.** 30

B. 15   **D.** 21

151. The volume of a cone is $\dfrac{\pi r^2 h}{3}$, where r is the radius of the cone base and h is the cone height. What is the volume, in cubic inches, of a cone of height 12 inches that has a base of radius 3 inches?

    A. 144π C. 72π E. 36π
    B. 108π D. 54π

Coordinate Geometry

Coordinate Axis System

The easiest way to understand the coordinate axis system is as an analog to the points of the compass. If we take a plot of land, we can divide it into quadrants:

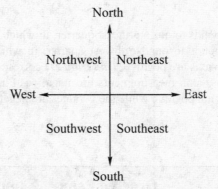

Now, if we add measuring units along each of the directional axes, we can actually describe any location on this piece of land by two numbers.

Example:

Point P is located at 4 units East and 5 units North. Point Q is located at 4 units West and 5 units North. Point R is located at 4 units West and 2 units South. Point T is located at 3 units East and 4 units South.

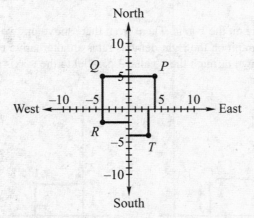

The coordinate system used in coordinate geometry differs from our map of a plot of land in that it uses x- and y-axes divided into negative and positive regions.

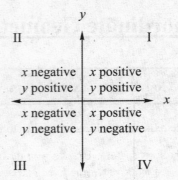

It is easy to see that *Quadrant I* corresponds to our Northeast quarter, in which the measurements on both the *x*- and *y*-axes are positive. *Quadrant II* corresponds to our Northwest quarter, in which the measurements on the *x*-axis are negative and the measurements on the *y*-axis are positive. *Quadrant III* corresponds to our Southwest quarter, in which both the *x*-axis measurements and the *y*-axis measurements are negative. Finally, *Quadrant IV* corresponds to our Southeast quarter, in which the *x*-values are positive while the *y*-values are negative.

Ordered Pairs

An *ordered pair* of coordinates has the general form (x, y). The first element refers to the *x-coordinate*: the distance left or right of the *origin*, or intersection of the axes. The second element gives the *y-coordinate*: the distance up or down from the origin.

Example:

Plot $(3, 2)$.

➤ Move to the positive 3 value on the *x*-axis. Then, from there move up two units on the *y*-axis, as illustrated by the graph on the left. The graph on the right demonstrates an alternative method: the point $(3, 2)$ is located at the intersection of a line drawn through the *x*-value 3 parallel to the *y*-axis and a line drawn through the *y*-value 2 parallel to the *x*-axis.

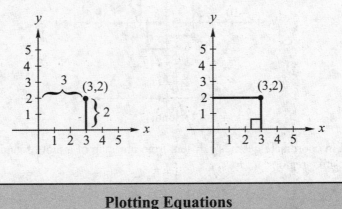

Plotting Equations

The coordinate axis system provides a framework for plotting equations. Simply plot several pairs of points for the given equation.

*Example*s:

1. Plot the equation $x = y$.

    ➢ This equation has an infinite number of solutions:

x	1	2	3	5	0	−3	−5	...
y	1	2	3	5	0	−3	−5	...

Plot these pairs of x and y on the axis system. Draw a line through them to produce a plot of the original equation. The complete picture of the equation $x = y$ is a straight line including all the real numbers such that x is equal to y.

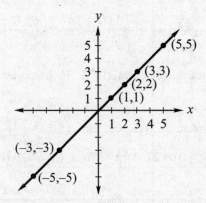

2. Plot the equation $y = 2x$.

    ➢ This equation has an infinite number of solutions:

x	−4	−2	−1	0	1	2	4	...
y	−8	−4	−2	0	2	4	8	...

After entering the points on the graph, complete the picture. It is a straight line, but it rises more rapidly than does $x = y$.

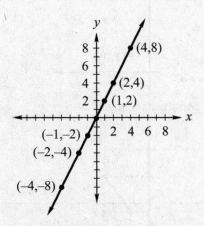

Midpoint of Line Segments

For a line segment between two points, (x_1, y_1) and (x_2, y_2), the **midpoint** $= \left(\dfrac{x_1 + x_2}{2}, \dfrac{y_1 + y_2}{2} \right)$. The x-coordinate of the midpoint is the average of the two x-axis endpoints and the x-coordinate of the midpoint is the average of the two y-axis endpoints.

*Example*s:

1. Find the midpoint between $(-5, 8)$ and $(11, 34)$.

   ➤ The midpoint is $\left(\dfrac{x_1 + x_2}{2}, \dfrac{y_1 + y_2}{2} \right) = \left(\dfrac{-5 + 11}{2}, \dfrac{8 + 34}{2} \right) = \left(\dfrac{6}{2}, \dfrac{42}{2} \right) = (3, 21)$.

2. One endpoint of a circle diameter is located at $(13, 1)$. If the center of the circle is $(15, 10)$, find the other endpoint.

   ➤ The midpoint of the diameter is $(15, 10)$, so $15 = \dfrac{x_1 + x_2}{2} = \dfrac{13 + x_2}{2}$ and $10 = \dfrac{y_1 + y_2}{2} = \dfrac{1 + y_2}{2}$.

   $x_2 = (15 \cdot 2) - 13 = 17$ and $y_2 = (10 \cdot 2) - 1 = 19$. Thus, $(x_2, y_2) = (17, 19)$.

Distance Between Two Points

To determine the distance between two points on a coordinate graph, consider points P and Q. For simplicity's sake, we will confine the discussion to the first quadrant, but the method generally works in all quadrants and even with lines covering two or more quadrants. Assign the value (x_1, y_1) to point P and (x_2, y_2) to point Q:

To find distance between points P and Q, construct a triangle:

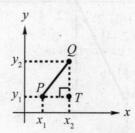

Point T now has the coordinates (x_2, y_1). To calculate the length of $\overline{PT}$, find the distance moved on the x-axis: $x_2 - x_1$ units. The y-coordinate does not change. Similarly, the length of $\overline{QT}$ will be $y_2 - y_1$ since the distance is purely vertical, moving up from y_1 to y_2, with no change in the x-value. Apply the Pythagorean theorem:

$$(PQ)^2 = (PT)^2 + (QT)^2 = (x_2 - x_1)^2 + (y_2 - y_1)^2 \Rightarrow PQ = \sqrt{(x_2 - x_1)^2 + (y_2 - y_1)^2}$$

Example:

In the following figure, what is the length of $\overline{PQ}$?

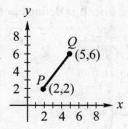

➤ Find the length of $\overline{PQ}$ by constructing a triangle:

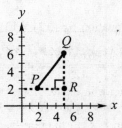

$\overline{QR}$ runs from $(5,6)$ to $(5,2)$, so it must be 4 units long. $\overline{PR}$ runs from $(2,2)$ to $(5,2)$, so it is 3 units long. Use the Pythagorean theorem: $\left(\overline{PQ}\right)^2 = \left(\overline{QR}\right)^2 + \left(\overline{PR}\right)^2 = 4^2 + 3^2 = 16 + 9 = 25$. Therefore, $\overline{PQ} = \sqrt{25} = 5$.

Therefore, you can find the length of any line segment drawn in a coordinate axis system between points (x_1, y_1) and (x_2, y_2) using this ***distance formula***: $d = \sqrt{(x_2 - x_1)^2 + (y_2 - y_1)^2}$. Notice that it does not actually matter which point is considered the start of the line and the end of the line, since the change in each coordinate is squared in the distance formula.

Example:

In the following figure, what is the distance between P and Q?

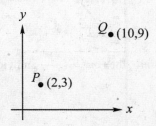

➤ The distance between P and Q is: $\sqrt{(x_2 - x_1)^2 + (y_2 - y_1)^2} = \sqrt{(10-2)^2 + (9-3)^2} = \sqrt{64+36} = \sqrt{100} = 10$.

Linear Functions

Slope-Intercept Form

If x and y are related by a linear equation, then y is a ***linear function***. Except for a vertical line, every line equation is a linear function that can be represented in ***slope-intercept form***: $y = mx + b$. m is the slope of the line and b is the y-intercept. The y-intercept is the y-coordinate of the point where the line intersects the y-axis, or where $x = 0$. The ***slope***, m, of a line describes the steepness of the line. It is defined as the change in y-values divided by the change in x-values, or rise over run: ***slope*** $= m = \dfrac{y_2 - y_1}{x_2 - x_1} = \dfrac{rise}{run}$.

Examples:

1. Find the slope of the line containing $(3,2)$ and $(8,22)$.

   ➤ $m = \dfrac{y_2 - y_1}{x_2 - x_1} = \dfrac{22 - 2}{8 - 3} = \dfrac{20}{5} = 4$.

2. Find the slope of the line given by the equation $6x + 12y = 13$.

   ➤ $6x + 12y = 13 \Rightarrow 12y = -6x + 13 \Rightarrow y = \dfrac{-6x + 13}{12} \Rightarrow y = -\dfrac{x}{2} + \dfrac{13}{12}$. Therefore, the slope is $-\dfrac{1}{2}$.

3. The points $(-5,12)$, $(0,7)$ and $(10,-3)$ lie on a line. What is the y-intercept of this line?

   ➤ The x-coordinate of the second point is 0. Therefore, this point's y-coordinate, 7, is the y-intercept of the line.

Parallel Lines

The equation of a line that is parallel to the x-axis is $y = k$, where is a constant. The equation of a line that is parallel to the y-axis is $x = c$, where c is a constant. If two lines are parallel, their slopes are equal and vice versa.

Example:

Find the equation for a line that passes through the point $(0,12)$ and is parallel to the line $y = 7x - 15$.

➤ A line has slope-intercept form $y = mx + b$. If the line passes through the y-axis at $(0,12)$, then the y-intercept $b = +12$. If the two lines are parallel, then the slopes are equal and $m = +7$. Therefore, the line equation is $y = mx + b \Rightarrow y = 7x + 12$.

Perpendicular Lines

If two perpendicular lines have slopes m_1 and m_2, then $m_1 = -\dfrac{1}{m_2}$ and vice versa.

Example:

The equation of a line is $y = \dfrac{x}{4} + 10$. If a second line is perpendicular to the line, what is the slope of this line?

➢ If two lines are perpendicular to one another, their slopes are opposite reciprocals of one another. Thus, if a line has a slope of $\dfrac{1}{4}$, then the line perpendicular to it has a slope of -4.

Quadratic Functions

If y is expressed in the form $y = ax^2 + bx + c$, where $a \neq 0$ and b is any real number, y is a *quadratic function*. Graphs of quadratic functions are called parabolas.

Example:

A quadratic function of the form $y = ax^2 + bx + c$ includes the following ordered pairs of (x, y): $(1,17)$, $(5,61)$, and $(7,95)$. What is the value of c for this quadratic function?

➢ Set up the system of three simultaneous equations that are generated by the three ordered pairs:

$$17 = a(1)^2 + b(1) + c \Rightarrow 17 = a + b + c$$
$$61 = a(5)^2 + b(5) + c \Rightarrow 61 = 25a + 5b + c$$
$$95 = a(7)^2 + b(7) + c \Rightarrow 95 = 49a + 7b + c$$

Use the method of solving simultaneous equations to determine the values of a, b, and c. Multiply the first equation by -1, and add it to the other two equations to eliminate c:

$$\begin{array}{ll} -1(17 = a + b + c) & \qquad -1(17 = a + b + c) \\ + \;\; 61 = 25a + 5b + c & \qquad + \;\; 95 = 49a + 7b + c \\ \hline \;\;\;\; 44 = 24a + 4b & \qquad \;\;\;\; 78 = 48a + 6b \end{array}$$

Now, combine these new equations to eliminate a. Multiply the first equation by -2, and add it to the second equation to eliminate a:

$$\begin{array}{l} -2(44 = 24a + 4b) \\ + \;\; 78 = 48a + 6b \\ \hline -10 = -2b \Rightarrow b = 5 \end{array}$$

Substitute 5 for b in either of the new equations and solve for a: $44 = 24a + 4(5) \Rightarrow 24a = 24 \Rightarrow a = 1$. Finally, substitute the values for a and b into any of the three original equations to solve for c. Since the first equation is simplest, we'll use that one: $17 = a + b + c \Rightarrow 17 = 1 + 5 + c \Rightarrow c = 11$.

Identifying Graphs of Functions

You may be asked simply to identify graphs of linear and quadratic functions. The graph of a linear function is a straight line, while the graph of a quadratic function is called a parabola and always has the shape of a curve about the

y-axis. The basic quadratic graph that you need to know is $f(x) = x^2$, as illustrated in the second of the following examples.

Examples:

1. The line of best fit for $y = f(x)$ for the ordered pairs $(-4, -18)$, $(1, 3)$, $(2, 6)$, $(3, 8)$, and $(4, 14)$ is best represented by which of the following graphs?

A. 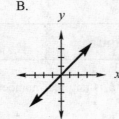 B. C. 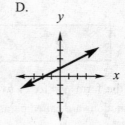 D. E.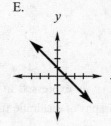

> The correct answer is (A). Both x and y increase in value for each ordered pair, so eliminate (C) and (E). You can eliminate (B) since the values of x and y in the given ordered pairs clearly indicate that $x \neq y$. Finally, eliminate (D) because when $x = 1$, $y = 3$, whereas in the graph of (D), $y < 3$ when $x = 1$.

2. Which of the following graphs depicts a quadratic function?

F. 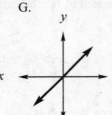 G. H. 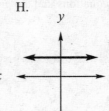 J. 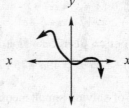 K.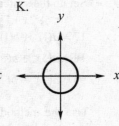

> All quadratic equations can be written in the form $y = ax^2 + bx + c$. (G) is a linear plot with the y-intercept equal to 0: $y = ax$. (H) is a constant value for y: $y = k$. (K) is a plot of a circle: $x^2 + y^2 = k$, where k is a constant. (J) is a complicated function without a standard form of equation. Only (F) is a quadratic equation: $y = ax^2$.

Functions can be also mathematical models of real-life situations. For example, an item might present information about the projected sales of a product at various prices and ask for a mathematical model in the form of a graph or equation that represents projected sales as a function of price.

Qualitative Behavior of Graphs

You should also understand how the graphs of functions behave qualitatively. Items on the exam might show the graph of a function in the xy-coordinate plane and ask for the number of values of x for which $f(x)$ equals a particular value. Alternatively, an item may present a graph with numerical values, requiring you to recognize the form of the graphed function.

*Example*s:

1. The following figure shows a graph of the function $y = x^2 + 2x + 6$. The smallest possible integer value of $y = ?$

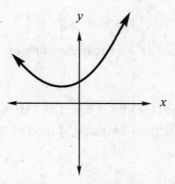

➤ The lowest point on the function occurs when $x < 0$. Find the symmetry by substitution: if $x = 1$, $y = 9$; if $x = 0$, $y = 6$; if $x = -1$, $y = 5$; if $x = -2$, $y = 6$; if $x = -3$, $y = 9$. The coordinates of these points are $(-3, 9)$, $(-2, 6)$, $(-1, 5)$, $(0, 6)$, and $(1, 9)$, respectively. Thus, the lowest point occurs at $(-1, 5)$. Alternatively, solve for the vertex using the properties of parabolas. The standard form of a parabola is: $y = a(x - h)^2 + k$, where the vertex is at (h, k). Write the equation in standard form: $y = (x^2 + 2x + 1) + 6 - 1 = (x + 1)^2 + 5 = [x - (-1)]^2 + 5$. Therefore, the vertex is at $(-1, 5)$.

2. What is the sum of all distinct integer x-values for the graph of the absolute value function in the following figure?

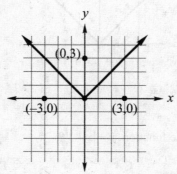

➤ Each negative x-value has a canceling positive x-value. Therefore, the answer is zero.

Transformation Effects on Graphs

When you alter a graph, you transform it. If you transform a graph without changing its shape, you translate it. Vertical and horizontal transformations are translations. Items on the exam may test knowledge of the effects of simple translations of graphs of functions. For example, the graph of a function $f(x)$ could be given and you might be asked items about the graph of the function $f(x + 2)$.

Vertical Translations

To move a function up or down, you add or subtract outside the function. That is, $f(x)+b$ is $f(x)$ moved up b units, and $f(x)-b$ is $f(x)$ moved down b units.

Example:

In order to obtain the graph of $y=(x+2)^2+6$ from the graph of $y=x^2+4x+11$, how should the graph of $y=x^2+4x+11$ be moved?

➢ Rewrite the original in the form $f(x)+b$: $y=x^2+4x+11 \Rightarrow y=x^2+4x+4+7=(x+2)^2+7$. Thus, to obtain the graph of $y=(x+2)^2+6$ from the graph of $y=(x+2)^2+7$, the graph must be moved one unit down.

Horizontal Translations

To shift a function to the left or to the right, add or subtract inside the function. That is, $f(x+b)$ is $f(x)$ shifted b units to the left, and $f(x-b)$ is $f(x)$ shifted b units to the right.

Example:

The following graph is of the function $y=|x|$.

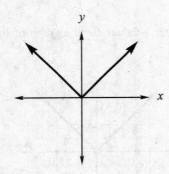

Which of the following is a graph of the function $y=|x+3|$?

A.   B.   C.   D.   E.

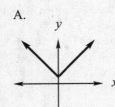   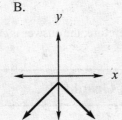   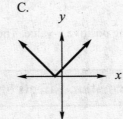   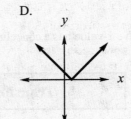   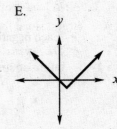

➢ By translation of the original graph from $y=|x|$ to $y=|x+3|$, the original graph is moved three units to the left, (C). Alternatively, substitute values for x and y: $y=0$ for $x=-3$. (C) is the only graph that contains the point $(-3,0)$.

Graphing Geometric Figures

You can also use the coordinate system for graphing geometric figures. The following figure is a graph of a square whose vertices are at coordinates $(0,0)$, $(4,0)$, $(4,4)$, and $(0,4)$.

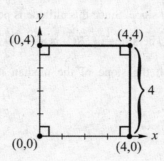

Each side of the square is equal to 4 since each side is 4 units long and parallel to either the *x*- or *y*-axis. Since every coordinate point is the perpendicular intersection of two lines, it is possible to measure distances in the coordinate system.

*Example*s:

1. In the following figure, what is the area of the circle?

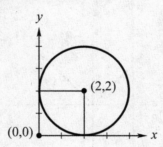

   ➤ To solve this problem, find the radius of the circle. The center of the circle is located at the intersection of $x = 2$ and $y = 2$, or the point $(2,2)$. Thus, the radius is 2 units long and the area is 4π.

2. $\triangle ABC$ has coordinates A, B, and C equal to $(5,3)$, $(19,7)$ and $(17,25)$, respectively. By how much does the largest slope for any median of $\triangle ABC$ exceed the largest slope for any altitude of $\triangle ABC$?

   ➤ The largest slope occurs for the steepest ascent for increasing values of *x*. Draw a figure of the given information in the coordinate plane:

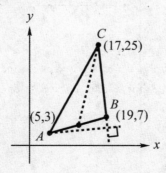

A median is drawn from one angle of a triangle to the midpoint of the opposite side. Of the three possible medians, the median that connects C to the midpoint of $\overline{AB}$ has the largest slope. The midpoint of $\overline{AB}$ is $\left(\dfrac{5+19}{2}, \dfrac{7+3}{2}\right) = (12, 5)$. Therefore, the slope of the median is $\dfrac{25-5}{17-12} = 4$. An altitude is drawn from one angle of a triangle to the opposite side at a right angle. Of the three possible altitudes, the altitude that connects A to $\overline{BC}$ has the largest slope. Since this altitude is perpendicular to $\overline{BC}$, its slope is the opposite reciprocal of the slope of $\overline{BC}$. The slope of $\overline{BC}$ is $\dfrac{25-7}{17-19} = \dfrac{18}{-2} = -9$, so the slope of the altitude $\dfrac{1}{9}$.

Therefore, the amount by which the slope of the median is larger than the slope of the altitude is:

$$4 - \frac{1}{9} = \frac{36}{9} - \frac{1}{9} = \frac{35}{9}.$$

Coordinate Geometry

DIRECTIONS: Choose the correct answer to each of the following items. Answers are on page 791.

1. Which of the following graphs represents a relation of which the domain is the set of all real numbers and the range is the set of all non-negative real numbers?

A.

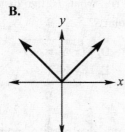

D.

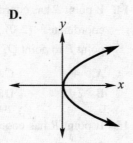

B.

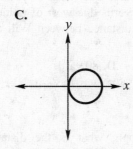

E.

C.

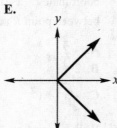

2. Which of the lettered points on the number line below could represent the result when the coordinate of point F is divided by the coordinate of point X?

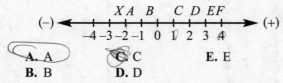

A. A

B. B

C. C

D. D

E. E

3. $\overline{AB}$ is the diameter of a circle whose center is point O. If the coordinates of point A are $(2,6)$ and the coordinates of point B are $(6,2)$, find the coordinates of point O.

A. $(4,4)$ C. $(2,-2)$ E. $(2,2)$

B. $(4,-4)$ D. $(0,0)$

4. $\overline{AB}$ is the diameter of a circle whose center is point O. If the coordinates of point O are $(2,1)$ and the coordinates of point B are $(4,6)$, find the coordinates of point A.

A. $\left(3,3\frac{1}{2}\right)$ C. $(0,-4)$ E. $\left(-1,-2\frac{1}{2}\right)$

B. $\left(1,2\frac{1}{2}\right)$ D. $\left(2\frac{1}{2},1\right)$

5. Find the distance from the point whose coordinates are $(4,3)$ to the point whose coordinates are $(8,6)$.

A. 5   C. $\sqrt{7}$ E. 15

B. 25   D. $\sqrt{67}$

6. The vertices of a triangle are $(2,1)$, $(2,5)$, and $(5,1)$. What is the area of the triangle?

A. 12   C. 8   E. 5

B. 10   D. 6

7. The area of a circle whose center is at $(0,0)$ is 16π. The circle does NOT pass through which of the following points?

A. $(4,4)$ C. $(4,0)$ E. $(0,-4)$

B. $(0,4)$ D. $(-4,0)$

8. What is the slope of a line that passes through $(0, -5)$ and $(8, 27)$?

   A. 4   C. $\frac{8}{32}$ E. -4

   B. 2   D. $-\frac{8}{32}$

9. The slope of a line that passes through points $(3, 7)$ and $(12, y)$ is $\frac{1}{3}$. What is the value of y?

   A. 2   C. $6\frac{2}{3}$ E. 10

   B. 4   D. $7\frac{1}{3}$

10. What is the slope of the line $y = 5x + 7$?

    A. 7   C. 2   E. $\frac{1}{5}$

    B. 5   D. $\frac{7}{5}$

11. A line passes through points $(3, 8)$ and $(w, 2k)$. If $w \neq 3$, what is the slope of the line?

    A. $\frac{8 - 2k}{3 + w}$ C. $\frac{2k - 8}{w - 3}$ E. $\frac{3}{8}$

    B. $\frac{2k + 8}{w + 3}$ D. $\frac{w - 3}{2k - 8}$

12. What is the equation of the line that passes through the point $(0, 13)$ and is parallel to the line $4x + 2y = 17$?

    A. $4x + 2y = 13$

    B. $4x + 2y = -13$

    C. $y = -2x + 13$

    D. $y = 2x + 13$

    E. Cannot be determined from the given information

13. A line passes through the point $(0, -5)$ and is perpendicular to the line $y = -\frac{x}{2} + 5$. What is the equation of the line?

    A. $y = -\frac{x}{2} - 5$

    B. $y = 2x - 5$

    C. $y = -2x - 5$

    D. $y = -\frac{x}{2} + 13$

    E. Cannot be determined from the given information

14. If point P has coordinates $(-2, 2)$ and point Q has coordinates $(2, 0)$, what is the distance from point P to point Q?

    A. -4 C. $4\sqrt{5}$ E. 6

    B. $2\sqrt{5}$ D. 4

15. If point R has coordinates (x, y) and point S has coordinates $(x + 1, y + 1)$, what is the distance between point R and point S?

    A. $\sqrt{2}$ D. $\sqrt{x^2 + y^2 + 2}$

    B. 2   E. $x + y + 1$

    C. $\sqrt{x^2 + y^2}$

16. Will is standing 40 yards due north of point P. Grace is standing 60 yards due west of point P. What is the shortest distance between Will and Grace?

    A. 20 yards   D. 80 yards

    B. $4\sqrt{13}$ yards   E. $80\sqrt{13}$ yards

    C. $20\sqrt{13}$ yards

17. On a coordinate graph, what is the distance between points $(5, 6)$ and $(6, 7)$?

    A. $\sqrt{2}$ C. 2   E. $6\sqrt{2}$

    B. 1   D. 4

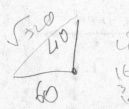

18. On a coordinate plane, point B is located 7 units to the left of point A. The x-coordinate of point A is x, and the y-coordinate of point A is y. What is the x-coordinate of point B?

    A. $x-7$
    B. $x+7$
    C. $y+7$
    D. $y-7$
    E. Cannot be determined from the given information

19. Point R is represented on the coordinate plane by (x,y). The vertical coordinate of point S is three times the vertical coordinate of point R and the two points have the same horizontal coordinate. The ordered pair that represents point S is:

    A. $(3x,y)$ C. $(x,y-3)$ E. $(x,3y)$
    B. $(x,y+3)$ D. $(3x,3y)$

20. A square is drawn in a coordinate plane. Which of the following transformations of the square will shift the square 7 units to the right and 5 units downward?

    A. Add 7 to each x-coordinate and add 5 to each y-coordinate.
    B. Multiply each x-coordinate by 7 and divide each y-coordinate by 5.
    C. Add 7 to each x-coordinate and subtract 5 from each y-coordinate.
    D. Subtract 7 from each x-coordinate and subtract 5 from each y-coordinate.
    E. Subtract 7 from each x-coordinate and add 5 to each y-coordinate.

21. In the rectangular coordinate system below, if $x = 4.2$, then y equals which of the following?

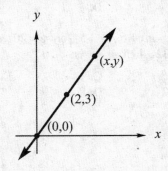

    A. 2.8   C. 4.8   E. 6.3
    B. 3.4   D. 6.2

22. Points $(x,-4)$ and $(-1,y)$ (not shown in the figure below) are in Quadrants III and II, respectively. If x and $y \neq 0$, in which quadrant is point (x,y)?

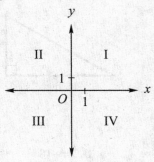

    A. I
    B. II
    C. III
    D. IV
    E. Cannot be determined from the given information

23. If Sam lives 8 miles west of Jeni, and Molly lives 10 miles north of Jeni, approximately how many miles less would Molly walk if she walks directly to Sam's house, rather than first to Jeni's house and then to Sam's house?

    A. 1   C. 3   E. 5
    B. 2   D. 4

24. If point B (not shown in the figure below) lies below the x-axis at point $(4,-4)$, what is the area of $\triangle ABC$?

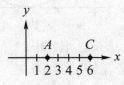

    A. 2   C. 6   E. 16
    B. 4   D. 8

25. On a coordinate graph, what is the distance between points $(-1,4)$ and $(2,8)$?

    A. 3   C. 5   E. 8
    B. 4   D. 6

26. In the figure below, $\overline{AB}$ is the base of a water ski ramp and is 18 feet long. The slope (rise divided by run) of the ramp is m. If the ramp is y feet high, then what is the value of y?

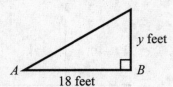

A. $\dfrac{m}{18}$ **C.** $18-m$ **E.** $m+18$

B. $18m$ **D.** $m-18$

27. What is the midpoint between $(-2,15)$ and $(8,17)$?

A. $(6,16)$ **C.** $(5,16)$ **E.** $(6,32)$

B. $(3,16)$ **D.** $(5,32)$

28. In the figure below, $\overline{AB}$ is the diameter of a circle whose center is at point P. What are the coordinates for point B?

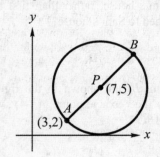

A. $(10,7)$ **C.** $(12,7)$ **E.** $(11,7)$

B. $(5,2.5)$ **D.** $(11,8)$

29. How many of the following graphs are graphs of linear functions?

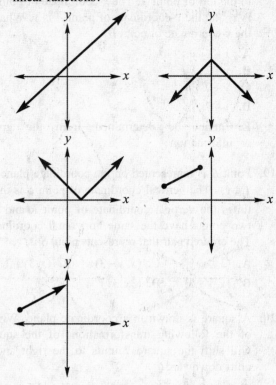

A. 1 **C.** 3 **E.** 5

B. 2 **D.** 4

30. In each of the following four sets, the three ordered pairs belong to a linear function. In how many of the four sets is the value of the variable x less than zero?

$\{(0,1), (-4,7), (x,0)\}$
$\{(0,2), (-5,52), (x,12)\}$
$\{(2,-5), (-2,-17), (x,13)\}$
$\{(6,17), (8,25), (x,4)\}$

A. 0 **C.** 2 **E.** 4

B. 1 **D.** 3

31. If $y=mx+b$, $x=5$ for $y=20$, and $x=9$ for $y=32$, then $m+b$ is:

A. 76 **C.** 14 **E.** 3

B. 52 **D.** 8

32. Which of the following graphs depicts the quadratic functions $y = \dfrac{x^2}{2}$ and $y = -\dfrac{x^2}{2}$?

A.

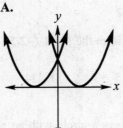

D.

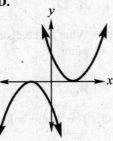

B.

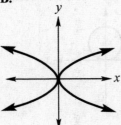

E.

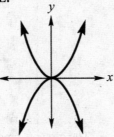

C.

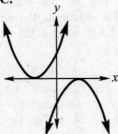

33. If $y = -2x^2 + 16x - 1$, what is the largest possible value for y?

   A. −1
   B. 13
   C. 31
   D. 32
   E. Cannot be determined from the given information

34. The graph of $y = 4x^2$ intersects the graph of $y = x^2 + 3x$ at how many points?

   A. 0   **C.** 2   **E.** 4
   B. 1   **D.** 3

35. A student noted that the graph of the following ordered points for (x, y) appeared to approximate a parabolic curve: $(1,7)$, $(-1,0)$, $(2,12)$, $(4,29)$, $(5,42)$. Which of the following equations best represents the curve?

   A. $y = x^2 + 6$

   B. $y = x^2 + 3x + 2$

   C. $y = 2x^2 + x + 4$

   D. $y = x^2 - x + 8$

   E. $y = 2x^2 + x + 4$

36. The graph of the following ordered pairs for (x, y) is approximately a straight line of the form $y = mx + b$: $(1,18)$, $(2,23)$, $(3,27)$, $(4,32)$, $(5,38)$. Which of the following best approximates the value of b?

   A. 13   **C.** 20   **E.** 25
   B. 18   **D.** 23

37. A scientist studying insect movement observes that in a day, each insect travels a particular geometric pattern and the distance traveled by each insect is directly proportional to the insect's length. The values for insect length and distance traveled in a day, in inches, for four insects are: $(1,1.57)$, $(1.5,2.36)$, $(2,3.14)$, and $(3,4.71)$. The geometric pattern traveled by the four insects is a:

   A. square
   B. equilateral triangle
   C. circle
   D. semicircle
   E. regular polygon of five sides

38. The figure below shows two parallel lines with coordinates of points as shown. What is the slope of the line passing through point $(6,0)$?

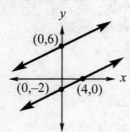

A. $\dfrac{1}{2}$ C. $\dfrac{1}{4}$ E. $\dfrac{1}{6}$

B. $\dfrac{1}{3}$ D. $\dfrac{1}{5}$

39. The center of a circle is located at $(19,7)$. One end of a diameter of the circle is located at $(4,6)$. The second end of the diameter is located at:

A. $(11.5, 6.5)$ C. $(34,8)$ E. $(38,8)$

B. $(11.5, 13)$ D. $(38,14)$

40. In the figure below, which is not necessarily drawn to scale, $ABCD$ is a square and $\angle FGH \cong \angle A$.

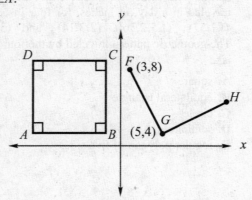

If points F and G have the coordinates as indicated in the figure, how many of the following four ordered pairs could possibly represent point H?

$(8,6), (9,6), (11,7), (13,8)$

A. 0   C. 2   E. 4

B. 1   D. 3

41. The line that passes through $(1,5)$ and $(-2,17)$ is parallel to the line that passes through $(17,6)$ and $(13, y)$. What is the value of y?

A. 10   C. 16   E. 22
B. 14   D. 18

42. What is the distance from the point $(-2,5)$ to the point $(7,-7)$?

A. 9   C. 15   E. 24
B. 12   D. 18

43. The figure below shows a circle with an area of 9π.

The circle is tangent to the x-axis at $(0,0)$ and the center of the circle lies on the y-axis. The constant function $y = k$ intersects the circle at exactly one point. If $k > 0$, what is the value of k?

A. 1   C. 3   E. 9
B. 2   D. 6

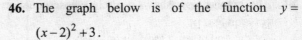

44. The figure below shows a graph of $y = \dfrac{12}{x^2 + 6x + 7}$. How many different integers for y are not a part of the graph of $y = \dfrac{12}{x^2 + 6x + 7}$?

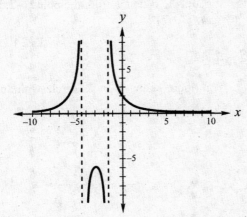

A. 2   **C.** 7   **E.** 13
B. 6   **D.** 12

45. The graph below shows two different parabola functions: $y = (x-1)^2 + 4$ and $y - 2 = -(x+5)^2$.

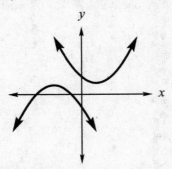

The values of y that are not on either of the parabolas are all values of y such that:

A. $-5 \le y \le 1$ **C.** $1 < y < 4$ **E.** $4 < y < 5$
B. $2 < y < 4$ **D.** $1 \le y \le 5$

46. The graph below is of the function $y = (x-2)^2 + 3$.

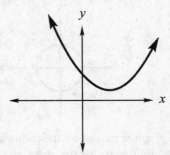

If a horizontal shift of four units to the left were performed on the original graph, at what point (x, y) would the transformed graph intersect the original graph?

A. $(2, 7)$ **C.** $(6, 3)$ **E.** $(0, 7)$
B. $(2, -1)$ **D.** $(-2, 3)$

47. The graph of $y = 3x^2$ can be produced from the graph of $y = x^2$ by performing a vertical stretch by a factor of three. The graph of $y = 2x^2 + 12x + 1$ can be produced from the graph of $y = x^2$ by performing a vertical stretch by a factor of two, a horizontal shift of three units to the left, and a vertical shift of:

A. 17 units down.
B. 12 units down.
C. 1 unit down.
D. 1 unit up.
E. 12 units up.

48. The following ordered pairs for (x, y) represent points on a graph: $(5, 15)$, $(10, 28)$, $(11, 27)$, $(25, 47)$, $(40, 76)$, $(50, 111)$, and $(60, 129)$. Which of the following equations represents the line of best fit (the line that most closely approximates the set of points)?

A. $y = \dfrac{x}{3}$ **C.** $y = 3x - 6$ **E.** $y = 5x - 4$

B. $y = \dfrac{x}{3} - 2$ **D.** $y = 2x + 3$

49. The graph below shows a circle whose equation is $x^2 + y^2 = 16$.

The graph is moved by the following transformations: four units to the right and two units up. Which of the following is the correctly transformed graph?

A.

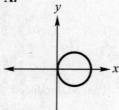

D.

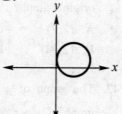

B.

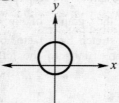

E.

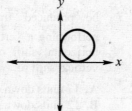

C.

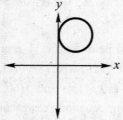

Story Problems

Story problems may test arithmetic, algebra, or geometry in the context of a "story." You should have everything you need to solve these problems. However, remember that if a math story item stumps you, you have the answer at hand. Simply work backwards from the answer choices—the right answer has to be one of the choices. Since quantitative (i.e., numerical value) choices are arranged in size order, starting with the middle answer choice will result in the fewest calculations.

In solving story problems, the most important technique is to read accurately. Be sure you clearly understand what you are asked to find. Then, evaluate the item in common sense terms to eliminate answer choices. For example, if two people are working together, their combined speed is greater than either individual speed, but not more than twice as fast as the fastest speed. Finally, be alert for the "hidden equation"—some necessary information so obvious that the item assumes that you know it.

Examples:

1. boys + girls = total class

2. imported wine + domestic wine = all wine

3. wall + floor = right angle (Pythagorean theorem)

Some of the frequently encountered types of problem-solving problems are described in this section, although not every item you may encounter will fall into one of these categories. However, thoroughly familiarizing yourself with the types of problems that follow will help you to develop the skills to translate and solve all kinds of verbal problems.

Coin Problems

For *coin problems*, change the value of all monies involved to cents before writing an equation. The number of nickels must be multiplied by 5 to give their value in cents; dimes must be multiplied by 10; quarters by 25; half-dollars by 50; and dollars by 100.

Example:

Richard has $3.50 consisting of nickels and dimes. If he has 5 more dimes than nickels, how many dimes does he have?

➢ Let x equal the number of nickels, $x + 5$ equal the number of dimes, $5x$ equal the value of the nickels in cents, $10(x + 5) = 10x + 50$ equal the value of the dimes in cents, and 350 equal the value of the money he has in cents. Thus, $5x + 10x + 50 = 350 \Rightarrow 15x = 300 \Rightarrow x = 20$. Therefore, Richard has 20 nickels and 25 dimes.

In an item such as this, you can be sure that 20 would be among the multiple-choice answers. You must be sure to read carefully what you are asked to find and then continue until you have found the quantity sought.

Number and Set Problems

Number problems can be story problems that require knowledge of the properties of numbers in order to solve the item. Typically, number problems involve ***consecutive integers*** or ***consecutive odd/even numbers***. Consecutive integers are one number apart and can be represented by x, $x+1$, $x+2$, etc. Consecutive even or odd integers are two numbers apart and can be represented by x, $x+2$, $x+4$, etc.

Example:

Three consecutive odd integers have a sum of 33. Find the average of these integers.

➢ Represent the integers as x, $x+2$, and $x+4$. Write an equation indicating the sum is 33: $x+x+2+x+4 = 3x+6 = 33 \Rightarrow 3x = 27 \Rightarrow x = 9$. Thus, the integers are 9, 11, and 13. In the case of evenly spaced numbers such as these, the average is the middle number, 11. Since the sum of the three numbers was given originally, all we really had to do was to divide this sum by 3 to find the average, without ever knowing what the numbers were.

Set problems test understanding of relationships between different sets of numbers or ***elements***. A ***set*** is a collection of things; e.g., the set of positive integers.

DEFINITIONS FOR WORKING WITH SETS

1. The ***number of elements*** in set P is: $n(P)$.

2. The ***union*** of two sets P and Q is the set of all elements in *either* P or Q, or both: $P \cup Q$.

3. The ***intersection*** of two sets P and Q is the set of all elements in *both* P and Q: $P \cap Q$.

4. The ***cardinal number theorem*** is used to find the number of elements in a union of two sets: $n(P \cup Q) = n(P) + n(Q) - n(P \cap Q)$

*Example*s:

1. Let $S = \{3, 5, x\}$. If exactly one subset of S contains two different elements whose sum is 12, what value(s) can x be?

   ➢ Since either $3 + x = 12$ or $5 + x = 12$, then $x = 9$ or $x = 7$.

2. In a class of 30 students, 15 students are learning French, 11 students are learning Spanish, and 7 students are learning neither French nor Spanish. How many students in the class are learning both French and Spanish?

   ➢ Use the cardinal number theorem:

   $$n(F \cup S) = n(F) + n(S) - n(F \cap S)$$
   $$30 - 7 = 15 + 11 - n(F \cap S)$$
   $$n(F \cap S) = 3$$

The cardinal number theorem is also known as the ***addition principle for counting*** and is the first of several useful methods for counting objects and sets of objects without actually listing the elements to be counted. According to the theorem, if set A contains m objects, set B contains n objects, and there are no objects common to the two sets, then the total number of objects in the two sets combined is $m + n$. However, if there are k objects common to the two sets, then the total in the combined set is $m+n-k$. In other words, you must take into account the double-counting of objects common to both sets.

Example:

Of a group of students at a campus cafe, 9 ate pizza and 5 had salad. If 3 had both pizza and salad, how many had either pizza or salad?

➤ The question describes two sets: one consisting of students that ate pizza (set P: $m=9$), and one consisting of students that had salad (set S: $n=5$). Since the question states that 3 students had both pizza and salad, the number of students common to the two sets is 3 ($k=3$). Therefore, the total in the combined set (number of students who had either pizza or salad) is: $m+n-k=9+5-3=11$.

This kind of situation involving sets that overlap is most easily handled by displaying the given information in a ***Venn diagram***.

Example:

Two circles are drawn on a floor. 20 people are standing in circle A. 15 people are standing in circle B. 9 people are standing in both circles. Find the total number of people standing in the two circles.

➤ The item can be symbolized with a Venn diagram:

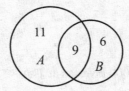

From the diagram, it can be seen that there are a total of $11+9+6$ or 26 people.

Age Problems

Age problems involve a comparison of ages at the present time, several years from now, or several years ago. A person's age x years from now is found by adding x to his present age. A person's age x years ago is found by subtracting x from his present age.

*Example*s:

1. Michelle was 12 years old y years ago. What is her age b years from now?

   ➤ Michelle's present age is $12+y$. In b years, her age will be $12+y+b$.

2. Logan is 5 years older than Florencia. Three years ago, Logan was twice as old as Florencia. How old is Logan?

   ➤ If you have trouble setting up the equations, use numbers. Suppose that Florencia is 11. If Logan is 5 years older than Florencia, then Logan must be $11+5=16$. Thus, if L is Logan's age and F is Florencia's age, $L=F+5$. Three years ago, Logan was $L-3$ and Florencia was $F-3$. So, since 3 years ago, Logan was twice as old as Florencia, $L-3=2(F-3) \Rightarrow L-3=2F-6 \Rightarrow L=2F-3$. Substitute $L=F+5 \Rightarrow F=L-5$ for F in the equation $L=2F-3$ to find Logan's current age: $L=2F-3=2(L-5)-3=2L-13 \Rightarrow L=13$.

Interest Problems

Simple Interest

Simple interest is computed on the principal (amount of initial investment) only. To calculate the amount of simple interest paid on an investment, multiply the principal invested by the rate (percent) of interest paid and the time of the investment: **Simple interest income = principal • rate • time.**

Examples:

1. If $4,000 is invested at 3% simple annual interest, how much interest is earned in 4 months?

   ➤ Since the annual interest is 3%, the interest for 1 year is: $4,000(0.03) = \$120$. Thus, the interest earned in 4 months, or $\frac{1}{3}$ of a year is: $\frac{\$120}{3} = \$40$.

2. Mr. Krecker invests $4,000, part at 6% and part at 7%; the first year return is $250. Find the amount invested at 7%.

   ➤ Let x equal the amount invested at 7%. Thus, $4,000 - x$ equals the amount invested at 6%; $0.07x$ equals the income from the 7% investment; and $0.06(4,000 - x)$ equals the income from the 6% investment. Therefore:

$$0.07x + 0.06(4,000 - x) = 250$$
$$7x + 6(4,000 - x) = 25,000$$
$$7x + 24,000 - 6x = 25,000$$
$$x = 1,000 \ (\$1,000 \text{ invested at } 7\%)$$

Compound Interest

Compound interest is computed on the principal as well as on any interest already earned. The interest already earned is determined as simple interest for each period that the interest is compounded with the principal increasing to include the previously earned interest. If annual interest is compounded for a given period, the interest rate for that period is only a fraction of the interest rate, as determined by the number of periods for which the interest is compounded.

Example:

If $2,000 is invested at 4% annual interest, compounded quarterly, what is the balance after 9 months?

➤ Since the interest is compounded quarterly, figure the interest for the four periods, with each successive interest computed for the principal plus all prior interest income. Since the interest rate is 4% annually, compounded four times a year, the interest rate for each period is 1%. The balance after the first 3 months (one-quarter of a year) would be: $2,000 + (\$2,000)(0.01) = \$2,000 + \$20 = \$2,020$. The balance after the second 3 months would be: $2,020 + (\$2,020)(0.01) = \$2,020 + \$20.20 = \$2,040.20$. The total balance after the final third 3 months would be: $2,040.20 + (\$2,040.20)(0.01) = \$2,040.20 + \$20.40 = \$2060.60$.

The previous example illustrates how if interest is compounded, the interest is computed on the principal as well as on any interest earned. The general formula for compounded interest follows:

$$\textbf{Final Balance} = \textbf{Principal} \cdot \left(1 + \frac{\textbf{interest rate}}{C}\right)^{(\textbf{time})(C)}$$

where C is the number of times the interest is compounded annually.

Example:

If $12,000 is invested at 8% annual interest, compounded semiannually, what is the balance after one year?

➤ The interest is compounded twice a year, so $C = 2$. Therefore, the final balance is $12,000\left(1 + \dfrac{0.08}{2}\right)^{(1)(2)} =$

$12,000(1.04)^2 = \$12,979.20$.

Mixture Problems

You should be familiar with two kinds of *mixture problems*. The first type is sometimes referred to as dry mixture, in which dry ingredients of different values, such as nuts or coffee, are mixed. For this type of problem, it is best to organize the data in a chart of three rows and three columns labeled as illustrated in the following problem.

Example:

A dealer wishes to mix 20 pounds of nuts selling for 45 cents per pound with some more expensive nuts selling for 60 cents per pound to make a mixture that will sell for 50 cents per pound. How many pounds of the more expensive nuts should he use?

➤ Create a table summarizing the provided information:

	No. of lbs. ×	Price/lb. =	Total Value
Original	20	0.45	0.45(20)
Added	x	0.60	0.60(x)
Mixture	$20 + x$	0.50	0.50($20 + x$)

The value of the original nuts plus the value of the added nuts must equal the value of the mixture:

$0.45(20) + 0.60(x) = 0.50(20 + x)$
$45(20) + 60(x) = 50(20 + x)$
$900 + 60x = 1,000 + 50x$
$10x = 100$
$x = 10$

Therefore, he should use 10 lbs. of 60-cent nuts.

The second type of mixture item deals with percents and amounts rather than prices and value.

Example:

How much water must be added to 20 gallons of solution that is 30% alcohol to dilute it to a solution that is only 25% alcohol?

➤ Create a table summarizing the provided information:

	No. of gals. ×	% alcohol =	Amt. alcohol
Original	20	0.30	0.30(20)
Added	x	0	0
Mixture	$20 + x$	0.25	0.25($20 + x$)

Note that the percentage of alcohol in water is zero. Had pure alcohol been added to strengthen the solution, the percentage would have been 100%. Thus, the amount of alcohol added (none) plus the original amount must equal the amount of alcohol in the new solution:

$$0.30(20) = 0.25(20 + x)$$
$$30(20) = 25(20 + x)$$
$$600 = 500 + 25x$$
$$100 = 25x$$
$$x = 4\,\text{gallons}$$

Motion Problems

The fundamental relationship in all *motion problems* is *distance = rate • time*. The problems at the level of this examination usually derive their equation from a relationship concerning distance. Most problems fall into one of three types.

Motion in Opposite Directions

When two objects moving at the same speed start at the same time and move in opposite directions, or when two objects start at points at a given distance apart and move toward each other with the same speed until they meet, then the distance the second travels will equal one-half the total distance covered. Either way, the total distance $= d_1 + d_2$:

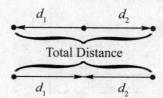

Motion in the Same Direction

This type of item is sometimes called the "catch-up" problem. Two objects leave the same place in the same direction at different times and at different rates, but one "catches up" to the other. In such a case, the two distances must be equal.

Round Trip

In this type of problem, the rate going is usually different from the rate returning. The times are also different. But if we go somewhere and then return to the starting point, the distances must be the same.

To solve any motion problem, it is helpful to organize the data in a box with columns for rate, time, and distance. A separate line should be used for each moving object. Remember that if the rate is given in *miles per hour*, the time must be in *hours* and the distance in *miles*.

*Example*s:

1. Two cars leave a restaurant at 1 p.m., with one car traveling east at 60 miles per hour and the other west at 40 miles per hour along a straight highway. At what time will they be 350 miles apart?

   ➤ Create a table summarizing the provided information:

	Rate	×	Time	=	Distance
Eastbound	60		x		$60x$
Westbound	40		x		$40x$

Notice that the time is unknown, since we must determine the number of hours traveled. However, since the cars start at the same time and stop when they are 350 miles apart, their times are the same: $60x + 40x = 350 \Rightarrow 100x = 350 \Rightarrow x = 3.5$. Therefore, in 3.5 hours, it will be 4:30 p.m.

2. Gloria leaves home for school, riding her bicycle at a rate of 12 miles per hour. Twenty minutes after she leaves, her mother sees Gloria's English paper on her bed and leaves to bring it to her. If her mother drives at 36 miles per hour, how far must she drive before she reaches Gloria?

   ➤ Create a table summarizing the provided information:

	Rate	×	Time	=	Distance
Gloria	12		x		$12x$
Mother	36		$x - \dfrac{1}{3}$		$36\left(x - \dfrac{1}{3}\right)$

The 20 minutes has been converted to $\dfrac{1}{3}$ of an hour. In this problem, the times are not equal, but the distances are: $12x = 36\left(x - \dfrac{1}{3}\right) = 36x - 12 \Rightarrow 12 = 24x \Rightarrow x = \dfrac{1}{2}$. Thus, if Gloria rode for $\dfrac{1}{2}$ hour at 12 miles per hour, the distance covered was 6 miles. So, Gloria's mother must drive 6 miles before she reaches her.

3. Nisha leaves home at 11 a.m. and rides to Andrea's house to return her bicycle. She travels at 12 miles per hour and arrives at 11:30 a.m. She turns right around and walks home. How fast does she walk if she returns home at 1 p.m.?

   ➤ Create a table summarizing the provided information:

	Rate	×	Time	=	Distance
Going	12		$\dfrac{1}{2}$		6
Return	x		$1\dfrac{1}{2}$		$\dfrac{3x}{2}$

The distances are equal: $6 = \dfrac{3x}{2} \Rightarrow 12 = 3x \Rightarrow x = 4$ miles per hour.

Rate and Work Problems

Rate Problems

We introduced rate problems in the section above on motion problems, since distance traveled per unit time is a rate. Anytime you compare two quantities with different units, you are finding a *rate*. To find a rate, look for the different units and their corresponding numbers. Rate problems can be solved by using ratios.

*Example*s:

1. If Save-A-Lot Grocery advertises 2 pounds of cherries for $2.20, how much would 3 pounds of cherries costs?

   ➢ Create two ratios corresponding to the different units and their corresponding numbers. Set the ratios equal to one another and solve for the unknown quantity. The rate in the question is quantity of cherries per price (or price per quantity of cherries), and the unknown is the cost of 3 pounds of cherries: $\frac{2 \text{ pounds}}{\$2.20} = \frac{3 \text{ pounds}}{x} \Rightarrow x = \frac{3}{2}(\$2.20) = \$3.30$.

2. During a 4-hour party, 5 adults consumed drinks costing $120. For the same drink costs per person per hour, what would be the cost of drinks consumed by 4 adults during a 3-hour party?

   ➢ The ratio in question is drink costs per person per hour, so equate two ratios and solve for the missing value: $\frac{\$120}{5 \text{ adults/4 hours}} = \frac{x}{4 \text{ adults/3hours}} \Rightarrow \frac{120 \cdot 4}{5} = \frac{x \cdot 3}{4} \Rightarrow x = \frac{120 \cdot 16}{15} = 8 \cdot 16 = \$128$.

Note that the following words are frequently used in rate problems: *for, in, per, to, each*. For example: $100 *for* 5 hours of work, 3 widgets produced *in* 5 minutes, 55 miles *per* hour, 13 floors *to* a building, 7 cards *to each* person.

Work Problems

Combined rate, or **work**, problems concern the speed with which work can be accomplished and the time necessary to perform a task, if the size of the workforce is changed. Thus, work problems involve combining individual rates into a combined rate.

Example:

If Tess alone can weed a garden in 3 days and Rio can weed the same garden in 5 days, how long will it take them to weed the garden if they work together?

➢ Let *x* equal number of days required if Tess and Rio work together to weed the garden and create a table summarizing the given information:

	Tess	Rio	Together
Days to weed garden	3	5	x
Part weeded in 1 day	$\frac{1}{3}$	$\frac{1}{5}$	$\frac{1}{x}$

Since the part done by Tess in one day plus the part done by Rio in one day equals the part done by both in one day, we have: $\frac{1}{3} + \frac{1}{5} = \frac{1}{x}$. Multiply each part of the equation by $15x$ to clear the fractions:

$\frac{1}{3}(15x) + \frac{1}{5}(15x) = \frac{1}{x}(15x) \Rightarrow 5x + 3x = 15 \Rightarrow 8x = 15 \Rightarrow x = 1\frac{7}{8}$ days.

From the previous example, we can see that the basic formula for solving work problems is: $\frac{1}{a} + \frac{1}{b} = \frac{1}{c}$, where *a* and *b* are the number of minutes, days, hours, etc. that it takes the two individuals, respectively, to complete a job when working alone, and *c* is the number of minutes, days, hours, etc. that it takes the two individuals to do the job when working together.

Example:

When working alone, Machine X can fill a production order in 4 hours, and Machine Y can fill the same order in y hours. When the two machines operate simultaneously to fill the production order, it takes them 2.5 hours to complete the job. What is the value of y?

➤ $\frac{1}{4}+\frac{1}{y}=\frac{1}{2.5} \Rightarrow \frac{1}{4}(10y)+\frac{1}{Y}(10y)=\frac{1}{2.5}(10y) \Rightarrow 2.5y+10=4y \Rightarrow \frac{3}{2}(y)=10 \Rightarrow y=\frac{20}{3}=6\frac{2}{3}$. Thus, working

alone, Machine Y can fill the production order in $6\frac{2}{3}$ hours.

Variation Problems

Variation in mathematics refers to the interrelationship of variables in such a manner that a change of value for one variable produces a corresponding change in another. There are three basic types of variation: *direct*, *inverse*, and *joint*.

Direct Variation

The expression "x varies directly with y" can be described by either of the following equations:

DIRECT VARIATION RELATIONSHIPS

$y = kx$, k is a constant

$$\frac{x_1}{y_1}=\frac{x_2}{y_2}$$

Two quantities are said to vary directly if they change in the same direction. As one increases, the other increases and their ratio is equal to the positive constant.

For example, the amount you must pay for milk varies directly with the number of quarts of milk you buy. The amount of sugar needed in a recipe varies directly with the amount of butter used. The number of inches between two cities on a map varies directly with the number of miles between these cities.

Example:

If x varies directly as y^2, and $x=12$ when $y=2$, what is the value of x when $y=3$?

➤ Notice that the variation involves the square of y. Therefore, $\frac{x_1}{y_1^2}=\frac{x_2}{y_2^2} \Rightarrow \frac{12}{2^2}=\frac{x}{3^2} \Rightarrow \frac{12}{4}=\frac{x}{9} \Rightarrow x=27$.

Inverse Variation

The expression "x varies inversely as y" can be described by either of the following equations:

INVERSE VARIATION RELATIONSHIPS

$xy = k$, k is a constant

$$\frac{x_1}{y_2} = \frac{x_2}{y_1}$$

Two quantities vary inversely if they change in opposite directions. As one quantity increases, the other quantity decreases.

For example, the number of people hired to paint a house varies inversely with the number of days the job will take. A doctor's stock of flu vaccine varies inversely with the number of patients she injects. The number of days a given supply of cat food lasts varies inversely with the number of cats being fed.

Example:

The time t to empty a container varies inversely with the square root of the number of men m working on the job. If it takes 3 hours for 16 men to do the job, how long will it take 4 men working at the same rate to empty the container?

➤ $\dfrac{t_1}{\sqrt{m_2}} = \dfrac{t_2}{\sqrt{m_1}} \Rightarrow t_1\sqrt{m_1} = t_2\sqrt{m_2} \Rightarrow 3\sqrt{16} = t\sqrt{4} \Rightarrow t = 3 \cdot \dfrac{\sqrt{16}}{\sqrt{4}} = 3\left(\sqrt{4}\right) = 3 \cdot 2 = 6$.

Joint Variation

The expression "x varies jointly as y and z" can be described by any of the following equations:

JOINT VARIATION RELATIONSHIPS

$$\frac{x}{yz} = k, \ k \text{ is a constant}$$

$$\frac{x_1}{y_1 z_1} = \frac{x_2}{y_2 z_2} \Leftrightarrow \frac{x_1}{x_2} = \left(\frac{y_1}{y_2}\right)\left(\frac{z_1}{z_1}\right)$$

Example:

The area, A, of a triangle varies jointly as the base b and the height h. If $A = 20$ when $b = 10$ and $h = 4$, what is the value of A when $b = 6$ and $h = 7$?

➤ $\dfrac{A_1}{b_1 h_1} = \dfrac{A_2}{b_2 h_2} \Rightarrow \dfrac{20}{(10)(4)} = \dfrac{A_2}{(6)(7)} \Rightarrow A_2 = 21$.

Percent Problems

Many problem-solving items involve percents as they apply to certain types of business situations.

Percent Increase or Decrease

Percent increase or decrease is found by putting the amount of increase or decrease over the original amount and changing this fraction to a percent.

Example:

> A company normally employs 100 people. During a slow spell, it fired 20% of its employees. By what percentage must it now increase its staff to return to full capacity?

> ➤ $20\% = \dfrac{1}{5} \cdot 100 = 20$. The company now has $100 - 20 = 80$ employees. If it then increases by 20 employees, the percentage increase is $\dfrac{20}{80} = \dfrac{1}{4}$, or 25%.

Discounts

A discount is expressed as a percent of the original price that will be deducted from that price to determine the sale price.

Examples:

> 1. Bill's Hardware offers a 20% discount on all appliances during a sale week. How much must Mrs. Russell pay for a washing machine marked at $280?

> ➤ $20\% = \dfrac{1}{5} \Rightarrow \dfrac{1}{5} \cdot \$280 = \$56$ discount $\Rightarrow \$280 - \$56 = \$224$ sale price. Alternatively, the following shortcut simplifies the solution: if there is a 20% discount, Mrs. Russell will pay 80% of the marked price: $80\% = \dfrac{4}{5} \Rightarrow \dfrac{4}{5} \cdot \$280 = \$224$ sale price.

> 2. A store offers a television set marked at $340 less consecutive discounts of 10% and 5%. Another store offers the same set marked at $340 less a single discount of 15%. How much does the buyer save buying at the better price?

> ➤ In the first store, the initial 10% discount means the buyer will pay 90%, or $\dfrac{9}{10}$ of $340, which is $306.

> Now, the second discount must be figured on the first sale price. The additional 5% discount means the buyer will pay 95% of $306, or $290.70. In the second store, the single discount of 15% means the buyer will pay 85% of $340, or $289. Thus, the second store will have a lower sale price, and the buyer saves $290.70 - \$289 = \$1.70$ buying at that better price.

Profit

Gross profit is equal to revenues minus expenses, that is, the selling price minus cost.

Example:

> A used car lot paid $5,000 for a trade-in car. At what price should the salesman sell the used car in order to make a gross profit of 60% of the cost of the car?

> ➤ The cost of the car is $5,000, so the gross profit is 60% of $5,000, or $0.6(5,000) = \$3,000$. Since the gross profit is equal to the selling price minus cost, the selling price of the car must be gross profit plus cost, or $\$3,000 + \$5,000 = \$8,000$.

Commission

Many salespeople earn money on a commission basis. In order to inspire sales, they are paid a percentage of the value of goods that they personally sell. This amount is called a commission.

Examples:

1. Mr. Saunders works at Brown's Department Store, where he is paid $80 per week in salary plus a 4% commission on all his sales. How much does he earn in a week in which he sells $4,032 worth of merchandise?

   ➤ Find 4% of $4,032 and add this amount to $80: $4,032 • 0.04 = \$161.28 \Rightarrow \$161.28 + \$80 = \$241.28$.

2. Bill Olson delivers newspapers for a dealer and keeps 8% of all money collected. In one month, he was able to keep $16. How much did he forward to the dealer?

   ➤ First, find how much he collected by asking $16 is 8% of what number: $\$16 = 0.08x \Rightarrow \$1,600 = 8x \Rightarrow x = \$200$. Then, subtract the amount Bill kept ($16) from the total collected ($200). Therefore, Bill forwarded $184 to the dealer.

Taxes

Taxes are a percent of money spent or money earned.

Examples:

1. Dane County collects a 7% sales tax on automobiles. If the price of a used Ford is $5,832 before taxes, what will it cost when the sales tax is added in?

   ➤ Find 7% of $5,832 to determine the amount of tax and then add that amount to $5,832. This can be done in one step by finding 107% of $5,832: $\$5,832 • 1.07 = \$6,240.24$.

2. If income is taxed at the rate of 10% for the first $10,000 of earned income, 15% for the next $10,000, 20% for the next $10,000, and 25% for all earnings over $30,000, how much income tax must be paid on a yearly income of $36,500?

   ➤ Find the income tax collected at each percentage rate and add them:

   $$
   \begin{array}{l}
   10\% \text{ of first } \$10,000 = \$1,000 \\
   15\% \text{ of next } \$10,000 = \$1,500 \\
   20\% \text{ of next } \$10,000 = \$2,000 \\
   + \ 25\% \text{ of next } \$6,500 = \$1,625 \\
   \hline
   \qquad \text{Total Tax} = \$6,125
   \end{array}
   $$

Measurement Problems

Some questions may involve different units of measure. For any problem requiring conversion from one unit of measure to another, other than for units of time, the relationship between those units will be given.

Example:

A car travels at a constant rate of 37 miles per hour. If 1 kilometer is equal to 0.62 miles, approximately how many kilometers does the car travel in 20 minutes?

➤ 1 kilometer equals 0.62 miles, so multiply the given speed by $\dfrac{1 \text{ kilometer}}{0.62 \text{ miles}}$ to convert it to kilometers per hour:

$\dfrac{37 \text{ miles}}{\text{hour}} \cdot \dfrac{1 \text{ kilometer}}{0.62 \text{ miles}} \approx 60$ kilometers per hour. Thus, in 20 minutes, or one-third of an hour, the car travels

$\dfrac{60}{3} = 20$ kilometers.

Counting Methods

The Multiplication Principle for Counting

The ***multiplication principle for counting*** states that if an object is to be chosen from a set of *m* objects and a second object is to be chosen from a different set of *n* objects, then the total number of ways of choosing both object simultaneously is *mn*. In other words, if an operation takes two steps and the first step can be performed in *m* ways, and if, for each of those ways, the second step can be performed in *n* ways, then the total number of ways of performing the operation is *mn*.

*Example*s:

1. A litter of boxer puppies contains 4 with brindle coloring and 5 with fawn coloring. In how many ways can one choose a pair of one brindle puppy and one fawn puppy from this litter of puppies?

   ➤ You have 4 choices for a brindle puppy and 5 choices for a fawn puppy. By the multiplication principle, the total number of possible pairs is: $4 \cdot 5 = 20$.

2. From a garden with 6 flower varieties, a bouquet of 3 different types of flowers is to be picked. How many different possible bouquets are there?

   ➤ Extend the multiplication principle to a three-step process: there are 6 choices of flower for the first pick of the bouquet, for each of which there are 5 choices for the second flower (because one flower type has been eliminated, having been picked as the first flower in the bouquet). Furthermore, for each of these pairs, there are 4 remaining flower choices for the third pick (because two flower types have been eliminated, having been picked as the first and second flowers in the bouquet). Therefore, the total number of possible bouquets is: $6 \cdot 5 \cdot 4 = 120$.

Permutations

A natural extension of the multiplication principle is the concept of ***permutations***, or orderings in distinct arrangements of *n* distinguishable objects in a row. If a set of *n* objects is to be ordered from 1st to n^{th}, then there are *n* choices for the first object, $n-1$ choices for the second object, $n-2$ choices for the third object, and so on, until there is only one choice for the nth object. Therefore, the number of ways of ordering the *n* objects, also called ***n factorial***, is as follows:

$$n! = n(n-1)(n-2)\ldots(3)(2)(1)$$

*Example*s:

1. If five spices (rosemary, oregano, basil, sage, and pepper) are arranged randomly on a shelf, what is the chance that they will be in alphabetical order from left to right?

> There are five distinguishable objects that can be arranged in $5! = 5 \cdot 4 \cdot 3 \cdot 2 \cdot 1 = 120$ ways. In only one of these ways will they be in alphabetical order. Therefore, the chance is $\dfrac{1}{120}$ that the spices will be arranged in alphabetical order from left to right.

2. In how many ways can five spices (rosemary, oregano, basil, sage, and pepper) be arranged on the shelf if the oregano and the basil must be next to each other?

> Since the oregano and the basil must be next to each other, treat the two together as one spice, thereby reducing the total number of spices to be arranged from five to four. These four spices—rosemary, oregano/basil, sage, and pepper—can be arranged in $4! = 4 \cdot 3 \cdot 2 \cdot 1 = 24$ ways. However, for each of these ways, we could have set up the "glued" spices in two sequences: oregano/basil or basil/oregano. Therefore, there is a total of $2 \cdot 24 = 48$ ways in which the spices can be arranged with the oregano and basil next to each other.

If you are asked to find the number of ways to arrange a smaller group that is being drawn from a larger group, you can use the following **permutation formula**:

$$P = \frac{n!}{(n-k)!}$$

where n is the number of elements in the larger set and k is the number of elements being arranged.

Example:

Five candidates are running for office. The candidates who come in first, second, and third place will be elected president, vice-president, and treasurer, respectively. How many outcomes for president, vice-president, and treasurer are there?

> Using the permutation formula: $P = \dfrac{n!}{(n-k)!} = \dfrac{5!}{(5-3)!} = \dfrac{5!}{2!} = \dfrac{5 \cdot 4 \cdot 3 \cdot 2 \cdot 1}{2 \cdot 1} = 5 \cdot 4 \cdot 3 = 60$. Notice that the formula is the same as applying the following logic: Any of the five candidates could come in first place, leaving four candidates who could come in second place, leaving three candidates who could come in third place, for a total of $5 \cdot 4 \cdot 3 = 60$ possible outcomes for president, vice-president, and treasurer.

Combinations

A **combination** problem is one in which the order or arrangement of the smaller group that is being drawn from the larger group does NOT matter. Rather than the permutation formula, use the following **combination formula**:

$$C = \frac{n!}{k!(n-k)!}$$

where n is the number of elements in the larger set and k is the number of elements being arranged.

Example:

How many different ways are there to choose four socks from a drawer containing nine socks?

> Since the order or arrangement of the four socks being drawn from the drawer containing nine socks does not matter, use the combination formula: $C = \dfrac{9!}{4!(9-4)!} = \dfrac{9!}{4! \cdot 5!} = \dfrac{9 \cdot 8 \cdot 7 \cdot 6 \cdot 5!}{4 \cdot 3 \cdot 2 \cdot 1 \cdot 5!} = \dfrac{9 \cdot 8 \cdot 7}{4} = 126$.

Probability

Single-Event Probability

Probability is concerned with experiments that have a finite number of outcomes. Probabilities occur in games, sports, weather reports, etc. The probability that some particular outcome or set of outcomes (called an *event*) will occur is expressed as a ratio. The numerator of a probability ratio is the number of ways that the event of interest can occur. The denominator is the total number of outcomes that are possible. This *probability ratio* is true for experiments in which all of the individual outcomes are equally likely:

$$\text{Probability of event} = \frac{\text{number of ways that event can happen}}{\text{number of outcomes possible}}$$

Example:

If a six-sided die is tossed, what is the probability that you will get a number greater than 4?

➤ There are a total of six ways a die can land: 1, 2, 3, 4, 5, or 6. Each of these six events are equally likely. There are two possible outcomes that are greater than 4: 5 or 6. Therefore, the probability of the die landing with a number greater than 3 is $\frac{2}{6} = \frac{1}{3}$.

Note that the probability that an event occurs is a number between 0 and 1, inclusive. If the event has no outcomes, then it is impossible and its probability is 0. If the event is the set of all possible outcomes, then it is certain to occur and its probability is 1.

Multiple-Event Probability

Another type of probability involves finding the probability of a certain outcome after multiple events. One type of *multiple-event probability* involves individual events that must occur a certain way. For these experiments, figure out the probability for each individual event and multiply the individual probabilities together.

Example:

If two marbles are randomly chosen from a jar with three red marbles and seven black marbles, what is the probability that both marbles will be red?

➤ Since three out of the ten marbles are red, the probability that the first marble chosen is red is $\frac{3}{10}$. After choosing one red marble, this leaves two red marbles in the jar out of nine. Therefore, the probability that the second marble chosen will also be red is $\frac{2}{9}$. The probability that both marbles chosen will be red is:

$$\frac{3}{10} \cdot \frac{2}{9} = \frac{6}{90} = \frac{1}{15}.$$

A second type of multiple-event probability involves individual events that can have different outcomes. For these experiments, create a probability ratio by dividing the number of desired outcomes by the total number of possible outcomes. The total number of possible outcomes is found by multiplying together the number of possible outcomes for each individual event. The number of desired outcomes can be determined by counting the possibilities.

Example:

If a dime is tossed three times, what is the probability that at least two of the three tosses will be heads up?

➤ There are two possible outcomes for each toss (heads or tails), so after three tosses there are a total of $2^3 = 2 \cdot 2 \cdot 2 = 8$ possible outcomes. Next, list all the possibilities where at least two of the three tosses are heads up: H, H, H; H, H, T; H, T, H; T, H, H. Thus, the total number of desired outcomes is four. Therefore, the probability that at least two of the three tosses will be heads up is: $\frac{4}{8} = \frac{1}{2}$.

Probabilities can also be determined for an experiment with two different events, A and B. The probability of A occurring is denoted by $P(A)$, and the probability of B occurring is denoted by $P(B)$. Given these two events, there are three additional events that can be defined. "Not A" is the set of outcomes that are not outcomes in A; "A or B" is the set of outcomes in A or B or both ($A \cup B$); "A and B" is the set of outcomes in both A and B ($A \cap B$). If the event "A and B" is impossible, then A and B are said to be ***mutually exclusive***. If the occurrence of either event A or B does not alter the probability that the other event occurs, then A and B are said to be ***independent***.

PROBABILITIES FOR MULTIPLE-EVENT EXPERIMENTS
(An experiment with events A and B)

1. "Not A": $P(\text{not } A) = 1 - P(A)$

2. "A or B": $P(A \text{ or } B) = P(A) + P(B) - P(A \text{ and } B)$

3. "A and B" (A and B are mutually exclusive): $P(A \text{ and } B) = 0$

4. "A and B" (A and B are independent): $P(A \text{ and } B) = P(A)P(B)$

Example:

If a six-sided die is tossed, what is the probability that you will a prime number or an even number?

➤ Let A be the event that the outcome is a prime number, $\{2, 3, 5\}$, and let B be the event that the outcome is an even number, $\{2, 4, 6\}$. Since 3 outcomes are prime, $P(A) = \frac{3}{6} = \frac{1}{2}$. Similarly, $P(B) = \frac{1}{2}$. $P(A$ and $B)$, or the

probability that the outcome is both even and prime, is $\frac{1}{6}$ since only 2 is both even and prime. Therefore,

$P(A$ or $B) = \frac{1}{2} + \frac{1}{2} - \frac{1}{6} = \frac{5}{6}$. Note that this is the same as reasoning that the set of prime and even numbers on

the die is $\{2, 3, 4, 5, 6\}$, so the probability of getting one of these numbers is $\frac{5}{6}$.

Geometric Probability

Some items on the exam may involve geometric probability. For example, if a point is to be chosen at random from the interior of a region, part of which is shaded, you might be asked to find the probability that the point chosen will be from the shaded portion of the region. Such an item might be presented in a specific context, such as throwing darts at a target.

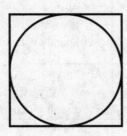

Examples:

1. The figure below shows a circle inscribed in a square. The area of the square is 324. If a point is selected at random in the interior of the square, what is the approximate probability that the point also lies in the interior of the circle?

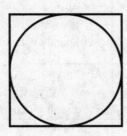

> ➤ Since the area of the square is 324, $A_{square} = s^2 \Rightarrow s = 18$. The side of the square is equal to the diameter of the circle, so the radius of the circle is $18 \div 2 = 9$. The area of the circle is: $A_{circle} = \pi r^2 = \pi(9)^2 = 81\pi$. Therefore, the probability that a point chosen at random in the interior of the square will also be in the interior of the circle is: $\dfrac{A_{circle}}{A_{square}} = \dfrac{81\pi}{324} = \dfrac{\pi}{4} \approx 0.785$.

2. The figure below shows a rectangle that is bounded by the two axes and two lines whose respective equations are $y = 8$ and $x = 6$. The shaded trapezoidal region is bounded on three sides by portions of three sides of the rectangle. The fourth unbounded side of the shaded trapezoidal region is a line segment that is a portion of the line whose equation is $2y = x + 4$. If a point is selected at random in the interior of the rectangle, what is the probability that the point also lies in the shaded region?

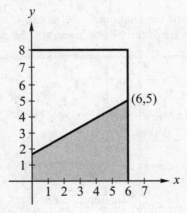

> ➤ For the line $2y = x + 4$, substitute values for x and solve for y. If $x = 0$, $2y = 0 + 4 \Rightarrow y = 2$. If $x = 6$, $2y = 6 + 4 \Rightarrow y = 5$. The parallel sides of the trapezoid have lengths of 2 and 5; the altitude of the trapezoid is 6. Therefore, the probability that the point will be in both the interior of the rectangle and the interior of the shaded region is: $\dfrac{A_{shaded}}{A_{rectangle}} = \dfrac{\frac{6(2+5)}{2}}{6 \cdot 8} = \dfrac{3 \cdot 7}{48} = \dfrac{21}{48} = \dfrac{7}{16}$.

Data Interpretation: Tables and Graphs

You are expected to be able to interpret data displayed in tables, charts, and graphs.

Example:

The tables below show the number, type, and cost of candy bars bought during one week at two local drugstores.

| | Number of Candy Bars Bought | | | | | |
| | Type A | | Type B | | Type C | |
	Large	Giant	Large	Giant	Large	Giant
Drugstore P	60	20	69	21	43	17
Drugstore Q	44	18	59	25	38	13

Cost per Candy Bar	Large	Giant
Type A	$0.45	$0.69
Type B	$0.45	$0.79
Type C	$0.55	$0.99

What is the total cost of all Type B candy bars bought at these two drugstores during the week?

➢ Total the cost of all Type B bars bought at the two drugstores: $69(0.45) + 21(0.79) + 59(0.45) + 25(0.79) = \$93.94$.

The test may also ask about the line of best fit for a scatterplot. A scatterplot is really just a plot of various data points for which a line of best fit can be drawn. For example, an item may require you to identify that a line of best fit for a scatterplot has a slope that is positive but less than 1. You are not expected to use formal methods for finding the equation of a line of best fit.

Example:

The points in the scatterplot below show the relationship between 14 students' test scores on a mid-term test and a final test. What is the approximate average (arithmetic mean) of the scores on the final test for all students who scored above 90 on the midterm test?

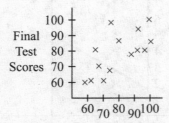

Mid-Term Test Scores

➢ Five students scored above 90 on the mid-term. Their marks are the five to the right on the scatterplot. The five corresponding scores on the final are approximately 80, 80, 85, 95, and 100. The average of these scores is approximately 88.

Story Problems

DIRECTIONS: Choose the correct answer to each of the following items. Answers are on page 792.

1. A suit is sold for $68 while marked at $80. What is the rate of discount?

    A. 15%   **C.** $17\frac{11}{17}\%$ **E.** 24%

    B. 17%   **D.** 20%

2. Lilian left home with $60 in her wallet. She spent $\frac{1}{3}$ of that amount at the supermarket, and she spent $\frac{1}{2}$ of what remained at the drugstore. If Lilian made no other expenditures, how much money did she have when she returned home?

    A. $10   **C.** $20   **E.** $50

    B. $15   **D.** $40

3. In the figure below, circle O and circle P are tangent to each other. If the circle with center O has a diameter of 8 and the circle with center P has a diameter of 6, what is the length of $\overline{OP}$?

    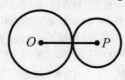

    A. 7   **C.** 14   **E.** 28

    B. 10   **D.** 20

4. A man buys a radio for $70 after receiving a discount of 20%. What was the marked price?

    A. $56   **C.** $87.50   **E.** $92

    B. $84.50   **D.** $90

5. Colin and Shaina wish to buy a gift for a friend. They combine their money and find they have $4.00, consisting of quarters, dimes, and nickels. If they have 35 coins and the number of quarters is half the number of nickels, how many quarters do they have?

    A. 5   **C.** 20   **E.** 36

    B. 10   **D.** 23

6. Willie receives $r\%$ commission on a sale of s dollars. How many dollars does he receive?

    A. rs **C.** $100rs$ **E.** $\dfrac{rs}{100}$

    B. $\dfrac{r}{s}$ **D.** $\dfrac{r}{100s}$

7. Three times the smallest of three consecutive odd integers is 3 more than twice the largest. Find the largest integer.

    A. 9   **C.** 13   **E.** 17

    B. 11   **D.** 15

8. A refrigerator was sold for $273, yielding a 30% profit on the cost. For how much should it be sold to yield only a 10% profit on the cost?

    A. $210   **C.** $235   **E.** $241

    B. $231   **D.** $240

9. If 60 feet of uniform wire weigh 80 pounds, what is the weight, in pounds, of 2 yards of the same wire?

    A. $2\frac{2}{3}$ **C.** 80   **E.** 2,400

    B. 8   **D.** 120

10. What single discount is equivalent to two successive discounts of 10% and 15%?

    A. 25%   **C.** 24%   **E.** 22%

    B. 24.5%   **D.** 23.5%

11. Robert is 15 years older than Stan. However, y years ago Robert was twice as old as Stan. If Stan is now b years old and $b > y$, find the value of $b - y$.

    A. 13   C. 15   E. 17
    B. 14   D. 16

12. The net price of a certain article is $306 after successive discounts of 15% and 10% are taken off the marked price. What is the marked price?

    A. $408
    B. $400
    C. $382.50
    D. $234.09
    E. None of the above

13. A gear 50 inches in diameter turns a smaller gear 30 inches in diameter. If the larger gear makes 15 revolutions, how many revolutions does the smaller gear make in that time?

    A. 9   C. 20   E. 30
    B. 12   D. 25

14. If a merchant makes a profit of 20% based on the selling price of an article, what percent does he make on the cost?

    A. 15   C. 25   E. 45
    B. 20   D. 40

15. How many ounces of pure acid must be added to 20 ounces of a solution that is 5% acid to strengthen it to a solution that is 24% acid?

    A. $2\frac{1}{2}$ C. 6   E. 10

    B. 5   D. $7\frac{1}{2}$

16. If x men can do a job in h days, how long would y men take to do the same job?

    A. $\dfrac{x}{h}$ C. $\dfrac{hy}{x}$ E. $\dfrac{x}{y}$

    B. $\dfrac{xh}{y}$ D. xyh

17. A certain radio costs a merchant $72. At what price must he sell it if he is to make a profit of 20% of the selling price?

    A. $86.40   C. $90   E. $148
    B. $88   D. $144

18. A dealer mixes a pounds of nuts that cost b cents per pound with c pounds of nuts that cost d cents per pound. At what price should he sell a pound of the mixture if he wishes to make a profit of 10 cents per pound?

    A. $\dfrac{ab + cd}{a + c} + 10$

    B. $\dfrac{ab + cd}{a + c} + 0.1$

    C. $\dfrac{b + d}{a + c} + 10$

    D. $\dfrac{b + d}{a + c} + 0.10$

    E. $\dfrac{b + d + 10}{a + c}$

19. If a furnace uses 40 gallons of oil in a week, how many gallons, to the nearest gallon, does it use in 10 days?

    A. 57   C. 28   E. 4
    B. 44   D. 20

20. Nell invests $2,400 in the Security National Bank at 5%. How much additional money must she invest at 8% so that the total annual income will be equal to 6% of her entire investment?

    A. $4,400   C. $3,000   E. $1,200
    B. $3,600   D. $2,400

21. A baseball team has won 40 games out of 60 played. It has 32 more games to play. How many of these must the team win to make its record 75% for the season?

    A. 28   C. 30   E. 34
    B. 29   D. 32

22. A recipe requires 13 ounces of sugar and 18 ounces of flour. If only 10 ounces of sugar are used, how much flour, to the nearest ounce, should be used?

    A. 11   C. 13   E. 15
    B. 12   D. 14

23. Ivan left Austin to drive to Boxville at 6:15 p.m. and arrived at 11:45 p.m. If he averaged 30 miles per hour and stopped one hour for dinner, how many miles is Boxville from Austin?

    A. 120   C. 180   E. 190
    B. 135   D. 185

24. If prices are reduced 25% and sales increase 20%, what is the net effect on gross receipts?

    A. They increase by 5%.
    B. They decrease by 5%.
    C. They remain the same.
    D. They increase by 10%.
    E. They decrease by 10%.

25. If a car can drive 25 miles on two gallons of gasoline, how many gallons will be needed for a trip of 150 miles?

    A. 12   C. 16   E. 20
    B. 13   D. 17

26. A plane traveling 600 miles per hour is 30 miles from Kennedy Airport at 4:58 p.m. At what time will it arrive at the airport?

    A. 5:00 p.m.   C. 5:02 p.m.   E. 5:23 p.m.
    B. 5:01 p.m.   D. 5:20 p.m.

27. A salesperson earns a commission of 5% on all sales between $200 and $600, and 8% on all sales over $600. What is the commission earned in a week in which sales total $800?

    A. $20   C. $48   E. $88
    B. $36   D. $78

28. A school has enough bread to last 30 children 4 days. If 10 children are added, how many days will the bread last?

    A. $\frac{1}{3}$ C. $2\frac{1}{3}$ E. 3

    B. $1\frac{1}{3}$ D. $2\frac{2}{3}$

29. Mr. Bridges can wash his car in 15 minutes, while his son Dave takes twice as long to do the same job. If they work together, how many minutes will the job take them?

    A. 5   C. 10   E. 30

    B. $7\frac{1}{2}$ D. $22\frac{1}{2}$

30. A train travels from Madison to Chicago at an average speed of 50 miles per hour and returns immediately along the same route at an average speed of 40 miles per hour. Of the following, which is closest to the average speed, in miles per hour, for the round-trip?

    A. 43.0   C. 44.4   E. 45.0
    B. 44.0   D. 44.5

31. At c cents per pound, what is the cost of a ounces of salami?

    A. $\dfrac{c}{a}$ C. ac E. $\dfrac{16c}{a}$

    B. $\dfrac{a}{c}$ D. $\dfrac{ac}{16}$

32. If 3 miles are equivalent to 4.83 kilometers, then 11.27 kilometers are equivalent to how many miles?

    A. $2\frac{1}{3}$ C. 7   E. $7\frac{1}{2}$

    B. 5   D. $7\frac{1}{3}$

33. If 4 workers take an hour to pave a road, how long should it take 12 workers to pave the same road?

    A. $\frac{1}{4}$ hour   C. $\frac{1}{2}$ hour   E. 1 hour

    B. $\frac{1}{3}$ hour   D. $\frac{3}{4}$ hour

34. At a certain printing plant, each of m machines prints 6 newspapers every s seconds. If all machines work together but independently without interruption, how many minutes will it take to print an entire run of 18,000 newspapers?

    A. $\dfrac{180s}{m}$ C. $50ms$ E. $\dfrac{300m}{s}$

    B. $\dfrac{50s}{m}$ D. $\dfrac{ms}{50}$

35. If p pencils cost d dollars, how many pencils can be bought for c cents?

A. $\dfrac{100pc}{d}$　　C. $\dfrac{pd}{c}$　　E. $\dfrac{cd}{p}$

B. $\dfrac{pc}{100d}$　　D. $\dfrac{pc}{d}$

36. Gerard takes 6 hours to do a job. Leo takes 8 hours to do the same job. How many hours should it take Gerard and Leo working together to do the same job?

A. $\dfrac{7}{24}$　　C. 3　　E. 7

B. $2\dfrac{3}{7}$　　D. $3\dfrac{3}{7}$

37. There are two drains, Drain 1 and Drain 2, in a pool. If both drains are opened, the pool is emptied in 20 minutes. If Drain 1 is closed and Drain 2 is open, the pool will be emptied in 30 minutes. If Drain 2 is closed and Drain 1 is open, how many minutes will it take to empty the pool?

A. 20　　C. 50　　E. 120
B. 30　　D. 60

38. Working alone, Machines X, Y, and Z can do a certain job in 3, 5, and 6 hours, respectively. What is the ratio of the time it takes Machine X to do the job, working alone at its rate, to the time it takes Machines Y and Z to do the job, working together at their individual rates?

A. $\dfrac{11}{33}$　　C. $\dfrac{30}{33}$　　E. $\dfrac{30}{11}$

B. $\dfrac{11}{30}$　　D. $\dfrac{33}{30}$

39. If the number n of newspapers sold per week varies with the price p in dollars according to the equation $n = 40 - 3p$, what would be the total weekly revenue from the sale of $1 newspapers?

A. $30　　C. $35　　E. $40
B. $33　　D. $37

40. A car dealer who gives a customer a 20% discount on the list price of a car still realizes a net profit of 25% of cost. If the dealer's cost is $4,800, what is the usual list price of the car?

A. $6,000　　C. $7,200　　E. $8,001
B. $6,180　　D. $7,500

41. A candy manufacturer produces 400 bars of a certain chocolate each month at a cost to the manufacturer of 25 cents and all the produced chocolate bars are sold each month. What is the minimum selling price per bar that will ensure that the monthly profit on the sales of these chocolate bars will be at least $420?

A. $1.00　　C. $1.20　　E. $1.30
B. $1.10　　D. $1.25

42. Acme Auto Parts manufactures car parts for which the production costs consist of annual fixed costs totaling $120,000 and variable costs averaging $6 per item. If Acme Auto Parts sells each item for $12, how many items must it manufacture and sell to earn an annual profit of $60,000?

A. 6,000　　C. 15,000　　E. 30,000
B. 12,000　　D. 20,000

43. The variable m varies directly as the square of t. If m is 7 when $t = 1$, what is the value of m when $t = 2$?

A. 28　　C. 7　　E. 2

B. 14　　D. $3\dfrac{1}{2}$

44. 6 students in a class failed algebra, representing $16\dfrac{2}{3}$% of the class. How many students passed the course?

A. 48　　C. 33　　E. 28
B. 36　　D. 30

45. If the value of a piece of property decreases by 10% while the tax rate on the property increases by 10%, what is the effect on taxes?

A. Taxes increase by 10%.
B. Taxes increase by 1%.
C. There is no change in taxes.
D. Taxes decrease by 1%.
E. Taxes decrease by 10%.

46. The variable m varies jointly as r and l. If m is 8 when r and l are each 1, what is the value of m when r and l are each 2?

A. 64   C. 16   E. 2
B. 32   D. 4

47. Of the Coral Estates residents, 95% live in private homes. Of those, 40% live in air-conditioned homes. What percent of the residents of Coral Estates live in air-conditioned homes?

A. 3%   C. 30%   E. 38%
B. 3.8%   D. 34%

48. Exactly three years before the year in which Anna was born, the year was $1980 - x$. In terms of x, what is the year of Anna's twentieth birthday?

A. $1977 + x$ C. $2003 - x$ E. $2006 + x$
B. $1997 + x$ D. $2003 + x$

49. Mr. Carlson receives a salary of $500 a month and a commission of 5% on all sales. What must be the amount of his sales in July so that his total monthly income is $2,400?

A. $48,000   C. $7,600   E. $2,000
B. $38,000   D. $3,800

50. John can wax his car in 3 hours. Jim can do the same job in 5 hours. How long will it take them if they work together?

A. $\dfrac{1}{2}$ hour   C. 2 hours   E. 8 hours

B. $1\dfrac{7}{8}$ hours   D. $2\dfrac{7}{8}$ hours

51. In a run/walk marathon, Weber runs x miles in h hours, then walks the remainder of the marathon route, y miles, in the same number of hours. Which of the following represents Weber's average speed, in miles per hour, for the entire marathon?

A. $\dfrac{x - y}{h}$ C. $\dfrac{2(x + y)}{h}$ E. $\dfrac{x + y}{2h}$

B. $\dfrac{x - y}{2h}$ D. $\dfrac{2(x + y)}{2h}$

52. In the junior class at Shawnee High School, 168 students took the SAT test, 175 students took the ACT test, 80 students took both, and 27 students did not take either one. What is the total number of students in the junior class at Shawnee High School?

A. 440   C. 290   E. 248
B. 343   D. 282

53. Let $R = \{3, 5, 6, 7, 9\}$. How many different subsets of R with 1, 2, 3, or 4 elements contain one or more odd numbers?

A. 31   C. 29   E. 27
B. 30   D. 28

54. A survey of 51 students was conducted concerning each student's favorite flavors of ice cream. Of the 51 students, 10 students liked only vanilla, 12 students liked only strawberry, and 15 students liked only chocolate. Every student liked at least one of the three flavors. 7 students liked both vanilla and strawberry, and 9 students liked both vanilla and chocolate. The largest possible number of students who could have liked both chocolate and strawberry is:

A. 2   C. 7   E. 14
B. 3   D. 12

55. Sixty students are enrolled in French, Spanish, or German. Forty-five students are in French, 35 are in Spanish, and 20 are in German. Fifteen students are enrolled in all three of the courses. How many of the students are enrolled in exactly two of the courses?

A. 5   C. 12   E. 20
B. 10   D. 15

56. If there are 3 different roads from Seattle to Olympia and 4 different roads from Olympia to Portland, how many different routes are there from Seattle to Portland that pass through Olympia?

A. 1   C. 10   E. 24
B. 7   D. 12

57. Set X is the set of all positive integral multiples of 8: $X = \{8, 16, 24, 32, ...\}$. Set Y is the set of all positive integral multiples of 6: $Y = \{6, 12, 18, 24, ...\}$. The intersection of these two sets is the set of all positive integral multiples of:

A. 2   **C.** 14   **E.** 48
B. 4   **D.** 24

58. In how many arrangements can a theater usher seat 4 men and 3 women in a row of 7 seats if the men are to have the first, third, fourth, and seventh seats?

A. 6   **C.** 24   **E.** 840
B. 12   **D.** 144

59. Of the 50 children in a school sports program, 40% will be assigned to softball, and the remaining 60% to baseball. However, 70% of the children prefer softball and 30% prefer baseball. What is the least possible number of children who will NOT be assigned to the sport they prefer?

A. 10   **C.** 20   **E.** 35
B. 15   **D.** 30

60. Recipes are filed in a recipe book according to at least 12 different color codes. If combination of three different colors is chosen to represent each color code and if each color code is uniquely represented by that choice of three colors, what is the minimum number of colors needed for the coding? (Assume that the order of the colors in a combination does not matter.)

A. 3   **C.** 5   **E.** 10
B. 4   **D.** 6

61. If y varies directly with x and the constant of variation is 3, then $y = 12.3$ when $x = 4.1$. If y varies directly with x and $y = 6.72$ when $x = 4.2$, then what is the constant of variation?

A. 3.1   **C.** 2.52   **E.** 2.50
B. 4.2   **D.** 1.6

62. Each of the following choices is comprised of three equations relating x and y. Identify the set of equations that demonstrates direct variation, inverse variation, and neither direct nor inverse variation, respectively?

A. $y = 3x; x^2 + y^2 = x + 5; y = \dfrac{4}{x}$

B. $y = 3x; x^2 + y^2 = x + 5; y = \dfrac{x}{4}$

C. $x = \dfrac{y}{3}; xy = 7; x^2 + y^2 = \dfrac{x}{5}$

D. $y = 3x; y = \dfrac{4}{x}; x = 5y$

E. $y = \dfrac{2x}{3}; x = 5y; x^2 + y^2 = x + 7$

63. At a constant temperature, the resistance of a wire varies directly with length and inversely with the square of the wire diameter. A piece of wire that is 0.1 inch in diameter and 50 feet long has a resistance of 0.1 ohm. What is the resistance, in ohms, of a wire of the same material that is 9,000 feet long and 0.3 inches in diameter?

A. 0.3   **C.** 2   **E.** 9
B. 0.9   **D.** 3

64. Let y vary directly as x, and let w vary directly as the square of x. If $y = 10$ for $x = 1.25$ and $w = 8$ for $x = \sqrt{2}$, then for what positive value of x will $y = w$?

A. 1   **C.** 2   **E.** 5
B. $1\dfrac{1}{2}$ **D.** 4

65. The perimeter of a square varies directly as the length of one side of the square with a constant of variation of 4. The circumference of a circle varies directly as the circle's radius and a constant of variation equal to:

A. π **C.** 1   **E.** $\dfrac{1}{n}$
B. 2π **D.** 2

66. If x and y vary inversely, then for any ordered pair (x, y), the value of xy is a constant number. The ordered pairs $(-12, -3)$ and $(6, 6)$ represent an example of inverse variation for x and y. Which of the following graphs represents a possible inverse variation relationship between x and y?

A.

D.

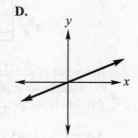

B.

E.

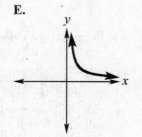

C.

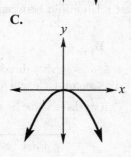

67. The formula for compound interest is $A = P(1 + \frac{r}{n})^{nt}$, where A is the final amount, P is the initial investment, r is the annual percentage interest rate, t is the time period, and n is the number of times per year that the interest is compounded. If an initial investment of \$10,000 accrues compound interest at a percentage rate of 4.16% and is worth \$10,424.02, \$10,866.03, \$11,326.77, and \$11,807.06 after 1, 2, 3, and 4 years, respectively, then n is approximately equal to:

A. 1   C. 4   E. 12
B. 2   D. 6

68. The simple interest earned on an investment is given by the formula $I = prt$, where I is the amount of interest, p is the amount invested, r is the yearly percentage rate of interest, and t is the number of years for the investment. What is the simple interest earned on an investment of \$1,000 for 2 years at a yearly percentage rate of interest of 6%?

A. \$6   C. \$60   E. \$600
B. \$12   D. \$120

69. The probability that an event will happen can be shown by the fraction $\dfrac{\text{winning events}}{\text{total events}}$ or $\dfrac{\text{favorable events}}{\text{total events}}$. From the 8-digit number 12,344,362, Helen selects a digit at random. What is the probability that she selected 4?

A. $\dfrac{1}{8}$ C. $\dfrac{1}{4}$ E. $\dfrac{4}{1}$

B. $\dfrac{1}{5}$ D. $\dfrac{1}{2}$

70. Last night, Dave and Kathy both arrived at Pizza Palace at two different random times between 10:00 p.m. and midnight. They had agreed to wait exactly 15 minutes for each other to arrive before leaving. What is the probability that Dave and Kathy were together at Pizza Palace last night between 10:00 p.m. and midnight?

A. $\dfrac{1}{8}$ C. $\dfrac{15}{64}$ E. $\dfrac{31}{64}$

B. $\dfrac{1}{4}$ D. $\dfrac{3}{8}$

71. George must select 1 pencil from 6 different pencils and 1 pen from 5 different pens. How many different combinations can George make?

A. 5   C. 30   E. 65
B. 11   D. 56

72. A letter is selected at random from the word "DAVID." What is the probability that the letter selected is "D"?

A. $\dfrac{1}{5}$ C. $\dfrac{1}{3}$ E. $\dfrac{3}{5}$

B. $\dfrac{1}{4}$ D. $\dfrac{2}{5}$

73. One of the letters in the alphabet is selected at random. What is the probability that the letter selected is a letter found in the word "MATHEMATICS"?

    A. $\dfrac{1}{26}$ **C.** $\dfrac{5}{13}$ **E.** $\dfrac{6}{13}$

    B. $\dfrac{4}{13}$ **D.** $\dfrac{11}{26}$

74. Two integers are to be randomly selected from the sets below, one integer from each set. What is the probability that the sum of the two integers will equal 11?

    $$X = \{2, 4, 5, 8, 9\}$$
    $$Y = \{2, 3, 4, 7\}$$

    A. 0.10   **C.** 0.20   **E.** 0.30
    B. 0.15   **D.** 0.25

75. If 5 books are lined up in random order on a shelf, what is the probability that the oldest book will be on the left end and the newest book will be on the right end?

    A. $\dfrac{1}{20}$ **C.** $\dfrac{1}{6}$ **E.** $\dfrac{1}{4}$

    B. $\dfrac{1}{8}$ **D.** $\dfrac{1}{5}$

76. If a fair coin is to be tossed 3 times, what is the probability that on at least 1 of the tosses the coin will turn up heads?

    A. $\dfrac{1}{8}$ **C.** $\dfrac{1}{2}$ **E.** $\dfrac{31}{64}$

    B. $\dfrac{1}{4}$ **D.** $\dfrac{7}{8}$

77. In the figure below, two sides of the rectangle $ABGF$ lie on two sides of the square $ACDE$. $\overline{AF} = 9$, $\overline{BC} = 8$, and $\overline{FE} = 1$.

    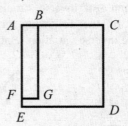

    If a point is chosen at random in the interior of the square, what is the probability that the point also lies in the interior of the rectangle?

    A. $\dfrac{1}{50}$ **C.** $\dfrac{7}{50}$ **E.** $\dfrac{11}{50}$

    B. $\dfrac{3}{50}$ **D.** $\dfrac{9}{50}$

78. The stronger the relationship between two variables, the more closely the points on a scatter plot will approach some linear or curvilinear pattern. Which of the scatter plots below represents the strongest relationship between the two variables?

    A.

    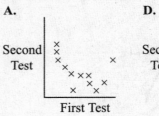

    D.

    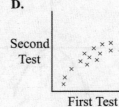

    B.

    E.

    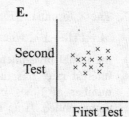

    C.

    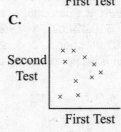

79. The table below shows the daily change in the weather temperatures for a certain city last week. What was the net change, in degrees Celsius, in the weather temperature for the week?

Day	Daily Change in Temperature (°C)
Sunday	+5.5
Monday	+1.7
Tuesday	−3.9
Wednesday	−3.3
Thursday	−0.5
Friday	+0.8
Saturday	−0.2

A. −5.7   C. 0.1   E. 5.7
B. −0.1   D. 5.3

80. The table below represents the number of voters in five counties that voted in a general election and the percent change in the number of voters from the previously held primary election. Which county had the greatest net increase in voters between the primary and the general elections?

County	Number of Voters in General Election (in millions)	Percent Change from Primary Election
M	5.67	−23%
N	2.34	+14%
O	1.25	−2%
P	4.56	+4%
Q	6.23	+8%

A. County M
B. County N
C. County O
D. County P
E. County Q

81. The table below shows the number of students in three sports at East High School. 8 students are in both basketball and tennis, 5 students are in both basketball and volleyball, and 3 students are in both volleyball and tennis. No student is in all three sports. What is the total number of students that participate only in basketball or tennis?

Sport	Number of Students
Basketball	35
Volleyball	15
Tennis	40

A. 22   C. 50   E. 75
B. 29   D. 51

Math Express Summary

Arithmetic

1. **Natural Numbers:** *Natural* numbers are the set of positive integers and are also referred to as counting numbers: $\{1, 2, 3, 4, 5, \ldots\}$.

2. **Whole Numbers:** *Whole* numbers are the numbers used for counting, plus the number zero: $(0, 1, 2, 3, 4, 5, \ldots)$.

3. **Integers:** *Integers* are positive or negative whole numbers.

   e.g., $-568, -45, 0, 6, 67, \dfrac{16}{2}, 345$

4. **Positive and Negative Integers:** When adding integers that have the *same* sign, add their values with positive signs, and give the result the same sign as the original values.

   e.g., 1. $4 + 8 = 12$

   2. $-5 + (-3) = -(5 + 3) = -8$

   When adding integers that have *opposite* signs, take their values with positive signs, subtract the smaller from the larger, and then give the result the sign of the integer with the larger positive value.

   e.g., 1. $-3 + 2 = -(3 - 2) = -1$

   2. $4 + (-6) = -(6 - 4) = -2$

   Subtracting an integer of any sign from another integer of any sign is the same as adding its opposite.

   e.g., 1. $4 - 8 = 4 + (-8) = -4$

   2. $-3 - 2 = -3 + (-2) = -5$

   3. $-5 - (-3) = -5 + 3 = -2$

   4. $7 - (-4) = 7 + 4 = 11$

5. **Even and Odd Integers:** An *even* integer is evenly divisible by 2, whereas an *odd* integer is not evenly divisible by 2. 0 is an even integer.

   e.g., 1. $-50, -4, 0, 2, 34$ are even integers.

   2. $-45, -3, 9, 15$ are odd integers.

   Important properties of even and odd integers:

even + even = even	e.g., $2 + 4 = 6$
even + odd = odd	e.g., $4 + 3 = 7$
odd + odd = even	e.g., $3 + 5 = 8$
odd + even = odd	e.g., $3 + 4 = 7$
even • even = even	e.g., $2 \cdot 4 = 8$
even • odd = even	e.g., $2 \cdot 3 = 6$
odd • odd = odd	e.g., $3 \cdot 5 = 15$
odd • even = even	e.g., $3 \cdot 2 = 6$

6. **Consecutive Integers:** *Consecutive* integers are in continuous sequence. If the first integer of a consecutive sequence is m, the sequence is m, $m + 1$, $m + 2$, etc.

   e.g., 1. $\{4, 5, 6, 7, \ldots\}$

   2. $\{-10, -9, -8, -7, \ldots\}$

   Consecutive *even* or *odd* integers are in continuous sequence of even or odd integers, respectively. An even or odd sequence is m, $m + 2$, $m + 4$, $m + 6$, etc.

   e.g., 1. $\{-4, -2, 0, 2, \ldots\}$

   2. $\{7, 9, 11, 13, \ldots\}$

7. **Real Numbers:** Real numbers are all the numbers on the number line, including integers, decimals, fractions, and radical numbers.

   e.g., $-\dfrac{1}{2}, 0, \dfrac{2}{3}, \sqrt{2}, \pi$

   A real number is *rational* if it can be written as the ratio of two integers, where the denominator does not equal zero. Natural numbers, whole numbers, integers, common fractions, and repeating decimals are examples of rational numbers.

e.g., $-\dfrac{1}{2}$, 0, $0.\overline{11}$, 0.75, $\dfrac{2}{3}$

A real number is *irrational* if it cannot be written as the ratio of two integers. Irrational numbers have infinite non-repeating decimal representations.

e.g., $\sqrt{2}$, π

Properties of real numbers:

$(+)(+) = (+)$
$(-)(-) = (+)$
$(+)(-) = (-)$
$(-)^2 = (+)$
$m + 0 = m$, where m is a real number
$m \cdot 0 = 0$, where m is a real number

e.g., 1. $\left(\dfrac{1}{2}\right)(4) = 2$

   2. $(-2)\left(-\dfrac{4}{5}\right) = \dfrac{8}{5}$

   3. $(2)(-4) = (-8)$

   4. $\left(-\dfrac{3}{4}\right)(4) = -3$

   5. $(-2)^2 = 4$

   6. $2 + 0 = 2$

   7. $(2)(0) = 0$

8. **Factor:** A *factor* is a number that divides evenly into another number.

   e.g., 1, 2, 3, 4, 6, and 12 are factors of 12

9. **Prime:** A *prime* number is any natural number (except 1) that is divisible only by 1 and itself.

   e.g., 2, 3, 5, 7, 11, 13, 17, and 19 are all prime numbers

10. **Prime Factors:** All natural numbers can be expressed as the product of prime numbers, which are called the *prime factors* of that number.

    e.g., 1. $3 = (3)(1)$

       2. $12 = (2)(2)(3)$

11. **Miscellaneous Symbols:**

    "=" means "is equal to"
    "≠" means "is not equal to"
    "<" means "is less than"
    ">" means "is greater than"
    "≤" means "is less than or equal to"
    "≥" means "is greater than or equal to"
    "| |" means "absolute value (always non-negative)"

    e.g., 1. $3 = 3$

       2. $\dfrac{3}{4} \neq \dfrac{5}{6}$

       3. $-3 < 6$

       4. $5 > 4$

       5. $m - 3 \leq -3$,
          for $m = \ldots, -3, -2, 0$

       6. $m + 3 \geq 3$,
          for $m = 0, 1, 2, 3, \ldots$

       7. $|-5| = 5$

12. **Terms:** The *sum* or *total* is the result of adding numbers together. The *difference* is the result of subtracting one number from another. The *product* is the result of multiplying numbers together. The *quotient* is the result of dividing one number by another. The *remainder* is the number remaining after one number is divided into another number.

    e.g., 1. The sum (or total) of 2 and 3 is 5: $2 + 3 = 5$.

       2. The difference between 5 and 2 is 3: $5 - 2 = 3$.

       3. The product of 2 and 3 is 6: $(2)(3) = 6$.

4. The quotient of 6 divided by 2 is 3:
$6 \div 2 = 3$.

5. The remainder of 7 divided by 3 is 1:
$7 \div 3 = 2$ plus a remainder of 1.

13. **Fractions:** When one whole integer is divided by another whole integer (other than zero) and the result is not a third whole integer, the result is a fraction, or ratio. The top number is called the *numerator*; the bottom number is called the *denominator*.

e.g., 2 divided by 3 results in a fraction, not a whole number: $2 \div 3 = \dfrac{2}{3}$.

Proper fractions have a numerator of lower value than the denominator and thus have a value less than 1.

e.g., $\dfrac{1}{2}$ and $\dfrac{3}{4}$ are both less than 1.

Improper fractions have a numerator of greater value than the denominator, and thus have a value greater than 1.

e.g., $\dfrac{3}{2}$ and $\dfrac{4}{3}$ are both greater than 1.

A *mixed number* consists of both a whole number and a fraction written together.

e.g., 1. $2\dfrac{1}{2} = 2 + \dfrac{1}{2}$

2. $3\dfrac{4}{5} = 3 + \dfrac{4}{5}$

To add, subtract, multiply, or divide fractions, convert mixed numbers to improper fractions as follows:

a. The new denominator is the denominator of the fractional part of the mixed number.

b. The new numerator is the whole number of the mixed number multiplied by the denominator of the fractional part and then added to its numerator.

e.g., 1. $3\dfrac{1}{4} = \dfrac{(3 \cdot 4) + 1}{4} = \dfrac{13}{4}$

2. $6\dfrac{2}{5} = \dfrac{(6 \cdot 5) + 2}{5} = \dfrac{32}{5}$

3. $2\dfrac{12}{13} = \dfrac{(2 \cdot 13) + 12}{13} = \dfrac{38}{13}$

To convert an improper fraction to a mixed number, reverse the process as follows:

a. Divide the denominator into the numerator. The integer part of the quotient becomes the whole number part of the mixed number.

b. With the same denominator, create a fraction with the numerator equal to the remainder of the first step.

e.g., 1. $\dfrac{29}{5} = 29 \div 5$

$= 5$ with a remainder of 4

$= 5\dfrac{4}{5}$

2. $\dfrac{31}{6} = 31 \div 6$

$= 5$ with a remainder of 1

$= 5\dfrac{1}{6}$

3. $\dfrac{43}{13} = 43 \div 13$

$= 3$ with a remainder of 4

$= 3\dfrac{4}{13}$

14. **Reducing Fractions:** It is conventional to reduce all fractions to lowest terms. To reduce a fraction to lowest terms, eliminate redundant factors that are in both the numerator and the denominator. Either factor or divide out the redundant factors from both.

e.g., $\dfrac{8}{16} = \dfrac{1(8)}{2(8)} = \dfrac{1}{2}$, or $\dfrac{8}{16} = \dfrac{8 \div 8}{16 \div 8} = \dfrac{1}{2}$

A fraction is expressed in *lowest terms* when there is no natural number (other than 1) that can be divided evenly into both the numerator and the denominator.

e.g., $\dfrac{8}{15}$ is in lowest terms, as there is no natural number (other than 1) that divides evenly into 8 and 15.

15. **Common Denominators:** A *common denominator* is a number that is a multiple of the denominators of two or more fractions.

   e.g., Since 12 is an even multiple of both 3 and 4, it is a common denominator for $\dfrac{1}{3}$ and $\dfrac{1}{4}$.

   Converting a fraction to another denominator is the reverse of reducing it to lowest terms. Multiplying the numerator and the denominator of a fraction by the same number is equal to multiplying it by 1, which means that the value is unchanged.

   e.g., 1. $\dfrac{1}{4} = \dfrac{(1)(3)}{(4)(3)} = \dfrac{3}{12}$

   2. $\dfrac{2}{3} = \dfrac{(2)(4)}{(3)(4)} = \dfrac{8}{12}$

16. **Complex Fractions:** A *complex fraction* is a fraction in which either the numerator or the denominator, or both, contains fractions. There are two methods for simplifying complex fractions.

   Method 1: Multiply the numerator by the reciprocal of the denominator and simplify.

   e.g., $\dfrac{\frac{1}{2}}{\frac{3}{4}} = \left(\dfrac{1}{2}\right)\left(\dfrac{4}{3}\right) = \dfrac{4}{6} = \dfrac{2}{3}$

   Method 2: Multiply both the numerator and the denominator by the least common denominator for the terms in the numerator and the denominator of the complex fraction and simplify.

   e.g., $\dfrac{\frac{1}{2}}{\frac{3}{4}} \cdot \dfrac{\frac{4}{1}}{\frac{4}{1}} = \dfrac{\frac{4}{2}}{\frac{12}{4}} = \dfrac{2}{3}$

17. **Adding Fractions:** The procedure for adding fractions varies depending on whether or not the fractions already share the same denominator.

   To add fractions with the same denominator, create a new fraction using the common denominator. The new numerator is the sum of the old numerators.

   e.g., $\dfrac{3}{7} + \dfrac{2}{7} = \dfrac{5}{7}$

   To add fractions with different denominators, find a common denominator and convert the fractions.

   e.g., 1. $\dfrac{1}{3} + \dfrac{1}{5} = \dfrac{1(5)}{3(5)} + \dfrac{1(3)}{5(3)} = \dfrac{5}{15} + \dfrac{3}{15} = \dfrac{8}{15}$

   2. $\dfrac{1}{3} + \dfrac{2}{7} = \dfrac{1(7)}{3(7)} + \dfrac{2(3)}{7(3)} = \dfrac{7}{21} + \dfrac{6}{21} = \dfrac{13}{21}$

   To add a fraction and a whole number, treat the whole number as a fraction with a denominator of 1.

   e.g., $2 + \dfrac{1}{5} + \dfrac{1}{2} = \dfrac{2}{1} + \dfrac{1}{5} + \dfrac{1}{2}$

   $= \dfrac{2(10)}{1(10)} + \dfrac{1(2)}{5(2)} + \dfrac{1(5)}{2(5)}$

   $= \dfrac{20}{10} + \dfrac{2}{10} + \dfrac{5}{10}$

   $= \dfrac{27}{10}$

   To add a fraction and a mixed number, change the mixed number to an improper fraction and then add.

   e.g., $2\dfrac{1}{3} + \dfrac{1}{3} = \dfrac{7}{3} + \dfrac{1}{3} = \dfrac{8}{3} = 2\dfrac{2}{3}$

18. **Subtracting Fractions:** Follow the same procedure for addition, except subtract rather than add.

   To subtract fractions with the same denominator, simply subtract the second numerator from the first.

   e.g., $\dfrac{5}{7} - \dfrac{2}{7} = \dfrac{3}{7}$

To subtract fractions with different denominators, first find a common denominator.

e.g., $\dfrac{7}{8} - \dfrac{3}{5} = \dfrac{7(5)}{8(5)} - \dfrac{3(8)}{5(8)} = \dfrac{35}{40} - \dfrac{24}{40} = \dfrac{11}{40}$

19. **"Flying-X" Method for Adding and Subtracting Fractions:** It is not necessary to find the least common denominator when adding or subtracting fractions if you reduce the result to lowest terms. Any common denominator will work—simply use the "flying-x" method.

$$\dfrac{a}{b} + \dfrac{c}{d} = \dfrac{a}{b} \overset{+}{\diagdown\diagup} \dfrac{c}{d} = \dfrac{ad + bc}{bd}$$

Step 1: Multiply the denominators together to get a new denominator.

Step 2: Multiply the numerator of the first fraction by the denominator of the second.

Step 3: Multiply the denominator of the first fraction by the numerator of the second.

Step 4: The new numerator is the sum (or difference) of the results of steps 2 and 3.

e.g., 1. $\dfrac{2}{7} + \dfrac{1}{5} = \dfrac{2}{7} \overset{+}{\diagdown\diagup} \dfrac{1}{5} = \dfrac{10 + 7}{35} = \dfrac{17}{35}$

  2. $\dfrac{3}{5} - \dfrac{1}{3} = \dfrac{3}{5} \overset{-}{\diagdown\diagup} \dfrac{1}{3} = \dfrac{9 - 5}{15} = \dfrac{4}{15}$

20. **Multiplying Fractions:** Multiplication of fractions does not require a common denominator. Just multiply numerators to create a new numerator, and multiply denominators to create a new denominator.

e.g., 1. $\dfrac{3}{4} \cdot \dfrac{1}{2} = \dfrac{(3)(1)}{(4)(2)} = \dfrac{3}{8}$

  2. $\dfrac{2}{3} \cdot \dfrac{2}{5} = \dfrac{(2)(2)}{(3)(5)} = \dfrac{4}{15}$

21. **Dividing Fractions:** To divide by a fraction, take the reciprocal of the divisor (the fraction doing the dividing) and then multiply the two terms.

e.g., 1. $2 \div \dfrac{1}{4} = 2 \cdot \dfrac{4}{1} = \dfrac{8}{1} = 8$

  2. $\dfrac{\frac{2}{3}}{\frac{5}{6}} = \dfrac{2}{3} \cdot \dfrac{6}{5} = \dfrac{12}{15} = \dfrac{4}{5}$

22. **Converting Fractions to Decimals:** If the fraction already has a denominator that is 10, 100, 1,000, etc., the conversion is easy. The numerator of the fraction becomes the decimal. The placement of the decimal point is governed by the number of zeros in the denominator.

e.g. Express $\dfrac{127}{1,000}$ in decimal form.

In the numerator, count three places—one for each zero in 1,000—to the left from the right of the last digit: $\dfrac{127}{1,000} = 0.127$.

If there are fewer numbers in the numerator than there are decimal places, add zeros to the left of the number until there are enough decimal places.

e.g., $\dfrac{3}{100} = 0.03$

To convert a proper fraction with a denominator other than 10, 100, etc., first convert the fraction to the equivalent form using a denominator such as 10, 100, etc. To determine which denominator to use, divide the denominator of the fraction into 10, then into 100, then into 1,000, until a denominator that is evenly divisible by the denominator of the original fraction is found.

e.g., 1. $\dfrac{2}{5} = \dfrac{(2)(2)}{(5)(2)} = \dfrac{4}{10} = 0.4$

  2. $\dfrac{1}{4} = \dfrac{(1)(25)}{(4)(25)} = \dfrac{25}{100} = 0.25$

  3. $\dfrac{3}{8} = \dfrac{(3)(125)}{(8)(125)} = \dfrac{375}{1,000} = 0.375$

To convert proper fractions to decimals, dividing the denominator into the numerator is usually easier.

e.g., 1. $\dfrac{2}{5} = 5\overline{)2.0}^{\,0.4} = 0.4$

2. $\dfrac{3}{8} = 8\overline{)3.000}^{\,0.375} = 0.375$

To convert a mixed number into a decimal, convert the fractional part of the mixed number to a decimal as just discussed, and then place the whole number part of the mixed number to the left of the decimal point.

e.g., 1. $6\dfrac{1}{10} = 6.1$

(Convert $\dfrac{1}{10}$ to 0.1 and then place the 6 to the left of the decimal point.)

2. $3\dfrac{7}{8} = 3.875$

(Convert $\dfrac{7}{8}$ to 0.875 and then place the 3 to the left of the decimal point.)

To convert an improper fraction to a decimal, convert it to a mixed number and follow the procedure just outlined.

e.g., $\dfrac{9}{4} = 2\dfrac{1}{4} = 2.25$

23. **Converting Decimals to Fractions:** The numerator of the fraction is the digit(s) to the right of the decimal point. The denominator is a 1 followed by the same number of zeros as the number of decimal places to the right of the decimal point.

e.g., $0.005 = \dfrac{5}{1,000} = \dfrac{1}{200}$

(0.005 has three decimal places, so the new denominator is 1 followed by 3 zeroes).

If a decimal has numbers to both the right and left of the decimal point, the conversion to a fraction results in a mixed number. The whole number part of the mixed number is the whole number part of the decimal.

e.g., 1. $1.75 = 1 + \dfrac{75}{100} = 1 + \dfrac{3}{4} = 1\dfrac{3}{4}$

2. $357.125 = 357 + \dfrac{125}{1,000} = 357 + \dfrac{1}{8} = 357\dfrac{1}{8}$

Memorize these decimal equivalents:

$\dfrac{1}{2} = 0.50 \qquad \dfrac{1}{3} = 0.\overline{33} \qquad \dfrac{1}{4} = 0.25$

$\dfrac{1}{5} = 0.20 \qquad \dfrac{1}{6} = 0.1\overline{6} \qquad \dfrac{1}{7} = 0.\overline{142857}$

$\dfrac{1}{8} = 0.125 \qquad \dfrac{1}{9} = 0.\overline{11} \qquad \dfrac{1}{10} = 0.10$

(Note: A bar over a digit or digits indicates that the digit or group of digits repeats.)

24. **Adding and Subtracting Decimals:** To add or subtract decimals, line up the decimal points, fill in the appropriate number of zeros, and then add or subtract.

e.g., $0.25 + 0.1 + 0.825 = $
$$
\begin{array}{r}
0.25 \\
0.1 \\
+\ 0.825 \\
\hline
= 0.250 \\
0.100 \\
+\ 0.825 \\
\hline
1.175
\end{array}
$$

25. **Multiplying Decimals:** To multiply decimals, first multiply as with whole numbers and then adjust the decimal point. Count the total number of decimal places in the numbers being multiplied, count that many places to the left from the right of the final digit in the product, and put the decimal point there.

e.g., 1. $(0.1)(0.2)(0.3) = 0.006$
($1 \cdot 2 \cdot 3 = 6$, and there are three decimal places in the multiplication.)

2. $(0.10)(0.10)(0.10) = 0.001000 = 0.001$
($10 \cdot 10 \cdot 10 = 1,000$, and there are six decimal places in the multiplication.)

26. **Dividing Decimals:** When the divisor (the quantity by which another quantity, the dividend, is to be divided) is a whole number, place a

decimal point in the quotient immediately above the decimal point in the dividend. Keep dividing until there is no remainder, adding zeros as needed to the right of the divisor.

$$
\begin{array}{r}
1.25 \\
\text{e.g., } 2.5 \div 2 = 2\overline{)2.50} \\
\underline{-\ 2} \\
0\ 5 \\
\underline{-\ 4} \\
10 \\
\underline{-\ 10} \\
0
\end{array}
$$

When the divisor is a *decimal*, "clear" the fractional part of the decimal by moving the decimal points of both the dividend and divisor, the same number of spaces to the right.

$$
\begin{array}{r}
2 \\
\text{e.g., } 5 \div 2.5 = 50 \div 25 = 25\overline{)50} \\
\underline{-\ 50} \\
0
\end{array}
$$

27. **Ratios:** A *ratio* is a statement about the relationship between two quantities. The ratio of two quantities, x and y, can be expressed as $x \div y$, x/y, or $x : y$.

e.g., 1. $\dfrac{2}{5} = 2 : 5$

2. $\dfrac{\text{boys}}{\text{girls}} = \text{boys} : \text{girls} = \text{ratio of boys to girls}$

3. $\dfrac{\text{miles}}{\text{hour}} = \text{miles} : \text{hour} = \text{miles per hour}$

28. **Proportions:** A *proportion* is a statement of equality between two ratios.

e.g., $\dfrac{3}{4} = \dfrac{9}{12}$

With *direct variation*, ratios are directly related: the more of one quantity, the more of the other, and vice versa.

e.g., If 12 donuts cost \$3.60, how much do 4 donuts cost?

$$
\frac{\text{Total Cost for } X}{\text{Total Cost for } Y} = \frac{X}{Y}
$$

$$
\frac{\$3.60}{Y} = \frac{12}{4}
$$

$$
\$3.60(4) = 12Y
$$

$$
Y = 3.60(4) \div 12 = \$1.20
$$

With *inverse variation*, ratios are inversely related: an increase in one quantity is a decrease in the other. Use this method to solve inverse variation problems: first, set up an ordinary proportion, making sure that you group like quantities; then, take the reciprocal of the proportion's right side; and finally, cross-multiply and solve for the unknown.

e.g., Traveling at a constant rate of 150 mph, a plane makes the trip from City P to City Q in four hours. How long will the trip take if the plane flies at a constant rate of 200 mph?

$$
\frac{\text{Speed } X}{\text{Speed } Y} = \frac{\text{Time } X}{\text{Time } Y}
$$

$$
\frac{150 \text{ mph}}{200 \text{ mph}} = \frac{4 \text{ hours}}{Y \text{ hours}}
$$

$$
\frac{150}{200} = \frac{Y}{4}
$$

$$
Y = 4(150) \div 200 = 3 \text{ hours}
$$

29. **Percentage Conversions:** *To change any decimal to a percent*, move the decimal point two places to the right and add a percent sign. To change a percent to a decimal, reverse the process.

e.g., 1. $0.275 = 27.5\%$

2. $0.03 = 3\%$

3. $0.02\% = 0.0002$

4. $120\% = 1.20$

To convert a fraction to a percent, first convert the fraction to a decimal. Reverse the process for converting percents to fractions.

e.g., 1. $\dfrac{3}{4} = 0.75 = 75\% = 0.75 = \dfrac{75}{100} = \dfrac{3}{4}$

MATH SKILLS REVIEW

2. $\dfrac{5}{8} = 0.625 = 62.5\% = \dfrac{625}{1,000} = \dfrac{5}{8}$

30. Common Percent Problems: All percent problems have the same three components: "is," "of," and %. Depending on the form of the question, one of these three components is the unknown variable.

"What is x% of that?"
"This is what percent of that?"
"This is x% of what?"

Percent problems can be solved using several different methods. Two methods are outlined below.

Method 1: Write the statement as an equation, rewrite the percent as $\dfrac{\%}{100}$, and solve for the unknown.

e.g., 5 is 20% of what number?

$$5 = \dfrac{20}{100}x$$
$$x = \dfrac{(5)(100)}{20} = 25$$
Thus, 5 is 20% of 25.

Method 2: Since there are three parts to all percent problems ("is," "of," and %), use the following equation to solve for the unknown: $\dfrac{\text{is}}{\text{of}} = \dfrac{\%}{100}$.

e.g., 1. 20 is what percent of 50?

$\% = x$, "is" $= 20$, "of" $= 50$
$$\dfrac{\text{is}}{\text{of}} = \dfrac{\%}{100}$$
$$\dfrac{20}{50} = \dfrac{x}{100}$$
$$x = \dfrac{(20)(100)}{50} = 40$$

2. What number is 20% of 25?

$\% = 20$, "is" $= x$, "of" $= 25$
$$\dfrac{\text{is}}{\text{of}} = \dfrac{\%}{100}$$
$$\dfrac{x}{25} = \dfrac{20}{100}$$
$$x = \dfrac{(20)(25)}{100} = 5$$

Another common percent item is *change in amount*.

$$\text{Percent Change} = \dfrac{|\text{New Amount} - \text{Original Amount}|}{\text{Original Amount}}$$

The absolute value allows for percent decreases as well.

e.g., An item's price is increased from $3 to $5. What is the percent increase in the price?

$$\dfrac{|\text{New Amount} - \text{Original Amount}|}{\text{Original Amount}} = \dfrac{5-3}{3}$$
$$= \dfrac{2}{3}$$
$$= 66\dfrac{2}{3}\%$$

31. Averages: To calculate an *average* (or mean), add together the quantities to be averaged; then divide that sum by the number of quantities added.

e.g., The average of 3, 7, and 8 is 6: $3 + 7 + 8 = 18$ and $18 \div 3 = 6$.

If solving for a *missing element* of an average, set up the average equation and solve for the unknown.

e.g., The average score on four tests is 90. If three scores are 89, 92, and 94, what is the fourth score?

$$\dfrac{89 + 92 + 94 + x}{4} = 90 \Rightarrow x = 85$$

In *weighted averages*, greater weight is given to one element than to another.

—459—

e.g., Four books cost $6.00 each and two books cost $3.00 each. What is the average cost of a book?

$$\frac{(4)(6)+(2)(3)}{4+2}=\frac{24+6}{6}=\frac{30}{6}=5$$

32. **Median:** The *median* is the middle value of a number set when arranged in ascending or descending order. The median of an even numbered set is the average of the two middle values, when the numbers are arranged in ascending or descending order.

e.g., The median of {8, 6, 34, 5, 17, 23} is: $\frac{8+17}{2}=12.5$.

33. **Mode:** The value that appears most frequently in a set of numbers is the *mode*.

e.g., The mode of {4, 5, 3, 4, 5, 1, 2, 3, 6, 4, 6} is 4.

34. **Counting Principle:** To determine the number of ways that particular events can occur, multiply the number of ways that each event can occur.

e.g., 1. How many ways can you select one boy and one girl from a class of 15 girls and 13 boys?

$(15)(13)=195$ ways

2. In how many ways can 5 students sit in a row with 5 chairs?

$(5)(4)(3)(2)(1)=120$ ways

3. In how many ways can you fill three chairs given five students?

$(5)(4)(3)=60$ ways

35. **Probability Principle:** The probability that an event will happen can be found from the fraction $\frac{\text{winning events}}{\text{total events}}$ or $\frac{\text{favorable events}}{\text{total events}}$.

e.g., From the set {−4, −3, −2, 0, 1, 6, 8, 1002}, a number is selected at random. What is the probability that the selected number is an even integer?

In the set, there are six even integers (-4, -2, 0, 6, 8, and 1002) of a total of eight integers, so the probability is: $\frac{6}{8}=\frac{3}{4}$.

Algebra

1. Basic Operations:

Addition: $n + n = 2n$

  $n + m = n + m$

Subtraction: $3n - 2n = n$

  $n - m = n - m$

Multiplication: $n \cdot m = (n)(m) = nm$

  $(n)(0) = 0$

Division: $n \div m = \dfrac{n}{m}$

  $n \div 0 = \text{undefined}$

2. Powers: A *power* of a number indicates repeated multiplication.

e.g., 3 raised to the fifth power is equal to: $3^5 = (3)(3)(3)(3)(3) = 243$.

3. Exponents: An *exponent* is a number that indicates the operation of repeated multiplication. Exponents are notated as superscripts. The number being multiplied is the *base*.

e.g., 1. $2^3 = (2)(2)(2) = 8$

2. $5^4 = (5)(5)(5)(5) = 625$

Exponent Rules:

a. $x^m \cdot x^n = x^{m+n}$

b. $x^m \div x^n = x^{m-n}$

c. $\left(x^m\right)^n = x^{mn}$

d. $(xy)^m = x^m y^m$

e. $\left(\dfrac{x}{y}\right)^m = \dfrac{x^m}{y^m}$

f. $x^1 = x$, for any number x

g. $x^0 = 1$, for any number x, such that $x \neq 0$

h. 0^0 is undefined.

e.g., 1. $\left(2^3\right)\left(2^2\right) = (2 \cdot 2 \cdot 2)(2 \cdot 2) = 2^{3+2} = 2^5$

2. $\left(3^2\right)\left(3^3\right)\left(3^5\right) = 3^{2+3+5} = 3^{10}$

3. $2^4 \div 2^2 = \dfrac{(2)(2)(2)(2)}{(2)(2)} = 2^{4-2} = 2^2$

4. $\left(2^2\right)^3 = (2 \cdot 2)^3$

  $= (2 \cdot 2)(2 \cdot 2)(2 \cdot 2)$

  $= 2^{(2)(3)}$

  $= 2^6$

5. $(2 \cdot 3)^2 = (2 \cdot 3)(2 \cdot 3)$

  $= (2 \cdot 2)(3 \cdot 3)$

  $= 2^2 \cdot 3^2$

  $= 4 \cdot 9$

  $= 36$

6. $\left(2^3 \cdot 3^2\right)^2 = 2^{3 \cdot 2} \cdot 3^{2 \cdot 2} = 2^6 \cdot 3^4$

7. $\left(\dfrac{2}{3}\right)^2 = \dfrac{2^2}{3^2} = \dfrac{4}{9}$

8. $\left(\dfrac{3^3 \cdot 5^5}{3^2 \cdot 5^2}\right)^2 = \left(3^{3-2} \cdot 5^{5-2}\right)^2$

  $= \left(3^1 \cdot 5^3\right)^2$

  $= \left(3^2\right)\left(5^6\right)$

A negative exponent signifies a fraction, indicating the *reciprocal* of the base.

e.g., 1. $x^{-1} = \dfrac{1}{x}$

2. $2x^{-1} = 2\left(\dfrac{1}{x}\right) = \dfrac{2}{x}$

3. $4^{-2} = \left(\dfrac{1}{4}\right)^2 = \dfrac{1}{16}$

4. Roots: The *root* of a number is a number that is multiplied a specified number of times to give the original number. Square root $= m^{\frac{1}{2}} = \sqrt{m}$. Cube root $= m^{\frac{1}{3}} = \sqrt[3]{m}$.

e.g., 1. $\sqrt{4} = 4^{\frac{1}{2}} = 2$

2. $\sqrt[3]{8} = 8^{\frac{1}{3}} = 2$

3. $\sqrt{125} = 125^{\frac{1}{2}}$

$= (25 \cdot 5)^{\frac{1}{2}}$

$= (25)^{\frac{1}{2}} (5)^{\frac{1}{2}}$

$= \left(\sqrt{25}\right)\left(\sqrt{5}\right)$

$= 5\sqrt{5}$

4. $\sqrt{\frac{4}{9}} = \left(\frac{4}{9}\right)^{\frac{1}{2}} = \frac{4^{\frac{1}{2}}}{9^{\frac{1}{2}}} = \frac{\sqrt{4}}{\sqrt{9}} = \frac{2}{3}$

5. Basic Algebraic Operations: Algebraic operations are the same as for arithmetic, with the addition of unknown quantities. Manipulate operations in the same way, combining (adding and subtracting) only like terms. Like terms have the same variables with the same exponents.

e.g., 1. $x^2 - 3x + 5x - 3x^2 = -2x^2 + 2x$

2. $\left(x^2\right)\left(x^3\right) = x^{2+3} = x^5$

3. $4x^3 y^4 \div 2xy^3 = 2x^2 y$

4. $\frac{5}{x} + \frac{3}{x} = \frac{5+3}{x} = \frac{8}{x}$

5. $\left(\frac{x^2 y^3}{z}\right)\left(\frac{x^3 y^2}{wz}\right) = \frac{x^5 y^5}{wz^2}$

6. Multiplying Polynomials: A *polynomial* is an algebraic expression with more than one term. A binomial is a polynomial consisting of exactly two terms. When multiplying two binomials, use the *FOIL* (First, Outer, Inner, Last) *method*:

$$(x+y)(x+y) = ?$$

Multiply the *first* terms: $x \cdot x = x^2$
Multiply the *outer* terms: $x \cdot y = xy$
Multiply the *inner* terms: $y \cdot x = yx = xy$
Multiply the *last* terms: $y \cdot y = y^2$
Combine like terms: $(x+y)(x+y) = x^2 + 2xy + y^2$

e.g., $(x-y)(x-y) = ?$

First: $(x)(x) = x^2$
Outer: $(x)(-y) = -xy$
Inner: $(-y)(x) = -xy$
Last: $(-y)(-y) = y^2$
Combine: $x^2 - xy - xy + y^2 = x^2 - 2xy + y^2$

If the two polynomials are not binomials, do the following:

e.g., $(x+y)\left(x^2 + 2xy + y^2\right)$

$= x\left(x^2\right) + x(2xy) + x\left(y^2\right) + y\left(x^2\right) + y(2xy) + y\left(y^2\right)$

$= x^3 + 2x^2 y + xy^2 + x^2 y + 2xy^2 + y^3$

$= x^3 + 3x^2 y + 3xy^2 + y^3$

Memorize these common patterns:

$(x+y)^2 = (x+y)(x+y) = x^2 + 2xy + y^2$
$(x-y)^2 = (x-y)(x-y) = x^2 - 2xy + y^2$
$(x+y)(x-y) = x^2 - y^2$

7. Factoring: *Factoring* is the reverse of multiplication. There are three common factoring situations.

a. If all of the terms in an expression contain a common factor, then it can be factored out of each term. Do this first, if possible.

e.g., 1. $ab + ac + ad = a(b + c + d)$

2. $x^2 + x^3 + x^4 = x^2\left(1 + x + x^2\right)$

3. $3xy + xz + 4x = x(3y + z + 4)$

b. Algebraic expressions are often one of three common patterns.

e.g., 1. $x^2 + 2xy + y^2 = (x + y)(x + y)$
$$= (x + y)^2$$

2. $x^2 - 2xy + y^2 = (x - y)(x - y)$
$$= (x - y)^2$$

3. $x^2 - y^2 = (x - y)(x + y)$

c. Occasionally, expressions do not fall into one of the two categories above. To factor the expression, which is usually in the form $ax^2 + bx + c$, set up the following blank diagram: ( )( ). Fill in the diagram by answering the following questions:

- What factors produce the first term, ax^2?
- What factors produce the last term, c?
- Which of the possible factors, when added together, produce the middle term, bx?

e.g., 1. $x^2 + 3x + 2 = (x + 2)(x + 1)$

2. $x^2 + 4x - 12 = (x + 6)(x - 2)$

8. **Solving Linear Equations:** An equation that contains variables only of the first power is a linear equation. You can add, subtract, multiply, and divide both sides of an equation by the same value without changing the statement of equality. (You cannot multiply or divide by zero.) To find the value of a variable, isolate the variable on one side of the equation and solve.

e.g., 1.
$$4x + 2 = 2x + 10$$
$$4x + 2 - 2x = 2x + 10 - 2x$$
$$2x + 2 = 10$$
$$2x + 2 - 2 = 10 - 2$$
$$2x = 8$$
$$\frac{2x}{2} = \frac{8}{2}$$
$$x = 4$$

2.
$$\frac{2x + 6}{2} = 9$$
$$\left(\frac{2x + 6}{2}\right)(2) = 9(2)$$
$$2x + 6 = 18$$
$$2x + 6 - 6 = 18 - 6$$
$$2x = 12$$
$$\frac{2x}{2} = \frac{12}{2}$$
$$x = 6$$

9. **Solving Quadratic Equations:** Equations that involve variables of the second power are called quadratic equations and may have zero, one, or two real solutions.

a. If possible, take the square root of both sides.

e.g., $x^2 = 25$
$$x = \pm 5$$

b. Otherwise, arrange all terms on the left side of equation so that the right side of equation is zero: $ax^2 + bx + c = 0$. Factor the left side of the equation and set each binomial equal to zero. Solve for the unknown.

e.g., 1. If $x^2 - 2x = 3$, what is x?

$$x^2 - 2x - 3 = 0$$
$$(x - 3)(x + 1) = 0$$
$$x = \{-1, 3\}$$

2. If $x^2 - 3x = 4$, what is x?

$$x^2 - 3x - 4 = 0$$
$$(x - 4)(x + 1) = 0$$
$$x = \{-1, 4\}$$

c. The quadratic formula, $x = \dfrac{-b \pm \sqrt{b^2 - 4ac}}{2a}$, may also be used to solve quadratic equations.

e.g., If $3 - x = 2x^2$, what is x?

$$2x^2 + x - 3 = 0; \ a = 2; \ b = 1; \ c = -3$$

$$x = \frac{-b \pm \sqrt{b^2 - 4ac}}{2a}$$

$$= \frac{-1 \pm \sqrt{1^2 - 4(2)(-3)}}{2(2)}$$

$$= \frac{-1 \pm \sqrt{1 + 24}}{4}$$

$$= \frac{-1 \pm 5}{4}$$

$$= \left\{ -\frac{3}{2}, 1 \right\}$$

10. **Solving Simultaneous Equations:** Given two equations with two variables, the equations may be solved simultaneously for the values of the two variables. There are several methods for solving simultaneous equations.

Method 1—Substitution: Solve one equation for one variable and substitute this into the other equation to find the other variable. Plug back into the first equation.

e.g., If $2x - y = 6$ and $3x + 2y = 16$, what is x and y?

Solve for y: $\quad 2x - y = 6$
$$-y = 6 - 2x \Rightarrow y = 2x - 6$$

$$3x + 2y = 16$$
Substitute: $\quad 3x + 2(2x - 6) = 16$
$$3x + 4x - 12 = 16$$
$$7x = 28$$
$$x = 4$$

Substitute: $\quad y = 2x - 6 = 2(4) - 6 = 2$

Method 2—Elimination: Make the coefficients of one variable equal and then add (or subtract) the two equations to eliminate one variable.

e.g., If $2x - y = 6$ and $3x + 2y = 16$, what is x and y?

Combine: $\quad 2[2x - y = 6]$
$$\underline{+ \ 3x + 2y = 16}$$
$$7x = 28$$
$$x = 4$$

$$2x - y = 6$$
Substitute: $\quad 2(4) - y = 6$
$$y = 2$$

11. **Inequalities:** The fundamental rule for working with inequalities is similar to that for working with equalities. The same value may be added or subtracted to each side of an inequality without changing the inequality. Each side may be multiplied or divided by the same *positive* value without changing the direction of the inequality.

e.g., 1. $5 > 2$
$$5 + 25 > 2 + 25$$
$$30 > 27$$

2. $24 > 20$
$$24(2) > 20(2)$$
$$48 > 40$$

3. $24 > 20$
$$24 \div 4 > 20 \div 4$$
$$6 > 5$$

To multiply or divide by a *negative* number, reverse the direction of the inequality.

e.g., 1. $4 > 2$
$$4(-2) < 2(-2)$$
$$-8 < -4$$

2. $4 > 2$
$$4 \div (-2) < 2 \div (-2)$$
$$-2 < -1$$

12. **Slope:** The *slope*, m, of a line describes its steepness. It is defined as the change in y-values divided by the change in x-values, or rise over run.

$$m = \frac{\Delta y}{\Delta x} = \frac{y_2 - y_1}{x_2 - x_1} = \frac{\text{rise}}{\text{run}}$$

e.g., The slope of the line containing points $(-3, 5)$ and $(2, 7)$ is equal to: $m = \dfrac{y_2 - y_1}{x_2 - x_1} =$

$$\dfrac{7 - 5}{2 - (-3)} = \dfrac{2}{5}.$$

13. Linear Equations:

Slope-Intercept Form: $y = mx + b$;

Slope: $m = \dfrac{\Delta y}{\Delta x} = \dfrac{y_2 - y_1}{x_2 - x_1}$

Point-Slope Form: $y - y_1 = m(x - x_1)$

Standard Form: $ax + by = c$, $m = -\dfrac{a}{b}$

14. Distance Formula:
The distance between two points can be found using the *distance formula*:

$$d = \sqrt{(x_2 - x_1)^2 + (y_2 - y_1)^2}$$

where (x_1, y_1) and (x_2, y_2) are the given points.

e.g., What is the distance between points $(-1, 4)$ and $(7, 3)$?

$$d = \sqrt{[7 - (-1)]^2 + (3 - 4)^2} = \sqrt{64 + 1} = \sqrt{65}$$

15. Midpoint Formula:
The midpoint between two points, (x_1, y_1) and (x_2, y_2), is found using the *midpoint formula*:

$$\text{midpoint} = \left(\dfrac{x_1 + x_2}{2}, \dfrac{y_1 + y_2}{2} \right)$$

e.g., The midpoint between points $(-3, 6)$ and $(4, -9)$ is equal to: $\left(\dfrac{x_1 + x_2}{2}, \dfrac{y_1 + y_2}{2} \right) =$

$$\left(\dfrac{-3 + 4}{2}, \dfrac{6 + (-9)}{2} \right) = \left(\dfrac{1}{2}, -\dfrac{3}{2} \right).$$

16. Functions:
A function is a set of ordered pairs (x, y) such that for each value of x, there is exactly one value of y. The set of x-values for which the set is defined is called the domain of the function. The set of corresponding values of y is called the range of the function.

e.g., What is the domain and range for the function $f(x) = x^2$?

f represents the function and x represents values in the domain of the function. $f(x)$ represents values in the range of the function. Since x can be any real number, the domain is the set of all real numbers. We square the value of x to obtain $f(x)$. Squaring any real number yields a number of zero or more. Thus, the range is the set of all non-negative numbers.

Common Equations

1. **Distance:** Distance = (Rate)(Time). Given two of the three values, any unknown may be solved for by rearranging the equation.

   e.g., After driving constantly for four hours, Olivia reached her destination: 200 miles from where she started. What was her average rate of travel?

   $$\text{Distance} = (\text{Rate})(\text{Time})$$
   $$\text{Rate} = \frac{\text{Distance}}{\text{Time}} = \frac{200 \text{ miles}}{4 \text{ hours}} = 50 \text{ mph}$$

2. **Simple Interest:** $I_{simple} = Prt$, where P is the principal, r is the rate, and t is the time period.

   e.g., With a principal of $1,200 and a rate of 10 percent per year, what was the interest earned over one month?

   $$I_{simple} = Prt$$
   $$= (\$1,200)\left(\frac{0.10}{\text{year}}\right)\left(\frac{1 \text{ year}}{12 \text{ months}}\right) = \$10$$

3. **Compound Interest:** $I_{compound} = P\left(1+\dfrac{r}{C}\right)^{tC} - P$, where P is the principal, r is the rate, and t is the time period, and C is the number of times the interest is compounded annually.

   e.g., A principal of $1,000, compounded with interest of 15% per year, earns how much compound interest over 5 years?

   $$I_{compound} = P\left(1+\frac{r}{C}\right)^{tC} - P$$
   $$= \$1,000\left(1+\frac{0.15}{1}\right)^{5 \cdot 1} - \$1,000$$
   $$\approx \$2,011 - \$1,000 = \$1,011$$

4. **Combined Work Rates:** $Rate_1 + Rate_2 = Rate_3$

   e.g., Machine A washes four loads in 60 minutes and Machine B washes one load in 30 minutes. How many loads will both machines together wash in 20 minutes?

   $$\frac{x \text{ loads}}{20 \text{ min.}} = \frac{4 \text{ loads}}{60 \text{ min.}} + \frac{1 \text{ load}}{30 \text{ min.}}$$
   $$= \frac{4 \text{ loads}}{60 \text{ min.}} + \frac{2 \text{ loads}}{60 \text{ min.}}$$
   $$x = 20\left(\frac{4}{60} + \frac{2}{60}\right)$$
   $$= \frac{6(20)}{60}$$
   $$= 2 \text{ loads}$$

5. **Mixed Denominations:** When an item gives information that involves *mixed denominations* (e.g., different prices for same item, tickets, colors, etc.), set up simultaneous equations and solve the system of equations for the desired unknown quantity.

   e.g., The store sold apples for $0.20 and oranges for $0.50 each. A total of 50 apples and oranges were bought for $19. How many apples and how many oranges were bought?

   If x equals the number of apples and y the number of oranges, $x = 50 - y$. Therefore:

   $$(0.20)x + (0.50)y = 19$$
   $$0.2(50 - y) + 0.5y = 19$$
   $$10 - 0.2y + 0.5y = 19$$
   $$0.3y = 9$$
   $$y = 30$$
   $$x = 50 - y$$
   $$= 50 - 30$$
   $$= 20$$

6. **Mixture of Concentrations or Values:** A *mixture item* is one in which two quantities of different items with different concentrations or values are mixed together and a new quantity (the sum of the two) and concentration or value are created.

   $$Q_1C_1 + Q_2C_2 = (Q_1 + Q_2)C_3$$

e.g., How many liters of a juice that is 10% orange juice must be added to three liters of another juice that is 15% orange juice to produce a mixture that is 12% orange juice?

$$Q_1 C_1 + Q_2 C_2 = (Q_1 + Q_2) C_3$$
$$Q(0.10) + (3)(0.15) = (Q + 3)(0.12)$$
$$0.1Q + 0.45 = 0.12Q + 0.36$$
$$0.45 - 0.36 = 0.12Q - 0.1Q$$
$$0.09 = 0.02Q$$
$$Q = 4.5$$

7. **Markup, Cost, and Revenue:** $R = (1 + M)C$, where R is revenue, M is markup, and C is cost.

e.g., The revenue from an item marked up 25% is $120. What was the original cost?

$$C = \frac{R}{1 + M} = \frac{120}{1 + 0.25} = \$96$$

Geometry

1. Lines and Angles:

a. Symbols:

$\overline{AB}$: line segment with endpoints A and B

$\overrightarrow{AB}$: infinite ray from A through B

$\overleftrightarrow{AB}$: infinite line through both A and B

$l_1 \| l_2$: parallel lines

$\perp$: perpendicular

▛: right angle

b. Facts About Lines and Angles:

Vertical angles are equal:

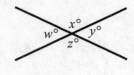

$$w = y; \ x = z$$

Two extended lines that do not intersect regardless of length are *parallel* to each other:

Parallel lines intersected by a third line, the transversal, create the following angles:

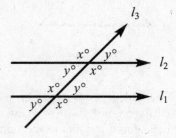

$$x = x, \ y = y, \ x + y = 180$$

Two lines *perpendicular* to the same line are parallel to each other:

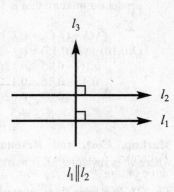

$$l_1 \| l_2$$

There are 180° in a *straight line*:

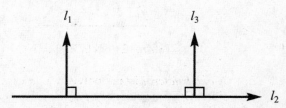

$$x + y = 180°$$

There are 90° in a *right angle* and two right angles form a straight line:

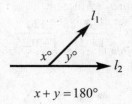

An angle less than 90° is an *acute angle*. In the following figure, $\angle PQR$ is an acute angle:

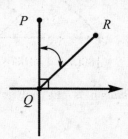

An angle greater than 90° is an *obtuse angle*. In the following figure, ∠PQR is an obtuse angle:

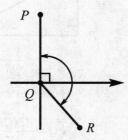

2. **Polygons:** A *polygon* is a closed figure created by three or more lines. The sum of the interior angles of any polygon is $180(n-2)$, where $n=$ the number of sides of the polygon. The sum of the measures of the exterior angles of a polygon is 360° for all polygons.

A *triangle* is any polygon with exactly three sides.

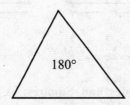

$$180(n-2) = 180(3-2) = 180$$

A *quadrilateral* is any polygon with exactly four sides. Opposite sides of a *parallelogram* are equal and parallel.

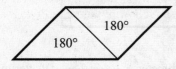

$$180(n-2) = 180(4-2) = 360$$

A *pentagon* is any polygon with exactly five sides.

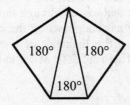

$$180(n-2) = 180(5-2) = 540$$

A *hexagon* is any polygon with exactly six sides.

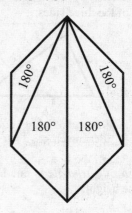

$$180(n-2) = 180(6-2) = 720$$

3. **Triangles:** A *triangle* is a 3-sided figure. Within a given triangle, the larger the angle, the longer the opposite side; conversely, the longer the side, the larger the opposite angle.

A triangle with two equal sides is an *isosceles* triangle. A triangle with three equal sides is an *equilateral* triangle.

Within a given triangle, if two sides are equal, their opposite angles are equal, and vice versa:

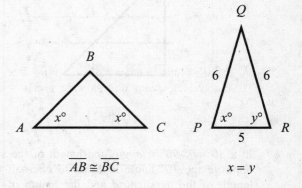

$$\overline{AB} \cong \overline{BC} \qquad\qquad x = y$$

The sides of every right triangle follow the *Pythagorean theorem*: the square of the hypotenuse is equal to the sum of the squares of the other two sides.

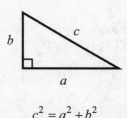

$$c^2 = a^2 + b^2$$

The *perimeter of a triangle* is the sum of the lengths of the three sides:

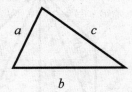

$$\text{Perimeter}_{\text{triangle}} = a + b + c$$

The *area of a triangle* is one-half times the base times the height:

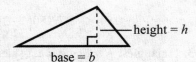

$$\text{Area}_{\text{triangle}} = \frac{1}{2}(bh) = \frac{bh}{2}$$

In a *45°-45°-90° triangle*, the length of the hypotenuse is equal to the length of either leg multiplied by the square root of two:

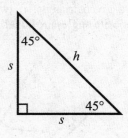

$$h = (s)\left(\sqrt{2}\right)$$

In a *30°-60°-90° triangle*, the length of the side opposite the 30° angle is equal to one-half the length of the hypotenuse and the length of the side opposite the 60° angle is equal to one-half the length of the hypotenuse multiplied by $\sqrt{3}$:

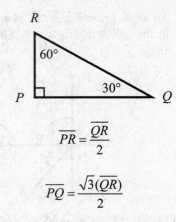

$$\overline{PR} = \frac{\overline{QR}}{2}$$

$$\overline{PQ} = \frac{\sqrt{3}(\overline{QR})}{2}$$

4. **Parallelograms and Trapezoids:** Again, a *parallelogram* is a quadrilateral in which both pairs of opposite sides are parallel. A *trapezoid* is a quadrilateral with only two parallel sides.

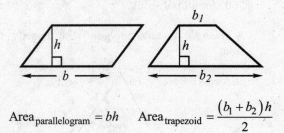

$$\text{Area}_{\text{parallelogram}} = bh \qquad \text{Area}_{\text{trapezoid}} = \frac{(b_1 + b_2)h}{2}$$

5. **Rectangles and Squares:** A *rectangle* is any four-sided figure that has four right angles. A *square* is a rectangle with four equal sides:

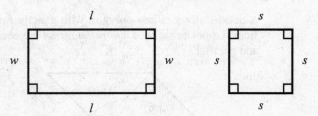

$$\text{Perimeter}_{\text{rectangle}} = 2(w + l) \qquad \text{Perimeter}_{\text{square}} = 4s$$

$$\text{Area}_{\text{rectangle}} = lw \qquad \text{Area}_{\text{square}} = s^2$$

6. **Circles:** The distance from the center of a circle to any point on the circle is the *radius*. A line segment that passes through the center of a circle and that has endpoints on the circle is called the *diameter*. The diameter of a circle is twice the radius. There are 360° of *arc* in a circle:

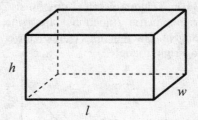

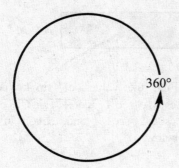

An angle inscribed in a circle intercepts an arc that is twice its measure:

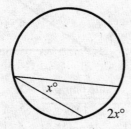

An angle whose vertex is at the center of a circle intercepts an arc of the same measure:

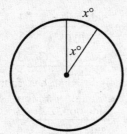

The *circumference of a circle* is the radius times 2π. The *area of a circle* is the radius squared times π.

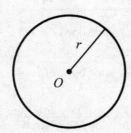

$$\text{Circumference}_{\text{circle}} = 2\pi r$$

$$\text{Area}_{\text{circle}} = \pi r^2$$

7. **Solid Geometry:** Solid geometry refers to three-dimensional figures. *Volume* is a three-dimensional quantity. The *volume of a rectangular solid* is the length times the width times the height:

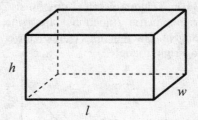

$$\text{Volume}_{\text{solid}} = lwh$$

The *volume of a cylinder* is the height times the radius squared times π.

$$\text{Volume}_{\text{cylinder}} = h(\pi r^2)$$

The *volume of a right circular cone* is one-third of the height times the radius squared times π.

$$\text{Volume}_{\text{right circular cone}} = \frac{h\left(\pi r^2\right)}{3}$$

The *surface area of a sphere* is four times π times the radius squared. The *volume of a sphere* is four-thirds times π times the radius cubed.

$$\text{Area}_{\text{surface of sphere}} = 4\pi r^2$$

$$\text{Volume}_{\text{sphere}} = \frac{4\pi r^3}{3}$$

Trigonometry

1. **Basic Trigonometric Functions:** The three basic trigonometric functions are sine, cosine, and tangent. The functions can be viewed in relationship to a right triangle.

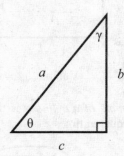

The *hypotenuse* is the side opposite the right angle. The *side opposite* is the side opposite the referenced angle. The *side adjacent* is the side next to the referenced angle, but not the hypotenuse.

Memorize these trigonometric definitions:

sine: $\sin\theta = \dfrac{\text{side opposite } \angle\theta}{\text{hypotenuse}} = \dfrac{b}{a}$

cosine: $\cos\theta = \dfrac{\text{side adjacent } \angle\theta}{\text{hypotenuse}} = \dfrac{c}{a}$

tangent: $\tan\theta = \dfrac{\sin\theta}{\cos\theta} = \dfrac{\text{side opposite } \angle\theta}{\text{side adjacent } \angle\theta} = \dfrac{b}{c}$

cosecant: $\csc\theta = \dfrac{1}{\sin\theta} = \dfrac{\text{hypotenuse}}{\text{side opposite } \angle\theta} = \dfrac{a}{b}$

secant: $\sec\theta = \dfrac{1}{\cos\theta} = \dfrac{\text{hypotenuse}}{\text{side adjacent } \angle\theta} = \dfrac{a}{c}$

cotangent: $\cot\theta = \dfrac{1}{\tan\theta} = \dfrac{\text{side adjacent } \angle\theta}{\text{side opposite } \angle\theta} = \dfrac{c}{b}$

SOH-CAH-TOA can be used to memorize the sine, cosine, and tangent ratios.

e.g., Find the values of $\sin A$, $\cos A$, $\tan A$, $\csc A$, $\sec A$, $\cot A$, $\sin C$, $\cos C$, $\tan C$, $\csc C$, $\sec C$, and $\cot C$ in the triangle below.

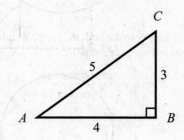

$\sin A = \dfrac{\text{side opp. } \angle A}{\text{hyp.}} = \dfrac{3}{5}$

$\sin C = \dfrac{\text{side opp. } \angle A}{\text{hyp.}} = \dfrac{4}{5}$

$\cos A = \dfrac{\text{side adj. } \angle A}{\text{hyp.}} = \dfrac{4}{5}$

$\cos C = \dfrac{\text{side adj. } \angle C}{\text{hyp.}} = \dfrac{3}{5}$

$\tan A = \dfrac{\text{side opp. } \angle A}{\text{side adj. } \angle A} = \dfrac{3}{4}$

$\tan C = \dfrac{\text{side opp. } \angle C}{\text{side adj. } \angle C} = \dfrac{4}{3}$

$\csc A = \dfrac{\text{hyp.}}{\text{side opp. } \angle A} = \dfrac{5}{3}$

$\csc C = \dfrac{\text{hyp.}}{\text{side opp. } \angle C} = \dfrac{5}{4}$

$\sec A = \dfrac{\text{hyp.}}{\text{side adj. } \angle A} = \dfrac{5}{4}$

$\sec C = \dfrac{\text{hyp.}}{\text{side adj. } \angle C} = \dfrac{5}{4}$

$\cot A = \dfrac{\text{side adj. } \angle A}{\text{side opp. } \angle A} = \dfrac{4}{3}$

$\cot C = \dfrac{\text{side adj. } \angle C}{\text{side opp. } \angle C} = \dfrac{4}{3}$

e.g., In the right triangle below, $\sin x = 0.75$. What is the length of $\overline{AC}$?

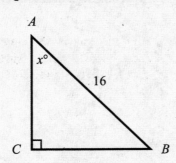

$$\sin x = \frac{\text{side opposite } \angle x}{\text{hypotenuse}}$$

$$\frac{3}{4} = \frac{\overline{BC}}{16}$$

$$\overline{BC} = \frac{3(16)}{4}$$

$$= 12$$

Therefore, using the Pythagorean theorem:

$$\left(\overline{AB}\right)^2 = \left(\overline{AC}\right)^2 + \left(\overline{BC}\right)^2$$

$$16^2 = \left(\overline{AC}\right)^2 + 12^2$$

$$\left(\overline{AC}\right)^2 = 256 - 144$$

$$= 112$$

$$\overline{AC} = \sqrt{112}$$

$$= \sqrt{16(7)}$$

$$= 4\sqrt{7}$$

2. Useful Trigonometric Relationships:

$$\sin x = \frac{1}{\csc x}$$

$$\cos x = \frac{1}{\sec x}$$

$$\tan x = \frac{\sin x}{\cos x} = \frac{1}{\cot x}$$

$$\sin^2 x + \cos^2 x = 1$$

$$1 + \cot^2 x = \csc^2 x$$

$$\tan^2 x + 1 = \sec^2 x$$

Note: $\sin^2 x$ is the equivalent of $\left(\sin x\right)^2$.

e.g., If $\sin x = \frac{3}{5}$ and $\cos x = \frac{4}{5}$, what is the value of $\tan x$, $\csc x$, $\sec x$, and $\cot x$?

$$\tan x = \frac{\sin x}{\cos x} = \frac{\frac{3}{5}}{\frac{4}{5}} = \frac{3}{4}$$

$$\csc x = \frac{1}{\sin x} = \frac{1}{\frac{3}{5}} = \frac{5}{3}$$

$$\sec x = \frac{1}{\cos x} = \frac{1}{\frac{4}{5}} = \frac{5}{4}$$

$$\cot x = \frac{1}{\tan x} = \frac{1}{\frac{3}{4}} = \frac{4}{3}$$

e.g., If $\sin^2 x = \frac{1}{4}$, what is the value of $\cos^2 x$?

$$\cos^2 x = 1 - \sin^2 x = 1 - \frac{1}{4} = \frac{3}{4}$$

3. Graphing Using Trigonometry: Frequently, trigonometry is used in graphing. Angles on a graph are customarily measured in a counterclockwise manner from the positive x-axis.

e.g., 1. In the figure below, the angle shown has a measure of 210°: $90° + 90° + 30° = 210°$.

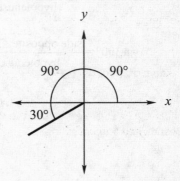

2. Without using a calculator, determine the values of $\cos 300°$ and $\sin 300°$.

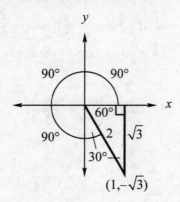

Notice that after drawing the angle, we create a right triangle by drawing a perpendicular from the end of the angle to the x-axis. The hypotenuse of any such triangle is always considered to be positive. However, the point at the end of the original angle may not always have positive coordinates. You may make up any length desired for one side of the triangle. Then, use geometry or trigonometry with the angles inside the triangle to get the remaining lengths. In this example, we let the hypotenuse equal 2 and used geometry or trigonometry to get 1 and $\sqrt{3}$ as shown on the figure. Notice that the point at the end of our original 300° angle has a positive x-coordinate, 1, and a negative y-coordinate, $-\sqrt{3}$. We must use those signed values. The 300° angle leaves us 60° from the closer x-axis. Thus, $\cos 300°$ uses the 60° angle:

$$\cos 300° = \frac{\text{side adjacent } \angle 300°}{\text{hypotenuse}} = \frac{1}{2}$$

$$\sin 300° = \frac{\text{side opposite} \angle 300°}{\text{hypotenuse}} = -\frac{\sqrt{3}}{2}$$

Formula Summary

ARITHMETIC, ALGEBRA, AND COORDINATE GEOMETRY

$$\text{Average} = \frac{x_1 + x_2 + x_3 + \ldots + x_n}{n} \,;\; x_1,\, x_2,\, x_3,\, \ldots,\, x_n = \text{values}\,;\; n = \text{total numbers}$$

$$\text{Finding Percent:} \;\; \frac{\text{is}}{\text{of}} = \frac{\%}{100}$$

$$\text{Percent Change} = \frac{\left| \text{New Amount} - \text{Original Amount} \right|}{\text{Original Amount}}$$

$$\text{Distance} = \text{Rate} \cdot \text{Time}$$

$$\text{Combined Work Rate:} \;\; \text{Rate}_3 = \text{Rate}_1 + \text{Rate}_2$$

$$\text{Mixture Problems:} \;\; (Q_1 + Q_2)C_3 = Q_1 C_1 + Q_2 C_2; \; Q = \text{quantities}; \; C = \text{concentrations}$$

$$\text{Interest}_{\text{simple}} = \text{Principal} \cdot \text{Rate} \cdot \text{Time}$$

$$\text{Interest}_{\text{compound}} = (\text{Principal})\left(1 + \frac{\text{Rate}}{\text{\# of Times Compounded Annually}}\right)^{(\text{Time Period})(\text{\# of Times Compounded Annually})} - \text{Principal}$$

$$\text{Revenue} = (1 + \text{Markup})(\text{Cost})$$

$$\text{Slope-Intercept Linear Equation:} \;\; y = mx + b$$

$$\text{Slope of a Line:} \;\; m = \frac{y_2 - y_1}{x_2 - x_1}$$

GEOMETRY

$$\text{Perimeter}_{\text{square}} = 4s \text{; } s = \text{side}$$

$$\text{Perimeter}_{\text{rectangle}} = 2l + 2w \text{; } l = \text{length} \text{; } w = \text{width}$$

$$\text{Perimeter}_{\text{triangle}} = a + b + c \text{; } a, b, \text{ and } c \text{ are the sides}$$

$$\text{Circumference}_{\text{circle}} = 2\pi r \text{; } \pi \approx 3.14 \text{; } r = \text{radius}$$

$$\text{Area}_{\text{square}} = s^2 \text{; } s = \text{length of side}$$

$$\text{Area}_{\text{rectangle}} = lw \text{; } l = \text{length} \text{; } w = \text{width}$$

$$\text{Area}_{\text{parallelogram}} = bh \text{; } b = \text{base} \text{; } h = \text{height}$$

$$\text{Area}_{\text{trapezoid}} = \frac{(b_1 + b_2)h}{2} \text{; } b = \text{base} \text{; } h = \text{height}$$

$$\text{Area}_{\text{triangle}} = \frac{bh}{2} \text{; } b = \text{base} \text{; } h = \text{height}$$

$$\text{Area}_{\text{circle}} = \pi r^2 \text{; } \pi \approx 3.14 \text{; } r = \text{radius}$$

SOLID GEOMETRY

$$\text{Volume}_{\text{cube}} = s^3 \text{; } s = \text{side}$$

$$\text{Volume}_{\text{rectangular solid}} = lwh \text{; } l = \text{length} \text{; } w = \text{width} \text{; } h = \text{height}$$

$$\text{Volume}_{\text{cylinder}} = \pi r^2 h \text{; } \pi \approx 3.14 \text{; } r = \text{radius} \text{; } h = \text{height}$$

$$\text{Volume}_{\text{cone}} = \frac{\pi r^2 h}{3} \text{; } \pi \approx 3.14 \text{; } r = \text{radius} \text{; } h = \text{height}$$

$$\text{Area}_{\text{surface of sphere}} = 4\pi r^2 \text{; } \pi \approx 3.14 \text{; } r = \text{radius}$$

$$\text{Volume}_{\text{sphere}} = \frac{4\pi r^3}{3} \text{; } \pi \approx 3.14 \text{; } r = \text{radius}$$

POLYGONS

45°-45°-90° Triangle: $h = s\sqrt{2}$; h = hypotenuse; s = length of either leg

30°-60°-90° Triangle: $a = \dfrac{h}{2}$; a = side opposite $\angle 30°$; h = hypotenuse

30°-60°-90° Triangle: $b = \dfrac{\sqrt{3}(h)}{2}$; b = side opposite $\angle 60°$; h = hypotenuse

Pythagorean Theorem (Right Triangles): $c^2 = a^2 + b^2$; c = hypotenuse; a and b = legs

Sum of Interior Angles of Polygon: $S = 180(n-2)$; n = number of sides of the polygon

---

TRIGONOMETRY

$$\sin\theta = \frac{\text{side opposite } \angle\theta}{\text{hypotenuse}}$$

$$\cos\theta = \frac{\text{side adjacent } \angle\theta}{\text{hypotenuse}}$$

$$\tan\theta = \frac{\sin\theta}{\cos\theta} = \frac{\text{side opposite } \angle\theta}{\text{side adjacent } \angle\theta}$$

$$\csc\theta = \frac{1}{\sin\theta} = \frac{\text{hypotenuse}}{\text{side opposite } \angle\theta}$$

$$\sec\theta = \frac{1}{\cos\theta} = \frac{\text{hypotenuse}}{\text{side adjacent } \angle\theta}$$

$$\cot\theta = \frac{1}{\tan\theta} = \frac{\text{side adjacent } \angle\theta}{\text{side opposite } \angle\theta}$$

$$\sin^2\theta + \cos^2\theta = 1$$

$$1 + \cot^2\theta = \csc^2\theta$$

$$\tan^2\theta + 1 = \sec^2\theta$$

Glossary of Terms

Absolute Value—the value of a number when the sign is not considered; the distance on the number line between the number and 0

Acute Angle—an angle with a measure of less than 90°

Adjacent Angles—angles that share a common side and a common vertex

Area—the space within a closed plane figure, measured in square units

Binomial—an algebraic expression with two terms

Circle—the set of all points in a plane that are equidistant from a center point

Circumference—the distance around a circle

Coefficient—the number in front of a term

Complementary Angles—two angles with a sum of 90°

Composite Numbers—a number that can be divided evenly by more than itself and one

Cube (1)—a six-sided solid with all six faces being equal-sized squares

Cube (2)—the result when a number is multiplied by itself twice

Cube Root—a number that when raised to the third power will yield a second given number

Denominator—the bottom term of a fraction

Diameter—a line segment extending from one side of a circle to the opposite, through the center point

Difference—the result of subtraction

Domain—the set of all x-values for a function

Equilateral Triangle—a triangle with all three sides equal and all three angles being 60°

Evaluate—to determine the value of an expression

Exponent—used to indicate the operation of repeated multiplication

Factor—an integer that divides into another integer equally

Function—ordered pairs (x, y) with exactly one y-value for any x-value

Hypotenuse—the side opposite the right angle of a right triangle

Improper Fraction—a fraction where the numerator is larger than the denominator

Integers—the set of numbers divisible by one without producing a remainder

Irrational Numbers—any number that cannot be expressed as a fraction

Isosceles Triangle—a triangle with two equal sides and equal opposite angles

Least Common Denominator—the smallest natural number that can be divided evenly by all denominators in the equation

Legs—in a right triangle, the two sides that are not the hypotenuse

Mean—the sum of all items divided by the number of items

Median—in a set of numbers arranged in order, the middle value or the mean of the two middle values

Mixed Number—a term that has both a whole number part and a fractional part

Mode—the most commonly occurring value in a set of values

Monomial—an algebraic expression with only one term

Natural Numbers—the set of positive integers starting with 1

Numerator—the top term of a fraction

Obtuse Angle—an angle with a measure between 90° and 180°

Origin—the intersection between the x- and y-axes of a coordinate graph

Parallel Lines—lines that never intersect regardless of how far they are extended

Parallelogram—a four-sided closed figure with opposite sides that are parallel and of equal length

Percentage—a fraction with a denominator of 100

Perimeter—the total distance around the outside of a polygon

Perpendicular Lines—two lines that intersect at a 90° angle

Polygon—a multi-sided closed plane figure

Polynomial—an algebraic expression with two or more terms

Power—used to indicate repeated multiplication

Prime Numbers—numbers that are evenly divisible only by themselves and one

Product—the result of multiplication

Proper Fraction—a fraction where the denominator is larger than the numerator

Quadrants—the four sections of a coordinate graph

Quadrilateral—a four-sided closed plane figure

Quotient—the result of division

Radius—a line segment extending from the center of a circle to any point on the circle

Range (1)—the difference between the largest and smallest numbers in a set

Range (2)—the set of all *y*-values for a function

Rational Number—any number that can be expressed as a fraction

Real Numbers—the set of rational and irrational numbers

Rectangle—a four-sided plane closed figure with opposite sides equal and 90° angles

Right Triangle—a triangle with a 90° angle

Root—a number that when raised to a certain power will yield a second given number

Scientific Notation—a number written as the product of a real number between 1 and 10 and a power of 10

Set—a group of numbers, elements, objects, etc.

Square (1)—the result when a number is multiplied by itself

Square (2)—a four-sided plane closed figure with all four sides equal and 90° angles

Square Root—a number that when raised to the second power will yield a second given number

Sum—the result of addition

Supplementary Angles—two angles with a sum of 180°

Term—an expression, either numerical or literal

Triangle—a three-sided closed plane figure

Variable—a symbol that is used to stand for a number

Vertex—a point at which two rays or sides of a polygon meet to form an angle

Volume—the space inside a solid, measured in cubic units

Whole Numbers—the set of positive integers including zero

X-axis—the horizontal axis of a coordinate graph

Y-axis—the vertical axis of a coordinate graph

Reading Skills Review

**COURSE
CONCEPT
OUTLINE**

What You Absolutely Must Know

Honing Your Reading Skills

When you move from reading materials that entertain to reading literature that requires higher levels of critical reading ability and that tests your ability to comprehend complex arguments, you must develop an aptitude for reading carefully and deliberately.

To read a densely written passage carefully for comprehension, there are five major reading elements you should consider when examining the written materials.

Understand the Five Elements of Reading Passages

Content

The content of a passage is made up of the information, data, images, and descriptions found in the text. The author uses words, phrases, and sentences to build the basic facts, figures, illustrations, and examples of a passage. He or she writes to communicate the basic "who," "what," "where," and "when" of the literary piece.

As a reader, you discover the content by asking, "What is the author attempting to tell, show, or explain to me?"

Case

The case (think of a legal case) of the author establishes the reasoning, arguments, or explanations for the content's purpose. The author is attempting to demonstrate that the main point of the content is meaningful, logical, emotionally moving, or important. Even in fictional works, narratives, or poetic literature, authors regularly point directly or indirectly to some reason or explanation for their views.

You discover the case in the passage by asking, "What evidence, arguments, explanations, or reasons does the author use to prove his or her point?"

Cause

The cause (or the "because") is the point of view or perspective from which the author writes. An author may or may not directly tell you his or her point of view. As a critical reader, you may need to "read between the lines" to discover some experience, perspective, background, personal view, opinion, or set of ideas that influence an author to write about specific content or argue in a certain manner.

You discover the cause by asking, "Why is this author exploring this specific content, arguing in this particular style, or writing in this particular manner?"

Context

The context refers to the time and place from which the author writes. All authors write from particular surroundings that influence their understanding of culture, science, history, social structures, etc. For example, an author writing in Spain during the sixteenth century would have a significantly different context than an author writing in New York City during the twenty-first century.

You discover the context by asking, "From when and where did the author write this passage, and how might it influence his or her point of view?"

Character

The character of the passage is the general mood or feeling that an author attempts to communicate. An author may write logically, emotionally, passionately, humorously, whimsically, sarcastically, or in a variety of other styles that project a particular mood.

You discover the character of a passage by asking, "How does the author use his or her style (words, phrases, sentence structure, paragraph patterns, images, illustrations, etc.) to communicate the general mood or feeling of the passage?"

The following strategies will assist you in reading all the previously described reading passage elements. The chart below illustrates how the reading elements correspond to the reading strategies.

Reading Element	Question to Ask	Reading Strategy
Content	"What is the author attempting to tell, show, or explain to me?"	• Clearly identify the main idea. • Determine the outline employed to develop the passage. • Locate the important specific details.
Case	"What evidence, arguments, explanations, or reasons does the author use to prove his or her point?"	• Analyze the arguments or persuasive devices.
Cause	"Why is this author exploring this specific content, arguing in this particular style, or writing in this particular manner?"	• Consider the author's point of view.
Context	"From when and where did the author write this passage and how might it influence his or her point of view?"	• Consider the author's point of view.
Character	"How does the author use his or her style (words, phrases, sentence structure, paragraph patterns, images, illustrations, etc.) to communicate the general mood or feeling of the passage?"	• Probe the mood of the passage.

Use the Six Strategies for Reading Carefully and Comprehensively

In the following section, you will learn the six basic strategies of reading passages more seriously, carefully, and comprehensively.

1. Clearly identify the main idea of the written material.
2. Determine the outline employed to develop the passage.
3. Locate the important specific details.
4. Analyze the arguments or persuasive devices.
5. Consider the author's point of view.
6. Probe the mood of the passage.

Identify the Main Idea (Main Theme) of the Passage

In presenting content, an author typically begins writing with a main idea in mind. This may also be called the main theme or the thesis of the passage. All other ideas, examples, facts, or illustrations in the passage are meant to support the main idea.

You discover the main theme by asking the following type of questions:

- What is the primary purpose of this paragraph or passage?

- What is the principle idea or central concept within this particular passage?

- What one statement or sentence best summarizes this reading material?

- What major idea or theme is the author attempting to communicate?

As you read, be careful not to confuse the arguments, examples, or the specific details with the main theme of the passage. The arguments, examples, and details are presented in a passage to support the main theme.

Example:

Though I love planet Earth with her snow-capped mountains, sand blown deserts, and deep blue oceans, as a scientist and a philosopher, I believe that humanity cannot live here forever. Colonization of
5   other planets, like the red planet Mars, will be necessary. With human population growing so quickly, there will simply not be enough room for all of us on earth by 2050. By that year, food and water will become extremely scarce for all but the most
10   powerful and wealthy, and many will suffer from drought and famine. Because of the growing problems at that time, the governments of nations around the world will need to band together soon to support a long-term plan to colonize other planets by sending
15   humans to live there by 2050. Personally, I am too nervous to be a pioneer on a distant planet, but it will be necessary that some humans undertake this great adventure.

What is the primary purpose of this paragraph?

➢ The main idea of this passage is that colonization of other planets will be necessary by the year 2050. The writer describes why colonization of other planets will be increasingly necessary by 2050. Though the author provides other arguments about why colonization will become necessary and includes thoughts about his or her own nervousness with space travel, the primary purpose is to communicate the coming need to colonize other planets by 2050.

TIP: One practical strategy for determining the main idea is to rephrase the passage into a single, concise sentence that summarizes the entire passage.

Determine the Outline Employed to Develop the Passage

Once you identify the main idea, you need to determine how the author develops that theme using logical arguments, examples, illustrations, facts, or details. A good way to understand the development of a passage is to outline the key ideas, statements, or arguments in that passage. A simple outline provides a way to line up the content in a thoughtful, logical, or sequential manner.

When outlining a passage, find the key statements or thoughts the author uses to support his or her main idea. Ask these questions to help determine the outline:

- What is the main idea of the passage?

- What are the supporting ideas that are used to confirm or strengthen the main idea?

- What primary facts or arguments does the author use to support the main theme?

- What order of ideas or information does the author use to communicate those facts or arguments?

An author may order his or her writing using, among others, one of the following styles:

- *Temporal:* time ordered (e.g., past to present, morning to evening, hours in a day)

- *Sequential:* ordered intervals (e.g., smallest to largest, simplest to most complex, least to most)

- *Categorical:* parts of a system (e.g., classification of animal kingdom, types of stars)

- *Geographical:* locations (e.g., east to west, floor to ceiling, inside to outside)

- *Logical:* rational order (e.g., *x* to *y* and *y* to *z*, *x* logically follows *y*)

- *Emotional:* feeling related (e.g., least impacting to most impacting, saddest time to happiest time)

Review the following reading passage and outline.

Example:

     First-year college students should be required to provide five hours of community service each week. This requirement would greatly benefit the surrounding community. A recent survey shows that
5 communities need more volunteer help. An interview with the mayor demonstrates that her city needs immediate help from more volunteers. This requirement would greatly benefit the student as well. Research demonstrates that students who participate
10 in community service make better grades than those who do not participate in community service. Also, students who participate in community service make more friends than those who do not participate in community service.

Main Idea: First-year college students should be required to provide five hours of community service each week.

1. Fact One: This requirement would greatly benefit the surrounding community.
   a. Argument One: A recent survey shows that communities need more volunteer help.
   b. Argument Two: An interview with the mayor demonstrates that her city needs immediate help from more volunteers.

2. Fact Two: This requirement would greatly benefit the student as well.
   a. Argument One: Research demonstrates that students who participate in community service make better grades than those who do not participate in community service.
   b. Argument Two: Students who participate in community service make more friends than those who do not participate in community service.

Review the following outline that uses a temporal flow (earliest period to latest period).

Example:

Main Idea: A historical overview of book printing

1. Era One: Printing before the invention of movable type
   a. The Egyptian printing methods
   b. The Greco-Roman printing methods
   c. The printing methods of the Middle Ages

2. Era Two: Printing immediately after the invention of movable type
   a. Contemporary practices at the time of Gutenberg's printing press
   b. European printing after Gutenberg's press

3. Era Three: Modern innovations in printing
   a. Innovations before computer technology
   b. Innovations after computer technology

Review the following outline that uses a categorical outline.

Example:

Introduction to Human Anatomy

1. The Digestive System

2. The Reproductive System

3. The Nervous System

4. The Skeletal System

5. The Muscular System

Locate the Important Specific Details

Authors add specific details to a passage to provide necessary information, define terms, add color, or give examples. To skillfully comprehend reading passages, you must locate the most important specific details in a passage.

TIP: One way to identify the most important details is to look for verbal signals. Verbal signals are words or phrases that the author uses to draw attention to significant facts or information.

Prompting Words

Authors use prompting words to clue you that something very important will soon be communicated. Look for words like "significantly," "importantly," "considerably," "vitally," "critically," "notably," or "essentially."

Defining Words

Authors use defining words to introduce a specific meaning of a word, phrase, or idea. A defining word can be as simple as the word "is" (e.g., A totem "is" a Native American religious symbol carved from wood). Other defining words or phrases include "means," "is defined as," or "that is." Regardless of whether an author uses one of these defining words or phrases, you should take special note whenever he or she provides a definition of a word, phrase, or idea.

Similarity Words

Similarity words make comparisons between a known idea and an unknown idea. "Like" is the most familiar similarity word (e.g., A plant cell is "like" an animal cell since both have cell walls and genetic material inside those cell walls). Other similarity words or phrases include "comparable," "similar," "equal to," or "related to."

Contrast Words

The word "but" is an extremely important verbal signal. It sets up a contrast between the "prototype" and the "model." Since prototype means the first example, you should expect it to be fairly primitive and the later versions to be more sophisticated (e.g., The Ohio River traffics many shipping barges "but" not nearly to the extent of the Mississippi River). Other similar verbal clues include "in contrast," "as opposed to," "although," or "unlike."

Example Words

The phrase "for example" serves as a verbal signal that a specific illustration or pattern will follow. The author uses one or more illustrations to support the given argument. Other similar verbal clues include "illustration," "for instance," "model," or "lesson."

Specific details may come in a variety of forms. A detail may be a number, a date, a quote, a definition, a color, a time, a location, etc. Again, a specific detail is not the main idea of the passage, but may play an important supporting role in making the passage more understandable or more readable. Specific details help readers to better understand the meaning of a passage.

Analyze the Arguments or Persuasive Devices

An author may employ a number of persuasive tools or arguments to attempt to prove his or her main ideas. As a critical reader, you will want to note what persuasive tools or arguments are used. In addition, you will want to analyze whether those arguments are valid and truly support the author's ideas.

To discover and analyze the arguments or persuasive devices, ask the following questions:

- How does the author support the main ideas (or supportive ideas) in his or her passage?

- What arguments does the author make for his or her conclusions?

- Is the supporting evidence valid, logical, or reasonable?

- Do the arguments make sense?

The following are various types of evidence or support that an author may use to prove or advance his or her arguments:

- Scientific data or research

- Statistics

- Historical facts

- Quotations from prominent individuals

- Personal experiences

- Logic

- Statements or ideas from other experts

- Emotional statements or stories

TIP: Authors may give direct cues when persuasive tools are used. Look for key words or phrases like "because," "for this reason," "due to," "in order that," "since," "as an example," or "for instance." When not given direct cues, you will need to infer when and how an author argues for his or her propositions.

Consider the Author's Point of View

When considering an author's point of view in a passage, you determine underlying intentions or assumptions of the author. You uncover the reasons why the author wrote on a particular topic using a particular line of reasoning or style of presentation. The author may directly state some of these reasons within the written materials or the author may leave other reasons unstated or hidden. You will need to infer the more implied or hidden reasons from the passage.

An author generally writes from a position of expertise or experience. An author who writes without true expertise in a given area may be writing merely opinion at best or fabrication at worst. This is important to recognize. You should attempt to determine the level of expertise and experience of a writer when reading a passage.

Here are some questions to consider in uncovering an author's point of view:

- What is the author's background (e.g., nationality, economic status, education)?

- What are the author's credentials (e.g., certifications, titles, degrees)?

- What are the author's biases (e.g., strong likes, dislikes, prejudices)?

- What positive/negative experiences have flavored the author's point of view?

- Did the author write simply to inform (e.g., a textbook, factual passages, brochure), or did the author write to persuade?

- What side of the issue does the author take?

- What does the author ultimately want you to believe?

- Why is the author passionate about this issue?

- How did the time or period when the author wrote influence the author?

- How did the place or location of the author influence the writing of the passage?

- To whom was the author writing and how did that influence the passage?

- How did the circumstances of the author's surroundings influence his or her ideas?

Probe the Mood of the Passage

You must take into account the overall mood of a passage. In short, mood is the feeling or tone of a passage. The mood of a passage will provide you with cues about the author's intent in writing the passage. An author's mood can be upbeat, sad, humorous, angry, depressed, analytical, entertaining, informational, academic, confused, scholarly, etc.

Here are some questions you may use to increase awareness of the mood of a passage:

- What is the overall feeling of the passage?

- What ideas does the author use to show he or she is passionate or dispassionate about the topic?

- What does the author want the reader to do after reading the passage (e.g., act in a certain way, think more deeply, understand concepts)?

- What emotional words, images, stories, or examples does the author use?

Summarize the Main Idea

DIRECTIONS: For each of the following passages, choose the statement that best rephrases and summarizes the material. Answers are on page 793.

1. The city of St. Louis has been called the "Gateway to the West" because it was the launching point for many of the trails used during the great westward migration. Many pioneers who ended their migrations as far west as California began their journey in this Missouri river town.

    A. St. Louis is a Missouri river town where many traveling from the west found safety.
    B. Many trails went to California from points east of St. Louis.
    C. St. Louis was the starting location for many migrants who were heading to the western U.S.
    D. Many people from the eastern U.S. traveled to St. Louis to see the "Gateway to the West."

2. Recreational hot air ballooning is restricted to short day trips, so there is little need for navigational instruments. On the other hand, multiple day hot air ballooning requires a significant amount of sophisticated navigational devices.

    F. The length of the flight determines the amount of navigational devices on hot air balloons.
    G. Recreational hot air ballooning is restricted to trips that last fewer than four days.
    H. Navigational equipment is necessary for all types of hot air ballooning.
    J. Due to the need for sophisticated navigational devices, rarely do balloons ever attempt longer trips.

3. As new strains of bacteria emerge that have developed immunity to antibiotics, researchers are constantly challenged to discover new treatments that will be effective. It is this constant need for increasing amounts of research that drives up the cost of effective drugs.

    A. Because researchers must constantly find antibiotics for new bacteria, the cost of drugs constantly increases.
    B. Because bacteria are being constantly discovered, researchers need new tools.
    C. Antibiotics are never effective in treating diseases caused by new strains of bacteria.
    D. Bacteria emerge due to effective research.

4. Carbon monoxide, a potentially deadly gas, has no color or odor. Thus, local municipalities now require all new homes to have carbon monoxide detectors that warn homeowners when this gas is leaking from heating units or piping.

    F. Carbon monoxide has the ability to leak from heating units and pipes in newer homes.
    G. Local cities are now requiring new homes to have detectors for leaking carbon monoxide, a potentially deadly gas.
    H. As a potentially deadly gas, carbon monoxide has a strong potential for becoming odorless and colorless.
    J. Leaking homes rarely detect carbon monoxide before serious injury occurs to the owner.

5. During the colonial period, the town of New Amsterdam, which was later to become New York City, was founded by the Dutch as a trading post. At the same time, Halifax, which is located in what is now Nova Scotia, Canada, housed a trading post and military fort for the British.

A. New Amsterdam and Halifax are names of cities in New York.

B. Traders often made their base of operations trading posts like New Amsterdam and Nova Scotia.

C. New Amsterdam was once a Dutch trading post for U.S. colonies.

D. The British and the Dutch both established trading posts in North America during the colonial period.

Determine the Main Idea

DIRECTIONS: For each of the following passages, determine what answer best describes the main idea or main theme of the paragraph. Answers are on page 793.

1. College professors are currently facing a major problem in their classes. While their students are studying as hard as students did ten to fifteen years ago, these same students are failing more classes. After forming a special committee to investigate why students were failing, one college arrived at an intriguing reason. They discovered that students are using more text messaging to communicate, and thus are less practiced writing in a formal and grammatically acceptable manner.

   A. Colleges should use special committees to investigate failing students.

   B. College professors should teach students proper English grammar.

   C. College students are failing more classes because they no longer practice using formal English grammar.

   D. College students should be persuaded not to use text messaging.

2. Twenty years ago, the African elephant population was declining at an alarming rate due primarily to poaching that supplied a large, illegal trade in ivory. Total elephant numbers declined by as much as 50 percent in the 1970s and 1980s. The Convention on International Trade in Endangered Species (CITES) enacted an international moratorium on the buying and selling of ivory, which was quickly followed by significant declines in ivory trading and in the rate of elephant poaching. Elephant populations in many African countries have since stabilized.

   F. CITES is an organization that helps endangered elephants, especially those who were born prior to 1970.

   G. Though twenty years ago the African elephant population was declining due to illegal hunting, it has now stabilized.

   H. Selling elephant ivory is very profitable.

   J. If trends continue, in twenty years, African elephants will no longer exist.

3. A flood is an overflow of water that covers lands that are normally not covered by water. A flood occurs, for example, when a stream or river overflows its banks. Small streams are subject to flash floods—that is, the very rapid increases in water that may last only a few minutes. In larger streams, floods usually last from several hours to a few days, and a series of storms might keep a river above flood stage for several weeks.

   A. Floods are natural occurrences that result in negative consequences for people.

   B. Rivers sometimes flood.

   C. Small streams are often subject to flash floods that last only a few minutes.

   D. A flood occurs when an overflow of water covers lands not normally covered by water.

4. If I could change one important thing about my country, it would be to have a mandatory service requirement. I mean that everyone who is able would be required to serve his or her country for a one- or two-year period following high school graduation. People would be given a choice about what kind of service they would do. They could choose to enter the military, to work in a poor area in a city, or to serve in a national park.

F. All high school graduates should be required to spend one or two years fulfilling a mandatory service requirement.
G. Because my country is not perfect, I would change one thing.
H. Military service is more important than working in a city or at a national park.
J. People should be given a choice about what kind of mandatory service they would enjoy, whether working in the military, in an urban area, or in a national park.

5. Like Shakespeare's King Richard, the woman had experienced a winter of discontent when life itself felt cold, wind blown, and gray. She longed for spring to come to her soul, when she would experience a warming of her moods. But sadness overtook her, like a blizzard covering a street with racing pillows of snow. No matter how hard she tried, she could not force spring before the proper time, but simply endured this season of sadness.

A. Blizzards caused the woman to become sad, much like they did for King Richard.
B. The woman experienced a sadness that she could not force to go away.
C. In winter, the woman experienced cold wind and clouds.
D. The woman desired for her soul to experience the type of winter that Shakespeare experienced.

6. The great Shawnee chief Tecumseh feared that contact between white and Indian civilizations would mean the eventual destruction of the Indian civilization. When the Delawares were pushed out of lands guaranteed to them by treaty, they turned to Tecumseh for leadership. Tecumseh attempted to block the advance of white settlers into the Old Northwest Territory by forming a federation of Indian tribes that reached all the way from Alabama to Minnesota. He met with tribes and explained that he hoped that the white settlers would withdraw peaceably; but if they did not, it was his plan to drive them out by using superior force.

F. Treaties were often negotiated with a federation of Indian tribes.
G. Tecumseh believed that white settlers would withdraw peaceably, but if they didn't, he would ask tribes like the Delawares to abandon their lands.
H. White settlers sought the help of Tecumseh as they entered the Old Northwest Territory.
J. Tecumseh was a key leader in attempting to block the advance of white settlers into the Old Northwest Territory.

7. According to many current theories of adolescent development, intellectually, young adolescents are exploring values and ideas in a new way. They are beginning to form abstractions, to generalize, and to think about thinking itself. This intellectual development enables them to shift away from an authoritarian and childlike sense of right and wrong to a more open and complex approach to value formation. They begin to struggle with conflicting concepts like individual rights and the overriding social good.

A. As adolescents develop intellectually, they think with more sophistication about moral values.
B. Individual rights and the overriding social good cause adolescents to struggle.
C. A childlike sense of right and wrong is a natural phase in early adolescence.
D. All adolescents learn to think critically about thinking itself.

8. The history of western medicine can be traced to Hippocrates, a Greek physician who lived on the island of Cos. Few particulars are known about the life of Hippocrates, but the establishment of the school of medicine on Cos is regarded as his most important achievement. The school emphasized reason and observation and regarded disease as having natural, not supernatural, causes. In addition to a systematized body of empirical knowledge free of superstition, the school of Hippocrates evolved into a tradition of the highest standards of conduct.

    F. The life of Hippocrates can be traced to the island of Cos.

    G. The text of the Hippocratic Oath is regularly used by modern doctors.

    H. Hippocrates is the father (founder) of modern medicine.

    J. Superstitions during the time of Hippocrates caused many illnesses to be wrongly treated.

9. Geothermal energy offers enormous potential for many applications. This new renewable source relies on the Earth's own natural energy to heat or cool a house or multi-family dwelling directly. It does not waste energy by needing to convert energy to steam or other high-temperature fluids to create heating and cooling potential. This ultimately brings great cost savings to producers and consumers of heating and cooling energy.

    A. Geothermal energy is better for multi-family dwellings than other forms of energy.

    B. Steam can be used to generate energy for heating and cooling.

    C. Geothermal energy has potentially positive benefits for those who produce and consume it.

    D. Energy always costs producers and consumers a great deal of money.

10. In 1848, gold was discovered in California, and newspapers quickly spread the word. President James K. Polk confirmed the discovery in his 1848 State of the Union message to Congress. The president's words were enough to trigger the greatest national mass migration in U.S. history and a global gold fever. People used their life savings, mortgaged their homes, and sold everything they had to travel to California in hopes of becoming wealthy.

    F. President James K. Polk delivered his State of the Union message in 1948.

    G. Global gold fever is typically started by newspaper announcements.

    H. People will spend their life savings, mortgage their homes, and sell everything in order to become rich.

    J. The California gold discovery of 1848 led to a large migration of people to California.

Outlining Passages

DIRECTIONS: For each of the following passages, write an outline that follows the author's development of the content. Examples of outlines are on page 793.

Passage 1

Speaking unscientifically, we say that lightning strikes an object on the ground; but from a scientific point of view, this language is inaccurate. Cloud-to-ground lightning begins when complex meteorological
5 processes cause a tremendous electrostatic charge to build up within a cloud. Typically, the bottom of the cloud is negatively charged. When the charge reaches 50 to 100 million volts, air is no longer an effective insulator, and lightning occurs within the cloud itself.
10 Approximately 10 to 30 minutes after the onset of intra-cloud lightning, negative charges called stepped leaders emerge from the bottom of the cloud, moving toward the Earth in 50-meter intervals at speeds of 100 to 200 kilometers per second, creating an ionized
15 channel. As the leaders near the Earth, their strong electric field causes streamers of positively charged ions to develop at the tips of pointed objects connected directly or indirectly to the ground. These positively charged streamers flow upward.

20 When the distance, known as the striking distance, between a stepped leader and one of the streamers reaches 30 to 100 meters, the intervening air breaks down completely and the leader is joined to the Earth via the streamer. Now, a pulse of current known
25 as a return stroke ranging from thousands to hundreds of thousands of amperes moves at one tenth to one third the speed of light from the Earth through the object from which the streamer emanated and up the ionized channel to the charge center within the cloud.
30 An ionized channel remains in the air and additional negative charges called dart leaders will quickly move down this path resulting in further return strokes. It is this multiplicity that causes the flash to flicker. The entire event typically lasts about one second. The
35 return stroke's extremely high temperature creates the visible lightning and produces thunder by instantly turning moisture into steam.

PASSAGE OUTLINE

Passage 2

Twenty years ago, the African elephant population was declining at an alarming rate due primarily to poaching that supplied a large, illegal trade in ivory. Total elephant numbers declined by as much
5 as 50 percent in the 1970s and 1980s. The Convention on International Trade in Endangered Species (CITES) enacted an international moratorium on the buying and selling of ivory, which was quickly followed by significant declines in ivory trading and in the rate of
10 elephant poaching. Elephant populations in many African countries have since stabilized.

U.S. involvement in African elephant conservation, through both its import control provisions and its grant programs, remains important.
15 One of the earliest projects funded was a cooperative effort with the Central African Republic and the World Wildlife Fund. A cooperative effort was underway to establish a reserve in the southeastern portion of that country. While funds for gating the reserve were
20 anticipated, no funds were available for basic equipment and operations of anti-poaching patrols— hired from local communities—until a cooperative project was implemented using funds provided by the United States. When the first patrols were put into
25 place, the only signs of elephants in a local clearing within the park were the carcasses of several poached animals. Today, more than 2,000 individual elephants, young and old, have been identified as using that clearing.

30 In Senegal, the westernmost population of elephants in Africa is now secure. Through an African elephant conservation fund grant, an anti-poaching program has provided local community employment and protection for the remaining elephant population.
35 For the first time in years, baby elephants are now seen in this small but genetically valuable population. Similar to the projects described above, funds have been provided to augment anti-poaching and management support in Cameroon, Congo, Eritrea,
40 Gabon, Mali, Senegal, Tanzania, Zambia, and Zimbabwe.

PASSAGE OUTLINE

Locate Verbal Signs

DIRECTIONS: In the following passage, underline and identify any prompting, defining, similarity, contrast, or example verbal signals. Answers are on page 793.

A flood is an overflow of water that covers lands that are normally not covered by water. A flood occurs, for example, when a stream or river overflows its banks. Small streams are subject to flash floods—that
5 is, the very rapid increases in water that may last only a few minutes. In larger streams, floods usually last from several hours to a few days, and a series of storms might keep a river above flood stage for several weeks.

Floods can occur at any time, but weather
10 patterns have a strong influence on when and where floods happen. Cyclones—similar in structure to tornadoes—bring moisture inland from the ocean, causing floods in the spring in the western United States. Thunderstorms are relatively small but intense
15 storms that cause flash floods in smaller streams during the summer in the Southwest. Frontal storms at the edge of large, moist air masses moving across the country cause floods in the northern and eastern parts of the United States during the winter.

20 The magnitude of a flood is described by a term called the recurrence interval, which is based upon long-term study of flow records for a stream. A five-year flood is one that would occur, on the average, once every five years. Although a 100-year flood is
25 expected to happen only once in a century, it is important to remember that there is a one percent chance that a flood of that size could happen during any given year.

Of course, the frequency and magnitude of floods
30 can be altered if changes are made in the drainage basin of a stream or river. Significantly, harvesting timber or changing land use from farming to housing can cause the runoff to increase, resulting in an increase in the magnitude of flooding. On the other
35 hand, dams can protect against flooding by storing storm runoff. Although the same volume of water must

eventually move downstream, the peak flow can be reduced by temporarily storing water and then releasing it when water levels have fallen.

Locate Specific Details

DIRECTIONS: After reading each of the following passages, select the best answer about the specific details. Answers are on page 794.

Items #1–3 are based on the following passage.

Fraktur is a uniquely American folk art rooted in the Pennsylvania Dutch (Pennsylvania German) culture. In German, *fraktur* refers to a particular typeface used by printers. Derived from the Latin
5 *fractura*, "breaking apart," *fraktur* suggests that the letters are broken apart and reassembled into designs. Fraktur as a genre of folk art refers to a text (usually religious) that is decorated with symbolic designs.

1. Pennsylvania Dutch is the same term as which of the following?

    A. Pennsylvania Irish
    B. Pennsylvania Scottish
    C. Pennsylvania German
    D. Pennsylvania Mennonite

2. The word *fractura* in Latin means:

    F. breaking apart.
    G. forging together.
    H. artful lettering.
    J. German lettering.

3. Fraktur would generally appear in what type of text?

    A. Latin
    B. Dutch
    C. Broken
    D. Religious

Items #4–6 are based on the following passage.

Lightning is basically an electrical discharge of immense proportions. Some 80 percent of lightning occurs within clouds; about 20 percent is cloud-to-ground lightning; and an extremely small percentage is
5 cloud-to-sky lightning.

4. According to the passage, lightning is:

    F. an immense proportion.
    G. an electrical discharge.
    H. a natural occurrence for clouds.
    J. always within clouds.

5. What percentage of lightning occurs within clouds?

    A. 10%
    B. 20%
    C. 80%
    D. 100%

6. According to the passage, 20 percent of lightning travels from clouds to:

    F. ground.
    G. sky.
    H. clouds.
    J. electricity.

Items #7–10 are based on the following passage.

We are now in the throes of a third transformation in communications, although when it began exactly is difficult to say. One might choose that evening of 1844 when Samuel Morse telegraphed the message "What
5 has God wrought!" Or possibly one could point to the invention by Charles Babbage of the "Analytic Engine," a mechanical device that prefigured (came before) the modern electronic computer. Or perhaps this third transformation began with the ENIAC
10 computer developed during World War II as the first digital electronic computer. In any case, it is estimated that it took about 150,000 years for human knowledge to first double, then 1,500 years for it to double again, and that it now doubles every 15 years or less.

7. What computer was developed during World War II?

   A. ENIAC
   B. Morse Code
   C. The Analytic Engine
   D. Charles Babbage

8. Who invented the "Analytic Engine"?

   F. Samuel Morse
   G. Charles Babbage
   H. The ENIAC Company
   J. No one can say.

9. How frequently does knowledge currently double?

   A. Every 150,000 years
   B. Every 1,500 years
   C. Every 15 years or less
   D. All of the above

10. According to the passage, the era in communications we are currently experiencing is the:

   F. first transformation.
   G. digital computer age.
   H. doubling of information age.
   J. third transformation.

Analyze the Arguments

DIRECTIONS: Read the following passages and then answer the corresponding items. Answers are on page 794.

Items #1–2 are based on the following passage.

Alcohol abuse and dependence are serious problems affecting 10 percent of adult Americans, and the toll is high: 3 out of 100 deaths in the United States can be linked directly to alcohol. In addition to traffic
5 crashes, injuries in the home and on the job, and serious long-term medical consequences, alcohol abuse has been implicated in aggression and crime. The cost of alcohol abuse and alcohol dependence is estimated to be as high as $1 trillion annually.

1. In the paragraph above, the author argues that alcohol abuse and dependence are serious problems. Which of the following reasons does he NOT use to support his main idea?

   A. Three out of 100 deaths in the United States can be linked directly to alcohol.
   B. Aggression and crime can be correlated to alcohol abuse.
   C. The cost of alcohol abuse and dependence is as high as $1 trillion annually.
   D. Ten percent of adult Americans experience traffic crashes, injuries in the home and on the job due to alcohol abuse.

2. In the paragraph above, what type of evidence or support does the author use to prove his or her argument?

   F. Historical quotation
   G. Statistics
   H. A personal story
   J. A statement from an expert

Items #3–4 are based on the following passage.

Regardless of where the hopeful migrants originated, the months-long trip to the California gold country was perilous. A journey across the continent meant rough conditions and possibly attacks by Indians
5 or by other emigrants. Those coming by sea from Europe and the eastern United States had to travel around stormy Cape Horn. The sea journey could be shortened by going overland through the jungles of the Isthmus of Panama, but it was a region rife with
10 cholera and other diseases. From San Francisco, getting to the mining areas was difficult. There was little housing, disease was rampant, and food prices were astronomically high.

3. According to the author, journey to the California gold country was perilous. What dangers does the author suggest that migrants might have experienced?

   A. Attacks by other emigrants
   B. Jungle diseases
   C. Sea storms
   D. All of the above

4. The author claims that when emigrants arrived in California gold country, there was little housing, much disease, and high food prices. What does the author infer?

   F. Even upon arrival at their destination, the emigrants continued to experience great peril.
   G. Many emigrants returned home before arriving in California.
   H. Conditions were less difficult in San Francisco.
   J. Travel by sea was less costly than travel over inland trails.

Items #5–8 are based on the following passage.

During the past decade, the problem of gang-related crime has become a significant policy issue in the United States. According to recent estimates, more than 16,000 gangs are active in this country, with at
5 least half a million members who commit more than 600,000 crimes each year.

Gang membership leads to criminal behavior. The study mentioned in your textbook reported that 80 percent of individual gang members said that they had
10 stolen cars, but only 10 percent of at-risk youths were not gang members. Gang members were also more involved with selling drugs.

The study reports similar contrasts for violent crimes. About 40 percent of gang members had
15 participated in a drive-by shooting, compared with 2 percent of at-risk youths. Gang members were far likelier to own guns, and the guns they owned were of a larger caliber.

Most gang members join for security and a sense
20 of belonging. As for security, research demonstrates that the benefits of avoiding gang membership far outweigh those of joining. For example, gang members are five times as likely to suffer a violent death as are at-risk youths who are not gang members. As for the
25 sense of belonging, creative prevention that fosters feelings of belonging in the community as a whole might dissuade many of these youths from joining gangs.

5. According to the author, gang membership has become a serious policy issue because:

A. gang members long for a sense of belonging.
B. drive-by shootings are becoming far too frequent.
C. gang members are more likely to be involved in violent crime.
D. gang members are less frequently found to be involved in illegal drug use.

6. The author reasons that gang members are wrong in thinking they will be more secure by joining a gang. Which of the following statements best describes the author's argument?

F. Gang members do not join gangs for security but for a sense of belonging.
G. A gang member is five times as likely to suffer a violent death as those not affiliated with a gang.
H. Research demonstrates that gang members do indeed feel more secure after joining a gang.
J. None of the above

7. The author argues that gang members are more likely to participate in which of the following?

A. Drive-by shootings
B. Selling drugs
C. Gun ownership
D. All of the above

8. The author suggests that potential gang members may be dissuaded from joining a gang if:

F. they owned their own weapons.
G. they felt more of a sense of belonging in their own communities.
H. the government created new policies that punish violent criminals.
J. gang membership did not lead to criminal behavior.

Items #9–10 are based on the following passage.

The Amazon River of South America is the most environmentally important river in the entire world. By pure volume of water, it is the largest river in the world. In fact, by simple calculation of the total flow of
5   water from river to ocean, the Amazon River disperses more water into the ocean than the other ten largest rivers flowing into the ocean combined. By percentage, the Amazon River expels 20 percent of all the freshwater discharge into the oceans. Though officially
10 the Nile River is the longest in the world, by volume of water and percentage of freshwater discharge, the Amazon River is the queen of the rivers.

9. The author argues that the Amazon River is the most environmentally important river in the entire world. What statement does he or she use to support his or her position?

   A. The Amazon River discharges 20 percent of all freshwater into the oceans.
   B. The Nile is the longest river in the world.
   C. The Amazon River is in South America.
   D. Scientists can calculate the volume of the Amazon River.

10. What persuasive device does the author use to support his or her opinion?

   F. Famous quotations
   G. Life experiences
   H. Scientific facts
   J. Emotional stories

Consider the Author's Point of View

DIRECTIONS: Read the following passages and then answer the corresponding questions. Answers are on page 794.

Items #1–6 are based on the following passage.

The history of western medicine can be traced to Hippocrates, a Greek physician who lived on the island of Cos. Few particulars are known about the life of Hippocrates, but the establishment of the school of
5 medicine on Cos is regarded as his most important achievement. The school emphasized reason and observation and regarded disease as having natural, not supernatural, causes. Reason and observation are important elements of modern medicine. In addition to
10 a systematized body of empirical knowledge free of superstition, the school of Hippocrates evolved a tradition of the highest standards of conduct. Today, the Hippocratic Oath, which defines the duties and moral obligations of a physician, is taken by all
15 medical students upon completion of their training.

As a physician myself, I believe all medical students must accept and endorse the methodology of Hippocrates—reason and observation—prior to being admitted to medical school. As one of the older
20 professors in a highly prestigious medical school, I have grown tired of students who desire to be doctors only for fame and fortune and fail to understand the rich scientific foundations of the profession.

1. Who is the author?

   physician

2. Does the author have expertise or experience regarding this particular subject?

   yes

3. What are the author's likes or dislikes?

   fame and fortune

4. Why did the author write this passage?

   To inform.

5. What does this author want you to believe?

   He was a client western medicin.

6. What is the passage mainly about?

   Hipocras medicin.

Items #7–11 are based on the following passage.

After spending 30 years in the American banking industry, I have come to believe strongly that government bailouts of failing banks are harmful because they create incentives that aggravate the
5 underlying economic problems. Indeed, I have seen first-hand how moral hazard incentives are the villains in the recent, unprecedented wave of financial system collapses. Banks willingly and knowingly take on more risks—especially default risks—than they would if
10 they were not protected by government safety nets. In extreme cases, banking collapses lead to the fiscal insolvency of governments that bail out banks and to exchange rate collapse. As one of the first female members of Congress, I wrote legislation that would
15 have kept the government from bailing out failed banks. Unfortunately, few listened to my cogent arguments and instead they foolishly allowed themselves to be deceived by the banks.

7. Who is the author?

works in a Bank

8. Does the author have expertise or experience regarding this particular subject?

30 year of experiens

9. What are the author's likes or dislikes?

↓ Gornment

10. Why did the author write this passage?

To Informe and talk about how her legisratd migh help.

11. What does this author want you to believe?

It helps all the people

Items #12–14 are based on the following passage.

The following letter from a citizen was written to the editor of a newspaper in a developing nation in Africa in the 1990s. This nation had recently moved from a military dictatorship to a democratic form of government.

    If I could change one important thing about my country, it would be to have a mandatory service requirement. I mean that everyone who is able would be required to serve his or her country for a one- or
5 two-year period. People would be given a choice about what kind of service they would do. You could choose the military, but you would not have to. You could be assigned to work in a poor area in the city or in a rural area. In addition, you could be a carpenter, or a teacher,
10 or whatever. I think that this requirement would be good for three reasons.

    First, required service would be good for the people who do it. I have seen many people come back from military service who went in as children but
15 became adults. I think this is because they were treated like adults and asked to do adult things. Also, they learned to work well with other people on a team, and they even learned some valuable skills.

    Second, the service would be good for the people
20 who are served. Just think about the different things people could do. One group of people could restore run-down housing in a poor neighborhood and make a place for people to live. Some other people could work in a farm area and help people raise crops. Some other
25 people could be teachers and work in schools. And everyone who was served would benefit.

    Third, the service would make being a citizen more valuable. We too often take our citizenship for granted. Many people don't even bother to vote.
30 Perhaps that is because if it's free, people don't think that it's worth very much. If people had to "buy" their citizenship with their time, they would think that it was more important.

12. How did the time or period when the author wrote influence the author?

    poor country so he wanted to do something to help

13. How did the place or location of the author influence the writing of the passage?

    Africa

14. How did the circumstances of the author influence the writing of the passage?

    he is comparing with other and telling what is right to do

Items #15–17 are based on the following passage.

In this passage, a professor of sociology at a large public university in Los Angeles writes on the criminal behavior of gang members. The article was written in 1978.

During the past decade, the problem of gang-related crime has become a significant policy issue in the United States. According to recent estimates, more than 16,000 gangs are active in this country, with at
5 least half a million members who commit more than 600,000 crimes each year.

Gang membership leads to criminal behavior. The study mentioned in your textbook reported that 80 percent of individual gang members said that they had
10 stolen cars, but only 10 percent of at-risk youths were not gang members. Gang members were also more involved with selling drugs.

The study reports similar contrasts for violent crimes. About 40 percent of gang members had
15 participated in a drive-by shooting, compared with 2 percent of at-risk youths. Gang members were far likelier to own guns, and the guns they owned were of a larger caliber.

Most gang members join for security and a sense
20 of belonging. As for security, research demonstrates that the benefits of avoiding gang membership far outweigh those of joining. For example, gang members are five times as likely to suffer a violent death as are at-risk youths who are not gang members. As for the
25 sense of belonging, creative prevention that fosters feelings of belonging in the community as a whole might dissuade many of these youths from joining gangs.

15. How did the time or period when the author wrote influence the author?

_____

_____

_____

16. How did the place or location of the author influence the writing of the passage?

_____

_____

_____

17. How did the circumstances of the author influence the writing of the passage?

_____

_____

_____

Probe the Mood of the Passage

DIRECTIONS: Read the following passage and then answer the corresponding questions. Answers are on page 795.

The following is a passage from Jonathan Swift's "A Modest Proposal."

It is a melancholy object to those, who walk through this great town, or travel in the country, when they see the streets, the roads and cabin-doors crowded with beggars of the female sex, followed by three, four, 5 or six children, all in rags, and importuning every passenger for an alms. These mothers instead of being able to work for their honest livelihood, are forced to employ all their time in strolling to beg sustenance for their helpless infants who, as they grow up, either turn 10 thieves for want of work, or leave their dear native country, to fight for the Pretender in Spain, or sell themselves to the Barbadoes.

I think it is agreed by all parties, that this prodigious number of children in the arms, or on the 15 backs, or at the heels of their mothers, and frequently of their fathers, is in the present deplorable state of the kingdom, a very great additional grievance; and therefore whoever could find out a fair, cheap and easy method of making these children sound and useful 20 members of the common-wealth, would deserve so well of the public, as to have his statue set up for a preserver of the nation.

But my intention is very far from being confined to provide only for the children of professed beggars: it 25 is of a much greater extent, and shall take in the whole number of infants at a certain age, who are born of parents in effect as little able to support them, as those who demand our charity in the streets.

1. What is the mood of the passage?

_____

_____

_____

2. How does the author demonstrate the mood of the passage?

_____

_____

_____

EXERCISE 9

Bonus Passages

The following bonus passages are provided so that you can practice all of the "Honing Your Reading Skills" strategies comprehensively.

DIRECTIONS: Each passage below is followed by a number of items. Answer each item based upon the content of the passage. Answers are on page 795.

Items #1–10 are based on the following passage.

In 1848, gold was discovered in California, and newspapers quickly spread the word. President James K. Polk confirmed the discovery in his 1848 State of the Union message to Congress. The president's words
5 and the knowledge that taking the precious metal was completely unregulated in California were enough to trigger the greatest national mass migration in U.S. history and a global gold fever. People used their life savings, mortgaged their homes, and sold everything
10 they had to travel to California in hopes of becoming wealthy. At the time gold was discovered, there were approximately 11,000 non-Native Americans living in California. Between the discovery and 1852, some 300,000 people, mostly young and male, traveled to
15 California from all quarters.

Regardless of where the hopeful travelers originated, the months-long trip was perilous. A journey across the continent meant rough conditions and possibly attacks by Indians or by other emigrants.
20 Those coming by sea from Europe and the eastern United States had to travel around stormy Cape Horn. The sea journey could be shortened by going overland through the jungles of the Isthmus of Panama, but it was a region rife with cholera and other diseases. From
25 San Francisco, getting to the mining areas was difficult. There was little housing, disease was rampant, and food prices were astronomically high.

There were tales of people finding thousands of dollars of gold in only a few weeks, but most miners
30 just encountered hard times. To survive, some left mining or worked for wages in other men's operations. The problem for many was that they couldn't afford to return home, and any news of other people striking it

rich would renew hope. Many people lost, but a few
35 lucky ones won. By 1860, approximately $600 million in gold had been mined—more than $10 billion today.

1. In line 5, the word *precious* most nearly means:

   A. legal.
   B. scarce.
   C. beautiful.
   D. valuable.

2. The author mentions that 300,000 people moved to California in order to:

   F. demonstrate that many people became wealthy.
   G. underscore the size of the migration.
   H. show that they came from all over the world.
   J. explain why so many miners failed to find gold.

3. It can be inferred that some people mortgaged their homes in order to:

   A. get money to travel to California.
   B. ensure a place to return to.
   C. provide insurance against failure.
   D. purchase gold from California.

4. It can be inferred that travelers who crossed the Isthmus of Panama:

   F. generally came from the eastern U.S.
   G. arrived in California after the Gold Rush.
   H. avoided the trip around Cape Horn.
   J. paid less than others for their trip.

5. In line 24, the word *rife* most nearly means:

    A. devoid.
    B. filled.
    C. immune.
    D. suspected.

6. The author mentions all of the following as difficulties facing travelers when they arrived in San Francisco EXCEPT:

    F. high food prices.
    G. a housing shortage.
    H. widespread disease.
    J. lack of work.

7. In line 17, the word *perilous* most nearly means:

    A. dangerous.
    B. lengthy.
    C. uneventful.
    D. expensive.

8. In line 32, the phrase "couldn't afford" most nearly means:

    F. weren't able to sell their gold.
    G. couldn't find transportation.
    H. had no money.
    J. didn't want.

9. According to the selection, why did so many people move to California?

    A. They hoped to become rich by mining gold.
    B. President Polk encouraged them to go.
    C. They wanted to open stores to sell goods to miners.
    D. They had no homes of their own.

10. What is the main focus of the selection?

    F. The conditions in San Francisco during the California Gold Rush
    G. The various modes of transportation available during the mid-1800s
    H. The demographic characteristics of the people who came to California
    J. The California migration triggered by the discovery of gold

Items #11–16 are based on the following passage.

Geothermal energy offers enormous potential for direct, low-temperature applications. Unlike indirect applications, this new technology relies on the Earth's natural thermal energy to heat or cool a house or multi-
5 family dwelling directly without the need to convert steam or other high-temperature fluids into electricity using expensive equipment.

A geothermal system consists of a heat pump and exchanger plus a series of pipes, called a loop, installed
10 below the surface of the ground or submerged in a pond or lake. Fluid circulating in the loop is warmed and carries heat to the home. The heat pump and exchanger use an electrically powered vapor compression cycle—the same principle employed in a
15 refrigerator—to concentrate the energy and to transfer it. The concentrated geothermal energy is released inside the home at a higher temperature, and fans then distribute the heat to various rooms through a system of air ducts. In summer, the process is reversed: excess
20 heat is drawn from the home, expelled to the loop, and absorbed by the Earth.

Geothermal systems are more effective than conventional heat pumps that use the outdoor air as their heat source (on cold days) or heat sink (on warm
25 days) because geothermal systems draw heat from a source whose temperature is more constant than that of air. The temperature of the ground or groundwater a few feet beneath the Earth's surface remains relatively stable—between 45°F and 70°F. In winter, it is much
30 easier to capture heat from the soil at a moderate 50°F than from the atmosphere when the air temperature is below zero. Conversely, in summer, the relatively cool ground absorbs a home's waste heat more readily than the warm outdoor air.

35 The use of geothermal energy through heat pump technology has almost no adverse environmental consequences and offers several advantages over conventional energy sources. Direct geothermal applications are usually no more disruptive of the
40 surrounding environment than are normal water wells. Additionally, while such systems require electricity to concentrate and distribute the energy collected, they actually reduce total energy consumption by one-fourth to two-thirds, depending on the technology used. For
45 every 1,000 homes with geothermal heat pumps, an electric utility can avoid the installation of two to five megawatts of generating capacity. Unfortunately, only a modest part of the potential of this use for geothermal

energy has been developed because the service industry
50 is small and the price of competing energy sources is low.

11. The author regards the new technology as:

  A. promising but underutilized.
  B. dependable but costly.
  C. inexpensive but unreliable.
  D. unproven but efficient.

12. The passage implies that a rise in the cost of conventional energy would result in:

  F. a decrease in the cost for installing geothermal heating and cooling equipment.
  G. an economic incentive in favor of the use of conventional energy sources.
  H. an expanded reliance on direct geothermal technology for climate control of smaller structures.
  J. a decrease in the number of new homes constructed using geothermal heating.

13. Which of the following would be the most logical continuation of the passage?

  A. A listing of geological features of the Earth such as geysers and volcanoes that might be potential geothermal energy sources
  B. A review of the history of the use of geothermal energy and associated technologies
  C. A description of experimental techniques for converting geothermal energy into electricity
  D. A discussion of some ways of expanding reliance on geothermal energy for direct, low-temperature applications

14. The author refers to a refrigerator in line 15 in order to:

  F. demonstrate the feasibility of geothermal technology.
  G. provide the reader with a familiar example of heat pump technology.
  H. illustrate the distinction between direct and indirect geothermal technology.
  J. prove that geothermal energy can cool as well as heat.

15. In line 33, *waste* most nearly means:

    A. inefficient.
    B. unused.
    C. recycled.
    D. unwanted.

16. Which of the following helps to illustrate why the new technology can be used for air conditioning as well as heating homes?

    F. A pool of still water freezes faster than a running stream.
    G. A drink of well water tastes cool on a hot summer day.
    H. Clothes on a line dry more quickly on a dry day than on a day with high humidity.
    J. It feels colder on a windy winter day than on a day with the same temperature and no wind.

Careful Reading of Item Stems

After surveying thousands of students, we found that up to one-third of the time an item was answered incorrectly because the student misinterpreted the item. In other words, students could have answered the item correctly had they understood what the test writers were really asking. You must read the item carefully and correctly or you will get it wrong.

It may seem that this sort of error would only affect your ability to correctly answer Reading items. In fact, if you cannot read with enough precision to comprehend the exact item that is being asked, you are also limiting your potential to correctly answer English, Mathematics, and Science items. An inability to focus on the actual question means that you would most likely have problems in all sections of the exam.

The following exercises are designed to reinforce careful reading of the item stems on the actual test. Although some of the items in these exercises may seem to require knowledge of basic verbal, math, and science concepts, it will not be necessary to "solve" an item. Do not be confused by distracting terminology or by an answer that "might" qualify as a correct restatement of the item stem. The correct answer choice to a Careful Reading item is the most specifically accurate, and therefore the *best*, restatement of the question that is being asked by the test-writers.

Careful Reading of English Item Stems

The following exercise will help you focus on the exact question that is being asked by English item stems that correspond to passages on the ACT English Test. There is no need for you to see the entire selection as it would appear on the actual exam. When you have become proficient at careful reading, you will no longer waste valuable time on an individual item trying to determine the exact question that is being asked.

DIRECTIONS: For each of the following items, determine which of the given answer choices is the best restatement of the original item stem. Answers are on page 795.

1. Which of the following represents the most logical sequence for the paragraphs?

    A. In what order should the paragraphs be arranged?
    B. Which of the following sequences is illogical?
    C. In what order should the paragraphs not be arranged?
    D. Which paragraph would not be represented in the most logical sequence?

2. Is the author's quote of D.H. Lawrence in the last paragraph appropriate?

    F. Is the quote made by the author appropriate to the passage?
    G. Does D.H. Lawrence's quote belong in a different paragraph?
    H. Is the quote made by D.H. Lawrence appropriate to the passage?
    J. Does the author correctly quote D.H. Lawrence?

3. The author's intended audience is most likely:

    A. Who is most like the author's intended audience?
    B. Whom does the author intend to address?
    C. Which audience does the author most like?
    D. Whom does the author not intend to address?

4. How might the author have developed the essay so that it was more interesting?

    F. What would make the essay more interesting?
    G. How could the author have written a less developed essay?
    H. What would make the essay less interesting?
    J. How could the author have written a more developed essay?

5. Which of the following best describes the overall character of the essay?

    A. What is the main idea of the essay?
    B. Which character in the essay best describes the overall theme?
    C. What best describes the main character in the essay?
    D. Which of the following best describes the characteristics of the essay in general?

6. Which of the following is most probably the author's opinion rather than a fact?

    F. Which fact is not an opinion held by the author?
    G. Which of the author's views could be argued as fact?
    H. Which fact is presented by the author?
    J. What is indicative of the author's viewpoint?

7. What would be the most logical continuation of the essay?

    A. Logically, how might the author begin the essay?

    B. Logically, how might the author end the essay?

    C. Logically, how might the author continue the essay?

    D. Logically, how might the author continue the first paragraph?

8. What might logically have preceded this essay?

    F. What type of passage would logically come before this essay?

    G. What is the precedent for a logically structured essay?

    H. What type of passage would logically come after this essay?

    J. What always precedes a logically structured essay?

9. This essay is most probably taken from a:

    A. What is this essay about?

    B. How might this essay be continued?

    C. What might be the source of this essay?

    D. What might have preceded this essay?

10. What would strengthen the author's contention that con games rank first in heartlessness?

    F. What weakens the author's argument that con games are not heartless?

    G. What supports the author's argument that con games are not heartless?

    H. What strengthens the author's argument that con games are the most heartless?

    J. What weakens the author's argument that con games are the most heartless?

11. Which of the following would most strengthen the essay?

    A. What would not make the essay weaker?

    B. What would make the essay stronger?

    C. What would not make the essay stronger?

    D. What would make the essay weaker?

12. Is the final sentence of the passage an appropriate ending?

    F. Would the final sentence be a more appropriate beginning?

    G. Does the final sentence appropriately end the passage?

    H. Is the fifth line an appropriate ending to the second paragraph?

    J. Is the final sentence an appropriate statement?

13. What assumption is the essay's author making?

    A. What does the author know to be true?

    B. What does the author accept to be true?

    C. What do you, as a reader, know to be true about the author?

    D. What do you, as a reader, assume to be true about the essay?

14. Where might you find this essay published?

    F. Where are most essays published?

    G. Where would you publish this essay?

    H. In what type of publication might this essay have been published?

    J. Under what conditions might such an essay have been published?

15. Which of the following is not a strategy the author uses to make his/her point?

    A. What does the author use to make the point?

    B. What doesn't the author use to make the point?

    C. What would not be effective in demonstrating the author's point?

    D. What is the author's point?

16. Which of the following would most strengthen the author's argument that Shakespeare is the poet of human nature?

    F. What least weakens the author's argument?

    G. What most weakens the author's argument?

    H. What doesn't least strengthen the author's argument?

    J. What most strengthens the author's argument?

17. The author most likely wrote this essay for which of the following audiences?

   A. Who most influenced the author?
   B. Which audience would not read this essay?
   C. For whom did the author write this essay?
   D. Who most enjoyed the author's essay?

18. The author relies on which of the following to develop the passage?

   F. What device is used to develop the passage?
   G. What is the author's point of view?
   H. What is the author's tone in the passage?
   J. What conclusion does the author make in the passage?

19. The author probably quotes St. Augustine in order to:

   A. What is the author's view of St. Augustine?
   B. Why does the author refer to St. Augustine?
   C. Why does the author quote St. Augustine?
   D. What is St. Augustine's quote?

Careful Reading of Mathematics Item Stems

The following exercise will help you focus on the exact question that is being asked by Mathematics item stems on the ACT Mathematics Test. It is not necessary to worry about your math skills; these skills are addressed in the Math Skills Review. When you have become proficient at careful reading, you will no longer waste valuable time on an individual item trying to determine the exact question that is being asked.

DIRECTIONS: For each of the following items, determine which of the given answer choices is the best restatement of the original item stem. Answers are on page 795.

1. If a machine produces 240 thingamabobs per hour, how many minutes are needed for the machine to produce 30 thingamabobs?

   A. How many minutes does it take to make 270 thingamabobs?
   B. How many minutes does it take to make 8 sets of 30 thingamabobs each?
   C. How many minutes does it take to make 240 thingamabobs at 30 thingamabobs per hour?
   D. How many minutes does it take to make 30 thingamabobs at 240 thingamabobs per hour?

2. After a 20% decrease in price, the cost of an item is D dollars. What was the price of the item before the decrease?

   F. What was the original price of the item?
   G. What was the price before the 80% decrease?
   H. What was the price before the $20 decrease?
   J. What was the price before the 80% increase?

3. If the price of candy increases from 5 pounds for $7 to 3 pounds for $7, how much *less* candy, in pounds, can be purchased for $3.50 at the new price than at the old price?

   A. How much less candy can be purchased for $3.50 at the old price?
   B. How much candy can be purchased for $3.50 at the new price?
   C. How much less candy can be purchased for $3.50 at the new price?
   D. How much candy can be purchased for $3.50 at the old price?

4. A jar contains 24 white marbles and 48 black marbles. What percentage of the marbles in the jar are black?

   F. What percentage of the 72 marbles in the jar are white?
   G. How many more black marbles than white marbles are in the jar?
   H. What percentage of all the marbles in the jar are not black?
   J. Of the 72 white and black marbles in the jar, what percentage are not white?

5. Twenty students attended Professor Rodriguez's class on Monday, and twenty-five students attended on Tuesday. The number of students who attended on Tuesday was what percentage of the number of students who attended on Monday?

   A. 45 students is what percentage of 20 students?
   B. 45 students is what percentage of 25 students?
   C. 25 students is what percentage of 20 students?
   D. 20 students is what percentage of 25 students?

6. Willie's monthly electric bills for last year were as follows: $40, $38, $36, $38, $34, $34, $30, $32, $34, $37, $39, and $40. What was the mode?

   F. What number is the average of the series?
   G. What number occurs least frequently?
   H. What number occurs most frequently?
   J. What number is the median of the series?

7. If 4.5 pounds of chocolate cost $10, how many pounds of chocolate can be purchased for $12?

   A. At the given price, how much more chocolate can be purchased for $12 than $10?
   B. At the given price, what is the cost of 12 pounds of chocolate?
   C. At the given price, how many pounds can be purchased for $12?
   D. At the given price, how many pounds can be purchased for $10?

8. At Star Lake Middle School, 45% of the students bought a yearbook. If 540 students bought yearbooks, how many students did NOT buy a yearbook?

   F. How many students bought a yearbook?
   G. How many students did not buy a yearbook if 45% bought yearbooks?
   H. How many of the 540 students bought a yearbook if 45% bought yearbooks?
   J. How many of the 540 students did not buy a yearbook?

9. Walking at a constant rate of 4 miles per hour, it took Jill exactly 1 hour to walk home from school. If she walked at a constant rate of 5 miles per hour, how many minutes did the trip take?

   A. How long was the trip if Jill walked at a rate of 1 mile per hour when it takes 4 hours to walk home at a rate of 5 miles per hour?
   B. How long was the trip if Jill walked at a rate of 4 miles per hour when it takes 1 hour to walk home at a rate of 5 miles per hour?
   C. How long was the trip if Jill walked at a rate of 5 miles per hour when it takes 1 hour to walk home at a rate of 4 miles per hour?
   D. How long was the trip if Jill walked at a rate of 5 miles per hour when it takes 4 hours to walk home at a rate of 1 mile per hour?

10. If the sum of 5 consecutive integers is 40, what is the smallest of the 5 integers?

   F. What is the smallest of 5 integers that equal 40 when added together?
   G. What is the smallest of 10 consecutive integers that equal 40 when added together?
   H. What is the largest of 5 consecutive integers that equal 40 when added together?
   J. What is the smallest of 5 consecutive integers that equal 40 when added together?

11. Which of the following equations correctly describes the relationship between the values x and y in the table?

   A. According to the table, what is the relationship between x and y as expressed in an equation?
   B. How much larger than x is y?
   C. How much smaller than x is y?
   D. According to the table, what is the relationship between x and z?

12. The quadratic equation $x^2 - 3x = 4$ can be solved by factoring. Which of the following states the complete solution?

   F. What is the complete solution to the quadratic equation $x^2 - 4x = 3$?
   G. What is the complete solution to the quadratic formula?
   H. What is the complete solution to the quadratic equation $x^2 - 3x = 4$?
   J. What is one of the values of x for the given quadratic equation?

13. In a card game, a player had five successful turns in a row, and after each one the number of points added to his total score was double what was added the preceding turn. If the player scored a total of 465 points, how many points did he score on the first turn?

   A. How many points did he score on the fifth turn?
   B. How many total points did he score after all five turns?
   C. How many points did he score after the first turn?
   D. On the first turn, how many points did the player score?

14. At a certain firm, d gallons of fuel are needed per day for each truck. At this rate, g gallons of fuel will supply t trucks for how many days?

   F. How many t trucks will g gallons supply for d days?
   G. d gallons will supply t trucks for how many days if g gallons of fuel are needed per day for each truck?
   H. g gallons will supply t trucks for how many days if d gallons of fuel are needed per day for each truck?
   J. g gallons and d gallons together will supply t trucks for how many days?

15. A merchant increased the price of a $25 item by 10%. If she then reduces the new price by 10%, the final result is equal to which of the following?

   A. What is the final price of a $25 item after its price has been decreased by 10% and the resulting price is then increased by 10%?
   B. What is 10% of 10 $25 items?
   C. What is the final price of a $25 item after its price has been increased by 10% and the resulting price is then decreased by 10%?
   D. How much is 20% of a $25 item?

16. If a train travels m miles in h hours and 45 minutes, what is its average speed in miles per hour?

   F. How long does it take the train to travel 45 miles?
   G. What is the average speed if a train travels h miles in m hours and 45 minutes?
   H. What is the average speed, in miles per hour, if a train travels 45 miles in h hours and m minutes?
   J. What is the average speed if a train travels m miles in h hours and 45 minutes?

17. In a right isosceles triangle, the hypotenuse is equal to which of the following?

   A. What is the hypotenuse of a right triangle?
   B. What is the hypotenuse of a right triangle in which two sides are equal?
   C. What is the hypotenuse of an isosceles triangle in which all three sides are equal?
   D. What is the hypotenuse of a 30°-60°-90° triangle?

18. If a line intersects two points that are plotted at (3,6) and (7,9), what is its slope?

   F. What are the slopes of two lines that include points (3,6) and (7,9), respectively?
   G. What is the slope of a line that includes points (3,6) and (7,−9)?
   H. What is the slope of a line that includes points (6,3) and (9,7)?
   J. What is the slope of a line that includes points (3,6) and (7,9)?

19. The average of 8 numbers is 6; the average of 6 other numbers is 8. What is the average of all 14 numbers?

   A. What is the average of the 8 numbers?
   B. What is the average of all 14 numbers?
   C. What is the average of 8 numbers plus the other average of 6 numbers?
   D. What is the average of the other 6 numbers?

20. If the fourth term in a geometric sequence is 125 and the sixth term is 3,125, what is the second term of the sequence?

   F. What is the second term in the periodic sequence?
   G. What value is represented between the first and third terms in the geometric sequence?
   H. What geometric term represents the process that is necessary to determine the value of the given sequence?
   J. What is the difference between 3,125 and 125?

Careful Reading of Reading Item Stems

The following exercise will help you focus on the exact question that is being asked by Reading item stems that correspond to passages on the ACT Reading Test. There is no need for you to see the entire selection as it would appear on the actual exam. When you have become proficient at careful reading, you will no longer waste valuable time on an individual item trying to determine the exact question that is being asked.

DIRECTIONS: For each of the following items, determine which of the given answer choices is the best restatement of the original item stem. Answers are on page 796.

1. What is the main idea of the passage?

   A. What is the central theme of the passage?
   B. Which specific detail is mentioned in the first paragraph of the passage?
   C. Which idea is always stated in the last paragraph of the passage?
   D. Which idea is a supporting detail in the passage?

2. According to the passage, which of the following was true of the presidential election of 1796?

   F. What did not happen in the presidential election of 1796?
   G. What does the passage say about the presidential election of 1792?
   H. What could have happened in the presidential election of 1796?
   J. What actually happened in the presidential election of 1796?

3. According to the passage, Hamilton's plan did not include which of the following?

   A. What was the focus of Hamilton's plan?
   B. Who opposed Hamilton's plan?
   C. What was not a part of Hamilton's plan?
   D. Which of Hamilton's plans did not succeed?

4. The tone of this passage can best be described as:

   F. What is the main point made by the author?
   G. What is the author's definition of tone?
   H. How does this passage make you feel?
   J. How does the author feel about the topic of the passage?

5. According to the passage, all of the following are true of the Republicans EXCEPT:

   A. What is true of the Republicans?
   B. What is true ONLY of the Republicans?
   C. What is not true of the Republicans?
   D. What is not true ONLY of the Republicans?

6. It can be inferred from the passage that the term "Monocrats" means:

   F. What does the term "Monocrats" mean?
   G. What does the author infer about Monocrats?
   H. Why does the author use the term "Monocrats" in the passage?
   J. Where does the author refer to Monocrats in the passage?

7. Unlike the sublittoral zone, the littoral zone has which of the following features?

   A. What is a definition of the sublittoral zone?
   B. How does the littoral zone differ from the sublittoral zone?
   C. Which characteristic isn't true of either zone?
   D. How are the two zones similar to each other?

8. It can be inferred that Miss Hephzibah views the day's coming events with:

   F. What events occur on this particular day?
   G. Is Miss Hephzibah inferring how the day's events will occur?
   H. How does Miss Hephzibah feel about the day's coming events?
   J. What does Miss Hephzibah infer about the day's coming events?

9. Mrs. Gay's primary quality seems to be her:

   A. How does Mrs. Gay seem to others?
   B. What does Mrs. Gay's primary quality seem to be?
   C. Are the quality views of Mrs. Gay not primarily consistent?
   D. What doesn't the primary quality of Mrs. Gay seem to be?

10. According to the passage, the Republican Party appealed primarily to:

    F. What was the Republican Party's primary appeal?
    G. Who won the Republican Party primary?
    H. Who appealed primarily to the Republican Party?
    J. Who liked the Republican Party?

11. According to the author, most authorities regard the Biarni narrative as:

    A. How do all authorities regard the Biarni narrative?
    B. How do most authorities regard the Biarni narrative?
    C. How does the author regard the Biarni narrative?
    D. How does the author agree with the authorities in regarding the Biarni narrative?

12. According to the passage, radar will have difficulty locating an airplane under which of the following conditions?

    F. What is the ideal condition for radar to function properly?
    G. Under which condition is it impossible to use radar for detecting airplanes?
    H. Under which condition should airplanes not be permitted to fly?
    J. Under which condition will radar have difficulty detecting airplanes?

13. The relationship between the frequency and wavelength of a wave is:

    A. What is the wave's relationship to its frequency?
    B. The frequency and wavelength of a wave have what sort of relationship?
    C. What is the relationship between a wave and its wavelength?
    D. How frequently do wavelengths exhibit a relationship to their respective waves?

14. Since radio waves will not penetrate the ionosphere but microwaves will, would you expect X-rays to penetrate the ionosphere?

    F. Do X-rays penetrate the ionosphere?
    G. Do microwaves penetrate the ionosphere?
    H. Do radio waves penetrate the ionosphere?
    J. Since radio waves penetrate the ionosphere when microwaves do, would you expect X-rays to do the same?

15. Which factor would be most important in order for radar to detect and track storms?

    A. Which is the only important factor in order for radar to detect and track storms?
    B. Which factor is deemed least important for radar to detect and track storms?
    C. The ability of radar to detect and track storms depends most upon which of the following factors?
    D. What is the most important factor for radar to function properly?

16. Which of the following points out a serious weakness in the passage's reasoning?

    F. What would least strengthen the reasoning?
    G. What would most strengthen the reasoning?
    H. What would least weaken the reasoning?
    J. What would most weaken the reasoning?

17. Each of the following could help explain the apparent contradiction EXCEPT:

    A. What is the contradiction?
    B. Why is the contradiction apparent?
    C. What does not help explain the contradiction?
    D. What helps explain the contradiction?

18. Which of the following would most weaken the conclusion?

    F. What would strengthen the conclusion?
    G. What is the weakness of the conclusion?
    H. What is the weakest conclusion?
    J. What would most weaken the conclusion?

19. The passage makes which of the following assumptions?

    A. Which assumption is made by the author?
    B. What is the passage about?
    C. Which of the choices is an assumption?
    D. Which assumption is not made by the author?

20. If the statements are true, which of the following could also be true?

    F. What is not true of the statements?
    G. What could be true of the statements?
    H. What is true all of the time?
    J. What could be true if the statements are true?

21. Which of the following would be the most logical continuation of the passage?

    A. Which ending is the best ending of the passage?
    B. What is the best way to continue the passage?
    C. What is the logical ending of the passage?
    D. What would be the most illogical continuation of the passage?

22. The speaker implies that:

    F. What does the speaker say is implied?
    G. What does the speaker say that could be implied?
    H. What does the speaker imply in the passage?
    J. What doesn't the speaker imply in the passage?

23. The passage assumes that:

    A. What assumption can be made by the reader of the passage?
    B. What is the conclusion of the passage?
    C. What is the main idea of the passage?
    D. What does the author assume in the passage?

24. Which of the following, if true, would best help to explain the apparent contradiction?

    F. Which truth best explains the contradiction?
    G. What is the contradiction?
    H. Why is the contradiction apparently true?
    J. Which contradiction is true?

25. The argument relies primarily on:

    A. Which statement primarily supports the argument?
    B. What is the passage primarily about?
    C. Is the argument of the passage primarily about reliance?
    D. What is the primary argument?

26. Which of the following statements is logically inconsistent with the passage?

    F. Which statement is inconsistently logical?
    G. Which statement is both logical and consistent with the passage?
    H. Which statement is both illogical and inconsistent with the passage?
    J. Which statement does not logically fit within the passage's structure?

27. The main point of the passage is:

    A. What is the main point of the second paragraph?
    B. What is the main idea of the passage?
    C. Which point is a specific detail in the passage?
    D. Which of the following points is not mentioned in the passage?

Careful Reading of Science Item Stems

The following exercise will help you focus on the exact question that is being asked by Science item stems that correspond to passages on the ACT Science Test. There is no need for you to see the entire selection as it would appear on the actual exam. It is also not necessary to worry about your science skills; these skills are addressed in the Science Skills Review. When you have become proficient at careful reading, you will no longer waste valuable time on an individual item trying to determine the exact question that is being asked.

DIRECTIONS: For each of the following items, determine which of the given answer choices is the best restatement of the original item stem. Answers are on page 796.

1. Which of the following would be good animals to use for the experiment?

   A. Which animals are best suited for the experiment?
   B. Which experiment would be most appropriate to determine whether animals are good or bad?
   C. What subject other than animals would be best suited for the experiment?
   D. Which procedure would necessarily follow an experiment on animals?

2. What was the control for temperature in Experiment 5?

   F. What did Experiments 1 through 5 use as the control for temperature?
   G. What was used to control the temperature in Experiment 5?
   H. What was the temperature in Experiment 5?
   J. What did Experiment 5 use as the control for temperature?

3. Which of the following conclusions is consistent with the data presented in the table?

   A. The information provided in the table conforms with which determination?
   B. Which conclusions are consistent with the data presented in the table?
   C. The data provided in the table is not consistent with which conclusion?
   D. Which element of data in the table is most consistent with the following conclusion?

4. Which statement is supported by the results of Experiment 1 alone?

   F. The results of Experiment 1 exclusively support which statement?
   G. Which statement is exclusively supported by the results of Experiment 1?
   H. Without the results of Experiment 1, the results of which experiment would support the statement?
   J. Which statement about Experiment 1 is supported by the results of the other experiments?

5. Which hypothesis best explains the observation that the agar plates never appear clear beyond a 2-inch area surrounding the soaked paper disks?

   A. The observation that the agar plates appear clear beyond a 2-inch area surrounding the soaked paper disks is best explained by which hypothesis?
   B. The condition of the agar plates within a 2-inch area surrounding the soaked paper disks is best explained by which hypothesis?
   C. The condition of the agar plates beyond a 2-inch area surrounding the soaked paper disks is best explained by which hypotheses?
   D. The condition of the agar plates beyond a 2-inch area surrounding the soaked paper disks is best explained by which hypothesis?

6. Which of the following changes in the experiments would have permitted a test of the hypothesis that the quality of a fossil imprint depends on the pressure applied?

   F. A test of the hypothesis that the quality of a fossil imprint does not depend on the pressure applied would have been permitted by which changes in the experiments?
   G. A test of the hypothesis that the quality of a fossil imprint depends on the pressure applied would not have been permitted by which changes in the experiments?
   H. A test of the hypothesis that the quantity of a fossil imprint depends on the pressure applied would have been permitted by which changes in the experiments?
   J. A test of the hypothesis that the quality of a fossil imprint depends on the pressure applied would have been permitted by which changes in the experiments?

7. A scientist seeking to explain why Theory 2 has more predictive power than Theory 1 might argue that:

   A. What might a scientist argue to explain why Theory 2 has more predictive power than Theory 1?
   B. What might a scientist argue to explain why Theory 2 has less predictive power than Theory 1?
   C. What might a scientist argue to explain why Theory 1 has less predictive power than Theory 2?
   D. What might a scientist argue to explain why Theory 1 has more predictive power than Theory 2?

8. Which of the following is the strongest argument that Scientist 1 could use to counter Scientist 2's suggested mechanism for the origin of life?

   F. In order to support Scientist 2's suggested mechanism for the origin of life, which of Scientist 1's arguments is the strongest?
   G. What is Scientist 2's suggested mechanism for the origin of life?
   H. In order to counter Scientist 1's suggested mechanism for the origin of life, which of Scientist 2's arguments is the strongest?
   J. In order to counter Scientist 2's suggested mechanism for the origin of life, which of Scientist 1's arguments is the strongest?

9. According to the graph, female moths are most sensitive to sounds between:

   A. Within what range of sounds do female moths exhibit the least sensitivity?
   B. Within what range of sounds do female moths exhibit the highest sensitivity?
   C. Within what range of sounds do male moths exhibit the highest sensitivity?
   D. Within what range of sounds do male moths exhibit the least sensitivity?

10. It is thought that some species of birds "learn" to fly. This belief is based on observations of young birds fluttering and flapping their wings at the nest until they reach the age when flight is possible. In Species X, nestlings were kept in harmless, but tight, plastic tubes in which they could not carry out such "practice movements." They were released when they reached the age of flight. Viewpoint 1 predicts that the birds will fly:

F. What does Viewpoint 1 predict about all birds' ability to fly?
G. Regarding Species X, what does Viewpoint 1 predict about their ability to fly?
H. Regarding all species of birds other than Species X, what does Viewpoint 1 predict about their ability to fly?
J. What does Viewpoint 1 predict about Species X that Viewpoint 2 also predicts?

11. What is the minimum number of points where two circumferences from two seismic stations, both measuring the same earthquake, can meet?

A. Two circumferences can meet at what maximum number of points?
B. What is the minimum number of earthquakes that two seismic stations can measure?
C. Two circumferences can meet at what minimum number of points?
D. What is the minimum number of seismic stations required to measure an earthquake?

12. Was the site most recently above or below water?

F. Was the site below water?
G. Was the site recently above water?
H. Will the site be above water or below water?
J. As of late, was the site below water or above water?

13. What assumption is made to relate the fossil record to the environment?

A. What relates the fossil record to the environment?
B. What assumption about the fossil record can also be made about the environment?
C. The fossil record is related to the environment based on what assumption?
D. What assumption can be made about the relationship between fossil records and the environment?

14. With which explanation of the similar biochemistry of all life on Earth would Scientist 2 most likely agree?

F. How would Scientist 1 most likely explain the similar biochemistry of all life on Earth?
G. How would Scientist 2 most likely explain the similar biochemistry of all life on Earth?
H. How would Scientist 2 most likely explain the dissimilar biochemistry of all life on Earth?
J. Why does Scientist 2 not agree with the explanation that the biochemistry of all life on Earth is similar?

15. According to the diagram, the trophic level with the largest relative biomass is the:

A. Which diagram depicts the trophic level with the largest relative biomass?
B. How much is the largest relative biomass that is represented by the given trophic levels?
C. According to the diagram, which trophic level has the largest biomass in relationship to the other trophic levels?
D. According to the diagram, why is the trophic level with the largest relative biomass greater than the others?

16. In Experiment 1, gravity accelerates the stone as it falls from the cliff, causing it to pick up speed as it drops. Which of the following series of pictures most resembles how the stone appears as it drops?

    F. The falling stone in Experiment 2 most resembles which group of pictures?

    G. Which group of pictures most resembles the stone as it appears before it is dropped from the cliff in Experiment 1?

    H. Which group of pictures most resembles the decelerating stone as if falls from the cliff in Experiment 1?

    J. The falling stone in Experiment 1 most resembles which group of pictures?

Coding of Reading Item Stems

Most students are pressed for time on the Reading items. You can save time by looking for the correct answers to items as you read the passage for the first time. Reading a passage and answering several corresponding items at the rate of less than one item per minute requires a very different skill than what you would typically use when reading a book, newspaper, or magazine.

For Reading items, you must not only read the item correctly, but you must also correctly identify the item-type. Each Reading item, regardless of the corresponding passage format, will be one of seven basic types. You can avoid memorizing information that is not needed to answer an item by focusing only on the information that is needed to answer the question that is being asked by that specific item-type. Remember that many more questions could be asked about any given passage than are actually asked. If you do not identify the correct item-type, then there is a good chance that you will not use the appropriate strategy for finding the correct answer. You must, therefore, know the characteristics of the correct answer that are associated with each item-type.

Reading items are designed to test three levels of comprehension: appreciation of the general theme, understanding of specific points, and evaluation of the text. This section is designed to help you immediately recognize both the level of comprehension and the item-type that are being tested based on the wording of the item stem. Each of the three levels of comprehension is represented by at least one of the seven types of Reading items. The following descriptions summarize the three levels of reading comprehension and the item-types associated with each.

General Theme

The first level of reading—appreciation of the general theme—is the most basic. *Main Idea* items about the overall theme and development of the selection test whether you understand the passage at the most general level. The first and/or last sentences of paragraphs may be helpful in understanding either the content of a particular paragraph or the general theme of the passage.

Specific Points

The second level of reading—understanding specific points—takes you deeper into the selection. *Explicit Detail* items, items about the meanings of words (*Vocabulary*), and items about the logical roles of details (*Development*) help you understand specific points in the passage and test your ability to read carefully.

Evaluation

The third level of reading—evaluation of the text—takes you even deeper into the selection. *Implied Idea*, *Application*, and *Voice* items require, in addition to an understanding of the material, a judgment or an evaluation of what you have read. As a result, these items tend to be the most difficult.

SEVEN TYPES OF READING ITEMS

Main Idea – What is the unifying theme?

Explicit Detail – What is explicitly mentioned?

Vocabulary – How are certain words used?

Development – How are the ideas constructed and arranged?

Implied Idea – What can be inferred?

Application – How can the information be applied to new situations?

Voice – What does the writer reveal through attitude, voice, or tone?

When taking the test, approach the Reading items in the following way: first, preview the item; second, identify the item-type; third, code each item according to its respective level of reading comprehension; and, finally, think of the characteristics of the correct answer before you begin to read the passage.

Read each passage carefully as you search for clues that will help answer each item. Also, do not "speed-read" or skim through the passage. The faster you read the passage, the less likely you are to pick the correct answer choice. Most answer choices require careful reading, analysis, and application of the facts to the exact question that is being asked.

Comprehension Level Coding

DIRECTIONS: Code each of the following Reading item stems according to one of the three levels of comprehension: General Theme (GT), Specific Points (SP), or Evaluation (E). Answers are on page 796.

1. According to the passage, tears and laughter have all of the following in common EXCEPT:

   _____

2. The author implies that animals lack the ability to:

   _____

3. The word *ludicrous* in line 15 most nearly means:

   _____

4. The author develops the passage primarily by:

   _____

5. In the second paragraph, the author:

   _____

6. Which of the following titles best describes the content of the selection?

   _____

7. The author is primarily concerned with discussing the:

   _____

8. The passage states that the open government statute is intended to accomplish all of the following EXCEPT:

   _____

9. The passage most strongly supports which of the following conclusions about a decision that is within the authority of the executive director of an agency?

   _____

10. In the final paragraph, the author discusses:

    _____

11. The author makes all of the following points about the rules governing the commission EXCEPT:

    _____

12. It can be inferred from the passage that the executive director is authorized to make certain purchases costing less than $5,000 in order to:

    _____

13. Which of the following statements about a "review and comment" session can be inferred from the selection?

    _____

14. According to the passage, all of the following are true of metamorphic rock EXCEPT:

_____

15. As described by the selection, the sequence of events leading to the present landscape was:

_____

16. The author regards the explanation he gives as:

_____

17. The author provides information that defines which of the following terms?

_____

18. The author would most likely agree with which of the following statements?

_____

19. The passage supports which of the following conclusions about the writings of Yevgeny Zamyatin?

_____

20. The author's treatment of James Burnham's writing can best be described as:

_____

21. The statement that Burnham inverted the logical priority of the individual over the state means that Burnham believed that:

_____

22. The author criticized Burnham for:

_____

Item-Type Coding

DIRECTIONS: Code each of the following Reading item stems according to one of the seven item-types: Main Idea (MI), Explicit Detail (ED), Vocabulary (VCB), Development (D), Implied Idea (II), Application (A), or Voice (VCE). Answers are on page 796.

1. According to Burnham, in the completely autocratic state, history will have come to an end because:

2. It can be inferred from the passage that the physical features of a galaxy that do not belong to a rich cluster are determined primarily by the

3. The author implies that the currently accepted theories on galaxy formation are:

4. According to the passage, a cluster with a central, supergiant galaxy will:

5. According to the passage, the outcome of a collision between galaxies depends on which of the following?

6. According to the passage, as a galaxy falls inward toward the center of a cluster, it:

7. According to the passage, a star such as our sun would probably not be found in a cluster such as Virgo because:

8. The phrase "nature never became a toy to the wise spirit" means which of the following?

9. The author implies that the difference between farms and the landscape is primarily a matter of:

10. The author uses the word *property* in the phrase "property in the horizon" (line 20) to mean:

11. The phrase "color of the spirit" in line 25 means:

12. The main purpose of this passage is to:

13. The passage provides information that defines which of the following terms?

14. The author uses all of the following techniques EXCEPT:

15. The author mentions the two high mountains in order to show that it is unlikely to be true that:

_____

16. It can be inferred that the author regards the historicity of the Biarni narrative as:

_____

17. According to the passage, Wineland was characterized by which of the following geographical features?

_____

18. It can be inferred from the passage that scholars who doubt the authenticity of the Biarni narrative make all of the following objections EXCEPT:

_____

19. Which of the following best explains the relationship between the first paragraph and the second paragraph of the passage?

_____

20. All of the following are mentioned as similarities between Leif Erikson's voyage and Biarni's voyage EXCEPT:

_____

21. Which of the following best explains the distinction between a life circumstance and a life event?

_____

22. The author's attitude toward the Aleuts can best be described as one of:

_____

Vocabulary Skills Review

VI. Vocabulary List (p. 655)

Building Vocabulary with Sentence Completions

This Vocabulary Skills Review can be used either in preparation for a specific exam or as a general tool for building vocabulary and reading skills. Whether your objective is to perform well on an exam or to improve your vocabulary and reading skills, you will find the exercises in this review useful.

A good way to build your vocabulary and reading skills is with *sentence completion* items. These items will help to improve your knowledge of sentence structures, transitions, logic, and vocabulary. Sentence completions are also called *completions* or *fill-in-the-blanks.*

Studies have shown that people don't need to hear every word that is said in order to understand the point of what was said. If you think about it, these findings make sense. For example, you could be talking to someone on a cell phone in an area with poor reception and hear: "On your way back to the house, please pick up a medium ------- with mushrooms on it but no anchovies." The most important word in the sentence is missing, but you understand that you're supposed to pick up a pizza. Of course, most sentence completions are not so simple. Consider the following examples of sentence completions:

Examples:

1. To compensate for the funds that will no longer be available due to a decline in the value of the endowment's portfolio, the university will need to find an ------- sum from another source.

    A. anticipated
    B. equivalent
    C. unofficial
    D. unstated
    E. inconsequential

(B) is the correct answer choice. Since funds will no longer be available from the present source, it will be necessary to replace those funds: to do so, the university will need to find an equivalent sum from another source.

2. Although the mobster's efforts to appear mentally unstable and therefore unable to stand trial were ------- and even -------, the defense lawyers, through clever strategies, were able to postpone the criminal proceedings for several years.

    A. unrelenting . . predictable
    B. contrived . . convincing
    C. unpersuasive . . ludicrous
    D. predictable . . amusing
    E. ill-advised . . heroic

(C) is the correct answer choice. The "were ------- and even -------" tells you that the second substitution word makes a more extreme statement than the first. Also, the conjunction "although" at the beginning of the sentence tells you that the substitutions describe an effort that seemed unlikely to work, but that in fact resulted in partial success for the lawyers.

Sentence Completion Difficulty Factors			

There are two difficulty factors involved in every sentence completion item. The first factor is vocabulary. The second factor is context or sentence structure.

Vocabulary

Vocabulary can determine if a sentence completion item is easy or difficult. Compare the two sets of answer choices that follow each of the item stems in the following examples:

Examples:

1. After working together for several years, members of the crew had developed specialized terms for the tools they used, a(n) ------- only they could understand.

A. procedures	vs.	A. procedures
B. customs		B. customs
C. jargon		C. argot
D. appetite		D. appetite
E. rhythm		E. rhythm

   (C) is the correct answer in both sets of answer choices. A specialized vocabulary is called "jargon" or, less commonly, "argot." Although (C) is the answer in both cases, the difficulty level is not. The second set of answer choices is more difficult because "argot" is a less familiar word. So, the difficulty of a sentence completion item can depend upon the vocabulary in the answer choices.

2. Awed by the credentials of the reviewing committee, the doctoral candidate set forth the central thesis of the paper tentatively and answered questions with -------.

A. confidence	vs.	A. aplomb
B. delight		B. relish
C. uncertainty		C. diffidence
D. recklessness		D. abandon
E. directness		E. imperviousness

   (C) is the correct answer in both sets of answer choices. The candidate was awed and set forth the argument tentatively (i.e., not confidently). We can logically assume that the candidate would answer questions in a similar manner, so "uncertainty" is the best word to complete the sentence. Similarly, "diffidence" would also be the best answer here since it means "reserve, shyness, or modesty." Again, although (C) is the answer in both cases, the difficulty level is not. Note too that all of the answer choices in the second column are expressed in less familiar vocabulary. As you can see, an entire set of answer choices that consists of more difficult vocabulary words makes for an even more difficult item.

Complexity

Sentence structure can also determine if a sentence completion item is easy or difficult. In short, more difficult items will involve more difficult sentence structures. Compare the following two item stems:

Example:

Every society has a concept of justice, but what counts as
a just or an unjust act is -------.

vs.

The concept of justice is universal, found in every
society from the most primitive to the most advanced;
but the actions to which these terms attach are -------.

A. variable
B. laudable
C. foreseeable
D. crucial
E. implicit

(A) is the correct answer choice in both cases. In either sentence, the "but" sets up a contrast between an idea in the first part of the sentence and an idea in the second part of the sentence. The important idea in the first part is universality, so the important idea in the second part must be the opposite (i.e., uniqueness or variability).

Of course, the most difficult sentence completion items will include both unfamiliar vocabulary as well as a complex sentence structure. Consider the following example, which is presented with two different sentence structures and sets of answer choices:

Example:

Although the Best in Show was awarded to a dog owned by a relative of the judge, the decision was entirely -------.

A. wrong
B. happy
C. biased
D. pleasant
E. justified

vs.

Although the Best in Show was awarded to a dog owned by a relative of the judge, it cannot be argued that the decision was -------.

A. warranted
B. inconclusive
C. acceptable
D. appropriate
E. unjustified

(E) is the correct answer choice for both items. The conjunction "although" sets up a contrast between the two parts of the sentence. The first part of the sentence explains that the prize was awarded to a relative of the judge, which might suggest unfairness. However, "although" signals that the opposite is true; in other words, the judging was fair. So, (E) is the correct answer choice in both cases. It is more difficult to arrive at the correct answer in the second column, though, for the reasons mentioned above. Specifically, the vocabulary in the second column is less familiar. Also, the sentence structure in the second column is more complicated. As you'll see, sentence structures can be more complicated for several reasons, including the presence of extra clauses, parenthetical notes, or "negative" sentence constructions (i.e., "it can<u>not</u> be argued that the decision was <u>un</u>justified" instead of "the decision was entirely justified").

Sentence Completion Strategies

Anticipation

The first step when solving a sentence completion item is to read the sentence for meaning. Read the sentence at normal speed, as though someone were speaking to you. Then, identify one or two words that could complete the sentence successfully. If you're lucky, one of your words will appear in the list of answer choices. If that does not happen, look for the answer choice that is most similar to what you anticipated and that completes the sentence successfully.

Examples:

1. After his novel was rejected by six publishers, John became embittered and -------, so much so that his friends feared for his sanity.

    A. gentle
    B. wary
    C. morose
    D. pacified
    E. prudent

The question stem establishes that John was embittered, which is a negative state of emotion. So, you want to select the answer choice that also describes a negative emotional state. You might have anticipated words such as "disappointed," "angry," "depressed," or "sullen" to complete the sentence. These words do not appear in the list of answer choices, but "morose" is a negative emotional state consistent with feeling embittered. So, (C) is the correct answer choice.

2. Given the rapidly changing nature of today's technological society, schools can no longer hope to teach eternal principles, for by tomorrow, today's knowledge is -------.

    A. enriched
    B. reproduced
    C. adequate
    D. precarious
    E. obsolete

The question stem sets up a contrast between "eternal principles" and knowledge that is not eternal. You might have anticipated words such as "temporary," "outdated," or "transient" to complete the sentence. These words do not appear in the list of answer choices, but "obsolete" has a similar meaning. So, (E) is the best answer choice.

3. Retiring by nature and ------- even in private, Eleanor hardly ever spoke in public.

    A. confident
    B. taciturn
    C. preoccupied
    D. untamed
    E. courageous

The question stem tells you that Eleanor was unwilling to speak. So, the sentence could be completed with words such as "quiet" or "silent." Those words do not appear in the list of answer choices, but "taciturn" has a similar meaning. So, (B) is the correct answer choice.

Analysis

When reading a sentence completion item, pay attention to verbal signals. Verbal signals will tell you how the parts of a sentence fit together. For example, they can tell you:

- if one part of a sentence clarifies or adds detail to another;

- if a later element contradicts an earlier element; and

- if one idea is qualified or overruled by another.

Examples:

1. It is a rare individual who bothers to examine his or her fundamental ethical beliefs; indeed, the effort required ------- most people from even starting.

    A. cautions
    B. discourages
    C. sustains
    D. recalls
    E. withdraws

In this item, "indeed" is an important verbal signal. It indicates that the second part of the sentence supports or underscores the first part. So, if the first part states that few people bother to examine their beliefs, the second part goes one step further and says that the effort required "discourages" most people from doing so. Therefore, the correct answer is (B).

2. Although ------- in her criticism of the minutest details, she often ------- the larger picture; so her input was incomplete.

    A. understated . . conspired
    B. sparing . . omitted
    C. exhaustive . . overlooked
    D. creative . . presented
    E. meticulous . . emphasized

In this item, "although" is an important verbal signal. It indicates that the second part of the sentence will contrast with the first part. As a result, the two substitutions must be opposites or express dissimilar ideas. One would not expect someone described as "exhaustive" to have "overlooked" any detail, so (C) is the correct answer.

Finally, the following table has two columns. The first column is a list of signal words that are frequently used in sentence completion items. The second column explains the function of each signal word (i.e., it summarizes the logical relationship that is suggested or established by the signal word) and should be helpful when reviewing answer choices for sentence completions items.

Signal Word	What to Look for in Sentence Completion
therefore, thus, consequently, so, as a result	a further conclusion, the effect of a cause, an expected outcome
if, since, because	a premise of a logical argument, a cause leading to an effect, a condition or conditions leading to an outcome
and, additionally, further, moreover, similarly, likewise	further extension of a thought, a parallel or similar idea, added emphasis
although, though, while, but, rather, however, despite, unlike, yet, not	contrasting ideas, an exception, a reversal of thinking
indeed, in fact	an example, an idea for added emphasis
(:) colon	enumeration, clarification, further detail

This list of signal words is not exhaustive, but it highlights the type of verbal clue that can be very important in sentence completion items.

Substitution

In the end, some items still might seem too difficult to solve. The sentence structure might be too complex; the vocabulary might be too unfamiliar; or, even after evaluating verbal signals, the logic of the sentence might not make sense to you. If this happens, try substituting or plugging the answer choices into the sentence. You might find that, in the end, this simple step will help you to locate the correct answer choice.

Anticipating Sentence Completions

DIRECTIONS: For items #1–10, read each sentence through for meaning. Then, in the space provided, write a few possible words that you anticipate could be used to complete the sentence. Answers are on page 797.

1. Stress is the reaction an individual feels when he believes the demands of a situation ------- his ability to meet them.

   _____

   _____

   _____

2. The ------- of his career, capturing the coveted "Most Valuable Player" award, came at a time of deep personal sadness.

   _____

   _____

   _____

3. Martin's opponent is a(n) ------- speaker who is unable to elicit a reaction from a crowd on even the most emotional of issues.

   _____

   _____

   _____

4. The cold weather caused ------- damage to the Florida citrus crop, prompting growers to warn that the reduced yield is likely to result in much higher prices.

   _____

   _____

   _____

5. The report is so ------- that it covers all of the main points in detail and at least touches on everything that is even remotely connected with its topic.

   _____

   _____

   _____

6. The Constitution sets up a system of checks and balances among the executive, the legislative, and the judicial branches to ensure that no one branch can establish ------- control over the government.

   _____

   _____

   _____

7. The females of many common species of birds have dull coloring that ------- them when they are sitting on a nest in a tree or other foliage.

_____

_____

8. She was one of the most ------- criminals of the 1930s, her name a household word and her face in every post office.

_____

_____

9. Although he had not been physically injured by the explosion, the violence of the shock left him temporarily -------.

_____

_____

10. Good teachers know that study habits learned as a youngster stay with a student for life, so they try to find ways to ------- enthusiasm for studies.

_____

_____

DIRECTIONS: For items #11–20, read each sentence through for meaning. Then, in the space provided, enter your anticipated completion. Finally, match your anticipated completion to one of the answer choices for that item. Answers are on page 797.

11. Even those who vigorously disagreed with the goals of the plan ------- admitted that it had been well designed.

_____

   A. erroneously
   B. valiantly
   C. successfully
   D. defiantly
   E. grudgingly

12. The so-called "road rage" is just one more example of a more general ------- that includes disrespect for rules, traditions, and institutions.

_____

   A. incivility
   B. caution
   C. curiosity
   D. passion
   E. apprehension

13. Random noises have been shown to ------- sleep cycles, causing fatigue and irritability in test subjects.

_____

   A. reinforce
   B. disrupt
   C. solidify
   D. undermine
   E. fracture

14. Increasingly, state legislatures have enacted laws that use a standardized exam as the sole ------- by which the success or failure a school system is to be judged.

A. prediction
B. guarantee
C. actuality
D. criterion
E. aspiration

15. A fine public servant with an otherwise untarnished reputation has become the latest ------- in a war being waged by unscrupulous journalists against those who espouse principles they reject.

A. happenstance
B. victory
C. casualty
D. detriment
E. fiasco

16. The new bookstore, with its coffee bar and classical music, hopes that its literature selections will appeal to a ------- clientele.

A. sophisticated
B. conventional
C. provocative
D. restrictive
E. passive

17. The corporation's spokesperson ------- the report as junk science and accused the researchers of pursuing a political agenda.

A. highlighted
B. denounced
C. withdrew
D. fomented
E. inscribed

18. By the terms of the extremely ------- curriculum, all students at the academy were required to take two years of Latin, two years of algebra, and two years of fine arts.

A. industrious
B. fractured
C. provocative
D. valiant
E. regimented

19. The polite veneer that John exhibits in public ------- a violent temper that frequently erupts in private, especially when his authority is challenged.

A. condemns
B. belies
C. validates
D. queries
E. presages

20. Long hours of ------- rehearsal ensured that the orchestra performed the difficult piece flawlessly.

A. arduous
B. spontaneous
C. influential
D. jubilant
E. temporary

Analyzing Sentence Completions

DIRECTIONS: For items #1–10, analyze each sentence by underlining a few words or phrases that provide clues for the completion of the sentences. Then, write down a few possible words that you anticipate could be used to complete the sentence. Answers are on page 797.

1. The survivors had been drifting for days in the lifeboat, and in their weakness, they appeared to be ------- rather than living beings.

   _____

   _____

   _____

2. The guillotine was introduced during the French Revolution as a(n) -------, an alternative to other less humane means of execution.

   _____

   _____

   _____

3. Because of the ------- nature of the chemical, it cannot be used near an open flame.

   _____

   _____

   _____

4. The Mayor's proposal for a new subway line, although a(n) -------, is not a final solution to the city's transportation needs.

   _____

   _____

   _____

5. In a pluralistic society, policies are the result of compromise, so political leaders must be ------- and must accommodate the views of others.

   _____

   _____

   _____

6. The committee report vigorously expounded the bill's strengths but also acknowledged its -------.

   _____

   _____

   _____

7. Because there is always the danger of a power failure and disruption of elevator service, high-rise buildings, while suitable for younger persons, are not recommended for -------.

   _____

   _____

   _____

8. For a child to be happy, his day must be very structured; when his routine is -------, he becomes nervous and irritable.

_____

_____

_____

9. The current spirit of ------- among different religions has led to a number of meetings that their leaders hope will lead to better understanding.

_____

_____

_____

10. Our modern industrialized societies have been responsible for the greatest destruction of nature and life; indeed, it seems that more civilization results in greater -------.

_____

_____

_____

DIRECTIONS: For items #11–20, answer each sentence completion using verbal signals to analyze the logical structure of the sentence. Circle the letter of your answer choice. Answers are on page 797.

11. When Ghana achieved independence from colonial domination in 1957, the first country in sub-Saharan Africa to do so, it ------- economic and political advantages unrivaled elsewhere in tropical Africa.

A. demanded
B. enjoyed
C. proclaimed
D. denounced
E. incited

12. Fraktur, a genre of folk art that has its roots in the Rhine Valley, is ------- to the Pennsylvania Dutch region, though Russian-German Mennonites produced similar but ------- ornamental drawings.

A. endemic . . characteristic
B. inherent . . distinct
C. native . . unusual
D. reduced . . inconsequential
E. unique . . unrelated

13. The Free Trade Zone law was enacted in order to ------- legal issues left open by the Supreme Court case of California v. Bond.

A. resolve
B. undermine
C. redress
D. present
E. nullify

14. Scholars often speak of an early and a late Heidegger, but a more careful reading reveals only a(n) ------- shift rather than a radical ------- in his thought.

A. evolutionary . . bent
B. discernible . . consistency
C. inevitable . . temper
D. unpredictable . . change
E. gradual . . discontinuity

15. Van Gogh was virtually ------- at the time of his death: his agent, brother Theo, had sold only one of his paintings.

    A. unknown
    B. famous
    C. wealthy
    D. victorious
    E. adored

16. Legalized gambling seems to offer unlimited governmental revenue without the need to raise taxes; however, experience shows that casino gambling is not the financial ------- claimed by its proponents.

    A. panacea
    B. calamity
    C. incentive
    D. predicament
    E. validation

17. Low on supplies and badly in need of fresh troops, General Burgoyne's ------- and even ------- decision to push ahead resulted in disaster at Saratoga.

    A. reflective . . conscientious
    B. valorous . . cowardly
    C. rash . . foolhardy
    D. ill-advised . . calculated
    E. victorious . . generous

18. Although the Ford Edsel of the 1950s is commonly thought of as a "lemon," the car was actually -------; it was the victim of marketing, not ------- failures.

    A. attractive . . sales
    B. well-made . . engineering
    C. high-priced . . design
    D. desirable . . advertising
    E. well-known . . manufacturing

19. No reasonable trade-off between unemployment and inflation can be achieved by either monetary or fiscal policy alone; rather, both must be regarded as ------- tools for managing the economy.

    A. complementary
    B. intelligible
    C. unnecessary
    D. delicate
    E. unlimited

20. Professional schools assemble a(n) ------- student body not for the sake of enriching extracurricular life, but for the variety of personal and academic backgrounds that enhance the learning experience.

    A. homogeneous
    B. knowledgeable
    C. elite
    D. unexceptional
    E. diverse

Substituting Sentence Completions

DIRECTIONS: For items #1–12, select an appropriate completion for the corresponding blank in the following paragraph. Answers are on page 798.

Today, the Surgeon General announced the findings of a new ------- that concludes that smoking

represents a serious ------- to non-smokers as well as to

-------. According to the Surgeon General, disease risk
3

due to ------- of tobacco smoke is not limited to the
4

------- who is smoking, but it can also extend to those
5

who ------- tobacco smoke in the same room. Simple
6

------- of smokers and non-smokers within the same
7

airspace may reduce, but does not -------, exposure of
8

non-smokers to environmental smoke. A spokesperson

for the tobacco industry ------- the report, saying the
9

available ------- does not support the conclusion that
10

environmental tobacco smoke is a hazard to non-

smokers. On the other hand, the Coalition for

Smoking on Health, an anti-smoking organization,

------- the report and called for ------- government
11   12

action to ensure a smoke-free environment for all non-

smokers.

1. A. movie
    B. election
    C. report
    D. advertisement
    E. scholarship

2. A. consciousness
    B. hazard
    C. remedy
    D. possibility
    E. adaptation

3. A. cigarettes
    B. fumes
    C. alcoholics
    D. non-smokers
    E. smokers

4. A. observation
    B. criticism
    C. improvement
    D. inhalation
    E. incorporation

5. A. individual
    B. corporation
    C. doctor
    D. campaign
    E. reporter

6. A. create
    B. breathe
    C. enjoy
    D. ban
    E. exhibit

7. A. encouragement
    B. prohibition
    C. separation
    D. intermingling
    E. cooperation

8. A. imagine
   B. increase
   C. prepare
   D. intimidate
   E. eliminate

9. A. purchased
   B. prepared
   C. understood
   D. criticized
   E. underscored

10. A. alibi
    B. publicity
    C. evidence
    D. reaction
    E. conversation

11. A. praised
    B. rejected
    C. prolonged
    D. denied
    E. criticized

12. A. minimal
    B. immediate
    C. reactionary
    D. uncontrolled
    E. eliminating

DIRECTIONS: For items #13–17, answer each sentence completion using substitution. Circle the letter of your answer choice. Answers are on page 798.

13. The Senator frequently ------- other members of the chamber with unwarranted attacks on their personal lives.

    A. provokes
    B. analyzes
    C. enhances
    D. deprives
    E. elevates

14. Clyde's ------- occasionally astonished even his closest friends who knew full-well that his had been a(n) ------- childhood.

    A. sophistication . . extended
    B. naiveté . . sheltered
    C. wit . . precocious
    D. knowledge . . difficult
    E. wisdom . . uneducated

15. Research into sleep suggests that there are several ------- states between sleeping and waking and that it is difficult to determine where one ends and another begins.

    A. serious
    B. permissive
    C. predetermined
    D. unalterable
    E. intermediate

16. The playwright took a story so sublime that it has offered the ultimate challenge to composers, choreographers, and writers for centuries and, with a wanton heavy-handedness, gave the audience a hackneyed version that descended into -------.

    A. confusion
    B. bathos
    C. inattention
    D. significance
    E. indecision

17. Sensing his position was all but lost, the speaker launched into -------, hoping to save the day by rhetoric rather than reason.

    A. rationalization
    B. recapitulation
    C. dramatization
    D. exactitude
    E. peroration

EXERCISE 4

Building Vocabulary with Sentence Completions

DIRECTIONS: Each of the following sentences has one or two blanks. Choose the word or phrase for each blank that best fits the meaning of the sentence in its entirety. Circle the letter of your answer choice. Answers are on page 798.

1. While the fame of musical geniuses like Mozart and Beethoven endures for centuries, the idols of pop music quickly fade into -------.

   A. obscurity
   B. disbelief
   C. permanence
   D. poverty
   E. notoriety

2. In order to prevent an increase in the number of unemployed people, the economy must expand to ------- new jobs to offset those lost to factories in other countries.

   A. extinguish
   B. create
   C. prolong
   D. conceal
   E. avoid

3. In order to protect her privacy, the former employee spoke to reporters about the safety violations only after they guaranteed her -------.

   A. compensation
   B. publicity
   C. representation
   D. anonymity
   E. loyalty

4. In the State of Nature, described by Thomas Hobbes in *Leviathan* as a state of war, one against all others, no individual has sufficient physical strength to be assured of personal security, so all rely on -------.

   A. animosity
   B. premeditation
   C. principles
   D. prowess
   E. allies

5. Members of the Research and Development Council had been warned that the prototype was extremely -------, but were pleasantly surprised to see a model with many ------- usually incorporated only much later in the design process.

   A. crude . . refinements
   B. flexible . . advances
   C. rudimentary . . deficiencies
   D. unreliable . . trappings
   E. casual . . advantages

6. Although the developmental sequence of the reproductive cycle in insects is similar for many species, the timing can ------- greatly in regard to the beginning and duration of each stage.

   A. endure
   B. accelerate
   C. vary
   D. proceed
   E. coincide

7. The "framers' original intent" theory of Constitutional interpretation, though now ------- within academic circles, still has considerable practical effect because it is ------- by many sitting judges.

   A. propounded . . accepted
   B. disseminated . . rejected
   C. corroborated . . critiqued
   D. dismissed . . espoused
   E. encapsulated . . emphasized

8. Proponents of a flat tax hope to substitute a single federal revenue-raising measure for the ------- of convoluted and even self-contradictory provisions of the present tax code.

   A. tapestry
   B. concordance
   C. cacophony
   D. duplicity
   E. welter

9. An examination of the psychological forces that shape the personality of the title character of *The Magus* naturally invites closer study of its form, as story content and form are carefully ------- by Fowles in the novel.

   A. delineated
   B. anticipated
   C. integrated
   D. determined
   E. reserved

10. The broadcast of the story has seriously compromised the credibility of the entire news department: the key piece of information, though not ------- on the one particular point, is expected to support a vast ------- of implications for which no other proof is offered.

    A. fabricated . . contradiction
    B. unconvincing . . superstructure
    C. persuasive . . convocation
    D. inextricable . . skein
    E. conclusive . . facsimile

11. By and large, Wittgenstein's treatment of language in *The Philosophical Investigations* will be ------- to the lay person, but the more ------- points will be grasped only by specialists in the philosophy of language.

    A. granted . . general
    B. accessible . . esoteric
    C. concrete . . ingenious
    D. alien . . technical
    E. attractive . . abstract

12. For many years, the cost of faculty salaries and benefits rose faster than tuition and contributions to endowments so that some ------- were in danger of becoming -------.

    A. colleges . . expensive
    B. universities . . insolvent
    C. students . . dropouts
    D. unions . . superfluous
    E. teachers . . replaceable

13. In an effort to render as accurately as possible ------- lighting conditions, French Impressionist Claude Monet worked on several paintings at once, frantically changing canvases as ------- alterations in illumination created almost imperceptible new visual effects.

    A. essential . . unimportant
    B. transitory . . subtle
    C. momentary . . evident
    D. prototypical . . minute
    E. classical . . improbable

14. During the 1980s, fortunes were made on a seemingly daily basis by ------- traders who ------- conventional wisdom on investing in the stock market.

    A. maverick . . flouted
    B. rogue . . applied
    C. impoverished . . acknowledged
    D. devious . . promulgated
    E. renegade . . propounded

15. A fire in the Peoples Republic of China destroyed the factory responsible for producing most of the world's RAM memory components; the ensuing shortage was so ------- that computer users came to believe that the high prices were the result of ------- by suppliers.

    A. prolonged . . coddling
    B. insignificant . . touting
    C. ineffectual . . directing
    D. severe . . gouging
    E. unpredictable . . misleading

16. The idea that a single individual can alter the course of history is not mere speculation; in fact, well-documented instances are not even -------.

    A. established
    B. confirmable
    C. conceivable
    D. actualized
    E. exceptional

17. Some proponents of an author's lending royalty plan argue that borrowing a book from a library is a form of ------- since the reader enjoys the intellectual property without ------- the author.

    A. theft . . acknowledging
    B. piracy . . protecting
    C. contract . . paying
    D. servitude . . releasing
    E. larceny . . compensating

18. Though it seemed that director Robert Altman had firmly established his artistic reputation with the nomination of *Nashville* for Best Film of 1970, the 1979 film *Quintet*, perhaps the ------- of his career, earned him only the ------- of the critics.

    A. nadir . . disapprobation
    B. continuation . . notice
    C. denouement . . acclaim
    D. climax . . commentary
    E. low point . . recommendation

19. Albert's advanced degree in urban planning made him the most qualified person on the committee, but his status as the junior member made his criticism of transportation policy seem ------- even though his remarks were always -------.

    A. unwarranted . . superficial
    B. opportunistic . . spontaneous
    C. presumptuous . . incisive
    D. vapid . . insincere
    E. practical . . inappropriate

20. The professor's ------- treatment of students in the classroom contrasted with her behavior in the office, where those who sought advice found her to be genuinely ------- to their problems.

    A. supercilious . . sympathetic
    B. arrogant . . indifferent
    C. cavalier . . calloused
    D. cautious . . attentive
    E. inconsistent . . hardened

21. Legal positivists deny that international law can properly be called law because international organizations can only ------- prohibited conduct but do nothing to ------- it.

    A. investigate . . review
    B. identify . . encourage
    C. provoke . . rectify
    D. outline . . satisfy
    E. define . . punish

22. Following the ------- emotional pleas for passage of the bill by members known for rambling speeches, the ------- argument for its rejection was a welcome relief for the House.

    A. protracted . . trenchant
    B. lengthy . . specious
    C. flowery . . ornate
    D. undisguised . . deceiving
    E. blatant . . unfocused

23. In his treatment of science, Ernst Cassirer rejects the traditional ------- of fact and theory, approvingly quoting Goethe as saying "All fact is theory."

 A. asymmetry
 B. dichotomy
 C. frequency
 D. conjunction
 E. dysfunction

24. Although Jacques Derrida's writings held considerable theoretical promise, deconstructionism in America quickly deteriorated into a ------- as academics of limited intellectual ability mimicked its style without ------- its secrets.

 A. farce . . plumbing
 B. battle . . understanding
 C. burlesque . . concealing
 D. comedy . . purporting
 E. pretense . . sharing

25. Students had become so ------- to the principal's capriciousness that they greeted the announcement of yet another dress code with complete indifference.

 A. receptive
 B. inured
 C. sensitive
 D. attuned
 E. evasive

26. Recent journalistic reports of respected researchers ------- experimental results favorable to their own theories ------- the popular conception of science as a pure search for the truth.

 A. manufacturing . . supports
 B. presenting . . belies
 C. finding . . reinforces
 D. fabricating . . contradicts
 E. concealing . . undermines

27. A recurring theme in science fiction is the contest between good and evil for control over technology that is, in itself, -------.

 A. productive
 B. ill-conceived
 C. independent
 D. amoral
 E. inconsequential

28. In *The Ontology of Political Violence*, Professor Nogarola argues that so-called ------- evidence often dismissed as unreliable would be admissible in a court of law as testimony and has value in the political arena as well.

 A. anecdotal
 B. practical
 C. sensational
 D. collaborative
 E. probative

29. Ironically, the modern Olympic games, which are held up as the ideal of amateur athletics, originated with games in honor of Athena in which winners were rewarded not with laurel wreaths of little ------- worth but oil-filled amphorae with considerable ------- value.

 A. practical . . sentimental
 B. financial . . honorific
 C. market . . aesthetic
 D. capital . . sacrificial
 E. intrinsic . . economic

30. Supply creates its own demand; and advertising, if sufficiently -------, can convince consumers to ------- products for which they have little desire and even less need.

 A. strident . . approve
 B. pervasive . . purchase
 C. unscrupulous . . honor
 D. distasteful . . disregard
 E. vehement . . anticipate

31. In an effort to ------- the strike, the mediators suggested a compromise that they thought would be ------- to both the union and the company.

   A. shorten . . unpalatable
   B. resolve . . satisfactory
   C. end . . unacceptable
   D. extend . . acceptable
   E. accelerate . . puzzling

32. Because of the tremendous magnifying power of the Hubble Telescope, astronomical features that were before ------- are now resolved into fine detail.

   A. indistinguishable
   B. inapplicable
   C. intractable
   D. inalienable
   E. invaluable

33. Paradoxically, the more the audiences applauded his performances and critics praised his artistic accomplishments, the more ------- Isaac felt about his ability as a musician.

   A. decisive
   B. insecure
   C. confident
   D. reluctant
   E. assertive

34. An important goal of Black History Month is to ensure that African-Americans who have often received too little credit for their achievements in fields ranging from literature to physics are more widely -------.

   A. sustained
   B. acknowledged
   C. embellished
   D. retained
   E. envied

35. The directors who favored the plan to diversify overseas operations, though in ------- following their failed experiment on the domestic side, constituted a sufficiently ------- political force on the Board to gain a favorable vote.

   A. retreat . . cohesive
   B. disarray . . ineffective
   C. control . . powerful
   D. abeyance . . contentious
   E. disfavor . . fragmented

36. Our relegation of the fairy tale to the status of bedtime reading for children has resulted in the ------- of the goriest details from the Grimm tales.

   A. ratification
   B. reinsertion
   C. accentuation
   D. expurgation
   E. codification

37. For all of his outlandish costumes and immoderate behavior on-stage, rock musician Arlen Quigby was, in his private life, a(n) ------- person who was described by associates as a simple businessman.

   A. enigmatic
   B. famous
   C. conventional
   D. unstable
   E. flamboyant

38. As vaccines have become increasingly -------, cases of Haemophilius influenza among children under the age of five dropped nearly 99% in the last ten years, and the disease has been nearly -------.

   A. routine . . eradicated
   B. virile . . annihilated
   C. innocuous . . obliterated
   D. problematic . . rampant
   E. inefficacious . . contained

39. The script writers for the stage version of Kipling's *Just So Stories* wisely decided to make only ------- use of the author's original diction; the occasional flashes of alliteration are charming but overdone; their arcane sound would quickly have become ------- to the modern ear.

    A. judicious . . familiar
    B. intermittent . . inaudible
    C. sporadic . . cloying
    D. exacting . . familiar
    E. limited . . dissonant

40. Several highly publicized disagreements within the scientific community have become so ------- that many lay people now wonder whether the scientific process is a search for the truth or a contest of -------.

    A. repetitive . . platitudes
    B. egregious . . wills
    C. cacophonous . . theories
    D. acrimonious . . egos
    E. exuberant . . resources

Building Vocabulary with Antonyms

Antonym items ask you to find a word that means the opposite of the given word.

Example:

ACCEPT:

A. desire
B. pretend
C. reject
D. inquire
E. trap

(C) is the correct answer choice because to reject something is the opposite of to accept something.

Antonym items on standardized tests tend to be arranged in order of increasing difficulty since they test variations on meaning. Consider another example:

Example:

CULTIVATED:

A. treacherous
B. prepared
C. worried
D. insightful
E. uncultured

"Cultivated" can function as a verb or an adjective. To determine what part of speech is being tested, examine all of the answer choices. (B) and (C) can be verbs or adjectives. (A), (D), and (E) can only be adjectives. So, in this case, the item stem ("CULTIVATED") should be treated as an adjective. The primary definition of the adjective "cultivated" is "of, or relating to the preparation of land." You might anticipate an adjective like "fallow" as a possible antonym; however, no such word appears in the answer choices. Instead, the secondary definition of the adjective "cultivated" ("cultured" or "highly developed") is being tested. For example, a person may have cultivated or refined tastes. Therefore, (E) is the correct answer choice because "uncultured" means the opposite of "cultivated."

The two definitions of the adjective "cultivated" are not unrelated, and you should be able to see that the literal idea of cultivating land resembles the more figurative idea of cultivating or refining one's taste. Both definitions involve the idea of refinement or improvement. Such relationships between definitions are referred to as "echoes". Correctly answering antonym items often depends on the ability to hear these echoes.

In the following example, the meaning of a word varies based on whether it's used as a noun or a verb. As a result, the antonym item is more difficult.

Example:

AIR:

- A. vacate
- B. remind
- C. take
- D. conceal
- E. pose

The word "air" typically functions as a noun, which means "atmosphere." Again, though, review all of the answer choices to determine the part of speech being tested. All of the answer choices function only as verbs except for (E), which can also function as a noun. So, the item stem ("AIR") should be treated as a verb. The verb "air" can mean either "to expose to air" or "to make public." Both of these definitions involve the idea of exposure. Therefore, (D) is the correct answer choice because to conceal, which means "to hide," is the opposite of to publicize.

Building Vocabulary with Analogies

Analogy items, like antonym items, test your ability to understand relationships between vocabulary words. The most helpful example of an analogy is a mathematical proportion:

$$\frac{2}{3} = \frac{10}{15}$$

This mathematical statement asserts that 2 has the same relationship to 3 that 10 has to 15. This parallelism is an important feature of all analogies. We find the same parallelism in the following verbal analogy:

PULVERIZE : DUST :: SHATTER : SHARDS

The colons in the verbal analogy serve the same function as the slashes in the mathematical proportion. Also, the double colon in the verbal analogy serves the same function as the equals sign in the mathematical proportion:

$$\frac{\text{PULVERIZE}}{\text{DUST}} = \frac{\text{SHATTER}}{\text{SHARDS}}$$

This verbal analogy asserts that "pulverize" has the same relationship to "dust" as "shatter" has to "shards." To pulverize something is to reduce it to dust, and to shatter something is to reduce it to shards.

Verbal analogies are also often characterized by a secondary feature. To pulverize and to shatter are *both* means of destruction, and dust and shards are *both* the results of destruction. Such secondary relationships can often help you answer analogy items more quickly and accurately.

Building Vocabulary through Context

Unlike other vocabulary books that provide random lists of words and their definitions, this program builds vocabulary by helping you to learn the meaning of words in the context of short stories, essays, and other types of reading selections.

Students often believe that if they don't know what a word means, they won't be able to answer correctly an item that includes that word. This is simply not true. This section will help you to recognize word parts, become more familiar with challenging vocabulary words, and use context clues to determine what difficult words mean. This section will also help you to understand the logical structure of a sentence and how to use that understanding to anticipate appropriate words in vocabulary-related items.

The exercises in this section will enrich and build your vocabulary skills. You will learn vocabulary words in the context of a reading selection (vocabulary-in-context and sentence completion items) so you can actually learn them rather than simply memorize them. Additionally, antonym and analogy items will build your awareness of "echoes" or secondary relationships—a skill that will also strengthen your vocabulary and reading skills.

Building Vocabulary through Context

DIRECTIONS: The following passage is followed by several items. Read the passage and choose the best answer for each item based on what is stated or implied in the passage. You may refer to the passage as often as necessary to answer the items. Answers are on page 798.

SOCIAL SCIENCE: The following passage is an excerpt from a history of the political career of Thomas Jefferson, the author of the "Declaration of Independence."

"Heartily tired" from the brutal, almost daily conflicts that erupted over questions of national policy between himself and Alexander Hamilton, Thomas Jefferson resigned his position as Secretary of State in
5 1793. Although his Federalist opponents were convinced that this was merely a strategic withdrawal to allow him an opportunity to plan and promote his candidacy for the Presidency should Washington step down in 1796, Jefferson insisted that this retirement
10 from public life was to be final.

But even in retirement, the world of politics pursued him. As the election grew nearer and it became apparent that Washington would not seek a third term, rumors of Jefferson's Presidential ambitions grew in
15 intensity. Reacting to these continuous insinuations in a letter to James Madison, Jefferson allowed that while the idea that he coveted the office of chief executive had been originated by his enemies to impugn his political motives, he had been forced to examine his
20 true feelings on the subject for his own peace of mind. In so doing he concluded that his reasons for retirement—the desire for privacy, and the delight of family life—coupled with his now failing health were insuperable barriers to public service. The "little spice
25 of ambition" he had in his younger days had long since evaporated and the question of his Presidency was forever closed.

Jefferson did not actively engage in the campaign on his own behalf. The Republican party, anticipating
30 modern campaign tactics, created grass roots sentiment for their candidate by directing their efforts toward the general populace. In newspapers, Jefferson was presented as the uniform advocate of equal rights among the citizens while Adams was portrayed as the
35 champion of rank, titles, heredity, and distinctions. Jefferson was not certain of the outcome of the election until the end of December. Under the original electoral system established by the Constitution, each Presidential elector cast his ballot for two men without
40 designating between them as to office. The candidate who received the greater number of votes became the President; the second highest, the Vice President. Jefferson foresaw on the basis of his own calculations that the electoral vote would be close. He wrote to
45 Madison that in the event of a tie, he wished for the choice to be in favor of Adams. In public life, the New Englander had always been senior to Jefferson; and so, he explained, the expression of public will being equal, Adams should be preferred for the higher honor.
50 Jefferson, a shrewd politician, realized that the transition of power from the nearly mythical Washington to a lesser luminary in the midst of the deep and bitter political divisions facing the nation could be perilous, and he had no desire to be caught in
55 the storm that had been brewing for four years and was about to break. "This is certainly not a moment to covet the helm," he wrote to Edward Rutledge. When the electoral vote was tallied, Adams emerged the victor. Rejoicing at his "escape," Jefferson was completely
60 satisfied with the decision. Despite their obvious and basic political differences, Jefferson genuinely respected John Adams as a friend and compatriot. Although Jefferson believed that *Adams* had deviated from the course set in 1776, in Jefferson's eyes he
65 never suffered diminution; and Jefferson was quite confident that Adams would not steer the nation too far from its Republican tack. Within two years, Jefferson's views would be drastically altered as measures such as the Alien and Sedition Acts of 1798 convinced him of
70 the need to wrest control of the government from the Federalists.

1. In line 1, the word *heartily* most nearly means:

   A. sincerely.
   B. vigorously.
   C. zealously.
   D. completely.

2. In line 10, the word *public* most nearly means:

   A. communal.
   B. open.
   C. official.
   D. people.

3. In line 10, the word *final* most nearly means:

   A. last.
   B. closing.
   C. ultimate.
   D. conclusive.

4. In line 16, the word *allowed* most nearly means:

   A. permitted.
   B. admitted.
   C. tolerated.
   D. granted.

5. In line 29, the word *anticipating* most nearly means:

   A. expecting.
   B. presaging.
   C. awaiting.
   D. inviting.

6. In line 33, the word *uniform* most nearly means:

   A. standard.
   B. unchanging.
   C. militant.
   D. popular.

7. In line 35, the word *champion* most nearly means:

   A. victor.
   B. opponent.
   C. colleague.
   D. defender.

8. In line 47, the word *senior* most nearly means:

   A. older in age.
   B. higher in rank.
   C. graduate.
   D. mentor.

9. In line 52, the word *luminary* most nearly means:

   A. bright object.
   B. famous person.
   C. office holder.
   D. candidate.

10. In line 65, the word *diminution* most nearly means:

    A. foreshortening.
    B. shrinkage.
    C. abatement.
    D. degradation.

EXERCISE 6

Vocabulary Builder: Prose Fiction Passages

DIRECTIONS: Each passage in this exercise is followed by sets of sentence completion, vocabulary-in-context, antonym, and analogy items for building vocabulary through context. In addition to using the passages to infer word meanings, you may use a dictionary or refer to the Vocabulary List beginning on page 655.

The first set of items following each passage are sentence completion items based on words from the passage. Each sentence has one blank. Choose the word that best fits the meaning of the sentence in its entirety.

The second set of items following each passage are vocabulary-in-context items based on words from the passage. Choose the best answer for each item based on what is stated or implied in the passage.

The third set of items following each passage are antonym items based on words from the passage. For each item, choose the word that has a meaning most nearly opposite of the capitalized word.

The fourth set of items following each passage are analogy items based on words from the passage. For each item, find the pair of words that expresses a relationship most like that expressed by the capitalized words.

Answers are on page 798.

Passage I

PROSE FICTION: This passage is adapted from Edgar Allan Poe's "The Oval Portrait."

The portrait was that of a young girl. It was a mere head and shoulders, done in what is technically termed a vignette manner; much in the style of the favorite heads of Sully. The arms, the bosom, and even
5 the ends of the radiant hair, melted imperceptibly into the vague yet deep shadow, which formed the background of the whole. The metallic yellow frame was a valuable oval, richly gilded and filigreed in exquisitely fine detail. As a thing of art nothing could
10 be more admirable than the painting itself. But it could have been neither the execution of the work nor the immortal beauty of the countenance, which had so suddenly and so vehemently moved me. Least of all could it have been that my fancy, shaken from its half
15 slumber, had mistaken the head for that of a living person. I saw at once that the peculiarities of the design, of the vignetting, and of the frame, must have instantly dispelled such ideas—must have prevented even its momentary entertainment. Thinking earnestly
20 upon these points, I remained, for an hour perhaps, half sitting, half reclining, with my vision riveted upon the portrait. At length, satisfied with the true secret of its

effect, I fell back within the bed. I had found the spell of the picture in an absolute *life-likeness* of expression,
25 which at first startling, finally confounded, subdued, and appalled me. With deep and reverent awe, I replaced the candelabrum in its former position. The cause of my deep agitation being thus shut from view, I sought eagerly the volume which discussed the
30 paintings and their histories. Turning to the number which designated the oval portrait, I there read the vague and quaint words which follow:

"She was a maiden of rarest beauty, and not more lovely than full of glee. And evil was the hour when
35 she saw, and loved, and wedded the painter. He, passionate, studious, austere, and having already a bride in his Art; she all light and smiles and frolicsome as the young fawn; loving and cherishing all things: hating only the Art which was her rival; dreading only
40 the palette and brushes and other untoward instruments which deprived her of the countenance of her lover. It was thus a terrible thing for this lady to hear the painter speak of his desire to portray even his young bride. But she was humble and obedient, and sat meekly for many
45 weeks in the dark high turret-chamber where the light dripped upon the pale canvas only from overhead. But he, the painter, took glory in his work, which went on from hour to hour from day to day. And he was a

passionate and moody man, who became lost in
50 reveries; so that he *would* not see that the light which
fell so ghastly in that lone turret withered the health
and the spirits of his bride, who pined visibly to all but
him. Yet she smiled on and still on, uncomplainingly,
because she saw that the painter (who had great
55 renown) took a fervid and burning pleasure in his task,
and wrought day and night to depict her who so loved
him, yet who grew daily more dispirited and weak.
And in sooth some who beheld the portrait spoke of its
resemblance in low words, as of a mighty marvel, and
60 a proof not less of the power of the painter than of his
deep love for her, whom he depicted so surpassingly
well. But at length, as the labor drew nearer to its
conclusion, there were admitted none into the turret;
for the painter had grown wild with the ardor of his
65 work, and turned his eyes from the canvas rarely, even
to regard the countenance of his wife. And he would
not see that the tints which he spread on the canvas
were drawn from the cheeks of her who sat beside him.
And when many weeks had passed, but little remained
70 to do, save one brush upon the mouth and one tint upon
the eye, the spirit of the lady again flickered up as the
flame within the socket of the lamp. And then the brush
was given, and the tint was placed; and for one
moment, the painter stood entranced before the work
75 which he had wrought but in the next, while he yet
gazed, he grew tremulous and very pallid, and aghast,
and crying with a loud voice, 'this is indeed *Life* itself!'
turned suddenly to regard his beloved—*She was dead!*"

1. The physical differences between the fraternal
   twins were so ------- that only their family
   members were able to tell them apart.

   A. apparent
   B. invisible
   C. detectable
   D. imperceptible
   E. noticeable

2. Many Republicans are ------- opposed to fighting
   climate change with legislation, charging that the
   Democrat's current bill would drastically raise
   costs for the average American family.

   A. impassively
   B. sarcastically
   C. vehemently
   D. ironically
   E. humbly

3. To help control the rapidly increasing national
   debt, the Finance Minister recently announced a
   very ------- set of economic measures that
   drastically cut government services.

   A. mysterious
   B. lackadaisical
   C. lenient
   D. inept
   E. austere

4. The critic wrote in her review of the ballet that
   the ------- and conviction with which the dancers
   performed excused any minor imperfections in
   the overall performance.

   A. doubt
   B. ardor
   C. flawlessness
   D. indifference
   E. deliberation

5. When the animal control officer cornered the
   stray dog in an attempt to catch it, the dog bristled
   and whined in a low ------- tone.

   A. tremulous
   B. confident
   C. unexpected
   D. erratic
   E. passive

6. It can be inferred that the word *vignette*, as it is
   used in line 3, primarily refers to:

   A. a brief incident or scene.
   B. a particular style of brushstroke.
   C. a short musical composition.
   D. a picture with no definite border, shading off
      gradually at its edges.

7. In line 8, *gilded* is best understood to mean:

   A. sponsored.
   B. overlaid with gold.
   C. entangled.
   D. overfilled.

8. In line 8, *filigreed* is best understood to mean:

   A. excessive greed or avarice.
   B. characterized by lack of taste.
   C. adorned with delicate ornamentation.
   D. to be unfounded.

9. As it is used in line 12, the word *countenance* most nearly means:

   A. facial features.
   B. approval.
   C. pretense.
   D. motif.

10. In context, *designated* (line 31) most nearly means:

    A. delegated.
    B. indicated.
    C. appointed.
    D. delivered.

11. In line 40, *untoward* most nearly means:

    A. appropriate.
    B. disorderly.
    C. fortunate.
    D. troublesome.

12. It can be inferred that the word *reveries*, as it is used in line 50, primarily refers to:

    A. indifferences.
    B. daydreams.
    C. certainties.
    D. reverences.

13. As it is used in line 52, the word *pined* most nearly means:

    A. longed for.
    B. increased.
    C. wasted away.
    D. imagined.

14. In line 55, *renown* is best understood to mean:

    A. fame.
    B. aptitude.
    C. obscurity.
    D. perseverance.

15. As it is used in line 56, the word *wrought* most nearly means:

    A. hammered.
    B. wreaked havoc.
    C. worked with great care.
    D. operated carelessly.

16. WITHER:

    A. embarrass
    B. ignore
    C. nurture
    D. produce
    E. limit

17. CONFOUND:

    A. announce
    B. beckon
    C. ridicule
    D. welcome
    E. clarify

18. PALLID:

    A. colorful
    B. ancient
    C. private
    D. talkative
    E. excellent

19. APPALLING:

    A. visible
    B. pleasing
    C. widening
    D. knowing
    E. humane

20. AGITATE:

A. remind
B. select
C. list
D. delete
E. quiet

21. ENTRANCE:

A. elongate
B. bore
C. reward
D. accept
E. withdraw

22. SUBDUED:

A. active
B. hidden
C. queer
D. perfect
E. wooden

23. DISPEL:

A. wince
B. correct
C. assemble
D. attempt
E. grin

24. FERVID:

A. cool
B. sad
C. enjoyable
D. incomplete
E. reckless

25. QUAINT:

A. homey
B. current
C. stiff
D. backward
E. likable

26. ENTERTAIN : PROPOSAL ::

A. suppress : revival
B. sign : form
C. invite : retaliation
D. consider : suggestion
E. address: conference

27. EXECUTE : PLAN ::

A. punish : criminal
B. obey : refusal
C. deny : hope
D. accept : question
E. fulfill : dream

28. PORTRAY : CHARACTER ::

A. act : role
B. describe : drama
C. direct : orchestrate
D. perform : actor
E. write : report

29. CHERISH : DEAR ::

A. reject : suitor
B. enable : law
C. hoard : jewel
D. treasure : valuable
E. deposit : money

30. AWE : DREAD ::

A. concern : delight
B. fright: reassure
C. fear : alarm
D. invitation : beckon
E. agreement: negotiate

Passage II

PROSE FICTION: This passage is adapted from Arthur Conan Doyle's "The Adventure of the Devil's Foot."

In recording from time to time some of the curious experiences and interesting recollections, which I associate with my long and intimate friendship with Mr. Sherlock Holmes, I have continually been
5 faced with difficulties caused by his own aversion to publicity. To his sombre and cynical spirit all popular applause was always abhorrent, and nothing amused him more at the end of a successful case than to hand over the actual exposure to some orthodox official, and
10 to listen with a mocking smile to the general chorus of misplaced congratulation. It was indeed this attitude upon the part of my friend and certainly not any lack of interesting material, which has caused me of late years to lay very few of my records before the public. My
15 participation in some of his adventures was always a privilege, which entailed discretion and reticence upon me.

It was in the spring of the year 1897 that Holmes's iron constitution showed some symptoms of
20 giving way in the face of constant hard work of a most exacting kind, aggravated perhaps by occasional indiscretions of his own. In March of that year Dr. Moore Agar, of Harley Street, whose dramatic introduction to Holmes I may some day recount, gave
25 positive injunctions that the famous private agent lay aside all his cases and surrender himself to complete rest if he wished to avert an absolute breakdown. The state of his health was not a matter in which he himself took the faintest interest, for his mental detachment
30 was absolute, but he was induced at last, on the threat of being permanently disqualified from work, to give himself a complete change of scene and air. Thus, it was that in the early spring of that year we found ourselves together in a small cottage near Poldhu Bay,
35 at the further extremity of the Cornish peninsula.

It was a singular spot, and one peculiarly well suited to the grim humor of my patient. From the windows of our little whitewashed house, which stood high upon a grassy headland, we looked down upon the
40 whole sinister semicircle of Mounts Bay, that old death trap of sailing vessels, with its fringe of black cliffs and surge-swept reefs on which innumerable seamen have met their end. With a northerly breeze it lies placid and sheltered, inviting the storm-tossed craft to tack into it
45 for rest and protection.

Then come the sudden swirl round of the wind, the blustering gale from the south-west, the dragging anchor, the lee shore, and the last battle in the creaming breakers. The wise mariner stands far out from that evil
50 place.

On the land side our surroundings were as sombre as on the sea. It was a country of rolling moors, lonely and dun-colored, with an occasional church tower to mark the site of some old-world village. In every
55 direction upon these moors were traces of some vanished race, which has passed utterly away, and left as its sole record strange monuments of stone, irregular mounds which contained the burned ashes of the dead, and curious earthworks which hinted at prehistoric
60 strife. The glamour and mystery of the place, with its sinister atmosphere of forgotten nations, appealed to the imagination of my friend, and he spent much of his time in long walks and solitary meditations upon the moor. The ancient Cornish language had also arrested
65 his attention, and he had, I remember, conceived the idea that it was akin to Chaldean, and had been largely derived from the Phoenician traders in tin. He had received a consignment of books upon philology and was settling down to develop this thesis when
70 suddenly, to my sorrow, and to his unfeigned delight, we found ourselves, even in that land of dreams, plunged into a problem at our very doors which was more intense, more engrossing, and infinitely more mysterious than any of those which had driven us from
75 London. Our simple life and peaceful, healthy routine were violently interrupted, and we were precipitated into the midst of a series of events, which caused the utmost excitement not only in Cornwall but throughout the whole west of England. Many of my readers may
80 retain some recollection of what was called at the time "The Cornish Horror," though a most imperfect account of the matter reached the London press. Now, after some thirteen years, I will give the true details of this inconceivable affair to the public.

31. Due to her strong moral ------- to eating animals or animal-by-products, Maggie has been a life-long vegetarian.

A. adversity
B. aversion
C. sympathy
D. confliction
E. upbringing

32. Trafficking in human beings and other contemporary forms of slavery constitute a(n) ------- violation of the dignity and rights of human beings.

    A. alluring
    B. laudatory
    C. docile
    D. abhorrent
    E. pedestrian

33. J. D. Salinger was best known for his 1951 novel *The Catcher in the Rye*, as well as his ------- and reclusive nature following his withdrawal from public life in 1965.

    A. arrogance
    B. experience
    C. loquaciousness
    D. nervousness
    E. reticence

34. The governor stepped down from office after his ------- were made public and the state assembly demanded his resignation.

    A. decisions
    B. prudence
    C. indiscretions
    D. responsibilities
    E. virtues

35. In his book, *The Great Crash, 1929*, John Kenneth Galbraith argued that the 1929 stock market crash was ------- by rampant speculation and the belief of participants that they could become rich without work.

    A. considered
    B. precipitated
    C. protracted
    D. belabored
    E. delivered

36. In line 9, *orthodox* is best understood to mean:

    A. conventional.
    B. original.
    C. eccentric.
    D. personal.

37. The word *recount* (line 24) most nearly means to:

    A. conceal facts.
    B. calculate.
    C. reimburse.
    D. tell a story in detail.

38. Based on the use of the word *injunctions* in line 25, it can be inferred that *injunction* primarily refers to a(n):

    A. command.
    B. embargo.
    C. ruling.
    D. reprimand.

39. In line 36, *singular* is closest in meaning to:

    A. simular.
    B. allegorical.
    C. individual.
    D. remarkable.

40. As it is used in line 43, the word *placid* most nearly means:

    A. flabby.
    B. calm.
    C. noisy.
    D. appeasable.

41. It can be inferred that the word *tack*, as it is used in line 44, primarily means to:

    A. deal fairly.
    B. fasten.
    C. change course.
    D. attack.

42. It can be inferred that the word *lee*, as it is used in line 48, primarily refers to:

    A. the side sheltered from the wind.
    B. the rear of a boat.
    C. a breeze from the west.
    D. the far side of an object.

43. As it is used in line 68, the word *consignment* most likely refers to:

    A. a meeting or appointment.
    B. a homework assignment.
    C. items in a shipment.
    D. an error in communication.

44. In line 70, *unfeigned* most nearly means:

    A. affected.
    B. legitimate.
    C. insincere.
    D. genuine.

45. In line 80, *recollection* refers to a(n):

    A. collection of items.
    B. recalled memory.
    C. religious contemplation.
    D. act of recoiling.

46. SOMBRE:

    A. lacking movement
    B. brightly colored
    C. overly long
    D. completely finished
    E. high overhead

47. INTIMATE:

    A. stranger
    B. official
    C. bungler
    D. drunkard
    E. author

48. POPULAR:

    A. incorrect
    B. improper
    C. unknown
    D. righteous
    E. welcome

49. ARREST:

    A. back up
    B. start up
    C. move up
    D. slow up
    E. accelerate

50. EXACTING:

    A. faithful
    B. vengeful
    C. hopeful
    D. desirous
    E. lenient

51. SURRENDER:

    A. resist
    B. invite
    C. renew
    D. follow
    E. mistreat

52. INDUCED:

    A. exhaled
    B. reminded
    C. confirmed
    D. discouraged
    E. started

53. BLUSTERING:

    A. content
    B. quiet
    C. fearful
    D. sad
    E. determined

54. IMPERFECT:

    A. complete
    B. flowery
    C. wishful
    D. contrived
    E. aged

55. MEDITATE:

   A. remember
   B. foresee
   C. act
   D. deny
   E. understand

56. PHILOLOGY : LANGUAGE ::

   A. biology : physics
   B. astrology : astronomy
   C. archaeology : relics
   D. learning : study
   E. geology : geography

57. AGGRAVATE : CONDITION ::

   A. inform : announcement
   B. confirm : doubt
   C. relax : play
   D. insist : option
   E. worsen: problem

58. SINISTER : EVIL ::

   A. threatening : danger
   B. entertaining : drama
   C. fanciful : book
   D. conclusive : end
   E. protective : help

59. SOLITARY : CROWDED ::

   A. confined : locked
   B. comfortable : padded
   C. empty : occupied
   D. fortunate : lucky
   E. medical : healthy

60. DETACHED : CONNECTION ::

   A. harmful : fear
   B. unconscious : awareness
   C. permanent : foundation
   D. rewarding : profit
   E. gloomy : health

Passage III

PROSE FICTION: This passage is adapted from a letter written by the playwright George Bernard Shaw in response to critics of his plays.

There is a good reason, however, why I should take this haughty attitude towards those representative critics whose complaint is that my plays, though not unentertaining, lack the elevation of sentiment and
5 seriousness of purpose of Shakespeare and Ibsen. They can find, under the surface brilliancy for which they give me credit, no coherent thought or sympathy, and accuse me, in various terms and degrees, of an inhuman and freakish wantonness; of preoccupation
10 with "the seamy side of life"; of paradox, cynicism, and eccentricity, reducible, as some contend, to a trite formula of treating bad as good, and good as bad, important as trivial, and trivial and important, serious as laughable, and laughable as serious and so forth. As
15 to this formula I can only say that if anyone is simple enough to think that even a good comic opera can be produced by it, I invite him to try his hand, and see whether anything remotely resembling one of my plays will result.

20 I could explain the matter easily enough if I chose, but the result would be that people who misunderstand the plays would misunderstand the explanation ten times more. The particular exceptions taken are seldom more than symptoms of the
25 underlying fundamental disagreement between the romantic morality of the critics and the realistic morality of the plays. For example, I am quite aware the Swiss officer in *Arms and the Man* is not a conventional stage soldier. He suffers from want of
30 food and sleep; his nerves go to pieces after three days under fire, ending in the horrors of a rout and pursuit; he has found by experience it is more important to have a few bits of chocolate to eat than cartridges for his revolver. When many of my critics rejected these
35 circumstances as fantastically improbable and cynically unnatural, it was not necessary to argue them into common sense; all I had to do was to brain them, so to speak, with the first half-dozen military authorities at hand. But when it proved that such unromantic facts
40 implied to them a denial of the existence of courage, patriotism, faith, hope, and charity, I saw it was not really mere matter of fact at issue between us.

The real issue between us is whether idealism can survive the general onslaught, which is implicit in
45 *Arms and the Man* and other realistic plays. For my part, I hope not; for idealism, which is only a flattering name for romance in politics and morals, is as obnoxious to me as romance is in ethics or religion. I can no longer be satisfied with fictitious morals and
50 fictitious good conduct, shedding fictitious glory on overcrowding, disease, crime, drink, war cruelty, infant mortality, all the other commonplaces of civilization which drive men to the theater to make foolish pretenses. These things are progress, science, morals,
55 religion, patriotism, imperial supremacy, national greatness, and all the other names the newspapers call them.

On the other hand, I see plenty of good in the world working itself out as fast as the idealists will
60 allow it; if they would only leave it alone and learn to respect reality, which would include the beneficial exercise of respecting themselves, and incidentally respecting me, we should all get along much better and faster. At all events, I do not see moral chaos and
65 anarchy as the alternative to romantic convention; furthermore, I am not going to pretend that I do just to please the less clear-sighted people who are convinced the world is only held together by the force of unanimous, strenuous, eloquent, trumpet-tongued
70 lying. To me, the tragedy and comedy of life lie in the consequences, sometimes terrible, sometimes ludicrous, of the persistent attempts to found our institutions on the ideas suggested to our imaginations by our half-satisfied passions, instead of on a genuinely
75 scientific natural history.

61. Dazed by the explosion, nothing Fredrick said was -------; he babbled about the need for lace curtains on the machine shop windows.

    A. illogical
    B. coherent
    C. adequate
    D. sensitive
    E. informal

62. The suspect drove his car at 60 miles per hour through the school zone, demonstrating a(n) ------- disregard for the safety of the school-children.

   A. justifiable
   B. moral
   C. ambitious
   D. lucid
   E. wanton

63. The aviation magnate Howard Hughes is remembered for his ------- behavior and reclusive lifestyle in later life, caused in part by a worsening obsessive-compulsive disorder.

   A. gregarious
   B. customary
   C. eccentric
   D. habitual
   E. extroverted

64. The politician claimed that he would ------- middle-class income taxes by eliminating wasteful government spending and fraud.

   A. enhance
   B. augment
   C. increase
   D. reduce
   E. maintain

65. Arguably one of the most ------- presidents in American history, John F. Kennedy delivered an inaugural address in 1961 that was an inspirational call to action.

   A. inarticulate
   B. reticent
   C. taciturn
   D. belligerent
   E. eloquent

66. Based on the use of the word *elevation* in line 4, it can be inferred that *elevate* means to:

   A. decrease or drop.
   B. raise or lift up.
   C. assess or estimate.
   D. intensify or accelerate.

67. As it is used in line 10, the word *seamy* most nearly means:

   A. wholesome
   B. feeble
   C. unpleasant
   D. vigorous

68. In line 10, *paradox* is best understood to mean a(n):

   A. contradiction
   B. insincerity
   C. intricacy
   D. obscurity

69. The word *cynicism* (line 10) refers to the belief that:

   A. there are not absolute truths about the world.
   B. negative perceptions are the cause of negative realities.
   C. people and events are inherently good.
   D. human nature and motives cannot be trusted.

70. As the word *realistic* is used in line 26, it can be inferred that *realism* refers to the principle of:

   A. representation through generalization.
   B. representation without idealization.
   C. reproduction by individualization.
   D. change through moderate action.

71. In line 43, *idealism* refers to behavior or thought based on:

   A. a conception of things as one wishes them to be, rather than as they actually are.
   B. a conception of how things actually are.
   C. a conception of people motivated only by greed or some other selfish motive.
   D. delusion of persecution or extreme fear.

72. It can be inferred that the word *onslaught*, as it is used in line 44, primarily refers to a(n):

A. apology.
B. justification.
C. attack.
D. excuse.

73. Based on the use of the word *pretenses* in line 54, it can be inferred that *pretense* refers to all of the following EXCEPT:

A. a charade.
B. pretension.
C. candor.
D. a false claim.

74. In line 61, *beneficial* most nearly means:

A. bountiful.
B. helpful.
C. extensive.
D. refreshing.

75. As it is used in line 65, *anarchy* can be inferred to mean:

A. lawlessness.
B. order.
C. transformation.
D. reformation.

76. HAUGHTY:

A. angry
B. ignorant
C. trustworthy
D. above
E. humble

77. BRILLIANCY:

A. honor
B. dullness
C. travel
D. drama
E. entertainment

78. TRITE:

A. long
B. outspoken
C. fresh
D. confused
E. limp

79. REMOTE:

A. calm
B. firm
C. near
D. exact
E. simple

80. EXCEPTION:

A. bargain
B. condition
C. comfort
D. agreement
E. fatigue

81. ROUT:

A. orderly retreat
B. vicious bite
C. careless planning
D. quick march
E. long delay

82. IMPROBABLE:

A. hopeful
B. caring
C. thrown
D. flat
E. likely

83. OBNOXIOUS:

A. pleasant
B. harmful
C. uninteresting
D. inflated
E. required

84. FICTITIOUS:

    A. invented
    B. real
    C. warm-blooded
    D. self-contained
    E. outmaneuvered

85. CHAOS:

    A. defeat
    B. script
    C. order
    D. doom
    E. openness

86. SYMPTOMATIC : SYMBOLIC ::

    A. apparent : real
    B. diseased : healthy
    C. indicative : representative
    D. endearing : suggestive
    E. obvious : hidden

87. CHARITY : LOVE ::

    A. benevolence : kindness
    B. giving : receiving
    C. donation : deduction
    D. target : aim
    E. outrage : affection

88. FREAKISH : CHANGE ::

    A. concerned : humiliate
    B. annoying : please
    C. whimsical : vary
    D. controlled : worry
    E. tearful : work

89. IMPERIAL : AUTHORITY ::

    A. supreme : control
    B. needy : privilege
    C. legal : crime
    D. master : slave
    E. resentful : gift

90. LUDICROUS : LAUGHABLE ::

    A. careful : reckless
    B. completion : start
    C. absurd : ridiculous
    D. outlandish : believable
    E. sweet : sour

Vocabulary Builder: Social Science Passages

DIRECTIONS: Each passage in this exercise is followed by sets of sentence completion, vocabulary-in-context, antonym, and analogy items for building vocabulary through context. In addition to using the passages to infer word meanings, you may use a dictionary or refer to the Vocabulary List beginning on page 655.

The first set of items following each passage are sentence completion items based on words from the passage. Each sentence has one blank. Choose the word that best fits the meaning of the sentence in its entirety.

The second set of items following each passage are vocabulary-in-context items based on words from the passage. Choose the best answer for each item based on what is stated or implied in the passage.

The third set of items following each passage are antonym items based on words from the passage. For each item, choose the word that has a meaning most nearly opposite of the capitalized word.

The fourth set of items following each passage are analogy items based on words from the passage. For each item, find the pair of words that expresses a relationship most like that expressed by the capitalized words.

Answers are on page 799.

Passage I

SOCIAL SCIENCE: This passage is adapted from an essay entitled "Animal Images in Human History" in an art history and philosophy anthology.

Among the first images created by man were those of animals, and over the centuries mankind's preoccupation with the nonhuman inhabitants of the earth has never abated. Even when at pains to prove
5 how different he was from the beast, man has depended on the animal world for the imagery by which to explain his interior being as well as his relationship to the cosmos. Endowed with a vitality in common with man, yet following the dictates of an intelligence not
10 readily definable by human reason, the animal, whether wild or domesticated, threatening attacker or docile prey, has remained something of an enigma and often the subject of wonder. To reconstruct the history of religion, philosophy, or art without reference to the
15 animal image would be impossible. Although in our satisfied moment of sophistication, we no longer depend on the literal imagery of hawk-headed gods or rulers with the body of a lion, we still strut like a peacock and search ardently for the dove of peace.

20 No one knows for sure why the painters in prehistoric times represented bison on the walls of caves, but it is significant that the animals were rendered with more care and completeness than the human creatures. Whatever their utility, the swiftly
25 moving, rhythmic figures show an appreciation for animal beauty that can still be understood with sympathy. "Animal beauty" is a term we tend to use when we wish to describe some particularly adroit and rhythmic coordination of muscles and movement that
30 magnificently fulfills a prescribed act, an act that seems to be accomplished as answer to an interior impulse untrammeled by rational restraint or an imposed pattern of behavior. There is something magical in an artistic form expressive of such pure vitality, which seems
35 purposive and yet has no rational end. It is as if this summons from far back in the mind a cherished memory of simply being, of existing in a vital continuity not qualified by reason nor limited by concept of time. This particular kind of vital beauty is
40 not the exclusive property of any particular animal; it belongs no less to the hare than to the lion. That remarkable art known as the "animal style," which spread in the early centuries from Central Asia across China and westward through Europe, carried its animal
45 magic through forms that often lose all specific identity. However, the taut, curving forms live with

animal exuberance and transform any object they adorn
into a living thing. Significantly enough, this intensive
vitality was rarely associated with images of human
50 beings. Possibly the human image was not considered
to have the same magical power as the animal to
bestow perpetual life on the inanimate.

Quite probably there are two levels of appeal in
this kind of animal beauty in art. One is the promise of
55 an otherwise unattainable sense of muscular triumph,
of physical freedom. To run like an antelope or spring
like a lion has its reward, even though experienced
vicariously. Prudence is not a matter of concern when
we identify ourselves with the image of a charging
60 horse or the streamlined form of a plunging hawk.
Possibly there is even an element of envy in man's
admiration of the animal in which beauty and utility are
inseparable, and form and act seem to be one. Blessed
with the faculty to cogitate and rationalize conclusions,
65 we seem also to need moments in which we can live
beyond thought.

The intuitive basis for action is the other appeal
of that beauty we identify as peculiar to the animal and
possibly explains in part why animals have so often
70 become cosmic symbols. When in doubt about his own
power or the direction of his thinking, man has looked
upon the animal as more closely attuned to the
universe, living within a natural cycle from which man
has been alienated by an excess of his own thought. It
75 is not that most thinking human beings would want to
become animals, but the image presented by the animal
becomes the foundation upon which a different
ordering of the universe can be conceived.

1. Hayley was a very ------- child, naturally inclined
to be calm and agreeable.

   A. noisy
   B. feral
   C. orderly
   D. docile
   E. sensitive

2. After thirty years of incarceration, the prisoner
was exonerated and released, finally free and
-------.

   A. untrammeled
   B. confined
   C. restrained
   D. intractable
   E. unruly

3. In spite of his nervousness, Will finally ------- the
courage to telephone Kate and ask her to the
prom.

   A. invited
   B. summoned
   C. eliminated
   D. condensed
   E. disparaged

4. The nylon rope was ------- as the rock climber's
weight pulled it hard against the cliff.

   A. taunt
   B. slack
   C. pliant
   D. elastic
   E. taut

5. Always late, George ------- misses his bus and is
never on time to appointments.

   A. momentarily
   B. perpetually
   C. temporarily
   D. randomly
   E. briefly

6. In context, *abated* (line 4) most nearly means:

   A. increased.
   B. commenced.
   C. continued.
   D. diminished.

7. As it is used in line 6, the word *imagery* most nearly means:

    A. mental images.
    B. paintings.
    C. instruction.
    D. reflections.

8. It can be inferred that the word *endowed*, as it is used in line 8, most nearly means to:

    A. be indebted or owing money.
    B. donate goods or services.
    C. have talent or be gifted.
    D. be engaged or betrothed.

9. In line 8, *vitality* is best understood to mean:

    A. lethargy.
    B. life's energy.
    C. humor.
    D. habitat.

10. Based on the word *ardently* as it is used in line 19, *ardent* means to be:

    A. aggressive.
    B. indifferent.
    C. passionate.
    D. persuasive.

11. Based on the word *rendered* as it is used in line 23, *render* means to:

    A. repeat.
    B. tear apart.
    C. raise up.
    D. represent or depict.

12. In line 28, *adroit* is closest in meaning to all of the following EXCEPT:

    A. gauche.
    B. skillful.
    C. dexterous.
    D. clever.

13. In context, *prescribed* (line 30) most nearly means:

    A. spontaneous.
    B. imagined.
    C. donated.
    D. required.

14. As used in line 58, *vicariously* most nearly means:

    A. for a short time.
    B. to behave scandalously.
    C. through imagined participation.
    D. feeling extreme pleasure.

15. In line 67, *intuitive* most nearly means:

    A. intruding.
    B. demanding immediate attention.
    C. conscious reasoning.
    D. possessing insight.

16. ALIENATED:

    A. discussed
    B. prolonged
    C. derived
    D. focused
    E. attracted

17. PREOCCUPATION:

    A. disinterest
    B. knowledge
    C. discipline
    D. livelihood
    E. want

18. IMPOSE:

    A. combine
    B. adjust
    C. relieve
    D. return
    E. suppose

19. ATTUNED:

    A. out of step with
    B. from another country
    C. in training for
    D. without shame
    E. under a shadow

20. PURPOSIVE:

    A. acceptable
    B. unguided
    C. generous
    D. quarrelsome
    E. angry

21. CONTINUITY:

    A. break
    B. tie
    C. scratch
    D. usefulness
    E. income

22. EXCLUSIVE:

    A. rich
    B. simple
    C. shared
    D. friendly
    E. cuddly

23. EXUBERANCE:

    A. ignorance
    B. depression
    C. zeal
    D. forwardness
    E. looseness

24. BESTOW:

    A. send out
    B. ask for
    C. take back
    D. move over
    E. lie to

25. STRUT:

    A. jump
    B. announce
    C. amass
    D. slink
    E. pretend

26. RECONSTRUCT : PICTURE ::

    A. deduce : conclusion
    B. prepare : consume
    C. withhold : money
    D. fulfill : dream
    E. deny : enemy

27. IMPULSE : MOTION ::

    A. cause : effect
    B. trembling : fear
    C. wealth : riches
    D. harm : danger
    E. action : thought

28. UNATTAINABLE : ACHIEVE ::

    A. unavailable : present
    B. untoward : unfortunate
    C. unhealthy : ill
    D. unfinished : work
    E. unproductive : foolish

29. INSEPARABLE : APART ::

    A. bound : tied
    B. intertwined : together
    C. married : wed
    D. indivisible : split
    E. beloved : worshipped

30. DICTATES : COMMANDS ::

    A. advertisements : products
    B. directions : refusals
    C. warnings : dangers
    D. announcements : news
    E. instructions : orders

Passage II

SOCIAL SCIENCE: This passage is adapted from an essay entitled "More on Animal Images in Human History" in an art history and philosophy anthology.

There are aspects of animal beauty other than those of transcendent vitality and natural unity that have a long history of appeal. The gorgeous plumage, intricate patterns, and luxurious fur of the birds and
5 beasts set the standards, and often provided the materials—for man's raiment and domestic decoration from the beginning of history. Although the use of skins might be considered to a degree utilitarian, a more persistent dependence on the animal world was
10 for spectacular adornment, especially for ritualistic occasions. In almost every early culture, most significant decoration has been inseparable from animal inspiration. On the whole, flora played a poor second to fauna in the beginning, although it too had its
15 role to play. It was the animal that taught man to live beyond himself. As theorists have pointed out, only man had to dress himself and felt the need to give decorative meaning to his environment; to meet this peculiarly human need, he depended enthusiastically
20 on the elegant examples provided by his animal associates.

If man has liked to adorn himself in imitation of the animals, he has also found it instructive and useful to depict animals as people, using them as
25 embodiments of human traits or projecting human patterns on their actions. Aesop's fables, the *Panchatantra*, and folk tales from almost every culture put moral judgments in the mouths of animals, as if certain kinds of lessons can best be learned when
30 experienced in a non-human context. Furthermore, we take special pleasure in seeing ourselves—or at least our neighbors—tellingly characterized in the animal world. The cartoon of an irascible duck underscores human traits in a universal way that the likeness of a
35 habitually angry person would not, and a porcine puppet conveys more about some aspects of our life and times than any simple human character could, becoming a kind of popular heroine in the process. The figures of animals have carried much of the social
40 satire in historic times, being immune to the social restrictions that might inhibit our speaking ill of our fellows. Is it our fault a particularly fat man looks like a toad?—or rather, that a picture of a toad is immediately recognized as a likeness of a fat man? Not
45 only has the animal world served to sublimate and

personify our aspirations, it also has acted as a mirror to our foibles and a tutor to our ethical behavior.

Aside from everything else, man has usually wanted to be liked by animals, as if their affection, or
50 at least recognition, was a mark of special acceptance. Of course, he has also wanted to dominate them, but the compassionate dog, the contented cat, or the wise, devoted parrot make contributions that no amount of dominating can win. In such a relationship, who is the
55 teacher and who is taught?

It is good to know the long traditions of mystery, humor, and wisdom associated with animals have not been entirely lost to modern craftsmen. Even today, we find works that run the full gamut from mysterious
60 symbol to gentle satire. In fact, in recent years, with increasing domination of the man-made and oppressive blunting of sensibility by the preference for generalization over the particular, the threatened animal has assumed an even more poignant role. Perhaps animal
65 imagery can serve to remind us of this important point.

31. Colorado has a very rich -------, with over 3,200 species of seed plants collected, documented, and described by botanists since the first botanical exploration by Edwin James in 1819.

    A. culture
    B. history
    C. flora
    D. entourage
    E. fauna

32. Carl Linnaeus, Sweden's most famous natural scientist, catalogued the country's animal life, or -------, in 1746.

    A. flora
    B. society
    C. agriculture
    D. geography
    E. fauna

33. The 1938 Disney cartoon, *Self Control*, features the ------- Donald Duck as he attempts to manage his anger when some pesky insects make it difficult for him to maintain composure.

 A. easygoing
 B. irascible
 C. mysterious
 D. blasé
 E. anxious

34. Although the Russian writer Anton Chekhov sketched his characters with compassionate good-humor, he never abstained from highlighting their ------- and human weaknesses.

 A. talents
 B. accomplishments
 C. traditions
 D. foibles
 E. predilections

35. The novel *Old Yeller*, written by Fred Gipson in 1956, is arguably one of the most disturbing children's stories ever, mainly due to the ------- and emotionally devastating ending.

 A. dispassionate
 B. esoteric
 C. poignant
 D. hackneyed
 E. abstruse

36. In context, *transcendent* (line 2) most nearly means:

 A. extraordinary.
 B. transparent.
 C. conventional.
 D. observable.

37. As it is used in line 6, the word *raiment* most nearly means:

 A. narrative.
 B. evolution.
 C. shelter.
 D. clothing.

38. In line 8, *utilitarian* is best understood to indicate stressing the importance of:

 A. beauty over function.
 B. function over beauty.
 C. free will over fate.
 D. individual freedom.

39. Based on the use of the word *embodiments* in line 25, it can be inferred that *embodiment* refers to the:

 A. deprivation of property or title.
 B. representation of a deity or spirit in earthly form.
 C. concrete expression of some abstract idea or concept.
 D. abstract expression of real objects.

40. Based on the use of the word *projecting* in line 25, it can be inferred that *project* most nearly means to:

 A. imagine.
 B. protect.
 C. build.
 D. predict.

41. It can be inferred that the word *porcine*, as it is used in line 35, primarily refers to something:

 A. related to mushrooms.
 B. made from ceramic.
 C. homemade.
 D. pig-like.

42. In line 45, *sublimate* most nearly means to:

 A. submerge in liquid.
 B. reduce in quality or value.
 C. bring under control or conquer.
 D. make nobler or purer.

43. In context, *gamut* (line 59) most nearly means:

 A. an obstacle course.
 B. the entire range or extent of something.
 C. a division within a classification system.
 D. a collection of many items.

44. In line 61, *oppressive* is closest in meaning to:

A. uplifting.
B. tyrannical.
C. tolerant.
D. exacting.

45. In line 62, *sensibility* most nearly means the:

A. inability to feel or perceive emotions.
B. state of being aware of oneself.
C. capacity for feeling pain or stimulation.
D. capacity for being affected emotionally or intellectually.

46. GORGEOUS:

A. fat
B. plain
C. studious
D. lovely
E. wealthy

47. COMPASSIONATE:

A. wise
B. delightful
C. foolish
D. unfeeling
E. realistic

48. ADORN:

A. release
B. strip
C. control
D. sell
E. open

49. LUXURIATE:

A. hate
B. tire
C. waste
D. defend
E. report

50. ELEGANT:

A. tasteless
B. timid
C. sincere
D. new
E. incurable

51. INHIBIT:

A. grind
B. plod
C. promote
D. flatten
E. mark

52. HABITUALLY:

A. earnestly
B. likely
C. properly
D. occasionally
E. openly

53. BLUNT:

A. accept
B. sharpen
C. enforce
D. respond
E. correct

54. TELLING:

A. unimportant
B. rash
C. bold
D. unstable
E. pleasurable

55. UNDERSCORE:

A. invite
B. downplay
C. renew
D. attempt
E. succeed

56. TRAIT : CHARACTER ::

    A. feature : face
    B. behavior : norm
    C. desire : prayer
    D. endurance : strength
    E. pressure: deadline

57. THEORIST : HYPOTHESIS ::

    A. singer : microphone
    B. linguist : language
    C. thinker : explanation
    D. painter : easel
    E. teacher : student

58. PLUMAGE : FEATHER ::

    A. foliage : leaf
    B. lake : river
    C. fur : mammal
    D. marriage : couple
    E. bird : flight

59. SATIRE : RIDICULE ::

    A. parody : humor
    B. drama : comedy
    C. education : books
    D. learning : school
    E. imitation : flattery

60. ASPECT : ANGLE ::

    A. sight : eye
    B. light : vision
    C. view : perspective
    D. total : part
    E. record : report

Passage III

SOCIAL SCIENCE: This passage is adapted from an article entitled "Early Adolescence and Human Development" in a sociology journal.

Early adolescence is the second most rapid time of growth and change in human development. Only infancy exceeds early adolescence in velocity of growth. Physically, young adolescents are experiencing
5 a growth spurt and the onset of puberty. They have special health, nutritional, and mental health needs in relation to these physical changes. These needs have implications for school curricula. Emotionally and socially, young adolescents are exploring a sense of
10 uniqueness and belonging, of separation and commitment, future goals and their personal pasts. For the first time in their lives, they see themselves as having a personal and a social destiny, and as being part of a generation. Again, these have curricular
15 implications. Intellectually, young adolescents are exploring values and ideas in a new way. Some are beginning to form abstractions, to generalize, to think about thinking. This intellectual development makes it possible for some to become engaged with concepts,
20 imagery, contingencies, logical arguments, and even philosophical speculation. It also enables them to shift from an authoritarian sense of right and wrong to a more open and complex approach to value formation, both personal and social. This cognitive shift makes it
25 possible for young adolescents to struggle for the first time with conflicting concepts like individual rights and "the greater social good"—the underpinnings of democracy. This change in cognitive style has import for curriculum and teaching techniques.

30 And so, early adolescence is a critical time in human development; critical to the individual, and to the social order. We tend to be fearful of this stage of development. While acknowledging the plasticity of this stage, we anticipate that young adolescents are
35 more receptive to negative than to positive influences. We are apprehensive that the great majority who maneuver their way successfully through a time of life requiring considerable coping skills will "catch" the "diseases" of our "new epidemics"—pregnancy,
40 running away, dropping out of school, alcoholism, drug addiction, violence, and suicide. I do not mean to belittle the personal pain or social risk of such behaviors, but rather to insist that most young adolescents, for many reasons, most of which we do
45 not know, manage to cope with amazing stability through such a demanding period of life. Partly because of our fears, we label the age group "transitional" and put young adolescents on hold. By doing so, we fail to assign our talents and financial
50 resources to an extremely vulnerable and impressionable age group.

61. To prepare for every -------, the space authorities developed emergency evacuation plans for the International Space Station crew.

   A. criteria
   B. option
   C. inclination
   D. inconsistency
   E. contingency

62. The conference was intended to provide the scientists with a forum to engage in ------- about the origins of the universe and humanity's ultimate destiny.

   A. recklessness
   B. absolution
   C. abolition
   D. speculation
   E. accusation

63. The ------- government maintained its control over the people by severely punishing anyone who even attempted to question its policies.

   A. deposed
   B. authoritarian
   C. antediluvian
   D. bacchanalian
   E. laissez-faire

64. While ------- that he often turned in homework late, the student argued that this did not merit a failing grade in the course.

   A. denying
   B. ignoring
   C. believing
   D. repudiating
   E. acknowledging

65. Since the South African government disbanded the police force's endangered species unit in 2003, black rhinos have become extremely ------- to poaching by organized crime gangs.

A. impermeable
B. invincible
C. amenable
D. vulnerable
E. manageable

66. Based on the use of the word *curricula* in line 8, it can be inferred that *curriculum* refers to:

A. a building code.
B. a required course of study.
C. an underground passage.
D. a standard on which a decision is based.

67. Based on the use of the word *abstractions* in line 17, it can be inferred that *abstraction* most nearly means:

A. a causal or logical relation or sequence.
B. the mental act of contemplating the parts of an object as separate from the object itself.
C. a condition of being clogged or blocked.
D. an unrestrained expression of feelings.

68. As it is used in line 20, the word *arguments* refers to:

A. fights or quarrels.
B. disputed statements.
C. persuasive reasoning or discussions.
D. indications or suggestions.

69. The word *underpinnings* (line 27) most nearly means:

A. growth.
B. attenuation.
C. hidden opinions.
D. foundation.

70. It can be inferred that the word *import*, as it is used in line 28, primarily means to have:

A. significance.
B. futility.
C. foreign origins.
D. urgency.

71. In line 29, the word *techniques* refers to:

A. attitudes.
B. methods.
C. technologies.
D. designs.

72. As it is used in line 34, the word *anticipate* most nearly means to:

A. expect.
B. disperse.
C. prevent.
D. argue.

73. In line 36, *apprehensive* is closest in meaning to:

A. inexperienced.
B. assured.
C. confident.
D. fearful.

74. In line 39, the word *epidemics* refers to:

A. characteristics of a particular region.
B. required courses of study.
C. outbreaks of sudden rapid growth or development.
D. cultures or histories.

75. In line 42, *belittle* most nearly means to:

A. pay tribute.
B. treat as having little importance.
C. give emphasis.
D. express deep regret or remorse.

76. UNIQUE:

A. forward
B. warped
C. factual
D. undeniable
E. ordinary

77. GENERATE:

A. destroy
B. quiet
C. slice
D. stun
E. grope

78. PLASTICITY:

A. emotionalism
B. youthfulness
C. security
D. resistance
E. conformity

79. RECEPTIVE:

A. in favor of
B. inclined to
C. indifferent to
D. ignorant of
E. anxious to

80. TRANSITIONAL:

A. permanent
B. footloose
C. generous
D. captive
E. gentle

81. IMPRESSIONABLE:

A. exact
B. hard
C. timid
D. favorable
E. content

82. SPURT:

A. hold tight
B. lean over
C. fill up
D. rain heavily
E. flow steadily

83. COPE:

A. renew
B. surrender
C. plead
D. accept
E. help

84. INFANCY:

A. childhood
B. maturity
C. age
D. graduation
E. life

85. MANEUVER:

A. pray
B. drift
C. prevent
D. allow
E. point

86. VALUE : PRICE ::

A. product : cost
B. profit : markup
C. esteem : worth
D. donation : gift
E. debt : interest

87. ADOLESCENCE : YOUTHFUL ::

A. childhood : aged
B. adulthood : mature
C. seniority : old
D. parent : middle-aged
E. puberty : offspring

88. ASSIGN : PROJECT ::

   A. delegate : duty
   B. enforce : law
   C. require : demand
   D. insist : compliance
   E. renew: license

89. ADDICTION : RELY ::

   A. depression : enjoy
   B. pressure : relax
   C. failure : assist
   D. dependence : need
   E. intention: succeed

90. VELOCITY : MOTION ::

   A. structure : condition
   B. sincerity : honor
   C. change : circumstance
   D. failure : requirement
   E. speed : movement

Passage IV

SOCIAL SCIENCE: This passage is adapted from a chapter in an agricultural science textbook exploring modern agricultural problems.

Rapid increases in human population have steadily intensified pressures to augment the productivity of existing grazing and agricultural land.

5   Grazing land in the Indian subcontinent and isolated islands in the Philippines have a relatively low carrying capacity and are currently capable of sustaining only marginal levels of subsistence. Overexploitation has not only decreased their productivity, but is continuously destroying the fertility and stability

10 of affected soils. The problem is particularly injurious in areas of Pakistan and Northeast India, where overgrazing is resulting in desertification. In the Luni blocks of Rajasthan, most pastures now have only 10 to 15 percent of their original carrying capacity and the

15 forage deficit is met by expansion into standing vegetation. Within a twenty-year period, infecund sand cover has increased from 25 to 33 percent of the area.

In most Asian countries, rice is the principal food crop. Increased cultivation has barely met the demands

20 of the growing populations. In the Philippines, while food production has increased slightly faster than the size of population, even greater increases in per capita food demand have created new shortfalls. Indonesia, once an important rice exporter, has been dependent on

25 imported rice for several years. Most countries are merely keeping up with their current needs and gross shortages can be anticipated.

The intensified agricultural production required in these countries has potential adverse side effects on

30 other resources. The disruptive effects of the large-scale reservoirs needed for irrigation of more land are self-evident. Some other problems include waterlogging and salinity, soil erosion, increased populations of pests, and agricultural pollution.

35 Waterlogging and salinity can be a problem wherever surface water is applied to irrigated land with inadequate underground drainage. Water will rise to within a few feet of the surface, vitiating the growth of deep-rooted crops and allowing a concentration of

40 minerals and salt to build up near the surface. This has been seen in China, India, and Pakistan. Control projects involving the construction of new wells and drainage systems have been successful in reversing some of the deleterious effects, but at prodigious costs.

45 The establishment of broad area monoculture, primarily irrigated riceland, can result in difficult pest management problems. Recently, Indonesia has had some destructive and noisome pest outbreaks that have reduced rice yields up to 60 percent in the last two

50 years. Double-cropping does not allow dry-season pest population enervation, and their numbers are therefore maintained. An integrated pest management program is needed to realize increased productivity. This program must be done assiduously, not on an intermittent

55 schedule.

Soil erosion is occurring in hilly and mountainous areas, which often constitute the only remaining land available for cultivation. With the monsoon rains, erosion is inevitable unless there is an extensive

60 terracing system. The rivers of Nepal annually carry over 240 million cubic meters of soil to India. This deprivation has been called Nepal's "most dear export."

91. In the nineteenth century, expanding European-American settlement of the United States forced large numbers of Native Americans onto ------- lands.

   A. valuable
   B. sustentative
   C. precarious
   D. central
   E. marginal

92. Michael Pollan argues in *The Botany of Desire* that while ------- may offer economic advantages, it invites serious environmental risks because a field of identical plants will always be vulnerable to all the forces of nature.

   A. agriculture
   B. monoculture
   C. nomenclature
   D. polyculture
   E. permaculture

93. The neighbors of the confined animal feeding operation complained about the ------- odors and groundwater pollution.

    A. harmless
    B. noisome
    C. helpful
    D. noisy
    E. benign

94. Donna tended her garden -------, taking care to weed every other day and to fertilize with every watering.

    A. inconsistently
    B. strenuously
    C. assiduously
    D. irreverently
    E. respectfully

95. Although a ceasefire had been signed, ------- and sporadic gunfire disturbed the silence of the desert night.

    A. constant
    B. incipient
    C. contented
    D. intermittent
    E. deliberate

96. It can be inferred that the word *augment*, as it is used in line 2, means to:

    A. decrease.
    B. increase.
    C. remain constant.
    D. cease.

97. In context, *subsistence* (line 7) most nearly means:

    A. extinction.
    B. productivity.
    C. wastefulness.
    D. survival.

98. It can be inferred that the word *desertification* (line 12) refers to the process by which:

    A. land becomes wet and humid.
    B. land becomes dry and arid.
    C. air becomes wet and humid.
    D. air becomes dry and arid.

99. As it is used in line 16, the word *infecund* most nearly means:

    A. offensive smelling.
    B. infectious.
    C. unproductive.
    D. fertile.

100. In line 29, *adverse* is best understood to mean:

    A. unfavorable.
    B. constructive.
    C. poisonous.
    D. beneficial.

101. The word *salinity* (line 33) most nearly means:

    A. sourness.
    B. sweetness.
    C. saltiness.
    D. bitterness.

102. As it is used in line 38, the word *vitiating* most nearly means:

    A. assisting or helping.
    B. energizing or strengthening.
    C. depriving of oxygen.
    D. making faulty or defective.

103. It can be inferred that the word *deleterious*, as it is used in line 44, most nearly means:

    A. delicious.
    B. harmless.
    C. involuntary.
    D. destructive.

104. In line 44, *prodigious* most nearly means:

A. enormous.
B. marginal.
C. average.
D. luxuriant.

105. The word *enervation* (line 51) refers to:

A. weakening.
B. strengthening.
C. extinction.
D. animation.

106. INTENSIFY:

A. relax
B. improve
C. shorten
D. claim
E. wipe out

107. DEFICIT:

A. loss
B. debt
C. excess
D. sinful
E. calm

108. SUSTAIN:

A. collapse
B. prolong
C. bear
D. carry
E. fulfill

109. EXPLOITED:

A. cautious
B. weary
C. tremendous
D. unused
E. unprotected

110. DISRUPT:

A. implant
B. restore
C. simplify
D. create
E. dampen

111. INTEGRATED:

A. proper
B. simple
C. stolen
D. piecemeal
E. golden

112. PRINCIPAL:

A. wholesome
B. dietetic
C. unimportant
D. declining
E. serious

113. REALIZE:

A. fail
B. offer
C. deny
D. avoid
E. remind

114. INEVITABLE:

A. blank
B. unlikely
C. late
D. hurried
E. advanced

115. DEPRIVATION:

A. taking away
B. giving back
C. sending out
D. withholding from
E. pushing ahead

116. RESERVOIR : WATER ::

    A. highway : automobile
    B. den : lion
    C. silo : grain
    D. library : reader
    E. land : farming

117. TERRACED : STAIRS ::

    A. sunken : mound
    B. roofed : yard
    C. leveled : door
    D. sheer : wall
    E. rolling : mountains

118. IRRIGATED : WATER ::

    A. fertilized : nutrients
    B. farmed : crops
    C. produced : vegetables
    D. eroded : soil
    E. polluted : water

119. FORAGE : SEARCH ::

    A. hide : seek
    B. garden : plant
    C. harvest : sell
    D. water : weed
    E. hunt : pursue

120. CROP : CUT ::

    A. reduce : increase
    B. plant : harvest
    C. trim : snip
    D. sew : fit
    E. wheat : corn

Passage V

SOCIAL SCIENCE: This passage is adapted from an introductory economics course textbook.

The function of payment systems is to provide means for conducting exchanges of values. These values usually involve goods, services, financial obligations, or ownership records on one side, which
5 are exchanged for money from the other party in the transaction. However, in recent years, surrogates for money, such as checks or credit, have received increasing acceptance. Since they facilitate the exchange process, payment systems have become all-
10 persuasive and essential to the operation of modern society. All of us make use of one or more of these systems so easily and casually almost daily, we are seldom aware of the process.

Payment systems have a long history. One of the
15 first steps in organizing any nation is the enactment and promulgation of laws to provide for and regulate the value of some form of money and to enforce, to the greatest extent possible, its universal acceptance. Without widespread use and acceptance of a standard-
20 ized medium of exchange, the growth of industry and commerce would be stunted.

In early times, coins were the most prevalent form of money and are still widely used for many types of transactions; in fact, during the last two decades,
25 coin transactions have enjoyed a resurgence. The impetus for this increased reliance on coins was the spread of coin-operated vending machines. The development of paper currency provided a more convenient alternative to coins for all except low-value
30 transactions and facilitated the spread of commercial activity. More recently, the large-scale acceptance of checks provided a still better means for making many types of payments, especially those that have to be made over a distance; thus, their growth has been rapid.

35 A host of other, more specialized instruments have also been developed. Travelers' checks, a widely-accepted and convenient medium of exchange for those away from home, are safer than cash. Letters of credit, which are employed for similar reasons by businesses,
40 usually involve larger amounts than those for which travelers' checks are used. Money orders offer a means for individuals without checking accounts to effect safe and rapid payments at a distance. Telegraph transfers of money can be relied on where speed is critical. Each
45 system has other distinctive characteristics. Some offer greater safety from loss or theft than do others; some are more susceptible to fraud or misuse. Thus, we can choose among a wide range of options to suit our needs.

50 The importance of efficient payment mechanisms is amplified by their close relationship to another key social activity—the granting of credit. This relationship derives from the fact that the decision to extend credit is often based to a large extent on the past performance
55 of the recipient in making payments on prior credit offerings. This characteristic makes records of past payments an important component in the credit-granting process.

The most important factor, in social and
60 economic terms, has been the rapid growth in the extension of consumer credit as part of the process of conducting retail sales transactions. Both merchants and financial institutions offering credit—as well as those who receive it—have perceived benefits from the
65 frequent use of short-term credit systems, so a variety of means for providing such credit has arisen in recent years. This has led to a wide-spread and increasing use of credit cards provided by merchants, banks, and independent operators as a substitute for cash or checks
70 when making retail purchases.

Initially, however, credit cards were almost always associated with specific purchases (often from the single company issuing the card), and the grant of credit terminated upon the presentation of a monthly
75 bill. In this forum of use, the dominant features of value to the card-user were the convenience provided when making purchases, the greater safety of carrying smaller amounts of cash, and the possibility of aggregating a number of smaller payments into a single
80 large payment. More recently, and arising primarily from the introduction of bank credit cards, some systems provide extended credit, automatic use of credit when a checking account becomes overdrawn, and opportunities to borrow money unrelated to
85 specific purchases. These features can become more important than the convenience, security, and payments aggregation characteristics. In the process, payments and credit have grown still more tightly related, and the two elements have become increasingly difficult to
90 disentangle.

121. In the United States, the ------- of federal laws occurs upon signing by the President or overriding of a presidential veto.

    A. dissimilation
    B. promulgation
    C. proscription
    D. extension
    E. destruction

122. To suggest that jazz enjoyed a(n) ------- in the 1980s is to imply that it fell out of favor in the 1970s—a proposition with which many jazz fans would take issue.

    A. resurgence
    B. acquiescence
    C. insurgence
    D. disappearance
    E. importance

123. After the comptroller was caught embezzling funds from government accounts, her appointment was immediately -------.

    A. delegated
    B. initiated
    C. relegated
    D. renegotiated
    E. terminated

124. According to Leo Tolstoy, history—that is to say the collective life of the ------- of human beings—turns each moment of a monarch's life to account, and bends kings to its own ends.

    A. faction
    B. aggregate
    C. entourage
    D. separation
    E. range

125. Because she wrote checks totaling more than the available balance, Jill's bank account became -------.

    A. solvent
    B. accessible
    C. overhauled
    D. financed
    E. overdrawn

126. In context, *transaction* (line 6) primarily refers to a(n):

    A. performance.
    B. alteration.
    C. transition.
    D. business deal.

127. As it is used in line 6, the word *surrogates* refers to:

    A. descendants.
    B. replications.
    C. recipients.
    D. substitutes.

128. It can be inferred that the word *facilitate*, as it is used in line 8, most nearly means to:

    A. inhibit or slow down.
    B. make briefer.
    C. make less difficult.
    D. complicate.

129. In line 18, *universal* is best understood to mean:

    A. used by everyone.
    B. the state of being excluded.
    C. limited in availability.
    D. better than average.

130. According to the passage, the word *prevalent* (line 22) is used to refer to something:

    A. exceptional.
    B. absent.
    C. widespread.
    D. current.

131. The word *impetus* (line 26) most nearly means:

    A. inertia.
    B. stimulus.
    C. lethargy.
    D. insolence.

132. It can be inferred that the word *currency*, as it is used in line 28, primarily refers to a:

A. prevalent trend.
B. technique for making money.
C. record-keeping device.
D. medium of trade or exchange.

133. In line 47, *susceptible* most nearly means:

A. insensitive.
B. easily affected.
C. suspicious.
D. accessible.

134. In line 53, *derives* most nearly means:

A. comes from a source.
B. creates from new.
C. depart from an established course.
D. expresses contempt.

135. In line 57, *component* refers to a(n):

A. aggregate.
B. role or position.
C. substitute.
D. part.

136. CASUAL:

A. light
B. preplanned
C. homey
D. valuable
E. rare

137. STANDARDIZED:

A. involuntary
B. official
C. widespread
D. new
E. variable

138. HOST:

A. one of something
B. matched set
C. living tissue
D. wide appeal
E. moment in time

139. SPECIALIZED:

A. timely
B. free
C. general
D. quiet
E. victorious

140. DISTINCTIVE:

A. open-ended
B. poorly defined
C. keenly felt
D. easily seen
E. properly dressed

141. EXTEND:

A. trick
B. relax
C. withdraw
D. correct
E. lengthen

142. RETAIL:

A. wholesale
B. stored
C. shipping
D. cheap
E. insignificant

143. ASSOCIATED:

A. trapped
B. unrelated
C. worn
D. trained
E. insulted

144. ISSUE:

   A. argue about
   B. walk out on
   C. invite discussion
   D. feel out
   E. take back

145. DISENTANGLE:

   A. cut off
   B. tie up
   C. wear down
   D. look forward
   E. pull down

146. OBLIGATION : PAY ::

   A. promise : perform
   B. duty : ignore
   C. honor : defend
   D. virtue : reward
   E. taxes : evade

147. VENDOR : SELLER ::

   A. machine : coin
   B. goods : delivery service
   C. purchaser : buyer
   D. manufacturer : user
   E. banker : clerk

148. RECIPIENT : ACCEPT ::

   A. donor : give
   B. creator : destroy
   C. enforcer : violate
   D. informant : lie
   E. priest : confess

149. OPTIONS : CHOOSE ::

   A. routes : travel
   B. courses : enroll
   C. alternatives : select
   D. possibilities : realize
   E. rooms : inhabit

150. MERCHANT : TRADE ::

   A. clerk : advertisement
   B. manager : store
   C. businessperson : commerce
   D. director : stock
   E. seller : purchase

Passage VI

SOCIAL SCIENCE: This passage is adapted from an essay entitled "Customs and Opinions of Ancient Nations" in an introductory sociology textbook.

Nature being everywhere the same, men must necessarily have adopted the same verities, and fallen into the same delusions, in regard to those things which are the immediate objects of sense, and the most
5 striking to the imagination. They simply have ascribed the noise and effects of thunder to some superior being inhabiting the air. The people bordering upon the ocean, seeing great tides inundate their coasts at the time of the full moon, must naturally have imputed to
10 the moon the vicissitudes which attended her cyclical phases.

Among animals, the serpent must have appeared to them to be endowed with superior intelligence; because, seeing it sometimes cast its skin, they had
15 reason to think it became young again. It might, then, by this process of rejuvenation always remain youthful and therefore immortal. In Egypt and Greece, it was the symbol of immortality. The larger serpents found in proximity to fountains deterred the timorous from
20 approaching them, hence they were imagined to be guardians of hidden treasure. Serpents were also found to be mischievous animals, but as they were supposed to possess something divine, nothing less than a deity was imagined capable of destroying them.

25 Dreams too much have introduced the same superstitions all over the earth. If while awake, I am uneasy for my wife's or son's health, and in my sleep I see them in the agonies of death, should they die a few days later, it cannot be denied the gods sent me this
30 warning. If my dream is not fulfilled? It was a fallacious representation, with which the gods wished to terrify me. Or a woman applies to the oracles to know whether her husband will die within the year. One answers yes, the other no. It is certain that one of
35 them must be correct, and she will proclaim all over the city the wisdom of the one whose prognostication was fulfilled.

The origin of good and evil is a more philosophical question. The first theologians must have
40 put the same question which we all do from the age of fifteen or so: Why is there any evil in the world? It was taught in India, that Adimo, the daughter of Brahma, brought forth from the navel, the just from her right side and the unjust from her left; it was from this left

45 side that evil was originally introduced. We know of Pandora of the Greeks. This is the finest of all the allegories which antiquity has handed down to us.

So too all peoples have provided for the expiation of wrongdoing, for where was the man or woman who
50 had not been guilty of some injury against society? Who had not profaned the gods? Who had not debased himself? Where was the person whose natural instinct did not prompt a feeling of remorse? Water cleanses the body and our apparel, and fire purifies metal. It was
55 natural then that water and fire should purge the soul of its guilt, and in every temple were found holy water and sacred fire.

Men plunged themselves into the Ganges, the Indus, and the Euphrates when it was the noon moon.
60 This immersion expiated their sins. If they did not purify themselves in the Nile, it was only fear that the penitents might have been devoured by crocodiles. However, the priests who purified themselves on the people's behalf immersed themselves in large tubs of
65 water. The Greeks had in all of their temples sacred baths as well as sacred fires, which were universal symbols for all men of the purity of their souls.

151. The authorship of the ancient Sanskrit epic *Mahabharata*, a major text of Hinduism and cornerstone of Hindu mythology, is traditionally ------- to Vyasa.

A. subscribed
B. ascribed
C. delivered
D. propelled
E. transmitted

152. The inability of the Congress to pass any legislation was ------- to the Republicans for their perceived refusal to attempt negotiations with the Democrats.

A. demoted
B. transferred
C. promoted
D. imputed
E. donated

153. Because Elizabeth was so ------- and lacking in confidence, she was an easy target for every peddler and door-to-door salesperson.

A. brave
B. timorous
C. confrontational
D. outgoing
E. devious

154. The irony of the Nobel Peace Prize bearing the name of the inventor of dynamite has given rise to the myth that Alfred Nobel established the award as a way to ------- his guilty conscience.

A. augment
B. idealize
C. scrutinize
D. justify
E. expiate

155. We hoped that the media would not ------- the memory of our deceased father by reporting the malicious gossip and rumors surrounding his death.

A. profane
B. sustain
C. abolish
D. inflate
E. defend

156. As it is used in line 2, the word *verities* refers to:

A. methods.
B. truths.
C. histories.
D. falsehoods.

157. In context, *inundate* (line 8) most nearly means to:

A. dehydrate.
B. capitulate.
C. overflow.
D. emphasize.

158. In line 10, the word *vicissitudes* refers to:

A. changes in fortune.
B. mental confusion.
C. alteration of plans.
D. fierceness or aggression.

159. It can be inferred that the word *rejuvenation*, as it is used in line 16, primarily refers to the:

A. ending of life.
B. appearance of illusion.
C. personification of characteristics.
D. restoration of youth.

160. The word *proximity* (line 19) is used to indicate:

A. agility.
B. probability.
C. relevance.
D. nearness.

161. Based on the use of the word *oracles* in line 32, it can be inferred that *oracle* primarily refers to a(n):

A. public speech or debate.
B. person believed to foretell the future.
C. organization or coalition.
D. person making a donation.

162. As it is used in line 36, the word *prognostication* refers to a:

A. delay.
B. responsibility.
C. prediction.
D. perception.

163. Based on the use of the word *allegories* in line 47, it can be inferred that *allegory* primarily refers to a(n):

A. unsupported assertion.
B. symbolic story about human existence.
C. musical composition.
D. pledge of allegiance.

164. In line 53, *remorse* is closest in meaning to:

A. shame.
B. arrogance.
C. humility.
D. compassion.

165. In line 60, *immersion* most nearly means to:

A. absorb excess liquid.
B. confront one's emotions.
C. rise up from or come into view.
D. completely cover with liquid.

166. DELUSION:

A. true belief
B. unproved assumption
C. worthless notion
D. widely held opinion
E. crafty plan

167. SUPERIOR:

A. complete
B. lower
C. intense
D. practical
E. stronger

168. DETER:

A. prevent
B. encourage
C. remain
D. omit
E. sort

169. MISCHIEVOUS:

A. youthful
B. corrupt
C. forgiving
D. tarnished
E. well behaved

170. DIVINE:

A. holy
B. angelic
C. human
D. immortal
E. perfect

171. UNEASY:

A. reckless
B. foreboding
C. relaxed
D. frightful
E. worthwhile

172. FALLACIOUS:

A. probably
B. inconceivable
C. particular
D. correct
E. loud

173. PROCLAIM:

A. suppress
B. contend
C. presuppose
D. terrify
E. renew

174. DEBASE:

A. victimize
B. relate
C. concentrate
D. lift up
E. tear down

175. PURGE:

A. remove
B. stain
C. reline
D. wash
E. prevent

176. CYCLICAL : REPETITION ::

A. artificial : genuine
B. truthful : evident
C. circular : continuity
D. applicable : question
E. tremendous : strength

177. PENITENT : REPENT ::

A. musician : play
B. acrobat : fall
C. judgment : pronounce
D. guilty party : defend
E. confessant : admit

178. THEOLOGY : RELIGION ::

A. botany : plants
B. biology : human beings
C. archaeology : history
D. numerology : letters
E. geology : poetry

179. EAT : DEVOUR ::

A. feed : accept
B. drink : sip
C. consume : gobble
D. cook : prepare
E. plant : pick

180. PLUNGE : ENTER INTO ::

A. cover : take out of
B. fall : go down
C. ascend : cross over
D. return : go on
E. exit : remain within

Vocabulary Builder: Humanities Passages

DIRECTIONS: Each passage in this exercise is followed by sets of sentence completion, vocabulary-in-context, antonym, and analogy items for building vocabulary through context. In addition to using the passages to infer word meanings, you may use a dictionary or refer to the Vocabulary List beginning on page 655.

The first set of items following each passage are sentence completion items based on words from the passage. Each sentence has one blank. Choose the word that best fits the meaning of the sentence in its entirety.

The second set of items following each passage are vocabulary-in-context items based on words from the passage. Choose the best answer for each item based on what is stated or implied in the passage.

The third set of items following each passage are antonym items based on words from the passage. For each item, choose the word that has a meaning most nearly opposite of the capitalized word.

The fourth set of items following each passage are analogy items based on words from the passage. For each item, find the pair of words that expresses a relationship most like that expressed by the capitalized words.

Answers are on page 800.

Passage I

HUMANITIES: This passage is adapted from an essay discussing the epic poem *Kalevala*, compiled by Elias Lönnrot from Finnish folklore in the nineteenth century.

Those who enjoyed the *Star Wars* films would probably fall under the spell of the Finnish epic, *Kalevala*. Though first published nearly 150 years ago, many of the adventures in this epic could easily be
5 scripted into scenes for our modern fantasy adventure films. Instead of battling with advanced technological gadgets such as rockets and lasers, however, the heroes of *Kalevala* engage in bouts of wisdom and magic, casting spells of enchantment over their foes. Thus,
10 when wise old Vainamoinen, the greatest singer of the runes, is challenged by a young up-start, Joukahainen, it takes but a few magical charms to cause the young man to sink neck-deep into the seemingly solid ground. The thoroughly intimidated Joukahainen offers his
15 sister, Aino, as ransom for his release, and Vainamoinen accepts. The young girl, dismayed at the prospect of marriage to such an old man, drowns herself and becomes a fish. Vainamoinen later catches the fish, but he fails to recognize her and she escapes,
20 leaving him to grieve.

These fantastic adventures of charm-chanting heroes and sorcerers were known to illiterate Finnish singers for many hundreds of years. The episodes were sung as individual songs by traditional singers who
25 lived in isolated villages along the Finnish-Russian frontier. They became known to the educated, urban Finns only after the texts of some songs were set down on paper. Although a few of the songs had been sporadically recorded since the eighteenth century, it
30 was primarily the work of one individual—Elias Lönnrot—that clearly demonstrated the richness of these oral traditions. A medical doctor by profession, but an avid folklore collector by avocation, Lönnrot logged many miles on foot in the early 1830s, writing
35 down as many variants as he could find of the songs about Vainamoinen, Lemminkainen, Llmarinen, and others. Instead of publishing the songs as individual pieces, however, he arranged them into a linear story line.

40 In 1835, he published the *Kalevala* as an epic—the Finnish counterpart to the Nordic *Edda*, the Germanic *Nibelungenlied*, the Scottish Ossian poems, and harkening back to the classics, the Greek *Iliad* and *Odyssey*.

For Finland, the publication of songs sung by the ordinary folk in the hinterlands of their country served as a major stimulus to the building and fostering of a distinct national identity. Until then, the Finnish language and identity were held in rather low esteem; Finland's educated, urban elite had accepted, for the most part, the language, culture, and traditions of the governing Swedes. Through Lönnrot's *Kalevala*, the intelligentsia began to awaken to the richness of the Finnish heritage.

Although it took some time, the *Kalevala* helped to kindle national aspirations that eventually culminated in the establishment of an independent Finland. For the Finnish people, much under the sway of the general Romantic trends of the times, the *Kalevala* presented a past of which they could be proud. Scholars argued about the historicity of the heroes and engaged in discussion about the evolution of the songs through time. It became required reading in secondary schools, and playwrights, composers, and other artists were soon using its themes and motifs for their own creative ventures.

The *Kalevala* was indeed something of which to be proud, for soon after its publication in Finnish, it was translated into Swedish, French, German, and Russian. In America, the work received considerable publicity when Longfellow published his *Song of Hiawatha* in 1885, and critics accused him of plagiarizing the Finnish epic. Longfellow admitted that he was acquainted with the work through German translation and that he purposely copied the meter of the *Kalevala* in order to imbue his work with a certain ancient and noble tone and cadence. Prompted by the controversy, the English translation appeared in 1889. Since those times, translations have been printed in 30 languages. The *Kalevala* is probably the best known Finnish literary work throughout the world.

1. Because the dog barked ------- for no apparent reason, we decided he was not a very reliable watchdog.

   A. quietly
   B. callously
   C. temporarily
   D. sporadically
   E. shyly

2. A passionate skateboarder, Jonathan is planning a regional tour of neighborhood community centers to share his ------- love of the sport with underprivileged teens.

   A. apathetic
   B. average
   C. unreasonable
   D. aversive
   E. avid

3. The schedule for the six-week acting workshop indicates it will ------- in the final presentation of a one-act play to the entire student body.

   A. initiate
   B. converge
   C. culminate
   D. founder
   E. corroborate

4. From all around the country, young men with no work and ------- with patriotism rushed to serve in World War I.

   A. subdued
   B. withered
   C. placated
   D. imbued
   E. diminished

5. The high school concert band marched to a swift ------- played by the rhythmic drum section.

   A. dalliance
   B. irreverence
   C. cadence
   D. silence
   E. insurgence

6. In context, *prospect* (line 17) most nearly means:

   A. trust or confidence.
   B. mental consideration.
   C. a declaration.
   D. condition of success.

7. As it is used in line 33, the word *avocation* most nearly means:

   A. hobby.
   B. training.
   C. birth.
   D. job.

8. It can be inferred that the word *hinterlands*, as it is used in line 46, primarily refers to:

   A. areas close to big cities or towns.
   B. areas far from big cities or towns.
   C. capital cities.
   D. elevated or mountainous lands.

9. In line 53, *intelligentsia* is best understood to refer in general to the:

   A. educated class.
   B. uneducated class.
   C. university academic employees.
   D. farmers and peasants.

10. In line 54, *heritage* is best understood as referring to:

    A. innovations.
    B. political systems.
    C. landscape.
    D. customs and traditions.

11. The word *aspirations* (line 56) most nearly means:

    A. failures.
    B. realities.
    C. ambitions.
    D. legends.

12. It can be inferred that the word *establishment*, as it is used in line 57, most nearly means:

    A. destruction.
    B. formation.
    C. interpretation.
    D. purchase.

13. As it is used in line 58, the word *sway* most nearly means:

    A. freedom.
    B. support.
    C. influence.
    D. overindulgence.

14. In line 61, *historicity* most nearly means:

    A. authenticity.
    B. humility.
    C. exaggeration.
    D. origin.

15. In line 65, *motifs* is closest in meaning to:

    A. impulses.
    B. replications.
    C. main elements.
    D. mechanisms.

16. ELITE:

    A. lofty
    B. ordinary
    C. verbal
    D. continuous
    E. brief

17. ESTEEM:

    A. despise
    B. allow
    C. protrude
    D. complete
    E. insure

18. ILLITERATE:

    A. well known
    B. well read
    C. well worn
    D. well supplied
    E. well fought

19. DISMAYED:

A. confused
B. courageous
C. mournful
D. pretentious
E. dangerous

20. KINDLE:

A. preserve
B. assure
C. import
D. dampen
E. renew

21. INTIMIDATE:

A. suggest
B. postpone
C. study
D. encourage
E. exile

22. FOSTER:

A. crush
B. uphold
C. withdraw
D. respond
E. rotate

23. STIMULUS:

A. disorder
B. quiet
C. restraint
D. approval
E. joy

24. LINEAR:

A. random
B. elongated
C. worthwhile
D. consistent
E. gorgeous

25. EPIC:

A. factual
B. insignificant
C. tiresome
D. modern
E. useful

26. PLAGIARIZE : WRITING ::

A. condemn : criminal
B. release : information
C. steal : property
D. pay : dividend
E. perform : drama

27. NATIONS : FRONTIER ::

A. lots : boundaries
B. highways : cities
C. immigrants : citizens
D. governments : leaders
E. Earth : space

28. FANTASTIC : IMPOSSIBLE ::

A. unrealistic : inconceivable
B. dramatic : thinkable
C. logical : workable
D. scientific : speculative
E. permanent : movable

29. VENTURE : RISK ::

A. heroism : actor
B. confidence : disbelief
C. favoritism : choice
D. real : honest
E. gamble : danger

30. ENCHANT : CHARMED ::

A. put off : offended
B. describe : known
C. forego : delighted
D. insist : free
E. proceed : finished

Passage II

HUMANITIES: This passage is adapted from an essay discussing an anthology of American songs based on the classic, "Tie a Yellow Ribbon."

In 1972, Irwin Levine and L. Russell Brown copyrighted a song with the title of "Tie a Yellow Ribbon Round the Ole Oak Tree," and it was recorded by some 30 different vocalists in the late 1970s and
5 sold millions of copies. The hit version was recorded by the popular group Dawn, featuring Tony Orlando. In 1949, Aigosy Pictures released a motion picture starring John Wayne and Joanne Dru, called *She Wore a Yellow Ribbon*. The picture was popular and the
10 theme song, "Round Her Neck She Wore a Yellow Ribbon," became a hit. Not surprisingly, the lyrics make reference to the characters and events in the film. In one form or another, this song antedates both the movie and the hit tune. It has been registered for
15 copyright a number of times, the earliest claim for it being the composition of George Norton in 1917. Norton gave as his title "Round Her Neck She Wears a Yeller Ribbon."

It has also been reported as a college song of the
20 1920s in which environment it displayed considerable variation, both in its symbolism and in its suitability for public expression. A verse typical of the college type:

Around her knee, she wore a purple garter;
She wore it in the Springtime, and in the month of
25   May.
And if you asked her why the Hell she wore it,
She wore it for her William's man who's far, far
    away.

Other emblematic appurtenances of the young
30 lady include a baby carriage and a shotgun-wielding father. The color of the ribbon or garter could be varied in order to implicate a student of an appropriate college: crimson for Harvard, orange for Princeton, and so on. It was a slightly refined version of this college
35 tradition, rather than the movie theme song, which became a great favorite on the early 1960s, television show, "Sing Along with Mitch." It appears on pages 22 and 24 of the *Sing Along with Mitch Songbook*, where an accompanying headnote describes it as an "old army
40 marching song (based on a traditional theme)." Although the second verse is essentially the "purple garter" type, the first verse begins, "Around her neck, she wore a yellow ribbon."

It seems likely that Mitch Miller's popular
45 printing, a decade after the motion picture, helped foster the perhaps erroneous idea that wearing a yellow ribbon as a token of remembrance was a custom of the Civil War era, but the song does not appear in any known anthology of Civil War songs. Although it is
50 plausible that the families of Union army troops did adopt such a token, prudent historiography would demand evidence from a diary, photograph, or source contemporary to the war. Without such evidence, it seems likely that distant recollections of the Civil War
55 have subsequently been grafted onto the symbolism of a much later popular motion picture. Occurrences of this sort are often noticed in the study of folk balladry in which the anachronistic combinations are among the more interesting features of the genre.

60 Whether Levine and Brown were consciously or unconsciously influenced by *She Wore a Yellow Ribbon* is not known. If they were, it would be worth noting that the George Norton song that influenced them has a pedigree that stretches far beyond the
65 college environment of the 1920s. A similar song was heard in minstrel shows in this country around 1838: "All Round My Hat," which is unquestionably the ancestor of the later "Round Her Neck She Wore a Yellow Ribbon," with all of its variants and imitations.
70 Likewise, in *Othello*, Shakespeare has Desdemona refer to an earlier version of the song.

In its long descent from Tudor lyric to Cockney ballad to American minstrel ditty to ribald college song to motion picture theme to popular recording, we see
75 garters and ribbons of every hue—and the symbol of constancy in love has been anything but constant itself.

31. Dove releases are traditional following marriage ceremonies because the life-long pairing of doves is ------- of what the state of human marriage should be.

A. antagonistic.
B. sympathetic.
C. phobic.
D. empiric.
E. emblematic

32. The Innocence Project is comprised of law professors and their students who re-investigate and challenge the evidence in convictions of murder defendants whose claims of innocence seem -------.

    A. plausible
    B. deniable
    C. expected
    D. unlikely
    E. incredible

33. The mayoral candidate is campaigning on a platform of reigning in government expenditures, stressing that he is fiscally ------- and a friend of the business community.

    A. insensible
    B. furtive
    C. intensive
    D. prudent
    E. supple

34. Mel Brooks' 1974 film *Blazing Saddles*, set in the Wild West in 1874, contains many ------- props from the 1970s, including a stylish Gucci costume for the sheriff and an automobile.

    A. suitable
    B. decorous
    C. mundane
    D. anticlimactic
    E. anachronistic

35. There are a number of criteria by which one may classify musical -------, including the distinction between popular and traditional, regional and national differences, influences, and origins.

    A. instruments
    B. plots
    C. genres
    D. arrangements
    E. conflagrations

36. The word *antedates* (line 13) most nearly means:

    A. anticipates.
    B. precedes.
    C. prevents.
    D. follows.

37. Based on the use of the word *appurtenances* in line 29, it can be inferred that *appurtenance* refers to something:

    A. exaggerated or embellished.
    B. resembling a particular characteristic.
    C. subordinate to another, more important thing.
    D. fundamental in existence.

38. Based on the use of the word *wielding* in line 30, it can be inferred that *wield* means to:

    A. give up.
    B. handle or carry something.
    C. produce or bring forth.
    D. conceal

39. In line 32, *implicate* is best understood to mean to:

    A. make a copy of something.
    B. set about or attempt.
    C. indicate and set apart for a purpose.
    D. involve with or show a connection between things.

40. In line 34, *refined* most nearly means:

    A. defined essential characteristics.
    B. lowered in status or quality.
    C. cultivated or freed from coarseness.
    D. abbreviated or cut short.

41. It can be inferred that the word *anthology*, as it is used in line 49, primarily refers to:

    A. the study of human nature.
    B. an autobiographical account.
    C. an inventory of stock.
    D. a collection of songs.

42. It can be inferred that the word *historiography*, as it is used in line 51, primarily refers to the:

    A. scholarly study of history.
    B. process of producing images.
    C. science of drawing maps.
    D. deliberate display of emotion for effect.

43. Based on the use of the word *grafted* in line 55, it can be inferred that *graft* most nearly means to:

    A. work without compensation.
    B. attach or join together.
    C. obtain legally.
    D. duplicate or reproduce.

44. It can be inferred that the word *ditty*, as it is used in line 73, primarily refers to a(n):

    A. previously mentioned word.
    B. means of production.
    C. simple song.
    D. epic poem.

45. In line 73, *ribald* most nearly means:

    A. refined.
    B. popular.
    C. vulgar.
    D. mediocre.

46. LYRICAL:

    A. dramatic
    B. flexible
    C. repetitious
    D. short
    E. active

47. VOCAL:

    A. odd
    B. interesting
    C. forgetful
    D. silent
    E. powerful

48. TOKEN:

    A. false idea
    B. genuine article
    C. loved one
    D. wanted criminal
    E. known amount

49. TRADITIONAL:

    A. innovative
    B. well suited
    C. long winded
    D. zealous
    E. learned

50. CONTEMPORARY:

    A. modern
    B. outdated
    C. ill-advised
    D. well conceived
    E. nearby

51. COMPOSED:

    A. aloud
    B. intentional
    C. early
    D. upset
    E. qualified

52. ADOPT:

    A. believe
    B. select
    C. reject
    D. insist
    E. fulfill

53. ERR:

    A. tilt
    B. fold
    C. correct
    D. gladden
    E. find

54. CONSTANCY:

A. disloyalty
B. validity
C. construction
D. humility
E. rivalry

55. CIVIL:

A. impolite
B. chief
C. rigorous
D. required
E. new

56. SUBSEQUENT : LATER ::

A. onetime : long term
B. former : earlier
C. brief : permanent
D. historical : important
E. predicted : reported

57. COPYRIGHT : WRITING ::

A. royalty : work
B. composition : ownership
C. patent : invention
D. brand : trademark
E. violation : duplicate

58. ENVIRONMENT : CONTEXT ::

A. location : movement
B. transportation : commute
C. place : home
D. surroundings : locale
E. building : land

59. MINSTREL : SINGER ::

A. evangelist : preacher
B. gardener : reaper
C. lawyer : defender
D. actor : scene
E. runner : marathon

60. HEADNOTE : FOOTNOTE ::

A. beginning : opening
B. end : closing
C. top : bottom
D. face : hand
E. cover : book

Passage III

HUMANITIES: This passage is adapted from an introductory textbook on the history of American music.

Harmonica, mouth organ, French harp, harp—there are dozens of appellations in American English for this simple instrument, evidence of the local and regional level of its widespread appeal. The ubiquitous
5 little music maker may seem homely when compared with more cultivated species, but the hardy perennial has taken root in our musical landscape, and has been owned and played by more Americans than any other instrument. This wildflower has long been mistaken for
10 a weed by stodgy and established musical experts; consequently, there has been little scholarly writing devoted to it.

Like many familiar domestic blooms, the harmonica is an Old World transplant. The ancestral
15 rootstock of the free-reed family, to which the mouth harp belongs, comes from Asia where according to myth, the Chinese female sovereign Nyn-Kwa invented the *sheng* or mouth organ about 3000 B.C. Written descriptions of the instrument date from a thousand
20 years later, and examples and representations of *sheng* have been found at grave sites in central China dating from the 5th century B.C. Although its invention has been credited to several people, the first patent for the familiar mouth harmonica was filed in Berlin by
25 Friedrich Buschmann in 1821. Within ten years of its invention, the European mouth organ was being produced commercially in Austria, Switzerland, and the German kingdom of Saxony.

In the second half of the nineteenth century,
30 German manufacturers began the mass production of harmonicas with an eye to the huge export market. Towards the end of the century, German factories were producing up to ten million instruments a year, and more than half were sold in the United States.
35 Popularity of the instrument peaked between the world wars, when it was used for music education in public schools, on the vaudeville stage, and on early blues and "hillbilly" recordings. In the late 1940s, electric "city" blues bands featured amplified harmonicas as lead
40 instruments, and their records, though less popular in black communities since the mid-1960s, continue to be a strong influence on popular music both here and abroad.

With millions of mouth organs imported each
45 year for over a century, the harmonica is the most popular musical instrument in our nation's history. Why, then, the dearth of literature on the harmonica? One explanation is the type of sound produced by the instrument. In reed instruments such as the saxophone
50 or oboe, a flexible sliver of reed is vibrated against something. Once the reed is vibrating, the length of a resonating column of air is varied to produce different pitches. Free-reed instruments, like the harmonica, have reeds that vibrate without touching anything else.
55 As the vibrations of the free reeds are unhindered, the resulting sounds are dense with overtones, producing a timbre alternately described as mellifluous or irritating, according to the tastes of the listener. However, the same may also be said of a "serious" instrument such
60 as the violin. A more likely explanation is the simplicity and cost of the harmonica. Small and cheap, it has been the instrument of choice for children, working people, and vagabonds. Thus, the social status of the most visible harp players has not encouraged the
65 attention of students of "serious" music.

Fortunately, critical neglect has not prevented harmonica players from making good music, much of it endemic to the U.S. Harmonica tune books from the 1920s suggest the instrument's repertory embraced
70 familiar dance tunes, popular songs, and sentimental favorites of the preceding half-century. Prominent among early recordings are entertaining solo pieces in which harmonica virtuosos imitate the sounds of animals, crying babies, electric pumps, and railroads.
75 Train whistles and fox chases pervaded the recorded harmonica repertory.

Other virtuoso pieces make use of "note bending" to make sounds and play pitches which are, in theory, impossible to play on the instrument. The technique, as
80 yet unexplained by acoustic physicists, makes possible the distinctively fluid phrasing and wailing sound of the blues harmonica. By deflecting air with the mouth, the player can "bend" or flatten a note, almost to the tonal value of the next lower-pitched reed. This
85 technique was widely employed by blues players of the 1920s. In some solo recordings, the player sings a line, then uses the mouth harp to play an improvised instrumental response.

It is difficult to generalize about an instrument
90 used in making so many different kinds of music, except to say the differences in style between individuals are stronger than most regional characteristics. There is an intimate relationship be-

tween player and harp; the resulting music reflects
95 experience, outlook, and even mood more than with
most instruments. While limited in range, the
harmonica can speak with a very personal voice.
Perhaps its versatile adaptability is the real key to the
small instrument's large role in the musical life of
100 America.

61. The ------- presence of the extremely demanding
and critical factory owner made the workers
fearful for their jobs.

    A. vacuous
    B. ubiquitous
    C. distant
    D. ambiguous
    E. dubious

62. A(n) ------- of certified teachers has forced the
school board to hire teachers who are still
working on their certification.

    A. abundance
    B. compliment
    C. cooperation
    D. indictment
    E. dearth

63. Although Peter was just over five and half feet
tall, when he spoke you had to be impressed by
the deep, ------- quality of his voice.

    A. faint
    B. resonant
    C. vulnerable
    D. irreproachable
    E. commendable

64. Articulated in his smooth and ------- prose, the
English novelist Colin Thubron's eye for detail
and command of scope make for an absorbing,
complex read.

    A. callous
    B. terse
    C. temperamental
    D. mellifluous
    E. sarcastic

65. The ------- of the assembly hall were very poor,
making it difficult to hear the speaker past the
tenth row of seats.

    A. semantics
    B. ballistics
    C. aesthetics
    D. antics
    E. acoustics

66. Based on the use of the word *appellations* in line
2, it can be inferred that *appellation* most nearly
means:

    A. name.
    B. appearance.
    C. destination.
    D. manifestation.

67. It can be inferred that the word *perennial*, as it is
used in line 6, primarily refers to something that
is:

    A. original.
    B. rude in behavior.
    C. continuous.
    D. annoying.

68. As it is used in line 10, the word *stodgy* most
nearly means:

    A. substantial.
    B. boring.
    C. unaffected.
    D. lively.

69. In line 17, *sovereign* is best understood to mean:

    A. ruler.
    B. traveler.
    C. explorer.
    D. supplicant.

70. It can be inferred that the word *timbre*, as it is used in line 57, primarily refers to:

   A. a nervous characteristic.
   B. the wood of growing trees.
   C. a short, simple song.
   D. the quality of sound.

71. In line 68, *endemic* most nearly means:

   A. widespread or rapid growth.
   B. characteristic of a particular region.
   C. a long poetic composition.
   D. external to one's country or origin.

72. In line 69, *repertory* most nearly refers to a(n):

   A. musical play or production.
   B. entire collection of works.
   C. place where something is kept safe.
   D. history of development.

73. Based on the use of the word *virtuosos* in line 73, it can be inferred that *virtuoso* primarily refers to a(n):

   A. student.
   B. amateur.
   C. expert.
   D. entertainer.

74. In line 87, *improvised* most nearly means:

   A. skillful or accomplished.
   B. made up or performed spontaneously.
   C. immediately pertinent.
   D. dramatic monologue.

75. Based on its use in line 98, *versatile* can be defined as all of the following EXCEPT:

   A. adaptable.
   B. multipurpose.
   C. resourceful.
   D. inflexible.

76. HOMELY:

   A. powerless
   B. clean
   C. fancy
   D. timely
   E. happy

77. CULTIVATED:

   A. witty
   B. sad
   C. aloof
   D. uncultured
   E. tardy

78. AMPLIFY:

   A. simplify
   B. lift
   C. announce
   D. empower
   E. improve

79. DOMESTIC:

   A. simple
   B. far-fetched
   C. complete
   D. afraid
   E. imported

80. UNHINDERED:

   A. restrained
   B. blameworthy
   C. satisfied
   D. qualified
   E. preferred

81. NEGLECT:

   A. attention
   B. rejection
   C. consent
   D. wariness
   E. excuse

82. PERVASIVE:

    A. calm
    B. new
    C. limited
    D. roomy
    E. marvelous

83. FEATURED:

    A. collected
    B. opposed
    C. suppressed
    D. allowed
    E. widened

84. CRITICAL:

    A. wasteful
    B. unthinking
    C. scholarly
    D. evasive
    E. quiet

85. PROMINENT:

    A. famous
    B. anonymous
    C. youthful
    D. popular
    E. cautious

86. PITCH : SCALE ::

    A. word : page
    B. letter : alphabet
    C. person : crowd
    D. strand : rope
    E. closing : speech

87. VAGABOND : WANDER ::

    A. traveler : destination
    B. hobo : migrate
    C. voyager : home
    D. tramp : work
    E. worker : search

88. OVERTONE : SUGGEST ::

    A. echo : remind
    B. satisfaction : displease
    C. package : return
    D. victor : war
    E. expert : repair

89. DEFLECT : REFLECT ::

    A. set free : imprison
    B. turn aside : turn back
    C. throw out : take in
    D. move forward : move sideways
    E. lift up : set down

90. COMMERCE : TRADE ::

    A. property : sale
    B. business : exchange
    C. profit : motive
    D. enterprise : owner
    E. purchase : delivery

Passage IV

HUMANITIES: This passage is adapted from an essay about *La Gioconda*, the painting by Leonardo da Vinci more commonly known as the "Mona Lisa." The actual person in the painting may have been Lisa, the third wife of Francesco del Giocondo.

La Gioconda is, in the truest sense, Leonardo's masterpiece; the revealing paradigm of his mode of thought and work. We all know the face and hands of the figure, set in its marble chair, in that circle of
5 fantastic rocks, as in some faint light under the sea. Perhaps of all ancient pictures, time has chilled it least.

As often happens with works in which genius seems to surpass its limit, there is an element in it transmitted by, but not invented by, the master. In that
10 inestimable folio of drawings, once in the possession of Vasari, were certain designs by Verrocchio, faces of such impressive beauty that Leonardo, in his boyhood copied them many times. It is difficult not to see these designs of the elder master as the germinal principle of
15 that unfathomable smile, with its touch of something sinister, which infects all Leonardo's work.

Besides, the picture is a portrait. From childhood, we see this image defining itself on the fabric of his dreams, and were it not for explicit historical
20 testimony, we might fancy this was his ideal lady, embodied and beheld at last.

What was the relationship of a living Florentine to the creature of his thought? By what strange affinities had the dream and the person grown up so
25 apart, and yet so close? Present from the first incorporeal ideas in Leonardo's brain, dimly traced in the designs of Verrocchio, she is found present at last in Il Giocondo's house.

To be sure, it is a portrait, a painting, and legend
30 has it that mimes and musicians were used to protract that smile. Was it in four months or as by a stroke of magic the image was projected?

The presence that rises so strangely beside the waters is expressive of what after a thousand years men
35 had come to desire. Hers is the head upon all "the ends of the world are come," and the eyelids are a little weary. It is a beauty brought out from within and deposited upon the flesh, bit by bit, cell by cell— strange thoughts and fantastic reveries and exquisite
40 passions. Set it for a moment beside one of those Greek statues of beautiful women of antiquity. How they would be troubled by this beauty, into which the soul with all of its maladies had been passed! All the thoughts and experience of the world are etched and
45 molded there: the animalism of Greece, the lust of Rome, the mysticism of the Middle Ages with its spiritual ambition and imaginative loves, the return of the pagan world, the sins of the Borgias.

She is older than the rocks among which she sits.
50 Like the vampire, she has been dead many times, and learned the secrets of the grave; and has submerged herself in deep seas and kept their fallen day about her; and trafficked for some strange webs with Easter merchants and as Leda, the mother of Helen of Troy,
55 and as Saint Anne, the mother of Mary. All of this has been to her but as the sound of lyres and flutes, and lives only in the delicacy with which it has molded the changing lineaments and tinged the eyelids and the hands.

91. The established and successful member-owned cooperative served as a(n) ------- for the small, locally-owned food markets that have recently sprung up in the region.

   A. benefit
   B. substitution
   C. paradigm
   D. affliction
   E. anomaly

92. There is such a strong ------- between new cars made by rival automakers today that the casual observer cannot tell them apart.

   A. dissimilarity
   B. competition
   C. deterioration
   D. affinity
   E. variation

93. The notion that there is a(n) ------- realm of existence that is distinct from the material universe is fundamental to the belief in a divine being.

    A. physical
    B. logistical
    C. imaginary
    D. substitute
    E. incorporeal

94. In order to ------- the telephone call long enough to put a trace on it, the detective kept the caller engaged in seemingly pointless conversation.

    A. distract
    B. mitigate
    C. protract
    D. contract
    E. interrupt

95. Katya's memory of the moment was ------- with sorrow; while her voice was firm, it was obviously touched with grief.

    A. confused
    B. tipped
    C. prolonged
    D. tinged
    E. arranged

96. In context, *masterpiece* (line 2) most nearly refers to an artist's:

    A. most important work.
    B. beginning stages of a piece.
    C. posthumously published work.
    D. rehearsal or practice pieces.

97. As it is used in line 2, the word *mode* most nearly refers to a(n):

    A. sound.
    B. feeling.
    C. asset.
    D. method.

98. In line 10, *folio* is best understood to refer to a(n):

    A. duplicate.
    B. burial.
    C. booklet.
    D. painting.

99. It can be inferred that the word *germinal*, as it is used in line 14, refers to the:

    A. overriding themes.
    B. early stages.
    C. destructive elements.
    D. tutorial process.

100. The word *explicit* (line 19) most nearly means:

    A. clearly expressed.
    B. involved or entwined.
    C. embedded or contained.
    D. brought out.

101. In line 39, *exquisite* most nearly means characterized by:

    A. an even temperament.
    B. expensive taste.
    C. mind-numbing detail.
    D. intense emotions.

102. It can be inferred that the word *antiquity*, as it is used in line 41, most nearly means belonging to:

    A. modern culture.
    B. ancient times.
    C. the future.
    D. prehistory.

103. In line 43, *maladies* is best understood to refer to:

    A. dreams.
    B. sicknesses.
    C. painful emotions.
    D. memories.

104. In line 46, *mysticism* refers to:

    A. the historical record.
    B. exciting curiosities.
    C. the beliefs of mystics.
    D. a political system.

105. It can be inferred that the word *lineaments*, as it is used in line 58, refers to:

    A. skin ointments.
    B. descendants from a common ancestor.
    C. facial features.
    D. ground plans.

106. ANCIENT:

    A. classical
    B. modern
    C. worthless
    D. changing
    E. revered

107. GENIUS:

    A. uninspired
    B. continued
    C. hated
    D. tremendous
    E. practical

108. INESTIMABLE:

    A. boring
    B. worthless
    C. unstable
    D. required
    E. important

109. DESIGN:

    A. events
    B. history
    C. present
    D. denial
    E. chance

110. DEPOSIT:

    A. add to
    B. put down
    C. throw away
    D. pick up
    E. ask for

111. LUST:

    A. attract
    B. follow
    C. reject
    D. treat
    E. provoke

112. AMBITIOUS:

    A. uncaring
    B. forward
    C. clownish
    D. large
    E. worrisome

113. IMAGINATIVE:

    A. fantastic
    B. ordinary
    C. crude
    D. youthful
    E. drastic

114. SUBMERGE:

    A. pass over
    B. enter into
    C. slide along
    D. go down
    E. take out of

115. DELICACY:

    A. strength
    B. error
    C. trick
    D. emotion
    E. water

116. SURPASS : TOP ::

    A. fail : completion
    B. exceed : limit
    C. leap : speed
    D. claim : right
    E. adjust : center

117. INFECT : FEELING ::

    A. invent : story
    B. name : child
    C. fill : emotion
    D. confuse : love
    E. demand : answer

118. TESTIMONY : WITNESS ::

    A. proof : evidence
    B. defendant : accuser
    C. prosecutor : jury
    D. guilty : innocence
    E. account : reporter

119. MIME : SILENCE ::

    A. painter : canvas
    B. author : novel
    C. dancer : music
    D. playwright : drama
    E. actor : stage

120. PAGAN : RELIGION ::

    A. heathen : belief
    B. believer : worship
    C. creed : tenet
    D. minister : sermon
    E. convert : belief

Passage V

HUMANITIES: This passage is adapted from an essay about Joseph Turner's 1840 oil painting entitled "Slavers throwing overboard the Dead and Dying—Typhoon coming on," or more commonly, "The Slave Ship."

I think the noblest sea that Turner has ever painted, and so the noblest ever painted by man, is that of "The Slave Ship." It is a sunset on the Atlantic after a prolonged storm, but the storm is partially lulled, and
5 the torn and streaming rain clouds are scudding across the sky in scarlet lines to dissipate into the hollow of the night. The whole surface of the sea comprised within the canvas is divided into two ridges of enormous swell, not high, nor local, but a low, broad
10 heaving of the whole ocean, like the lifting of its bosom by a deep-drawn breath after the torture of the storm. Between these two ridges, the fire of the sunset falls along the trough of the sea, dyeing it with an awful but glorious light, the intense and lurid splendor
15 which burns like gold and bathes like blood.

Along this fiery path and valley, the tossing waves by which the swell of the sea is restlessly divided, lift themselves in the dark, indefinite, fantastic forms, each casting a faint and ghastly shadow behind
20 it along the illumined foam. They do not rise everywhere, but three or four together in wild groups, fitfully and furiously, as the under-strength of the swell compels or permits them; leaving between them treacherous spaces of level and whirling water, now
25 lighted with green lamp-like fire, now flashing back the gold of the declining sun, now fearfully dyed from above with the indistinguishable images of the burning clouds, which fall upon them in flakes of crimson and scarlet and give to the reckless waves the added motion
30 of their own fiery flying.

Purple and blue, the lurid shadows of the hollow breakers are cast upon the mist of night, which gathers cold and low, advancing like the shadow of death upon the guilty ship as it labors amidst the lighting of the
35 sea, its thin masts written upon the sky in lines of blood, girded with condemnation in that fearful hue which signs the sky with horror and mixes its flaming flood with the sunlight, and cast far along the desolate heave of the sepulchral waves, incarnadines the
40 multitudinous sea.

I believe, if I were reduced to rest Turner's immortality upon any single work, I should choose this. Its daring conception—ideal in the highest sense of the word—is based upon the purest truth and
45 wrought out with the concentrated knowledge of a life; its color is absolutely perfect, not one false or morbid hue in any part or line, and so modulated that every square inch of canvas is a perfect composition; its drawing as accurate as it is fearless, the ship buoyant,
50 bending, and full of motion; its tones as true as they are wonderful; and the whole picture dedicated to the most sublime of truths which we have shown to be formed by Turner's works—the power, majesty, and a depth of the open, deep, illimitable sea.

121. The morning fog was quickly ------- by the rays of the sun, allowing us to see the mountains far in the distance.

    A. condensed
    B. extended
    C. accumulated
    D. dissipated
    E. illuminated

122. Known for its sensationalism, the tabloid newspaper reported the horrendous crime in all of its ------- detail.

    A. exquisite
    B. lurid
    C. insipid
    D. ingenuous
    E. modest

123. With a ------- fascination, people flocked to the bombing scene from outer areas to catch a glimpse of the devastation.

    A. intelligent
    B. healthy
    C. cheery
    D. poignant
    E. morbid

124. Towards the end of the song, the Webb sisters' voices began to ------- into pitch-perfect harmony.

A. vary
B. intensify
C. stratify
D. modulate
E. displace

125. Although Marie had only known Martin for six months, she felt that her feelings for him were vast and -------.

A. illimitable
B. controlled
C. confidential
D. definable
E. inapt

126. As it is used in line 4, the word *lulled* most nearly means to have become:

A. tense.
B. calm.
C. irate.
D. defeated.

127. Based on the use of the wording *scudding* in line 5, it can be inferred that *scud* most nearly means to:

A. fall quietly.
B. pass rapidly.
C. expand quickly.
D. slow to a halt.

128. In context, *comprised* (line 7) most nearly means:

A. pressed together.
B. prohibited.
C. exposed to suspicion.
D. included.

129. As it is used in line 13, *trough* is best understood to refer to:

A. a receptacle for feeding animals.
B. low point of a business cycle.
C. an area of low barometric pressure.
D. a depression between two waves.

130. The word *ghastly* (line 19) most nearly means:

A. shockingly frightful.
B. lacking in substance.
C. spiritual.
D. pleasant.

131. As it is used in line 20, the word *illumined* most nearly means:

A. educated.
B. extinguished.
C. lit up.
D. cast a shadow.

132. It can be inferred that the word *condemnation*, as it is used in line 36, primarily refers to:

A. praise.
B. discord.
C. appeasement.
D. judgment.

133. It can be inferred that the word *sepulchral*, as it is used in line 39, primarily means:

A. joyous.
B. weakening.
C. overpowering.
D. dismal.

134. Based on the use of the word *incarnadines* in line 39, it can be inferred that *incarnadine* most nearly means to make:

A. alive.
B. red.
C. dead.
D. dark.

135. The word *immortality* (line 42) most nearly means:

    A. enduring fame.
    B. immediate demise.
    C. infamous reputation.
    D. collection of works.

136. PROLONG:

    A. give back
    B. cut short
    C. add to
    D. move back
    E. win over

137. SWELL:

    A. depression
    B. castle
    C. raft
    D. draft
    E. wire

138. LOCAL:

    A. trapped
    B. hurried
    C. barren
    D. widespread
    E. wise

139. TREACHEROUS:

    A. loyal
    B. excitable
    C. tremendous
    D. boorish
    E. fruitful

140. FITFUL:

    A. probable
    B. regular
    C. sincere
    D. doubtful
    E. plentiful

141. INDISTINGUISHABLE:

    A. well done
    B. well read
    C. well defined
    D. well informed
    E. well bred

142. ADVANCE:

    A. speak
    B. retreat
    C. confide
    D. sense
    E. announce

143. LABOR:

    A. refuse
    B. pass over
    C. call forth
    D. prevent
    E. send out

144. MULTITUDINOUS:

    A. singular
    B. complex
    C. required
    D. deniable
    E. hopeful

145. DEDICATE:

    A. share
    B. rent
    C. provide
    D. persuade
    E. hold out

146. RIDGE : LINE ::

    A. mountain : valley
    B. box : cube
    C. hill : dot
    D. river : water
    E. cloud : sky

147. WHIRL : CIRCULAR ::

    A. drill : spiral
    B. recall : memorial
    C. question : answerable
    D. raise : horizontal
    E. cross : limited

148. GIRD : BELT ::

    A. hand : hat
    B. wear : coat
    C. wrap : bandage
    D. wash : garment
    E. remove : cloak

149. HUE : VISION ::

    A. tone : hearing
    B. race : training
    C. painting : easel
    D. vessel : sea
    E. danger : warning

150. BUOYANT : CHEERFUL ::

    A. confined : freed
    B. lazy : busy
    C. endearing : hopeless
    D. lighthearted : glad
    E. reasonable : silly

Vocabulary Builder: Natural Science Passages

DIRECTIONS: Each passage in this exercise is followed by sets of sentence completion, vocabulary-in-context, antonym, and analogy items for building vocabulary through context. In addition to using the passages to infer word meanings, you may use a dictionary or refer to the Vocabulary List beginning on page 655.

The first set of items following each passage are sentence completion items based on words from the passage. Each sentence has one blank. Choose the word that best fits the meaning of the sentence in its entirety.

The second set of items following each passage are vocabulary-in-context items based on words from the passage. Choose the best answer for each item based on what is stated or implied in the passage.

The third set of items following each passage are antonym items based on words from the passage. For each item, choose the word that has a meaning most nearly opposite of the capitalized word.

The fourth set of items following each passage are analogy items based on words from the passage. For each item, find the pair of words that expresses a relationship most like that expressed by the capitalized words.

Answers are on page 801.

Passage I

NATURAL SCIENCE: This passage is adapted from an article entitled "Cosmic Evolution" in a popular cosmology journal.

Through the centuries, man has unceasingly searched the firmament for clues to his destiny. His imagination has been captivated by the stars, his mind challenged by the mystery of their origin and extent,
5 and his spirit imbued with a thirst for some understanding of his role in the cosmos.

Scientific discoveries in fields as diverse as astronomy and molecular biology in the course of the last 15 years have brought us closer to solving three
10 timeless enigmas: How did the universe begin? How did life originate and evolve? What is our place and destiny in the universe?

This burst of interdisciplinary discoveries has given rise to new concepts of the origin of life from
15 inanimate material on primitive Earth, the formation of planets and stars, the synthesis of fundamental particles of matter, and the beginnings of the universe itself. All seem to be founded on the same basic laws of chemistry and physics. The conclusion that the origin

20 and evolution of life is inextricably interwoven with the origin and evolution of the cosmos seems ineluctable. Taken in its totality, this pathway, from fundamental particles to advanced civilizations, constitutes the essence of the concept of cosmic
25 evolution.

To be sure, the sequence from primordial fireball to matter, to stars, to planets, to prebiotic chemistry, to life, and to intelligence, is fragmented and even controversial in some particulars. A broad picture,
30 however, is emerging: a picture that is both imaginative and illuminating.

Man appeared very late in this sequence of events, and with his increased intelligence came civilization, science, and technology. Cultural
35 evolution began and has proceeded very rapidly in the last few millennia. An infinitesimal fraction of the matter of the universe has been converted into the organic matter of the human brain. As a result, one part of the universe can now reflect upon the whole process
40 of cosmic evolution leading to the existence of human cognition. We wonder whether this process is a frequent occurrence in the universe; in doing so, we come to the postulate that life is widespread in the universe and at least in some cases, this life may have

45 evolved to the stage of intelligence and technological civilizations that it did on Earth.

Some of these civilizations may have learned to communicate with each other and achieved major advances in their own evolution as a result. Can we 50 detect them? Although many gaps, puzzles, and uncertainties remain, this unifying concept, in which the expansion of the universe, the birth and death of galaxies and stars, the formation of planets, the origins of life, and the ascent of humans are all explained by 55 the process of cosmic evolution, provides a sound scientific rationale on which to base a program to search for extraterrestrial intelligence.

1. The new Biomedical Research Center, which coordinates many aspects of the university's research, has developed ------- working relationships with the Neuroscience and Medical Physics departments.

   A. adversary
   B. disciplinary
   C. evolutionary
   D. interdisciplinary
   E. reactionary

2. Linus Pauling, winner of the Chemistry Nobel Prize in 1954, was an advocate of high doses of vitamin C, since it is vital to the ------- of collagen, the body's main connective tissue protein.

   A. destruction
   B. analysis
   C. substitution
   D. combination
   E. synthesis

3. An atheist is a person without a belief in, or who does not ------- the existence of, a god or deities.

   A. deny
   B. calculate
   C. postulate
   D. warrant
   E. feign

4. The liberals' ------- for universal health care is that access to high-quality health care is a human right, while the conservatives argue that coverage is a market commodity best left to the free market.

   A. protection
   B. substitution
   C. disagreement
   D. apology
   E. rationale

5. Until Congress canceled its funding, the NASA Deep Space Network used radio dishes to detect non-natural radio emissions from locations outside our solar system in an attempt to discover ------- civilizations.

   A. extraterrestrial
   B. ancient
   C. modern
   D. terrestrial
   E. foreign

6. It can be inferred that the word *firmament*, as it is used in line 2, primarily refers to:

   A. a thin thread or strand.
   B. hell or the underworld.
   C. the heavens.
   D. the earth or material world.

7. It can be inferred that the word *cosmos*, as it is used in line 6, primarily refers to the:

   A. planets.
   B. sky.
   C. universe.
   D. earth.

8. In context, *enigmas* (line 10) most nearly means:

   A. solutions.
   B. puzzles.
   C. doubts.
   D. certainties.

9. Based on the use of the word *inextricably* in line 20, it can be inferred that *inextricable* most nearly means:

   A. indescribable.
   B. incontrollable.
   C. inseparable.
   D. unexplainable.

10. In line 22, *ineluctable* is best understood to mean:

   A. unsolvable.
   B. inescapable.
   C. unappeasable.
   D. avoidable.

11. It can be inferred that the word *primordial*, as it is used in line 26, most nearly means existing:

   A. in the future.
   B. in modern times.
   C. in outer space.
   D. from the beginning of time.

12. It can be inferred that the word *prebiotic*, as it is used in line 27, most nearly means:

   A. existing before the origin of life.
   B. containing beneficial bacteria.
   C. inhibiting bacterial growth.
   D. pertaining to life.

13. The word *millennia* (line 36) refers to:

   A. millions of years.
   B. thousands of years.
   C. hundreds of years.
   D. tens of years.

14. As it is used in line 36, the word *infinitesimal* most nearly means:

   A. extending indefinitely.
   B. immeasurably tiny.
   C. enormous.
   D. calculable.

15. In line 41, *cognition* refers to:

   A. knowledge.
   B. misunderstanding.
   C. unawareness.
   D. existence.

16. CONTROVERT:

   A. revise
   B. understand
   C. agree
   D. believe
   E. ridicule

17. ILLUMINATE:

   A. instruct
   B. burden
   C. obscure
   D. flatten
   E. decline

18. SEQUENTIAL:

   A. random
   B. broad
   C. unintentional
   D. confined
   E. dull

19. ASCENT:

   A. miracle
   B. decline
   C. harbor
   D. enforcement
   E. fortune

20. INANIMATE:

   A. lively
   B. confused
   C. refined
   D. victorious
   E. satisfied

21. PRIMITIVE:

    A. unhappy
    B. lengthy
    C. sophisticated
    D. determined
    E. obvious

22. REFLECTION:

    A. width
    B. settlement
    C. fulfillment
    D. resentment
    E. absorption

23. CONSTITUTE:

    A. affirm
    B. remain
    C. lift
    D. take apart
    E. move in

24. ESSENTIAL:

    A. extra
    B. clever
    C. pointed
    D. motionless
    E. rancid

25. DESTINED:

    A. prepared
    B. free
    C. alone
    D. divided
    E. current

26. CAPTIVATE : INTEREST ::

    A. liberate : chains
    B. hold : attention
    C. return : investment
    D. prefer : favorite
    E. define : term

27. UNIFORM : DIVERSIFY ::

    A. identifiable : point
    B. intense : involve
    C. assured : dictate
    D. cool : test
    E. constant : vary

28. PARTICULAR : DETAIL ::

    A. window : casement
    B. fragment : piece
    C. closet : room
    D. age : maturity
    E. hope : despair

29. SOUND : UNRELIABLE ::

    A. healthy : new
    B. constant : afraid
    C. certain : lacking
    D. errorless : doubtful
    E. garbled: understandable

30. CONVERSION : CONTINUE ::

    A. transformation : maintain
    B. death : evolve
    C. civilization : advance
    D. evolution : emerge
    E. intelligence : learn

Passage II

NATURAL SCIENCE: This passage is adapted from an essay entitled "Antarctic Exploration" in an introductory earth sciences textbook.

At 3:29 p.m. on November 28, 1929, a heavily laden Ford Trimotor bounced down the rough ice runway of 'Little America' and clawed its way through an Antarctic overcast—embarking on an epic flight that
5 was anything but routine. The little plane, called the Floyd Bennett, weighed only 6,000 pounds. With its four-man crew, extra gasoline, food, and survival gear, it was carrying more than seven tons. The plane's three engines put out 975 horsepower; cruising speed was
10 just over 100 miles per hour. For navigating the desolate wastes, there were two drift meters and a sun-compass. The only other scientific instrument aboard was a bulky 100-pound aerial camera. Eighteen hours and 37 minutes (and 1,600 miles) later, the Floyd
15 Bennett touched back down on the Little America landing strip, mission completed. Richard E. Byrd and his crew were the first to conquer the South Pole by air, and their historic journey, the consummation of years of work and meticulous planning, had opened a new
20 era of scientific exploration.

Simply establishing the Little America base camp a year earlier was a triumph of logistics. Byrd's men unloaded and hauled several hundred tons of food, fuel, and equipment (including three airplanes) over the
25 crumbling ice barrier on dog sleds. The dismantled all-metal Ford Trimotor was stored that winter in a hangar made of snow blocks. After the long months of darkness set in, Byrd and his companions began final planning for their aerial assault on the South Pole. The
30 1,600-mile-long flight involved unprecedented features. For hundreds of miles, they would fly over a barren, rolling surface, then climb a mountain rampart 14,000 feet high, with a 10,500-foot pass, and continue the journey across a 10,000-foot plateau. Factors of
35 speed, horsepower, rate of climb, and other engineering problems entailed endless hours of tedious and complicated calculations.

Excavated from its snow cave in early November, the Floyd Bennett was reassembled in temperatures
40 that reached 50 degrees below zero. Without photographer Ashley McKinley and his equipment and survival gear, the plane could fly to the South Pole and back with no problem. To Byrd, McKinley's task was the crux of the plan: to photograph every mile of the
45 flight and to make a permanent record available to

science. Since the extra weight would make a nonstop trip impossible, it would be necessary to cache gasoline and food near the base of the mountain range that bordered the high Antarctic plateau. The aircraft would
50 then land and refuel during the return leg of the flight. Even so, weight and fuel consumption calculations were critical. The Floyd Bennett had to be light enough by the time it reached the Queen Maud Mountains to climb 11,000 feet and slip through the pass at the head
55 of the Axel Heiberg glacier.

On November 19, Byrd and his crew flew 400 miles to reconnoiter the jagged mountain barrier, then landed to establish their forward camp. On November 28, a geological party radioed that the weather over the
60 mountains was excellent, so that afternoon the Floyd Bennett headed south toward the pole. As the plane neared the Axel Heiberg glacier with its 10,500-foot pass, the men sighted another glacier which seemed low enough and wide enough to cross. The decision
65 had to be made quickly: to tackle the Axel Heiberg, altitude known but air currents unknown—the bordering peaks might be so high that air currents would dash the plane to the ground—or to take the unknown glacier, which looked feasible?

70 Byrd opted for the unknown glacier. As powerful air currents tossed the plane about, the pilot fought to gain altitude. Suddenly, the wheel turned loosely in his hands. The pass loomed ahead, but the Floyd Bennett would go no higher. If gasoline were jettisoned, it
75 would be impossible to reach the pole and return. If food were thrown overboard, all lives would be endangered in the event of a forced landing. "A bag of food overboard," ordered Byrd. The plane responded immediately and began to climb, but the fast-
80 approaching glacier was higher. Byrd gestured and another 150-pound bag of food careened through the trapdoor of the aircraft. Byrd reported "those were the slowest minutes we ever spent. Finally, we reached the pass. We ambled over—a few hundred yards to spare."

85 The vast Antarctic plateau ranged from 11,000 to 7,000 feet, sloping toward the South Pole. Cruising at only 90 miles per hour against a brisk headwind, Byrd navigated carefully over the jumbled terrain. At 1:14 a.m. on November 29, the big moment had come. The
90 crew dropped an American flag.

Flying at 2,500 feet over the snow, the plane then angled back over the original line of flight to cross again over the pole and make certain the feat was

accomplished. Then, the aircraft veered north toward
95 Little America. Byrd's navigation was unerring.

Several hours later, the weary crew spotted the
Axel Heiberg glacier in the distance. This time the
lightened plane soared through the pass with no
difficulty. After landing and refueling, Byrd and his
100 crew resumed the flight. At 10:10 a.m., the Floyd
Bennett touched down at Little America. "We were
deaf from the roar of the motor," according to Byrd,
"tired from the strain of the flight, but we forgot all that
in the tumultuous welcome of our companions."

105 The welcome echoed far beyond the cluster of
huts at Little America. Congratulations poured in from
all over the world. Byrd was a national hero. His
dramatic adventure had captured the imagination of
millions of Americans, and Antarctica was etched on
110 the national consciousness.

31. The overly ------- drill sergeant even required the
troops to polish the soles of their boots.

A. solicitous
B. careless
C. audacious
D. meticulous
E. cautious

32. Though previously the locals remained neutral,
recently there has been a(n) ------- surge of
support for the fundamentalists that can only be
attributed to the U.S. invasion of Afghanistan.

A. unremarkable
B. predictable
C. unprecedented
D. conventional
E. predetermined

33. While the negotiators claim there are several
issues as stake, the ------- of the matter is really
the President's refusal to agree to a reduction in
military aid to Latin America.

A. detail
B. outcome
C. adage
D. crux
E. mandate

34. In the backyard of the suspect's suburban home,
under a doghouse, the police found a ------- of
counterfeit bills.

A. manifesto
B. cache
C. exposé
D. deficit
E. wealth

35. A roar greeted the appearance of the legendary
guitarist on the stage, and the ------- applause did
not subside for over twenty minutes.

A. peaceful
B. diplomatic
C. lackadaisical
D. aggressive
E. tumultuous

36. As it is used in line 11, the word *desolate* most
nearly means:

A. without human inhabitants.
B. hopeless.
C. marked by indulgence.
D. densely populated.

37. It can be inferred that the word *aerial*, as it is
used in line 13, most nearly means:

A. pertaining to radio.
B. a small area between things.
C. of, in, or produced by the air.
D. a level piece of ground.

38. In context, *consummation* (line 18) most nearly
means:

A. antithesis.
B. completion.
C. conservation.
D. utilization.

39. In line 22, *logistics* refers to:

A. defense of an encampment.
B. analysis of data.
C. planning and coordination of operation de-tails.
D. the formal principles of knowledge.

40. In line 25, *dismantled* most nearly means:

A. violently shattered.
B. deprived of courage.
C. taken apart and stripped of essential parts.
D. dismissed or discharged.

41. The word *rampart* is used in line 32 to refer to:

A. extravagance or absence of restraint.
B. low place in mountain range.
C. a way of entrance or exit.
D. a wall-like ridge or dirt embankment.

42. In line 57, *reconnoiter* most nearly means to:

A. restore.
B. explore.
C. climb.
D. contemplate.

43. Based on the use of the word *jettisoned* in line 74, it can be inferred that *jettison* most nearly means to:

A. throw overboard.
B. burn or extinguish.
C. overflow.
D. illuminate.

44. In line 81, *careened* most nearly means:

A. exploded.
B. wedged.
C. lurched.
D. poked.

45. In line 109, *etched* most nearly means:

A. misused.
B. engraved.
C. irritated.
D. erased.

46. LADE:

A. hurry
B. unload
C. defy
D. consent
E. tune

47. EMBARK:

A. conclude
B. deny
C. insist
D. extend
E. open

48. BARREN:

A. helpful
B. doubtful
C. gigantic
D. premature
E. fertile

49. BRISK:

A. lively
B. dull
C. wet
D. clever
E. difficult

50. RESUME:

A. discontinue
B. overlook
C. pronounce
D. warm
E. undo

51. EXCAVATE:

    A. bury
    B. admit
    C. return
    D. avoid
    E. welcome

52. ROUTINE:

    A. helpful
    B. distant
    C. worn
    D. unusual
    E. living

53. DASHING:

    A. beautiful
    B. new
    C. knowledgeable
    D. withdrawn
    E. constant

54. AMBLE:

    A. stroll
    B. dash
    C. please
    D. tire
    E. erode

55. CLUSTER:

    A. turn back
    B. hold tight
    C. spread out
    D. wish for
    E. move aside

56. GEOLOGY : EARTH ::

    A. biology : organisms
    B. history : government
    C. military : war
    D. geography : politics
    E. chemistry : physics

57. PLATEAU : CLIMB ::

    A. approval : failure
    B. level : progress
    C. disappointment : search
    D. insight : focus
    E. garden: plant

58. GESTURE : IDEA ::

    A. repay : loan
    B. announce : information
    C. bury : scandal
    D. propose : date
    E. stare : sight

59. VAST : LIMITED ::

    A. frank : generous
    B. lengthy : extended
    C. hopeful : expectant
    D. extensive : narrow
    E. powerful: strong

60. TEDIOUS : TIRESOME ::

    A. refreshing : exhausting
    B. prolonged : delightful
    C. annoying : irksome
    D. relaxing : boring
    E. caring : hateful

Passage III

NATURAL SCIENCE: This passage is adapted from a discussion on the application of science and technology in the field of meteorology.

We can think of science as the attempt to comprehend the workings of nature, and of technology as the practical application of this knowledge. There are three major steps in applying science and
5 technology: experimental observation, analysis, and utilization.

There are two aspects of the experimental observation phase. One is the observation of natural phenomena as they occur. The second is the
10 observation of controlled experiments. The former has necessarily been the way of the past. However, with sounding rockets and satellites, the second became feasible and is being more extensively used.

The observation of natural phenomena as they
15 occur involves the development of sensors to observe important phenomena, and the collection of results into a data inventory that is readily accessible to all. For example, in meteorology, this involves a ground activity of assembling temperature, humidity, wind
20 velocity and direction, and other weather data. This information is observed at myriad locations throughout the world and forwarded regularly to central data collection stations. The development of a wide variety of sensors will be used for continued weather satellite
25 observations to provide an even wider variety of data— daily and on a global scale. A very significant meteorological observation activity now underway is the Global Atmospheric Research Program (GARP). This activity involves a large number of countries
30 throughout the world, cooperating to gather weather data of unprecedented scope on a global scale to help in the understanding of weather systems and phenomena throughout the world and the major factors that control their origin, development, and movement.

35 The observation of controlled experiments involves the development and use of techniques for conducting both passive and active experiments with natural phenomena and observation of the results. An example of the passive approach is the barium cloud
40 experiment, in which a sounding rocket was used to disperse a quantity of fine barium powder high above the atmosphere in the earth's magnetic field. In this case, the natural phenomena were undisturbed, and the barium cloud was used to chart with considerable

45 definition the earth's magnetic-field lines. An example of an active experiment is the injection of silver iodide pellets in cloud formations to induce rainfall.

In the analysis phase, basic relationships and trends are discerned and a better understanding of the
50 phenomena evolves. From the observed relationships and growing understanding, theories are developed and models of the phenomena are postulated. These theories and models are intended to help understand the complex cause and effect interactions among the many
55 variables involved. Definitive experiments are then sought to test the validity of the theories and models. Such experiments often entail further observations to obtain critical elements of data. It is via progressive iterative steps between experimental observation and
60 analysis that models evolve sufficiently for use on an operational basis. Using meteorology as an example, we currently have general models of weather system behavior. Although these models are limited to very crude weather forecasting, continued satellite
65 observations—together with programs like GARP— can lead to improvements in our global weather models, our understanding, and our ability to predict it.

In the utilization phase, all of the understanding from observations made and models analytically
70 developed is employed to predict what can or will happen under a specified set of conditions. Weather prediction is a typical example of how models are used in conjunction with current observation to develop forecasts for public use. It is the combination of an
75 ability to monitor and forecast events, together with an understanding of the basic mechanisms which cause predicted events—be they natural events or those created by man—that eventually will lead to global systems for management of our resources and control
80 of our environment in ways that best suit the needs of man.

61. Knowledge of the concentration of elements is important in managing a nuclear reactor and requires constant ------- of neutron activation.

A. distention
B. consumption
C. disclosure
D. exploitation
E. analysis

62. The ------- of low-cost recycled material in the production process allowed the manufacturing plant to increase profits by over 35 percent.

   A. elimination
   B. depreciation
   C. utilization
   D. accumulation
   E. capitulation

63. The plan to build a new highway on the north side of the city is -------, but it will be necessary to raise taxes.

   A. feasible
   B. imaginary
   C. impossible
   D. argumentative
   E. temporary

64. There are ------- small tasks required to keep an airplane in safe condition, so most pilots keep a detailed log of maintenance and safety checks.

   A. moderate
   B. generous
   C. effusive
   D. useful
   E. myriad

65. Accustomed to the frequent outbursts of their coach, the team members listened ------- as he shouted at them during half-time.

   A. actively
   B. passionately
   C. favorably
   D. passively
   E. aggressively

66. In context, *phenomena* (line 9) refers to:

   A. unobservable events or facts.
   B. observable events or facts.
   C. unrecorded events or facts.
   D. recorded events or facts.

67. In context, *data* (line 17) refers to:

   A. unobservable events or facts.
   B. observable events or facts.
   C. unrecorded events or facts.
   D. recorded events or facts.

68. As used in line 17, the word *inventory* refers to a(n):

   A. discovery or finding.
   B. secure place of storage.
   C. division for classification.
   D. organized list of collected information.

69. In line 17, *accessible* most nearly means:

   A. easily used.
   B. valuable.
   C. capable of being estimated.
   D. unobtainable.

70. It can be inferred that the word *disperse*, as it is used in line 41, most nearly means to:

   A. separate or divide.
   B. distribute or scatter.
   C. set on fire.
   D. replace or drive out.

71. Based on the use of the word *discerned* in line 49, it can be inferred that *discern* most nearly means to:

   A. ignore.
   B. analyze.
   C. identify.
   D. eliminate.

72. In line 56, *validity* is best understood to mean:

   A. error.
   B. illusion.
   C. accuracy.
   D. strength.

73. As it is used in line 57, the word *entail* most nearly means to:

    A. cause to be ineffective.
    B. plan or carry out with great care.
    C. indicate or set apart.
    D. cause or involve by necessity.

74. It can be inferred that the word *iterative*, as it is used in line 59, most nearly means:

    A. extreme or outermost.
    B. involving repetition.
    C. traveling from place to place.
    D. obligatory or necessary.

75. In line 73, *conjunction* most nearly means:

    A. contradiction.
    B. combination.
    C. exclusion.
    D. estimation.

76. FORWARD:

    A. remove
    B. remind
    C. return
    D. reopen
    E. relive

77. GLOBAL:

    A. light
    B. even
    C. local
    D. moving
    E. open

78. COMPREHENSIVE:

    A. partial
    B. early
    C. useful
    D. humorous
    E. special

79. UNDERWAY:

    A. centered
    B. connected
    C. young
    D. concealed
    E. planned

80. UNDISTURBED:

    A. planted
    B. proved
    C. stopped
    D. changed
    E. covered

81. DEFINITIVE:

    A. terrible
    B. temporary
    C. quiet
    D. long
    E. burning

82. INJECT:

    A. withdraw
    B. untie
    C. rethink
    D. proceed
    E. fall back

83. EXTENSIVE:

    A. far-reaching
    B. little known
    C. limited
    D. startling
    E. sudden

84. MONITOR:

    A. watch
    B. ignore
    C. send
    D. withhold
    E. trim

85. PROGRESSIVE:

   A. lacking interest
   B. moving backward
   C. opening up
   D. watching for
   E. pulling into

86. SENSORS : OBSERVE ::

   A. eyes : see
   B. nose : face
   C. hands : throw
   D. mouth : open
   E. neck : throat

87. METEOROLOGY: WEATHER ::

   A. history : geography
   B. language : speech
   C. music : performance
   D. anthology : ants
   E. psychology : thinking

88. FORMATION : ARRAY ::

   A. arrangement : order
   B. military : company
   C. permission : idea
   D. backyard : front yard
   E. dunce : teacher

89. COOPERATE : RESIST ::

   A. follow : include
   B. accept : deny
   C. move : rely
   D. retain : keep
   E. withstand : hold

90. CHART : REGION ::

   A. show : animal
   B. map : area
   C. present : plan
   D. wait : date
   E. insist : money

Passage IV

NATURAL SCIENCE: This passage is adapted from a lecture entitled "Memory and Learning."

Long-term learning—positive and negative—is made possible by the fact that the mind is able to remember virtually all it was ever aware of, including the most trivial details. However, there are several
5 conditions to this process of retention.

One condition is that such memory (learning) is situational: It is determined in part by the nature of the situation in which the learning occurs. Students "pay attention" in school and learn things tied to a concrete,
10 not abstract, teaching/learning situation; they learn something solely for the purpose of earning a grade. Consequently, since most school situations have no counterparts outside of school, a student often develops amnesia and is unable to recall information learned in
15 another context. Memory is like a filing system, in which an item is stored to be retrieved with a code keyed to that specific situation. If the situation eliciting that particular code is not encountered again, the filed item remains untouched and unused. It is important to
20 remember the filed item is not transient; it does not fade or die. It is merely dormant during the time it is not in use.

A second condition of "memory" learning is it appears to be bound to the state of arousal that existed
25 for the original learning. The ability to remember, therefore, depends to some degree on the ability to recreate or re-enter the formative state of arousal: the feeling, tone, or affective quality that characterized the brain at the time of learning. Thus, since there is
30 always some subjective element, some aura of feeling that accompanies all we ever learn, it is simply not enough to consider what so-called objective content or skill is being taught. The student's feelings while or after learning takes place will determine whether
35 learning will be effective.

Since students are often in a classroom for hours, it seems reasonable to assert that teachers must be concerned with the ambience of the classroom. Perhaps teachers should also be more aware of their
40 countenance; even a temporary lapse into boredom or irritation can place the students in a situation which makes learning unnecessarily onerous.

91. The new secretary was so consumed by petty office politics and ------- matters that she failed to take care of the tasks that were vital to the company's daily operations.

    A. vital
    B. voluble
    C. trivial
    D. relevant
    E. complicated

92. The teacher used fun games to aid the students in their ------- of the important concepts, dates, and facts that would be crucial for a passing grade on the exam.

    A. rejection
    B. deletion
    C. miscomprehension
    D. retention
    E. management

93. The general of the American army met with his ------- in the British forces, and they quickly realized that while their uniforms were different, their perspectives were similar.

    A. advisor
    B. prototype
    C. partner
    D. counterpart
    E. superior

94. Because they are ------- during hibernation, ground squirrels prepare for winter by building up a thick insulating layer of body fat during late summer and fall.

    A. active
    B. efficient
    C. dormant
    D. occupied
    E. vigorous

95. The aide had not researched the question completely, but his personal and ------- impression was that the governor should veto the bill.

    A. informed
    B. objective
    C. educated
    D. impartial
    E. subjective

96. In context, *virtually* (line 3) most nearly means:

    A. nearly.
    B. completely.
    C. exclusively.
    D. superficially.

97. As it is used in line 9, the word *concrete* most nearly means:

    A. insubstantial.
    B. significant.
    C. particular or specific.
    D. abstract.

98. In line 12, *consequently* most nearly means:

    A. in addition.
    B. regardless.
    C. for the reason.
    D. as a result.

99. As it is used in line 16, the word *retrieved* most nearly means:

    A. repeated.
    B. recovered.
    C. withdrawn.
    D. deleted.

100. Based on the use of the word *eliciting* in line 17, it can be inferred that *elicit* most nearly means to:

    A. make unlawful.
    B. evoke.
    C. offer.
    D. misplace.

101. It can be inferred that the word *transient*, as it is used in line 20, most nearly means:

    A. easily seen through.
    B. altered.
    C. temporary.
    D. transferrable.

102. In line 28, *affective* most nearly means:

    A. useful.
    B. stern.
    C. aloof.
    D. emotional.

103. It can be inferred that the word *aura*, as it is used in line 30, most nearly means:

    A. of or relating to the ear or sense of hearing.
    B. of, in, or pertaining to air.
    C. distinctive and persuasive quality or atmosphere.
    D. an observable luminous phenomenon.

104. In line 38, *ambience* primarily refers to the:

    A. mood or feeling associated with a place.
    B. decoration and furnishings of a room.
    C. surrounding influences or environment.
    D. structure or foundation of a room.

105. In line 42, *onerous* most nearly means:

    A. effortless.
    B. costly.
    C. burdensome.
    D. mistaken.

106. CONDITIONED:

    A. strong
    B. comfortable
    C. exact
    D. unqualified
    E. rare

107. SPECIFIED:

A. tight
B. unnamed
C. wishful
D. confessed
E. winning

108. KEY:

A. disconnect
B. reinforce
C. prolong
D. decide
E. complete

109. BOUND:

A. lost
B. free
C. secure
D. private
E. interesting

110. AROUSE:

A. kindle
B. shape
C. conceal
D. dampen
E. whitewash

111. SYSTEMATIC:

A. haphazard
B. orderly
C. temporary
D. competent
E. pressured

112. RECREATE:

A. destroy
B. finish
C. copy
D. redo
E. outdo

113. EFFECTIVE:

A. simple
B. full
C. useless
D. tempting
E. equal

114. ENCOUNTER:

A. establish
B. avoid
C. tell
D. repay
E. stand

115. RECALL:

A. classify
B. expect
C. triumph
D. send
E. gamble

116. FORMATIVE : MOLD ::

A. developing : shape
B. aging : growth
C. working : employ
D. expressive : shout
E. precious : dislike

117. OBJECTIVE : UNBIASED ::

A. conclusive : incomplete
B. final : continuing
C. accurate : factual
D. avoidable : delayed
E. sweetened : tart

118. AMNESIA : MEMORY ::

A. hearing : sense
B. blindness : sight
C. motion : legs
D. lungs : air
E. teeth : mouth

119. LAPSE : INTENTIONAL ::

    A. slip : planned
    B. force : controlled
    C. renew : overdue
    D. operate : stolen
    E. work : paid

120. ASSERT : STATE ::

    A. announce : listen
    B. question : ask
    C. paint : remodel
    D. close : continue
    E. waken : sleep

Passage V

NATURAL SCIENCE: This passage is adapted from a science news article about the Infrared Astronomical Satellite.

The birth of new stars and the death of old ones will be witnessed by a new Earth-orbiting instrument that will probe through space in quest of celestial phenomena that are invisible to our eyes but glow in
5 the infrared portion of the light spectrum. The instrument's array of infrared detectors will also lift the veil of thick dust clouds that block starlight streaming from the center of our galaxy and sharply limit our study of the densest and most active part of the Milky
10 Way. It will provide a new chart of the universe, mapping perhaps a million infrared sources for future study and will radically transform our concept of the universe. The new instrument is the Infrared Astronomical Satellite (IRAS), and it will be operated
15 by an international team of scientists and engineers.

Infrared astronomy is a recent development in astrophysics because most infrared radiation from space never reaches Earth's surface. Water vapor and other gases in the atmosphere absorb it, hence the
20 importance of situating the telescope above the atmosphere in Earth's orbit. Most infrared observations have been obtained by the use of balloons, sounding rockets, and high-altitude aircraft. The view has been highly circumscribed compared to the broad vista that
25 will be opened to IRAS.

Astronomers have received some tantalizing hints about what may be out there. An exciting example came from a brief survey of infrared objects by the Cambridge Laboratory. It found that some highly
30 evolved stars apparently shed a large percentage of their mass to the interstellar medium. This had not been observed with optical instruments (those that see only visible light). Those highly evolved stars are quite bright at infrared wavelengths, but are only dim specks
35 in conventional star photographs.

The theory of star formation accorded general acceptance today says that vast clouds of dust and gas float in space until some mechanism, which is not yet fully understood, triggers gravitational collapse. Over
40 hundreds of thousands of years each mote of dust, each atom of gas, attracts other motes and atoms until a huge, spinning globe is formed. When gravitational pressure is sufficient and when temperatures at the center of the globe soar high enough—about ten

45 million degrees—thermonuclear reactions commence, and the star begins to glow.

From the time the incipient star is a tenuous dust cloud until soon after the nuclear reactions begin, the heat produced by gravitational collapse is emitted as
50 infrared radiation. That is one of the most exciting prospects of IRAS' mission: the possibility of attending the birth of a star. What appears to be the first nascent star ever observed is buried deep within the nebula or gas cloud in the sword of the constellation Orion, a
55 small dot that while dim by optical measurements, is bright in infrared.

Millions or billions of years after they are born, stars approach their moment of death, when all their nuclear fuel is exhausted. As it begins to die, the star
60 ejects a cloud of dust, and the faint visible light from the moribund star is absorbed by the dust shell and then reemitted as infrared. With IRAS, scientists hope to observe the maternity wards and graveyards of the universe.

121. Though she complained every step of the way, Millie agreed that the panoramic ------- was well worth the four-hour hike to the top of the mountain pass.

    A. angle
    B. dead end
    C. opinion
    D. descent
    E. vista

122. The ------- descriptions of the products are designed to lure in customers and motivate them to buy what otherwise seems unnecessary.

    A. uninspiring
    B. disturbing
    C. reassuring
    D. tantalizing
    E. mundane

123. The artist was multitalented and worked in an assortment of -------, including watercolor, oil and acrylic, and sculpture.

    A. resources
    B. locations
    C. incentives
    D. processes
    E. mediums

124. Because the defendant's hold on reality was so -------, the judge ruled that she was not competent to stand trial.

    A. firm
    B. discernible
    C. tenuous
    D. humble
    E. convincing

125. The ------- grassroots "tea party" movement is more popular with many conservatives than the long-established Grand Old Party.

    A. struggling
    B. nascent
    C. obsolete
    D. mature
    E. prosaic

126. It can be inferred that the word *quest*, as it is used in line 3, most nearly means:

    A. discovery.
    B. deliberation.
    C. rotation.
    D. search.

127. It can be inferred that the word *celestial*, as it is used in line 3, pertains to the:

    A. ancient civilization or world.
    B. modern civilization or world.
    C. sky or heavens.
    D. earth or material world.

128. In context, *radically* (line 12) most nearly means:

    A. momentarily.
    B. fundamentally.
    C. unsubstantially.
    D. temporarily.

129. In line 17, *astrophysics* is best understood to refer to the:

    A. science of the behavior and physical properties of stars.
    B. divination of supposed influences of stars on human affairs.
    C. study of objects within the earth's atmosphere.
    D. science of the physical properties of the earth's surface.

130. As it is used in line 22, the word *obtained* most nearly means:

    A. eliminated.
    B. acquired.
    C. undermined.
    D. negotiated.

131. The word *circumscribed* (line 24) most nearly means:

    A. limited.
    B. traveled around.
    C. surrounded.
    D. cut off.

132. In line 40, *mote* is best understood to refer to a:

    A. method.
    B. feeling.
    C. small particle.
    D. small creature.

133. It can be inferred that the word *incipient*, as it is used in line 47, most nearly means:

    A. lacking taste.
    B. in an initial stage.
    C. dull or uninteresting.
    D. brightly burning.

134. As it is used in line 47, the word *tenuous* most nearly means:

    A. sturdy.
    B. dense.
    C. unsubstantial.
    D. harmless.

135. It can be inferred that the word *moribund*, as it is used in line 61, most nearly means:

    A. sinking.
    B. glowing.
    C. thriving.
    D. dying.

136. VEIL:

    A. disallow
    B. return
    C. install
    D. deny
    E. reveal

137. ATTEND:

    A. remind
    B. win
    C. close
    D. impart
    E. ignore

138. NEBULOUS:

    A. spatial
    B. important
    C. beautiful
    D. clear
    E. cramped

139. EXHAUSTED:

    A. filled
    B. ruined
    C. torn
    D. angry
    E. incapable

140. TRANSFORM:

    A. reinforce
    B. deduct
    C. remind
    D. believe
    E. permit

141. COMMENCE:

    A. prove
    B. turn
    C. end
    D. part
    E. wonder

142. CONVENTIONAL:

    A. solid
    B. scientific
    C. unusual
    D. borrowed
    E. true

143. EMIT:

    A. absorb
    B. denounce
    C. confess
    D. let in
    E. hope for

144. ACCORD:

    A. deceive
    B. deny
    C. denounce
    D. deprive
    E. delete

145. FAINT:

    A. weak
    B. ineffective
    C. complete
    D. brilliant
    E. irate

146. MATERNITY : MOTHER ::

    A. paternity : father
    B. brotherhood : sister
    C. family : members
    D. priesthood : congregation
    E. faculty : student

147. OPTICAL : ILLUSION ::

    A. eyesight : object
    B. heard : deafness
    C. visual : mistake
    D. perceived : sight
    E. eyeball: vision

148. COLOR : SPECTRUM ::

    A. rung : ladder
    B. cow : herd
    C. carpet : floor
    D. painting : frame
    E. puddle : rain

149. ASTRONOMY : STARS ::

    A. chemistry : physics
    B. biology : politics
    C. history : war
    D. botany : plants
    E. geology: farming

150. CONSTELLATION : STARS ::

    A. space : moon
    B. formation : intelligence
    C. box : marbles
    D. school : fish
    E. seating arrangement : guests

Passage VI

NATURAL SCIENCE: This passage is adapted from an essay entitled "The Growth of Intelligence" in an introductory life science textbook.

There is a wide variety of opinions on what evolutionary factors were responsible specifically for hominid intelligence; probably many were important. One theory is that intraspecific warfare plays an
5 important role. War seems to require rapid invention. Strategy discussions that are connected with the planning of warfare tend to involve a kind of verbal competition which requires resourcefulness. Furthermore, intraspecific conflict makes special demands on
10 organisms that their battle with the environment does not: the difference is between intelligence versus intelligence on the one hand, and intelligence versus mere non-intelligence on the other. Finally, warfare involves the young organisms as well, and organisms
15 not suited to it suffer the consequences in that their genes are eliminated from the breeding population. As attractive as the theory is, it is far from having been conclusively proven. Territoriality is a common trait, and some social mammals, such as man and the hyena,
20 exhibit, as a form of territorial behavior, organized violent conflict between social groups. However, territoriality is not a basic biological trait; many species are not afflicted with the desire to make war.

More likely, the most important stimuli to the
25 development of intelligence in early hominids were the demands of communication and language. About three million years ago, the rate of evolution in the brain accelerated, and was correlated with the increased use of stone tools. Such artifacts are evidence of complex
30 social structures, which in turn improved communication. At minimum, the techniques for manufacturing the articles had to be transmitted from one generation to the next. Some of the hominids' increased cranial capacity may have been related to a general increase in
35 motor coordination. The notion that man is a puny beast is a spurious one. He is actually fantastically powerful and yet possessing extreme dexterity, possessed as he is with subtle and accurate motor control of the hands and limbs. He also has very
40 complex feedback mechanisms that allow him to determine accurately the course of a thrown projectile with little practice.

There is general agreement that the need to adopt a predatory lifestyle on the savannah stimulated at least
45 the early development of manipulative ability, motor coordination, and the complex social organization in the hominids. The arboreal environment of the jungle could not have produced these traits. No monkey or ape can control a thrown projectile the way a man can;
50 independent finger control is a uniquely hominid characteristic. Moreover, chimpanzees and other apes, though they use natural objects such as sticks for tools, have never developed a systematic tool-making ability.

Thus, the demands of the savannah environment
55 were probably responsible for the development of intelligence and technological society in man, but it does not follow that this type of environment is a prerequisite to the development of these characteristics. It is possible such characteristics could have developed
60 in entirely different circumstances, nor were the environmental challenges themselves sufficient to produce this result. It was crucial that an animal well-adapted to live in the complex forest environment be pre-adapted to a new ecological niche on the savannah
65 and therefore able to invade it successfully.

151. My dogs are very -------: they bark and act aggressively whenever another dog walks by our yard.

    A. passive
    B. territorial
    C. terrestrial
    D. nonchalant
    E. dormant

152. Advocates of the "war on drugs" argue that strong drug enforcement in the United States is ------- with dramatic reductions in crime, drug use, and drug addiction rates.

    A. disassociated
    B. correlated
    C. motivated
    D. demonstrated
    E. unconnected

153. The new study published in *Genetics and Biotechnology* identifies a mechanism that plays a key role in how mutations are ------- from one generation to the next.

A. borrowed
B. disconnected
C. transmitted
D. isolated
E. inflated

154. Recent discoveries in South America and Asia suggest that Tyrannosaurus rex, the largest meat-eating ------- dinosaur, had a range much greater than originally thought.

A. ambulatory
B. predatory
C. satisfactory
D. reactionary
E. precursory

155. Very different animals occupy the same ecological ------- in different continents: for example, the bison is the largest land herbivore in America, while in Australia it is the kangaroo.

A. destination
B. imperative
C. prospect
D. cache
E. niche

156. It can be inferred that the word *hominid*, as it is used in line 3, refers to all forms, both extinct and living, of:

A. primate.
B. animal.
C. flora.
D. insect.

157. In context, *intraspecific* (line 4) most nearly means:

A. eliminating specific characteristics.
B. mutually joined or related.
C. occurring between members of the same species.
D. occurring between members of different species.

158. As it is used in line 23, the word *afflicted* most nearly means:

A. acted upon.
B. accomplished by.
C. inclined toward.
D. troubled with.

159. In line 29, *artifacts* is best understood to mean:

A. clever or artful skills.
B. evidence.
C. tools used by animals.
D. human-made objects.

160. It can be inferred that the word *cranial*, as it is used in line 33, pertains to the:

A. body.
B. skull.
C. lungs.
D. environment.

161. The word *spurious* (line 36) most nearly means:

A. genuine.
B. hypocritical.
C. false.
D. improbable.

162. It can be inferred that the word *dexterity*, as it is used in line 37, most nearly means:

A. gentleness.
B. agility.
C. clumsiness.
D. loquaciousness.

163. The word *savannah* (line 44) refers to:

A. grassland with scattered trees.
B. tropical rainforest.
C. an area far from cities or big towns.
D. temperate hardwood forest.

164. The word *arboreal* (line 47) most nearly means:

A. native.
B. flexible.
C. sheltered.
D. treelike.

165. In line 58, *prerequisite* most nearly means a(n):

A. requirement.
B. option.
C. development.
D. opportunity.

166. VERBAL:

A. wordy
B. physical
C. contained
D. dense
E. tremendous

167. RESOURCEFUL:

A. rugged
B. overbearing
C. incompetent
D. crowded
E. underhanded

168. SUFFER:

A. avoid
B. control
C. receive
D. supply
E. return

169. EXHIBIT:

A. insist
B. hide
C. wash
D. berate
E. crow

170. CONCLUSIVE:

A. final
B. rash
C. firm
D. poor
E. open

171. ACCELERATE:

A. rush
B. slow
C. return
D. widen
E. pull back

172. SUBTLE:

A. charming
B. clumsy
C. mental
D. poisonous
E. deadly

173. MINIMUM:

A. necessity
B. guilty
C. work
D. most
E. little

174. PUNY:

A. concerned
B. victorious
C. correct
D. robust
E. valiant

175. INVADE:

    A. withdraw
    B. conquer
    C. lose
    D. battle
    E. negotiate

176. STRATEGY : PLAN ::

    A. war : battle
    B. hostilities : win
    C. tactics : fight
    D. victory : surrender
    E. soldier : army

177. PROJECTILE : THROW ::

    A. bullet : wound
    B. rocket : land
    C. car : drive
    D. discus : leap
    E. stone : sling

178. MANIPULATION : CONTROLS ::

    A. punishment : criminals
    B. exploitation : workers
    C. handling : instruments
    D. abuse : people
    E. joyfulness : hearts

179. MOTOR : MUSCLES ::

    A. mental : mind
    B. past : present
    C. physical : emotions
    D. prepared : product
    E. threatening : harm

180. MANUFACTURE : PRODUCT ::

    A. strengthen : steel
    B. prefer : favorite
    C. contain : pressure
    D. remind : memory
    E. weave : fabric

Word Parts List

It isn't necessary to memorize vocabulary words in order to do well on vocabulary-related items. However, it can be helpful to make yourself familiar with the prefixes, suffixes, and vocabulary words on the following list. Each prefix or suffix is followed by a definition as well as one or two words that incorporate the prefix or suffix. Each vocabulary word is followed by a definition.

Prefixes

a, ab, abs—from, away
    abrade—wear off
    absent—away, not present
a, an—lacking, not
    asymptomatic—showing no symptoms
    anaerobic—able to live without air
ad, ac, af, ag, al, an, ap, ar, as, at—to, toward
    accost—approach and speak to
    adjunct—something added to
    aggregate—bring together
ambi, amphi—around, both
    ambidextrous—using both hands equally
    amphibious—living both in water and on land
ana—up, again, anew, throughout
    analyze—loosen up, break up into parts
    anagram—word spelled from letters of other word
ante—before
    antediluvian—before the Flood, extremely old
anti—against
    anti-war—against war
arch—first, chief
    archetype—first model
auto—self
    automobile—self-moving vehicle

bene, ben—good, well
    benefactor—one who does good deeds

circum—around
    circumnavigate—sail around
com, co, col, con, cor—with, together
    concentrate—bring closer together
    cooperate—work together
    collapse—fall together
contra, contro, counter—against
    contradict—speak against
    counterclockwise—against the clock

de—away from, down, opposite of
    detract—draw away from
di—twice, double
    dichromatic—having two colors
dia—across, through
    diameter—measurement across
dis, di—not, away from
    dislike—to not like
    digress—turn away from the subject
dys—bad, poor
    dyslexia—poor reading

equi—equal
    equivalent—of equal value
ex, e, ef—from, out
    expatriate—one living outside a native country
    emit—send out
extra—outside, beyond
    extraterrestrial—from beyond the earth

fore—in front of, previous
    forecast—tell ahead of time
    foreleg—front leg

homo—same, like
    homophonic—sounding the same
hyper—too much, over
    hyperactive—overly active
hypo—too little, under
    hypothermia—having too little body heat

in, il, ig, im, ir—not
    innocent—not guilty
    ignorant—not knowing
    irresponsible—not responsible
in, il, im, ir—on, into, in
    impose—place on
    invade—go into

intra, intro—within, inside
    intrastate—within a state

mal, male—bad, wrong, poor
    maladjusted—poorly adjusted
    malevolent—ill-wishing
mis—badly, wrongly
    misunderstand—understand incorrectly
mis, miso—hatred
    misogyny—hatred of women
mono—single, one
    monorail—train that runs on a single rail

neo—new
    Neolithic—of the New Stone Age
non—not
    nonentity—a nobody

ob—over, against, toward
    obstruct—stand against
omni—all
    omnipresent—present in all places

pan—all
    panorama—a complete view
peri—around, near
    periscope—device for seeing all around
poly—many
    polygonal—many-sided
post—after
    postmortem—after death
pre—before, earlier than
    prejudice—judgment in advance

pro—in favor of, forward, in front of
    proceed—go forward
    pro-war—in favor of war

re—back, again
    rethink—think again
    reimburse—pay back
retro—backward
    retrospective—looking backward

se—apart, away
    seclude—keep away
semi—half
    semiconscious—half conscious
sub, suc, suf, sug, sus—under, beneath
    subscribe—write underneath
    suspend—hang down
    suffer—undergo
super—above, greater
    superfluous—beyond what is needed
syn, sym, syl, sys—with, at the same time
    synthesis—a putting together
    sympathy—a feeling with

tele—far
    television—literally, a machine for seeing far off
trans—across
    transport—carry across a distance

un—not
    uninformed—not informed

vice—acting for, next in rank to
    vice president—second in command

Suffixes

able, ble—able, capable
    acceptable—able to be accepted
acious, cious—characterized by, having the quality of
    spacious—having the quality of space
age—sum, total
    mileage—total number of miles
al—of, like, suitable for
    theatrical—suitable for theater
ance, ancy—act or state of
    disturbance—act of disturbing
ant, ent—one who
    defendant—one who defends himself

ary, ar—having the nature of, concerning
    military—relating to soldiers
    polar—pertaining to the poles of the earth

cy—act, state, or position of
    presidency—position of president
    ascendancy—state of being raised up

dom—state, rank, that which belongs to
    wisdom—state of being wise

ence—act, state, or quality of
    dependence—state of depending

er, or—one who, that which
  doer—one who does
  conductor—that which conducts
escent—becoming
  obsolescent—becoming obsolete

fy—to make
  pacify—make peaceful

ic, ac—of, like
  demonic—of or like a demon
il, ile—having to do with, like, suitable for
  civil—having to do with citizens
  tactile—having to do with touch
ion—act or condition of
  operation—act of operating
ious—having, characterized by
  anxious—characterized by anxiety
ish—like, somewhat
  foolish—like a fool
ism—belief or practice of
  racism—belief in racial superiority
ist—one who does, makes, or is concerned with
  scientist—one concerned with science
ity, ty, y—character or state of being
  amity—friendship
  jealousy—state of being jealous
ive—of, relating to, tending to
  destructive—tending to destroy

logue, loquy—speech or writing
  monologue—speech by one person
  colloquy—conversation

logy—speech, study of
  geology—study of the earth

ment—act or state of
  abandonment—act of abandoning
mony—a resulting thing, condition, or state
  patrimony—trait inherited from one's father

ness—act or quality
  kindness—quality of being kind

ory—having the quality of, a place or thing for
  compensatory—quality of compensation
  lavatory—place for washing
ous, ose—full of, having
  glamorous—full of glamour

ship—skill, state of being
  horsemanship—skill in riding
  ownership—state of being an owner
some—full of, like
  frolicsome—playful

tude—state or quality of
  rectitude—state of being morally upright

ward—in the direction of
  homeward—in the direction of home

y—full of, like, somewhat
  wily—full of wiles

Roots

acr—bitter
  acrid, acrimony
act, ag—do, act, drive
  action, react, agitate, agent
acu—sharp, keen
  acute, acumen
agog—leader
  pedagogue, demagogic
agr—field
  agronomy, agriculture
ali—other
  alias, alienate, inalienable
alt—high
  altitude, contralto

alter, altr—other, change
  alternative, altercation, altruism
am, amic—love, friend
  amorous, amiable
anim—mind, life, spirit
  animism, animate, animosity
annu, enni—year
  annual, superannuated, biennial
anthrop—man
  anthropoid, misanthropy
apt, ept—fit
  apt, adapt, ineptitude
aqu—water
  aquatic, aquamarine

arbit—judge
   arbiter, arbitrary
arch—chief
   anarchy, matriarch
arm—arm, weapon
   army, armature, disarm
art—skill, a fitting together
   artisan, artifact, articulate
aster, astr—star
   asteroid, disaster, astral
aud, audit, aur—hear
   auditorium, audition, auricle
aur—gold
   aureate, aureomycin
aut—self
   autism, autograph

bell—war
   anti-bellum, belligerent
brev—short
   brevity, abbreviation, abbreviate

cad, cas, cid—fall
   cadence, casualty, accident
cand—white, shining
   candid, candle, incandescent
cant, chant—sing, charm
   cantor, recant, enchant
cap, capt, cept, ceipt, cept, cip—take, seize, hold
   capable, captive, accept, incipient
capit—head
   capital, decapitate, recapitulate
cede, ceed, cess—go, yield
   secede, exceed, process, intercession
cent—hundred
   century, percentage, centimeter
cern, cert—perceive, make certain, decide
   concern, certificate, certain
chrom—color
   monochrome, chromatic
chron—time
   chronometer, anachronism
cide, cis—cut, kill
   genocide, incision, suicide
cit—summon, impel
   cite, excite, incitement
civ—citizen
   uncivil, civilization
clam, claim—shout
   clamorous, proclaim, claimant
clar—clear
   clarity, clarion, declare

clin—slope, lean
   inclination, recline
clud, clus, clos—close, shut
   seclude, recluse, closet
cogn—know
   recognize, incognito
col, cul—prepare
   colony, cultivate, agriculture
corp—body
   incorporate, corpse
cosm—order, world
   cosmetic, cosmos, cosmopolitan
crac, crat—power, rule
   democrat, theocracy
cre, cresc, cret—grow
   increase, crescent, accretion
cred—trust, believe
   credit, incredible
crux, cruc—cross
   crux, crucial, crucifix
crypt—hidden
   cryptic, cryptography
cur, curr, curs—run, course
   occur, current, incursion
cura—care
   curator, accurate

dem—people
   demographic, demagogue
dent—tooth
   dental, indentation
derm—skin
   dermatitis, pachyderm
di, dia—day
   diary, quotidian
dic, dict—say, speak
   indicative, edict, dictation
dign—worthy
   dignified, dignitary
doc, doct—teach, prove
   indoctrinate, docile, doctor
domin—rule
   predominate, domineer, dominion
dorm—sleep
   dormitory, dormant
du—two
   duo, duplicity, dual
duc, duct—lead
   educate, abduct, ductile
dur—hard, lasting
   endure, obdurate, duration
dyn—force, power
   dynamo, dynamite

equ—equal
  equation, equitable
erg, urg—work, power
  energetic, metallurgy, demiurge
err—wander
  error, aberrant
ev—time, age
  coeval, longevity

fac, fact, fect, fic—do, make
  facility, factual, perfect, artifice
fer—bear, carry
  prefer, refer, conifer, fertility
ferv—boil
  fervid, effervesce
fid—belief, faith
  infidelity, confidant, perfidious
fin—end, limit
  finite, confine
firm—strong
  reaffirm, infirmity
flect, flex—bend
  reflex, inflection
flor—blossom
  florescent, floral
flu, fluct, flux—flow
  fluid, fluctuation, influx
form—shape
  formative, reform, formation
fort—strong
  effort, fortitude
frag, fract—break
  fragility, infraction
fug—flee
  refuge, fugitive

gam—marry
  exogamy, polygamous
ge, geo—earth
  geology, geode, perigee
gen—birth, kind, race
  engender, general, generation
gest—carry, bear
  gestation, ingest, digest
gon—angle
  hexagonal, trigonometry
grad, gress—step, go
  regress, gradation
gram, graph—writing
  cryptogram, telegraph
grat—pleasing, agreeable
  congratulate

grav—weight, heavy
  grave (situation), gravity
greg—flock, crowd
  gregarious, segregate

habit, hibit—have, hold
  habitation, inhibit, habitual
heli—sun
  helium, heliocentric, aphelion
her, hes—stick, cling
  adherent, cohesive
hydr—water
  dehydration, hydrofoil

iatr—heal, cure
  pediatrics, psychiatry
iso—same, equal
  isotope, isometric
it—journey, go
  itinerary, exit

ject—throw
  reject, subjective, projection
jud—judge
  judicial, adjudicate
jug, junct—join
  conjugal, juncture, conjunction
jur—swear
  perjure, jurisprudence

labor—work
  laborious, belabor
leg—law
  legal, illegitimate
leg, lig, lect—choose, gather, read
  illegible, eligible, select, lecture
lev—light, rise
  levity, alleviate
liber—free
  liberal, libertine
liter—letter
  literate, alliterative
lith—rock, stone
  Neolithic, lithograph
loc—place
  locale, locus, allocate
log—word, study
  logic, biology, dialogue
loqu, locut—talk, speech
  colloquial, loquacious, interlocutor
luc, lum—light
  translucent, pellucid, illumine

lud, lus—play
allusion, ludicrous, interlude

magn—large, great
magnificent, magnitude

mal—bad, ill
malodorous, malady

man, manu—hand
manifest, manicure, manuscript

mar—sea
maritime, submarine

mater, matr—mother
matrilocal, maternal

medi—middle
intermediary, medieval

ment—mind
demented, mental

merg, mers—plunge, dip
emerge, submersion

meter, metr, mens—measure
chronometer, metronome, geometry

micr—small
microfilm, micron

min—little
minimum, minute

mit, miss—send
remit, admission, missive

mon, monit—warn
admonish, monument, monitor

mor—custom
mores, immoral

mor, mort—death
mortify, mortician

morph—shape
amorphous, anthropomorphic

mov, mob, mot—move
removal, automobile, motility

mut—change
mutable, transmute, mutation

nasc, nat—born
native, natural, nascent, innate

necr—dead, die
necropolis, necrosis

neg—deny
renege, negative

nom, noun, nown,—name, order, rule
anonymous, antinomy, misnomer

nam, nym, nomen, nomin—name
nomenclature, cognomen, nominate

nomy—law, rule
astronomy, antinomy

nov—new
novice, innovation

ocul—eye
binocular, oculist

onym—name
pseudonym, antonym

oper—work
operate, cooperation, inoperable

ora—speak, pray
oracle, oratory

orn—decorate
adorn, ornate

orth—straight, correct
orthodox, orthopedic

pan—all
panacea, pantheon

pater, patr—father
patriot, paternity

path, pat, pass—feel, suffer
telepathy, patient, compassion

ped—child
pedagogue, pediatrics

ped, pod—foot
pedestrian, impede, tripod

pel, puls—drive, push
impel, propulsion

pend, pens—hang
pendulous, suspense

pet, peat—seek
petition, impetus, repeat

phil—love
philosopher, Anglophile

phob—fear
phobic, agoraphobia

phon—sound
phonograph, symphony

phor—bearing
semaphore, metaphor

phot—light
photograph, photoelectric

pon, pos—place, put
component, repose, postpone

port—carry
report, portable, deportation

pot—power
potency, potential

press—press
pressure, impression

prim, proto, prot—first
primal, proton, protagonist

psych—mind
  psychic, metempsychosis

quer, quir, quis, ques—ask, seek
  query, inquiry, inquisitive, quest

reg, rig, rect—straight, rule
  regulate, dirigible, corrective

rid, ris—laugh
  deride, risible, ridiculous

rog—ask
  rogation, interrogate

rupt—break
  erupt, interruption, rupture

sanct—holy
  sacrosanct, sanctify, sanction

sci, scio—know
  nescient, conscious, omniscience

scop—watch, view
  horoscope, telescopic

scrib, script—write
  scribble, proscribe, description

sed, sid, sess—sit, seat
  sediment, sedate, session

seg, sect—cut
  segment, section, intersect

sent, sens—feel, think
  nonsense, sensitive, sentient

sequ, secut—follow
  sequel, consequence, consecutive

sol—alone
  solitary, solo, desolate

solv, solu, solut—loosen
  dissolve, soluble, absolution

somn—sleep
  insomnia, somnolent

son—sound
  sonorous, unison

soph—wise, wisdom
  philosophy, sophisticated

spec, spic, spect—look
  specimen, conspicuous, spectacle

spir—breathe
  spirit, conspire, respiration

stab, stat—stand
  unstable, status, station

stead—place
  instead, steadfast

string, strict—bind
  astringent, stricture, restrict

stru, struct—build
  construe, structure, destructive

sum, sumpt—take
  presume, consumer, assumption

tang, ting, tact, tig—touch
  tangent, contingency, contact

tax, tac—arrange, arrangement
  taxonomy, tactic

techn—skill, art
  technique, technician

tele—far
  teletype, telekinesis

tempor—time
  temporize, extemporaneous

ten, tain, tent—hold
  tenant, tenacity, retention

tend, tens, tent—stretch
  contend, extensive, intent

tenu—thin
  tenuous, attenuate

test—witness
  attest, testify

the—god
  polytheism, theologist

tom—cut
  atomic, appendectomy

tort, tors—twist
  tortuous, torsion, contort

tract—pull, draw
  traction, attract, protract

trib—assign, pay
  attribute, tribute, retribution

trud, trus—thrust
  obtrude, intrusive

turb—agitate
  perturb, turbulent, disturb

umbr—shade
  umbrella, penumbra

urb—city
  urbane, suburb, urban

vac—empty
  vacuous, evacuation

vad, vas—go
  invade, evasive

val, vail—strength, worth
  valid, avail, prevalent

ven, vent—come
  advent, convene, prevention

ver—true
  aver, veracity, verity

verb—word
  verbose, adverb, verbatim

vert, vers—turn
revert, perversion, versatile
vest—dress
vestment
vid, vis—see
video, evidence, vision, revise
vinc, vict—conquer
evince, convict, victim
viv, vit—life
vivid, revive, vital
vo, voc, vok, vow—call
vociferous, provocative, equivocate
vol—wish
involuntary, volition
volv, volut—roll, turn
involve, convoluted, revolution
vulg—common
divulge, vulgarity

zo—animal
zoologist, Paleozoic

Vocabulary List

The following list is composed of words that students may find challenging on standardized tests. The list is divided into three difficulty levels. Familiarity with the Vocabulary List can only improve your chances of answering items correctly.

Difficulty Level 1

abstraction—mental act of contemplating the parts of a complex object as separate from the object itself

accelerate—to bring about at an earlier time; to cause to move faster

accessible—easily approached, entered, or used

accord—to bring into agreement

acknowledge—admit, grant, accept

acoustic—pertaining to the sense of hearing

addiction—compulsive physiological and psychological need for a habit-forming substance; the condition of being habitually or compulsively occupied with or involved in something

adolescence—the state or process of growing up

adopt—to take by choice into a relationship, especially to take voluntarily as one's own child; to take up and practice or use

adorn—to enhance the appearance of, especially with beautiful objects

advance—to accelerate the growth or progress of

aerial—pertaining to the air

affective—influencing the emotions, emotional

aggravate—to make worse, more serious, or more severe

alienate—to make unfriendly, hostile, or indifferent

ambience—environment, surroundings

ambitious—having a desire to achieve a particular goal

amnesia—loss of memory due usually to brain injury, shock, fatigue, repression, or illness

amplify—to make larger or greater (as in amount, importance, or intensity)

analysis—careful study of a situation or problem by examining all parts of the situation or problem

ancient—having had an existence of many years

anthology—collection of poems, songs

anticipate—foresee, expect

apprehensive—fearful, worried

argument—logical reasoning, a reasoned, persuasive discussion

arouse—to awaken from sleep

arrest—to bring to a stop; to take or keep in custody by authority of law

artifact—an object made by human hands

ascent—the act of rising or mounting upward

aspect—appearance to the eye or mind

assert—to state or declare positively and often forcefully or aggressively

assign—to appoint to a post or duty

associate—to join as a partner, friend, or companion

astronomy—the study of objects and matter outside the earth's atmosphere and of their physical and chemical properties

astrophysics—science of the physical properties of the stars

attend—to pay attention to

aura—an invisible atmosphere surrounding a person, halo

avid—very eager

awe—an emotion variously combining dread, veneration, and wonder that is inspired by authority or by the sacred or sublime

beneficial—helpful

blunt—slow or deficient in feeling

blustering—to talk or act with noisy and swaggering threats

bound—intending to go

brilliancy—very bright

brisk—keenly alert; sharp in tone or manner

casual—occurring without regularity; done without serious intent or commitment

celestial—pertaining to the heavens or sky

chaos—a state of utter confusion

charity—generosity and helpfulness especially toward the needy or suffering

chart—a sheet giving information in tabular form

cherish—to hold dear

civil—adequate in courtesy and politeness

cluster—a number of similar things that occur together

coherent—consistent, holding together

color—a phenomenon of light (i.e., red, brown, pink, or gray) or visual perception that enables one to differentiate otherwise identical objects

commence—to have or make a beginning

commerce—the exchange or buying and selling of commodities on a large scale involving transportation from place to place

compassionate—possessing a sympathetic consciousness of others' distress along with a desire to alleviate it

component—part or ingredient

composed—free from agitation

comprehensive—covering completely or broadly

comprise—include

conclusive—putting an end to debate or question especially by reason of irrefutability

concrete—particular or specific, not general or abstract

conditioned—brought or put into a specific state

consequence—effect, result, outgrowth

constellation—a configuration of stars

constitute—to appoint to an office, function, or dignity

conventional—formed by agreement or compact

conversion—to bring over from one belief, party, or view to another

cooperate—to act or work with another or others

cope—to deal with and attempt to overcome problems and difficulties

copyright—the exclusive legal right to reproduce, publish, sell, or distribute the matter and form of something

correlated—to be related, occurring together

cosmos—the universe and all that exists

counterpart—person or thing corresponding to another person or thing

cranial—pertaining to the skull

critical—of, relating to, or being a turning point or specially important juncture

crop—a plant, animal, or plant or animal product that can be grown and harvested extensively for profit or subsistence

culminated—reached the high point in development

currency—a medium of trade or exchange

curriculum—required course of study or courses in a school

cyclical—of, relating to, or being in a cycle

cynicism—belief that people are motivated only by greed or some other selfish motive

dashing—marked by vigorous action

data—observed events, facts, or occurrences

delicacy—the quality or state of being luxurious

delusion—something that is falsely or delusively believed or propagated

deposit—to place especially for safekeeping or as a pledge

deprivation—to take something away from

designated—indicated, specified

design—to create, fashion, execute, or construct according to plan

destine—to decree beforehand

detached—standing by itself

dismantle—to take apart and strip of essential parts

disperse—to break up, to scatter, to spread

disrupt—to break apart

distinctive—something marked as separate or different

ditty—a short, simple song

divine—of, relating to, or proceeding directly from God or a god; supremely good

domestic—living near or about human limitations

eat—to take in through the mouth as food

effective—producing a decided, decisive, or desired effect

elegant—of a high grade or quality

elevation—the act of raising up

elite—the choice part

eloquent—persuasive, well spoken

enchant—to influence by or as if by charms and incantation

encounter—to meet as an adversary or enemy

entertain—to show hospitality to; to keep, hold, or maintain in the mind

entrance—the means or place of entry

environment—the circumstances, objects, or conditions by which one is surrounded

epic—extending beyond the usual or ordinary especially in size or scope

epidemic—an outbreak of sudden rapid growth or development

essential—of the utmost importance

etch—to engrave

exception—a case in which a rule does not apply

exclusive—limiting or limited to possession, control, or use by a single individual or group

execute—to carry out fully

exhaust—to consume entirely

exhibit—to present to view

exploit—to make use of meanly or unfairly for one's own advantage

extend—to spread or stretch forth

extensive—having wide or considerable range

exuberance—joyously unrestrained and enthusiastic

facilitate—to ease, to make less difficult

faint—lacking courage or spirit, dim or weak, or to lose consciousness

featured—displayed, advertised, or presented as a special attraction

formation—an act of giving form or shape to something; group

formative—giving or capable of giving form

forward—near, at, or belonging to the forepart; strongly inclined

freakish—markedly strange or abnormal

genius—extraordinary intellectual power

genre—type, kind, category

geology—a science that deals with the history of the earth and its life especially as recorded in rocks

gesture—a movement of the body or limbs that expresses or emphasizes an idea, sentiment, or attitude

global—of, relating to, or involving the entire world

gorgeous—splendidly or showily brilliant or magnificent

heritage—something handed down from one's ancestors; customs and traditions

host—one who receives or entertains guests in a social or official capacity

hue—gradation of color

illiterate—unable to read or write

illuminate—to brighten with light

imagery—representations, pictures

imaginative—devoid of truth

immerse—to place in and completely cover with liquid

imperfect—not perfect

imperial—of, relating to, befitting, or suggestive of an empire or an emperor

impose—to establish or apply by authority

impressionable—easily influenced

improbable—unlikely to be true or occur

improvise—to make up or perform spontaneously and on the spur of the moment

impulse—a force so communicated as to produce motion suddenly

inanimate—not endowed with life or spirit

indistinguishable—indeterminate in shape or structure

inestimable—incapable of being measured

inevitable—unable to be avoided or evaded

infancy—a beginning or early period of existence

infect—to contaminate with a disease-producing substance or agent

inhibit—to prohibit from doing something

inject—to introduce into something forcefully

inseparable—seemingly always together

intensify—to make stronger, more acute

intimate—belonging to or characterizing one's deepest nature

intimidate—to make timid or fearful

invade—to enter for conquest or plunder

inventory—a stock or store of something, also an itemized list of goods

irrigate—to supply land or crops with water by artificial means

issue—a vital or unsettled matter

key—something that gives an explanation or identification or provides a solution

labor—expenditure of physical or mental effort especially when difficult or compulsory

linear—of, relating to, resembling, or having a straight line

local—of, relating to, or characteristic of a particular place; not general or widespread

lull—subside, become calm

lust—an intense longing

luxuriate—to thrive; to indulge oneself

lyrical—expressing deep personal emotion or observations

maneuver—evasive movement or shift of tactics

manipulate—to change by artful or unfair means so as to serve one's purpose

manufacture—to make from raw materials by hand or by machinery

masterpiece—an artist's most important work

maternity—the quality or state of being a mother

meditate—to engage in contemplation or reflection

merchant—a buyer and seller of commodities for profit

meteorology—a science that deals with the atmosphere and its phenomena and especially with weather and weather forecasting

mime—an ancient dramatic entertainment where scenes from life are represented silently and usually in a ridiculous manner

minimum—the least quantity assignable, admissible, or possible

mischievous—able or tending to cause annoyance, trouble, or minor injury

mode—way, method, or form

monitor—one that warns or instructs

morbid—diseased, or with a tendency to dwell on unwholesome matters

motor—one that imparts motion; engine

neglect—to give little attention or respect to

objective—factual; unbiased

obligation—a commitment to a course of action

obnoxious—highly offensive, objectionable

obtain—to acquire, to get

optical—of or relating to vision

options—things that may be chosen

overdrawn—having written a check for more than is in an account

particular—of, relating to, or being a single person or thing

passive—not acting; receiving impressions

placid—quiet, tranquil

plagiarize—to steal the words of another and pass off as one's own

plateau—an extensive flat area; a place or region of little or no change

plunge—to cause to penetrate or enter quickly and forcibly into something

popular—suitable to the majority

portray—to depict; to describe in words

preoccupation—extreme or excessive concern with something

prescribed—required, directed

pretense—a false claim or a false show of something

prevalent—widespread, generally accepted

primitive—of or relating to the earliest age or period

principal—most important, consequential, or influential

proclaim—to declare publicly

profane—to treat with irreverence or impiety

progressive—making use of or interested in new ideas, findings, or opportunities

projectile—an object propelled by external force

project—to see mentally or to imagine

prolong—to lengthen in time

prominent—readily noticeable

proximity—nearness

puny—slight or inferior in power, size, or importance

purge—to clear of guilt; to get rid of; to remove

purposive—serving or effecting a useful function

quest—search, inquiry

rationale—the fundamental reason for something

realize—to bring into concrete existence; to understand

recall—to bring back to mind

receptive—open and responsive to ideas

recipient—one that receives

reconstruct—to establish or assemble again

recreate—to give new life or freshness to

reduce—to consolidate, to diminish in size

refined—purified of coarse elements

reflection—the production of an image by or as if by a mirror

remorse—a deep sense of guilt

remote—separated by an interval or space greater than usual

renown—fame, reputation

resourceful—capable of devising ways or means

resume—to assume or take again

retail— to sell in small quantities directly to the consumer

retrieve—recover, call to mind

ridge—a range of hills or mountains

routine—a regular course or procedure

satire— a literary work holding up human vices to ridicule or scorn

seamy—unattractive, unpleasant

sensor—a device that responds to a physical stimulus and transmits a resulting impulse

sequential—of or relating to a continual series

singular—unusual, remarkable

sinister—singularly evil

solitary—being, living, or going alone or without companions

sound—free from injury or disease; showing good judgment or sense

specialized—designed, trained, or fitted for one particular purpose or occupation

specified—to name or state explicitly or in detail

spurt—to gush forth

standardized—to bring into conformity

stimulus—something that rouses or incites to activity

strategy—a careful plan or method

strut—to walk with a proud gait

submerge—to put under water

subsequent—following in time, order, or place

subtle—delicate, elusive

suffer— to submit to or be forced to endure

summons—a call or order to perform some action

superior—of higher rank, quality

surpass—to become better, greater, or stronger than

surrender—to yield to the power, control, or possession of another upon compulsion or demand

sustain—to give support or relief to

sway—influence or control

swell—to expand beyond a normal or original limit

taut—tightly stretched, tense

technique—method, procedure

terminate—to come to an end

theology—the study of religious faith, practice, and experience *traditional*—an inherited, established, or customary pattern of thought, action, or behavior

trait—a distinguishing quality

transaction—business deal

transform—to change in composition or structure

transitional—passing from one state, stage, subject, or place to another

trivial—unimportant, insignificant

unattainable—impossible to achieve

underway—no longer at rest; in progress

undisturbed—untroubled by interference

uneasy—lacking a sense of security; apprehensive

unhindered—not slowed or interfered with

uniform—showing a single form in all occurrences

unique—being the only one of its kind

universal—used or intended for use by everyone

utilitarian—stressing the importance of function over beauty

utilization—use

value—the worth of something

vast—very great in size or amount

veil—a cover of cloth

velocity—quickness of motion

vendor—one that sells

venture—to undertake risks and dangers of; an undertaking involving uncertainty

verbal—of, relating to, or consisting of words

versatile—able to do many things

vital—living, manifesting life, necessary or essential to life

vocal—uttered by the voice

vulnerable—capable of being injured or wounded

whirl—to move in a circle especially with force or speed

Difficulty Level 2

abacus—a frame with beads or balls used for doing or teaching arithmetic

abash—disconcert; to make embarrassed and ill at ease

abated—lessened, diminished

abate—to deduct; to make less

abduction—to carry off by force

aberration—a deviation from the normal or the typical

abeyance—temporary suspension

abhor—to detest; to shrink from in disgust or hatred

abhorrence—loathing; detestation

abhorrent—hateful, loathsome

abide—to stay; stand fast; remain

abjure—recant; to give up (opinions) publicly

abominate—to loathe; to dislike very much

abrade—to scrape or rub off

abridge—to shorten; to reduce in scope or extent

abrogate—to cancel; call off

abscond—to go away hastily and secretly

absolve—to acquit; to pronounce free from guilt or blame

abstinence—the act of voluntarily doing without pleasures

abstruse—hard to understand; deep; recondite

absurdity—nonsense

abyss—chasm; a deep fissure in the earth; bottomless gulf

acclaim—to greet with loud applause or approval

accretion—growth in size by addition or accumulation

acerbic—sharp, bitter, or harsh in temper and language

acquisition—something or someone acquired or added

acrimony—asperity; bitterness or harshness of temper, manner, or speech

acute—shrewd; keen or quick of mind

adapt—to adjust; to make fit or suitable by changing

adjunct—connected or attached in a secondary or subordinate way

adorn—ornament; to put decorations on something

adroit—expert; clever; skillful in a physical or mental way

adulterate—to make something inferior, false, or impure

adversary—opponent; a person who opposes or fights against another

adverse—contrary to one's interest, undermining otherwise good results

advocate—a person who pleads another's cause

aesthete—a person who artificially cultivates artistic sensitivity or makes a cult of art and beauty

aesthetic—artistic; sensitive to art and beauty

affable—gentle and kindly

affinity—close connection, resemblance, or relationship

afflicted—troubled with, suffering from, burdened by

afflict—to cause pain or suffering to; to distress very much

affluent—plentiful; abundant; flowing freely

aggrandize—to make seem greater

agitate—to move with irregular, rapid, or violent action; to trouble the mind or feelings of

alias—an assumed name

allegiance—loyalty or devotion

alleviate—to reduce or decrease; to lighten or relieve

allocate—to allot; to distribute in shares or according to a plan

alloy—the relative purity of gold or silver; fineness

allude—to refer in a casual or indirect way

altercation—an angry or heated argument

amalgamate—to unite; to combine

ambiguous—not clear; having two or more possible meanings

ambivalence—simultaneously conflicting feelings toward a person or thing

amble—to go easily and unhurriedly; to stroll

ameliorate—to improve; to make or become better

amenable—willing to follow advice or suggestion; answerable

amiable—good-natured; having a pleasant and friendly disposition

amicable—peaceable; showing good will

amphibious—able to live both on land and in water

anagram—a word or phrase made from another by rearranging its letters

analogy—partial resemblance; similarity in some respects between things otherwise unlike

anarchy—the complete absence of government

anathema—a thing or person greatly detested

anatomist—a person who analyzes in great detail

anecdote—a short, entertaining account of some happening

anhydrous—without water

animosity—hostility; a feeling of strong dislike or hatred

annexation—attachment; adding on

anomalous—abnormal; deviating from the regular arrangement, general rule, or usual method

anthology—a collection of poems, stories, songs, or excerpts

antidote—a remedy to counteract a poison

antigen—a protein, toxin, or other substance to which the body reacts by producing antibodies

antipathy—strong or deep-rooted dislike

antiquity—belonging to ancient times

anvil—an iron or steel block on which metal objects are hammered into shape

apathetic—feeling little or no emotion; unmoved

apocryphal—not genuine; spurious; counterfeit; of doubtful authorship or authenticity

appall—to overcome with consternation, shock, or dismay

appease—to satisfy or relieve

appellation—name or title

appraise—to set a price for; to decide the value of

apprehension—an anxious feeling of foreboding; dread

apprentice—novice; any learner or beginner

arabesque—a complex and elaborate decorative design

arbitrary—unreasonable; unregulated; despotic

arbitrate—to decide a dispute

arboreal—of or like a tree

arcane—hidden or secret

ardor—devotion, passion, emotional warmth

arduous—difficult to do; laborious; onerous

arid—dry and barren; lacking enough water for things to grow

aromatic—smelling sweet or spicy; fragrant or pungent

arouse—to awaken, as from sleep

articulate—expressing oneself easily and clearly

artisan—craftsman; a worker in a skilled trade

ascribe—to attribute to (as a cause)

aspiration—desire, hope, or wish for something, especially an honor or advancement

aspiration—strong desire or ambition

assail—to assault; to attack physically and violently

assay—an examination or testing

assert—to state positively, declare, or affirm

assimilate—to absorb and incorporate into one's thinking

astound—to amaze; to bewilder with sudden surprise

astute—cunning; having or showing a clever or shrewd mind

atrocity—brutality; a very displeasing or tasteless thing

attune—to bring into harmony

auditor—a hearer or listener

augment—to enlarge; to make greater, as in size, quantity, or strength

auspicious—successful; favored by fortune

austere—forbidding, severe, harsh, rigid, stern

authoritarian—characterized by unquestioned obedience to authority

aversion—intense dislike

avid—eager and enthusiastic

avocation—hobby

avow—to declare openly or admit frankly

ballad—a romantic or sentimental song

banal—commonplace; dull or stale because of overuse

bane—ruin; death; deadly harm

barrage—a heavy, prolonged attack of words or blows

barren—empty; devoid; unable to produce offspring

barrio—in Spanish-speaking countries, a district or suburb of a city

bask—to warm oneself pleasantly, as in the sunlight

baste—to sew with long, loose stitches; to moisten food while cooking

beacon—any light for warning or guiding

bedazzle—to dazzle thoroughly

bedizen—to dress or decorate in a cheap, showy way

belated—tardy; late or too late

belittle—to treat as having little importance

belligerent—at war; showing a readiness to fight or quarrel

beneficent—doing good

benevolence—a kindly, charitable act or gift

benign—good-natured; kindly

bequeath—to hand down; pass on

berate—to scold or rebuke severely

bestow—to be put to use; to convey as a gift

bewilder—to puzzle; to confuse hopelessly

bias—a mental leaning or inclination; partiality; bent

bilge—the bulge of a barrel or cask

bilk—to cheat or swindle; to defraud

blandishment—a flattering act or remark meant to persuade

blatant—obvious

blithe—carefree; showing a gay, cheerful disposition

boisterous—rowdy; noisy and unruly

bolster—a long, narrow cushion or pillow; to support

boon—blessing; welcome benefit

boor—a rude, awkward, or ill-mannered person

bourgeois—a person whose beliefs, attitudes, and practices are conventionally middle-class

brazen—like brass in color, quality, or hardness; impudent

breach—a breaking or being broken

breadth—width; lack of narrowness

brevity—the quality of being brief

buoyant—capable of floating

buttress—a projecting structure built against a wall to support or reinforce it

cadence—flow of rhythm, regularity of beat

cadet—a student at a military school

cadge—to beg or get by begging

cajole—to coax with flattery and insincere talk

callous—unfeeling; lacking pity or mercy

camaraderie—loyal, warm, and friendly feeling among comrades

candid—honest or frank

capacious—roomy; spacious

caprice—whim; a sudden, impulsive change

capricious—erratic; flighty; tending to change abruptly

caption—a heading or title, as of an article

careen—to cause to lean sideways, to tip or tilt

carping—tending to find fault

cartographer—a person whose work is making maps or charts

castigate—to punish or rebuke severely

catalyst—a person or thing acting as the stimulus in bringing about or hastening a result

catapult—a slingshot or type of launcher

catastrophe—any great and sudden disaster or misfortune

caustic—corrosive; that which can destroy tissue by chemical action

cavern—a cave

cerebral—intellectual; appealing to the intellect rather than the emotions

charlatan—a person who pretends to have expert knowledge or skill

chary—careful; cautious

chasten—to punish; to refine; to make purer in style

chide—to scold

chivalrous—gallant; courteous; honorable

circuitous—roundabout; indirect; devious

circumlocution—an indirect way of expressing something

circumscribed—narrow, restricted, limited

circumspect—cautious; careful

circumvent—to go around

citizenry—all citizens as a group

clairvoyant—having the power to perceive that which is outside of the human senses

clamor—a loud outcry; uproar

clamorous—noisy; loudly demanding or complaining

clandestine—kept secret or hidden

cleave—to split; to divide by a blow

cliché—an expression or idea that has become trite

coalesce—to grow together; to unite or merge

coddle—to treat tenderly

codicil—an appendix or supplement

coerce—to enforce; to bring about by using force

coeval—of the same age or period

cognition—thinking or thought

cognizance—perception or knowledge

cognizant—aware or informed

coherent—clearly articulated; capable of logical, intelligible speech and thought

colloquial—conversational; having to do with or like conversation

combustion—the act or process of burning

commend—to praise; to express approval of

commensurate—proportionate; corresponding in extent or degree

commingle—to intermix; to blend; to mingle together

commodity—anything bought and sold

communicable—that which can be communicated

compassion—deep sympathy; sorrow for the sufferings of others

compatible—that which can work well together, get along well together, combine well

compelling—captivating; irresistibly interesting

competent—well qualified; capable; fit

complacency—quiet satisfaction; contentment

complacent—self-satisfied; smug

complaisant—willing to please; obliging

compliance—agreement, conformance, or obedience; a tendency to give in readily to others

compliant—yielding; submissive

comprehend—to understand fully

comprise—to include; to contain

compulsion—that which compels; driving force

computation—calculation; a method of computing

concession—an act or instance of granting or yielding

conciliatory—tending to reconcile

concise—brief and to the point; short and clear

concoct—to devise, invent, or plan

condemnation—judgment, doom

condemn—to censure; to disapprove of strongly

condescension—a patronizing manner or behavior

condolence—expression of sympathy with another in grief

condone—to forgive, pardon, or overlook

conduit—a channel conveying fluids; a tube or protected trough for electric wires

confiscate—to seize by authority

conformity—action in accordance with customs, rules, and prevailing opinion

confound—to bring into ruin

congregation—a gathering of people or things

congruent—in agreement; corresponding; harmonious

conjoin—to join together, unite, or combine

conjunction—a joining together, union, or association

consensus—an opinion held by all or most

consignment—items in a shipment

conspire—to plan and act together secretly

constancy—steadfastness of mind under duress

consternation—great fear or shock that makes one feel helpless or bewildered

constituent—component; a necessary part or element

consummate—supreme; complete or perfect in every way; to finish; to complete

contemn—to scorn; to view with contempt

contemporaneous—existing or happening in the same period of time

contemporary—happening, existing, living, or coming into being during the same period of time

contemptuous—scornful; disdainful

contentious—always ready to argue; quarrelsome

contentment—the state of being satisfied

context—the whole situation, background, or environment relevant to a particular event, personality, or creation.

contingency—possible, accidental, or chance event

continuity—uninterrupted connection, succession, or union

contrite—penitent; feeling sorry for sins

controvert—to dispute or oppose by reasoning

contumacious—disobedient; obstinately resisting authority

conventional—customary; typical

conversion—a change from one belief, religion, doctrine, or opinion to another

convey—to make known; to carry

conviction—a strong belief

convoluted—extremely involved; intricate; complicated

copious—very plentiful; abundant

coronation—act or ceremony of crowning a sovereign

corpuscle—a very small particle

corroborate—to confirm; to make more certain the validity of

countenance—facial expression; composure

coup—a sudden, successful move or action

covert—concealed; hidden; disguised

covet—to want ardently; to long for with envy

crass—tasteless; insensitive; coarse

craven—very cowardly; abjectly afraid

credence—belief, especially in the reports or testimony of another

credulity—a tendency to believe too readily

crescendo—any gradual increase in force, intensity

criterion—a standard on which judgment can be based

critique—a critical analysis or evaluation

crux—essential or most important point

cryptic—mysterious; having a hidden or ambiguous meaning

culmination—climax; the highest point

culpable—deserving blame; blameworthy

cultivate—to prepare; to grow

cultivated—refined; educated

cumulative—accumulated; increasing in effect, size, or quantity.

cunning—skillful or clever

curator—a person in charge of a museum or library.

cynical—sarcastic; sneering

daunt—to intimidate; to make afraid or discouraged

dearth—any scarcity or lack

debacle—an overwhelming defeat

debase—to cheapen; to make lower in value, quality, character, or dignity

debilitate—to make weak or feeble

decelerate—to reduce speed; to slow down

decipher—to decode; to make out the meaning of

decisive—showing determination or firmness

decry—to denounce; to speak out against strongly and openly

dedicate—to commit to a goal or way of life; to set apart for a definite use

deference—courteous regard or respect

defiance—open, bold resistance to authority or opposition

defiant—openly and boldly resisting

deficit—a lack; an absence

definitive—final; authoritative

deflect—to turn aside especially from a straight course or fixed direction

defunct—no longer living or existing; dead or extinct

defuse—to render harmless

degenerate—having sunk below a former or normal condition

delegate—to send from one place to another; appoint; assign

deleterious—injurious; harmful to health or well-being

delineate—to describe; to depict in words

delirium—uncontrollably wild excitement or emotion

demagogue—a leader who gains power using popular prejudices and false claims; a leader of the common people in ancient times

demise—a ceasing to exist; death

demure—affectedly modest or shy; coy

denouement—the outcome, solution, unraveling, or clarification of a plot in a drama, story

denounce—to condemn strongly

derive—to come from a source

desertification—process by which land becomes dry and arid

desolate—without inhabitants, lonely

despotic—of or like a despot; autocratic; tyrannical

destitute—living in complete poverty

desuetude—disuse; the condition of not being used

deter—to turn aside, discourage, or prevent from acting

detonate—to explode violently and noisily

detumescence—a gradual shrinking of a swelling

devastate—to make helpless; to overwhelm

devious—not straightforward or frank

dictate—to speak or act domineeringly

diction—manner of expression in words

diminutive—very small; tiny

disabuse—to rid of false ideas or misconceptions

discern—to make out clearly

discern—to see, perceive, or recognize

discombobulate—to upset the composure of

discomfit—to make uneasy

disconcert—to embarrass; to confuse

discordant—disagreeing; conflicting

discord—disagreement; conflict

discourteous—impolite; rude; ill-mannered

discrepancy—difference; inconsistency

disentangle—to free from entanglement

disinter—to bring to light

dismay—to cause to lose courage or resolution

disparage—to show disrespect for; to belittle

dispel—to drive away by or as if by scattering

dissident—not agreeing

distillate—the essence; purified form

distraught—extremely troubled

divergence—a separation; a difference

divergent—deviating; different

diverse—different; dissimilar

diversion—distraction of attention

divination—the art of foretelling future events; clever conjecture

docile—easily disciplined, easily led

doggerel—trivial, awkward, satirical verse

dogma—a doctrine; tenet; belief

dolt—a stupid, slow-witted person; blockhead

dormant—inactive, idle, sleeping

dross—waste matter; worthless stuff; rubbish

drub—to defeat soundly in a fight or contest

dubious—feeling doubt; hesitating; skeptical

dulcet—sweet-sounding; melodious

duress—constraint by threat; imprisonment

eccentricity—irregularity; oddity

eccentric—peculiar, odd

eclectic—selecting from various systems, doctrines, or sources

efficacious—having the intended result; effective

effusive—expressing excessive emotion

eject—to throw out, to expel

elicit—to draw forth, to bring out, to evoke

embark—to make a start

embellish—to decorate by adding detail; to ornament

emblematic—symbolic

embodiment—the concrete expression of some abstract idea or concept

emend—to correct or improve

eminent—rising above other things or places

emissary—a person sent on a specific mission

emit—to throw or give off or out

emollient—softening; soothing

empathy—ability to share in another's emotions, thoughts, or feelings

emulate—to imitate

enamor—to fill with love and desire; to charm

encroach—to trespass or intrude

endowed—provided with talent or virtue

enigma—riddle; a perplexing and ambiguous statement

enmity—hostility; antagonism

entail—to necessitate; to logically require

enthrall—to captivate; to fascinate

enumerate—to count; to determine the number of

epigram—a short poem with a witty point

epithet—a descriptive name or title

epitome—a person or thing that shows typical qualities of something

equipoise—state of balance or equilibrium

equivocal—having two or more meanings

equivocate—to be deliberately ambiguous

eradicate—to wipe out; to destroy; to get rid of

erroneous—mistaken; wrong

err—to stray; to make a mistake

espionage—the act of spying

espouse—to support or advocate

esteem—the regard in which one is held

euphoria—feeling of vigor or well-being

evocation—calling forth

ewe—female sheep

exacting—tryingly or unremittingly severe in making demands

exalt—to elevate; to praise; to glorify

exasperate—to irritate or annoy very much; to aggravate

excavate—to form a cavity or hole in

excoriate—to denounce harshly

exemplary—serving as a model or example

explicit—plain, clear, obvious

expunge—to erase or remove completely

exquisite—characterized by intense emotion

extant—still existing; not extinct

extol—to praise highly

extrapolate—to arrive at conclusions or results

extraterrestrial—originating outside of the earth

exuberance—high spirits; joy; energy

faddish—having the nature of a fad

fallacious—misleading or deceptive

famine—hunger; a withering away

fantastic—marked by extravagant fantasy or extreme individuality

fauna—animals or animal life

feasible—workable, possible

feckless—weak; ineffective

feint—a false show; sham

feral—untamed; wild

fervent—hot; burning; glowing

fervid—impassioned; fervent; hot; burning

fictitious—not genuinely felt; false

finite—having measurable or definable limits; not infinite

fissure—a long, narrow, deep cleft or crack

fitful—having an erratic or intermittent character

flippant—frivolous and disrespectful; saucy

flora—plants or plant life

florid—highly decorated; gaudy; showy; ornate

flout—to show scorn or contempt

folio—book or booklet

forage—to search for food or provisions

forbearance—patience

forbid—to not permit; to prohibit

forensics—debate or formal argumentation

forge—a furnace for heating metal to be wrought; to advance; to craft;

forlorn—without hope; desperate

formidable—causing fear or dread

forthright—straightforward; direct; frank

fortify—to strengthen

foster—to nurture; affording, receiving, or sharing nurture or parental care though not related by blood or legal ties

fracas—a noisy fight or loud quarrel; brawl

fractious—hard to manage; unruly

fraught—emotional; tense; anxious; distressing

frenetic—frantic; frenzied

frieze—ornamental band formed by a series of decorations

froward—not easily controlled; stubbornly willful

fulsome—offensively flattering

futile—ineffectual; trifling or unimportant

gamut—the entire range or extent of anything

generate—to bring into existence

genial—cheerful; friendly; sympathetic

germinate—to start developing or growing

ghastly—horrible, frightening, terrible

gilded—overlaid with gold

gird—to encircle or bind

glib—done in a smooth, offhand fashion

goad—to drive on; to spur

gouge—to scrape or hollow out

gourmand—a glutton; one who indulges to excess

graft—to attach so that two things grow together

gregarious—fond of the company of others; sociable

gristle—cartilage found in meat

grouse—to complain; to grumble

grovel—to behave humbly or abjectly

habitually— usually; doing, practicing, or acting in some customary manner

hackney—to make trite by overuse

hapless—unfortunate; unlucky; luckless

haste—the act of hurrying; quickness of motion

haughty—blatantly and disdainfully proud; arrogant

headnote—a prefixed note of comment or explanation

heed—to take careful notice of

hence—thereafter; subsequently

herbaceous—like a green leaf in texture, color, shape

heroine—girl or woman of outstanding courage and nobility

hew—to chop or cut with an ax or knife; to hack or gash

hierarchy—an arrangement in order of rank, grade, class

hindsight—ability to see, after the event, what should have been done

hirsute—hairy; shaggy; bristly

historicity—authenticity

homely—unaffectedly natural

homogeneous—of the same race or kind

hone—to perfect; to sharpen;

hoodwink—to mislead or confuse by trickery

hue—a particular shade or tint of a given color

humble—not proud; not self-assertive; modest

humdrum—lacking variety; dull; monotonous

humility—absence of pride or self-assertion

hybrid—anything of mixed origin; unlike parts

hypocrisy—pretending to be what one is not

hypothesis—unproved theory

idealism—behavior or thought based on a conception of things as they should be or one wished them to be, rather than as they actually are

idealist—visionary or dreamer

idiosyncrasy—personal peculiarity or mannerism

idolatrous—given to idolatry or blind adoration

idolatry—worship of idols

idol—object of worship; false god

illimitable—boundless, infinite

illumined—lit up

imbued—filled, inspired with feeling

immaculate—perfectly clean; unsoiled

immortality—unending life; everlasting fame

impart—to make known; to tell or reveal

impeccable—without defect or error; flawless

impede—to obstruct or delay

impenitent—without regret, shame, or remorse

imperceptibly—not obviously, hardly noticeably

imperturbable—cannot be disconcerted, disturbed, or excited; impassive

impervious—not affected

impetuous—moving with great, sudden energy

impinge—to make inroads or encroach

impious—lacking respect or dutifulness

implacable—unable to be appeased or pacified; relentless

implicate—to involve; to show a connection between

import—weight, consequence

imposture—fraud; deception

inadvertent—not attentive or observant; heedless

incantation—chanted words or formula

incarcerate—to imprison; to confine

incessant—continual; never ceasing

incinerate—to burn up; to cremate

incongruous—lacking harmony or agreement

incontrovertible—not disputable or debatable

incorrigible—unable to be corrected, improved, or reformed

incumbent—lying, resting on something; imposed as a duty

indignation—righteous anger

indignity—unworthiness or disgrace

indiscernible—imperceptible

indiscretion—imprudence, rashness, error

indiscriminate—confused; random

indispensable—absolutely necessary or required

indomitable—not easily discouraged, defeated, or subdued

induced—moved by persuasion or influence

industrious—diligent; skillful

ineffable—too overwhelming to be expressed in words

inefficacious—unable to produce the desired effect

ineluctable—unavoidable, inescapable

inextricable—incapable of being disentangled or untied

infallible—incapable of error; never wrong

infamy—bad reputation; notoriety; disgrace

infinitesimal—extremely small, immeasurably tiny

ingratiate—to achieve one's good graces by conscious effort

inimical—hostile; unfriendly

injunction—command, order

innate—existing naturally rather than through acquisition

innocuous—harmless; not controversial, offensive, or stimulating

inquisitor—harsh or prying questioner

insipid—not exciting or interesting; dull

insouciant—calm and untroubled; carefree

insularity—detachment; isolation

integrated—combined or added parts that make a unified whole

intelligible—clear; comprehensible

intemperate—lacking restraint; excessive

interdisciplinary—involving several different fields of study

intermittent—stopping and starting, irregular

interstellar—between or among the stars

intuitive—characterized by a knowing that is immediate, without conscious reasoning
inundate—to overflow, to spread over as a flood
inveterate—habitual; of long standing; deep-rooted
irascible—easily angered; quick-tempered
iterative—characterized by repetition

jaunty—gay and carefree; sprightly; perky
jubilant—joyful and triumphant; elated; rejoicing
jurisprudence—a part or division of law

kernel—the most central part; a grain
kindle—to start a fire burning

lackluster—lacking energy or vitality
lambaste—to scold or denounce severely
lament—to mourn or grieve
languid—without vigor or vitality; drooping; weak
lapse—a slight error typically due to forgetfulness or inattention
laudable—praiseworthy; commendable
laudatory—expressing praise
lee—the side sheltered from the wind
legion—a large number; multitude
lethargic—abnormally drowsy or dull; sluggish
limerick—nonsense poem of five anapestic lines
limn—to describe
lineament—feature of the face
lionize—to treat as a celebrity
listless—spiritless; languid
literati—scholarly or learned people
lithe—bending easily; flexible; supple
litigant—a party to a lawsuit
liturgy—ritual for public worship in any of various religions or churches
livid—grayish-blue; extremely angry
logistics—the science of moving supplies
loquacious—fond of talking
loquacity—talkativeness
lucid—transparent
ludicrous—amusing or laughable through obvious absurdity
lummox—a clumsy, stupid person
lurid—vivid in a shocking way, startling

magnanimous—noble in mind
magnitude—greatness; importance or influence
malevolence—malice; spitefulness; ill will
malfeasance—wrongdoing or misconduct
malinger—to pretend to be ill to escape duty or work; to shirk
marginal—of only slight value
masque—dramatic composition

maverick—a person who takes an independent stand
maxim—statement of a general truth
mazurka—a lively Polish folk dance
meager—thin; lean; emaciated
medieval—characteristic of the Middle Ages
medium—surrounding substance
mellifluous—sounding sweet and smooth; honeyed
menace—to threaten harm or evil
mercenary—motivated by a desire for money or other gain
merriment—gaiety and fun
metamorphose—to transform
metaphor—a figure of speech containing an implied comparison
methodology—system of procedures
meticulous—extremely careful with small points, very detailed
millennia—thousands of years
minatory—menacing; threatening
minstrel—a medieval musical entertainer
miser—a greedy, stingy person
mitigate—to make less rigorous or less painful; to moderate
mnemonic—helping, or meant to help, the memory
modicum—small amount
modulate—to adjust or adapt to a certain proportion
monarch—hereditary head of a state
monoculture—a single, undiversified crop
mordant—biting; cutting; caustic; sarcastic
moribund—dying
morose—ill-tempered; gloomy
mote—a small particle
motif—main element or idea
myriad—consisting of very large numbers
mysticism—doctrines or beliefs of mystics
mythical—imaginary; fictitious

narcissism—self-love
negate—to make ineffective
nexus—a connected group or series
nib—point of a pen
nocturnal—active during the night
noisome—having a bad odor; foul-smelling
nomad—one who has no permanent home, who moves about constantly
nostalgia—a longing for things of the past
notoriety—prominence or renown, often unfavorable
novice—apprentice; beginner
nuance—a slight or delicate variation

obliterate—to erase; to efface
obsequious—compliant; dutiful; servile
obsolete—no longer in use or practice

obstinate—unreasonably determined to have one's own way; stubborn

obtuse—not sharp or pointed; blunt

occult—secret; esoteric

odium—disgrace brought on by hateful action

officious—ready to serve; obliging

ominous—threatening; sinister

omnipotent—unlimited in power or authority

onerous—burdensome; laborious

onslaught—attack, furious assault

oppressive—weighing heavily on the mind or spirit, causing distress

opulent—very wealthy or rich

oracle—a place where, or a medium by which, a deity is consulted; also, a person believed to be in communication with a deity, and one who can foretell the future

oration—a formal public speech

orator—eloquent public speaker

ornate—heavily ornamented or adorned

orthodox—conventional, proper, correct

oscillate—to be indecisive in purpose or opinion; to vacillate

ossify—to settle or fix rigidly

ostracism—rejection or exclusion by general consent

overtone—a secondary effect, quality, or meaning

overwrought—overworked; fatigued

paean—a song of joy, triumph, praise

pagan—one who has little or no religion and who delights in pleasures and material goods

palliate—to relieve without curing; to make less severe

pallid—deficient in color

palpable—tangible; easily perceived by the senses

pantomime—action or gestures without words as a means of expression

paradigm—example or model

paradox—seeming contradiction

paramount—ranking higher than any other

parch—to dry up with heat

pariah—outcast

parody—a poor or weak imitation

pathology—conditions, processes, or results of a particular disease

peccadillo—minor or petty sin; slight fault

pellucid—transparent or translucent; clear

penchant—strong liking or fondness

penitent—expressing pain or sorrow for sins or offenses; truly sorry

peremptory—intolerantly positive or assured

perennial—continually present, perpetual, never failing

peril—exposure to harm or injury; danger

peripheral—outer; external; lying at the outside

perpetual—unceasing, never ending

pervade—to become prevalent throughout

pervasive—diffusing throughout every part

petrous—of or like rock; hard

petulant—peevish; impatient or irritable

phenomena—events, facts, or occurrences

philistine—a person smugly narrow and conventional in views and tastes

philology—the study of literature and of disciplines relevant to literature or to language as used in literature

pinion—to confine or shackle

pitch—degree of slope; top, zenith

placate—to stop from being angry; to appease

plasticity—capacity for being molded or altered

platitude—commonplace, flat, or dull quality

plausible—conceivable, possible

plethora—overabundance; excess

plumage—the feathers of a bird

poignant—sharp or painful to the feelings

poseur—a person who assumes attitudes or manners merely for their effect upon others

postulate—to claim; to demand; to require

pragmatic—busy or active in a meddlesome way; practical

prebiotic—on the verge of having life

precipitated—brought on, caused to happen

preclude—to shut out; to prevent

precocious—exhibiting premature development

predatory—living by robbing or preying on others

predilection—preconceived liking; partiality or preference

prerequisite—required before, a necessary condition for a further occurrence

presage—sign or warning of a future event; omen

prescience—foreknowledge

preside—to exercise control or authority

prig—annoyingly pedantic person

proclivity—natural or habitual inclination

procure—to obtain; to secure

prodigious—enormous, huge

profane—to show disrespect for sacred things; irreverent

profuse—generous, often to excess

proliferate—to reproduce (new parts) in quick succession

prolific—turning out many products of the mind

prolix—wordy; long-winded

propagate—to reproduce; to multiply

propinquity—nearness of relationship; kinship

propriety—properness; suitability

prosaic—matter of fact; ordinary

prose—ordinary speech; dull

prospect—mental consideration

protracted—drawn out in time

protuberance—projection; bulge

provocative—stimulating; erotic

prudent—cautious, sensible

pugnacious—eager and ready to fight; quarrelsome

pundit—actual or self-professed authority

punitive—inflicting, concerned with, or directed toward punishment

quaff—to drink deeply in a hearty or thirsty way

quaint—unusual or different in character or appearance

quell—to crush; to subdue; to put an end to

querulous—full of complaint; peevish

quotidian—everyday; usual or ordinary

radical—fundamental, basic, important

ramify—to divide or spread out into branches

rancor—deep spite or malice

rapacious—taking by force; plundering

rasp—rough, grating tone

ratify—to approve or confirm

raucous—loud and rowdy

realism—behavior or thought based on a conception of how things actually are; in literature the attempt to picture people and things as they really are

reciprocate—to cause to move alternately back and forth

recluse—secluded; solitary

recollection—the act of remembering something

recompense—to repay; to compensate

recount—to relate, tell, describe in detail

regale—to delight with something pleasing or amusing

rejuvenation—the process of making young again, restoring youth

relegate—to exile or banish

relinquish—to give up; to abandon

remedial—providing a remedy

render—to represent or depict

reparation—restoration to good condition

repertory—collection, stock, store

replete—well-filled or plentifully supplied

reprieve—to give temporary relief to, as from trouble or pain

reprobate—to disapprove of strongly

repugnant—contradictory; inconsistent

requiem—musical service for the dead

reservoir—a large or extra supply of something

resonating—vibrating, resounding

resplendent—dazzling; splendid

restitution—return to a former condition or situation

resurgence—revival, new force

retention—remembering, memory

reticent—habitually silent; reserved

rhapsodize—to describe in an extravagantly enthusiastic manner

rogue—a rascal; scoundrel

rubric—a category or section heading, often in red; any rule or explanatory comment

ruffian—brutal, violent, lawless person

ruse—trick or artifice

sacred—holy; of or connected with religion

salinity—saltiness

salutary—healthful; beneficial

salutation—greeting, addressing, or welcoming by gestures or words

salve—balm that soothes or heals

sanctimonious—pretending to be very holy

sanction—support; encouragement; approval

savannah—grassland with only scattered trees

savant—learned person; eminent scholar

scrupulous—having principles; extremely conscientious

scud—to pass or skim rapidly

scurvy—low; mean; vile; contemptible

semaphore—system of signaling

seminal—important; critical;

sensibility—the capacity for being affected emotionally or intellectually

serene—calm; peaceful; tranquil

servile—humbly yielding or submissive; of a slave or slaves

shroud—to cover, protect, or screen; veil; shelter

signatory—joined in the signing of something

sinister—wicked; evil; dishonest

sinuous—not straightforward; devious; twisting

slake—to make less intense by satisfying

snide—slyly malicious or derisive

sodden—filled with moisture; soaked

solace—comfort; consolation; relief

soluble—able to be dissolved

somber—dark and gloomy or dull

sombre—shaded as to be dark and gloomy

soporific—pertaining to sleep or sleepiness

sovereign—supreme ruler, highest authority

speculation—intellectual examination or analysis

sporadically—occasionally, irregularly

spurious—not true or genuine; false

squalid—foul or unclean

stealth—secret, furtive, or artfully sly behavior

stigma—mark or sign indicating something not considered normal or standard

stint—to restrict or limit

stolid—unexcitable; impassive

stymie—to obstruct or frustrate

subdued—lacking in vitality, intensity, or strength

subjectivity—pertaining to thoughts or emotions of the person thinking, as opposed to the actual situation or reality

subliminal—on the threshold of consciousness; under the surface

submission—resignation; obedience; meekness

subsistence—survival, state of remaining alive

suffice—to be adequate

sully—to soil or stain; to tarnish by disgracing

sunder—to break apart, separate, or split

superfluous—excessive

supine—sluggish; listless; passive

surfeit—too great an amount or supply; excess

surreptitious—acting in a secret, stealthy way

surrogate—a substitute

susceptible—easily affected, open to

symbiosis—relationship of mutual interdependence

symptomatic—having the characteristics of a particular disease

syntax—orderly or systematic arrangement of words

synthesis—the joining of elements to make a new whole

systematic—presented or formulated as a coherent body of ideas or principles

tactile—perceived by touch; tangible

tangible—having actual form and substance

tantalizing—teasing, interesting

tawdry—cheap and showy; gaudy; sleazy

tedious—tiresome because of length or dullness

tedium—tediousness

telling—carrying great weight and producing a marked effect

tempt—to persuade, induce, or entice

tenet—principle, doctrine, or belief held as a truth

tenuous—unsubstantial, slight, flimsy

terrestrial—worldly; earthly

territorial—characterized by behavior associated with the defense of a territory

testimony—firsthand authentication of a fact

throng—crowd

timorous—fearful, timid

tinge—to give a slight trace of color

token—an outward sign or expression

toupee—a man's wig

tractable—easily worked; obedient; malleable

tranquil—calm; serene; peaceful

transcendent—surpassing, excelling, or extraordinary

transgress—to go beyond a limit

transient—temporary, passing, not permanent

translucent—partially transparent or clear

transmit—to pass; to send on

transmute—to transform; to convert

treacherous—likely to betray trust; untrustworthy; insecure

treachery—perfidy; disloyalty; treason

trepidation—fearful uncertainty; anxiety

trite—not fresh or original

troubadour—minstrel or singer

trough—depression between two waves

truncate—to cut short

tumultuous—noisy, disorderly, boisterous

turgid—swollen; distended

turmoil—commotion; uproar; confusion

tyranny—very cruel and unjust use of power or authority

uncanny—inexplicable; preternaturally strange; weird

underling—one in a subordinate position; inferior

underpinnings—supports, foundation

underscore—to make evident

unfeigned—genuine, sincere, real

unfetter—to free from restraint; to liberate

unification—state of being unified

unintelligible—unable to be understood; incomprehensible

unity—oneness; singleness

univocal—unambiguous

unprecedented—new, novel, never done before

unscrupulous—not restrained by ideas of right and wrong

untenable—indefensible; incapable of being occupied

untoward—unfortunate, unfavorable, troublesome

unwitting—not knowing; unaware

upbraid—to rebuke severely or bitterly

uproarious—loud and boisterous

usury—interest at a high rate

utilitarian—stressing usefulness over beauty

utopia—idealized place

vacillate—to sway to and fro; to waver or totter

vacuum—completely empty space

vagabond—a person without a permanent home who moves from place to place; wandering

vagrant—a person who lives a wandering life

valiant—brave

validity—accuracy, factualness

vapid—tasteless; flavorless; flat

variegate—to vary; to diversify

veer—to change direction; to shift

vehement—acting or moving with great force

venerate—to show feelings of deep respect; to revere

vengeance—revenge

verity—truth

vestige—a trace of something that once existed

vex—to distress; to afflict; to plague

vicariously—by substitution, through imagined participation

villainous—evil; wicked

virtually—for all practical purposes, in effect

virtuoso—expert, highly skilled person

vitality—power to live or survive, mental or physical energy

vitiate—to spoil; to corrupt

vivacious—full of life and animation; lively

vocation—trade; profession; occupation

volatile—flying or able to fly

voluble—talkative

voluminous—large; bulky; full

voracious—ravenous; gluttonous

waft—to float, as on the wind

wane—to grow dim or faint

wary—cautious; on one's guard

welter—to become soaked; stained; bathed

wheedle—to coax; to influence or persuade by flattery

whet—to make keen; to stimulate

wield—to use as a tool; to carry

wile—sly trick

wither—to dry up or shrivel

witty—cleverly amusing

wrath—intense anger; rage; fury

wrench—sudden, sharp twist or pull

wrought—made by artistry or effort, worked

yacht—small vessel for pleasure cruises or racing

yearn—to have longing or desire

yielding—submissive; obedient

zeal—intense enthusiasm

zenith—highest point; peak

Difficulty Level 3

allegory—parable

abstemious—exercising moderation; self-restraint

adroit—skilled, clever

aggregate—to collect into a sum

alacrity—cheerful promptness; eagerness

ambient—surrounding

amorphous—shapeless; formless

anachronistic—the representation of something as existing at an impossible or inappropriate time

antedate—to precede, to come before in time

antediluvian—before the flood; antiquated

apostate—fallen from the faith

appurtenance—a thing pertaining to or connected with something else

arboreal—pertaining to trees

arrogate—to claim or seize as one's own

ascetic—practicing self-denial; austere

ascribe—to attribute to a cause

asperity—having a harsh temper; roughness

assiduous—diligent

assiduously—diligently, carefully

assuage—to lessen; to soothe

attenuation—a thinning out

august—great dignity or grandeur

aver—to affirm; to declare to be true

bacchanalian—drunken

baleful—menacing; deadly

beguile—to deceive or cheat; to charm or coax

beleaguer—to besiege or attack; to harass

belie—to misrepresent; to be false to

bellicose—belligerent; pugnacious; warlike

bombastic—pompous; puffed up with conceit; using inflated language

bovine—resembling a cow; placid or dull

bucolic—rustic; pastoral

burgeon—to grow forth; to send out buds

cache—to store or to hide; a hidden supply

cacophony—harsh or discordant sound; dissonance

calumny—slander

capitulate—to surrender

cathartic—purgative; inducing a figurative cleansing

cavil—to disagree; to nit-pick; to make frivolous objections

celerity—swiftness

chassis—framework and working parts of an automobile

chimerical—fantastically improbable; highly unrealistic

churlish—rude; surly

circumscribe—to limit

cogent—convincing

collusion—conspiring in a fraudulent scheme

comely—attractive; agreeable

compendium—brief, comprehensive summary

concord—harmony

confluence—flowing or coming together

consecrate—to induct into a religious office; to declare sacred

consonance—agreement; harmony

contrite—penitent; repentant; feeling sorry for sins

contumely—an insult; contemptuous treatment

conundrum—a riddle; difficult problem

cosset—to pamper

countenance—face, expression, features

cupidity—excessive desire for money; avarice

cursory—hasty; done without care

decimate—to destroy a great number

defer—to yield; to delay

deleterious—destructive, injurious

demur—to take exception; to object

denigrate—to blacken someone's reputation or character

derision—ridicule

desiccate—to dry up; to drain

desultory—aimless; unmethodical; unfocused

dexterity—skill in using one's hands or body

diaphanous—translucent; see-through

diatribe—speech full of bitterness

didactic—intended primarily to instruct

diffidence—modesty; shyness; lack of confidence

dilatory—given to delay or procrastination

dilettante—aimless follower of the arts; amateur; dabbler

din—loud confusing noise

disaffection—lack of trust; to cause discontent

disarming—charming; peaceable; able to remove hostility

discursive—rambling; passing from one topic to another

disingenuous—deceitful; lacking in candor; not frank

disparate—basically different; unrelated

disputatious—argumentative

disquietude—uneasiness; anxiety

dissemble—to conceal true motives; to pretend

dissipate—to dissolve, to fade

dissolute—loose in morals or conduct

dissonant—lacking in harmony; discordant

dogmatic—adhering to a tenet

dolorous—sorrowful; having mental anguish

duplicity—deception by pretending to feel and act one way while acting another; bad faith; double dealing

ebullient—greatly excited

edify—to instruct; to correct morally

efface—to erase; to obliterate as if by rubbing it out

efficacy—power to produce desired effect

effrontery—shameless boldness; impudence; temerity

egregious—notorious; shocking

encomium—glowing praise

encumber—to hinder

endemic—belonging to, or found only in a certain nation or region

enervation—process of depriving of strength, weakening

engender—to cause; to produce

enigma—riddle, puzzle

ensconce—to settle in; to hide or conceal

ephemeral—fleeting; short-lived

equanimity—calmness; composure

erudite—learned; scholarly

eschew—to shun

esoteric—hard to understand

etymology—study of word parts

evanescent—tending to vanish like vapor

evince—to show clearly

exacerbate—to worsen; to embitter

exculpate—to clear from blame

execrable—detestable

exegesis—explanation, especially of biblical passages

exhort—to urge

exigency—urgent situation

expatriate—one choosing to live abroad

expiate—to atone for

facile—easily accomplished; ready or fluent

fatuous—foolish or inane

fealty—loyalty; allegiance

felicitous—well chosen; apt; suitable

ferment—to agitate;

fetid—malodorous

filial—pertaining to a son or daughter

filigree—delicate, lacelike ornamentation

firmament—the sky, the heavens

flaccid—flabby

foible—small moral or character weakness

foment—to stir up; to instigate

fortuitous—accidental; by chance

fulminate—to thunder; to explode

fungible—capable of being used in place of something else

gainsay—to contradict; to speak or act against

galvanize—to stimulate by shock; to stir up; to revitalize

gambol—to romp; to skip about

garrulous—loquacious; wordy; talkative

germinal—beginning, of the first stages

gossamer—sheer, like cobwebs

gratuitous—free; unnecessary; without reason

guile—slyness and cunning

hackles—hairs on back and neck

halcyon—calm; peaceful

harbinger—one that announces or foreshadows what is coming; precursor; portent

hedonist—one who believes pleasure is sole aim in life

hegemony—dominance, especially of one nation over another

heinous—atrocious; hatefully bad

hermetic—obscure and mysterious; relating to the occult

hinterland—area far from big cities or towns

historiography—the scholarly study of history

hominid—all forms of man, both extinct and living

hubris—arrogance; excessive self-conceit

hummock—small hill

humus—substance formed by decaying vegetable matter

iconoclastic—attacking cherished traditions

ignominious—dishonorable; disgraceful

imbroglio—complicated situation

immolate—to offer as a sacrifice; to destroy by fire

immutable—unchangeable

impalpable—imperceptible; intangible

impecunious—without money

impetus—stimulus, incentive

importune—to urge repeatedly

impuissance—powerlessness; feebleness

impunity—freedom from punishment or harm

impute—to attribute to (as a fault or crime)

incarnadines—to make red, especially blood or flesh-colored

inchoate—recently begun; rudimentary

incipient—beginning, in the first stages

incisive—sharply expressive

incorporeal—without physical existence, not having a material body

inculcate—to impress on the mind by admonition

incursion—temporary invasion

indelible—not able to be removed or erased

indemnify—to make secure against loss

indigent—poor

indite—to write or compose

indolent—lazy

ineluctable—irresistible; not to be escaped

inexorable—not to be moved by entreaty; unyielding; relentless

infecund—not fertile, barren

iniquitous—wicked; immoral

insidious—deceitful; treacherous

intelligentsia—people regarded as the learned class

internecine—mutually destructive

interpolate—to insert between other things

intractable—stubborn

intransigence—refusal to compromise

intraspecific—pertaining to or occurring between or among members of the same species

intrepid—brave

inure—to make accustomed to something difficult

invective—abuse

inveigh—to condemn; to censure

irascible—easily irritated, easily angered

jaundice—prejudice; envy; yellow discoloring of skin or tissue

jettison—to throw overboard

jocose—given to joking

jocund—merry

juggernaut—irresistible, crushing force

juxtapose—to place side by side

ken—range of knowledge

kinetic—producing motion

kismet—fate

knell—tolling of a bell

knoll—little round hill

lachrymose—producing tears

laconic—using few words

lade—to put a load or burden on or in

largess—liberal giving; generous gift

lascivious—lustful

lassitude—weariness; debility

latent—potential but undeveloped; dormant

laxity—carelessness

legerdemain—sleight of hand

licentious—amoral; lewd and lascivious

Lilliputian—extremely small

limpid—clear

lugubrious—mournful, often to an excessive degree

maelstrom—whirlpool

maladroit—clumsy; bungling

malady—sickness, disease, illness

malediction—curse

malignant—growing worse

malleable—capable of being shaped

maraud—to rove in search of plunder

martinet—one who issues orders

masticate—to chew

maudlin—effusively sentimental

megalomania—mania for doing grandiose things

melee—a fight

mellifluous—flowing sweetly and smoothly

mendacity—untruthfulness

mendicant—beggar

mercurial—volatile; changeable; fickle

meretricious—flashy; tawdry

miasma—a poisonous atmosphere

misanthrope—a person who hates mankind

miscreant—villain

mollify—to soothe

monolithic—consisting of a single character; uniform; unyielding

moribund—dying

multitudinous—existing in or consisting of innumerable elements or aspects

munificent—generous

myopic—nearsighted; lacking foresight

nadir—lowest point

nascent—in the process of being born

nebulous—indistinct or vague; hazy or cloudy

necromancy—black magic; dealing with the dead

nefarious—wicked

niche—a place particularly well suited to the thing occupying it

noisome—hurtful, harmful

nostrum—questionable medicine

nubile—marriageable

nugatory—futile; worthless

obdurate—stubborn; unyielding

obfuscate—to make obscure; to confuse

obloquy—slander; disgrace; infamy

obstreperous—unruly; boisterous; noisy

obviate—to make unnecessary

occlude—to shut or close

odious—hateful; vile

oligarchy—government by a privileged few

onerous—burdensome

opprobrium—infamy; vilification

ostensible—apparent; showing outwardly; professed

panegyric—formal praise

paradigm—model or pattern

paragon—model of perfection

parlance—language; idiom

parlay—to exploit successfully

parsimonious—stingy

paucity—scarcity

pecuniary—obsessed by money

pedantic—bookish

pejorative—negative in connotation; having a tendency to make worse; disparaging

penurious—marked by penury; stingy

perdition—eternal damnation; complete ruin

perfidy—treacherous; betrayal of trust

perfunctory—indifferent; done merely as a duty; superficial

pernicious—fatal; very destructive or injurious

perspicacious—having insight; penetrating; astute

perspicuous—plainly expressed

phlegmatic—calm; not easily disturbed

piebald—of different colors; mottled; spotted

piety—devoutness; reverence for God

pillory—to criticize or ridicule

pined—wasted away, grew thin

piquancy—something that stimulates taste; tartness

pithy—essential; brief and to the point

polemic—controversy; argument in support of a point of view

polyglot—speaking several languages

porcine—pig-like

portent—sign; omen; something that foreshadows a coming event

postulate—assumption or supposition

precipitous—abrupt or hasty

primordial—first in time, existing from the beginning

probity—honesty; integrity

prodigal—wasteful; reckless with money

prodigious—marvelous; enormous

profligate—dissolute; reckless; loose in morals; wanton

profundity—intellectual depth

prognostication—prediction, prophesy

promulgate—to announce publicly, especially a law

propitious—favorable; timely

proscribe—to outlaw, ostracize, or banish

protract—to prolong in time or space; to extend or lengthen

puerile—childish; lacking in maturity

pungent—stinging; sharp in taste; caustic

pusillanimous—cowardly

quiescent—at rest; dormant; temporarily inactive

quixotic—idealistic but impractical

raconteur—someone who is skilled at telling stories or anecdotes

raffish—vulgar; crude

raiment—clothing or dress

rampart—an embankment of earth

recalcitrant—stubborn; refractory; reluctant; unwilling; refusing to submit

recidivism—habitual return to crime

recondite—abstruse; profound; secret

reconnoiter—to survey, examine, or explore

recumbent—reclining; lying down

redolent—suggestive of an odor; fragrant

redoubtable—formidable; causing fear

refractory—stubborn; obstinate

remand—to order back; to return to service

remonstrate—to object; to protest

remunerative—compensating; rewarding for service

repine—to complain, mourn, or fret

reticence—silence, reserve, reluctance to speak

reveries—dreamy thinking, daydreaming

ribald—irreverent or coarse

rout—a crowd of people; an overwhelming defeat; to defeat overwhelmingly

sagacious—perceptive; shrewd; having insight

salacious—lustful; lecherous; lascivious

salient—standing out conspicuously; prominent

salubrious—healthful

sanguine—having a ruddy complexion; cheerful; hopeful

sardonic—sneering; sarcastic; cynical

sartorial—tailored

saturnine—sullen; sardonic; gloomy

sedition—resistance to authority

sedulous—diligent; persevering

sententious—terse; concise; aphoristic

sepulchral—pertaining to burial and the grave, hence dismal, gloomy, tomblike

sophistry—seemingly plausible but fallacious reasoning

specious—seeming reasonable but incorrect

spendthrift—one who spends money extravagantly

splenetic—bad-tempered; irritable

spurious—false, counterfeit

static—showing a lack of motion

stentorian—powerful in sound; extremely loud

stodgy—dull, tedious, uninteresting

stringent—vigorous; rigid; binding

sublimate—to purify or refine

succor—aid; assistance; comfort

supercilious—contemptuous; arrogant

sycophant—one who seeks favor by flattering; a parasite

taciturn—quiet; habitually silent

tack—to change course, to zigzag

tangential—peripheral; only slightly connected

temerity—foolish or rash boldness

temporal—not lasting forever; limited by time

tenacity—holding fast

timbre—distinguishing quality of a sound

toady—servile flatterer; a "yes man"

tome—large book

torpor—lack of activity; lethargy

tortuous—winding; full of curves

traduce—to speak falsely

transcendent—exceeding usual limits; incomparable; beyond ordinary existence; peerless

tremulous—trembling, fearful, timid

trenchant—effective; thorough; cutting; keen

truculent—threatening; aggressively self-assertive; savage

turbid—muddy

turpitude—depravity

ubiquitous—seemingly present everywhere, widespread

unctuous—oily; suave

undulating—moving with a wavelike motion

unequivocal—plain; obvious

untrammeled—unconfined, not shackled

vacuity—emptiness

vainglorious—boastful

vanguard—forerunner; advance forces

vehemently—violently, intensely

venal—capable of being bribed

venial—forgivable; trivial

veracious—truthful

verbose—wordy

verdant—green; lush in vegetation

verisimilitude—appearance of truth

veritable—actual; being truly so

vicissitude—change of fortune

vignette—a picture with no definite border, shading off gradually at its edges

viscid—having a cohesive and sticky fluid

vista—view, outlook

vitiating—spoiling, tending to make weak or faulty

vitriolic—corrosive; sarcastic

vituperative—abusive; scolding

vociferous—clamorous; noisy

vouchsafe—to bestow condescendingly; to guarantee

waggish—mischievous; humorous; tricky

wanton—uncalled for; without regard for what is right; unrestrained

winnow—to sift; to separate good parts from bad

winsome—agreeable; gracious

wizen—to wither; to shrivel

xenophobia—fear or hatred of foreigners

zealous—fervent; enthusiastic

zephyr—gentle breeze; west wind

Science Skills Review

COURSE CONCEPT OUTLINE

What You Absolutely Must Know

IV. Presentation of Conflicting Viewpoints (p. 721)

Introduction

The purpose of most science sections of standardized tests is to examine your ability to read and understand scientific information. Rather than testing your knowledge of science facts, the items will measure your science reasoning and problem-solving skills. These science tests emphasize the ability to reason using the skills of a scientist, not the recall of scientific content or specific mathematical skills that are used in science.

Studying and completing the activities in the Science Skills Review will enhance your science reasoning abilities. This review will examine how an experiment is set up, provide guidelines for organizing data collected by observation and experimentation, and present a list of terms that are often found in the passages and corresponding items.

Science Passages

The scientific skills that are measured on the ACT test are tested by items that ask about scientific information presented in three different types of passages: Data Representation, Research Summary, and Conflicting Viewpoints. The scientific information in all three types of passages is obtained through observation and experimentation. While more commonly found in Data Representation passages, any Science passage may include information that is organized in the form of charts, diagrams, figures, graphs, illustrations, and tables like those found in science journals and textbooks. Typically, on the test, you will be asked to read, interpret, and analyze data presented in these forms.

Data Representation Passages

The **Data Representation** passages present scientific information in the form of graphs, tables, and figures. In Data Representation passages, you may be asked to select a conclusion that can be supported by the data, determine the relationship between two variables, or select an explanation for a given experimental result. You may also be required to determine if a conclusion is consistent with the information given or apply the given data to a new situation.

Research Summary Passages

The **Research Summary** passages consist of descriptions of how specific experiments were carried out and a summary of the experimental results. In the Research Summary passages, you may be required to identify the differences in the design of the experiments, predict the outcome based on the results of an experiment, or predict the outcome of an experiment if the design is changed. You may also be required to identify a hypothesis that is being tested, select a hypothesis supported by the results of an experiment, determine the conclusion supported by the given results of an experiment, or select an experiment that could be conducted in order to test another hypothesis.

Conflicting Viewpoints Passages

The **Conflicting Viewpoints** passages present differing hypotheses, theories, or viewpoints of two or three scientists. In the Conflicting Viewpoints passages, you may be required to determine each scientist's position, select the evidence that supports the viewpoints of one or more of the scientists, or determine the similarities and differences of the various scientists' viewpoints. You may also be asked to determine the strengths and weaknesses of the viewpoints, figure out how new information would affect one or more of the viewpoints, or predict evidence that would support a scientist's viewpoint.

Science Vocabulary List

The following list consists of terms that are commonly found in the passages and corresponding items. Understanding the definitions and uses of these terms will help you to better understand the material in which they are used.

absolute—existing independent of any other cause

accuracy—freedom from mistake; exactness; the relationship between the gradation on a measuring device and the actual standard for the quantity being measured

adverse—acting against or in an opposite direction

analogous—similar or comparable in certain respects

analyze—to study the relationship of the parts of something by analysis

application—ability to put to a practical use; having something to do with the matter at hand

approximately—nearly; an estimate or figure that is almost exact

argument—a reason for or against something

assumption—something accepted as true

comprehend—to understand fully

concentration—the ratio of the amount of solute to the amount of solvent or solution

conclusion—a final decision based on facts, experience, or reasoning

confirm—to make sure of the truth of something

consequence—something produced by a cause or condition

consistent—in agreement; firm; changeless

constant—remaining steady and unchanged

contradiction—a statement in opposition to another

control group—experimental group in which conditions are controlled

controlled experiment—one in which the condition suspected to cause an effect is compared to one without the suspected condition

controlled variable—a factor in an experiment that remains constant

correlation—a close connection between two ideas or sets of data

criticism—a finding of fault; disapproval

definitive—most nearly complete or accurate

demonstrate—to explain by use of examples or experiments

dependence—a state of being controlled by something else

dependent variable—result or change that occurs due to the part of an experiment being tested (positioned on the vertical y-axis)

diminish—to make smaller or less; decrease in size

direct relationship—the connection between two variables that show the same effect (i.e., both increase or both decrease)

effective—producing or able to produce a desired condition

estimation—forming a calculation based on incomplete data

ethical—following accepted rules of behavior

evaluation—the result of a finding; estimating the value of something

evidence—that which serves to prove or disprove something

examine—to look at or check carefully

expectation—the extent of a chance that something will occur

experiment—a test made to find something out

experimental design—the plan for a controlled experiment

experimental group—the experimental part in which all conditions are kept the same except for the condition being tested

explanation—a statement that makes something clear

extrapolation—estimating a value for one characteristic that is beyond the range of a given value of another characteristic

figure—a picture that explains

fundamental—a basic part

generalization—something given as a broad statement or conclusion

hypothesis— testable explanation of a question or problem

illustrate—to make clear by using examples

imply—to suggest rather than to say plainly

inconsistent—not in agreement

incorporate—to join or unite closely into a single body

independent variable—in a controlled experiment, the variable that is being changed (positioned on the horizontal *x*-axis)

indication—the act of pointing out or pointing to something

indicator—any device that measures, records, or visibly points out; any of various substances used to point out, such as, a cause, treatment, or outcome on an action

ingredient—any of the components of which something is made

interpolation—estimating a value that falls between two known values; a "best-fit line" on a graph

interpretation—the act of telling the meaning of; explanation

inverse (indirect) relationship—the connection between two variables that shows the opposite effect (i.e., when the value of one variable increases, the value of the other variable deceases)

investigate—to study by close and careful observation

irregular—not continuous or coming at set times

issue—something that is questioned

judgment—an opinion formed by examining and comparing

justify—to prove or show to be right or reasonable

legend—a title, description, or key accompanying a figure or map

maximum—as great as possible in amount or degree

measurement—the act of finding out the size or amount of something

mechanism—the parts or steps that make up a process or activity

minimum—as small as possible in amount or degree

model—a pattern or figure of something to be made

modify—to make changes in something

observation—the act of noting and recording facts and events

opinion—a belief based on experience and on seeing certain facts

optimum—the best or most favorable degree, condition, or amount

pattern—a model, guide, or plan used in making things; definite direction, tendency, or characteristics

perform—to carry out; accomplish

phenomenon—an observable fact or event

precision—the quality of being exactly stated; exact arrangement

predict—to figure out and tell beforehand

preference—a choosing of or liking for one thing rather than another

probability—the quality of being reasonably sure but not certain of something happening or being true

procedure—the way in which an action or actions is carried out

proponent—one who supports a cause

proportional—any quantities or measurements having the same fixed relationship in degree or number

reasonable—showing or containing sound thought

refute—to prove wrong by argument or evidence

relationship—the state of being connected

replicate—to copy or reproduce

revise—to look over again; to correct or improve

simulation—the act or process of simulating a system or process

study—a careful examination and investigation of an event

suggest—to offer as an idea

summarize—to state briefly

support—to provide evidence

theory—a general rule offered to explain experiences or facts

translate—to change from one state or form to another

treatment—to expose to some action

underlying—to form the support for something

unit—a fixed quantity used as a standard of measurement

validity—based on evidence that can be supported

value—the quantity or amount for which a symbol stands

variable—that which can be changed

viewpoint—opinion; judgment

Basics of Experimental Design

The Science passages describe scientific methods that may be unfamiliar to you, but are commonly used by scientists to interpret and analyze scientific information. You need to be familiar with these basics of experimental design in order to understand the complete meaning of the passages and items.

Types of Research

Scientists regularly attempt to identify and solve problems by investigating the world around them. Different scientists may use different approaches to conduct their investigations. *Qualitative*, or descriptive, research is based generally on observable data only.

Example:

A field biologist may observe coral reefs in order to determine if the loss of this habitat would threaten the extinction of many species that live in the coral reefs.

Quantitative research is based on the collection of numerical data—usually by counting or measuring.

Example:

A laboratory biologist may investigate the factors that affect the flow of substances across cell membranes. Numerical data is collected by measuring the change in mass of a cellophane bag that is filled with a sugar solution and then placed in a beaker of pure water.

Forming and Testing Hypotheses

Scientists normally *form a hypothesis* and then test it through observation, experimentation, and/or prediction. A hypothesis is defined as a possible explanation of a question or problem that can be formally tested. A hypothesis can be thought of as a prediction about why something occurs or about the relationship between two or more variables.

Scientists describe an experiment as a procedure that *tests a hypothesis* by the process of collecting information under controlled conditions. Based on the experimental results, scientists can determine whether or not the hypothesis is correct or must be modified and re-tested. Testing hypotheses through experiments is at the core of scientific investigations and studies.

An important part of testing a hypothesis is identifying the *variables* that are part of an experiment. A variable is any condition that can change in an experiment. Controlled experimentation is carried out by keeping all the variables constant, except the one under study. The variable under study is called the *independent variable* and is determined by the experimenter. This variable can be changed independently of the other variables, and it is the only variable that can affect the outcome of an experiment by causing a change that can be observed or measured. The changed conditions are called the *dependent variables* because they are the result of, or dependent upon, the changes in the independent variable.

Scientists attempt to test only one independent variable at a time so that he or she knows which condition produced the effect. *Controlled variables*, or controls, are conditions that could affect the outcome of an experiment but do not, because they are held constant. Controls are used to eliminate the possibility that conditions other than those that are a part of an experiment may affect the outcome of the experiment.

The statement of a testable hypothesis must be structured so that it will demonstrate how a change in the independent variable can cause an observed or measured change in the dependent variable. A hypothesis may be typically structured as follows: the independent variable will describe how the variable under study is changed; the dependent variable will describe the effect of those changes.

Example:

> In a controlled experiment, in order to determine the effect of a high protein diet on the growth rate of rats, the independent variable would be the exposure to a high protein diet, while the dependent variable would be the effect on the growth rate. A possible hypothesis for this experiment may be stated as follows: When the amount of protein is increased in the diet of rats, then their growth rate will increase.

Design of Controlled Experiments

The design of controlled experiments involves two groups: the **control group** and the **experimental group**. In the control group, all variables are kept the same. In the experimental group, all conditions are kept the same as the control group except the condition that is being tested, the independent variable.

The control group and the experimental group must be as similar as possible at the beginning of a controlled experiment. The only difference in the design of the two groups is the addition of the independent variable that is tested in the experimental group. It is common in a controlled experiment to have more than one experimental group to represent the possible variations in the conditions of the independent variable. All other variables that could affect the outcome of the experiment are held constant.

Example:

> In the previous experiment about the effect of a high protein diet on the growth rate of rats, a large test population of commonly similar rats would be randomly divided into two smaller groups of equal number—the control group and the experimental group.

The rats in the above experiment are randomly divided to ensure that both groups are representative samples of the original population. If the test group is not representative of the original population, other uncontrolled conditions could affect the outcome of the experiment. If there are any uncontrolled conditions in either group, it could be argued that any experimental results would be due to differences in the composition of the different test groups instead of a result of the independent variable.

Continuing the development of the experiment, we see that the establishment of certain conditions makes this a controlled experiment.

Example:

> The rats in the control group are exposed to the same environmental conditions as the rats in the experimental group, except for the amount of protein in their diet. The control group rats are given a diet with the normal amount of protein. The rats in the experimental group are exposed to a high protein diet (independent variable), in addition to exposure to the same environmental conditions as the control group. (It would be possible to have more than one experimental group with each having a greater amount of protein.) The other conditions that could change, such as the temperature, amount of food and water, and amount of living space, are held constant for both groups of rats.

➢ These conditions are the controls necessary for this experiment to be considered a controlled experiment. The data collected can be used to determine if the hypothesis is correct, and it will ultimately lead to the forming of a conclusion. The following table summarizes the design of this experiment:

Test Population (number of test subjects)	Controlled Variables (conditions that are kept the same in both groups)	Independent Variables (conditions that vary between the two groups)	Dependent Variables (conditions that result from the experiment)
Control Group (50 rats)	sunlight, temperature, amount of water	normal protein diet	growth rate
Experimental Group (50 rats)	sunlight, temperature, amount of water	high protein diet	growth rate

(Note: It is possible to determine an experiment's effect on multiple dependent variables.)

Basics of Experimental Design

DIRECTIONS: Read the description of the following controlled experiment and answer the accompanying items. Answers are on page 802.

An experiment was carried out to determine the effect of temperature on the heart rate of frogs. In the experiment, 100 frogs were removed from a large 25°C enclosure and separated randomly into four equal groups: A, B, C, and D. Each group was maintained in a separate container at a different constant temperature: Group A at 5°C; Group B at 15°C; Group C at 25°C; and Group D at 35°C. All other conditions, such as the size, type, age, and number of the frogs, as well as the size of the container and the amount of light, were the same for all groups of frogs.

1. The purpose of the experiment is to: _____

_____

_____

2. The independent variable is: _____

_____

_____

3. The dependent variable is: _____

_____

_____

4. The controlled variables are: _____

_____

_____

5. The control group(s) is (are): _____

_____

_____

6. The experimental group(s) is (are): _____

_____

_____

7. Write a possible hypothesis by filling in the blanks in the following sentence:

When the _____ is _____,
    (independent variable) (describe how it is changed)

then the _____ will _____.
    (dependent variable)   (describe the effect)

Data Organization and Analysis in Controlled Experiments

After collecting data, a scientist must determine the most appropriate way to present the information so that it can be easily interpreted and analyzed. The two most common ways that scientists report their data are tables and graphs. These pictorial representations are easy ways to show where a pattern, trend, or relationship exists. The tables and graphs can be organized in a variety of ways, but there are some generally accepted basic guidelines.

Tables

As the name implies, a *table* presents data in the form of rows and columns. The number of vertical columns and horizontal rows depends on the kind and amount of data collected. In the most basic tables, there is a column for both the independent variable and the dependent variable. When relevant, units of measurement for the variables are included. A heading or title is included to communicate the purpose of the experiment.

And here is how to "read" a table: the data needed to answer questions are located by referencing column and row. The descriptive information is always very important.

Example:

Deaths Due to High Cholesterol Intake					
			Smoking Habit		
				Current	
Occupational Class	Never	Former	1–14 g/day	14–24 g/day	> 24 g/day
Agricultural Workers, Unskilled Workers	1,926	2,013	2,334	2,765	3,109
Manual Workers, Skilled Workers	1,507	1,822	2,002	2,209	2,813
Industrial Foremen, Non-Manual Workers	1,022	1,233	1,448	1,548	1,999
Civil Servants, Management	936	1,051	1,109	1,278	1,560
Professionals, Executives	722	801	855	942	1,088
Total	6,113	6,920	7,748	8,742	10,569

In this case, the title tells you that the table is a summary of deaths due to high cholesterol intake. The first column indicates that the deaths are itemized according to occupational class. The remaining columns show the impact of smoking habit on the number of deaths per occupational class due to high cholesterol intake. Note that while the smoking habit is given in units of grams per day, the numbers listed still refer to the number of deaths. Based on the information given in the table, we can see several general trends: the number of deaths due to high cholesterol intake increases as worker skill level decreases regardless of smoking habit; furthermore, the number of deaths across all occupational classes is directly correlated to smoking habit.

In complex tables, the columns may be subdivided to represent additional variations in the conditions of the independent and dependent variables. The rows include the data from repeated trials under the same experimental setup. When recording data in a table, the values of the independent variable are arranged in an ordered manner—numerical values are arranged from the largest to the smallest or from the smallest to the largest.

Relationships between variables may be direct, indirect (inverse), or constant. A *direct relationship* occurs when one variable increases as the other increases, or when one variable decreases as the other decreases. An *indirect*, or inverse, *relationship* occurs when one variable increases as the other decreases. A *constant relationship* occurs when a change in one variable has no effect on the other variable.

Example:

The table below makes it easy to see that there is a direct relationship between the temperature and the heart rate of frogs.

The Effect of Temperature on Frog Heart Rates		
Group	*Temperature (°C)* (independent variable)	*Average Heart Rate(per minute)* (dependent variable)
A	5	10
B	15	20
C	25	30
D	35	40

As the temperature increases, so does the heart rate of the frog. If the heart rate had decreased as the temperature increased, then there would have been an indirect relationship between the two variables. If the heart rate had remained the same as the temperature was increased or decreased, then the relationship would have been considered constant.

Graphs

Scientists often collect large amounts of data while performing experiments. It may not be possible to clearly present the data in the form of a table. The arrangement of the data in a table may not easily or adequately show a pattern, trend, or relationship. Usually, a well-constructed *graph* can communicate experimental results more clearly than a data table. Generally, when the values of the variables are arranged in a graph, the patterns, trends, and relationships are more apparent than when those same values are arranged in a table.

Four of the most common kinds of graphs are line, bar, cumulative bar, and circle graphs. In a line graph, value is determined by the distance from the base line to the intersection of the line and the scale reading. A bar graph is easy to identify because it uses bars to represent value. In a cumulative bar graph, each bar portion represents a percentage of the whole bar. A circle graph is easy to recognize and commonly called a pie chart because the division of the circle into sectors resembles a pie cut into pieces.

Line Graphs

A *line graph* has four basic parts: *horizontal axis* (*A*), *vertical axis* (*B*), *line* (*C*), and *heading* or *title* (*D*). A line graph is used to show the relationship between two variables. The variables being compared are positioned on the two axes of the graph. As with a table, the heading or title communicates the purpose of the experiment.

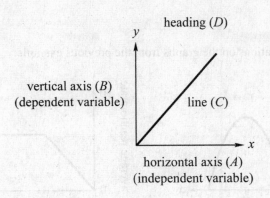

heading (*D*)

vertical axis (*B*)
(dependent variable)

line (*C*)

horizontal axis (*A*)
(independent variable)

The *independent variable* is always positioned on the horizontal axis, called the *x-axis*. The experimenter can change the value of the independent variable and those values are marked off along the horizontal axis.

The *dependent variable* is always positioned on the vertical axis, the *y-axis*. The dependent variable, such as the rate of a chemical reaction, is any change that results from changing the value of the independent variable. Values of the dependent variable are marked off along the vertical axis.

The data that describe the relationship between the variables appear on the graph as dots, connected to form a line or curve. Each dot, or plot, represents the relationship that exists between a measurement on the vertical axis and a measurement on the horizontal axis. The slope of the line that is created by the connected points represents the relationship between the two variables. If more than one line appears on the same graph, each line represents different independent variable conditions. Additionally, the lines may be curved rather than straight. However, typically, this does not affect the general relationship illustrated.

Example:

The slopes of the lines in the following three graphs illustrate the typical kinds of relationships between variables shown in a line graph:

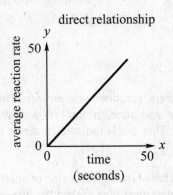

direct relationship

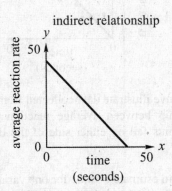

indirect relationship

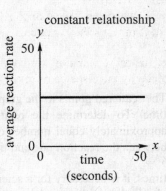

constant relationship

The first graph illustrates a *direct relationship*—as time increases, the reaction rate increases. The second graph illustrates an *indirect relationship*—as time increases, the reaction rate decreases. The third graph illustrates a *constant relationship*—as time increases, the rate of reaction remains the same; that is, time had no effect on the rate of reaction.

Example:

The following graphs illustrate variations on the graphs from the previous example:

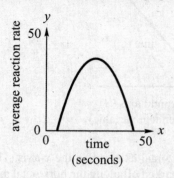 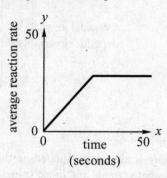

The first graph indicates that as time increases, the reaction rate increases to an ***optimum***, or best rate, and then decreases. The second graph indicates that as time increases, the reaction rate increases, and then becomes constant.

Since the collection of experimental data is often subject to error, data points plotted on a line may not be directly connected. The graph may show only scattered points so that a smooth line may not be constructed. As a result, another type of line graph is required to illustrate an estimate of a value that falls among the known values on the graph. A ***best-fit*** line, a line that comes close to all of the points, must be constructed. This process is called ***interpolation***.

Example:

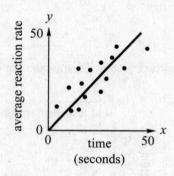

The scattered points in the graph above illustrate data collected from several reactions over an increasing period of time. To determine the relationship between average reaction rate and time, a line is drawn so that an approximately equal number of points fall on either side of the line. This graph indicates a direct relationship between the reaction rate and time.

Sometimes, it is necessary for a scientist to estimate a value for one variable based on a given value of another variable that is beyond the limits of the available data shown on the graph. The scientist must then extend the line on the graph based on the data given. The process is called ***extrapolation***.

Example:

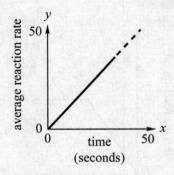

If the line is relatively straight, as shown in the graph above, the line can be extended far enough so that the values called for can be included. Suppose the scientist wanted to determine the reaction rate at a time of 50 seconds. By extending the line to follow the apparent pattern, it is possible to predict the reaction rate.

When using the technique of extrapolation, a scientist must be careful not to make the possible false assumption that the relationship will continue unchanged indefinitely. It is possible that beyond a certain time, an unexpected change in the independent variable will result in an unpredicted change in the dependent variable. When the graph line is a curve, it is necessary to use one's best judgment to extend the line to follow the apparent pattern.

Example:

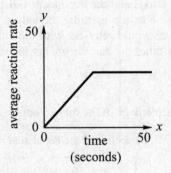

In the graph above, if the data collection had stopped after about 15 units of time, the scientist may have inaccurately predicted that the reaction rate would continue to increase.

Note that occasionally a line graph will show a "break" in the scale. This is done to conserve space and only when no values fall into the deleted part.

Example:

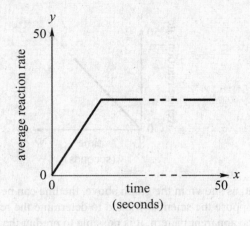

Bar Graphs

A ***bar graph*** is similar to a line graph, but it is better for making simple comparisons. This type of graph is typically used to display data that does not continuously change. Bar graphs present related data side by side so the data can be easily compared. A heading describing the presented data accompanies the graph.

The basic setup of a bar graph is similar to a line graph in that there is a horizontal *x*-axis and a vertical *y*-axis. The independent ***variable*** is positioned on the *x*-axis and the dependent variable is on the *y*-axis. Thick bars rather than data points show relationships among data. The bars representing the values of the independent variable, on the *x*-axis, are drawn up to an imaginary point where they would intersect with the values of the dependent variable on the *y*-axis if these values were extended. Generally, the taller the bar, the greater the value it represents.

Example:

The following bar graph shows the percentage of the human population having each of the four blood types:

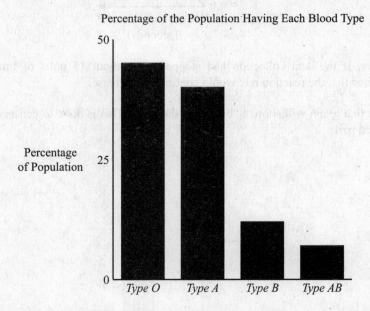

The independent variable is the different blood types found in the population. The dependent variable is the percentage of each blood type. The graph shows that the most common blood type is Type O, while the least common is Type AB.

Note that the bars in a graph do not necessarily have to be oriented vertically. They can be oriented horizontally with the base line on the left or the right. In a horizontal configuration, the longer the bar, the greater the value it represents.

Example:

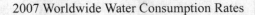

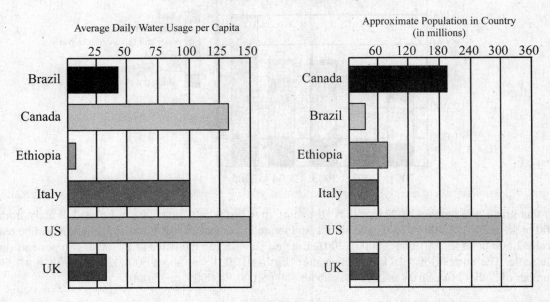

Here you have two related bar graphs. In each, the magnitude of a reading is represented by the length of the bar. For example, the average daily water usage per capita in the United States was 150 gallons: you can read the value "150" from the scale below the bar. But what gives the bar the value 150 is the length of the bar: it runs from the base line (or zero) to the value of 150 on the scale. Similarly, the average daily water usage per capita in Italy was 100, and the bar for Italy is 100 units long, running from the base line (zero) to 100 on the scale.

The graph on the right is also a bar graph and is read in the same way, but notice the additional information provided: the populations are graphed in terms of millions. Thus, the total population in Italy is not 60, but 60,000,000.

Cumulative Bar Graphs

The key feature of the cumulative bar graph is that only the bottom component and the total are read from the base line. All other components are read from the top of the component immediately below to the bottom of the component immediately above (or the top of the bar in the case of the topmost component).

Example:

Number of Live Births in County X by Year

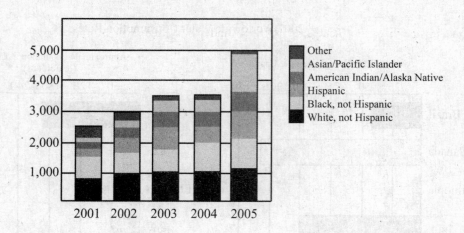

In this graph, the number of "white (not Hispanic)" live births in County X can be read directly from the scale: 900 or so in 2001, 1,000 in 2002, and so on. And the total number of live births in County X can be read from the scale: 2,500 or so in 2001 and 3,000 in 2002. But you *cannot* read the value of the other components directly from the scale. The number of "black (not Hispanic)" births in 2001 was about 600 ($1,500 - 900$), not 1,500; and the number of "other" live births in 2005 was about 100 ($5,000 - 4,900$), not 5,000.

Note that for questions based on cumulative bar graphs, you can make the mistake of attempting a reading directly from the scale rather than correctly finding the length of that component of the bar.

Circle Graphs

Circle graphs use a circle divided into sections to display data. A circle graph is sometimes called a pie graph or pie chart because it looks like a pie cut up into pieces. Each section of the graph represents one of the categories of a particular subject. The whole circle represents 100% of the data for all of the categories. The bigger the section, the larger the value it represents. Circle graphs are typically used to illustrate information that is collected by observation rather than by experimentation.

Example:

The following circle graph represents the amount of organisms in a sample of soil:

Organisms in the Soil
(by mass)

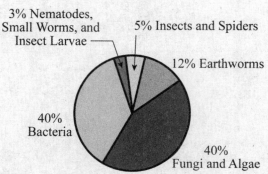

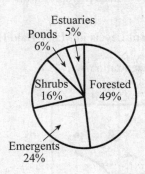

As indicated in the graph, bacteria and fungi and algae are the most common organisms in the soil. Each group makes up 40% of the total amount of organisms.

In a circle graph, the size of the sector represents value, and usually a value is attached to each sector. Additionally, a circle graph, without supplemental information, does not give a real value, as opposed to a percent or a share. For that, you need to know the total value represented by the graph, and this is often given in a note.

Example:

Composition of Wetland Area, 2004
(Total area = 108 million acres)

Estuaries 5%
Ponds 6%
Shrubs 16%
Forested 49%
Emergents 24%

In this case, the percentages are given and you could, if asked, compare those directly, e.g., there is a little more than twice as much forested wetlands (49%) as emergent wetlands (24%). And because you have the total area of wetlands for the entire graph (108 million acres), you can calculate values for each sector. For example, the total number of acres of estuary wetlands is 5% of 108 million, or 5.4 million acres.

Note that a single circle graph can only show one time period, size, source, etc. (e.g., year, acreage, country, etc.). So when a graph includes multiple elements such as both a bar graph and a circle graph, the circle graph applies to only one of the bars in the bar graph—not to all of them. The following examples illustrate how information might be presented using multiple elements:

Example:

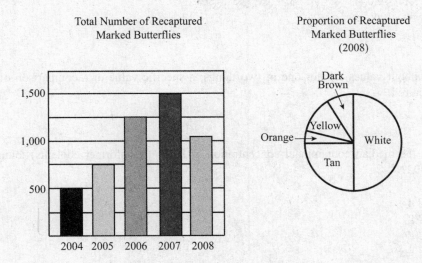

Total Number of Recaptured
Marked Butterflies

Proportion of Recaptured
Marked Butterflies
(2008)

Dark Brown
Yellow
Orange
White
Tan

In this case, inclusion of the bar and circle graphs allows for the question: "Of the recaptured marked butterflies in 2008, about how many more were marked white than tan?" The bar graph indicates that the total number of recaptured butterflies is a little more than 1,000. Based on the circle graph, 50% of the total, or a little more than

500, were marked white; and 25% of the total, or a little more than 250, were marked tan. Therefore, approximately $500 - 250 = 250$ more of the recaptured butterflies were marked white than tan.

Data Analysis Questions

Often questions based on tables and graphs require you to gather the data from the graph. These types of the questions fall into one of three major categories: reading values, manipulating values, and drawing inferences.

We'll look at examples of each category, but we'll need a graph for the examples:

Contaminant Levels in Maine Bald Eagle Eggs

Median Contaminant Concentration   Pesticide Contaminant Distribution, 2005

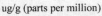

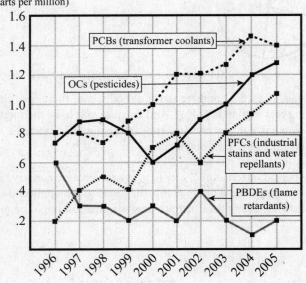

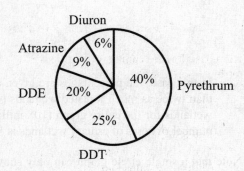

Reading Values

Questions that ask about values ask for one of two things: a specific value or a comparison of values. Typically, no calculations are required.

Examples:

1. What was the median contaminant concentration of PCBs (transformer coolants) found in Maine bald eagle eggs in 2002?

    A. 0.2 ug/g
    B. 0.7 ug/g
    C. 0.8 ug/g
    D. 1.2 ug/g

    ➤ The correct answer (D). Read the value of average contaminant concentration of PCBs for the year 2002: 1.2 ug/g.

2. In which year did the median contaminant concentration of PFCs (industrial stains and water repellants) found in Maine bald eagle eggs first exceed 0.6 ug/g (parts per million)?

   F. 1998
   G. 1999
   H. 2000
   J.   2001

> ➤ The correct answer is (H). Locate the line for PFCs and find the first year for which the line broke across the 0.6 mark: 2000.

3. For how many years shown was the median contaminant concentration of OCs (pesticides) found in Maine bald eagle eggs less than that of PFCs (industrial stains and water repellants)?

   A. 1
   B. 2
   C. 3
   D. 4

> ➤ The correct answer is (B). Those years were 2000 and 2001.

It's possible for reading values questions to be more complicated, but only because the question stem asks you to retrieve more data from the graph.

Example:

For how many years in which the median contaminant concentration of PCBs (transformer coolant) found in Maine bald eagle eggs was greater than that of OCs (pesticides) was the contaminant concentration of PFCs (industrial stains and water repellants) greater than that of PBDEs (flame retardants)?

   F. 6
   G. 7
   H. 8
   J.   9

> ➤ The correct answer is (G). This question requires you to first identify those years in which contaminant concentration of PCBs was greater than that of OCs: 1996, 1999, 2000, 2001, 2002, 2003, 2004, 2005. Next, identify those years in which contaminant concentration of PFCs was greater than that of PBDEs: 1997, 1998, 1999, 2000, 2001, 2002, 2003, 2004, 2005. Now compare the two, and count up the number of years that satisfy both: 1999, 2000, 2001, 2002, 2003, 2004, 2005.

Manipulating Values

The second group of questions require a calculation of some sort. Simple calculations involve basic manipulations such as addition and subtraction.

Examples:

1. What was the total median contaminant concentration found in Maine bald eagle eggs in 2002?

   A. 1.9 ug/g
   B. 2.4 ug/g
   C. 2.9 ug/g
   D. 3.1 ug/g

➢ The correct answer is (D). Locate the four individual contaminant concentrations for 2002 and add the numbers togetheer to get the total median contaminant concentration: $0.4 + 0.6 + 0.9 + 1.2 = 3.1$ ug/g.

2. In 2003, PCBs (transformer coolants) accounted for how much more contaminant concentration than PBDEs (flame retardants) in Maine bald eagle eggs?

    F. 0.1 ug/g
    G. 0.3 ug/g
    H. 1.1 ug/g
    J. 1.3 ug/g

➢ The correct answer is (H). Subtract the median contaminant concentration of PBDEs for 2003 from the median contaminant concentration of PCBs for the same year: $1.3 - 0.2 = 1.1$ ug/g.

3. In 1998, OCs (pesticides) and PCBs (transformer coolants) combined accounted for how much more median contaminant concentration found in Maine bald eagle eggs than PFCs (industrial stains and water repellants) and PBDEs (flame retardants) combined?

    A. 0.8 ug/g
    B. 1.0 ug/g
    C. 1.6 ug/g
    D. 2.4 ug/g

➢ The correct answer is (A). First, add together the contaminant concentrations for OCs and PCBs in 1998: $0.9 + 0.7 = 1.6$ ug/g. Second, add together the contaminant concentrations for PFCs and PBDEs in 1998: $0.5 + 0.3 = 0.8$ ug/g. Finally, subtract the second total from the first: $1.6 - 0.8 = 0.8$ ug/g.

More difficult manipulation questions require you to express some value as a fraction, a percentage, or in terms of a ratio.

Examples:

1. PBDEs (flame retardants) accounted for what approximately percent of the total median contaminant concentration found in Maine bald eagle eggs in 2002?

    F. 4%
    G. 13%
    H. 18%
    J. 23%

➢ The correct answer is (G). The total median contaminant concentration for 2002 was: $1.2 + 0.9 + 0.6 + 0.4 = 3.1$ ug/g. And $\dfrac{0.4}{3.1} = 0.13 = 13\%$.

2. In 1997, what was the ratio of median contaminant concentration of OCs (pesticides) to median contaminant concentration of PBDEs (flame retardants) found in Maine bald eagle eggs?

    A. 3:1
    B. 2:1
    C. 1:1
    D. 1:3

> The correct answer is (A): $\dfrac{0.9}{0.3} = \dfrac{3}{1} = 3:1$.

For questions that require manipulations, analyze the question stem to determine what data you need and make a note on your scratch paper. Then find the data on the graph and enter it on your note. Finally, do the required manipulation.

Drawing Inferences

The third common type of table and graph data analysis question requires you to draw an inference from the data. In other words, the first question type (read a value) just asks you to demonstrate that you know how to read the graph. The second question type (manipulate the values) requires you to manipulate the data in order to arrive at a solution. For this third type (draw an inference), you have to draw a further conclusion from the data explicitly given.

Example:

> In 2005, what percentage of the total median contaminant concentration found in Maine bald eagle eggs was due to DDE?
>
> F. 2.5%
> G. 3.0%
> H. 6.5%
> J. 9.0%

> ➤ The correct answer is (H). To get the answer, you have to see that the circle graph provides the breakdown for pesticide contaminants (OCs) in 2005. First, find the total median contaminant concentration for 2005: $1.4 + 1.3 + 1.1 + 0.2 = 4.0$ ug/g. From the circle graph, we see that DDE was responsible for 20% of the pesticide contaminants in 2005, or $(0.2)(1.3) = 0.26$ ug/g. Therefore, DDE was responsible for $\dfrac{0.26}{4.0} = 0.065 = 6.5\%$ of the total median contaminant concentration found in Maine bald eagle eggs in 2005.

Data Analysis Strategies

Data analysis of tables and graphs can be time-consuming, so fortunately there are three general shortcuts: approximation, simplification, and "meastimation."

Approximation

Some graph questions, as you have already seen, explicitly invite you to approximate. Question stems are particularly likely to include words such as "approximately" or "about" or "most nearly" when the graph uses large values and an exact value cannot reliably be read from the graph.

Example:

> A graph entitled "Total Microbial Bacteria Count by Elapsed Time" with values in the millions of cells/mL is not going to permit a reading of 1,197,268. Round off, usually to the nearest integer or tenth: 1.1 million.

Simplification

A second way to avoid doing arithmetic is to set up your solution and then simplify the numbers before doing the calculation.

Example:

Suppose that you are asked to find the difference between two populations, one that is 25% of the total population, and the other 40%, when the total population is 14,356,341. You'd round off the population to 14 million and set up your solution: $(40\% \text{ of } 14) - (25\% \text{ of } 14) = ?$ Instead of doing two multiplications and then a subtraction, you can subtract first ($40\% - 25\% = 15\%$) and then do one multiplication: 15% of 14 is 2.1, or 2,100,000.

"Meastimation"

A third shortcut is to use the picture itself to "meastimate" quantities. "Meastimate" is a made-up word that just indicates a combination of measuring and estimating.

Examples:

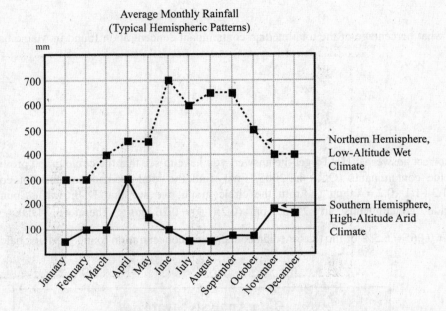

Average Monthly Rainfall
(Typical Hemispheric Patterns)

1. In which of the following months was the difference in rainfall between the low-altitude wet climate and the high-altitude arid climate the greatest?

   A. January
   B. June
   C. July
   D. December

   ➤ The correct answer is (B). You can "meastimate" the answer just by looking at the difference between the two lines: of the five months given, the difference between the two lines is greatest in June.

2. What was the difference between the northern climate rainfall and the southern climate rainfall in November?

   F. 150
   G. 200
   H. 220
   J. 300

   ➤ The correct answer is (H). You can get the answer by subtracting values taken from the graph or you can use a piece of scratch paper to measure the difference between the two values and then compare that difference to the left-hand scale for the graph. That way, you can used the principle that "distance equals value" to "meastimate" the answer.

The point here is that you can't answer a graph question with greater precision than the graph itself, so questions often invite you to approximate. And even when the question doesn't specifically call for an approximation, you'll save time if you use one of these shortcuts.

Note that when graphs are plotted on a logarithmic scale, in which each additional y-axis unit represents a tenfold increase in magnitude, you cannot measure distances and compare them to the scale to determine values. This is because the magnitude of the difference between points on the y-axis varies according to where on the scale those points fall.

Example:

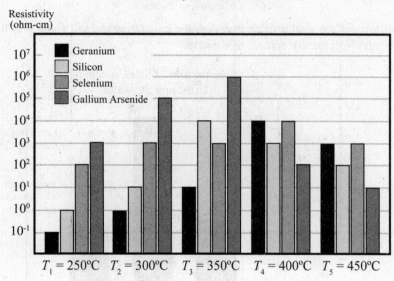

Resistivity of Semiconductors

How much more resistive is a silicon semiconductor at 350°C than a geranium semiconductor at the same temperature?

➤ If you failed to notice that this is a logarithmic graph, you might mistakenly assume that at 350°C the silicon semiconductor is twice as resistive as the geranium semicondcutor because its bar is twice as large. However, because the graph is logarithmic, you cannot compare the bars directly. Instead, you must read the values from the y-axis. The resistivity of silicon at 350°C is 10^4 ohm-cm; the resitivity of geranium at 350°C is 10^1 ohm-cm. Therefore, the silicon resistor is $\dfrac{10^4}{10^1} = 10^3 = 1,000$ times as resistive as the geranium semiconductor at 350°C.

Data Organization and Analysis in Controlled Experiments

DIRECTIONS: Read the descriptions of the following controlled experiments and data sets. Answer the accompanying items based on the information provided in the tables and graphs. Answers are on page 802.

Experimental Data Set 1

The following graph illustrates the results of an investigation comparing the salt content in the urine of two mammals (humans and kangaroo rats) with the salt content of seawater:

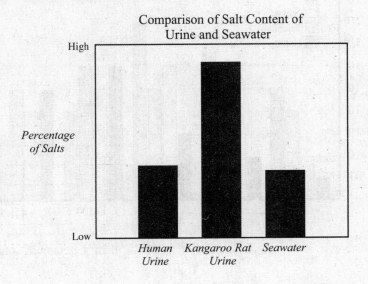

Comparison of Salt Content of Urine and Seawater

1. The independent variable is: _Salt content_.

2. The dependent variable is: _1/4_ .

3. The mammal with a percentage of salt in its urine closest to the percentage of salt in seawater is the:

   Human urine

Experimental Data Set 2

A laboratory investigation was performed to determine the length of time necessary to digest starch (carbohydrates). Ten grams of potato were added to 15 milliliters of an enzyme solution and placed in a test tube. The percentage of starch digested was recorded over a 24-hour period, as can be seen in the table below. A line graph is also provided to illustrate the relationship between the variables.

Carbohydrate Digestion over a 24-Hour Period	
Time (hours)	Percentage of Carbohydrates Digested
0	0
4	5
8	15
12	50
16	75
20	85
24	90

Carbohydrate Digestion over a 24-Hour Period

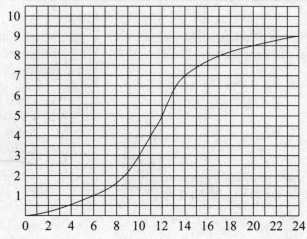

Percentage of Carbohydrates Digested

Time (Hours)

4. The independent variable is: _____ Time _____

5. The dependent variable is: _____ % _____

6. The independent variable is on the __X__ axis.

7. The dependent variable is on the __Y__ axis.

8. The slope of the line indicates that generally as the amount of time (increases, decreases, stays constant), the percentage of carbohydrates digested (increases, decreases, stays constant).

9. According to the data, during which four-hour period did the greatest amount of carbohydrate digestion occur?

   A.   0–4 hours
   B.   4–8 hours
   C.   8–12 hours
   D.   20–24 hours

Experimental Data Set 3

The following table summarizes the estimated population exposed to five major earthquakes. The Richter and Modified Mercalli scales are used to rate and compare the intensity of earthquakes. The Richter scale is a measure of the motion of the ground 100 kilometers from the earthquake's epicenter; each increase of 1 represents a tenfold increase in the motion of the ground. The Modified Mercalli scale is from I (not felt) to XII (extreme). It is subjective, as it describes and rates earthquakes in terms of human reactions and observations.

Estimated Population Exposed to Earthquake Shaking										
		Estimated Population Exposure (thousands)								
		Estimated Modified Mercalli Intensity								
Location (Date)	Richter Scale	I	II-III	IV	V	VI	VII	VIII	IX	X+
Coast of Central Peru (8/15/07)	8.0	—	—	527	2,285	7,875	1,297	449	0	0
Eastern Sichuan, China (5/12/08)	7.9	—	—	190,360	89,674	15,469	11,873	4,684	707	605
Pakistan (10/28/08)	6.4	—	—	10,340	2,308	332	98	42	7	0
Sulawesi, Indonesia (11/16/08)	7.3	—	1,272	2,242	835	611	120	0	0	0
Coast of Central Peru (2/2/09)	6.0	—	2,386	7,538	371	198	110	0	0	0

10. In 2008, what was the total population exposed to earthquake shaking in Eastern Sichuan, China?

    F.   313,372
    G.   3,133,720
    H.   31,337,200
    J.   313,372,000

11. What was the total population exposed to earthquake shaking on the coast of central Peru in 2009?

    A. 5,080,000
    B. 10,603,000
    C. 18,433,000
    D. 29,036,000

12. In 2008, what was the total population exposed to earthquake shaking of Mercalli intensity VIII or higher?

    F. 6,045,000
    G. 5,996,000
    H. 4,684,000
    J. 1,319,000

13. Of the following, which earthquake resulted in the greatest population exposed to earthquake shaking of Mercalli intensity V?

    A. Coast of central Peru, 2007
    B. Pakistan, 2008
    C. Sulawesi, Indonesia, 2008
    D. Coast of central Peru, 2009

14. What was the approximate total population exposed to earthquake shaking of Mercalli intensity III or lower for all five earthquakes?

    F. 1,300,000
    G. 2,400,000
    H. 3,000,000
    J. 3,700,000

15. For which of the following pairs of earthquakes was the ratio of Richter scale ratings the greatest?

    A. China (2008) : Pakistan (2008)
    B. Peru (2007) : Peru (2009)
    C. Peru (2009) : Peru (2007)
    D. Indonesia (2008) : Pakistan (2008)

Experimental Data Set 4

Soil is made up of rock and mineral particles, water, gases (air), dead plant and animal matter, and tiny living organisms. Water soaks in the ground from rain (and other forms of precipitation). Gases come from the air, plants, and animals. Soil also contains living organisms (such as bacteria, fungi, insects, etc.) that break down nonliving organic plants and animal matter in the soil, making it rich and healthy for plants to grow in. An experiment was conducted on soil samples collected from two different geological locations. The following graphs summarize the soil sample compositions by content:

Soil Composition by Sample Location
(Soil Sample Sizes = 100 grams)

Woodland

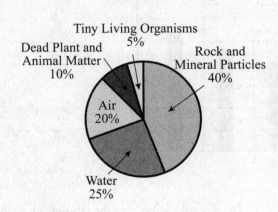

Meadow

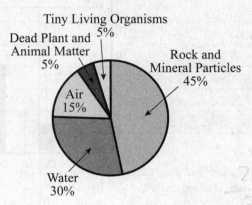

16. What was the total weight of rock and mineral particles in the meadow soil sample?

    F. 45 grams
    G. 40 grams
    H. 30 grams
    J. 25 grams

17. What component had the same weight in both of the soil samples?

    A. Rock and mineral particles
    B. Water
    C. Dead plant and animal matter
    D. Tiny living organisms

18. In the meadow soil sample, the weight of rock and mineral particles was most nearly equal to the combined weight of:

    F. water and dead plant and animal matter.
    G. water and air.
    H. air and dead plant and animal matter.
    J. air and tiny living organisms.

19. What is the ratio of the percentage of water in the woodland soil sample to the percentage of water in the meadow soil sample?

    A. $\dfrac{6}{5}$

    B. 1

    C. $\dfrac{5}{6}$

    D. $\dfrac{3}{4}$

20. How much heavier was the dead plant and animal matter in the woodland soil sample than in the meadow soil sample?

    F. 5 grams
    G. 10 grams
    H. 15 grams
    J. Cannot be determined from the given information

Experimental Data Set 5

The following graph summarizes the results of an experiment conducted to investigate the role that light plays in the growth and development of bean seedlings. Seedlings were grown in two conditions: light and dark. Seedling heights were measured at five-day intervals following planting and averaged across the total number of seedlings in each group.

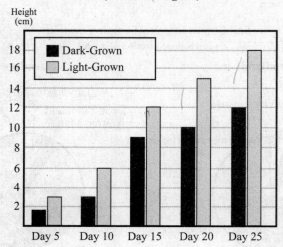

Median Height of Bean Seedlings
(*Phaseolus vulgaris*)

21. What was the median height for the dark-grown bean seedlings after 20 days?

    A. 3 cm
    B. 8 cm
    C. 10 cm
    D. 12 cm

22. For which day was the difference between the median height of light-grown and dark-grown bean seedlings the greatest?

    F. Day 10
    G. Day 15
    H. Day 20
    J. Day 25

23. What was the average of the median heights for the light-grown and dark-grown bean seedlings on Day 25?

    A. 12 cm
    B. 15 cm
    C. 18 cm
    D. 30 cm

24. For which day was the ratio of the median height of light-grown to dark-grown seedlings the greatest?

    F. Day 5
    G. Day 10
    H. Day 15
    J. Day 20

25. Which of the following statements can be inferred from the graph?

    I.   The smallest five-day increase in the median height of dark-grown bean seedlings was from Day 15 to Day 20.
    II. The greatest percentage increase in the median height of light-grown bean seedlings for the period shown on the graph was from Day 10 to Day 15.
    III. On Day 20, the median height of dark-grown bean seedlings was greater than that of light-grown seedlings.

    A. I only
    B. II only
    C. I and II only
    D. I and III only

Experimental Data Set 6

Plant growth hormones are chemicals naturally produced in plants that accelerate, inhibit, or otherwise affect the growth of a plant. The following graph summarizes the results of five trials, in each of which one plant growth hormone was fed supplementally to the plants in the trial. The effects of the hormone in each trial were categorized according to five different categories of increased plant growth.

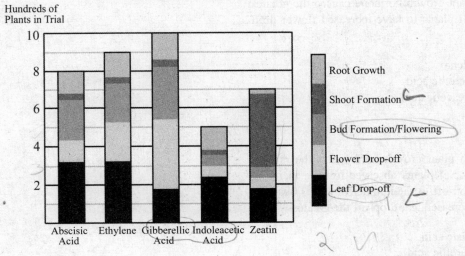

Plant Growth Trials
(by Plant Growth Hormone)

26. Approximately how many plants in the abscisic acid trial were observed to have increased leaf drop-off?

   F. 180
   G. 225
   H. 300
   J. 315

27. What was the total number of plants in the gibberellic acid trial?

   A. 700
   B. 950
   C. 1,000
   D. 3,300

28. Approximately how many plants in the ethylene trial were observed to have increased flower drop-off?

   F. 150
   G. 200
   H. 250
   J. 300

29. For which plant growth hormone was increased shoot formation observed for the greatest number of plants?

   A. Abscisic acid
   B. Ethylene
   C. Gibberellic acid
   D. Zeatin

30. Approximately what fraction of the plants involved in the ethylene trial were observed to have increased leaf drop-off?

   F. $\frac{1}{5}$

   G. $\frac{1}{4}$

   H. $\frac{1}{3}$

   J. $\frac{2}{3}$

31. In the indoleacetic acid trial, how many plants were observed to have increased flower drop-off?

    A. 6
    B. 60
    C. 300
    D. 370

32. Which plant growth hormone caused the greatest number of plants to have increased flower drop-off?

    F. Ethylene
    G. Gibberellic acid
    H. Indoleacetic acid
    J. Zeatin

33. For which plant growth hormone is the ratio of the number of plants observed to have increased flower drop-off to the number of plants observed to have increased leaf drop-off the greatest?

    A. Abscisic acid
    B. Gibberellic acid
    C. Indoleacetic acid
    D. Zeatin

34. For the zeatin trial, what is the approximate ratio of the number of plants observed to have increased shoot formation to the number of plants observed to have increased leaf drop-off?

    F. 3:1
    G. 2:1
    H. 3:2
    J. 6:5

35. Approximately how many more plants were observed to have increased bud formation/flowering in the gibberellic acid trial than in the indoleacetic acid trial?

    A. 420
    B. 350
    C. 300
    D. 220

Experimental Data Set 7

Amphibians (frogs, toads, and salamanders) occur in areas where fresh water breeding sites are susceptible to acidification (a reduction in pH to acidic levels) from man-made sources via acid rain, acid snowmelt, or other modes of pollution. Some species are more tolerant of acid conditions than others. Thus, depending on the species, the amount of acidity, and other environmental variables, amphibians may experience developmental deformities and increased mortality due to acidification. The following graph summarizes the results of an experiment studying the survival rate of two species of amphibian larvae (tadpoles) at varying pH levels:

Surviving Tadpole Populations

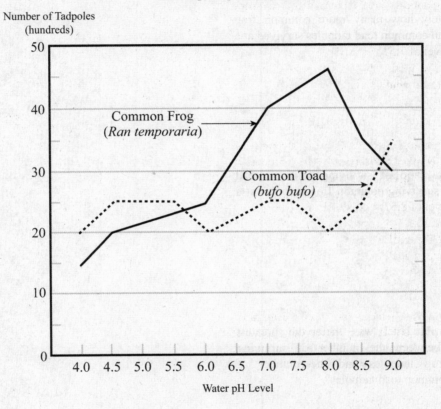

36. Approximately how many common frog tadpoles survived at a water pH level of 7.0?

    F.   25
    G.   40
    H. 2,500
    J. 4,000

37. Approximately how many common toad tadpoles survived at a water pH level of 4.0?

    A. 2,000
    B. 1,500
    C.   20
    D.   15

38. At a water pH level of 9.0, what was the total surviving tadpole population?

    F. 6,500
    G. 3,500
    H. 3,000
    J.   500

39. The smallest percent increase in the number of surviving common frog tadpoles occurred from:

    A. pH 4.0 to pH 4.5.
    B. pH 4.5 to pH 5.0.
    C. pH 6.0 to pH 6.5.
    D. pH 6.5 to pH 7.0.

40. For how many water pH levels shown did the number of surviving common toad tadpoles exceed the number of surviving common frog tadpoles?

    F. 3
    G. 4
    H. 5
    J. 6

41. Approximately how many more common frog tadpoles than common toad tadpoles survived at a water pH level of 7.5?

    A. 2,000
    B. 2,500
    C. 4,500
    D. 7,000

42. What is the ratio of surviving common toad tadpoles to surviving common frog tadpoles at a water pH level of 8.5?

    F. 1:2
    G. 5:7
    H. 7:5
    J. 14:5

43. At which pH level was there the greatest difference between the number of surviving common frog tadpoles and the number of surviving common toad tadpoles?

    A. 6.5
    B. 7.0
    C. 8.0
    D. 8.5

44. At which of the following pH levels was the number of surviving common toad tadpoles most nearly equal to the number of surviving common frog tadpoles?

    F. 4.0
    G. 5.5
    H. 6.0
    J. 8.0

45. What is the difference in pH between the optimum water pH level for common frog tadpole development and that for common toad tadpole development?

    A. 0.0
    B. 0.5
    C. 1.0
    D. 2.0

Experimental Data Set 8

The ionization energy of an atom is the minimum energy required to remove an electron from the ground state of the isolated gaseous atom. The first ionization energy, I_1, is the energy needed to remove the first electron from the atom, the second ionization energy, I_2, is the energy needed to remove the next (i.e., the second) electron from the atom, and so on. The higher the value of the ionization energy, the more difficult it is to remove the electron. The following table summarizes the first five ionization energies for five consecutive elements in the periodic table:

Ionization Energies by Element							
			Ionization Energy (kJ/mol)				
Number	Symbol	Name	I_1	I_2	I_3	I_4	I_5
11	Na	Sodium	496	4,562	6,910	9,543	13,354
12	Mg	Magnesium	738	1,451	7,733	10,543	13,630
13	Al	Aluminum	578	1,817	2,749	11,577	14,842
14	Si	Silicon	787	1,577	3,232	4,356	16,091
15	P	Phosphorus	1,012	1,907	2,914	4,964	6,274

46. According to the table, approximately what is the total ionization energy required for removing the first five electrons of a phosphorus atom?

F. 1,000 kJ/mol
G. 4,000 kJ/mol
H. 17,000 kJ/mol
J. 26,000 kJ/mol

47. The first ionization energy is most nearly equal for which two elements?

A. Sodium and magnesium
B. Magnesium and silicon
C. Sodium and aluminum
D. Aluminum and silicon

48. For sodium, the first ionization energy is approximately what percent of the second ionization energy?

F. 5%
G. 11%
H. 33%
J. 50%

49. The first ionization energy of phosphorus is approximately what fraction of the total ionization energy required for removing the first three electrons of a phosphorus atom?

A. $\frac{1}{6}$

B. $\frac{1}{4}$

C. $\frac{1}{3}$

D. $\frac{1}{2}$

50. In the table above, which element has smallest difference between the first and fifth ionization energies?

F. Sodium
G. Magnesium
H. Silicon
J. Phosphorus

Experimental Data Set 9

Greenhouse gas emissions come primarily from energy-related carbon dioxide emissions, resulting from the combustion of fossil fuels in energy use. Additional carbon dioxide emissions result from deforestation and decay of biomass. Another greenhouse gas, methane, comes from landfills, coal mines, oil and natural gas operations, and agriculture. Nitrous oxide is emitted through the use of nitrogen fertilizers and from industrial and waste management processes. Several human-made gases—hydrofluorocarbons (HFCs), perfluorocarbons (PFCs), and sulfur hexafluoride (SF$_6$)—are released as byproducts of industrial processes and through leakage.

Anthropogenic Greenhouse Gas Emissions, 2004

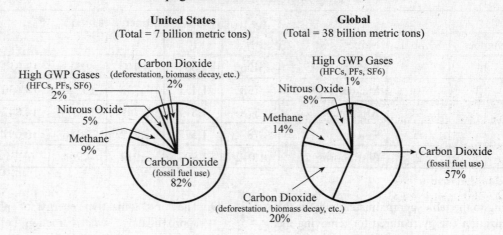

51. In terms of percent, emissions from methane gas in the United States was most nearly equal to emissions from which greenhouse gas globally?

    A. Methane
    B. Nitrous oxide
    C. Carbon dioxide (fossil fuel use)
    D. High GWP gases

52. How many metric tons of the greenhouse gases in the United States came from non-energy-related carbon dioxide emissions?

    F. 1.4 million
    G. 14 million
    H. 140 million
    J. 1.4 billion

53. The percentage of total global greenhouse gas emissions from energy-related carbon dioxide produced in the United States was approximately:

    A. 2%.
    B. 15%.
    C. 47%.
    D. 82%.

54. Total global greenhouse gas emissions from sources other than carbon dioxide weighed approximately:

    F. 1 billion metric tons.
    G. 10 billion metric tons.
    H. 20 billion metric tons.
    J. 40 billion metric tons.

55. What was the approximate fraction of global greenhouse gas emissions from non-energy-related carbon dioxide emissions?

A. $\dfrac{4}{5}$

B. $\dfrac{3}{5}$

C. $\dfrac{1}{4}$

D. $\dfrac{1}{5}$

56. What was the difference between nitrous oxide emissions in the United States and globally?

F. 0.35 billion metric tons
G. 1.25 billion metric tons
H. 2.69 billion metric tons
J. 3.04 billion metric tons

Experimental Data Set 10

Cell respiration refers to the process of converting the chemical energy of organic molecules into a form immediately usable by organisms. Peas undergo cell respiration during germination. Glucose may be oxidized completely if sufficient ozygen is availabe according to the following equation:

$$C_6H_{12}O_6 + 6\ O_2(g) \rightarrow 6\ H_2O + 6\ CO_2(g) + energy$$

The following graph summarizes the results of an expermient conducted to monitor the carbon dioxide produced by cell respiration of peas during germination at two different temperatures:

Carbon Dioxide Production by Germinating Peas

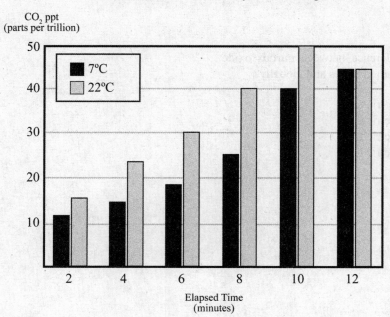

57. The ratio of CO_2 produced by germinating peas at 22°C to that produced by germinating peas at 7°C was greatest after how much elapsed time?

    A. 2 minutes
    B. 6 minutes
    C. 8 minutes
    D. 10 minutes

58. Total CO_2 produced by germinating peas at 7°C at 2 minutes, 4 minutes, and 6 minutes was approximately:

    F. 30 ppt.
    G. 36 ppt.
    H. 45 ppt.
    J. 52 ppt.

59. The average (arithmetic mean) of CO_2 produced by the germinating peas at 22°C for the six time periods shown was most nearly:

    A. 40 ppt.
    B. 34 ppt.
    C. 24 ppt.
    D. 20 ppt.

60. For how many of the elapsed time periods shown did CO_2 produced by germinating peas at 22°C exceed that produced by germinating peas at 7°C by more than 10 ppt?

F. 3
G. 2
H. 1
J. 0

61. Which of the following statements can be inferred from the graph?

I. After an elapsed time of 12 minutes, CO_2 produced by germinating peas at 7°C accounted for 100% of CO_2 produced by germinating peas at 7°C and 22°C combined.

II. After an elapsed time of 10 minutes, CO_2 produced by germinating peas at 7°C was less than 75% of CO_2 produced by germinating peas at 22°C.

III. After an elapsed time of 4 minutes, CO_2 produced by germinating peas at 22°C was 160% of CO_2 produced by germinating peas at 7°C.

A. I only
B. III only
C. I and III only
D. II and III only

Experimental Data Set 11

Insects are the most numerous group of animals on the planet, making up about 80% of all animals. In fact, there are more species of insects than all other species of living things. They play essential roles in the balance of nature as predators, food for other animals, and scavengers. The following graph summarizes the results of a backyard inventory of five general insect populations in five different locations, each measuring one square meter:

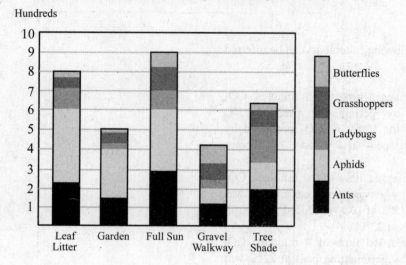

Backyard Inventory of Insect Populations (by Location)

62. What was the approximate number of ladybugs in the tree shade location?

    F. 510
    G. 360
    H. 210
    J. 150

63. In the full sun location, what was the total number of insects that were not ants?

    A. 510
    B. 610
    C. 770
    D. 1,190

64. The number of ants in the garden location was most nearly equal to the number of:

    F. ants in the full sun location.
    G. aphids in the gravel walkway location.
    H. ladybugs in the tree shade location.
    J. grasshoppers in the leaf litter location.

65. What was the approximate total number of grasshoppers in the five backyard locations combined?

    A. 360
    B. 460
    C. 520
    D. 600

66. Which of the following statements can be inferred from the graph?

    I.   In the five locations combined, the total number of aphids was greater than the total number of ladybugs.
    II. The number of butterflies in the gravel walkway location was less than the number of butterflies in the tree shade location.
    III. The largest number of aphids in the backyard was found in the leaf litter location.

    F. I only
    G. III only
    H. I and II only
    J. I and III only

Experimental Data Set 12

Harmful algal blooms caused by the rapid growth of algae, such as blue-green algae (cyanobacteria), can present problems for ecosystems and be extremely toxic to animals and humans. Daily water samples taken from a lake with algal bloom were analyzed for potentially toxin-producing cyanobacteria. The following graph presents the results:

Densities of Potentially Toxigenic Cyanobacteria in Water Samples

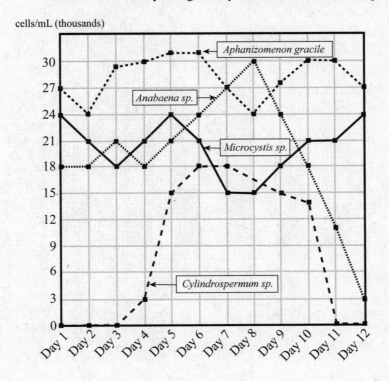

67. Water samples from which day had the greatest density of *Microcystis sp.*?

    A. Day 3
    B. Day 5
    C. Day 6
    D. Day 8

68. What was the total density of cyanobacteria in the water samples taken on Day 4?

    F. 75,000
    G. 72,000
    H. 58,000
    J. 30,000

69. For how many days was the density of *Microcystis sp.* greater than that of *Anabaena sp.*?

    A. 3
    B. 5
    C. 7
    D. 9

70. The difference between the densities of *Aphanizomenon gracile* and *Microcystis sp.* was greatest in the water samples taken on which day?

    F. Day 3
    G. Day 4
    H. Day 6
    J. Day 7

71. The greatest day-to-day percentage increase in the density of *Anabaena sp.* occurred from:

   A. Day 4 to Day 5.
   B. Day 5 to Day 6.
   C. Day 6 to Day 7.
   D. Day 8 to Day 9.

Experimental Data Set 13

A solar panel is essentially a battery charger that transforms sunlight into an electrical DC charge. This energy is then stored in a battery to be used at a later time. The following graph depicts the energy stored in two batteries by month of production from identical solar panels in two different locations:

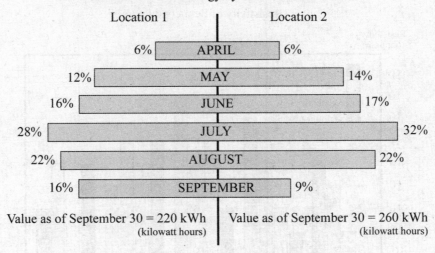

Stored Solar Panel Energy by Month of Production

72. For Location 1, the energy stored as of September 30 that was produced in June was most nearly:

    F. 15%.
    G. 16%.
    H. 17%.
    J. 34%.

73. During which of the following months and locations was the stored solar panel energy the greatest?

    A. May, Location 2
    B. June, Location 1
    C. June, Location 2
    D. August, Location 1

74. If the solar panel in Location 2 produced 50 kWh in June, how much of that energy was no longer stored in the battery on September 30?

    F. 5.8 kWh
    G. 11 kWh
    H. 16.5 kWh
    J. Cannot be determined from the given information

75. On May 31, how much energy was being stored by the battery for the solar panel in Location 2?

    A. 52 kWh
    B. 45 kWh
    C. 36 kWh
    D. Cannot be determined from the given information

76. Which of the following statements can be inferred from the graph?

    I. In December, the solar panel in Location 1 had less energy output than the solar panel in Location 2.
    II. The total energy stored by the battery for the solar panel in Location 2 for the period May through August was 221 kWh.
    III. In August, the battery for the solar panel in Location 2 stored 88 kWh more energy than the battery for the solar panel in Location 1.

    F. I only
    G. III only
    H. II and III only
    J. Neither I, II, nor III

Experimental Data Set 14

The resistivity of a semiconductor is defined as the resistance per unit area and unit length, expressed in ohm-cm, and is by definition the reciprocal of conductivity. In this experiment, the resistivity of the surface of four different semiconductor wafers was measured using a four-point resistivity probe at five different temperatures to determine how the resistivities vary over a range of temperatures. The data is summarized on the following logarithmic graph.

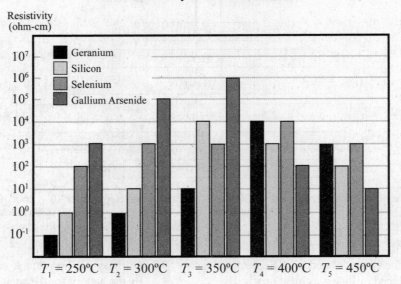

Resistivity of Semiconductors

77. At which temperature is the resistivity of geranium the highest?

    A. 300°C
    B. 350°C
    C. 400°C
    D. 450°C

78. What is the resistivity (in ohm-cm) of gallium arsenide at 300°C?

    F. 10^0
    G. 10^1
    H. 10^3
    J. 10^5

79. What is the ratio of the resistivity of selenium at 250°C to the resistivity at 350°C?

    A.   1:10
    B.   1:100
    C.   10:1
    D. 1,000:1

80. What is the difference in resistivity (in ohm-cm) of geranium and silicon at 350°C?

    F. 1,000
    G. 9,900
    H. 9,990
    J. 10,000

81. What is the average resistivity (in ohm-cm) of selenium for the five temperatures shown?

    A. 1,000
    B. 2,620
    C. 10,000
    D. 26,200

82. What is the net change of resistivity in gallium arsenide between 400°C and 450°C?

    F. An increase of 90%
    G. An increase of 10%
    H. A decrease of 10%
    J. A decrease of 90%

Presentation of Conflicting Viewpoints

In laboratory experiments, scientists study the characteristics of matter or energy and attempt to find factors that will affect these characteristics. In typical experiments, scientists get to manipulate or change the independent variable. The independent variable, sometimes called the "causal variable," is assumed to cause any resulting change in the dependent variable.

Many problems (dependent variables) studied by scientists cannot be studied in the lab. An example might be the cause of cancer in humans. Scientists cannot put humans in a lab and treat them with substances that cause cancer. Instead, they must look at groups of individuals who get cancer and groups that do not get cancer, and determine the "secret" independent variable that caused the problem from the collected data. "Cause" is a strong word in science, and it generally leads to arguments among scientists. Differences in opinions lead us to *conflicting viewpoints*.

Conflicting Viewpoints passages can always be recognized because they are labeled with names such as Scientist I and Scientist II. The scientists may be labeled with more specificity, for example, a chemistry passage may have Chemist I arguing with Chemist II about a chemistry problem; however, the argument is usually over the independent variable.

Example:

> Ask yourself the question, "Do cigarettes cause cancer?" Scientists from tobacco companies and doctors are certainly in disagreement over this issue. There is a warning on cigarette packaging; however, it does not say that cigarettes cause cancer. You may know many people who smoke who are cancer-free. Likewise, there are individuals that get lung cancer who never smoke.

Your job in reading these passages is to identify the problem (dependent variable) and determine the conflict of opinion over the cause (independent variable). Each scientist will provide you with data; some data will support only their respective position, and some data will support multiple positions. Some data may attempt to discredit the data of the other scientist. You need to sort out these matters.

Presentation of Conflicting Viewpoints

DIRECTIONS: Read the descriptions of the following conflicting viewpoints and answer the accompanying items. Answers are on page 803.

Two detectives are called to the scene of a crime at about 5:00 a.m. The neighbors called the police when they heard a noise at 4:30 a.m.; however, they thought it was a firecracker rather than a gun. The victim is a 25-year-old female with a gunshot wound to the head. There is a large bruise on the back of her head. The door to the apartment was locked and there is no sign of forced entry. Nothing appears to have been taken. There is a gun lying on the floor near the left hand of the woman. A check of the serial number found that the woman had recently purchased the weapon. There was a blood-soaked pillow just above the woman's head. The police could not find a suicide note. There did not appear to be any other physical evidence at the scene. Neighbors that were interviewed said that the woman had recently been divorced and that she had been noticeably upset by the divorce.

Detective I

Detective I believes that the death was a homicide and asks that the ex-husband be picked up for questioning.

Detective II

Detective II believes that the death was a suicide and asks that the ex-husband be notified.

1. The dependent variable (the problem) is: _____

_____

2. The conflicting viewpoint is: _____

_____

3. The independent variable causing the conflict is:

_____

4. Fill in the following table:

Data	More Consistent with Detective 1	More Consistent with Detective 2	Equally Consistent with Both Detectives 1 and 2
Gun Owned by Woman			
Bloody Pillow			
Bruise on Head			
Firecracker-like Noise			
No Forced Entry			
Locked Door			
No Suicide Note			
Divorced Victim			
Despondent Victim			

Science Passages

DIRECTIONS: Each passage is followed by several items. After reading a passage, choose the best answer to each item. You may refer to the passages as often as necessary. Answers are on page 803.

Passage I

Germination is the beginning of the growth of a seed after a period of inactivity. The following experiments were designed to compare the amount of time it takes for seeds of different vegetables to germinate.

Experiment 1

Radish seeds, soaked in water for 24 hours, were germinated at 25°C for 10 days. The results are shown in Graph 1.

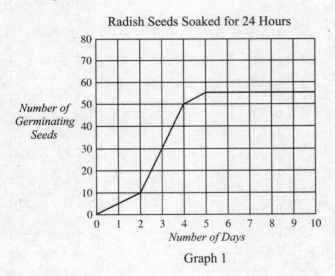

Radish Seeds Soaked for 24 Hours

Graph 1

Experiment 2

Bean seeds, soaked in water for 24 hours, were germinated at 25°C for 10 days. The results are shown in Graph 2.

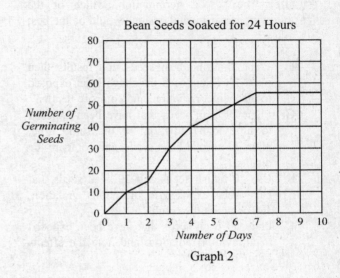

Bean Seeds Soaked for 24 Hours

Graph 2

1. Graphs 1 and 2 show that after 3 days:

   A. more radish seeds have germinated.
   B. more bean seeds have germinated.
   C. equal numbers of radish seeds and bean seeds have germinated.
   D. no radish seeds or bean seeds have germinated.

2. A generalization that can be made about the data is that:

   F. 24 hours is the best soaking period for both radish seeds and bean seeds.
   G. radish seeds germinate more rapidly than bean seeds.
   H. the bean seeds had a steady rate of germination.
   J. most bean seeds of this kind require 7 days to germinate.

3. Which factor is the independent variable in this experiment?

   A. The period of the soaking
   B. The dishes in which the seeds were planted
   C. The rate of germination
   D. The kind of seeds used

4. To test the hypothesis that ultraviolet radiation affects bean seed germination, which of the following experimental designs would be the best to use?

   F. Plant 20 normal bean seeds, note results; then plant 20 bean seeds that have been exposed to ultraviolet radiation, and compare results.
   G. Plant 20 bean seeds that have been exposed to ultraviolet radiation; at the same time, plant 20 normal bean seeds, and compare the results.
   H. Use 20 radish seeds and 20 bean seeds that have been exposed to ultraviolet violation, and compare the results.
   J. Plant 50 bean seeds that have been exposed to ultraviolet radiation, and note the effects of the radiation.

Passage II

A scientist wanted to determine the effects of different doses of an experimental drug called PCH. This drug was believed to help control weight gain. To test this hypothesis, four experimental groups, each with 100 rats, were given a daily dose with only sugar or a daily dose with sugar and a different amount of the drug. The rats were all fed the same kind and amount of food. After one year, the percentage of rats gaining weight was determined. The results of this experiment are presented in Table 1.

Table 1		
Group	Contents of Dose	% of Rats Gaining Weight
1	5 grams of sugar	19%
2	5 grams of sugar 1 gram of PCH	21%
3	5 grams of sugar 5 grams of PCH	19%
4	5 grams of sugar 10 grams of PCH	20%

5. Which was the control group in this experiment?

A. 1
B. 2
C. 3
D. 4

6. As the dose of PCH increases, the percentage of rats gaining weight:

F. increases.
G. decreases.
H. remains constant.
J. varies.

7. In order to interpret the results of this experiment, it would be most useful to know the:

A. characteristics of the rats in each group.
B. chemical composition of PCH.
C. kind of sugar used in the doses.
D. kind of food fed to the rats.

8. From the data showing the percentage of rats gaining weight, it could be concluded that:

F. PCH was effective in helping control the weight gain of the rats.
G. sugar was required for the PCH to be effective.
H. sugar alone was responsible for the weight gain of the rats.
J. PCH had no significant effect in helping control the weight gain of the rats.

Passage III

Atoms are considered the basic building blocks of matter. The atom consists of a positively charged center, or nucleus, surrounded by negatively charged electrons. The major kinds of particles in the nucleus are positively charged protons and neutrally charged neutrons. The number of protons, called the atomic number, identifies the element. The mass number of the atom represents the total number of protons and neutrons. Not all of the atoms of an element are identical. The different atoms of an element are called isotopes. The three carbon-isotopes are shown in Table 1.

Table 1				
Name	Protons	Neutrons	Electrons	Mass Number
Carbon-12	6	6	6	12
Carbon-13	6	7	6	13
Carbon-14	6	8	6	14

9. The atomic number of the element carbon is:

A. 6.
B. 7.
C. 12.
D. 34.

10. The three carbon-isotopes all have:

F. the same number of neutrons.
G. the same mass number.
H. an equal number of protons and electrons.
J. an equal number of neutrons and protons.

11. Carbon-13 has:

A. 6 protons and 7 electrons.
B. 7 protons and 6 electrons.
C. 6 protons and 7 neutrons.
D. 13 protons.

12. If the isotope of an element contains 8 protons, 9 neutrons, and 8 electrons, the atomic number and mass number would be, respectively:

F. 8 and 17.
G. 9 and 17.
H. 8 and 26.
J. 9 and 26.

Passage IV

Sodium chloride (table salt) is a crystal made up of rows of sodium (Na) ions and chloride (Cl) ions. Ions are atoms that are electrically charged. When sodium chloride is dissolved in water, it separates into its ions. The sodium ions and chloride ions are released from their positions in the crystal pattern and they move about freely. Other crystalline substances, such as sugar, do not produce ions when dissolved in water. When substances react with water to form ions, they are said to be ionized. The charged ions in the water are responsible for the conduction of electricity. Substances that conduct an electrical current when dissolved are called electrolytes. Substances that do not conduct an electric current are called non-electrolytes.

To study the electrical conductivity, an apparatus that measures the ability of substances to conduct electricity was used.

Experiment 1

Solid sodium chloride was tested and found to be a non-conductor. Pure water was also tested and found to be a non-conductor. When a teaspoon of sodium chloride was added to water, the solution was found to be a good conductor of electricity. Sugar did not conduct electricity as a solid or when dissolved in water.

Experiment 2

When a few crystals of sodium chloride were added to water, the solution showed a weak conduction of electricity. As additional sodium chloride was added, the ability of the solution to conduct electricity increased.

13. Experiment 1 indicates that sodium chloride conducts electricity when it:

  A. dissolves in alcohol.
  B. is tested as a solid.
  C. dissolves in water.
  D. is combined with sugar.

14. Which of the following graphs represents the relationship between the amount of sodium chloride dissolved in water and its conductivity?

F.
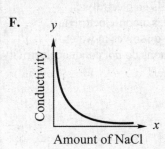

G.
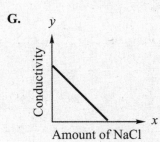

H.
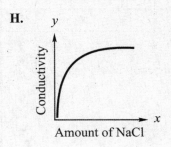

J.
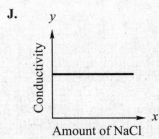

15. In order for a substance to be a conductor of electricity, the substance must have:

  A. rapidly moving molecules.
  B. charged particles that are free to move.
  C. ions in a crystalline form.
  D. been dissolved in a solvent.

16. Which of the following is NOT a characteristic of sugar?

    F.   Solid sugar is an electrolyte.
    G. Solid sugar is a non-electrolyte.
    H. Solid sugar dissolves in water.
    J.   Sugar solutions do not conduct electricity.

Passage V

In the United States, there are millions of cases of food poisoning reported each year. Food poisoning is due to deadly bacteria, such as Salmonella. Since the mid-1980s, the United States Food and Drug Administration has approved irradiation of a variety of foods. Food is irradiated to destroy the harmful bacteria. During irradiation, gamma rays passing through food break chemical bonds among atoms and destroy the genetic material of the bacteria, which prevents them from reproducing. Although the irradiation of food is becoming more widespread, the practice continues to be a controversial topic. The idea of an irradiated food supply is supported by some people and opposed by others.

Viewpoint 1

Proper preparation of food kills harmful bacteria in or on food. This means that irradiation is not necessary. According to some scientists, there is evidence that irradiation lessens the nutritional value of food by causing the loss of vitamins. Foods exposed to gamma rays have lost such vitamins as A, C, and E. One study found that animals that were fed irradiated food lost weight. Pregnant animals often miscarry, most likely due to reduced amounts of vitamin E in the irradiated food. Some chemicals in the food may be changed, resulting in the production of toxic by-products. While these unidentified toxic substances occur in small amounts, no one is certain what effect they will have as they accumulate in the body over a lifetime of consuming irradiated food.

Viewpoint 2

Food irradiation has significant value in destroying the bacteria that infect the food. Irradiated food has a much longer shelf life than traditionally treated food. Irradiation destroys nutrients but no more than is normally destroyed by cooking food. Food irradiated with 10,000 rads or less of gamma rays show little or no nutrient loss. According to the FDA, food exposed to greater than 10,000 rads exhibits nutrient loss that is generally no more than the loss that occurs in frozen and canned food. FDA scientists also admit that some by-products of the alteration of chemicals in the food are cancer-causing agents. However, they occurred in very small amounts in irradiated food. Most of these by-products turned out to be identical to naturally occurring food substances.

17. One of the principal differences between the viewpoints concerns:

   A. loss of nutritional value of food caused by irradiation.
   B. the effectiveness of food irradiation in destroying harmful bacteria.
   C. the accumulation of by-products of food irradiation in the body.
   D. the effect of gamma rays on the breakdown of vitamin A.

18. According to Viewpoint 1:

   F. the by-products of food irradiation are cancer-causing.
   G. the irradiation of food increases the nutritional value of food.
   H. the by-products of food irradiation are identical to naturally occurring food substances.
   J. the irradiation of food lessens the nutritional value of food.

19. These viewpoints are similar because they both suggest that food irradiation:

   A. is necessary to destroy harmful bacteria in food.
   B. is not necessary to destroy harmful bacteria in food.
   C. can lessen the nutritional value of food.
   D. can improve the nutritional value of food.

20. Which experimental information would NOT support Viewpoint 1?

   F. Food exposed to gamma rays loses much of vitamins A, C, and E.
   G. Food exposed to gamma rays does not lose much of vitamins A, C, and E.
   H. Toxic by-products of food alteration by gamma rays are accumulated in the body over a period of time.
   J. Irradiated food has a shelf life twice that of non-irradiated food.

Passage VI

Nuclear reactors release great amounts of nuclear energy through controlled chain reactions. For this reason, nuclear power has been considered a source of abundant energy. Nuclear power, however, poses several problems. The most serious problem is the radioactive waste produced by the use of nuclear energy. The waste is very dangerous and remains so for thousands of years. How and where to dispose of this waste safely is a dilemma that has not been resolved. In 1987, the U.S. Congress authorized the Department of Energy to study Yucca Mountain in the southern desert of Utah as a place to bury the highly radioactive nuclear fuel rods from nuclear power plants.

Geologist 1

The most feasible and safe method for disposing of highly radioactive material is to store it underground. Yucca Mountain was chosen because it is believed that the mountain rock could keep the radioactive waste isolated for thousands of years. This proposed site is located underneath a thick layer of volcanic ash. It is above the ground water of aquifers in order to reduce the danger of seepage. The area is very remote and almost uninhabited. It is located in an area with low rainfall, thus less water enters the ground. It is also an area where the ground is mostly composed of volcanic tuff that slows down the filtration of water into the ground. The volcanic activity near Yucca Mountain is mild, with minimal chance for a large eruption. The chance of a severe earthquake is also remote.

Geologist 2

Burial of radioactive waste is the best disposal method. Yucca Mountain, however, is not the best site because it is hydrologically and geologically active. Burial at this site poses the risk of radioactive materials leaking out and contaminating surrounding soil and ground water. If a leak did occur, ground water contamination would be a major problem. Many of the surrounding cities, including parts of Las Vegas, receive some of their water from the aquifers in the area. The area around Yucca Mountain has numerous faults and even a small volcano nearby. Any significant geological activity could disturb waste containers. If earthquakes or volcanic eruptions occurred, the radioactive material at the site could be carried to the surface, threatening the entire region.

21. According to Geologist 1:

    A. radioactive waste should not be buried underground.
    B. the geologic structure of Yucca Mountain would minimize geological activity.
    C. earthquake or volcanic activity is likely to occur near Yucca Mountain.
    D. the radioactive waste should be buried somewhere other than Yucca Mountain.

22. Both geologists agree that:

    F. the radioactive waste should be buried somewhere other than Yucca Mountain.
    G. hydrological and geological activity near Yucca Mountain is minimal.
    H. the best way to store radioactive waste is to bury it underground.
    J. the radioactive waste is likely to leak into ground water.

23. Which of the following would provide the strongest evidence for the position of Geologist 2?

    A. The site is both geologically stable and safe from the entry of water.
    B. Construction at the site has been found to be destructive to animal habitats.
    C. The rock formations of Yucca Mountain will keep the waste sufficiently isolated for thousands of years.
    D. There is a periodic upwelling of ground water at Yucca Mountain.

24. Which of the following would provide the strongest evidence for the position of Geologist 1?

    F. The rock formations of Yucca Mountain were formed by rainwater seeping downward, not by groundwater seeping upward.
    G. There is a large aquifer underneath Yucca Mountain.
    H. The Yucca Mountain site is affected by 32 known earthquake faults.
    J. Rainwater containing nuclear chemicals has reached the site level.

Writing Skills Review

COURSE CONCEPT OUTLINE

What You Absolutely Must Know

Planning an Essay

Understand the Assignment

Let the Prompt Be Your Topic

When presented with a prompt, always read it several times until you are completely familiar with the material. Sometimes it may be helpful to underline key words or phrases that are important.

Usually, the prompt is intended to be your topic and an inspiration to writing. If you pay careful attention to the language of the prompt, it can actually help you to get started.

Consider this sample essay prompt:

> Human beings are often cruel, but they also have the capacity for kindness and compassion. In my opinion, an example that demonstrates this capacity is ———.
>
> Complete the statement above with an example from current affairs, history, literature, or your own personal experience. Then write a well-organized essay explaining why you regard that event favorably.

This topic explicitly invites you to choose an example of kindness or compassion from history, current events, literature, or even personal experience. Thus, you could write about the end of a war (history), a mission of humanitarian aid (current events), the self-sacrifice of a fictional character (literature), or even about the day that your family helped a stranded motorist (personal experience). Remember that what you have to say is not as important as how you say it.

Develop a Point of View

Sometimes an essay prompt will invite you to present your opinion on an issue. When you encounter such prompts, you must decide whether you are in agreement or disagreement with the statement given.

Write Only on the Assigned Topic

While the types of prompts may differ among assignments or tests, the directions all agree on this point: You must write on the assigned topic. The assigned topic is often "open-ended," so you should have no problem coming up with something to write.

Organize Your Thoughts

Limit the Scope of Your Essay

The requirements of the writing assignment should determine the length and scope of your essay. Always remember to define the scope of an essay before beginning to write. This will improve your focus, and your essay will be more likely to accomplish only the assigned task, whether it is to defend a controversial position or to provide a definition. The more limited and specific your topic, the more successful your essay is likely to be since you will be better able to supply the specific details necessary to give depth and sophistication to your essay. You will also reduce the possibility of either straying onto tangential topics or under-developing a specific claim.

Develop a Thesis

A thesis statement provides the scope, purpose, and direction of an essay in one clear and focused statement. A thesis statement usually includes your claims or assertions and the reasoning and evidence you will use to support them. If possible, try to formulate the thesis of your composition in a single sentence during the pre-writing stage. When developing a thesis, keep in mind the following ideas:

IMPORTANT POINTS FOR DEVELOPING A THESIS

1. The thesis must not be too broad or too narrow.

2. The thesis must be clear to both you and the essay reader.

3. Everything in the essay must support your thesis.

4. Use specific details and examples rather than generalizations to support your thesis.

Identify Key Points

Identify the two or three (perhaps four) important points that you want to make. Then, decide on the order of presentation for those points.

Write an Outline

Once you gain a clear understanding of the assignment and its requirements, it is then important to organize the major points of your essay in a written outline. The purpose of an outline is to develop a logical structure to your arguments and to streamline your essay. An outline should include your thesis statement, the key points of your argument, and the concluding statement of your essay. A sample outline structure is presented below for your reference.

SAMPLE OUTLINE

I. Introduction: Thesis Statement

II. First Key Point
   A. Sub-Point 1
   B. Sub-Point 2

III. Second Key Point
   A. Sub-Point 1
   B. Sub-Point 2

IV. Third Key Point
   A. Sub-Point 1
   B. Sub-Point 2

V. Conclusion: Restatement of Thesis

Composition

Organize Ideas into Paragraphs

A good writer uses paragraphs effectively. Paragraphs are important because they provide the structure through which a writer conveys meaning. To illustrate this point with an analogy, imagine a grocery store in which items are not organized into sections. In this store, there is no fresh produce section, no canned goods section, no baked goods section, and no frozen foods section. Consequently, a single bin holds bunches of bananas, cans of beans, loaves of bread, and frozen turkeys. This lack of organization would make shopping very difficult. Likewise, essays without paragraphs (or with poorly organized paragraphs) are very difficult—if not impossible—to understand.

First, you will need to decide how many paragraphs you will write. Your essay should contain two to four important points that develop or illustrate your thesis. Each important point should be treated as its own paragraph.

Do not write simply to fill up space and make it seem like you have many ideas. This approach can result in repetition and wordiness, which is a sign of disorganization and unclear thinking. Write enough to demonstrate your writing ability and to prove your thesis. Five paragraphs (an introduction paragraph, three main body paragraphs, and a concluding paragraph) are usually sufficient.

Write the Essay

Many students become frustrated before they even begin to write. They sit and stare at the blank page and complain that they are "blocked." In other words, they can't think of anything to write. The secret to successfully beginning an essay is simple. After you have completed the pre-writing stage, just start writing. You may need to go back and revise some of your work, but this is the easiest way to avoid "writer's block." As you write your essay, follow this simple essay structure:

BASIC ESSAY STRUCTURE

I. Introduction: State the thesis of your essay.
   A. State your position clearly.
   B. State the elements that you will be using to support your position.

II. Body: Each paragraph in the body of your essay will be devoted to one of the supporting elements that are introduced in the introduction. Elaborate on the elements by using examples.

III. Conclusion: Summarize your position and the reasons for your position.

The Introduction

During the pre-writing stage, you analyzed the topic. Now, use the introduction (the first paragraph) to write clear and concise sentences that describe the topic, your point of view on it, and what you plan to say to back up your position. In general, an introduction should let the reader know what direction your essay will take. However, don't spend too much time on an introduction. The remainder of the essay will be where you'll explain your ideas and give your examples in more detail.

When writing your introduction, keep these points in mind:

WRITING AN INTRODUCTION

1. Focus on the essay topic presented in the prompt and clearly state your point of view on this topic.

2. Use a tone that is sincere, straight-forward, and clear. DO NOT be cute or funny, ironic or satiric, overly emotional or too dramatic.

3. DO NOT repeat the writing prompt word-for-word. Instead, paraphrase the prompt in your own words and then clearly state your point of view.

4. After stating your point of view, briefly state the evidence or arguments you will use to support your point of view.

Finally, an effective introduction often accomplishes one of the following tasks as well: it explains why readers should care about the topic at hand; or, it grabs the reader's attention by describing briefly an incident in real life that is related to the topic.

The Body

The heart of the essay is the development which takes place in the body paragraph(s). Here, the writer must attempt, in paragraph form, to support the main idea of the essay through illustrations, details, and examples. These body or developmental paragraphs must serve as a link in the chain of ideas and contribute directly to the essay's main idea or position.

Each paragraph should start with a transitional statement or phrase that describes the relationship of the paragraph to the previous paragraphs. The length of any one of these body paragraphs can vary, but each paragraph should only cover one main idea. You may do this through a style that is descriptive, narrative, or expository. You may take a factual or an anecdotal approach. Whatever approach you choose and whatever style you adopt, though, your writing must be coherent, logical, unified, and well-ordered.

When writing your essay, avoid the following common mistakes:

AVOID THESE COMPOSITION ERRORS

1. DO NOT use sentences that include irrelevant material. In each body paragraph, only include sentences that relate specifically to the argument being made in that paragraph.

2. DO NOT use sentences that disrupt logical development. In each body paragraph, make sure each sentence logically follows from the sentence that comes before it.

Transitions

A good writer uses transitional words or phrases to connect thoughts, to provide for a logical sequence of ideas, and to link paragraphs. The following list includes some transitions and the logical relationships they indicate:

TRANSITIONAL WORDS AND PHRASES

Addition
again
also
and
besides
both…and
finally
first, second, third
furthermore
in addition
likewise
moreover
not only…but (also)
similarly

Alternation
either…or
neither…nor
nor
or
so that

Cause/Effect/Purpose
accordingly
as
as a consequence
as a result
because
consequently
for
for this purpose
hence
since
therefore
so

Conditions
as if (as though)
if
once…then
unless

Contrast
all the same
although
but
even though
however
instead
nevertheless
on the contrary
on the other hand
otherwise
still
though
yet

Space
here
in the middle
nearby
next to
opposite to
there
to the left/right
where
wherever

Support
for example
for instance
in fact
in general
such as

Summary
as shown above
in other words
in brief
in conclusion
in general
in short
in summary
to sum up

Time
after (clause)
after (noun)
as soon as
at the present time
before (clause)
before (noun)
during
eventually
finally
in (month, year)
later
meanwhile
since (clause)
then
until (clause)
when
whenever
while (clause)

The Conclusion

A successful writer knows when and how to end an essay. To conclude your essay effectively, you should have a strong and clear concluding paragraph. This concluding paragraph should make a reader feel that your essay has made its point, that a thesis has been explained, and that your point of view has been supported by specific examples, ideas, or arguments. A concluding paragraph can be as short as three to six sentences. The following are some guidelines for writing a successful concluding paragraph:

EFFECTIVE METHODS FOR CONCLUDING AN ESSAY

1. Restate your point of view on the essay topic.

2. Summarize the main arguments and evidence you used to support your point of view.

3. If time permits, conclude with a brief statement as to why your point of view is more defensible than a different point of view on the essay topic. What are the positive consequences of holding your point of view? What are the negative consequences of holding the opposite point of view?

The following is a quick overview of ineffective methods for writing a conclusion:

INEFFECTIVE METHODS FOR WRITING A CONCLUSION

1. DO NOT apologize for being unable to present all possible arguments in a limited amount of time.

2. DO NOT complain that the topic was uninteresting. DO NOT complain that the topic was too broad.

3. DO NOT introduce new material that you won't have time to develop. DO NOT introduce irrelevant material.

Principles of Good Writing

While writing, keep the three principles of good writing in mind: write grammatically, punctuate and spell correctly, and write concisely and clearly. If you follow these conventions, you will communicate your ideas clearly and effectively.

Write Grammatically

When writing an essay, the following principles of good grammar should be observed:

CORRECT GRAMMAR AND EFFECTIVE ESSAYS

1. Each sentence must have a conjugated (main) verb that agrees with its subject.

2. Each pronoun must have a referent (antecedent) with which it agrees.

3. Similar elements in a sentence must appear in parallel form.

4. Modifiers must agree with what they modify. They must also make sense.

5. Each sentence should use clear and concise language.

Punctuate and Spell Correctly

In addition to writing grammatically, concisely, and formally (without using slang or other low-level usage language), you must punctuate and spell correctly. Since you are in charge of writing the essay, you can choose to avoid punctuation and spelling errors. If you are unsure about how to punctuate a particular construction or spell a particular word, choose an alternative.

Write Concisely and Clearly

Use simple and direct sentences. Avoid complex and convoluted sentences. In general, the most complicated sentence you should use is one with two independent clauses that are joined by a conjunction such as "and" or "but." Of course, you can also use sentences that include one dependent clause and one independent clause that are joined together by a conjunction such as "while" or "although." Again, though, try to express yourself simply and directly. Also, avoid using any unnecessary or wordy phrases, such as those illustrated in the following chart:

AVOID THESE UNNECESSARY AND WORDY PHRASES

Instead of: *Say:*

In my opinion, I believe that...................I believe that
In the event of an emergency.................In an emergency
On the possibility that it may.................Since it may
close to the point of ....close to
have need for ....need
with a view to ....to
in view of the fact that ....because
give consideration to..............................consider
mean to imply...imply
disappear from view ....disappear
in this day and age ....today
the issue in question...............................issue

Also, while neatness is not graded, it is almost certainly true that an illegible essay will not receive a good grade.

Revision and Scoring

Proofread Your Essay

Proofreading is an essential part of the writing process. The first draft of an essay usually will not be free of errors. This means that you will need to re-read the essay and correct any grammatical errors or logical inconsistencies. There are two categories of errors generally appear in essays: structural errors and mechanics/usage errors.

Proofread for Structural Errors

When proofreading, first consider the structural elements of an essay. The three most important structural factors in an essay are unity, coherence, and support. Essays are judged by how well they meet these basic requirements. To improve your essay, ask yourself the following questions:

UNITY, COHERENCE, AND SUPPORT

1. Does the essay have a main thesis that is clearly stated in the introduction? What is it? What is the essay's point of view on the essay topic?

2. Does the introduction clearly state the arguments and evidence that will support the essay's point of view?

3. Does each body paragraph have a topic sentence? A topic sentence is the first sentence of a paragraph, and it summarizes what will be argued or presented in that paragraph.

4. Does each body paragraph make a different argument to support the essay's point of view?

5. Do the other sentences in each body paragraph all support the topic sentence? In other words, do the other sentences all further the argument or present evidence related to the main point made in the topic sentence?

6. Do the body paragraphs include specific details or examples to make the argument more vivid and interesting?

7. Does the essay use transitional words or phrases that allow the reader to move easily from one idea or paragraph to the next?

8. Does the essay have a conclusion that clearly re-states the essay's point of view on the essay topic? Does the conclusion explain why this point of view is more defensible than a different point of view on the essay topic?

Proofread for Mechanics/Usage Errors

After reviewing the structures of your essay, look for mechanics/usage errors. Although these are less important, mechanics/usage errors can prevent readers from focusing on the substance of an essay. The following is a list of common mechanics/usage errors:

COMMON MECHANICS/USAGE ERRORS

1. Omission of words—especially "the," "a," and "an"

2. Omission of final letters in words

3. Careless spelling errors

4. Incorrect use of capital letters

5. Faulty punctuation

Scoring Rubric

The rubric (scoring guide) on the following page summarizes how your essay will likely be graded by the essay reader.

ESSAY SCORE QUALIFICATIONS

Score	_Essay Qualities_

Excellent
- demonstrates _clear and consistent competence_ though it may have occasional errors
- effectively and insightfully addresses the writing task
- is well-organized and fully developed
- uses appropriate and innovative examples to support ideas
- demonstrates a superior grasp of grammar and style, varies sentence structure, and uses a wide range of vocabulary

Superior
- demonstrates _reasonably consistent competence_ with occasional errors or lapses in quality
- effectively addresses the writing task
- is generally well-organized and adequately developed
- uses appropriate examples to support ideas
- demonstrates a competent grasp of grammar and style, employs some syntactic variety, and uses appropriate vocabulary

Good
- demonstrates _adequate competence_ with occasional errors and lapses in quality
- addresses the writing task
- is organized and somewhat developed
- uses examples to support ideas
- demonstrates an adequate but inconsistent grasp of grammar and style with minor errors in grammar and diction
- displays minimal sentence variety

Average
- demonstrates _developing competence_
- may contain one or more of the following weaknesses: inadequate organization or development; inappropriate or insufficient details to support ideas; and an accumulation of errors in grammar, diction, or sentence structure

Below Average
- demonstrates _some incompetence_
- is flawed by one or more of the following weaknesses: poor organization; thin development; little or inappropriate detail to support ideas; and frequent errors in grammar, diction, and sentence structure

Weak
- demonstrates _incompetence_
- is seriously flawed by one or more of the following weaknesses: very poor organization, very thin development, and usage or syntactical errors so severe that meaning is somewhat obscured

Sample Essay

DIRECTIONS: You have 30 minutes to plan and write an essay. Read the prompt carefully and make sure you understand the instructions. A successful essay will have the following features: it will take a position on the issue presented in the writing prompt; it will maintain a consistent focus on the topic; it will use logical reasoning and provide supporting ideas; it will present ideas in an organized manner; and, finally, it will include clear and effective language in accordance with the conventions of standard written English. Sample essay responses and analyses begin on page 804.

Teachers evaluate the work of students by grading exams, homework, and other assignments, as well as class participation. The end-of-term report card with its letter or numerical grades is a time-honored tradition. Now, some teachers and administrators suggest that students be given the opportunity to grade teachers. They point out that students are in a unique position to assess the effectiveness of their teachers because they spend so much time with the teachers in the classroom. Some of those favoring this idea propose that students complete forms, ranking teachers according to relevant criteria, such as "Preparedness" and "Ability to Communicate." Other teachers and administrators oppose this idea and argue that students lack the experience and perspective to determine what makes an effective teacher. They also express concern that the evaluation forms could be used by students to retaliate against teachers for personal reasons. In your opinion, should students be given the opportunity to grade their teacher?

In your essay, take a position on this issue. You can write about either point of view presented here, or you can present a different point of view on this topic. Support your position with relevant reasons and/or examples from your own experience, observations, or reading.

ESSAY OUTLINE

Appendix A:

Answers and Explanations

GRAMMAR AND MECHANICS SKILLS REVIEW

EXERCISE 1—PARTS OF SPEECH (p. 48)

1. taxi = noun
   traffic = noun
   it = pronoun
   hurried = verb
   airport = noun

2. movers = noun
   unloaded = verb
   and = conjunction
   it = pronoun
   in = preposition

3. dark = modifier
   clouds = noun
   blocked = verb
   our = pronoun
   and = conjunction

4. dinner = noun
   cleared = verb
   table = noun
   and = conjunction
   sat = verb

5. room = noun
   was filled = verb
   with = preposition
   authors = noun
   Polish = modifier

6. first = modifier
   shows = noun
   were = verb
   earlier = modifier
   programs = noun

7. waiter = noun
   arrived = verb
   Victor = noun
   ordered = verb
   and = conjunction

8. inspector = noun
   finally = modifier
   approved = verb
   and = conjunction
   allowed = verb

9. notified = verb
   in = preposition
   water = noun
   would be = verb
   hours = noun

10. band = noun
    finished = verb
    crowd = noun
    burst = verb
    loud = modifier

11. called = verb
    her = pronoun
    would be = verb
    their = pronoun
    date = noun

12. cat = noun
    slept = verb
    warmth = noun
    of = preposition
    sun = noun

13. train = noun
    pulled = verb
    called = verb
    name = noun
    and = conjunction

14. we = pronoun
    children = noun
    were = verb
    in = preposition
    rear = noun

15. they = pronoun
    leave = verb
    teach = verb
    hikers = noun
    and = conjunction

16. covered = verb
    steaming = modifier
    melted = modifier
    sticky = modifier
    syrup = noun

17. weekend = noun
    made = verb
    special = modifier
    brilliant = modifier
    beautiful = modifier

18. eventful = modifier
    wrote = verb
    but = conjunction
    his = pronoun
    unopened = modifier

19. barely = modifier
    make out = verb
    bus = noun
    as = conjunction
    it = pronoun

20. offered = verb
    us = pronoun
    or = conjunction
    were = verb
    delicious = modifier

EXERCISE 2—COMMON GRAMMATICAL ERRORS (p. 65)

1. A	5. C	9. A	13. B	17. A	21. D	25. A
2. J	6. J	10. H	14. G	18. J	22. J	
3. D	7. B	11. C	15. B	19. B	23. D	
4. H	8. G	12. J	16. J	20. G	24. H	

26. The adverb "slowly" is the correct answer choice.

27. The adverb phrase "really well" is the correct answer choice.

28. The adjective "polite" is the correct answer choice.

29. The adverb "well" is the correct answer choice.

30. The adjective "good" is the correct answer choice.

31. The adjective "terrible" is the correct answer choice.

32. The adjective "awful" is the correct answer choice.

33. The adverb "terribly" is the correct answer choice.

34. The adverb "well" is the correct answer choice.

35. The adverb "well" is the correct answer choice.

36. The adverb "hard" is the correct answer choice.

37. The adverb "fast" is the correct answer choice.

38. The adjective "near" is the correct answer choice.

39. The adverb "slowly" is the correct answer choice.

40. The adjective "healthy" is the correct answer choice.

41. The adjective "heavy" is the correct answer choice.

42. The plural subject "many people" requires the plural form "receive."

43. The plural subject "books" requires the plural form "were."

44. The plural subject "stores" requires the plural form "offer."

45. The plural subject "bottles" requires the plural form "remain."

46. The singular subject "tourist" requires the singular form "is."

47. The plural subject "several different species" requires the plural form "were."

48. The plural subject "young boys" requires the plural form "were."

49. The plural subject "several barrels" requires the plural form "have."

50. The plural subject "sponsors" requires the plural form "hope."

51. The plural subject "Dawn, Harriet, and Gloria" requires the plural form "are."

52. The singular subject "the mayor" requires the singular form "worries."

53. The plural subject "acts" requires the plural form "have been."

54. The plural subject "rock musicians" requires the plural form "lose."

55. The plural subject "the leaves" requires the plural form "fall."

56. The plural subject "the computer and the printer" requires the plural form "have."

57. The singular subject "Theresa" requires the singular form "was."

58. The singular subject "the film critic" requires the singular form "writes."

59. The plural subject "ingredients" requires the plural form "have."

60. The singular subject "the computer" requires the singular form "was."

61. The singular subject "support" requires the singular form "has."

62. The plural subject "Bill and Jean" requires the plural form "are."

63. The plural subject "several students" requires the plural form "were."

64. The singular pronoun "his or her" is the correct answer choice.

65. The singular pronoun "her" is the correct answer choice.

66. The singular subject "music" requires the singular form "is."

67. "My two daughters enjoy different TV shows; the older one watches game shows, while the younger one prefers talk shows."

68. "Her present instructor is the best of all the ones she has had so far."

69. "In the technology lab, I choose the computer with the greatest memory."

70. "According to the counselor, taking these classes in this order is much more beneficial than the other way around."

71. "Our school is unique in many aspects."

72. "The fraternity he joined is better than all other fraternities."

73. "Which of these three sections is best?"

74. "You will receive your grades no later than tomorrow at 2 p.m."

75. "There is no need for further negotiation."

76. "She is doing so badly in her art class that she could not do any worse."

77. "This exercise seems more difficult than all of the others."

78. "Jeff is taller than any other boy in his class."

79. "The heroine was unbelievably naive."

80. The original is correct.

EXERCISE 3—ANALYZING SENTENCE STRUCTURE (p. 79)

1. D	10. J	19. A	28. H	37. A	46. J	55. E
2. G	11. C	20. H	29. C	38. H	47. B	56. J
3. E	12. K	21. A	30. G	39. B	48. H	57. D
4. G	13. A	22. K	31. A	40. H	49. C	
5. A	14. K	23. C	32. J	41. C	50. G	
6. H	15. B	24. G	33. C	42. H	51. C	
7. D	16. K	25. D	34. J	43. D	52. J	
8. K	17. B	26. H	35. B	44. H	53. C	
9. C	18. K	27. E	36. F	45. B	54. J	

58. "When at school, he studies, goes to the library, and works on the computer."

59. "In order to get eight hours of sleep, the student prefers sleeping in late in the morning to going to bed early in the evening."

60. "He could not deliver the supplies because the roads had not yet been plowed."

61. "I still need to pass Math 252 and English 301 and return two overdue books before I am allowed to graduate."

62. The original is correct.

63. "Our instructor suggested that we study the assignment carefully, go to the library to research the topic extensively, and conduct a survey among 20 subjects."

64. "The increase of attrition among community college students is caused by a lack of family support and a limited income while attending school."

65. "Many non-smokers complained about the health risks associated with second-hand smoke; as a result, smoking is banned in the library and the cafeteria, and smokers have to leave the building to light a cigarette."

66. The original is correct.

67. "After talking to financial aid and seeing your advisor, return to the registrar's office."

68. "Professor Walker helped not only me, but many of my classmates as well."

69. "In his communications class, he can work either in groups or in pairs."

70. "I prefer that other geography class because of the clear explanations and numerous exercises in the textbook, as well as Mrs. Patrick's vivid teaching style."

71. "The question is whether to study tonight or to get up earlier tomorrow morning."

72. The original is correct.

73. "Reasons for the latest tuition increase are the upgraded computers, the new library, and the 6.5 percent inflation."

74. "If you want to succeed, you must be willing to work hard."
"If one wants to succeed, one must be willing to work hard."

75. "She likes tennis, golf, and swimming."

EXERCISE 4—PROBLEMS OF LOGICAL EXPRESSION (p. 91)

1. C	**5.** A	**9.** C	**13.** B	**17.** A	**21.** D	**25.** D
2. G	**6.** F	**10.** K	**14.** G	**18.** F	**22.** G	**26.** J
3. C	**7.** B	**11.** A	**15.** C	**19.** D	**23.** A	**27.** A
4. K	**8.** K	**12.** F	**16.** F	**20.** K	**24.** J	

28. "The life of my generation is easier than that of my parents."

29. The original is correct.

30. The original is correct.

31. "I am spending more time on the assignments in my management class than on those in all my other classes combined."

32. "Going to school, he tripped on a crack in the pavement."

33. "Only Mary failed the test; everyone else in her class passed."

34. "Did you see the film on television about the five people on the boat?"

35. "The police officer, in his patrol car, ordered the man to stop."

36. "When you picked up the phone, the noise became muted."

37. "While I was swimming, a fish nibbled on my toe."

38. "Of all his admirers, only his wife loved him."

39. The original is correct.

40. "When we entered the class, the blackboard came into view."

41. "The baby was in a stroller pushed by his mother."

42. "To get to school, we walked nearly two miles."

43. "Leaning out the window, she could see the garden below."

44. "The hotel room that we had reserved was clean and comfortable."

45. "This book is heavier than that one."

EXERCISE 5—IDIOMS AND CLARITY OF EXPRESSION (p. 105)

1. The adjective "principal" is the correct answer choice.

2. The verb "accept" is the correct answer choice.

3. The noun "weather" is the correct answer choice.

4. The preposition "into" is the correct answer choice.

5. The verb "advise" is the correct answer choice.

6. The conjunction "than" is the correct answer choice.

7. The phrase "all ready" is the correct answer choice.

8. The noun "stationery" is the correct answer choice.

9. The noun "effect" is the correct answer choice.

10. The verb "sit" is the correct answer choice.

11. The verb "lie" is the correct answer choice.

12. The adverb "altogether" is the correct answer choice.

13. The past tense verb "passed" is the correct answer choice.

14. The noun "dessert" is the correct answer choice.

15. The verb "lose" is the correct answer choice.

16. The verb "affect" is the correct answer choice.

17. The contraction "you're" is the correct answer choice.

18. "Used" is the correct answer choice.

19. The verb "rise" is the correct answer choice.

20. "Supposed" is the correct answer choice.

21. The possessive pronoun "its" is the correct answer choice.

22. The adjective "conscious" is the correct answer choice.

23. The verb "seem" is the correct answer choice.

24. The plural noun "allusions" is the correct answer choice.

25. The noun "complement" is the correct answer choice.

26. The adjective "later" is the correct answer choice.

27. The noun "build" is the correct answer choice.

28. The past tense verb "knew" is the correct answer choice.

29. The adjective "personal" is the correct answer choice.

30. The noun "course" is the correct answer choice.

31. The adjective "cloth" is the correct answer choice.

32. The verb "elude" is the correct answer choice.

33. The adverb "no" is the correct answer choice.

34. The prefix "ante" is the correct answer choice.

35. The noun "morale" is the correct answer choice.

36. The adjective "capital" is the correct answer choice.

37. The verb "faze" is the correct answer choice.

38. "Excess" is the correct answer choice.

39. The verb "proceed" is the correct answer choice.

40. The noun "forte" is the correct answer choice.

41. The verb "disperse" is the correct answer choice.

42. The adverb "formally" is the correct answer choice.

43. The adjective "averse" is the correct answer choice.

44. The noun "incidence" is the correct answer choice.

45. The adjective "dual" is the correct answer choice.

46. The verb "expend" is the correct answer choice.

47. The noun "discomfort" is the correct answer choice.

48. The noun "idol" is the correct answer choice.

49. The verb "emigrate" is the correct answer choice.

50. The noun "clique" is the correct answer choice.

51. The noun "prophecy" is the correct answer choice.

52. The noun "lightning" is the correct answer choice.

53. The adjective "whatever" is the correct answer choice.

54. The adjective "imminent" is the correct answer choice.

55. The verb "adapt" is the correct answer choice.

56. The noun "epitaphs" is the correct answer choice.

57. The preposition "among" is the correct answer choice.

58. The noun "benefit" is the correct answer choice.

59. The adverb "a lot" is the correct answer choice.

60. The noun "number" is the correct answer choice.

61. The adverb "almost" is the correct answer choice.

62. The adjective "all right" is the correct answer choice.

63. The verb "annoy" is the correct answer choice.

64. The singular noun "alumnus" is the correct answer choice.

65. The adverb "alongside" is the correct answer choice.

66. The conjunction "since" is the correct answer choice.

67. The adjective "eager" is the correct answer choice.

68. The verb "meet" is the correct answer choice.

69. The adverb "awhile" is the correct answer choice.

70. The adverb "about" is the correct answer choice.

71. "Couple of" is the correct answer choice.

72. "You and me" is the correct answer choice.

73. The adjective "continuous" is the correct answer choice.

74. "Seems unable" is the correct answer choice.

75. The verb "assume" is the correct answer choice.

76. The adjective "uninterested" is the correct answer choice.

77. "Just as" is the correct answer choice.

78. The conjunction "that" is the correct answer choice.

79. The pronoun "one another" is the correct answer choice.

80. The conjunction "whether" is the correct answer choice.

81. The plural noun "human beings" is the correct answer choice.

82. The verb "finalize" is the correct answer choice.

83. The past tense verb "flouted" is the correct answer choice.

84. The adjective "healthful" is the correct answer choice.

85. The noun "slander" is the correct answer choice.

86. "Regard" is the correct answer choice.

87. The adverb "regardless" is the correct answer choice.

88. The verb "lend" is the correct answer choice.

89. The singular verb "is" is the correct answer choice.

90. The preposition "off" is the correct answer choice.

91. The verb "stop" is the correct answer choice.

92. The conjunction "that" is the correct answer choice.

93. The verb "manage" is the correct answer choice.

94. The singular pronoun "his or her" is the correct answer choice.

95. "Any other" is the correct answer choice.

96. The conjunction "but" is the correct answer choice.

97. "Try to" is the correct answer choice.

98. "Whoever" is the correct answer choice.

99. The preposition "for" is the correct answer choice.

100. C	**107.** C	**114.** A	**121.** D	**128.** H	**135.** B	**142.** H
101. A	**108.** C	**115.** B	**122.** J	**129.** C	**136.** G	**143.** C
102. B	**109.** A	**116.** J	**123.** C	**130.** J	**137.** B	
103. B	**110.** B	**117.** B	**124.** J	**131.** B	**138.** G	
104. B	**111.** A	**118.** G	**125.** D	**132.** F	**139.** C	
105. C	**112.** B	**119.** A	**126.** J	**133.** A	**140.** G	
106. A	**113.** C	**120.** H	**127.** C	**134.** G	**141.** C	

EXERCISE 6—PUNCTUATION (p. 126)

1. He was not aware that you had lost your passport.

2. Did you report the loss to the proper authorities?

3. I suppose you had to fill out many forms.

4. What a nuisance!

5. I hate doing so much paper work!

6. Did you ever discover where the wallet was?

7. I imagine you wondered how it was misplaced.

8. Good for you!

9. At least you now have your passport.

10. What will you do if it happens again?

11. I don't know if they are coming, though I sent them an invitation weeks ago.

12. Neurology is the science that deals with the anatomy, physiology, and pathology of the nervous system.

13. Nursery lore, like everything human, has been subject to many changes over long periods of time.
    Nursery lore—like everything human—has been subject to many changes over long periods of time.

14. Bob read Joyce's *Ulysses* to the class; everyone seemed to enjoy the reading.

15. In order to provide more living space, we converted an attached garage into a den.

16. Because he is such an industrious student, he has many friends.

17. I don't recall who wrote *A Midsummer Night's Dream*.

18. In the writing class, students learned about coordinating conjunctions—and, but, so, or, yet, for, and nor.

19. "Those who do not complain are never pitied" is a familiar quotation by Jane Austen.

20. Howard and his ex-wife are on amicable terms.

21. Her last words were, "Call me on Sunday," and she jumped on the train.

22. He is an out-of-work carpenter.

23. This is what is called a "pregnant chad."

24. "Come early on Monday," the teacher said, "to take the exit exam."

25. The dog, man's best friend, is a companion to many.
    The dog—man's best friend—is a companion to many.

26. The winner of the horse race is, to the best of my knowledge, Silver.
    The winner of the horse race is—to the best of my knowledge—Silver.

27. Every time I see him, the dentist asks me how often I floss.

28. The officer was off-duty when he witnessed the crime.

29. *Anna Karenina* is my favorite movie.

30. Red, white, and blue are the colors of the American flag.

31. Stop using "stuff" in your essays; it's too informal.

32. She was a self-made millionaire.

33. The Smiths, who are the best neighbors anyone could ask for, have moved out.
    The Smiths—who are the best neighbors anyone could ask for—have moved out.

34. My eighteen-year-old daughter will graduate this spring.

35. Dracula lived in Transylvania.

36. The students were told to put away their books.

37. Begun while Dickens was still at work on *Pickwick Papers*, *Oliver Twist* was published in 1837 and is now one of the author's most widely read works.

38. Given the great difficulties of making soundings in very deep water, it is not surprising that few such soundings were made until the middle of this century.

39. Did you finish writing your thesis prospectus on time?

40. The root of modern Dutch was once supposed to be Old Frisian, but the general view now is that the characteristic forms of Dutch are at least as old as those of Old Frisian.

41. Moose, once scarce because of indiscriminate hunting, are protected by law, and the number of moose is once again increasing.
Moose—once scarce because of indiscriminate hunting—are protected by law, and the number of moose is once again increasing.

42. He ordered a set of books, several records, and a film almost a month ago.

43. Perhaps the most interesting section of New Orleans is the French Quarter, which extends from North Rampart Street to the Mississippi River.

44. Writing for a skeptical and rationalizing age, Shaftesbury was primarily concerned with showing that goodness and beauty are not determined by revelation, authority, opinion, or fashion.

45. We tried our best to purchase the books, but we were completely unsuccessful even though we went to every bookstore in town.

46. A great deal of information regarding the nutritional requirements of farm animals has been accumulated over countless generations by trial and error; however, most recent advances have come as the result of systematic studies at schools of animal husbandry.

47. *Omoo*, Melville's sequel to *Typee*, appeared in 1847 and went through five printings in that year alone.
Omoo—Melville's sequel to *Typee*—appeared in 1847 and went through five printings in that year alone.

48. "Go to Florence for the best gelato in all of Italy," said the old man to the young tourist.

49. Although the first school for African Americans was a public school established in Virginia in 1620, most educational opportunities for African Americans before the Civil War were provided by private agencies.

50. As the climate of Europe changed, the population became too dense for the supply of food obtained by hunting, and other means of securing food, such as the domestication of animals, were necessary.
As the climate of Europe changed, the population became too dense for the supply of food obtained by hunting, and other means of securing food—such as the domestication of animals—were necessary.

51. In Faulkner's poetic realism, the grotesque is somber, violent, and often inexplicable; in Caldwell's writing, it is lightened by a ballad-like, humorous, sophisticated detachment.

52. The valley of the Loire, a northern tributary of the Loire at Angers, abounds in rock villages; they occur in many other places in France, Spain, and northern Italy.
The valley of the Loire—a northern tributary of the Loire at Angers—abounds in rock villages; they occur in many other places in France, Spain, and northern Italy.

53. The telephone rang several times; as a result, his sleep was interrupted.

54. He has forty-three thousand dollars to spend; however, once that is gone, he will be penniless.

55. Before an examination, do the following: review your work, get a good night's sleep, eat a balanced breakfast, and arrive on time to take the test.

DIAGRAMMING SENTENCES SKILLS REVIEW

EXERCISE 1—SUBJECTS AND VERBS (p. 140)

1. Ducks quack.

   | Ducks | quack |

   The subject of the sentence is "ducks." The verb "quack" is in the present tense.

2. Mosquitoes are buzzing.

   | Mosquitoes | are buzzing |

   The subject of the sentence is "mosquitoes." The verb "are buzzing" is a progressive form of the present tense.

3. People have been talking.

   | People | have been talking |

   The subject of the sentence is "people." The verb "have been talking" is present-perfect progressive.

4. They will be captured.

   | They | will be captured |

   The subject of the sentence is "they," a personal pronoun. The verb "will be captured" is in the future tense, passive voice.

5. Money had been collected.

   | Money | had been collected |

   The subject of the sentence is "money." "Had been collected" is in the past-perfect tense, passive voice.

EXERCISE 2—MODAL AUXILIARY VERBS (p. 145)

1. You may stay.

   | You | may stay |

   The verb consists of the present modal auxiliary verb "may" and the basic present tense form of "stay."

2. They should be scolded.

| They | should be scolded |

The verb consists of the present modal auxiliary verb "should" and the basic present passive form of "scold."

3. She must have been delayed.

| She | must have been delayed |

The verb consists of the present modal auxiliary verb "must" and the basic present-perfect passive form of "delay."

4. That could have been done.

| That | could have been done |

The verb consists of the present subjunctive of the modal auxiliary verb "can" and the basic present-perfect passive form of "do."

5. They might be coming.

| They | might be coming |

The verb consists of the present subjunctive form of the modal auxiliary verb "may" and the basic present progressive form of "come."

EXERCISE 3—CONJUNCTIONS (p. 149)

1. Buses come and go.

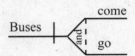

"Come and go" is a compound verb. Since it constitutes the entire predicate, it is also a compound predicate.

2. Deer were running and jumping.

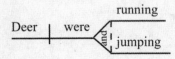

Together with the helping verb "were," the compound present participle "running and jumping" forms the past progressive.

3. Children run, jump, and play.

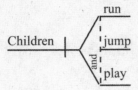

This compound predicate consists of three verbs.

4. Doctors and nurses are scurrying.

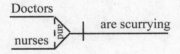

"Doctors and nurses" is a compound subject. The coordinating conjunction "and" joins the two nouns. The verb "are scurrying" is a progressive form of the present tense.

5. Bombs fell and people died.

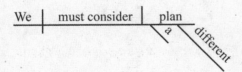

This is a compound sentence. In other words, it consists of two independent clauses joined by a coordinating conjunction.

EXERCISE 4—ARTICLES, ATTRIBUTIVE ADJECTIVES, AND DIRECT OBJECTS (p. 155)

1. We must consider a different plan.

We | must consider | plan / a \ different

"Plan" is a direct object. "Different" is an attributive adjective.

2. Either the county or the city must assume primary responsibility.

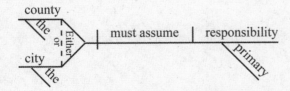

"Responsibility" is a direct object. "Either…or" is called a correlative conjunction.

3. The new store sells athletic clothing and equipment.

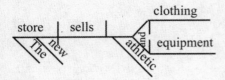

Since athletic modifies both "clothing" and "equipment," its line is attached to the part of the direct-object line that belongs to both objects.

4. Employers appreciate honest and diligent employees.

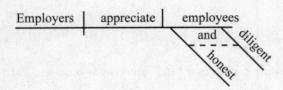

"Honest and diligent" is a compound attributive adjective.

5. She buys and restores old furniture.

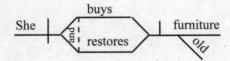

The verbs "buys" and "restores" have the same direct object: "furniture."

EXERCISE 5—ADVERBS (p. 160)

1. Angrily and inexorably the storm devastated the coastal regions.

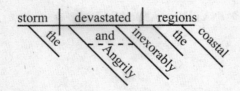

"Angrily and inexorably" is a compound adverb.

2. Not all Americans favor bigger and more expensive cars.

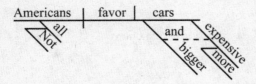

The adverbs "not" and "more" modify the attributive adjectives "all" and "expensive," respectively. "Bigger and more expensive" is a compound attributive adjective.

3. I did the assignment fast and inattentively.

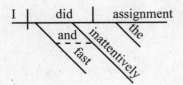

"Fast and inattentively" is a compound adverb.

4. She wrote an exceedingly but unexpectedly beautiful poem.

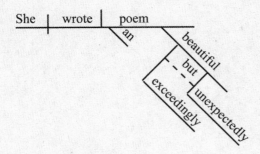

The compound adverb "exceedingly but unexpectedly" modifies the attributive adjective "beautiful."

5. This subdivision has about fifty residences.

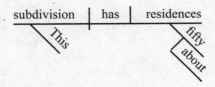

"This" is called a demonstrative adjective. "About" is an adverb modifying the adjective "fifty."

EXERCISE 6—SUBJECTIVE COMPLEMENTS: PREDICATE NOMINATIVES AND PREDICATE ADJECTIVES (p. 165)

1. Our waiter was both efficient and courteous.

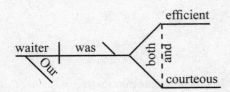

"Our" is a possessive pronoun. "Both" and "and" are correlative coordinating conjunctions.

APPENDIX A: ANSWERS AND EXPLANATIONS

2. She was feeling happy, but he was feeling sad.

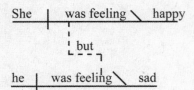

This is a compound sentence whose two main clauses are joined by the coordinating conjunction "but." "Was feeling" is a linking verb. "Happy" and "sad" are predicate adjectives.

3. He is a truly remarkable scholar but a lousy poet.

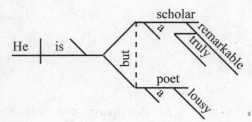

This sentence features a compound predicate nominative.

4. He became angry and silent and left the room.

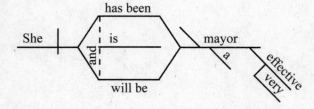

The first branch of the compound predicate contains a compound predicate adjective ("angry and silent"), the second a direct object ("room").

5. She has been, is, and will be a very effective mayor.

The compound, tripartite verb "has been, is, and will be" has "mayor" as its predicate nominative.

EXERCISE 7—APPOSITIVES (p. 169)

1. Her cousins Jack and Jill climbed a hill.

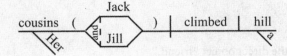

"Jack and Jill" is a compound restrictive appositive. It is in apposition with the subject "cousins."

2. J. J., a four-year band member, was chosen as the most outstanding musician.

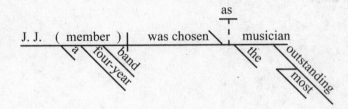

"Member," a nonrestrictive appositive, is in apposition with the subject "J. J." The passive verb "was chosen" functions as a linking verb. "Musician" is a predicate nominative, and "as" is an expletive.

3. The renters altered, that is, nearly destroyed, the apartment.

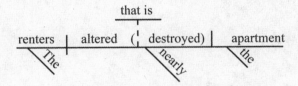

The verb phrase "nearly destroyed" is in apposition with the main verb "altered." "That is" is an expletive. Other such function words and phrases, which are sometimes called appositive conjunctions because they are not entirely devoid of meaning, are "especially," "for example," "in other words," and "or."

4. They have strength, speed, and mental toughness—the right qualities.

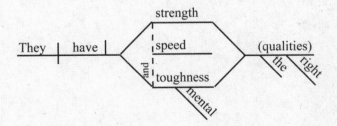

"Qualities" is in apposition with the compound direct object "strength, speed, and mental toughness."

5. Have you met my friend Marcy?

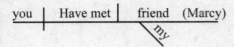

"Marcy" is a restrictive appositive. It is in apposition with the direct object "friend."

EXERCISE 8—PREPOSITIONAL PHRASES (p. 175)

1. Early in the week, friends of ours are coming for dinner.

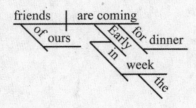

"In the week" and "for dinner" are adverbial prepositional phrases. The former modifies the adverb "early," and the latter modifies the verb "are coming." "Ours" is an absolute possessive.

2. They approach every new challenge with enthusiasm and determination.

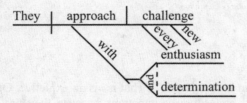

"With enthusiasm and determination" is a prepositional phrase containing a compound object.

3. We can go through the narrow tunnel or over the narrow bridge.

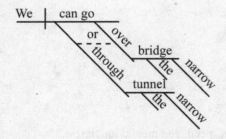

"Through the narrow tunnel or over the narrow bridge" is a compound prepositional phrase.

4. The principal is taking a group of teachers out for lunch.

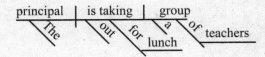

"Out for" is not a phrasal preposition. "Out" is an adverb in this sentence.

5. She acted in accordance with the express wishes of her clients.

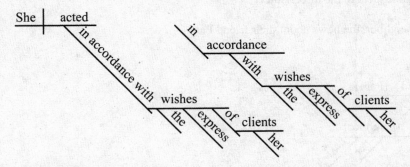

"In accordance with" can be considered a phrasal preposition; however, it can also be diagrammed as a prepositional phrase.

EXERCISE 9—INDIRECT OBJECTS AND OBJECTIVE COMPLEMENTS (p. 180)

1. John gave Judy an engagement ring.

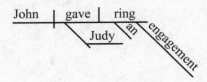

"Judy" (the person to whom something was given) is an indirect object. "Engagement" is a noun used as an adjective.

2. The governor gave each distinguished student and his or her mentor a monetary award.

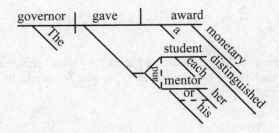

"Student" and "mentor" constitute a compound indirect object.

3. The rescue team found the campers alive and declared them extremely fortunate.

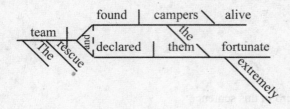

"Alive" cannot be recognized as an objective complement by asking "what"? Like all objective complements, it completes the action of the verb with respect to the direct object.

4. Jamie told Shanika, her next-door neighbor, the news about their friend Pam.

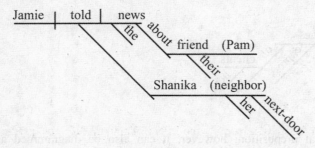

"Neighbor" is in apposition with "Shanika," an indirect object, while "Pam" is in apposition with "friend," the object of the preposition "about."

5. Humpty-Dumpty was found in pieces, and neither the king's horses nor the king's men could make him whole again.

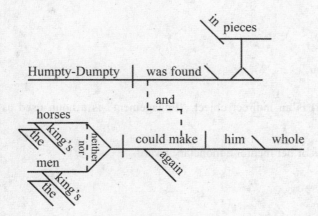

The passive verb "was found" functions here as a linking verb, and the prepositional phrase "in pieces" serves as a predicate adjective. If the first main clause were active ("they found him in pieces"), "in pieces" would be an objective complement, like "alive" in sentence 3 of this exercise.

EXERCISE 10—INFINITIVES (p. 189)

1. Their plan was to fly to Seattle and rent a car.

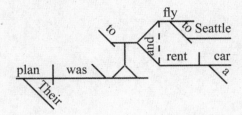

The compound infinitive phrase "to fly to Seattle and rent a car" serves as a predicate nominative.

2. That is easy to promise but hard to do.

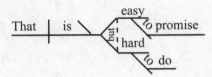

The infinitives "to promise" and "to do" function here as adverbial modifiers. They modify the predicate adjectives "easy" and "hard," respectively.

3. She spoke too softly to be understood.

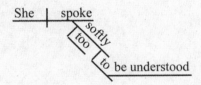

The present passive infinitive "to be understood" modifies the adverb "softly."

4. He walks three miles every day to stay cardiovascularly healthy.

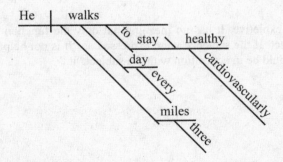

The infinitive phrase "to stay cardiovascularly healthy" functions as a modifier of the verb "walks"; it tells why he walks. "Miles" and "day" are adverbial objectives.

5. Domestic responsibilities compelled them to stay at home.

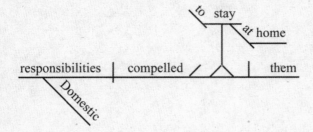

The infinitive phrase "to stay at home" functions here as an objective complement.

6. The students are to go immediately to their desks.

"To go" is a complementary infinitive. A verb and its complementary infinitive are, taken together, often equivalent to a verb phrase using a modal auxiliary verb or to a future-tense verb form. In this case, "are to go" can be expressed as "must go."

7. For them to become angry is not helpful to our cause.

The word "for" as used in this sentence can be called an expletive. It has no meaning but only the function of introducing an infinitive phrase and its objective-case subject. If the sentence were expressed as "It is not helpful to our cause for them to become angry," the "for" phrase would be in apposition with the subject "it."

8. To have to be told three times to behave is a sign of immaturity.

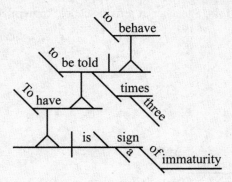

The infinitive phrase "to have to be told three times to behave" is the subject of the sentence, the infinitive phrase "to be told three times to behave" has a complementary function, and the infinitive "to behave" is a direct object.

9. She said for the children to be ready to leave in ten minutes.

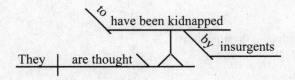

The infinitive phrase introduced by the expletive "for" is the direct object of "said." "Children" is the subject of the infinitive "to be."

10. They are thought to have been kidnapped by insurgents.

They | are thought \ to have been kidnapped / by insurgents

The present-perfect passive infinitive "to have been kidnapped," along with its modifying prepositional phrase, functions here as a predicate adjective. The passive verb "are thought" acts as a linking verb.

EXERCISE 11—GERUNDS (p. 195)

1. Ms. Shelby, a teacher at our school, calls her friendship with Mr. Moss, a teacher at a rival school, "fraternizing with the enemy."

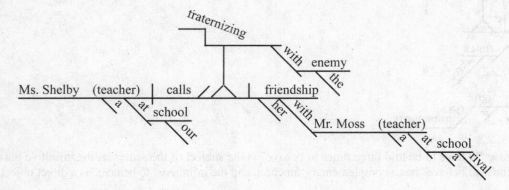

The gerund phrase "fraternizing with the enemy" is an objective complement, which is diagrammed here in the traditional manner.

2. Something worth quoting is worth quoting accurately.

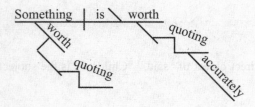

Each "quoting" is an adverbial objective. The first modifies an attributive adjective, the second a predicate adjective.

3. The landlord increased his profit by raising the rent and reducing the amenities.

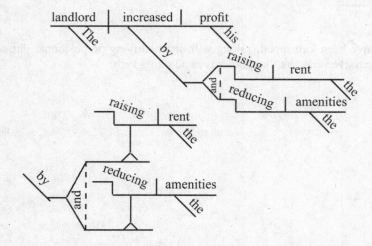

The compound gerund phrase "raising the rent and reducing the amenities" is the object of the preposition "by." The second diagram above is another way of diagramming the compound gerund phrase.

4. The men are playing golf and the women are going shopping.

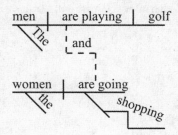

"Shopping" is a gerund used as an adverbial objective. It tells where the women are going. "Playing" and "going" are participial components of progressive verb forms.

5. The joylessness in Mudville is the result of Casey's not having hit a home run.

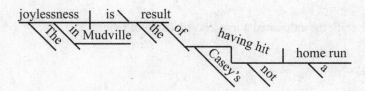

The gerund phrase "Casey's not having hit a home run" contains the adjectival modifier "Casey's" and the adverbial modifier "not." "Having hit" is a present-perfect active gerund.

EXERCISE 12—PARTICIPLES (p. 201)

1. Still running smoothly after twenty-five miles, she left the park and headed for the finish line.

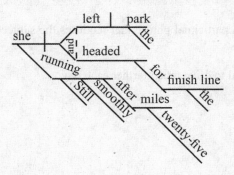

"Running" is a present participle. It introduces a participial phrase that modifies the subject of the sentence, "she." The sentence has a compound predicate.

2. Chewing, spitting, and occasionally talking, the three old-timers watched the people and the trains go by.

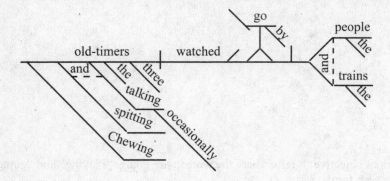

A compound participial phrase featuring three present participles modifies the subject of the sentence, "old-timers." "Go by" is a "*to*-less" infinitive phrase used as an objective complement. It is diagrammed here in the traditional way.

3. Having reached the end of her twelve-hour shift, the exhausted nurse heaved a sigh of relief.

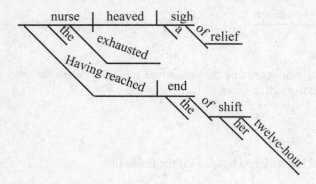

The present-perfect active participle "having reached" introduces a participial phrase that modifies the subject of the sentence, "nurse." "Exhausted" is a past participle.

4. The bridge having collapsed, some interstate commuters were forced to drive much farther each day.

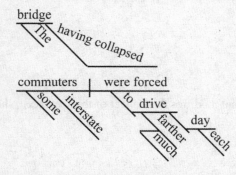

"The bridge having collapsed" is a nominative absolute. "Having collapsed" is a present-perfect participle.

5. Speaking of rascals, Oscar just knocked at the door.

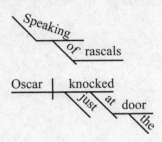

"Speaking of rascals" is an independent participial phrase.

EXERCISE 13—ADVERB CLAUSES (p. 209)

1. Although snow was expected later in the day, most schools were open.

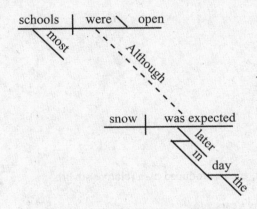

"Although" is a subordinating conjunction; such conjunctions introduce subordinate clauses. No matter where it may appear in a sentence, a subordinate clause is always diagrammed below the main clause.

2. She knows a lot about the world because she travels a lot.

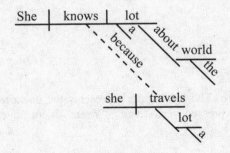

The subordinate clause "because she travels a lot" is introduced by the subordinating conjunction "because." The second "lot" is an adverbial objective.

3. When they entered the theater, they went to their seats immediately.

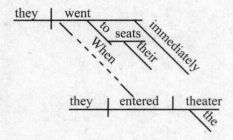

"When" is equivalent to two prepositional phrases: "at the time" and "at which," the second of which includes a relative pronoun. That "when" modifies both "went" and "entered" is shown in the diagram by the solid ends of the line upon which "when" rests.

4. She arrived after the party had begun but before the food had been served.

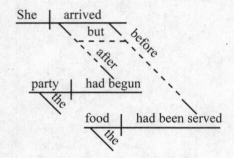

The coordinating conjunction "but" connects two adverb clauses, each introduced by a relative adverb.

5. Whenever she crossed the old bridge, she thought of a night many years ago.

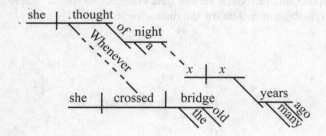

"Whenever" (*at any time at which*) is an indefinite relative adverb. The left-hand *x* represents the unexpressed relative pronoun "that," and the right-hand *x* represents the unexpressed verb "was." "Years" is an adverbial objective.

6. The more it rains, the faster the grass grows.

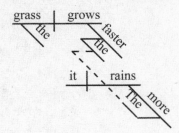

This sentence features the correlatives "the…the." Think: *the grass grows faster according to the extent to which it rains more*. "The" modifying "faster" is an ordinary adverb; "the" modifying "more" is a relative adverb.

7. It was so late that no more trick-or-treaters were expected.

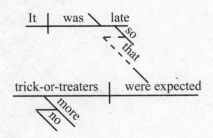

Think: it was late to a degree in which no more trick-or-treaters were expected.

8. After the guests arrive, but before the food is brought out, let's remind them of the reason for the party.

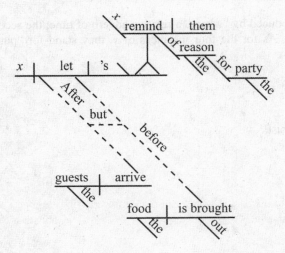

This complex sentence features two adverb clauses. The main clause is "let's remind them of the reason for the party."

9. He is kinder and more generous than his sister.

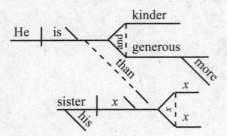

This comparative sentence contains a compound comparative adjective. The relative adverb is "than."

10. When our family does a jigsaw puzzle, the children always put in more pieces than the parents.

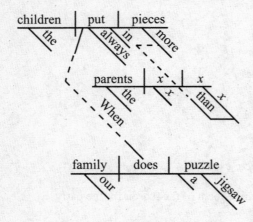

This sentence has two subordinate clauses: the first is introduced by "when," a relative adverb of time; the second is introduced by "than," a relative adverb of comparison. As for the four instances of *x*, they stand for "put in many pieces."

EXERCISE 14—ADJECTIVE CLAUSES (p. 215)

1. Choose carefully the person in whom you place your full trust.

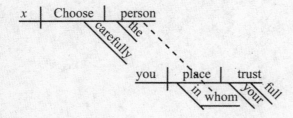

The relative pronoun "whom" is the object of the preposition "in." Its antecedent is "person."

2. The guy whose car is parked illegally may soon be looking for a ride.

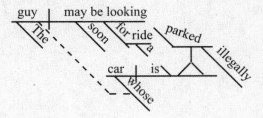

The relative pronoun "whose," a possessive modifier of the noun "car," has "guy" as its antecedent.

3. The accident happened on the day they arrived in Miami.

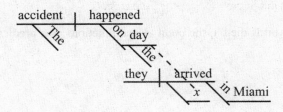

The relative pronoun "that," an adverbial objective, is unexpressed.

4. The other prizes will be given to whoever answers correctly.

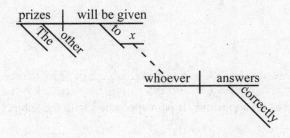

"Whoever" is the subject of the relative clause "whoever answers correctly." Its antecedent is the unexpressed object of the preposition "to."

5. I have already told you the reason I can't be there.

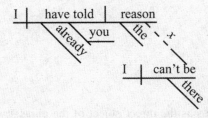

The noun "reason" is modified by "[why] I can't be there," an adjective clause introduced by the unexpressed relative adverb "why."

EXERCISE 15—NOUN CLAUSES (p. 220)

1. An unintended result of the experiment was that many birds died.

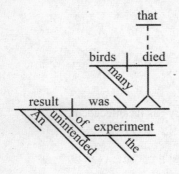

The expletive "that" introduces a noun clause ("that many birds died"); the noun clause functions as a predicate nominative.

2. It is a widespread belief that poinsettias are poisonous.

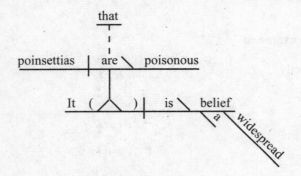

The noun clause "that poinsettias are poisonous" functions as an appositive. It is in apposition with the subject of the sentence, "it." "That" is an expletive.

3. The professor attempted to find out who damaged his car.

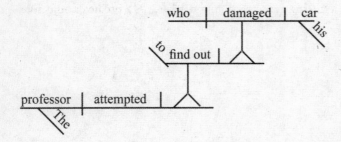

The interrogative pronoun "who" introduces a noun clause that functions as the direct object of the phrasal verb "find out."

4. The station manager claimed to be uncertain as to why the station had lost so many listeners.

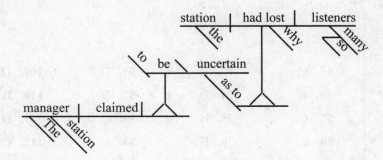

The noun clause introduced by the adverb "why" acts as the object of the phrasal preposition "as to."

5. How many angels could fit on the head of a pin was a question that some medieval theologians are said to have found intriguing.

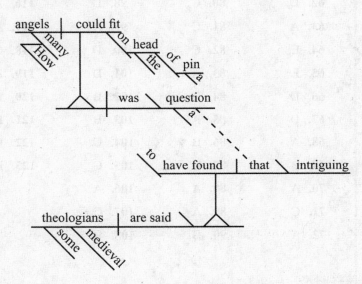

The noun clause introduced by the interrogative adverb "how" is the subject of the sentence. "That" is a relative pronoun. The passive verb "are said" functions as a linking verb, the infinitive phrase as a predicate adjective.

MATH SKILLS REVIEW

EXERCISE 1—NUMBERS (p. 253)

1. B	19. B	37. D	55. C	73. D	91. D	109. D
2. B	20. C	38. B	56. E	74. D	92. B	110. B
3. B	21. C	39. D	57. C	75. E	93. C	111. D
4. C	22. C	40. B	58. C	76. E	94. E	112. C
5. C	23. E	41. A	59. D	77. D	95. A	113. B
6. D	24. A	42. C	60. C	78. C	96. A	114. A
7. C	25. A	43. C	61. A	79. D	97. E	115. C
8. E	26. D	44. A	62. D	80. C	98. D	116. A
9. E	27. B	45. E	63. A	81. C	99. A	117. A
10. B	28. B	46. A	64. E	82. C	100. D	118. C
11. C	29. A	47. B	65. E	83. A	101. D	119. E
12. D	30. D	48. A	66. D	84. B	102. B	120. B
13. D	31. D	49. A	67. D	85. A	103. B	121. D
14. C	32. C	50. B	68. A	86. B	104. C	122. B
15. D	33. C	51. B	69. B	87. D	105. C	123. E
16. C	34. E	52. A	70. A	88. A	106. A	
17. C	35. B	53. C	71. C	89. A	107. C	
18. B	36. A	54. C	72. A	90. D	108. B	

EXERCISE 2—FRACTIONS (p. 268)

1. E	12. C	23. D	34. A	45. A	56. C	67. C
2. D	13. B	24. B	35. A	46. C	57. E	68. D
3. B	14. E	25. C	36. C	47. B	58. A	69. D
4. C	15. E	26. C	37. C	48. A	59. D	70. C
5. C	16. A	27. E	38. B	49. A	60. D	71. C
6. D	17. C	28. A	39. B	50. A	61. E	
7. A	18. C	29. B	40. A	51. D	62. A	
8. C	19. B	30. C	41. B	52. C	63. B	
9. E	20. E	31. D	42. A	53. A	64. E	
10. C	21. B	32. B	43. A	54. A	65. D	
11. B	22. B	33. D	44. B	55. E	66. A	

EXERCISE 3—DECIMALS (p. 282)

1. C	11. B	21. C	31. E	41. A	51. A	61. D
2. C	12. B	22. E	32. C	42. A	52. C	62. C
3. B	13. B	23. A	33. A	43. B	53. E	63. B
4. B	14. C	24. A	34. A	44. B	54. B	64. C
5. B	15. A	25. C	35. E	45. A	55. A	65. C
6. E	16. B	26. B	36. D	46. D	56. C	66. A
7. B	17. B	27. D	37. D	47. B	57. C	67. D
8. A	18. D	28. A	38. A	48. B	58. B	
9. D	19. B	29. B	39. B	49. B	59. D	
10. A	20. A	30. D	40. B	50. C	60. B	

EXERCISE 4—PERCENTS (p. 292)

1. E	20. C	39. A	58. B	77. D	96. C	115. D
2. A	21. C	40. A	59. C	78. C	97. E	116. E
3. B	22. D	41. D	60. D	79. C	98. D	117. C
4. B	23. E	42. A	61. D	80. C	99. A	118. E
5. C	24. D	43. E	62. C	81. D	100. D	119. A
6. A	25. D	44. A	63. B	82. C	101. D	120. C
7. C	26. B	45. B	64. B	83. C	102. C	121. D
8. B	27. C	46. D	65. B	84. C	103. B	122. D
9. A	28. A	47. A	66. B	85. A	104. A	123. C
10. A	29. C	48. B	67. E	86. D	105. C	124. B
11. B	30. A	49. A	68. C	87. D	106. C	125. B
12. B	31. B	50. A	69. D	88. C	107. E	126. D
13. A	32. E	51. C	70. B	89. D	108. C	127. A
14. A	33. D	52. C	71. B	90. E	109. E	128. A
15. A	34. B	53. B	72. D	91. C	110. D	129. C
16. C	35. D	54. B	73. C	92. D	111. D	
17. B	36. C	55. B	74. C	93. E	112. E	
18. D	37. D	56. B	75. D	94. A	113. D	
19. C	38. B	57. C	76. D	95. B	114. B	

EXERCISE 5—STATISTICAL MEASURES (p. 305)

1. A	9. E	17. E	25. B	33. D	41. B	49. C
2. D	10. A	18. A	26. C	34. A	42. B	50. B
3. C	11. E	19. D	27. B	35. C	43. E	51. D
4. B	12. B	20. D	28. E	36. C	44. D	
5. C	13. B	21. D	29. B	37. D	45. B	
6. E	14. A	22. E	30. B	38. B	46. C	
7. A	15. C	23. E	31. C	39. D	47. C	
8. C	16. D	24. B	32. D	40. A	48. E	

EXERCISE 6—RATIOS AND PROPORTIONS (p. 313)

1. B	9. B	17. E	25. B	33. B	41. D	49. B
2. A	10. D	18. D	26. C	34. A	42. B	50. E
3. D	11. D	19. D	27. D	35. D	43. C	
4. C	12. C	20. E	28. B	36. C	44. B	
5. A	13. B	21. C	29. E	37. B	45. D	
6. A	14. C	22. B	30. C	38. B	46. B	
7. D	15. D	23. C	31. D	39. C	47. A	
8. B	16. D	24. C	32. C	40. A	48. C	

EXERCISE 7—EXPONENTS AND RADICALS (p. 327)

1. E	9. A	17. E	25. D	33. D	41. D	49. D
2. D	10. A	18. D	26. A	34. B	42. B	50. E
3. E	11. B	19. C	27. C	35. B	43. D	51. E
4. B	12. C	20. C	28. B	36. C	44. A	
5. C	13. C	21. C	29. C	37. D	45. D	
6. E	14. B	22. A	30. C	38. B	46. C	
7. C	15. B	23. E	31. A	39. C	47. B	
8. A	16. C	24. A	32. A	40. E	48. A	

EXERCISE 8—ALGEBRAIC OPERATIONS (p. 341)

1. A	19. B	37. E	55. E	73. A	91. A	109. B
2. E	20. C	38. E	56. B	74. A	92. E	110. B
3. C	21. C	39. C	57. D	75. A	93. D	111. A
4. C	22. B	40. D	58. C	76. C	94. B	112. E
5. E	23. A	41. B	59. A	77. E	95. D	113. D
6. B	24. C	42. B	60. D	78. D	96. A	114. C
7. A	25. B	43. C	61. A	79. A	97. B	115. B
8. E	26. C	44. D	62. D	80. C	98. C	116. E
9. B	27. C	45. D	63. A	81. D	99. C	117. D
10. B	28. C	46. E	64. D	82. D	100. A	118. A
11. C	29. C	47. E	65. D	83. C	101. E	119. E
12. C	30. C	48. C	66. B	84. D	102. C	120. A
13. E	31. B	49. A	67. B	85. B	103. E	121. D
14. A	32. A	50. D	68. A	86. A	104. E	
15. E	33. C	51. D	69. B	87. C	105. B	
16. D	34. D	52. A	70. C	88. B	106. E	
17. D	35. A	53. D	71. B	89. C	107. A	
18. D	36. E	54. D	72. B	90. D	108. D	

EXERCISE 9—ALGEBRAIC EQUATIONS AND INEQUALITIES (p. 364)

1. C	18. A	35. C	52. E	69. A	86. A	103. C
2. C	19. B	36. B	53. C	70. D	87. D	104. C
3. C	20. C	37. D	54. B	71. E	88. B	105. D
4. B	21. B	38. A	55. A	72. D	89. E	106. B
5. E	22. B	39. C	56. C	73. A	90. D	107. A
6. E	23. A	40. E	57. D	74. B	91. D	108. B
7. D	24. C	41. A	58. E	75. B	92. D	109. D
8. B	25. B	42. C	59. C	76. B	93. E	110. C
9. D	26. A	43. E	60. D	77. A	94. C	111. B
10. C	27. E	44. B	61. E	78. A	95. D	112. B
11. A	28. C	45. B	62. B	79. E	96. E	113. E
12. D	29. B	46. A	63. A	80. A	97. A	114. A
13. D	30. B	47. C	64. C	81. E	98. D	115. D
14. E	31. D	48. A	65. D	82. D	99. E	116. E
15. E	32. D	49. D	66. C	83. D	100. B	117. B
16. D	33. D	50. D	67. E	84. E	101. A	118. A
17. C	34. C	51. D	68. C	85. A	102. A	119. E

EXERCISE 10—GEOMETRY (p. 388)

1. C	23. C	45. E	67. A	89. D	111. B	
2. D	24. E	46. E	68. E	90. A	112. A	134. B
3. C	25. D	47. C	69. C	91. C	113. B	135. C
4. B	26. B	48. C	70. D	92. D	114. D	136. C
5. E	27. B	49. D	71. C	93. C	115. B	137. B
6. A	28. A	50. D	72. B	94. D	116. E	138. C
7. E	29. D	51. B	73. B	95. B	117. E	139. C
8. D	30. E	52. C	74. E	96. C	118. E	140. D
9. B	31. B	53. B	75. A	97. C	119. E	141. A
10. A	32. B	54. A	76. B	98. B	120. A	142. C
11. B	33. C	55. D	77. A	99. C	121. C	143. E
12. B	34. C	56. A	78. A	100. A	122. C	144. C
13. A	35. B	57. A	79. A	101. C	123. C	145. E
14. C	36. A	58. E	80. B	102. C	124. D	146. A
15. A	37. D	59. B	81. B	103. C	125. C	147. C
16. A	38. C	60. C	82. D	104. B	126. B	148. D
17. C	39. B	61. E	83. C	105. C	127. A	149. E
18. E	40. D	62. C	84. D	106. D	128. D	150. C
19. E	41. D	63. B	85. A	107. E	129. C	151. E
20. C	42. B	64. A	86. B	108. C	130. A	
21. A	43. D	65. D	87. C	109. D	131. C	
22. C	44. D	66. B	88. E	110. A	132. C	

EXERCISE 11—COORDINATE GEOMETRY (p. 417)

1. B	8. A	15. A	22. B	29. C	36. A	43. D
2. A	9. E	16. C	23. E	30. C	37. D	44. B
3. A	10. B	17. A	24. D	31. D	38. A	45. B
4. C	11. C	18. A	25. C	32. E	39. C	46. E
5. A	12. C	19. E	26. B	33. C	40. D	47. A
6. D	13. B	20. C	27. B	34. C	41. E	48. D
7. A	14. B	21. E	28. D	35. B	42. C	49. D

EXERCISE 12—STORY PROBLEMS (p. 443)

1. A	13. D	25. A	37. D	49. B	61. D	73. B
2. C	14. C	26. B	38. D	50. B	62. C	74. B
3. A	15. B	27. B	39. D	51. E	63. C	75. A
4. C	16. B	28. E	40. D	52. C	64. C	76. D
5. B	17. C	29. C	41. E	53. C	65. B	77. D
6. E	18. A	30. C	42. E	54. D	66. E	78. D
7. D	19. A	31. D	43. A	55. B	67. E	79. C
8. B	20. E	32. C	44. D	56. D	68. D	80. E
9. B	21. B	33. B	45. D	57. D	69. C	81. D
10. D	22. D	34. B	46. B	58. D	70. C	
11. C	23. B	35. B	47. E	59. B	71. C	
12. B	24. E	36. D	48. C	60. D	72. D	

READING SKILLS REVIEW

EXERCISE 1—SUMMARIZE THE MAIN IDEA (p. 493)

1. C   2. F   3. A   4. G   5. D

EXERCISE 2—DETERMINE THE MAIN IDEA (p. 495)

1. C   3. D   5. B   7. A   9. C
2. G   4. F   6. J   8. H   10. J

EXERCISE 3—OUTLINING PASSAGES (p. 498)

Passage 1
 I. A tremendous electrostatic charge builds up within a cloud.
 II. Lightning occurs within the cloud itself.
 III. Negative charges called stepped leaders emerge from the bottom of the cloud, moving toward the Earth and creating an ionized channel.
 IV. A strong electric field causes streamers of positively charged ions to develop and flow upward.
 V. A return stroke moves through the object from which the streamer emanated and up the ionized channel to the charge center within the cloud.
 VI. An ionized channel remains in the air, and dart leaders will quickly move down this path, resulting in further return strokes.

Passage 2
 I. The efforts of the Convention on International Trade in Endangered Species
   a. An international moratorium was enacted on the buying and selling of ivory.
   b. The moratorium prompted significant declines in ivory trading and in the rate of elephant poaching.
 II. The cooperative effort of the U.S. with the Central African Republic and the World Wildlife Fund
   a. A reserve has been established in the southeastern portion of that country.
   b. Anti-poaching patrols were established using funds provided by the U.S.
 III. The efforts of Senegal's anti-poaching program
   a. An African Elephant conservation fund grant has provided protection for the elephant population.
   b. Similar protection projects have begun in Cameroon, Congo, Eritrea, Gabon, Mali, Senegal, Tanzania, Zambia, and Zimbabwe.

EXERCISE 4—LOCATE VERBAL SIGNS (p. 500)

A flood is an overflow of water that covers lands that are normally not covered by water (*defining*). A flood occurs, for example, when a stream or river overflows its banks (*example*). Small streams are subject to flash floods—that is, the very rapid increases in water that may last only a few minutes (*defining*). In larger streams, floods usually last from several hours to a few days, and a series of storms might keep a river above flood stage for several weeks.

Floods can occur at any time, but weather patterns have a strong influence on when and where floods happen. Cyclones—similar in structure to tornadoes (*similarity*)—bring moisture inland from the ocean, causing floods in the spring in the western United States. Thunderstorms are relatively small but intense storms that cause flash floods in smaller streams during the summer in the Southwest. Frontal storms at the edge of large, moist air masses moving across the country cause floods in the northern and eastern parts of the United States during the winter.

The <u>magnitude of a flood is described by a term called the recurrence interval</u> (***defining***) which is based upon long-term study of flow records for a stream. A <u>five-year flood is one that would occur, on the average, once every five years</u> (***defining***). Although <u>a 100-year flood is expected to happen only once in a century</u> (***defining***), it is <u>important to remember</u> (***prompting***) that there is a one percent chance that a flood of that size could happen during any given year.

Of course, the frequency and magnitude of floods can be altered if changes are made in the drainage basin of a stream or river. <u>Significantly, harvesting timber or changing land use from farms to housing can cause the runoff to increase</u> (***prompting***), resulting in an increase in the magnitude of flooding. <u>On the other hand, dams can protect against flooding</u> (***contrast***) by storing storm runoff. Although the same volume of water must eventually move downstream, the peak flow can be reduced by temporarily storing water and then releasing it when water levels have fallen.

EXERCISE 5—LOCATE SPECIFIC DETAILS (p. 501)

1. C	**3.** D	**5.** C	**7.** A	**9.** C
2. F	**4.** G	**6.** F	**8.** G	**10.** J

EXERCISE 6—ANALYZE THE ARGUMENTS (p. 503)

1. D	**3.** D	**5.** C	**7.** D	**9.** A
2. G	**4.** F	**6.** G	**8.** G	**10.** H

EXERCISE 7—CONSIDER THE AUTHOR'S POINT OF VIEW (p. 506)

1. The author claims to be both a physician and a professor at a prestigious medical school.

2. One could assume that the author, as a physician, has a working knowledge of the field of medicine. One could also assume that the author, as a professor at a prestigious medical school, is well-versed in the needs of the medical community and the status of students entering medical school.

3. The author most certainly has the highest respect for the application of the Hippocratic method of reason and observation within the medical practice. The author also dislikes, or holds in contempt, medical students who pursue medical careers for the reasons of fame and fortune.

4. The author is attempting to change what he or she perceives as problems in the attitudes and perceptions of medical students.

5. The author wants you to believe that the Hippocratic method of observation and reason is essential for medical students. He or she also wants you to believe that this perspective must be acquired prior to being admitted into medical school.

6. The passage discusses the origins of modern medicine; specifically, the passage is about Hippocrates in the role of father (or founder) of modern medicine.

7. The author has spent 30 years in the American banking industry, was one of the first female members of Congress, and wrote legislation regarding banking.

8. The author has 30 years of banking experience and knowledge regarding banking laws.

9. The author strongly dislikes or disagrees with the idea that government bailouts of failing banks are helpful to the economy.

10. The author writes to make a strong case for the government not to get involved in banking bailouts.

11. The author wants you to believe that government bailouts of banks have detrimental results to the economy as a whole.

12. Written in the 1990s, the author is certainly influenced by the democratic ideals of citizenship that have influenced many nations in the twentieth century.

13. Written in Africa, the author writes with the knowledge of a poorer, agrarian culture.

14. Moving from being a citizen under a military dictatorship to being a citizen within a democratic government has influenced the author to desire others to be more actively involved in the growth and development of his or her nation.

15. The author wrote this piece at a time when gang influence was having a detrimental effect on urban cultures and urban economies.

16. Since the location was Los Angeles, the author writes about gang issues in an urban center that was greatly affected by gang activity.

17. The author certainly writes with a negative point of view regarding gangs and gang members. He also appears to write from an outsider's view of gang involvement. As a sociologist, he is interested in the social aspects of gangs, but mostly from an academic viewpoint.

EXERCISE 8—PROBE THE MOOD OF THE PASSAGE (p. 510)

1. The mood of the passage is quite depressing and bleak. The passage might be described as somber or dark.

2. The author uses the terms "melancholy," "deplorable," and "helpless infants." He verbally paints a picture of begging mothers and children in need of charity.

EXERCISE 9—BONUS PASSAGES (p. 511)

1. D	4. H	7. A	10. J	13. D	16. G
2. G	5. B	8. H	11. A	14. G	
3. A	6. J	9. A	12. H	15. D	

EXERCISE 10—CAREFUL READING OF ENGLISH ITEM STEMS (p. 516)

1. A	4. F	7. C	10. H	13. B	16. J	19. C
2. H	5. D	8. F	11. B	14. H	17. C	
3. B	6. J	9. C	12. G	15. B	18. F	

EXERCISE 11—CAREFUL READING OF MATHEMATICS ITEM STEMS (p. 519)

1. D	4. J	7. C	10. J	13. D	16. J	19. B
2. F	5. C	8. G	11. A	14. H	17. B	20. G
3. C	6. H	9. C	12. H	15. C	18. J	

EXERCISE 12—CAREFUL READING OF READING ITEM STEMS (p. 523)

1. A	**5.** C	**9.** B	**13.** B	**17.** C	**21.** B	**25.** A
2. J	**6.** F	**10.** J	**14.** F	**18.** J	**22.** H	**26.** J
3. C	**7.** B	**11.** B	**15.** C	**19.** A	**23.** D	**27.** B
4. J	**8.** H	**12.** J	**16.** J	**20.** J	**24.** F	

EXERCISE 13—CAREFUL READING OF SCIENCE ITEM STEMS (p. 527)

1. A	**4.** G	**7.** A	**10.** G	**13.** C	**16.** J
2. J	**5.** D	**8.** J	**11.** C	**14.** G	
3. A	**6.** J	**9.** B	**12.** J	**15.** C	

EXERCISE 14—COMPREHENSION LEVEL CODING (p. 533)

1. SP	**5.** SP	**9.** E	**13.** E	**17.** SP	**21.** E
2. E	**6.** GT	**10.** SP	**14.** SP	**18.** E	**22.** SP
3. SP	**7.** GT	**11.** SP	**15.** SP	**19.** E	
4. SP	**8.** SP	**12.** E	**16.** E	**20.** E	

EXERCISE 15—ITEM-TYPE CODING (p. 535)

1. ED	**5.** ED	**9.** II	**13.** ED	**17.** ED	**21.** A
2. II	**6.** ED	**10.** VCB	**14.** D	**18.** II	**22.** VCE
3. II	**7.** ED	**11.** II	**15.** D	**19.** D	
4. ED	**8.** A	**12.** MI	**16.** II	**20.** ED	

VOCABULARY SKILLS REVIEW

EXERCISE 1—ANTICIPATING SENTENCE COMPLETIONS (p. 547)

1. exceed, surpass

2. climax, high point, zenith

3. boring, dull, uninspiring

4. serious, severe, large-scale

5. complete, comprehensive

6. complete, total, authoritarian

7. hides, camouflages, conceals

8. wanted, infamous, notorious

9. dazed, confused, disoriented

10. generate, spark, increase

11. E	**13.** B	**15.** C	**17.** B	**19.** B
12. A	**14.** D	**16.** A	**18.** E	**20.** A

EXERCISE 2—ANALYZING SENTENCE COMPLETIONS (p. 550)

1. dead, spirits, ghosts

2. reform, improvement

3. flammable

4. start, beginning

5. tolerant, understanding

6. weaknesses, shortcomings

7. the elderly, senior citizens

8. disrupted, interrupted

9. cooperation, accord

10. annihilation, death

11. B	**13.** A	**15.** A	**17.** C	**19.** A
12. E	**14.** E	**16.** A	**18.** B	**20.** E

EXERCISE 3—SUBSTITUTING SENTENCE COMPLETIONS (p. 553)

1. C	4. D	7. C	10. C	13. A	16. B
2. B	5. A	8. E	11. A	14. B	17. E
3. E	6. B	9. D	12. B	15. E	

EXERCISE 4—BUILDING VOCABULARY WITH SENTENCE COMPLETIONS (p. 555)

1. A	7. D	13. B	19. C	25. B	31. B	37. C
2. B	8. E	14. A	20. A	26. D	32. A	38. A
3. D	9. C	15. D	21. E	27. D	33. B	39. C
4. E	10. B	16. E	22. A	28. A	34. B	40. D
5. A	11. B	17. E	23. B	29. E	35. A	
6. C	12. B	18. A	24. A	30. B	36. D	

EXERCISE 5—BUILDING VOCABULARY THROUGH CONTEXT (p. 565)

1. D	3. D	5. B	7. D	9. B
2. C	4. B	6. B	8. B	10. D

EXERCISE 6—VOCABULARY BUILDER: PROSE FICTION PASSAGES (p. 567)

1. D	14. A	27. E	40. B	53. B	66. B	79. C
2. C	15. C	28. A	41. C	54. A	67. C	80. D
3. E	16. C	29. D	42. A	55. C	68. A	81. A
4. B	17. E	30. C	43. C	56. C	69. D	82. E
5. A	18. A	31. B	44. D	57. E	70. B	83. A
6. D	19. B	32. D	45. B	58. A	71. A	84. B
7. B	20. E	33. E	46. B	59. C	72. C	85. C
8. C	21. B	34. C	47. A	60. B	73. C	86. C
9. A	22. A	35. B	48. C	61. B	74. B	87. A
10. B	23. C	36. A	49. B	62. E	75. A	88. C
11. D	24. A	37. D	50. E	63. C	76. E	89. A
12. B	25. B	38. A	51. A	64. D	77. B	90. C
13. C	26. D	39. D	52. D	65. E	78. C	

EXERCISE 7—VOCABULARY BUILDER: SOCIAL SCIENCE PASSAGES (p. 579)

1. D	27. A	53. B	79. C	105. A	131. B	157. C
2. A	28. A	54. A	80. A	106. A	132. D	158. A
3. B	29. D	55. B	81. B	107. C	133. B	159. D
4. E	30. E	56. A	82. E	108. A	134. A	160. D
5. B	31. C	57. C	83. B	109. D	135. D	161. B
6. D	32. E	58. A	84. B	110. B	136. B	162. C
7. A	33. B	59. A	85. B	111. D	137. E	163. B
8. C	34. D	60. C	86. C	112. C	138. A	164. A
9. B	35. C	61. E	87. B	113. A	139. C	165. D
10. C	36. A	62. D	88. A	114. B	140. B	166. A
11. D	37. D	63. B	89. D	115. B	141. C	167. B
12. A	38. B	64. E	90. E	116. C	142. A	168. B
13. D	39. C	65. D	91. E	117. D	143. B	169. E
14. C	40. A	66. B	92. B	118. A	144. E	170. C
15. D	41. D	67. B	93. B	119. E	145. B	171. C
16. E	42. D	68. C	94. C	120. C	146. A	172. D
17. A	43. B	69. D	95. D	121. B	147. C	173. A
18. C	44. B	70. A	96. B	122. A	148. A	174. D
19. A	45. D	71. B	97. D	123. E	149. C	175. B
20. B	46. B	72. A	98. B	124. B	150. C	176. C
21. A	47. D	73. D	99. C	125. E	151. B	177. E
22. C	48. B	74. C	100. A	126. D	152. D	178. A
23. B	49. A	75. B	101. C	127. D	153. B	179. C
24. C	50. A	76. E	102. D	128. C	154. E	180. B
25. D	51. C	77. A	103. D	129. A	155. A	
26. A	52. D	78. D	104. A	130. C	156. B	

EXERCISE 8—VOCABULARY BUILDER: HUMANITIES PASSAGES (p. 603)

1. D	23. C	45. C	67. C	89. B	111. C	133. D
2. E	24. A	46. A	68. B	90. B	112. A	134. B
3. C	25. B	47. D	69. A	91. C	113. B	135. A
4. D	26. C	48. B	70. D	92. D	114. E	136. B
5. C	27. A	49. A	71. B	93. E	115. A	137. A
6. B	28. A	50. B	72. B	94. C	116. B	138. D
7. A	29. E	51. D	73. C	95. D	117. C	139. A
8. B	30. A	52. C	74. B	96. A	118. E	140. B
9. A	31. E	53. C	75. D	97. D	119. C	141. C
10. D	32. A	54. A	76. C	98. C	120. A	142. B
11. C	33. D	55. A	77. D	99. B	121. D	143. B
12. B	34. E	56. B	78. A	100. A	122. B	144. A
13. C	35. C	57. C	79. E	101. D	123. E	145. A
14. A	36. B	58. D	80. A	102. B	124. D	146. C
15. C	37. C	59. A	81. A	103. B	125. A	147. A
16. B	38. B	60. C	82. C	104. C	126. B	148. C
17. A	39. D	61. B	83. C	105. C	127. B	149. A
18. B	40. C	62. E	84. B	106. B	128. D	150. D
19. B	41. D	63. B	85. B	107. A	129. D	
20. D	42. A	64. D	86. B	108. B	130. A	
21. D	43. B	65. E	87. B	109. E	131. C	
22. A	44. C	66. A	88. A	110. D	132. D	

EXERCISE 9—VOCABULARY BUILDER: NATURAL SCIENCE PASSAGES (p. 623)

1. D	27. E	53. D	79. E	105. C	131. A	157. C
2. E	28. B	54. B	80. D	106. D	132. C	158. D
3. C	29. E	55. C	81. B	107. B	133. B	159. D
4. E	30. A	56. A	82. A	108. A	134. C	160. B
5. A	31. D	57. B	83. C	109. B	135. D	161. C
6. C	32. C	58. B	84. B	110. D	136. E	162. B
7. C	33. D	59. D	85. B	111. A	137. E	163. A
8. B	34. B	60. C	86. A	112. A	138. D	164. D
9. C	35. E	61. E	87. E	113. C	139. A	165. A
10. B	36. A	62. C	88. A	114. B	140. A	166. B
11. D	37. C	63. A	89. B	115. D	141. C	167. C
12. A	38. B	64. E	90. B	116. A	142. C	168. A
13. B	39. C	65. D	91. C	117. C	143. A	169. B
14. B	40. C	66. B	92. D	118. B	144. B	170. E
15. A	41. D	67. D	93. D	119. A	145. D	171. B
16. C	42. B	68. D	94. C	120. B	146. A	172. B
17. C	43. A	69. A	95. E	121. E	147. C	173. D
18. A	44. C	70. B	96. A	122. D	148. A	174. D
19. B	45. B	71. C	97. C	123. E	149. D	175. A
20. A	46. B	72. C	98. D	124. C	150. E	176. C
21. C	47. A	73. D	99. B	125. B	151. B	177. E
22. E	48. E	74. B	100. B	126. D	152. B	178. C
23. D	49. B	75. B	101. C	127. C	153. C	179. A
24. A	50. A	76. C	102. D	128. B	154. B	180. E
25. B	51. A	77. C	103. C	129. A	155. E	
26. B	52. D	78. A	104. A	130. B	156. A	

SCIENCE SKILLS REVIEW

EXERCISE 1—BASICS OF EXPERIMENTAL DESIGN (p. 686)

1. The purpose of the experiment is to <u>determine the effect of temperature on the heart rate of frogs</u>.

2. The independent variable is temperature. (The experimenter determined the temperature before the experiment started.)

3. The dependent variable is <u>heart rate</u>.

4. The controlled variables are <u>size, type, age, and number of frogs, as well as container size and amount of light</u>.

5. The control group is <u>Group C</u>. (Group C refers to the frogs in the container that is approximately the same temperature as the enclosure from which the frogs were removed).

6. The experimental groups are <u>Groups A, B, and D</u>.

7. When the <u>temperature</u> is <u>increased</u>, then the <u>heart rate of the frogs</u> will <u>decrease</u>.

EXERCISE 2—DATA ORGANIZATION AND ANALYSIS IN CONTROLLED EXPERIMENTS (p. 702)

1. The independent variable is <u>the source of salt</u>.

2. The dependent variable is <u>the percentage of salt</u>.

3. The mammal with a percentage of salt in its urine closest to the percentage of salt in seawater is <u>the human</u>.

4. The independent variable is <u>the amount of time (in hours) over which the experiment was conducted</u>.

5. The dependent variable is <u>the percentage of carbohydrate digested</u>.

6. The independent variable is on the <u>horizontal</u> axis.

7. The dependent variable is on the <u>vertical</u> axis.

8. The slope of the line indicates that generally as the amount of time <u>increases</u>, the percentage of carbohydrates digested <u>increases</u>.

9. C	17. D	25. C	33. B	41. A	49. A	57. B
10. J	18. G	26. J	34. G	42. G	50. J	58. H
11. B	19. C	27. C	35. D	43. C	51. B	59. B
12. F	20. F	28. G	36. J	44. G	52. H	60. G
13. B	21. C	29. D	37. A	45. C	53. B	61. B
14. J	22. J	30. H	38. F	46. H	54. G	62. J
15. B	23. B	31. B	39. B	47. B	55. D	63. B
16. F	24. G	32. G	40. H	48. G	56. H	64. H

65. A	**68.** G	**71.** A	**74.** F	**77.** C	**80.** H
66. J	**69.** C	**72.** G	**75.** D	**78.** J	**81.** B
67. B	**70.** J	**73.** D	**76.** J	**79.** A	**82.** J

EXERCISE 3—PRESENTATION OF CONFLICTING VIEWPOINTS (p. 722)

1. The dependent variable (the problem) is <u>the discovery of a dead woman</u>.

2. The conflicting viewpoint is <u>whether the death was a homicide or a suicide</u>.

3. The independent variable causing the conflict is <u>the lack of evidence indicating who shot the gun</u>.

4.

Data	More Consistent with Detective 1	More Consistent with Detective 2	Equally Consistent with Both Detectives 1 and 2
Gun Owned by Woman		✓	
Bloody Pillow			✓
Bruise on Head	✓		
Firecracker-like Noise			✓
No Forced Entry			✓
Locked Door		✓	
No Suicide Note	✓		
Divorced Victim	✓		
Despondent Victim		✓	

EXERCISE 4—SCIENCE PASSAGES (p. 723)

1. C	**5.** A	**9.** A	**13.** C	**17.** A	**21.** B
2. G	**6.** J	**10.** H	**14.** H	**18.** J	**22.** H
3. D	**7.** A	**11.** C	**15.** B	**19.** C	**23.** D
4. G	**8.** J	**12.** F	**16.** F	**20.** G	**24.** F

WRITING SKILLS REVIEW

EXERCISE 1— SAMPLE ESSAY (p. 744)

Above Average Response

Parents, educators, and government leaders are increasingly concerned about the quality of education in our schools. Recently, the government instituted a policy of comprehensive testing to ensure that all students are getting a quality education and that no child is left behind. The theory is that these tests show what students have learned. If the students in a particular school don't score high enough, then that school is deemed to be failing its students. At that point, special programs are made available to provide additional instruction and tutoring to the school's students. The additional opportunities are supposed to help students learn and then perform better on the tests.

If you think about the structure of education, you'll see that it involves teachers and students in a school setting. Teachers have always evaluated students. Periodically, teachers give us tests, and we get report cards to tell our parents how we are doing in school. The new government testing is designed to find out whether schools are doing a good job. But in all of this, no one is testing the teachers. I think that if everyone is serious about improving the quality of education, then it would be a good idea to have students give their teachers report cards.

From a school improvement standpoint, teacher evaluations would help administrators learn which teachers are doing a good job and which teachers are not. When a student performs poorly in math, everyone assumes that it is the student who is at fault. And with the new testing program, if the average math score is low, then it must be the school that is failing. But it might also be the case that a single bad teacher is the real cause. A teacher who can't make math concepts clear to students could easily have an entire class with students getting poor marks on their report cards. Parents will lecture their children but never realize that the whole class has the same problem. The school may get blamed for not providing a quality education, but maybe there are other classes in the school that don't have this problem. In other words, student evaluations could be a valuable tool for identifying the real problem.

Another advantage of student evaluations would be improving the quality of teaching. Let's say, for example, that a particular teacher speaks softly and is hard to hear. Students might not want to say anything about the teacher. If only one or two students complain, they may be considered trouble-makers. But if the entire class fills out an evaluation form and under "Ability to Communicate" says "The teacher is hard to hear," then the problem can be addressed. Administrators could meet with the teacher and go over the evaluations. They could suggest to the teacher to speak up more clearly.

The objection that students might retaliate personally is really just a red herring. Students are already permitted to vote for the "Outstanding Teacher" award (or similar awards) given by most schools. Additionally, it would be obvious from the tone of the evaluations if the teacher had been unfairly criticized. Statements like "A rotten teacher" or "Can't really help us" wouldn't carry much weight. Statements like "Speaks too softly" or "Doesn't answer questions about difficult topics" are useful. Finally, a structured evaluation would make it less likely that students would comment on irrelevant factors like a teacher's personal habits.

If you listen to the debate about education, you can't help but notice that the issues are complicated. A quality education is not a simple matter. You need the right setting, the proper tools, motivated students, effective teachers, and good administration. It's like a complex recipe that calls for good ingredients mixed up in the right proportions and cooked at the right temperature for the correct length of time. Student evaluations of teachers is not going to solve all of the education world's problems. But student evaluations could be an important part of a successful recipe.

Position on issue: The writer clearly states the position at the end of the second paragraph.

Topic development and essay organization: Although the structure of the essay isn't articulated in outline form (such as "Point 1"; "Point 2"; etc.), the structure is evident. The writer uses paragraphing and transitional phrases, such as "another advantage," to help the reader follow the train of thought. The writer develops the points within each paragraph. In the next-to-the-last paragraph, for example, the writer offers three reasons for believing that the danger of personal retaliation is not very significant.

Language usage, sentence structure, and punctuation: The essay might be subjected to two related criticisms. One, sometimes the examples seem to be a little abstract. The example of "math scores" never really gets very specific, though it is difficult to say exactly how the writer could improve on what is written.

Additionally, the prose, while effective, seems a little dry. It lacks zip. Even the recipe analogy in the last paragraph seems flat. Maybe the writer could have mentioned a specific dish, say gumbo, in which several ingredients have to be mixed together to get the desired result. Even that little flair would have lightened up the writing style.

Summary and conclusions: This is a very strong response. It would surely get at least a "5" and more likely a "6" from most readers.

Below Average Response

In my opinion, students should not get to evaluate teachers because it wouldn't mean anything, and it would just be a chance for some students to dump on teachers they don't like.

Teachers give students grades for a reason. Teachers know more than the students do because they've been to college. So when a teacher gives a test, that teacher knows the right answer and can mark the papers accordingly. This system makes sense. Students have not been to college. They don't have experience teaching classes. Most, if not all, students couldn't make up an exam to test a teacher's ability to teach. They wouldn't know which questions to ask on the exam and wouldn't know what the right answers are. So students really don't know how to grade a teacher on ability to teach.

Also, some, maybe even many, students would use the evaluation to take pot shots at teachers they don't like or have a grudge about. This would be especially dangerous if students got together to say the same thing. If only one student says a teacher is rude, then no one might care. If half the class says a teacher is rude, the principal would figure where there's smoke there's fire.

The evaluations could also be unfair to hard teachers. No students like to have a lot of homework, but homework is important. It's a given fact that some teachers give more homework than others. So would students give low marks to the teachers who gave the most homework? That seems like it might happen.

Even if there were an evaluation form with categories, this would still be a problem. Everyone could agree to mark low on "Preparedness" and "Ability to Communicate." That way, there wouldn't be any question asked about retribution. The students would be using the form.

Student evaluations of teachers is not a good idea. The whole thing won't help and it could really hurt some good teachers.

Position on issue: The writer conveys the position in the first sentence. Although the position is clearly stated, the prose used is not an effective manner in which to start the essay.

Topic development and essay organization: This essay is pretty rough, but it does contain some relevant ideas. The writer explains that the evaluations would have limited utility and further that the system could be abused. The second point is developed in greater detail than the first. The writer argues that students might conspire against an unpopular teacher and that the evaluations might be used to retaliate against taskmasters. The final point in this development—that the evaluation form itself might mask this phenomenon—is particularly interesting.

The essay lacks coherent structure. The writer fails to outline her ideas in the introductory paragraphs and does not use helpful transitional phrases.

Language usage, sentence structure, and punctuation: The essay suffers from informal language and glaring grammar errors.

Summary and conclusions: The prose is not polished. Nonetheless, it is an honest effort and addresses the topic. This essay would likely be a "3." Some readers might not score it quite that high, and it would be surprising if it were given a "4."

Appendix B:

Test Answer Sheets

PRE-ASSESSMENT
BUBBLE SHEET

Name

Student ID Number

Date

Instructor

Course/Session Number

TEST 1—ENGLISH

1 (A) (B) (C) (D)	16 (F) (G) (H) (J)	31 (A) (B) (C) (D)	46 (F) (G) (H) (J)	61 (A) (B) (C) (D)
2 (F) (G) (H) (J)	17 (A) (B) (C) (D)	32 (F) (G) (H) (J)	47 (A) (B) (C) (D)	62 (F) (G) (H) (J)
3 (A) (B) (C) (D)	18 (F) (G) (H) (J)	33 (A) (B) (C) (D)	48 (F) (G) (H) (J)	63 (A) (B) (C) (D)
4 (F) (G) (H) (J)	19 (A) (B) (C) (D)	34 (F) (G) (H) (J)	49 (A) (B) (C) (D)	64 (F) (G) (H) (J)
5 (A) (B) (C) (D)	20 (F) (G) (H) (J)	35 (A) (B) (C) (D)	50 (F) (G) (H) (J)	65 (A) (B) (C) (D)
6 (F) (G) (H) (J)	21 (A) (B) (C) (D)	36 (F) (G) (H) (J)	51 (A) (B) (C) (D)	66 (F) (G) (H) (J)
7 (A) (B) (C) (D)	22 (F) (G) (H) (J)	37 (A) (B) (C) (D)	52 (F) (G) (H) (J)	67 (A) (B) (C) (D)
8 (F) (G) (H) (J)	23 (A) (B) (C) (D)	38 (F) (G) (H) (J)	53 (A) (B) (C) (D)	68 (F) (G) (H) (J)
9 (A) (B) (C) (D)	24 (F) (G) (H) (J)	39 (A) (B) (C) (D)	54 (F) (G) (H) (J)	69 (A) (B) (C) (D)
10 (F) (G) (H) (J)	25 (A) (B) (C) (D)	40 (F) (G) (H) (J)	55 (A) (B) (C) (D)	70 (F) (G) (H) (J)
11 (A) (B) (C) (D)	26 (F) (G) (H) (J)	41 (A) (B) (C) (D)	56 (F) (G) (H) (J)	71 (A) (B) (C) (D)
12 (F) (G) (H) (J)	27 (A) (B) (C) (D)	42 (F) (G) (H) (J)	57 (A) (B) (C) (D)	72 (F) (G) (H) (J)
13 (A) (B) (C) (D)	28 (F) (G) (H) (J)	43 (A) (B) (C) (D)	58 (F) (G) (H) (J)	73 (A) (B) (C) (D)
14 (F) (G) (H) (J)	29 (A) (B) (C) (D)	44 (F) (G) (H) (J)	59 (A) (B) (C) (D)	74 (F) (G) (H) (J)
15 (A) (B) (C) (D)	30 (F) (G) (H) (J)	45 (A) (B) (C) (D)	60 (F) (G) (H) (J)	75 (A) (B) (C) (D)

TEST 2—MATHEMATICS

1 (A) (B) (C) (D) (E)	13 (A) (B) (C) (D) (E)	25 (A) (B) (C) (D) (E)	37 (A) (B) (C) (D) (E)	49 (A) (B) (C) (D) (E)
2 (F) (G) (H) (J) (K)	14 (F) (G) (H) (J) (K)	26 (F) (G) (H) (J) (K)	38 (F) (G) (H) (J) (K)	50 (F) (G) (H) (J) (K)
3 (A) (B) (C) (D) (E)	15 (A) (B) (C) (D) (E)	27 (A) (B) (C) (D) (E)	39 (A) (B) (C) (D) (E)	51 (A) (B) (C) (D) (E)
4 (F) (G) (H) (J) (K)	16 (F) (G) (H) (J) (K)	28 (F) (G) (H) (J) (K)	40 (F) (G) (H) (J) (K)	52 (F) (G) (H) (J) (K)
5 (A) (B) (C) (D) (E)	17 (A) (B) (C) (D) (E)	29 (A) (B) (C) (D) (E)	41 (A) (B) (C) (D) (E)	53 (A) (B) (C) (D) (E)
6 (F) (G) (H) (J) (K)	18 (F) (G) (H) (J) (K)	30 (F) (G) (H) (J) (K)	42 (F) (G) (H) (J) (K)	54 (F) (G) (H) (J) (K)
7 (A) (B) (C) (D) (E)	19 (A) (B) (C) (D) (E)	31 (A) (B) (C) (D) (E)	43 (A) (B) (C) (D) (E)	55 (A) (B) (C) (D) (E)
8 (F) (G) (H) (J) (K)	20 (F) (G) (H) (J) (K)	32 (F) (G) (H) (J) (K)	44 (F) (G) (H) (J) (K)	56 (F) (G) (H) (J) (K)
9 (A) (B) (C) (D) (E)	21 (A) (B) (C) (D) (E)	33 (A) (B) (C) (D) (E)	45 (A) (B) (C) (D) (E)	57 (A) (B) (C) (D) (E)
10 (F) (G) (H) (J) (K)	22 (F) (G) (H) (J) (K)	34 (F) (G) (H) (J) (K)	46 (F) (G) (H) (J) (K)	58 (F) (G) (H) (J) (K)
11 (A) (B) (C) (D) (E)	23 (A) (B) (C) (D) (E)	35 (A) (B) (C) (D) (E)	47 (A) (B) (C) (D) (E)	59 (A) (B) (C) (D) (E)
12 (F) (G) (H) (J) (K)	24 (F) (G) (H) (J) (K)	36 (F) (G) (H) (J) (K)	48 (F) (G) (H) (J) (K)	60 (F) (G) (H) (J) (K)

TEST 3—READING

1 (A) (B) (C) (D)	9 (A) (B) (C) (D)	17 (A) (B) (C) (D)	25 (A) (B) (C) (D)	33 (A) (B) (C) (D)
2 (F) (G) (H) (J)	10 (F) (G) (H) (J)	18 (F) (G) (H) (J)	26 (F) (G) (H) (J)	34 (F) (G) (H) (J)
3 (A) (B) (C) (D)	11 (A) (B) (C) (D)	19 (A) (B) (C) (D)	27 (A) (B) (C) (D)	35 (A) (B) (C) (D)
4 (F) (G) (H) (J)	12 (F) (G) (H) (J)	20 (F) (G) (H) (J)	28 (F) (G) (H) (J)	36 (F) (G) (H) (J)
5 (A) (B) (C) (D)	13 (A) (B) (C) (D)	21 (A) (B) (C) (D)	29 (A) (B) (C) (D)	37 (A) (B) (C) (D)
6 (F) (G) (H) (J)	14 (F) (G) (H) (J)	22 (F) (G) (H) (J)	30 (F) (G) (H) (J)	38 (F) (G) (H) (J)
7 (A) (B) (C) (D)	15 (A) (B) (C) (D)	23 (A) (B) (C) (D)	31 (A) (B) (C) (D)	39 (A) (B) (C) (D)
8 (F) (G) (H) (J)	16 (F) (G) (H) (J)	24 (F) (G) (H) (J)	32 (F) (G) (H) (J)	40 (F) (G) (H) (J)

TEST 4—SCIENCE

1 (A) (B) (C) (D)	9 (A) (B) (C) (D)	17 (A) (B) (C) (D)	25 (A) (B) (C) (D)	33 (A) (B) (C) (D)
2 (F) (G) (H) (J)	10 (F) (G) (H) (J)	18 (F) (G) (H) (J)	26 (F) (G) (H) (J)	34 (F) (G) (H) (J)
3 (A) (B) (C) (D)	11 (A) (B) (C) (D)	19 (A) (B) (C) (D)	27 (A) (B) (C) (D)	35 (A) (B) (C) (D)
4 (F) (G) (H) (J)	12 (F) (G) (H) (J)	20 (F) (G) (H) (J)	28 (F) (G) (H) (J)	36 (F) (G) (H) (J)
5 (A) (B) (C) (D)	13 (A) (B) (C) (D)	21 (A) (B) (C) (D)	29 (A) (B) (C) (D)	37 (A) (B) (C) (D)
6 (F) (G) (H) (J)	14 (F) (G) (H) (J)	22 (F) (G) (H) (J)	30 (F) (G) (H) (J)	38 (F) (G) (H) (J)
7 (A) (B) (C) (D)	15 (A) (B) (C) (D)	23 (A) (B) (C) (D)	31 (A) (B) (C) (D)	39 (A) (B) (C) (D)
8 (F) (G) (H) (J)	16 (F) (G) (H) (J)	24 (F) (G) (H) (J)	32 (F) (G) (H) (J)	40 (F) (G) (H) (J)

PRE-ASSESSMENT
ESSAY RESPONSE SHEET

Name _____

Student ID Number _____

Date _____

Instructor _____

Course/Session Number _____

Appendix C:
Progress Reports

CORE/TARGETED SKILLS
PROGRESS REPORTS

The progress reports on the following pages are designed to help you monitor your progress throughout the skills reviews in the "Core/Targeted Skills" part of volume 1 of the student text. Complete the assigned items by the due date given by your instructor. Correct your answers using the answers and explanations in Appendix A of this book*, and record both the number and percentage of items answered correctly on the *student copies* of the progress reports. Identify the date on which you completed each exercise. List the numbers of any items that you would like your instructor to review in class. Then, transfer this information to the corresponding *instructor copies* of the reports and give them to your instructor. Be sure to leave the last three columns of the *instructor copies* blank; these are for your instructor's use in evaluating your progress. (Note: In the first column of each report, the numbering refers to the exercises and the page numbers refer to the locations of those exercises in this book.)

*Consult with your instructor to determine whether you will use Appendix A to complete the Core/Targeted Skills Progress Reports.

GRAMMAR AND MECHANICS SKILLS REVIEW
(Student Copy)

Exercise	Total # of Items			% of Items Correct	Date Completed	Item #s to Review
	Possible	Assigned	Correct			
1. Parts of Speech (p. 48)	20					
2. Common Grammatical Errors (p. 65)	80					
3. Analyzing Sentence Structure (p. 79)	75					
4. Problems of Logical Expression (p. 91)	45					
5. Idioms and Clarity of Expression (p. 105)	143					
6. Punctuation (p. 126)	55					

DIAGRAMMING SENTENCES
SKILLS REVIEW

(Student Copy)

	Total # of Items			% of Items Correct	Date Completed	
Exercise	*Possible*	*Assigned*	*Correct*			*Item #s to Review*
1. Subjects and Verbs (p. 140)	5					
2. Modal Auxiliary Verbs (p. 145)	5					
3. Conjunctions (p. 149)	5					
4. Articles, Attributive Adjectives, and Direct Objects (p. 155)	5					
5. Adverbs (p. 160)	5					
6. Subjective Complements: Predicate Nominatives and Predicate Adjectives (p. 165)	5					
7. Appositives (p. 169)	5					
8. Prepositional Phrases (p. 175)	5					
9. Indirect Objects and Objective Complements (p. 180)	5					
10. Infinitives (p. 189)	10					
11. Gerunds (p. 195)	5					
12. Participles (p. 201)	5					
13. Adverb Clauses (p. 209)	10					
14. Adjective Clauses (p. 215)	5					
15. Noun Clauses (p. 220)	5					

MATH SKILLS REVIEW
(Student Copy)

Exercise	Total # of Items			% of Items Correct	Date Completed	Item #s to Review
	Possible	Assigned	Correct			
1. Numbers (p. 253)	123					
2. Fractions (p. 268)	71					
3. Decimals (p. 282)	67					
4. Percents (p. 292)	129					
5. Statistical Measures (p. 305)	51					
6. Ratios and Proportions (p. 313)	50					
7. Exponents and Radicals (p. 327)	51					
8. Algebraic Operations (p. 341)	121					
9. Algebraic Equations and Inequalities (p. 364)	119					
10. Geometry (p. 388)	151					
11. Coordinate Geometry (p. 417)	49					
12. Story Problems (p. 443)	81					

READING SKILLS REVIEW

(Student Copy)

Exercise	Total # of Items			% of Items Correct	Date Completed	Item #s to Review
	Possible	Assigned	Correct			
1. Summarize the Main Idea (p. 493)	5					
2. Determine the Main Idea (p. 495)	10					
3. Outlining Passages (p. 498)	2		N/A	N/A		N/A
4. Locate Verbal Skills (p. 500)	1		N/A	N/A		N/A
5. Locate Specific Details (p. 501)	10					
6. Analyze the Arguments (p. 503)	10					
7. Consider the Author's Point of View (p. 506)	17					
8. Probe the Mood of the Passage (p. 510)	2					
9. Bonus Passages (p. 511)	16					
10. Careful Reading of English Item Stems (p. 516)	19					
11. Careful Reading of Mathematics Items Stems (p. 519)	20					
12. Careful Reading of Reading Item Stems (p. 523)	27					
13. Careful Reading of Science Item Stems (p. 527)	16					
14. Comprehension Level Coding (p. 533)	22					
15. Item-Type Coding (p. 535)	22					

VOCABULARY SKILLS REVIEW
(Student Copy)

Exercise	Total # of Items			% of Items Correct	Date Completed	Item #s to Review
	Possible	Assigned	Correct			
1. Anticipating Sentence Completions (p. 547)	20					
2. Analyzing Sentence Completions (p. 550)	20					
3. Substituting Sentence Completions (p. 553)	17					
4. Building Vocabulary with Sentence Completions (p. 555)	40					
5. Building Vocabulary through Context (p. 565)	10					
6. Vocabulary Builder: Prose Fiction Passages (p. 567)	90					
7. Vocabulary Builder: Social Science Passages (p. 579)	180					
8. Vocabulary Builder: Humanities Passages (p. 603)	150					
9. Vocabulary Builder: Natural Science Passages (p. 623)	180					

SCIENCE SKILLS REVIEW
(Student Copy)

Exercise	Total # of Items			% of Items Correct	Date Completed	Item #s to Review
	Possible	Assigned	Correct			
1. Basics of Experimental Design (p. 686)	7					
2. Data Organization and Analysis in Controlled Experiments (p. 702)	82					
3. Presentation of Conflicting Viewpoints (p. 722)	4					
4. Science Passages (p. 723)	24					

WRITING SKILLS REVIEW
(Student Copy)

Exercise	Total # of Items			% of Items Correct	Date Completed	Item #s to Review
	Possible	Assigned	Correct			
1. Sample Essay (p. 744)	1		N/A	N/A		N/A

GRAMMAR AND MECHANICS
SKILLS REVIEW

(Instructor Copy)

Name _____   Student ID Number _____

Date _____ Instructor _____ Course/Session Number _____

Exercise	Total # of Items			% of Items Correct	Date Completed	Item #s to Review	Instructor Skill Evaluation (Check One Per Section)		
	Possible	Assigned	Correct				Mastered	Partially Mastered	Not Mastered
1. Parts of Speech (p. 48)	20								
2. Common Grammatical Errors (p. 65)	80								
3. Analyzing Sentence Structure (p. 79)	75								
4. Problems of Logical Expression (p. 91)	45								
5. Idioms and Clarity of Expression (p. 105)	143								
6. Punctuation (p. 126)	55								

DIAGRAMMING SENTENCES
SKILLS REVIEW
(Instructor Copy)

Name _____ Student ID Number _____

Date _____ Instructor _____ Course/Session Number _____

Exercise	Total # of Items			% of Items Correct	Date Completed	Item #s to Review	Instructor Skill Evaluation (Check One Per Section)		
	Possible	Assigned	Correct				Mastered	Partially Mastered	Not Mastered
1. Subjects and Verbs (p. 140)	5								
2. Modal Auxiliary Verbs (p. 145)	5								
3. Conjunctions (p. 149)	5								
4. Articles, Attributive Adjectives, and Direct Objects (p. 155)	5								
5. Adverbs (p. 160)	5								
6. Subjective Complements: Predicate Nominatives and Predicate Adjectives (p. 165)	5								
7. Appositives (p. 169)	5								
8. Prepositional Phrases (p. 175)	5								
9. Indirect Objects and Objective Complements (p. 180)	5								
10. Infinitives (p. 189)	10								
11. Gerunds (p. 195)	5								
12. Participles (p. 201)	5								
13. Adverb Clauses (p. 209)	10								
14. Adjective Clauses (p. 215)	5								
15. Noun Clauses (p. 220)	5								

MATH SKILLS REVIEW
(Instructor Copy)

Name _____   Student ID Number _____

Date _____   Instructor _____   Course/Session Number _____

Exercise	Total # of Items			% of Items Correct	Date Completed	Item #s to Review	Instructor Skill Evaluation (Check One Per Section)		
	Possible	Assigned	Correct				Mastered	Partially Mastered	Not Mastered
1. Numbers (p. 253)	123								
2. Fractions (p. 268)	71								
3. Decimals (p. 282)	67								
4. Percents (p. 292)	129								
5. Statistical Measures (p. 305)	51								
6. Ratios and Proportions (p. 313)	50								
7. Exponents and Radicals (p. 327)	51								
8. Algebraic Operations (p. 341)	121								
9. Algebraic Equations and Inequalities (p. 364)	119								
10. Geometry (p. 388)	151								
11. Coordinate Geometry (p. 417)	49								
12. Story Problems (p. 443)	81								

READING SKILLS REVIEW
(Instructor Copy)

Name _____ Student ID Number _____

Date _____ Instructor _____ Course/Session Number _____

Exercise	Total # of Items			% of Items Correct	Date Completed	Item #s to Review	Instructor Skill Evaluation (Check One Per Section)		
	Possible	Assigned	Correct				Mastered	Partially Mastered	Not Mastered
1. Summarize the Main Idea (p. 493)	5								
2. Determine the Main Idea (p. 495)	10								
3. Outlining Passages (p. 498)	2		N/A	N/A		N/A			
4. Locate Verbal Skills (p. 500)	1		N/A	N/A		N/A			
5. Locate Specific Details (p. 501)	10								
6. Analyze the Arguments (p. 503)	10								
7. Consider the Author's Point of View (p. 506)	17								
8. Probe the Mood of the Passage (p. 510)	2								
9. Bonus Passages (p. 511)	16								
10. Careful Reading of English Item Stems (p. 516)	19								
11. Careful Reading of Mathematics Items Stems (p. 519)	20								
12. Careful Reading of Reading Item Stems (p. 523)	27								
13. Careful Reading of Science Item Stems (p. 527)	16								
14. Comprehension Level Coding (p. 533)	22								
15. Item-Type Coding (p. 535)	22								

VOCABULARY SKILLS REVIEW

(Instructor Copy)

Name _____   Student ID Number _____

Date _____ Instructor _____ Course/Session Number _____

Exercise	Total # of Items			% of Items Correct	Date Completed	Item #s to Review	Instructor Skill Evaluation (Check One Per Section)		
	Possible	Assigned	Correct				Mastered	Partially Mastered	Not Mastered
1. Anticipating Sentence Completions (p. 547)	20								
2. Analyzing Sentence Completions (p. 550)	20								
3. Substituting Sentence Completions (p. 553)	17								
4. Building Vocabulary with Sentence Completions (p. 555)	40								
5. Building Vocabulary through Context (p. 565)	10								
6. Vocabulary Builder: Prose Fiction Passages (p. 567)	90								
7. Vocabulary Builder: Social Science Passages (p. 579)	180								
8. Vocabulary Builder: Humanities Passages (p. 603)	150								
9. Vocabulary Builder: Natural Science Passages (p. 623)	180								

SCIENCE SKILLS REVIEW
(Instructor Copy)

Name _____   Student ID Number _____

Date _____   Instructor _____   Course/Session Number _____

Exercise	Total # of Items			% of Items Correct	Date Completed	Item #s to Review	Instructor Skill Evaluation (Check One Per Section)		
	Possible	Assigned	Correct				Mastered	Partially Mastered	Not Mastered
1. Basics of Experimental Design (p. 686)	7								
2. Data Organization and Analysis in Controlled Experiments (p. 702)	82								
3. Presentation of Conflicting Viewpoints (p. 722)	4								
4. Science Passages (p. 723)	24								

WRITING SKILLS REVIEW
(Instructor Copy)

Name _____   Student ID Number _____

Date _____   Instructor _____   Course/Session Number _____

Exercise	Total # of Items			% of Items Correct	Date Completed	Item #s to Review	Instructor Skill Evaluation (Check One Per Section)		
	Possible	Assigned	Correct				Mastered	Partially Mastered	Not Mastered
1. Sample Essay (p. 744)	1		N/A	N/A		N/A			

CAMBRIDGE ACT® • PLAN® • EXPLORE® VICTORY, 10th EDITION
ERROR CORRECTION AND SUGGESTION FORM

Name/Location: _____ Day Phone: _____ E-mail Address: _____

Part of Materials:
☐ Student Text (Volume 1), Specify Subject: _____ Page: _____ Item: _____
☐ Student Text (Volume 2), Specify Subject: _____ Page: _____ Item: _____
☐ Teacher's Guide, Specify Subject: _____ Page: _____ Item: _____
☐ Test Explanations, Specify Year/Code: _____ Page: _____ Item: _____

Error/Suggestion: _____
_____
_____

Part of Materials:
☐ Student Text (Volume 1), Specify Subject: _____ Page: _____ Item: _____
☐ Student Text (Volume 2), Specify Subject: _____ Page: _____ Item: _____
☐ Teacher's Guide, Specify Subject: _____ Page: _____ Item: _____
☐ Test Explanations, Specify Year/Code: _____ Page: _____ Item: _____

Error/Suggestion: _____
_____
_____

Part of Materials:
☐ Student Text (Volume 1), Specify Subject: _____ Page: _____ Item: _____
☐ Student Text (Volume 2), Specify Subject: _____ Page: _____ Item: _____
☐ Teacher's Guide, Specify Subject: _____ Page: _____ Item: _____
☐ Test Explanations, Specify Year/Code: _____ Page: _____ Item: _____

Error/Suggestion: _____
_____
_____

Part of Materials:
☐ Student Text (Volume 1), Specify Subject: _____ Page: _____ Item: _____
☐ Student Text (Volume 2), Specify Subject: _____ Page: _____ Item: _____
☐ Teacher's Guide, Specify Subject: _____ Page: _____ Item: _____
☐ Test Explanations, Specify Year/Code: _____ Page: _____ Item: _____

Error/Suggestion: _____
_____
_____

Part of Materials:
☐ Student Text (Volume 1), Specify Subject: _____ Page: _____ Item: _____
☐ Student Text (Volume 2), Specify Subject: _____ Page: _____ Item: _____
☐ Teacher's Guide, Specify Subject: _____ Page: _____ Item: _____
☐ Test Explanations, Specify Year/Code: _____ Page: _____ Item: _____

Error/Suggestion: _____
_____
_____

Mail form to Cambridge Educational Services, Inc. or fax form to 1-847-299-2933. For teacher's assistance, call 1-800-444-4373 solutions@CambridgeEd.com. Visit our Web site at www.CambridgeEd.com.